WORLD TRADE ORGANIZATION

Dispute Settlement Reports

2002
Volume VII

Pages 2579-3042

CAMBRIDGE
UNIVERSITY PRESS

CAMBRIDGE UNIVERSITY PRESS

Cambridge, New York, Melbourne, Madrid, Cape Town, Singapore, São Paulo

Cambridge University Press
The Edinburgh Building, Cambridge CB2 2RU, UK

Published in the United States of America by Cambridge University Press, New York

www.cambridge.org
Information on this title: www.cambridge.org/9780521854665

First published 2005

Printed in the United Kingdom at the University Press, Cambridge

A catalogue record for this book is available from the British Library

ISBN-13 987-0-521-85466-5 hardback
ISBN-10 0-521-85466-0 hardback

THE WTO DISPUTE SETTLEMENT REPORTS

The *Dispute Settlement Reports* of the World Trade Organization (the "WTO") include panel and Appellate Body reports, as well as arbitration awards, in disputes concerning the rights and obligations of WTO Members under the provisions of the *Marrakesh Agreement Establishing the World Trade Organization*. The *Dispute Settlement Reports* are available in English, French and Spanish. Starting with 1999, the first volume of each year contains a cumulative index of published disputes.

This volume may be cited as DSR 2002:VII

TABLE OF CONTENTS

Page

United States- Section 129(c)(1) of the Uruguay Round Agreements Act (WT/DS221)

Report of the Panel 2581

Egypt – Definitive Anti-Dumping Measures on Steel Rebar from Turkey (WT/DS211)

Report of the Panel 2667

Cumulative Index of Published Disputes 3035

UNITED STATES – SECTION 129(c)(1) OF THE URUGUAY ROUND AGREEMENTS ACT

Report of the Panel
WT/DS221/R

Adopted by the Dispute Settlement Body
on 30 August 2002

TABLE OF CONTENTS

			Page
I.	PROCEDURAL BACKGROUND		2584
II.	FACTUAL ASPECTS		2586
	A.	Section 129 of the URAA	2586
	B.	The Retrospective Duty Assessment System of the United States	2589
III.	MAIN ARGUMENTS OF THE PARTIES		2590
	A.	Canada	2590
		1. Introduction	2590
		2. Description of Section 129(c)(1) of the URAA	2590
		3. Section 129(c)(1) is Inconsistent with the United States' Obligations Under the AD Agreement, the SCM Agreement, Article VI of the GATT 1994 and Article XVI:4 of the WTO Agreement	2592
		(a) Antidumping Cases	2593
		(b) Subsidy Cases	2594
		4. Section 129(c)(1) Mandates a Violation of the WTO Obligations of the United States	2595
		5. The Principle of Prospective Compliance	2599
		6. Differences Between Prospective and Retrospective Duty Assessment Systems	2602
		7. Date of Definitive Duty Determination and not Date of Entry of Imports is the Operative Date for Determining Compliance	2603
		8. Conclusion	2604
	B.	United States	2604
		1. Introduction	2604
		2. Description of Section 129(c)(1) of the URAA	2605

Page

3. Canada Has Failed to Establish that Section
    129(c)(1) Mandates Action Inconsistent with
    WTO Rules 2606

    (a) Canada Must Establish that Section
         129(c)(1) Mandates Action that is
         Inconsistent with the United States'
         WTO Obligations 2606

    (b) The Meaning of Section 129(c)(1) Is a
         Factual Question That Must Be Answered
         by Applying US Principles of Statutory
         Interpretation 2606

    (c) Canada Misinterprets what Section
         129(c)(1) Actually Requires 2607

    (d) Conclusion 2609

4. Section 129(c)(1) Is Consistent with the DSU,
    which Requires Prospective Remedies when a
    Measure is Found Inconsistent with WTO
    Obligations 2609

    (a) The Principle of Prospective Remedies in
         the Dispute Settlement Process 2609

         (i)   Textual Analysis of the DSU 2609

         (ii) Panel and Appellate Body
               Clarification of the DSU 2611

    (b) The Date of Entry is the Operative Date
         for Determining whether Relief is
         "Prospective" or "Retroactive" 2612

         (i)   Using the Date of Entry as the Basis
               for Implementation is Consistent
               with the AD and SCM Agreements 2612

         (ii) Using the Date of Definitive Duty
               Determination as the Basis for
               Implementation Could Lead to
               Unexpected Results 2614

    (c) There Should be no Distinction between
         Members with Retrospective Duty
         Assessment Systems and Members with
         Prospective Duty Assessment Systems 2615

         (i)   Canada's Position is Based on
               Artificial Distinctions Between
               Retrospective Duty Systems and
               Prospective Duty Systems 2615

Page

                (ii)   The WTO Obligations that Apply to Members with Retrospective and Prospective Systems are the Same 2616

                (iii)   Canada is Seeking to Create an Obligation for Members with Retrospective Systems to Provide a Retroactive Remedy in Cases Involving Antidumping and Countervailing Duty Measures............ 2617

        (d)   Conclusion... 2618

    5.   Conclusion 2619

IV.   MAIN ARGUMENTS OF THE THIRD PARTIES 2619

    A.   European Communities.. 2619

        1.   The Principle of Prospective Compliance................. 2619

        2.   The Temporal Scope of the Principle of Prospective Compliance... 2620

    B.   Japan 2621

V.   INTERIM REVIEW... 2624

    A.   Background 2624

    B.   Comments by Canada 2624

        1.   Terms of Reference.. 2624

        2.   Burden of Proof 2626

    C.   Comments by the United States 2627

VI.   FINDINGS 2627

    A.   Measure at Issue.. 2627

    B.   Claims and Arguments of the Parties and Analytical Approach of the Panel... 2628

        1.   Arguments of the Parties... 2628

        2.   Evaluation by the Panel 2631

    C.   Canada's Principal Claims.. 2633

        1.   Actions Identified by Canada as Required and/or Precluded by Section 129(c)(1) 2634

        2.   Meaning and Scope of Section 129(c)(1) 2636

            (a)   Examination of the URAA 2636

            (b)   Examination of Section 129(c)(1) as Interpreted by the SAA................................. 2637

                (i)   Arguments of the Parties 2638

                (ii)   Evaluation by the Panel...................... 2639

Page

3. Whether Section 129(c)(1) Requires and/or
Precludes any of the Actions Identified by
Canada 2642

4. Whether Section 129(c)(1) has the Effect of
Requiring and/or Precluding any of the Actions
Identified by Canada 2642

(a) Section 129(c)(1) as Enacted 2643

(i) Arguments of the Parties 2643

(ii) Evaluation by the Panel 2646

Methodology Cases 2646

Revocation Cases... 2651

Conclusion.. 2655

(b) Statement of Administrative Action 2655

(i) Arguments of the Parties 2656

(ii) Evaluation by the Panel 2657

(c) Application of Section 129(c)(1) to Date 2661

(i) Arguments of the Parties 2661

(ii) Evaluation by the Panel 2662

(d) Conclusion.. 2662

5. Whether Section 129(c)(1) Mandates the United
States to Take any of the Actions and/or not to
Take any of the Actions Identified by Canada........... 2663

6. Whether the Actions Identified by Canada, if
Taken or not Taken, would Infringe the WTO
Provisions that it has Invoked 2664

7. Overall Conclusion with Respect to Canada's
Principal Claims... 2664

D. Canada's Consequential Claims 2665

VII. CONCLUSION 2666

I. PROCEDURAL BACKGROUND

1.1 On 17 January 2001 Canada requested consultations with the United States pursuant to Article 4 of the Understanding on Rules and Procedures Governing the Settlement of Disputes (hereafter the "DSU"), Article XXII of the General Agreement on Tariffs and Trade 1994 (hereafter the "GATT 1994"), Article 30 of the Agreement on Subsidies and Countervailing Measures (hereafter the "SCM Agreement") and Article 17 of the Agreement on Implementation of Article VI of the General Agreement on Tariffs and Trade 1994 (hereafter the

"AD Agreement") regarding section 129(c)(1) of the US Uruguay Round Agreements Act (hereafter the "URAA")[1] and the Statement of Administrative Action (hereafter the "SAA")[2] accompanying the URAA.[3]

1.2   Consultations were held in Washington, D.C., on 1 March 2001, but did not lead to a mutually satisfactory resolution of the matter.

1.3   On 24 July 2001, Canada requested the Dispute Settlement Body (hereafter the "DSB") to establish a panel pursuant to Articles 4 and 6 of the DSU, Article XXIII of the the GATT 1994, Article 30 of the SCM Agreement and Article 17 of the AD Agreement. Canada's panel request referenced only section 129(c)(1) of the URAA as the measure at issue. Canada claimed that section 129(c)(1) of the URAA is inconsistent with Articles VI:2, VI:3 and VI:6(a) of the the GATT 1994; Articles 10, 19.4, 21.1, 32.1 and 32.5 of the SCM Agreement; Articles 1, 9.3, 11.1, 18.1 and 18.4 of the AD Agreement; Article XVI:4 of the Marrakesh Agreement Establishing the World Trade Organization (hereafter the "WTO Agreement"); and Articles 3.2, 3.7, 19.1, 21.1 and 21.3 of the DSU.[4]

1.4   At its meeting on 23 August 2001, the DSB established a panel pursuant to the request of Canada, in accordance with Article 6 of the DSU. The panel was established with standard terms of reference. The terms of reference are the following:

> To examine, in the light of the relevant provisions of the covered agreements cited by Canada in document WT/DS221/4, the matter referred to the DSB by Canada in that document, and to make such findings as will assist the DSB in making the recommendations or in giving the rulings provided for in those agreements.[5]

1.5   On 30 October 2001 the Panel was constituted as follows:

Chairperson: Ms. Claudia Orozco

Members: Mr. Simon Farbenbloom

             Mr. Edmond McGovern[6]

1.6   Chile, the European Communities, India and Japan reserved their rights to participate in the panel proceedings as a third party. The European Communities and Japan presented arguments to the Panel.

1.7   The Panel met with the parties on 18 and 19 February 2002 as well as on 26 March 2002. It met with the third parties on 19 February 2002. The Panel

---

[1]   Uruguay Round Agreements Act, Pub. L. No. 103-465, section 129(c)(1), 108 Stat. 4838, also codified at 19 U.S.C. 3538 (1994).

[2]   Statement of Administrative Action, in "Message from the President of the United States Transmitting the Uruguay Round Agreement, Texts of Agreements Implementing Bill, Statement of Administrative Action and Required Supporting Statements", H.R. Doc. No. 103-316, Vol. 1, pp. 656 *et seq.*

[3]   WT/DS221/1.

[4]   WT/DS221/4.

[5]   WT/DS221/5 (referring to WT/DSB/M/108).

[6]   *Ibid.*

issued its interim report to the parties on 22 May 2002. The Panel issued its final report to the parties on 12 June 2002.

II.   FACTUAL ASPECTS

2.1   This dispute concerns section 129(c)(1) of the URAA (hereafter "section 129(c)(1)").

2.2   This part of the Panel report reproduces relevant portions of section 129 of the URAA and, because section 129(c)(1) operates in the context of the US system of retrospective assessment of antidumping or countervailing duties, provides a description of the basic features of that system.

A.   *Section 129 of the URAA*

2.3   Section 129 of the URAA is entitled "Administrative Action Following WTO Panel Reports". It has five subsections, *viz.*, subsections (a) through (e). Subsections (a) through (d) are reproduced below in relevant part.[7]

(a)   ACTION BY UNITED STATES INTERNATIONAL TRADE COMMISSION.—

(1)   ADVISORY REPORT.— If a dispute settlement panel finds in an interim report under Article 15 of the Dispute Settlement Understanding, or the Appellate Body finds in a report under Article 17 of that Understanding, that an action by the International Trade Commission in connection with a particular proceeding is not in conformity with the obligations of the United States under the Antidumping Agreement, the Safeguards Agreement, or the Agreement on Subsidies and Countervailing Measures, the Trade Representative may request the Commission to issue an advisory report on whether title VII of the Tariff Act of 1930 or title II of the Trade Act of 1974, as the case may be, permits the Commission to take steps in connection with the particular proceeding that would render its action not inconsistent with the findings of the panel or the Appellate Body concerning those obligations. The Trade Representative shall notify the congressional committees of such request.

[…]

(4)   COMMISSION   DETERMINATION.—   Notwithstanding any provision of the Tariff Act of 1930 or title II of the Trade Act of 1974, if a majority of the Commissioners issues an affirmative report under paragraph (1), the Commission, upon the written request of the Trade Representative, shall issue a de-

---

[7]   Subsection (e) amends section 516A of the Tariff Act of 1930 to provide for judicial review by US courts and NAFTA binational panels of new Title VII determinations made by the US Department of Commerce or the International Trade Commission under section 129 that are implemented.

termination in connection with the particular proceeding that would render the Commission's action described in paragraph (1) not inconsistent with the findings of the panel or Appellate Body. The Commission shall issue its determination not later than 120 days after the request from the Trade Representative is made.

(5) CONSULTATIONS ON IMPLEMENTATION OF COMMISSION DETERMINATION.— The Trade Representative shall consult with the congressional committees before the Commission's determination under paragraph (4) is implemented.

(6) REVOCATION OF ORDER.— If, by virtue of the Commission's determination under paragraph (4), an antidumping or countervailing duty order with respect to some or all of the imports that are subject to the action of the Commission described in paragraph (1) is no longer supported by an affirmative Commission determination under title VII of the Tariff Act of 1930 or this subsection, the Trade Representative may, after consulting with the congressional committees under paragraph (5), direct the administering authority to revoke the antidumping or countervailing duty order in whole or in part.

[...]

(b) ACTION BY ADMINISTERING AUTHORITY.—

(1) CONSULTATIONS WITH ADMINISTERING AUTHORITY AND CONGRESSIONAL COMMITTEES.— Promptly after a report by a dispute settlement panel or the Appellate Body is issued that contains findings that an action by the administering authority in a proceeding under title VII of the Tariff Act of 1930 is not in conformity with the obligations of the United States under the Antidumping Agreement or the Agreement on Subsidies and Countervailing Measures, the Trade Representative shall consult with the administering authority and the congressional committees on the matter.

(2) DETERMINATION BY ADMINISTERING AUTHORITY.— Notwithstanding any provision of the Tariff Act of 1930, the administering authority shall, within 180 days after receipt of a written request from the Trade Representative, issue a determination in connection with the particular proceeding that would render the administering authority's action described in paragraph (1) not inconsistent with the findings of the panel or the Appellate Body.

(3) CONSULTATIONS BEFORE IMPLEMENTATION.— Before the administering authority implements any determination under paragraph (2), the Trade Representative shall consult with the administering authority and the congressional committees with respect to such determination.

(4) IMPLEMENTATION OF DETERMINATION.— The Trade Representative may, after consulting with the administering authority and the congressional committees under paragraph (3), direct the administering authority to implement, in whole or in part, the determination made under paragraph (2).

(c) EFFECTS OF DETERMINATIONS; NOTICE OF IMPLEMENTATION.—

(1) EFFECTS OF DETERMINATIONS.— Determinations concerning title VII of the Tariff Act of 1930 that are implemented under this section shall apply with respect to unliquidated entries of the subject merchandise (as defined in section 771 of that Act) that are entered, or withdrawn from warehouse, for consumption on or after—

(A) in the case of a determination by the Commission under subsection (a)(4), the date on which the Trade Representative directs the administering authority under subsection (a)(6) to revoke an order pursuant to that determination, and

(B) in the case of a determination by the administering authority under subsection (b)(2), the date on which the Trade Representative directs the administering authority under subsection (b)(4) to implement that determination.

(2) NOTICE OF IMPLEMENTATION.—

(A) The administering authority shall publish in the Federal Register notice of the implementation of any determination made under this section with respect to title VII of the Tariff Act of 1930.

(B) The Trade Representative shall publish in the Federal Register notice of the implementation of any determination made under this section with respect to title II of the Trade Act of 1974.

(d) OPPORTUNITY FOR COMMENT BY INTERESTED PARTIES.— Prior to issuing a determination under this section, the administering authority or the Commission, as the case may be, shall provide interested parties with an opportunity to submit written comments and, in appropriate cases, may hold a hearing, with respect to the determination.[8]

2.4 Under Section 129, the United States Trade Representative (hereafter the "USTR") may request the US International Trade Commission (hereafter the "ITC") or the US Department of Commerce (hereafter the "Department of Commerce") to take action "not inconsistent" with a panel report only if such action is

---

[8] Uruguay Round Agreements Act, Pub. L. No. 103-465, section 129(a)-(d), 108 Stat. 4836-4838.

in accord with US antidumping or countervailing duty law.[9] Section 129 does not apply in cases where implementation of an adverse DSB ruling requires a change in US antidumping or countervailing duty statutes.

B.   The Retrospective Duty Assessment System of the United States

2.5   In a US antidumping or countervailing duty investigation, the Department of Commerce determines whether the imports under investigation are being dumped or subsidized and the ITC determines whether the dumped or subsidized imports cause or threaten to cause material injury. If the final determinations of the Department of Commerce and the ITC establish that the imports under investigation are being dumped or subsidized and are causing (or threatening to cause) injury, the Department of Commerce issues an antidumping or countervailing duty order instructing the US Customs Service to (i) assess antidumping or countervailing duties on completion of a future administrative review and (ii) require the payment of a cash deposit of estimated duties on all future entries of the relevant product.[10]

2.6   The United States employs a "retrospective" duty assessment system under which definitive liability for antidumping or countervailing duties is determined after merchandise subject to an antidumping or countervailing duty measure enters the United States. The determination of definitive duty liability is made at the end of "administrative reviews" which are initiated by the Department of Commerce each year on request by an interested party (such as the foreign exporter or the US importer of the imports), beginning one year from the date of the order. In addition to calculating an assessment rate in respect of the entries under review, administrative reviews also determine the cash deposit rates for estimated antidumping or countervailing duties that will be required as a security on future entries, until subsequent administrative reviews are conducted with respect to those entries.

2.7   An administrative review entails a substantive legal and factual analysis of whether imports of the product during the period of review were dumped or subsidized and, if so, to what extent.[11] The facts pertaining to entries during the period under review are investigated for the first time during an administrative review. The law applied in an administrative review is the law as interpreted by the Department of Commerce at the time that it makes its administrative review decision. The Department of Commerce's interpretation of the underlying anti-

---

[9]   See section B.1.(c), third paragraph, of the Statement of Administrative Action, *supra*, p. 1023.

[10]   See section 351.211 of the Antidumping and Countervailing Duties Regulations, 19 C.F.R. Part 351 (exhibit CDA-5). Normally, if an administrative review is not requested, the Department of Commerce will instruct the US Customs Service to assess antidumping or countervailing duties at rates equal to the cash deposit of estimated antidumping or countervailing duties required on the relevant entries.

[11]   In administrative reviews, imports covered by the period under review are imports that entered the United States during the 12 to 18 months prior to the initiation of the review. The Department of Commerce does not issue its final determination in the administrative review until 12 to 18 months after the end of the review period.

dumping or countervailing duty laws or regulations may be different from the interpretation it applied in the original investigation or in previous administrative reviews.

2.8   At the conclusion of the administrative review, the Department of Commerce instructs the US Customs Service to assess definitive antidumping and countervailing duties in accordance with the determination of the Department of Commerce. To the extent that the definitive duties owed are less than the level of the cash deposits paid as security, any excess plus interest is returned to the importer. To the extent that the definitive liability is greater than the cash deposits, the importer must pay that additional amount.

III.   MAIN ARGUMENTS OF THE PARTIES

3.1   The main arguments, presented by the parties in their written submissions, oral statements, and in their written replies to written questions, are summarized below.

A.   Canada

3.2   This section summarizes the main arguments of **Canada**, i.e., the complaining party in this case.

1.   Introduction

3.3   Canada considers that the measure at issue in this dispute - section 129(c)(1) of the URAA - is inconsistent with the obligations of the United States under Article VI of the GATT 1994, the AD Agreement, the SCM Agreement, and the WTO Agreement.

3.4   The effect of section 129(c)(1) on imports subject to potential duty liability requires an understanding of certain procedural aspects of the US system of antidumping and countervailing duty assessment. Accordingly, Canada first discusses the US duty assessment system in order to provide context for understanding section 129(c)(1). Canada subsequently addresses the operation and substantive requirements of section 129(c)(1).

2.   Description of Section 129(c)(1) of the URAA

3.5   Section 129 of the URAA sets forth procedures under US law for the United States to comply with adverse DSB rulings concerning its obligations under the Agreement on Safeguards, the AD Agreement and the SCM Agreement in cases in which implementation can be achieved by administrative action without the need for statutory amendment.

3.6   Where a DSB ruling finds that an action by the ITC contravenes the obligations of the United States under the AD Agreement or the SCM Agreement, the USTR, pursuant to section 129(a)(1), "may request the Commission to issue an advisory report on whether Title VII of the Tariff Act of 1930 [...] permits the Commission to take steps [...] that would render its action not inconsistent with the findings of the panel or the Appellate Body". If the ITC issues a report confirming that it can rectify its actions in accordance with US law, section 129 then authorizes the USTR to request that the ITC issue a new determination to bring its actions into conformity with the findings of the DSB ruling. Absent such direction from the USTR, the ITC has no independent authority to revise its determination to make it "not inconsistent with" an adverse DSB ruling. In making its new determination, the ITC could (i) issue a new affirmative injury finding, or (ii) issue a new negative injury determination (finding no injury to a domestic industry) depending on which result was required to achieve compliance with the DSB ruling. Where the ITC makes a negative injury finding, under section 129(a)(6) the USTR may direct the Department of Commerce "to revoke the antidumping or countervailing duty order in whole or in part".

3.7   Where the DSB ruling finds that an action by the Department of Commerce is not in conformity with the obligations of the United States under the AD Agreement or the SCM Agreement, the USTR, pursuant to section 129(b)(1), must consult with the Department of Commerce and the relevant congressional committees on the matter. Section 129(b)(2) requires that, upon the request of the USTR, the Department of Commerce shall issue a new, WTO-consistent determination. Thereafter, pursuant to section 129(b)(4), the USTR may direct the Department of Commerce to implement, in whole or in part, its new determination.

3.8   Implementation of the new Department of Commerce antidumping or countervailing duty determination could result in (i) a new affirmative determination, or (ii) revocation of the original order if the Department of Commerce made a finding that there was no dumping or subsidization to support the original order. A new affirmative determination would set a new cash deposit rate for future entries. Revocation of an order would occur where the new determination results in negative findings with respect to dumping or subsidies to be offset. A new order would reflect any new cash deposit rate established.

3.9   The effect of section 129(c)(1) is that an original order is revoked or amended with respect to new entries imported into the United States on or after the date USTR directs implementation of a new determination (hereafter the "Implementation Date") but not in respect of prior unliquidated entries (that is, imports that entered the United States prior to the date on which the USTR directs implementation of a new determination pursuant to section 129(a)(6) or section 129(b)(4) of the URAA and in respect of which the Department of Commerce has not made a definitive determination of liability for antidumping or countervailing duties and directed the US Customs Service to liquidate those entries). Furthermore, with respect to new affirmative determinations, the new cash deposit rate will only be applied to future entries.

3.10   The Statement of Administrative Action ("SAA"), which accompanies the URAA, explains the result in greater detail. It states:

"[...] subsection 129(c)(1) provides that where determinations by the ITC or Commerce are implemented under subsections (a) or (b), such determinations have prospective effect only. That is, they apply to unliquidated entries of merchandise entered, or withdrawn from warehouse, for consumption on or after the date on which the Trade Representative directs implementation. Thus, *relief available under subsection 129(c)(1) is distinguishable from relief available in an action brought before a court or a NAFTA binational panel*, where, depending on the circumstances of the case, retroactive relief may be available. Under 129(c)(1), *if implementation of a WTO report should result in the revocation of an antidumping or countervailing duty order, entries made prior to the date of Trade Representative's direction would remain subject to potential duty liability.*"[12]

3.11   The SAA specifically addresses the situation where an antidumping or countervailing duty order is revoked based on a new determination by either the Department of Commerce or the ITC (i.e, based on negative injury, dumping or subsidy findings). It explains that "if implementation of a WTO report should result in the revocation of an [...] order, [unliquidated] entries made prior to the date of [the USTR's] direction [to implement] would remain subject to potential duty liability."[13] Thus the SAA confirms that: (1) the administrative review procedure for prior unliquidated entries will continue pursuant to an order that was found not to have been supported by WTO-consistent affirmative determinations of injury, dumping or subsidization and has been revoked; and (2) duty liability for these entries will be determined by the Department of Commerce without regard to the new WTO-consistent determination.

3.12   In some circumstances, following an adverse DSB ruling, the new determination may reflect a revised methodology (e.g., for calculating dumping duties or measuring a subsidy) and a new margin of dumping or rate of subsidy. Unless the final results of an administrative review for prior unliquidated entries establish duty liability at or below the rate established in the new determination, the United States would subject importers to greater liability than would be due under the new determination.

3.13   This necessarily means that the US Customs Service will retain certain cash deposits made by an importer pending an administrative review and that prior unliquidated entries will remain subject to excessive liability in a subsequent administrative review notwithstanding that there is no basis under the AD Agreement or the SCM Agreement for the Department of Commerce to take action against entries based upon an order which has been revoked or amended.

> 3.   *Section 129(c)(1) is Inconsistent with the United States' Obligations Under the AD Agreement, the SCM*

---

[12]   Statement of Administrative Action, *supra*, p. 1026 (emphasis added).
[13]   *Ibid.*

Agreement, Article VI of the GATT 1994 and Article XVI:4 of the WTO Agreement

(a)   Antidumping Cases

3.14   Section 129(c)(1) of the URAA violates Articles 1, 9.3, 11.1 and 18.1 of the AD Agreement and Articles VI:2 and VI:6(a) of the GATT 1994 by requiring the Department of Commerce to make administrative review determinations and to assess antidumping duties on prior unliquidated entries after the Implementation Date notwithstanding that the elements needed for the United States to make a finding of injurious dumping and to levy duties as provided in the original determination are no longer present.

3.15   Article VI:2 states that "[i]n order to offset or prevent dumping, a contracting party may levy on any dumped product an anti-dumping duty not greater in amount than the margin of dumping in respect of such product [...]". Thus, the imposition of antidumping duties exceeding the margin of dumping is inconsistent with Article VI:2. Article VI:6(a) precludes the levying of antidumping duties absent a determination that the imports concerned cause or threaten to cause material injury or materially retard the establishment of a domestic industry.

3.16   Article 1 of the AD Agreement requires that antidumping measures must meet the dumping and injury conditions of Article VI of the GATT 1994 and must be applied "pursuant to investigations initiated and conducted in accordance with the provisions of this Agreement." Consequently any antidumping duty must only be applied in those circumstances in which injury, dumping and causation determinations necessary to impose that duty are made in accordance with the AD Agreement. This requirement is supported by Article 9.1 of the AD Agreement which states that the "decision whether or not to impose an antidumping duty" and the "decision whether the amount of the anti-dumping duty to be imposed shall be the full margin of dumping or less" are left to the discretion of the Member. Article 18.1 states that "[n]o specific action against dumping of exports from another Member can be taken except in accordance with the provisions of the GATT 1994, as interpreted by this Agreement." As Article VI is the only provision in the GATT 1994 that specifically addresses dumping actions, both Articles 1 and 18.1 of the AD Agreement preclude a Member from taking action against dumping except in accordance with Article VI.

3.17   Accordingly, Articles 1 and 18.1 of the AD Agreement and Article VI:2 and VI:6(a) of the GATT 1994, read together with Article 9.1 of the AD Agreement, preclude a Member from (i) applying antidumping duties in the absence of a finding of injurious dumping in accordance with the provisions of the AD Agreement, and (ii) taking action against imports from another Member in an amount in excess of an amount equal to the margin of dumping determined in accordance with the AD Agreement. These provisions are violated by section 129(c)(1) by its requirement of the continued application (to prior unliquidated entries after the Implementation Date) of antidumping duty orders that have been either amended or revoked by the Department of Commerce. Where the Department of Commerce implements a new determination by revoking an order imposing potential duty liability on imports under section 129(a)(6) or under section 129(b)(4), it does so because the ITC made a negative injury determination or the Department of Commerce concluded that no dumping existed. In such circumstances, Articles 1 and 18.1 preclude the United States from applying a duty pursuant to the original determination because the requirements of Article VI:2 and VI:6(a) are not met. Similarly, if the Department of Commerce, in implementing a new determination pursuant to section 129(b)(4), were to amend an order imposing potential duty liability, it would do so because the new determination has established that the margin of dumping is lower or higher than the margin of dumping as established in the original determination. In such a situation, Articles 1 and 18.1 preclude the United States from taking "specific action against dumping" pursuant to the original determination because the requirement in Article VI:2 that the duty not exceed the margin of dumping is not met.

3.18   Article 9.3 states in part that "[t]he amount of anti-dumping duty shall not exceed the margin of dumping as established under Article 2" of the AD Agreement. Thus, Members may not impose duties that exceed the margin of dumping.

3.19   Article 11.1 states that "[a]n anti-dumping duty shall remain in force only as long as and to the extent necessary to counteract dumping which is causing injury". Accordingly, unless a Member can establish that the dumping in respect of which the antidumping duty was imposed continues to cause injury, there is no basis for that Member to continue to impose the duty.

(b)   Subsidy Cases

3.20   Section 129(c)(1) of the URAA also violates Articles 10, 19.4, 21.1 and 32.1 of the SCM Agreement, as well as Articles VI:3 and VI:6(a) of the GATT 1994, by requiring the Department of Commerce to make determinations regarding subsidization and impose final countervailing duties on prior unliquidated entries after the Implementation Date notwithstanding that the elements needed for the United States to make a finding of injurious subsidization and to levy duties as provided for in the original determination are no longer present.

3.21   Article VI:3 of the GATT 1994 provides that "[n]o countervailing duty shall be levied on any product [...] in excess of an amount equal to the estimated bounty or subsidy determined to have been granted." Pursuant to Article VI:6(a), a Member shall levy a countervailing duty on imports only if it determines "that the effect of the [...] subsidization [...] is such as to cause or threaten material injury to an established domestic industry, or is such as to retard materially the establishment of a domestic industry".

3.22   Articles 10 and 32.1 of the SCM Agreement must be read together with Article VI of the GATT 1994. Article 10 of the SCM Agreement provides that "Members shall take all necessary steps to ensure that the imposition of a countervailing duty on any product of the territory of any Member imported into the territory of another Member is in accordance with the provisions of Article VI of the GATT 1994 and the terms of this Agreement [...]". Article 32.1 of the SCM

Agreement states that "[n]o specific action against a subsidy of another Member can be taken except in accordance with the provisions of the GATT 1994, as interpreted by this Agreement". Thus, Articles 10 and 32.1 of the SCM Agreement and Article VI of the GATT 1994, read together, provide that a Member (i) may only take action if it determines that the effect of subsidization of imports is to cause or threaten to cause material injury to its domestic industry; and (ii) may not take action against imports from another Member in an amount in excess of an amount equal to the subsidy granted to those imports.

3.23   After a Member makes determinations of subsidization and injury, that Member may not levy a countervailing duty in excess of the amount of the subsidy. Article 19.4 of the SCM Agreement states that "[n]o countervailing duty shall be levied on any imported product in excess of the amount of subsidy found to exist, calculated in terms of subsidization per unit of the subsidized and exported product".

3.24   The requirement that the Department of Commerce continue to levy duties pursuant to the original order in administrative reviews also violates Article 21.1 of the SCM Agreement, which provides that "a countervailing duty shall remain in force only as long as and to the extent necessary to counteract subsidization which is causing injury" to a domestic industry. Accordingly, unless a Member can establish that injurious subsidization exists, there is no basis for that Member to continue to impose a duty. In circumstances in which the original order has been revoked, there is no basis on which the Department of Commerce could rule that the continued determinations of subsidization and the assessment of countervailing duties pursuant to that order is necessary, as is required pursuant to Article 21.1 of the SCM Agreement. In other cases, where the Department of Commerce has determined that there is a lower level of subsidization than originally established, section 129(c)(1) prevents the Department of Commerce from taking this new determination into account in respect of prior unliquidated entries.

3.25   Given the violations demonstrated by Canada of GATT Article VI and the provisions cited in the AD Agreement and the SCM Agreement, section 129(c)(1) is also inconsistent with Article 18.4 of the AD Agreement, Article 32.5 of the SCM Agreement and Article XVI:4 of the WTO Agreement. These provisions require that a Member's laws be in conformity with its WTO obligations as of the entry into force of the WTO Agreement.

4.   *Section 129(c)(1) Mandates a Violation of the WTO Obligations of the United States*

3.26   In its Second Submission, the United States raised a new defence. The United States claimed that section 129(c)(1) does not mandate a violation of the provisions of the AD Agreement, the SCM Agreement, the GATT 1994 and the WTO Agreement cited by Canada.

3.27   Canada suggests that, even if the Panel were to accept the United States' description of its laws, section 129(c)(1) would continue to mandate that the United States violate its WTO obligations in certain significant circumstances.

3.28   There are four key points that are relevant to the mandatory/discretionary doctrine in WTO and GATT jurisprudence and practice:

(a)   first, a member may challenge another Member's measure "as such", independent of any particular application of that measure;

(b)   second, a measure that is challenged "as such" is not inconsistent with a Member's WTO obligations unless it mandates that the Member take action inconsistent with those obligations;

(c)   third, a Member's measure need not mandate a violation in all circumstances to be inconsistent, as such, with that Member's WTO obligations; rather, it is sufficient that the measure mandate a violation in some circumstances; and

(d)   fourth, where the parties have disputed whether a measure mandates a violation of WTO rules, the practice of WTO panels has been to first determine the Member's obligations under the WTO Agreement and thereafter to determine whether the measure at issue contains sufficient discretion such that a violation of the Member's WTO obligations is not mandated in any circumstances.[14]

3.29   The mandatory nature of section 129(c)(1) can be demonstrated by considering two classes of cases – that is, methodology cases (those cases in which the implementation by the United States of an adverse DSB ruling does not require that the Department of Commerce revoke an antidumping or countervailing duty order but instead requires the Department of Commerce to make some change or amendment, such as a change in its methodology) and revocation cases (cases in which implementation of an adverse DSB ruling requires the Department of Commerce to revoke an antidumping or countervailing duty order).

3.30   Canada notes that the United States has not claimed that section 129(c)(1) would in no circumstances have the effect of precluding its implementation of the DSB ruling with respect to prior unliquidated entries. Indeed, the United States has conceded that prior unliquidated entries are subject to "potential duty liability" notwithstanding the revocation of an antidumping or countervailing duty order with respect to future entries.

3.31   The United States argues that section 129(c)(1) would not preclude the Department of Commerce from making final duty liability determinations in an administrative review on a basis consistent with a DSB ruling in *methodology cases*, even insofar as the determinations would apply to prior unliquidated entries. However, the US claim that the Department of Commerce has "administra-

---

[14]   See, for example, Panel Report, *United States - Measures Treating Export Restraints as Subsidies* ("*US - Export Restraints*"), WT/DS194/R and Corr.2, adopted 23 August 2001, DSR 2001:XI, 5767.

tive discretion" to change its interpretation is inconsistent with US principles of statutory construction, as well as the wording of the SAA.

3.32   As Canada understands US principles of statutory construction, the issue of whether the limitation in section 129(c)(1) could be nullified or ignored by the Department of Commerce in a subsequent administrative review would ultimately be decided by the US courts, and not by the Department of Commerce. As US courts have explained, a court "cannot presume that Congress intended [one result] with one hand, while reducing it to a veritable nullity with the other".[15] For this reason, US courts would be unlikely to afford deference to the Department of Commerce's interpretation of section 129(c)(1) in a subsequent administrative review. Although "[j]udicial deference to agency [Department of Commerce] interpretation is normally justified by the agency's expertise in the regulated subject matter [if the] issue is a pure question of statutory construction [it is an issue] for the courts to decide".[16]

3.33   The United States also argues that section 129(c)(1) has no effect with regard to any determinations made in another "segment" of the proceeding, particularly the definitive determination of duty liability made following an administrative review. However, this argument is contrary to the US principles of statutory construction.. Section 129(c)(1) states that determinations under section 129 shall apply with respect to entries on or after the Implementation Date. This would appear to preclude the Department of Commerce from taking action after the Implementation Date under section 129 consistent with a new determination in a subsequent separate segment of the proceeding with respect to prior unliquidated entries. Further, this argument is inconsistent with the SAA which states clearly, at page 1026, that the DSB ruling will not be implemented with regard to prior unliquidated entries.

3.34   The Department of Commerce, by complying with an adverse DSB ruling with respect to definitive duty determinations made after the Implementation Date for prior unliquidated entries, would materially undermine the wording in section 129(c)(1) and the SAA, which affirms that determinations to implement DSB rulings have prospective effect only. It seems unlikely that the US Congress would have created the limitation in section 129(c)(1) merely to permit the temporary retention of excess cash deposits that would be returned at the end of the

---

[15]   *Katie John* v. *United States*, 247 F.3d 1032, 1038 (9ᵗʰ Cir. 2001) ("*Katie John*") citing *Johnson* v. *United States R.R. Retirement Board*, 969 F.2d 1082, 1089 (D.C. Cir. 1992), which found that it was "unreasonable to conclude that Congress meant to create an entitlement with one hand and snatch it away with the other". See also *American Tobacco Co.* v. *Patterson*, 456 US 63, 71 (April 5, 1982) which stated that "[s]tatutes should be interpreted to avoid untenable distinctions and unreasonable results whenever possible".

[16]   *Katie John* at 1038 citing *Pension Benefit Guar. Corp.* v. *LTV Corp.*, 496 US 633, 651-2 (1990) which stated that "[a]gency expertise is one of the principal justifications behind Chevron defence"; *INS* v. *Cardoza-Fonseca* 480 US 421, 446 (1987), which stated that the issue "is a pure question of statutory construction for the courts to decide"; *Chevron, U.S.A., Inc.* v. *Natural Resources Defense Council, Inc.*, 467 US 837, 843 n. 9, which stated "[t]he judiciary is the final authority on issues of statutory construction; *Magana-Pizano* v. *INS*, 200 F.3d 603, 611 n. 11 (9ᵗʰ Cir. 1999), which stated that "[b]ecause the issue presented is a question of pure law and does not implicate agency expertise in any meaningful way, we need not defer under Chevron [...]."

administrative review process. Finally, the US assertion that the Department of Commerce could circumvent the limitation in section 129(c)(1) by using its 'administrative discretion' has not been tested in the US courts or in the Department of Commerce's administrative practice.

3.35   In *revocation cases*, a revocation of an order pursuant to section 129 will apply only to entries imported on or after the Implementation Date. The United States will retain the cash deposits with respect to the prior unliquidated entries, which will continue to be the subject of an administrative review. In conceding these points, the United States nevertheless argued that while the treatment to be accorded to prior unliquidated entries in a subsequent administrative review is uncertain, section 129(c)(1) nonetheless does not mandate treatment inconsistent with the United States' WTO obligations.

3.36   In cases in which compliance with a DSB ruling requires the Department of Commerce to revoke an order, the United States will be acting inconsistently with its WTO obligations by retaining cash deposits and holding administrative reviews of prior unliquidated entries. Further, even if the Department of Commerce, at the conclusion of the administrative review, were to terminate the order and return the cash deposits for entries (which is not provided for under US law), the United States will have acted inconsistently with its obligations under the AD Agreement and the SCM Agreement.

3.37   The United States has effectively conceded that, in cases in which compliance with a DSB ruling results in a new negative injury determination by the ITC, section 129(c)(1) precludes all but the occasional possibility of "accidental compliance". In a negative injury case, the antidumping or countervailing duty order would be revoked for all entries on or after the Implementation Date, but not for prior unliquidated entries. Based on the ITC determination, the Department of Commerce would terminate the order and issue instruction ending the requirement for cash deposits and bonds with respect to future entries but, because of section 129(c)(1), cash deposits for prior unliquidated entries would be retained. The United States provided no justification for making this distinction in a determination made by the Department of Commerce after the Implementation Date.

3.38   Further, the United States did not claim that section 129(c)(1) would never preclude the Department of Commerce from making determinations in administrative reviews consistently with the DSB ruling. Rather, the United States made a narrower claim that it is not obliged to implement a DSB ruling with respect to substantive duty determinations made after the Implementation Date with respect to prior unliquidated entries and, further, that section 129(c)(1) does not mandate a violation of its WTO obligations.

3.39   However, the US argument that section 129(c)(1) does not mandate violations of its WTO obligations is based on the United States' erroneous interpretation of its WTO obligations. The AD Agreement, the SCM Agreement, the GATT 1994, the WTO Agreement and the DSU do not authorize violations of the sort to which the United States tries to claim a right in defence of section 129(c)(1). Neither the DSU nor the principle of prospective compliance excuse the United States from complying with an adverse DSB ruling in determining duty liability after the Implementation Date with respect to prior unliquidated entries.

3.40   At most, the United States has asserted that the Department of Commerce might have some flexibility in circumventing the limitation in section 129(c)(1) in certain cases (for example, a change of interpretation of US law for other reasons, such as a direction from a US court). However, even if the Panel were to accept this US argument, section 129(c)(1) still mandates violations of the WTO obligations of the United States by (i) requiring the Department of Commerce to retain cash deposits and to conduct administrative reviews in circumstances inconsistent with the obligations of the United States under the AD Agreement and the SCM Agreement; and (ii) precluding the Department of Commerce from making final duty determinations consistent with the United States' WTO obligations as found by the DSB with respect to prior unliquidated entries.

5.   The Principle of Prospective Compliance

3.41   The fundamental issue in this case is what constitutes prospective compliance. Canada and the United States agree on the principle of prospective implementation of DSB rulings, but disagree on the meaning and application of prospective implementation in this case. In particular, Canada and the United States disagree whether the principle permits a Member to take WTO-inconsistent actions after the Implementation Date.

3.42   Canada is *not* seeking to have the Department of Commerce apply new section 129 determinations to liquidated entries.[17] This would be asking the United States to undo definitive duty determinations; clearly, this would be the retroactive application of an adverse DSB ruling. Rather, Canada considers that the principle of prospective implementation requires that definitive duty determinations made by a Member after the date established under the DSU for implementation of an adverse DSB ruling must be consistent with that ruling.

3.43   The United States argued that it is entitled to make determinations after the Implementation Date on a basis inconsistent with an adverse DSB ruling if those determinations affect prior unliquidated entries. By maintaining that the date of entry governs the application of the new WTO-consistent determinations of the ITC or the Department of Commerce, the United States claims the right to conduct administrative reviews and to make final legal determinations of duty liability for prior unliquidated entries on a WTO-inconsistent basis for months, and perhaps years, after the Implementation Date.

3.44   Canada sees no basis for this in the DSU or in the GATT/WTO tradition of prospective implementation. Section 129(c)(1) prevents the Department of Commerce from applying new section 129 determinations to prior unliquidated entries, which, as discussed above, violates the United States' obligations under

---

[17]   That is, entries for which, prior to the Implementation Date, the Department of Commerce made definitive duty determinations and instructed the US Customs Service to liquidate.

Article VI of the the GATT 1994, the AD Agreement and the SCM Agreement, as well as Article XVI:4 of the WTO Agreement.

3.45   In support of its position, the United States relied on various DSU provisions, cases and statements. However, none of these support the US proposition that prospective compliance is defined in terms of date of entry of imports, or the US argument that determinations made by the Department of Commerce after the Implementation Date are excused from compliance with an adverse DSB ruling with respect to prior unliquidated entries.

3.46   The principles enunciated in the report of the Appellate Body in *Brazil – Export Financing Programme for Aircraft – Recourse by Canada to Article 21.5 of the DSU*[18] are relevant. In that proceeding, Brazil argued that it should be free to continue to provide export subsidies on exports of aircraft made after the Implementation Date to the extent that it was implementing legal commitments entered into before the Implementation Date to provide subsidies on exports after the Implementation Date. The Appellate Body clearly stated that the issuance of bonds after the end of the reasonable period of time, on the same terms and conditions which had been previously found inconsistent with the SCM Agreement, was not consistent with Brazil's obligation to withdraw the illegal subsidies.[19]

3.47   In this case, the United States is trying to justify WTO-inconsistent action that it will take after the Implementation Date on grounds that the trade affected by its actions (namely, the prior unliquidated entries) occurs before the Implementation Date. Canada submits that this dispute presents a more serious case of infringement of WTO obligations than in *Brazil – Aircraft (Article 21.5 – Canada)* because new legal acts by the Department of Commerce and the ITC are at issue. Canada also submits that the reasoning in *Brazil – Aircraft (Article 21.5 – Canada)* applies in this case, and that the right claimed by the United States to conduct administrative reviews and make definitive legal determinations after the Implementation Date with respect to prior unliquidated entries has no basis in the WTO Agreement or any of the covered agreements.

3.48   In Canada's view, the principle of prospective implementation does not justify the United States making legal determinations after the Implementation Date on a WTO-inconsistent basis. The logical outcome of prospective implementation of an adverse DSB ruling in a retrospective duty assessment system is for the United States to apply new section 129 determinations to all prior unliquidated entries as well as future entries.

3.49   The principle of prospective implementation does not justify the United States continuing to make definitive duty determinations after the Implementa-

---

[18]   Appellate Body Report, *Brazil – Export Financing Programme for Aircraft – Recourse by Canada to Article 21.5 of the DSU* ("*Brazil – Aircraft (Article 21.5 – Canada)*"), WT/DS46/AB/RW, adopted 4 August 2000, DSR 2000:VIII, 4067, para. 46.
[19]   The Panel report is also relevant. The Panel stated that "[i]n our view, the obligation to cease performing illegal acts in the future is a fundamentally prospective remedy". See Panel Report, *Brazil – Export Financing Programme for Aircraft – Recourse by Canada to Article 21.5 of the DSU* ("*Brazil – Aircraft (Article 21.5 – Canada)*"), WT/DS46/RW, adopted 4 August 2000, as modified by the Appellate Body Report, WT/DS46/AB/RW, DSR 2000:IX, 4093, para. 6.15.

tion Date in respect of prior unliquidated entries on a WTO-inconsistent bases for months, or perhaps years, after the date on which it purportedly brought its measure into conformity with its WTO obligations. The United States has attempted to portray itself as the victim in this case. However, the United States is not being deprived of a right under the DSU or any other WTO agreement. Instead, the United States is seeking additional rights not provided in the WTO Agreement or the covered agreements, including the DSU.

3.50   In response to question 71 from the Panel, Canada suggested that the United States cannot apply a WTO-consistent methodology to prior unliquidated entries after the Implementation Date without refunding excess cash deposits. If the United States were to fail to refund excess cash deposits, the United States would violate both its domestic law and its WTO obligations.

3.51   First, under US law, cash deposits are considered as security against the final determination of liability. Where the final duty liability is less than the cash deposit, the difference must be refunded under US law. Sections 1671f and 1673f of the Tariff Act of 1930 provide for the refund of estimated antidumping and countervailing duty deposits which are in excess of the final determined duty liability.

3.52   Second, if the Department of Commerce was able to apply a new, WTO-consistent methodology to prior unliquidated entries which resulted in a final antidumping or countervailing duty that is lower than the cash deposits collected on the prior unliquidated entries, the United States would be required under WTO law to refund the excess cash deposits.[20] If the United States did not refund the excess cash deposits, the United States would violate its WTO obligations, in particular Article VI:2 and Article VI:3 of the GATT 1994, Articles 1 and 18.1 of the AD Agreement and Articles 10, 19.4 and 32.1 of the SCM Agreement.

3.53   Canada recalls that, in its view, the final legal determinations of duty liability established by the Department of Commerce after the Implementation Date must be in conformity with the adverse DSB ruling. The consequence of this is that, once the final amount of duty liability of entries has been established in an administrative review, any excess cash deposits collected in respect of those entries must be refunded by the United States. This is also consistent with the principle of prospective implementation of DSB rulings as applied by the Appellate Body in *Brazil – Aircraft (Article 21.5 – Canada)*.

3.54   In response to question 74 from the Panel, Canada expressed the view that in certain situations section 129(c)(1) results in the retention by the Department of Commerce of cash deposits for prior unliquidated entries in circumstances in which such retention is not justified in whole or in part. That is, the operation of section 129(c)(1) results in the retention by the Department of Commerce of cash deposits for prior unliquidated entries notwithstanding that (i) the ITC or the Department of Commerce makes a new determination which results in a revoca-

---

[20]   Canada recalls that it is not persuaded that the Department of Commerce could apply a new, WTO-consistent methodology to prior unliquidated entries in an administrative review held after the Implementation Date.

tion of the original antidumping or countervailing duty order, or (ii) the Department of Commerce makes a new determination amending the original antidumping or countervailing duty determination, which may result in a lower final antidumping duty or countervailing duty being assessed against those entries.

6. Differences Between Prospective and Retrospective Duty Assessment Systems

3.55 The United States argued that "[r]ecognizing the date of entry as the controlling date for determining the scope of a Member's implementation obligations in all cases avoids creating differences [between prospective and retrospective duty assessment systems] that are not contemplated in the Agreements".[21] However, Canada notes that the fact that the date of entry is the relevant date under a prospective duty assessment system for the purposes of determining final duty assessment is irrelevant to this case. Under the US retrospective duty assessment system, the end of the administrative review process is the relevant date for the purposes of determining final duty assessment.

3.56 Prospective and retrospective duty assessment systems are different approaches to determining antidumping and countervailing duty liability under the AD Agreement and the SCM Agreement. These differences give rise to certain advantages and disadvantages unique to each system. However, regardless of whether a Member chooses a retrospective or prospective duty assessment system, the Member must abide by its WTO obligations. The provisions of the AD Agreement, the SCM Agreement and the GATT 1994 are equally applicable to retrospective and prospective duty assessment systems. A Member must accept the consequences of whichever duty assessment system it chooses to adopt. A Member cannot argue, as the United States has done, that its retrospective duty assessment system permits it to make final duty determinations without regard to an adverse DSB ruling, in violation of its WTO obligations.

3.57 The United States asserted that Canada was advocating that Members with retrospective duty assessment systems be treated less favourably than Members with prospective duty assessment systems. The United States also stated that Canada was arguing that, unlike Members with retrospective duty assessment systems, "Members with prospective systems do not have an obligation to apply adverse DSB recommendations and rulings when conducting [...] reviews of pre-implementation entries."[22]

3.58 However, the United States has deliberately misconstrued Canada's argument. Canada is not arguing for a "special rule" in which only a Member with a retrospective duty assessment system must make determinations after the Implementation Date consistent with its WTO obligations. Canada accepts that a Member with a prospective duty assessment system has the same obligation. It is Canada's position that, notwithstanding the temporal differences in the making of

---

[21] US reply to Panel Question 17.
[22] US Second Submission, para. 27.

substantive duty determinations under a retrospective or a prospective duty assessment system, where a Member has agreed to implement an adverse DSB ruling, it must make all subsequent substantive duty determinations in accordance with that ruling following the expiration of the reasonable period of time.[23]

3.59   The United States also incorrectly implied that Canada would not implement an adverse DSB ruling in making a duty determination after the expiration of the reasonable period of time.[24] Canada considers that a Member, whether employing a prospective or retrospective duty assessment system, is not required to undo final duty determinations made before the expiration of the reasonable period of time. However, a redetermination made after the Implementation Date must be made in conformity with the DSB ruling notwithstanding that the redetermination would affect entries subject to a final determination made prior to the expiration of the reasonable period of time.[25]

7.   Date of Definitive Duty Determination and Not Date of Entry of Imports is the Operative Date for Determining Compliance

3.60   The United States argues that the date of entry of imports - and not the date of the definitive duty determination - is the operative date for determining prospective compliance. In essence, the United States argues that, having been found by the DSB to have violated its WTO obligations, it should be allowed to make duty determinations after the Implementation Date in a WTO-inconsistent manner.

3.61   The United States appeared to imply that the Department of Commerce's final determination of duty liability on imports was akin to a clerical act. This argument, however, disregards the importance of the administrative review process, which involves hearings, briefs and legal determinations. First, the law applied by the Department of Commerce in the administrative review process will reflect changes in policies and legal principles between the time of the original entry of imports and the time that the Department of Commerce makes its final definitive duty determination for those imports. Second, the substantive method-

---

[23]   Section 76.1 of Canada's Special Import Measures Act (the "SIMA") which provides the authority and procedure for the implementation of adverse DSB rulings, is the Canadian counterpart to section 129 of the URAA. Where section 76.1 of the SIMA has been invoked by Canada to implement a DSB ruling, substantive duty determinations after the expiration of the reasonable period of time would be made in compliance with that ruling.

[24]   US Second Submission, para. 26.

[25]   Canada's obligation under Article 9.3.2 of the AD Agreement to make provision for "prompt refund, upon request, of any duty paid in excess of the margin of dumping" is implemented in sections 57 to 59 of the SIMA. These sections provide for a redetermination of final duty liability so as to ensure that any antidumping or countervailing duty collected on goods does not exceed the actual margin of dumping or amount of subsidization for those goods. Section 60 of the SIMA provides that the "excessive" duty is to be returned forthwith to the importer. Unlike section 129(c)(1) of the URAA, there is nothing in section 76.1 or section 57 to 60 of SIMA to prevent Canada from making a redetermination after the expiration of the reasonable period of time which affects entries that occurred before that date.

ology used by the Department of Commerce in making its final definitive duty determination may be quite different from that applied in the original investigation or in previous administrative reviews.

3.62   The United States also attempted to minimize the significance of the legal and factual distinctions between cash deposits and definitive duty determinations.[26] However, under US law, the publication of an antidumping or countervailing duty order is merely the first step toward the final assessment of duties to be collected; the final assessment of those duties takes place in a subsequent administrative review where the final liability for payment of duties is determined and liquidation is carried out. Accordingly, the date of the definitive duty determination - and not the date of entry of imports - is the operative date for determining whether a Member with a retrospective duty assessment system has complied with its WTO obligations.

8.   Conclusion

3.63   Therefore, for the reasons set out above, Canada requests that the Panel:

(a)   find that section 129(c)(1) of the URAA is inconsistent with:

(i)   Article VI:2, VI:3 and VI:6(a) of the GATT 1994,

(ii)   Articles 1, 9.3, 11.1 and 18.1 and 18.4 of the AD Agreement,

(iii)   Articles 10, 19.4, 21.1, 32.1 and 32.5 of the SCM Agreement, and

(iv)   Article XVI:4 of the WTO Agreement, and

(b)   recommend that the United States bring section 129(c)(1) of the URAA into conformity with the SCM Agreement, the AD Agreement, the GATT 1994, and the WTO Agreement.

B.   United States

3.64   This section summarizes the main arguments of the **United States**, i.e., the responding party in this case.

1.   Introduction

3.65   In this dispute, Canada challenges section 129(c)(1) of the URAA as inconsistent with the WTO obligations of the United States. This provision of US law was enacted with the specific purpose of enabling the United States to implement WTO panel or Appellate Body decisions which find that the United States has taken antidumping or countervailing duty actions inconsistent with the AD Agreement or the SCM Agreement. Consistent with well-established GATT and WTO practice, section 129(c)(1) provides for such implementation on a prospective basis.

---

[26]   US reply to Panel Question 15.

3.66   Canada is seeking to require the United States to provide retroactive relief in cases involving antidumping and countervailing duty measures, despite the widely accepted principle that the dispute settlement process established in the DSU provides for prospective remedies. It is doing so by attempting to exploit the fact that the United States uses a "retrospective" system for calculating the amount of liability that an importer must pay when it imports merchandise that, at the time of entry, is subject to an antidumping or countervailing duty order.

3.67   Nothing in the text of the WTO agreements requires anything other than prospective implementation of adverse WTO panel or Appellate Body reports (hereafter "adverse WTO reports"). Just as importantly, nothing in the Agreements requires Members to apply adverse WTO reports not only to entries that take place after implementation, but also to entries that took place prior to implementation. Section 129(c)(1) is fully consistent with the WTO obligations of the United States. It ensures implementation of adverse WTO reports on a prospective basis, consistently with the United States' WTO obligations.

3.68   In any event, there is no need for the Panel to determine what constitutes "prospective" implementation in disputes involving antidumping and countervailing duty measures. Regardless of whether there is an obligation to implement adverse WTO reports with respect to entries that occurred prior to implementation, Canada, as the complaining party in this dispute, must establish that section 129(c)(1) would preclude the United States from doing so. Canada has failed to meet its burden of proof.

2.   Description of Section 129(c)(1) of the URAA

3.69   As previously noted, section 129 was enacted with the specific purpose of enabling the United States to implement WTO panel or Appellate Body decisions which find that the United States has taken actions inconsistent with the AD Agreement or the SCM Agreement. Section 129 provides the basic legal provisions through which the United States would make and implement new antidumping or countervailing duty determinations consistent with an adverse WTO report.

3.70   Section 129(c)(1), the specific provision that Canada is challenging, provides an effective date for new determinations by the Department of Commerce or the ITC which implement adverse WTO reports. Specifically, section 129(c)(1) provides that such determinations "shall apply with respect to unliquidated entries of the subject merchandise [...] that are entered, or withdrawn from warehouse, for consumption on or after" the date on which the USTR directs the Department of Commerce to revoke an antidumping or countervailing duty order or implement the new Department of Commerce determination.

3. *Canada Has Failed to Establish that Section 129(c)(1) Mandates Action Inconsistent with WTO Rules*

(a) Canada Must Establish that Section 129(c)(1) Mandates Action that is Inconsistent with the United States' WTO Obligations

3.71 Canada has challenged section 129(c)(1) "as such." Accordingly, the burden is on Canada to demonstrate that section 129(c)(1) mandates WTO-inconsistent action. If section 129(c)(1) does not mandate such action or preclude WTO-consistent action, there is no need for the Panel to determine the meaning of "prospective" implementation in WTO disputes involving antidumping and countervailing duty measures, because even if Canada is correct in asserting that the legal situation in effect at the time of the "final" determination controls, section 129(c)(1) does not mandate how the Department of Commerce must make such determinations.

3.72 It is well established under GATT and WTO jurisprudence that legislation of a Member violates that Member's WTO obligations only if the legislation *mandates* action that is inconsistent with those obligations or *precludes* action that is consistent with those obligations. If the legislation provides discretion to administrative authorities to act in a WTO-consistent manner, the legislation, as such, does not violate a Member's WTO obligations. The Appellate Body has explained that this concept "was developed by a number of GATT panels as a threshold consideration in determining when legislation as such - rather than a specific application of that legislation - was inconsistent with a Contracting Party's GATT 1947 obligations."[27]

3.73 Canada has not identified a scenario, and the United States is not aware of a scenario, particularly in light of this abstract case, in which section 129(c)(1) would mandate WTO-inconsistent action or preclude the United States from acting in a WTO-consistent manner.

(b) The Meaning of Section 129(c)(1) Is a Factual Question That Must Be Answered by Applying US Principles of Statutory Interpretation

3.74 The meaning of section 129(c)(1) as a matter of US law is a factual question that must be answered by applying US principles of statutory construction. In this regard, US courts and agencies must recognize the longstanding and elementary principle of US statutory construction that "an act of Congress ought never to be construed to violate the law of nations if any other possible construction remains".[28] While international obligations cannot override inconsistent requirements of domestic law, "ambiguous statutory provisions [...][should] be

---

[27] Appellate Body Report, *United States - Anti-Dumping Act of 1916* ("*US − 1916 Act*"), WT/DS136/AB/R, WT/DS162/AB/R, adopted 26 September 2000, DSR 2000:X, 4793, para. 88.
[28] *Murray v. Schooner Charming Betsy*, 6 U.S. (2 Cranch) 64, 118 (1804).

construed, where possible, to be consistent with international obligations of the United States."[29]

<h2 style="text-align:center">(c)   Canada Misinterprets what Section 129(c)(1) Actually Requires</h2>

3.75   Canada has failed to establish a *prima facie* case that section 129(c)(1) mandates action inconsistent with the AD Agreement, the SCM Agreement, or the GATT 1994, or precludes action consistent with those provisions.

3.76   Canada's failure to meet its burden of proof arises from its misinterpretation of the term "determination" as that term is used in section 129(c)(1). When the term is properly understood, it becomes clear that section 129(c)(1) only addresses the application of the *particular determination issued under the authority of section 129(c)(1)* to entries made after the date of implementation, and only with respect to that particular segment of the proceeding.[30] Section 129(c)(1) does not address what actions the Department of Commerce may or may not take in a *separate* determination in a *separate* segment of the proceeding, and thus does not mandate that the Department of Commerce take (or preclude it from taking) any particular action in any separate segment of the proceeding. This point applies in both of the scenarios that Canada has identified - "methodology" cases and "revocation" cases.

3.77   This point can be illustrated in "*methodology*" cases by considering a situation where a Member challenges a final dumping determination in an investigation. If a challenge to such a determination were successful, the Department of Commerce would make the necessary changes in its methodologies and issue a new, WTO-consistent determination. It would then apply that new determination by setting a new cash deposit rate, which would apply to all entries that took place on or after the implementation date. It is this new determination that is the "determination" referenced in section 129(c)(1).

3.78   If a company were then to request an administrative review of what Canada terms "prior unliquidated entries," the Department of Commerce would conduct the administrative review and issue a new determination in that segment of the proceeding. Since the administrative review determination would not be the "determination implemented under section 129(c)(1)," nothing in section 129(c)(1) would preclude the Department of Commerce from applying its new, WTO-consistent methodologies in the administrative review. Canada is

---

[29]   Restatement (Third) of the Foreign Relations Law of the United States, § 114 (1987).

[30]   Section 351.102 of the Department of Commerce's regulations defines a segment of a proceeding as follows:

> (1) *In general.* An antidumping or countervailing duty proceeding consists of one or more *segments.* "Segment of a proceeding" or "segment of the proceeding" refers to a portion of the proceeding that is reviewable under section 516A of the Act.
>
> (2) *Examples.* An antidumping or countervailing duty investigation or a review of an order or suspended investigation, or a scope inquiry under § 351.225, each would constitute a segment of a proceeding.

simply wrong, as a matter of fact, to claim that section 129(c)(1) would preclude the Department of Commerce from doing so.

3.79   The Department of Commerce has the authority to alter its statutory interpretations or its methodologies used to implement those interpretations, provided that it gives a reasonable explanation for doing so.[31] In an administrative review, the Department of Commerce would have the authority to alter its statutory interpretation or methodology from one announced prior to the implementation of the WTO panel report, and use the same, WTO-consistent interpretation or methodology adopted in the section 129 determination.[32] This would not, however, be an application of the section 129 determination to what Canada has termed "prior unliquidated entries."

3.80   Canada concedes that US administering authorities have the legal ability to change their interpretations or applications of statutes and regulations from one review to another and even that the Department of Commerce could do so in response to a WTO report that did not involve the United States as a party. Canada concludes, however, by stating that the Department of Commerce's ability to alter its interpretations "cannot override a statutory limitation such as section 129(c)(1)."[33] Canada did not identify any statutory or other basis in support of its assertions that a determination implemented under section 129(c)(1) limits the Department of Commerce's discretion in any other segment of the proceeding.

3.81   Indeed, section B.1.c.(2) of the SAA specifically notes that "it may be possible to implement the WTO report recommendations *in a future administrative review* under section 751 of the Tariff Act [...]". (emphasis added.) This language demonstrates the error in Canada's assertions that section 129(c)(1) would preclude the Department of Commerce from applying a WTO-consistent methodology to what they term "prior unliquidated entries" in a subsequent administrative review.

3.82   Similarly, if the United States were to implement an adverse WTO report by *revoking* an antidumping or countervailing duty order, section 129(c)(1) would ensure that the revocation would apply to all entries which took place on or after the date of revocation of the order, so the Department of Commerce would instruct the US Customs Service to stop requiring cash deposits as of that date. In any subsequent administrative review, the Department of Commerce would need to decide what to do with respect to entries that took place prior to the date of revocation.

---

[31]   See *INS v. Yang*, 519 U.S. 26, 32 (1996); *Atchison, Topeka & Santa Fe Ry v. Wichita Board of Trade*, 412 U.S. 800, 808 (1973); *British Steel, PLC v. United States*, 127 F.3d 1471, 1475 (Fed. Cir. 1997).

[32]   Where the international obligations of the United States have been clarified, for example through the adoption by the DSB of rulings and recommendations in a WTO panel or Appellate Body report involving a US methodology, the *Charming Betsy* principle, that "an act of Congress ought never to be construed to violate the law of nations if any other possible construction remains," might be relied upon by the Department of Commerce as a reasonable explanation for a change in its methodology in an administrative review determination distinct from a section 129 determination.

[33]   Canada's reply to Panel Question 70.

3.83   Canada has not challenged an actual application of section 129(c)(1) in such a scenario, and the Department of Commerce has not addressed such a scenario to date. The only impact of section 129(c)(1), however, is that the Department of Commerce would not determine the fate of those entries *in the revocation determination itself.* Section 129(c)(1) does not require the Department of Commerce to apply duties to those entries, it does not limit the Department of Commerce's discretion in deciding how to administer the law in separate proceedings with respect to those entries, it does not limit judicial review of the results of those separate proceedings, and it does not limit the Department of Commerce's obligation to implement the results of any such judicial proceedings. Even taking into account the language in the SAA, the most that can be said is that such entries would "remain subject to potential duty liability." Neither section 129(c)(1) itself, nor the provision as interpreted in light of the SAA, mandates any particular treatment of such entries in a separate segment of the proceeding.

(d)   Conclusion

3.84   In view of the above, the United States considers that Canada has failed to establish that section 129(c)(1) mandates a breach of any of the provisions of the AD Agreement, the SCM Agreement, or the GATT 1994 that Canada cites or precludes the United States from acting consistently with those provisions.

4.   *Section 129(c)(1) Is Consistent with the DSU, which Requires Prospective Remedies when a Measure is Found Inconsistent with WTO Obligations*

3.85   Even if section 129(c)(1) did mandate how the Department of Commerce is to treat what Canada terms "prior unliquidated entries," section 129(c)(1) would not breach the WTO obligations of the United States, because the DSU provides for prospective implementation of adverse WTO reports, and Members are under no obligation to implement such reports with respect to pre-implementation entries.

(a)   The Principle of Prospective Remedies in the Dispute Settlement Process

3.86   Canada fails to address the obligations imposed by the DSU, having abandoned all DSU claims raised in its panel request. Canada's decision to abandon these claims is not surprising, given that an examination of these provisions reinforces the prospective nature of WTO remedies. The fact that Canada has made no claim under the DSU should be sufficient for the Panel to find that they have failed to make a *prima facie* case.

(i)   Textual Analysis of the DSU

3.87   Language used throughout the DSU demonstrates that when a Member's measure has been found to be inconsistent with a WTO Agreement, the Member's obligation extends only to providing prospective relief, and not to remedying past transgressions. For example, under Article 19.1 of the DSU, when it has found a measure to be inconsistent with a Member's WTO obligations a panel or the Appellate Body "shall recommend that the Member concerned *bring the measure into conformity with that Agreement.*" The ordinary meaning of the term "bring" is to "[p]roduce as a consequence," or "cause to become."[34] These definitions give a clear indication of future action, supporting the conclusion that the obligation of a Member whose measure has been found inconsistent with a WTO agreement is to ensure that the measure is removed or altered in a prospective manner, not to provide retroactive relief.

3.88   Article 3.7 of the DSU also supports the conclusion that the obligation to implement DSB recommendations is prospective in nature. Article 3.7 states, "In the absence of a mutually agreed solution, the first objective of the dispute settlement mechanism is usually to secure the withdrawal of the measures concerned if these are found to be inconsistent with the provisions of any of the covered agreements." The focus of WTO dispute settlement is on withdrawal of the *measure*, and not on providing compensation for the measure's past existence.

3.89   In a WTO case challenging an antidumping or countervailing duty measure, the measure in question is a border measure. Accordingly, revoking a WTO-inconsistent antidumping or countervailing duty measure prospectively will constitute "withdrawal" of the measure within the meaning of Article 3.7 of the DSU.

3.90   Article 21.3 of the DSU provides further support for this conclusion. Under Article 21.3, when immediate compliance is impracticable, Members shall have a reasonable period of time in which to bring their measure into conformity with their WTO obligations. Nothing in Article 21.3 suggests that Members are obliged, during the course of the reasonable period of time, to suspend application of the offending measure, much less to provide relief for past effects. Rather, in the case of antidumping and countervailing duty measures, entries that take place during the reasonable period of time may continue to be liable for the payment of duties.

3.91   Articles 22.1 and 22.2 of the DSU confirm not only that a Member may maintain the WTO-inconsistent measure until the end of the reasonable period of time for implementation, but also that neither compensation nor the suspension of concessions or other obligations are available to the complaining Member until the conclusion of that reasonable period of time. Thus, the DSU imposes no obligation on Members to cease application of the WTO-inconsistent measure on entries occurring prior to the end of the reasonable period of time.

---

[34]   The New Shorter Oxford English Dictionary, Clarendon Press, Oxford, 1993.

(ii)   Panel and Appellate Body Clarification of the DSU

3.92   WTO panel reports addressing the implementation obligations of Members following an adverse WTO report confirm that such decisions be implemented in a prospective manner. In *European Communities – Regime for the Importation, Sale and Distribution of Bananas – Recourse to Article 21.5 of the DSU by Ecuador*[35], the panel discussed the prospective nature of the recommendations a panel or the Appellate Body can make under the DSU, stating, "we do not imply that the EC is under an obligation to remedy past discrimination." Rather, the principle of Article 3.7 of the DSU "requires compliance *ex nunc* as of the expiry of the reasonable period of time for compliance with the recommendations and rulings adopted by the DSB." In identifying three possible methods by which the European Communities could bring the measure into conformity, none of them involved providing a remedy for past transgressions.[36]

3.93   When panels and the Appellate Body have been asked to make recommendations for retroactive relief, they have rejected those requests, recognizing that a Member's obligation under the DSU is to provide prospective relief in the form of withdrawing a measure inconsistent with a WTO agreement, or bringing that measure into conformity with the agreement by the end of the reasonable period of time. In the six years of dispute settlement under the WTO agreements, no panel or the Appellate Body has ever suggested that bringing a WTO-inconsistent antidumping or countervailing duty measure into conformity with a Member's WTO obligations requires the refund of antidumping or countervailing duties collected on merchandise that entered prior to the date of implementation.

3.94   Canada's views on prospective application have been consistent with this view that the DSU only provides for prospective relief. Consistent with the concerns raised by many other Members, Canada has asserted that if Members' obligations under the DSU were to be retroactive, the language would have been explicit because "it was a significant departure from previous practice [...]."[37]

3.95   This case is about the dispute settlement system. The fact that Canada has made no claim under the DSU is very telling; it highlights Canada's desire to avoid the well-accepted principle that the DSU does not require retroactive remedies. Section 129(c)(1) ensures that adverse WTO decisions will be implemented, in a prospective manner, in accordance with the requirements of the DSU.

---

[35]   Panel Report, *European Communities – Regime for the Importation, Sale and Distribution of Bananas – Recourse to Article 21.5 of the DSU by Ecuador* (*"EC – Bananas III (Article 21.5 – Ecuador)"*), WT/DS27/RW/ECU, adopted 6 May 1999, DSR 1999:II, 803, para. 6.105.
[36]   *Ibid.*, paras. 6.155-6.158.
[37]   Minutes of DSB Meeting of 11 February 2000, WT/DSB/M/75, p. 8.

(b) The Date of Entry is the Operative Date for Determining whether Relief is "Prospective" or "Retroactive"

(i) Using the Date of Entry as the Basis for Implementation is Consistent with the AD and SCM Agreements

3.96   This case revolves around what it means to implement an adverse WTO report in a prospective manner. In the context of an antidumping or countervailing duty measure, "prospective" implementation requires a Member to ensure that the new determination applies to all merchandise that enters for consumption on or after the date of implementation. This conclusion flows from the fact that it is the legal regime in effect on the date of entry which determines whether particular entries are liable for antidumping and countervailing duties. The fact that pre-implementation entries may remain unliquidated after the date of implementation - due to domestic litigation or any other reason - does not overcome the fact that a Member is under no obligation to implement with respect to such entries.

3.97   Using the date of entry as the basis for implementation is consistent with the basic manner in which the AD and SCM Agreements operate. Throughout those agreements, the critical factor for determining whether particular entries are subject to the assessment of antidumping or countervailing duties is the date of entry.

3.98   For example, Article 10.1 of the AD Agreement states that provisional measures and antidumping duties shall only be applied to "products which **enter for consumption** after the time" when the provisional or final decision enters into force, subject to certain exceptions.[38] Similarly, Article 8.6 of the AD Agreement states that if an exporter violates an undertaking, duties may be assessed on products "**entered for consumption** not more than 90 days before the application of ... provisional measures, except that any such retroactive assessment shall not apply to imports **entered** before the violation of the undertaking."[39] In addition, Article 10.6 of the AD Agreement states that when certain criteria are met, "[a] definitive anti-dumping duty may be levied on products which were **entered for consumption** not more than 90 days prior to the date of application of provisional measures [...]."[40] However, under Article 10.8, "[n]o duties shall be levied retroactively pursuant to paragraph 6 on products **entered for consumption** prior to the date of initiation of the investigation."[41] Whenever the AD Agreement specifies an applicable date for an action, the scope of applicability is based on entries occurring on or after that date.

---

[38]   Emphasis added. See also Article 20.1 of the SCM Agreement, containing virtually identical language which applies to countervailing duty investigations.
[39]   Emphasis added. The equivalent provision in the SCM Agreement is Article 18.6.
[40]   Emphasis added. See also Article 20.6 of the SCM Agreement.
[41]   Emphasis added.

3.99   Canada has not identified anything in Articles 1, 9.3 and 18.1 of the AD Agreement, or Articles VI:2 and VI:6(a) of GATT 1994, that requires the implementation of adverse WTO reports with respect to entries that occurred prior to the end of the reasonable period of time and the date on which the measure was brought into conformity with the WTO.

3.100   Furthermore, section 129(c)(1) of the URAA implements adverse WTO reports in a way that ensures compliance with Articles 10 and 32.1 of the SCM Agreement, and Articles VI:3 and VI:6(a) of GATT 1994. First, where the implementation of an adverse WTO report results in a determination that the amount of the subsidy is less than originally determined, section 129(c)(1) of the URAA ensures that all entries that take place on or after the date of implementation will be subject to the revised cash deposit rate established in the new determination. Similarly, when the implementation of an adverse WTO report results in a negative injury determination or a finding that there was no subsidization during the original period of investigation, the countervailing duty order will be revoked with respect to all entries that take place on or after the date of implementation. Section 129(c)(1) of the URAA ensures that such adverse WTO reports will be implemented, in a prospective manner, in accordance with the requirements of the DSU. Canada has failed to make even a *prima facie* case that the WTO Agreements require Members to implement adverse WTO reports regarding antidumping or countervailing duty measures with respect to entries that have occurred prior to the conclusion of the reasonable period of time for implementation.

3.101   Canada's claim that section 129(c)(1) is inconsistent with Article 11.1 of the AD Agreement and Article 21.1 of the SCM Agreement is similarly without basis. As their titles and context make clear, the purpose of the two articles is to provide for the periodic review of antidumping and countervailing duty orders and price undertakings to determine whether they remain necessary to offset injurious dumping or subsidization. They do not cover administrative reviews conducted to determine the amount of final antidumping or countervailing duty liability on past entries. Footnote 21 of the AD Agreement makes this point clear by specifically differentiating between reviews to determine the amount of final antidumping liability, which are conducted pursuant to Article 9.3 of the AD Agreement, and reviews conducted pursuant to Article 11. Neither Article 11 of the AD Agreement nor Article 21.1 of the SCM Agreement has any bearing whatsoever on the extent of a Member's obligation to bring a WTO-inconsistent measure into conformity with an adverse WTO report.

3.102   A recent Appellate Body report, *United States – Definitive Safeguard Measures on Imports of Circular Welded Carbon Quality Line Pipe from Korea*,[42] also provides support for the idea that the critical issue is date of entry. In the aptly numbered paragraph 129 of that report, the Appellate Body stated that

---

[42]   Appellate Body Report, *United States – Definitive Safeguard Measures on Imports of Circular Welded Carbon Quality Line Pipe from Korea* ("*US – Line Pipe*"), WT/DS202/AB/R, adopted 8 March 2002.

"a duty [...] does not need actually to be enforced and collected to be 'applied' to a product. In our view, duties are 'applied against a *product*' when a Member imposes conditions under which that product can enter that Member's market [...]." Thus, when the Appellate Body analyzed when a duty is "applied," it focused not on what might occur at the time of enforcement or collection, but on the conditions that imports would face at the border.

> (ii) Using the Date of Definitive Duty Determination as the Basis for Implementation Could Lead to Unexpected Results

3.103 The United States considers that the scope of a Member's implementation obligations is governed by the situation in effect at the time of entry. If Canada is correct in arguing that the Member's obligation depends upon the legal rights in effect on the date that the final duty liability is determined (and not on the date of entry), then a Member that has received DSB authorization to suspend concessions would be permitted to do so with respect to unliquidated, pre-authorization entries.

3.104 On this point, however, Canada's argument conflicts with the reasoning of the panel in the *United States – Import Measures on Certain Products from the European Communities* case.[43] That panel stated that suspending concessions on pre-authorization entries would constitute a retroactive remedy at odds with GATT and WTO practice. Further, the panel stated, "the applicable tariff (the applicable WTO obligation, the applicable law for that purpose), must be the one in force on the day of importation, the day the tariff is applied."[44] For the panel, the date of entry controlled whether the remedy was prospective or retroactive. Canada's attempt to distinguish the panel report on *US – Certain EC Products* on the basis of when the "rate of duty is fixed" misses the point,[45] since its argument implies that a Member that "fixes" the rate of duty at some point after the date of entry could, in fact, suspend concessions on unliquidated, pre-authorization entries.

3.105 Moreover, Canada's position makes it necessary to define when a Member "imposes" or "assesses" or "levies" duties. But interpreting the Agreements as creating distinct rights and obligations depending on when a Member "assesses" or "levies" duties could lead to unexpected results.

3.106 For example, Article 17.4 of the AD Agreement states that a matter may be referred to the DSB only when "final action has been taken by the administering authority of the importing Member to levy definitive anti-dumping duties or accept price undertakings [...]." Canada has argued at various points in this dis-

---

[43] Panel Report, *United States – Import Measures on Certain Products from the European Communities* ("*US – Certain EC Products*"), WT/DS165/R and Add.1, adopted 10 January 2001, as modified by the Appellate Body Report, WT/DS165/AB/R, DSR 2001:II, 413.

[44] Panel Report, *US – Certain EC Products, supra*, para. 6.77.

[45] Canada's reply to Panel Question 37.

pute that the term "levy" does not apply "to the imposition of potential liability in a Member using a retrospective system" and that the Department of Commerce does not make its final duty determinations until the end of administrative reviews. If the Panel were to adopt Canada's interpretation, then under the terms of Article 17.4, a panel would not have jurisdiction to review the final results of an antidumping investigation conducted by a Member with a retrospective system. If a Member believed that its exporters were subject to a WTO-inconsistent antidumping investigation, the Member would need to wait to bring a challenge until the end of an administrative review, normally more than two years after the completion of the investigation.

3.107 The need to precisely define when a Member "imposes" or "assesses" or "levies" duties arises from Canada's attempt to make the time of the "final" determination relevant to determining the scope of a Member's implementation obligations. When it is properly recognized that date of entry controls under both prospective and retrospective systems, these terms, and the distinctions between them, become irrelevant to this dispute.

(c) There Should be no Distinction between Members with Retrospective Duty Assessment Systems and Members with Prospective Duty Assessment Systems

(i) Canada's Position is Based on Artificial Distinctions Between Retrospective Duty Systems and Prospective Duty Systems

3.108 Canada and the United States agree that for Members with prospective systems, the date of entry controls for purposes of determining what constitutes "prospective" implementation of an adverse WTO report. Canada and the United States disagree, however, on whether that same date also controls for Members with retrospective systems. Although the United States believes the date of entry controls in all situations, Canada claims the date of entry is irrelevant in determining "prospective" implementation in retrospective systems. Canada's position is premised on a false factual distinction between retrospective and prospective systems, and Canada has failed to provide a textual basis for its position.

3.109 Canada attempts to build its legal arguments around the concept of "finality"; however, Canada employs inconsistent definitions of finality in order to create artificial distinctions between retrospective and prospective systems. When Canada's labels are set aside, the similarities between the two duty assessment systems are striking and in both cases, the liability for antidumping or countervailing duties arises at the border, at the time of entry.

3.110 For instance, under the Canadian prospective system, if an adverse WTO report results in a determination that there was no dumping or subsidization in a particular case, the determination implementing the adverse WTO report is deemed by law to be a termination of the investigation.[46] While Canadian law allows for the cessation of the collection of duties if this occurs, it does not appear to provide for the refund of duties incurred on entries that took place before the date of implementation.[47] Thus, the outcomes under the two systems are essentially the same.

3.111 Furthermore, even under Canada's prospective duty assessment system, the determination of duty liability is not final on the date of entry. Assessment does not occur until 30 days after the date of entry. Further, the duty on the entry is subject to redetermination based upon an importer's request within 90 days of the entry. In addition, for up to two years after the date of entry, Canada may redetermine the normal value, the export price, or the amount of subsidy associated with any imported product. Judicial review may further extend these periods. Consequently, even under Canada's prospective system, a number of determinations may be made after implementation regarding pre-implementation entries.

(ii) The WTO Obligations that Apply to Members with Retrospective and Prospective Systems are the Same

3.112 There is no evidence in the text of the AD Agreement or the SCM Agreement that the rules are intended to promote or create advantages or disadvantages for one type of system over the other. The DSU provides only for prospective remedies. Regardless of whether a Member utilizes a retrospective or prospective system of duty assessment, the date of entry is the controlling issue for determining whether the implementation obligations apply to a particular entry. A Member's obligation is to remove or modify the border measure (the antidumping or countervailing duty measure) with respect to all entries made on or after the date set for implementation.

3.113 Notwithstanding this, Canada is attempting to establish a different and higher level of obligation for Members with retrospective duty assessment systems than for Members with prospective duty assessment systems, based on nothing more than an arbitrary, form over substance, description of when duties are purportedly "final" under the two systems.

3.114 More specifically, Canada is seeking to draw a line between reviews conducted pursuant to Article 9.3.1 of the AD Agreement (in retrospective systems) and reviews conducted pursuant to Article 9.3.2 of the AD Agreement (in prospective systems). In essence, Canada is arguing that Members with retrospective duty assessment systems have an obligation to apply adverse DSB recommendations and rulings when conducting Article 9.3.1 reviews of pre-implementation entries, while Members with prospective systems do not have an obligation to apply adverse DSB recommendations and rulings when conducting Article 9.3.2 reviews of pre-implementation entries. In actuality, neither Member

---

[46] Article 76.1(5)(b) of Canada's Special Import Measures Act ("SIMA").
[47] Articles 9.21 and 76.1 of the SIMA.

has such an obligation, because the date of entry determines what constitutes "prospective" implementation in both systems.

3.115 The inconsistency in Canada's claims is further evidenced in Canada's position with respect to judicial review. As the United States has noted, Members are obligated to maintain judicial, arbitral or administrative tribunals to review administrative actions. Canada would appear to be arguing that an administrative determination by a Member with a retrospective system of duty assessment is somehow less final, when subject to judicial review, than a comparable administrative determination by a Member with a prospective system of duty assessment, when subject to judicial review. Canada has not explained how the same terms regarding judicial review in Article 13 of the AD Agreement and Article 23 of the SCM Agreement must be read to create such disparate results between Members with retrospective duty assessment systems and Members with prospective duty assessment systems.

> (iii) Canada is Seeking to Create an Obligation for Members with Retrospective Systems to Provide a Retroactive Remedy in Cases Involving Antidumping and Countervailing Duty Measures

3.116 Canada has argued repeatedly during this dispute that its arguments do not amount to a claim for retroactive relief in cases involving antidumping and countervailing duty measures because it is only asking the United States to make its decisions *after* the implementation date in accordance with adverse WTO reports, even if those decisions relate to pre-implementation entries. Canada has sought to distinguish the obligations applying to Members with prospective systems by claiming that those Members assess and collect duties at the time of entry, so that there are no decisions "after" the reasonable period of time that need to be made.[48] In Canada's view, a Member would only violate WTO rules if it were to make a WTO-inconsistent decision *after* the reasonable period of time.

3.117 However, in the United States' view, by attempting to have adverse DSB recommendations and rulings apply to pre-implementation entries, Canada *is* seeking a retroactive remedy. If the Members had wanted to provide for the applicability of implementation actions to pre-implementation entries, they would have explicitly provided for that in the DSU or elsewhere in the WTO Agreements - through language explicitly providing for either retroactive or injunctive relief. They did not do so. Instead, what the Members agreed to was a reasonable period of time in which to bring inconsistent measures into conformity with a

---

[48] Canada's position appears to be that even though the completion of the refund proceeding or judicial review might occur as long as two or more years after the end of the reasonable period of time, Members with prospective systems would not be obligated to apply the new, WTO-consistent methodology in that refund proceeding because the entry occurred prior to the end of the reasonable period of time. Canada was unable to point to any textual basis for its belief that the implementation obligations of Members with prospective systems differ from those of Members with retrospective systems.

Member's WTO obligations, and, as discussed above, no consequences for maintaining the inconsistent measures in the interim period. Adopting Canada's position and thereby modifying this agreement would be inconsistent with Article 3.2 of the DSU since it would add to the rights and obligations provided in the WTO Agreements.

3.118 What is more, Canada has argued that the United States would be required to return cash deposits collected in respect of what Canada terms "prior unliquidated entries."[49] Thus, Canada believes that Members with retrospective systems are not only under an obligation to ensure that all future (post-implementation) actions conform to WTO rules; they are also under an obligation to undo *past* (pre-implementation) actions.

3.119 By making an issue of the effect that implementation has on prior unliquidated entries, Canada is ignoring the international obligation - which is to bring the border measure into conformity with the agreement - and instead, is trying to create a new obligation for Members to provide redress or compensation to private parties within their own jurisdictions. There is no basis in the WTO agreements for such an obligation. To require refunds of cash deposits collected on entries prior to the end of the reasonable period of time would be to require retroactive relief, inconsistent with GATT/WTO practice.

3.120 In addition, under the logic that Canada has applied to prospective systems, if a Member with a retrospective system took *no* action with respect to cash deposits after the implementation date, there would be no possibility of a WTO violation. Canada has failed even to attempt to explain how an obligation not to take WTO-inconsistent action after the implementation date can somehow be transformed into an affirmative obligation to *take* a certain action - namely, refunding cash deposits collected before the implementation date - when that "obligation" appears nowhere in the AD Agreement, the SCM Agreement, the GATT 1994, or the DSU.

3.121 Moreover, to read such an obligation into the agreements could have serious consequences for other Members. In the *Guatemala Cement* dispute, Guatemala argued that the panel should not order the refund of past duties, stating, "[I]f a panel were to suggest a retroactive remedy, this could interfere directly with the sovereignty of a Member by establishing a domestic right of action where there had been none previously."[50]

(d)   Conclusion

3.122 Nothing in the text of the WTO agreements requires anything other than prospective implementation of adverse WTO reports. Just as importantly, nothing in the agreements requires Members to apply adverse WTO reports not only to entries that take place after implementation, but also to entries that took place

---

[49]   Canada's reply to Panel Question 32.

[50]   Panel Report, *Guatemala – Anti-Dumping Investigation Regarding Portland Cement from Mexico* (*"Guatemala – Cement I"*), WT/DS60/R, adopted 25 November 1998, as modified by the Appellate Body Report, WT/DS60/AB/R, DSR 1998:IX, 3797.

prior to implementation. Without a basis to assert that implementation decisions must apply in any way but prospectively - i.e., to new entries only - Canada's specific claims of violation under Articles 1, 9.3, 11.1 and 18.1 of the AD Agreement; Articles 10, 19.4, 21.1 and 32.1 of the SCM Agreement; and Articles VI:2, VI:3 and VI:6(a) of the GATT 1994 are inapposite. Section 129(c)(1) is fully consistent with the aforementioned WTO obligations of the United States. It ensures implementation of adverse WTO reports on a prospective basis, consistently with the United States' aforementioned WTO obligations.

3.123 Canada can only establish that the United States has breached the obligations of Article 18.4 of the AD Agreement, Article 32.5 of the SCM Agreement, and Article XVI:4 of the WTO Agreement to the extent that it establishes that section 129(c)(1) is inconsistent with the other WTO obligations that it invokes in support of its complaint. For the reasons described above, section 129(c)(1) is consistent with those other WTO obligations of the United States and, therefore, there is no breach of Article 18.4 of the AD Agreement, Article 32.5 of the SCM Agreement, or Article XVI:4 of the WTO Agreement.

5.   Conclusion

3.124 For the foregoing reasons, the United States requests that the Panel find that Canada has failed to establish that section 129(c)(1) is inconsistent with Articles VI:2, VI:3, VI:6(a) of the GATT 1994, Articles 1, 9.3, 11.1, 18.1 and 18.4 of the AD Agreement, Articles 10, 19.4, 21.1, 32.1 and 32.5 of the SCM Agreement, and Article XVI:4 of the WTO Agreement.

IV.   MAIN ARGUMENTS OF THE THIRD PARTIES

4.1   The main arguments of those third parties to these proceedings which have made submissions to the Panel, i.e., the European Communities and Japan, are as follows:

A.   European Communities

4.2   This section summarizes the main arguments of the **European Communities**.

1.   The Principle of Prospective Compliance

4.3   Canada's claim is based on the assumption that WTO Members have to apply compliance measures to all subsequent legal acts irrespective of the date of importation. In this context, the European Communities recalls that in the past numerous GATT and WTO panels were faced with requests by the complainant to recommend a reimbursement of anti-dumping and countervailing duties. This was never granted. What is more, Article 19.1 of the DSU does not contain an obligation of WTO Members to apply compliance measures to entries before the implementation date.

4.4   The WTO dispute settlement system follows the principle of non-retroactivity of remedies. Thus, the DSU does not impose an obligation of Members to remedy past or consummated violations, but requires prospective compliance. This is clearly reflected in the wording of Article 19.1 of the DSU which imposes an obligation to "*bring* the measure into conformity with" the covered agreements. Several panels have confirmed this principle.[51]

4.5   Moreover, Articles 19 and 21 of the DSU reflect the principle of "minimum interference" in the choice of compliance measures by Members concerned.

4.6   The principle of prospective compliance is further corroborated by the concept of a reasonable period of time for implementation. Article 21.3 of the DSU implies that the obligation to comply does not embrace goods that entered before the expiry of the reasonable period of time. This is also clearly reflected in the wording of Article 22.2 of the DSU, which refers to the obligation of a Member "to bring the measure found to be inconsistent with a covered agreement into compliance therewith [...] within the reasonable period of time."

4.7   In addition, Article 3.2 of the DSU clarifies that the fundamental purpose of the WTO dispute settlement system is to provide "security and predictability to the multilateral trading system". Thus, WTO remedies shall ensure market opportunities for the future rather than providing reparation or compensation in the public international law sense. Members are not required to erase the consequences of an illegal measure occurring before the end of the reasonable period of time.

2.   *The Temporal Scope of the Principle of Prospective Compliance*

4.8   The European Communities notes that the date of entry serves as reference point for most of the substantive obligations of WTO Members. Thus, the obligation not to subject imported products to duties and other charges in excess of the bound rates under the relevant Schedule of tariff concessions relates to the time of importation, Articles II:1(b) and II:1(c) of the GATT 1994. This is further supported by the *Kyoto International Convention on the Simplification and Harmonization of Customs Procedures* and the *tempus regit actum* rule under public international law.

4.9   Similarly, the text of Article VI of the GATT 1994 suggests that the obligation not to impose an anti-dumping or countervailing duty contrary to the conditions set by WTO law, relates to the date of entry. Article VI:6(a) of the GATT 1994 clarifies the *ratione temporis* of this rule by stating in relevant part "no con-

---

[51]   Panel Report, *US – Certain EC Products, supra*, para. 6.106; Panel Report, *EC – Bananas III (Article 21.5 – Ecuador), supra*, para 6.105.

tracting party shall levy any anti-dumping or countervailing duty on the importation of any product [...]."

4.10   The preposition "on" textually implies not only a local but also a temporal element. Thus, Article VI:6(a) of the GATT 1994 does not simply refer to a "border measure". This can be derived from the Appellate Body report in *United States – Anti-Dumping Act of 1916* where the Appellate Body decided that criminal and civil remedies constitute "specific action against dumping" and fall, therefore, within the scope of Article VI of the GATT 1994.

4.11   This understanding would not be contradicted by the term "levy" in Article VI:6(a) of the GATT 1994. Even if the term "levy" were to be interpreted according to footnote 12 of the AD Agreement and footnote 51 of the SCM Agreement this does not entail that the duty must be levied, i.e. assessed and collected, at the time of importation. Rather, it means that the dutiable event is the moment of importation. The relevant point in time is when the obligation to pay a duty arises and not when the duty is levied. In this regard Article 10.1 of the Anti-Dumping Agreement provides that an anti-dumping duty shall only be applied to products, which enter for consumption after the imposition of the measure.

4.12   In this context, the European Communities would also refer to the transparency provisions under WTO law, which provide that a measure must be published in advance before the importation date. This demonstrates that the WTO obligations relate to the point of importation. The transparency provisions would be undermined if the temporal aspect were disregarded.

4.13   On the basis of these fundamental principles of WTO law the date of entry should be the general reference point to determine the temporal scope of the obligation to comply with a DSB ruling under Article 19.1 of the DSU.

4.14   The European Communities notes Canada's argument that Article 9.3 of the AD Agreement would require the United States to apply its revised methodology during administrative reviews following implementation whatever the date of importation. The European Communities does not take a position on this argument.

B.   Japan

4.15   This section summarizes the main arguments of **Japan**.

4.16   Japan generally agrees with Canada that section 129(c)(1) raises significant systemic concerns. AD and CVD measures (as well as safeguard measures) should be temporary measures, applied to provide domestic industries relief from imports under specifically defined circumstances. Although these measures are permitted under the WTO Agreements, these measures also stand the greatest chance of being abused by overzealous authorities. As such, the application of such measures must be carefully supervised by the Members, through such mechanism as the Dispute Settlement Body so as to ensure that sanctioned forms of trade protection, like AD and CVD measures, are applied only when authorized by the relevant WTO agreements.

4.17   For the dispute settlement system to work effectively, recommendations or rulings of the DSB must be given effect. Once the DSB ruling is adopted by the Dispute Settlement Body, it is final and must be observed per Article 21.3 of the DSU. Either immediately following the DSB ruling or following the expiry date of the reasonable period of time decided in accordance with Article 21.3 of the DSU, any imposition by the United States of AD and CVD duties - including those on entries that are yet to be liquidated after the United States Trade Representative directs implementation of a new determination pursuant to section 129(a)(6) and section 129(b)(4) of the URAA - must be consistent with the DSB ruling.

4.18   In this case, the unique features of the US AD and CVD laws create an unusual situation. By using a retrospective system that allows entries to take place based on estimated duties, and only later determining the actual duties owed, the United States effectively defers its decision on the application of duties. Section 129(c)(1) singled out DSB rulings for different treatment from the ordinary liquidation procedures. If a DSB ruling declares the duties to be improper, section 129(c)(1) requires that WTO-inconsistent treatment be applied to prior unliquidated entries even after the United States Trade Representative directs the administering authority to apply revised anti-dumping or countervailing duty.

4.19   The United States may not hide behind the unique legal system it has adopted. Under the US system, the US authorities can change the estimated duties however they want - after all, they are not yet final under the US legal system - but they must ignore any decision by the WTO with regard to prior unliquidated entries. Section 129(c)(1) affirmatively bars the authorities from considering at all such decisions.

4.20   At great length the United States argues that the remedy under the WTO dispute settlement system should be of prospective nature and not retrospective, in its attempt to mis-characterise Canada's argument. Canada's argument, however, does not go that far as making any general statement about retrospective remedy, nor does Japan's. More specifically, Canada clarifies in footnote 25 of its submission that "the actions at issue in this dispute are those taken by the United States after the date it implements any measure to bring itself into conformity with the findings in a WTO Report." Hence it is clear that neither Canada nor Japan argues for retroactive application, or reversal of past actions.

4.21   In this connection, the United States misunderstands Japan's statement on the *Australia – Automotive Leather II (Article 21.5 – US)* case at the Dispute Settlement Body.[52] The issue at the DSB meeting was the Panel report recom-

---

[52]   US First Submission, para.39 and footnote 38. Japan stated at the meeting of the Dispute Settlement Body on 11 February 2000:

"The representative of *Japan* said that the Panel Report had dealt with very important legal issues. The most important issue was the interpretation of the phrase

mending repayment of a WTO-inconsistent subsidy. Japan opposed to the report because the Panel recommended the reversal of past actions that had already been finalised, as against the actions yet to be finalised. The prior unliquidated entries that Canada identified in this dispute are those that are pending the finalisation of dumping duty, to be collected at the time of liquidation. Thus, it is inapposite to draw an analogy between the two cases.

4.22   The Unites States also dismisses as irrelevant a reference Canada makes to the system of applying revised anti-dumping margins under the US domestic judicial review and NAFTA. In Japan's view, however, the legal significance of Canada's reference lies not in the difference in time periods for which the revised dumping margins are to be applied under respective regimes, but in the very fact that the United States deliberately chose to frame the language of section 129(c)(1) so as to exclude the application of revised dumping margin to the entries of subject imports that remain unliquidated even after the issuance of a directive by the Untied States Trade Representative when those entries entered the United States before the issuance of the directive. Canada's claim is on the applicability of DSB rulings to liquidation decisions taking place after the United States Trade Representative has issued the directive, after the reasonable period of time during which the United States is entitled to maintaining WTO-inconsistent measure, has expired. The question of retroactive application could arise only with regard to an action that has already taken place prior to the expiry of the reasonable period of time, which is not at issue here.

4.23   Japan believes Canada has raised serious questions about the consistency of section 129(c)(1) with US obligations under the WTO Agreements. Japan urges the Panel to give this important dispute the detailed attention it deserves. To the extent section 129(c)(1) violates US WTO obligations, the Panel should not hesitate to so find and to urge the United States to repeal the WTO-inconsistent aspects of section 129(c)(1).

"withdraw the subsidy" in Article 4.7 of the SCM Agreement. Although the parties concerned had argued that an interpretation of Article 4.7 of the SCM Agreement which would allow a retroactive remedy was inconsistent with the relevant DSU provisions and customary practice under the GATT 1947 and the WTO, the Panel had rejected this argument and had concluded that the recommendation to "withdraw the subsidy" was not limited to prospective action only but might **encompass repayment of the prohibited subsidy**. It had further concluded that full repayment in this case was necessary in order to resolve this dispute. This interpretation developed by the Panel would have a significant impact on implementation of other subsidy-related disputes. Japan shared the view that the retroactive remedy was inconsistent with the relevant provisions of the DSU and the customary practice under the GATT 1947 and the WTO." (emphasis added)
Minutes of DSB Meeting of 11 February 2000, WT/DSB/M/75, p. 7.

V.   INTERIM REVIEW[53]

A.   Background

5.1   In letters dated 29 May 2002, Canada and the United States requested an interim review by the Panel of certain aspects of the interim report issued to the parties on 22 May 2002. Neither party requested an interim review meeting. As agreed by the Panel, both parties were permitted to submit further comments on the other party's interim review requests. The United States submitted further comments on 4 June 2002.

B.   Comments by Canada

1.   Terms of Reference

5.2   **Canada** considers that the Panel misconstrued its terms of reference. Canada argues that, in interpreting its terms of reference, the Panel unduly restricted its analysis of the effect of section 129(c)(1) to preclude any analysis of other provisions of US law.[54] In Canada's view, the terms of reference do not preclude the Panel from considering the provisions of title VII of the Tariff Act of 1930. According to Canada, the United States argued before the Panel that, notwithstanding that section 129 determinations cannot apply to "prior unliquidated entries", the Department of Commerce has other authority under title VII of the Tariff Act of 1930 to take any necessary actions with respect to such entries. Canada considers that this argument was raised by the United States as an affirmative defence and that it is, therefore, not relevant whether the authority relied on by the United States was within the Panel's terms of reference. Canada further submits that it was unnecessary, as a matter of WTO law, for Canada to have included the provisions of title VII of the Tariff Act of 1930 in the terms of reference of the Panel since Canada identified the provision of US law - namely, section 129(c)(1) - that prevents the Department of Commerce from taking the actions needed to apply section 129 determinations to "prior unliquidated entries" in accordance with the WTO obligations of the United States.

5.3   The **United States** responds that Canada's objections rest on a faulty premise. According to the United States, Canada incorrectly assumes that it had met its initial burden of demonstrating that section 129(c)(1) operated in the manner it had alleged. The United States considers that since the Panel found that, as a matter of US law, section 129(c)(1) does not have the effect of requiring or precluding any of the actions identified by Canada, Canada failed to meet its initial burden. In the view of the United States, the issue of whether the United States relied on an "affirmative defence" does not, therefore, arise. The

---

[53]   Pursuant to Article 15.3 of the DSU, the findings of the final panel report shall include a discussion of the arguments made at the interim review stage. This Section of the Panel report is therefore part of the Panel's findings.

[54]   Canada cites footnote 123, *infra*, as an example.

United States also notes that the Panel acted properly in not examining other potential "measures" that Canada did not include in its panel request.

5.4   The **Panel** does not agree with Canada that it has misconstrued its terms of reference. Indeed, in its interim review comments, Canada itself acknowledges that it has included section 129(c)(1) in the Panel's terms of reference, but not the provisions of title VII of the Tariff Act of 1930.[55] We see no need, therefore, to reconsider our finding that the only measure that is within our terms of reference is section 129(c)(1).[56]

5.5   Canada argues that the Panel's terms of reference do not preclude the Panel from "considering" or "analysing" the provisions of title VII of the Tariff Act of 1930 as part of its assessment of the WTO-consistency of section 129(c)(1). We agree and note that neither in footnote 123 nor elsewhere in our findings did we state that our terms of reference preclude us from doing so. As a matter of avoiding any misunderstanding in this regard, we made minor drafting changes to the last sentence of footnote 123, and also the last sentence of the similar footnote 112.

5.6   As an additional matter, we note that neither footnote 123 nor any other statement in our findings should be taken to mean that we somehow failed to "consider" or "analyse" title VII of the Tariff Act of 1930 or other relevant provisions of US law in determining the WTO-consistency of section 129(c)(1). In fact, we have carefully considered and analysed all relevant provisions of US law brought to the attention of the Panel by Canada and the United States. As part of that analysis, we have also considered the relationship between title VII of the Tariff Act of 1930 and section 129(c)(1). This is apparent both from the questions we put to the parties[57] and from our findings[58].

5.7   Our analysis of section 129(c)(1) - including its effect - was done taking into account all provisions of US law referred to by the parties. This allowed us to understand the meaning and operation of section 129(c)(1). Nonetheless, it does not follow that all the provisions of US law that are relevant to the Panel's analysis of section 129 become part of the terms of reference of the Panel. The only measure included in our terms of reference is section 129(c)(1). Consequently, we can only determine the WTO-consistency of *that* measure.

5.8   Accordingly, with the exception of the minor changes we made to footnotes 123 and 112, we did not modify our findings in response to Canada's arguments regarding our interpretation of the terms of reference.

---

[55]   See, *supra*, para. 5.2 (last sentence).
[56]   See, *infra*, para. 6.5.
[57]   E.g., Panel Questions 3, 5, 6, 20, 21, 42, 84, 91, 93 and 94.
[58]   See, e.g., paras. 2.5-2.8, 6.50 and accompanying footnote, 6.69 and accompanying footnote, 6.70-6.71 and 6.84 and accompanying footnote.

2. Burden of Proof

5.9   **Canada** asserts that the Panel misapplied the burden of proof. According to Canada, once Canada had shown that section 129 prevents the Department of Commerce from applying determinations implemented under section 129 to "prior unliquidated entries", it was for the United States to claim and demonstrate that it had some other authority whereby it could take any necessary actions with respect to "prior unliquidated entries". Although Canada accepts that it was up to Canada to demonstrate that section 129 mandates the United States to take WTO-inconsistent action or not to take action which is required by its WTO obligations, in Canada's view, this obligation cannot extend so far as to require it to carry the burden of disproving the effect of measures other than the measure about which it has complained. Canada notes, in this regard, that since the United States raised the affirmative defence that measures other than section 129 would permit the Department of Commerce to take the necessary actions with regard to "prior unliquidated entries", it was for the United States   - and not Canada - to discharge the burden of proving the effect of those measures.

5.10   The **United States** responds that if Canada believes that a particular measure of a WTO Member "as such" fails to meet an alleged obligation to implement adverse WTO reports with respect to what Canada terms "prior unliquidated entries", the burden is on Canada to establish that the measure mandates action inconsistent with that alleged obligation. According to the United States, Canada failed to meet this burden with respect to section 129(c)(1). In the view of the United States, the issue of whether the United States relied on an "affirmative defence" and whether the Panel misapplied the burden of proof does not, therefore, arise.

5.11   The **Panel** is unable to agree with Canada's assertion that it has misapplied the burden of proof in this case. As we have stated at para. 6.23 below, it was for Canada to demonstrate, *inter alia*, that section 129(c)(1) mandates the United States to take or not take the action identified by Canada. Contrary to what Canada would have the Panel believe, however, Canada cannot discharge that burden merely by demonstrating that determinations made and implemented under section 129 are not applicable to "prior unliquidated entries". As is clear from our findings, the fact that section 129 determinations do not apply to "prior unliquidated entries" does not, in itself, establish that section 129(c)(1) requires (or has the effect of requiring) any of the actions listed in para. 6.31 or precludes (or has the effect of precluding) any of the actions listed in para. 6.32.[59] As a result, on a correct application of the burden of proof, the burden of proof did *not* shift to the United States, as Canada suggests, once Canada had shown that section 129 determinations do not apply to "prior unliquidated entries".

5.12   Canada's additional argument that the Panel inappropriately required Canada to carry the burden of disproving the effect of measures about which Canada did not complain is misplaced. Canada did not identify a single paragraph in our findings to support this assertion. In fact, it could not do so, as our

---

[59]   See, *infra*, in particular paras. 6.55, 6.68-6.69 and 6.83-6.84.

findings make it clear that we required Canada to prove the effect of section 129(c)(1), and not to disprove the effect of measures about which Canada did not complain.[60]

5.13   In the light of the foregoing considerations, we are not convinced that there is a need to change our findings in response to Canada's arguments regarding our application of the burden of proof. We should note, however, that our review of the relevant parts of our findings resulted in a minor drafting change at para. 6.73.

C.   Comments by the United States

5.14   All of the comments submitted by the **United States** related to typographical errors.

5.15   The **Panel** made appropriate corrections.

VI.   FINDINGS

A.   Measure at Issue

6.1   The **Panel** recalls that its terms of reference are as follows:

> To examine, in the light of the relevant provisions of the covered agreements cited by Canada in document WT/DS221/4, the matter referred to the DSB by Canada in that document, and to make such findings as will assist the DSB in making the recommendations or in giving the rulings provided for in those agreements.[61]

6.2   Document WT/DS221/4 is Canada's request for the establishment of a panel in this case. It states that "[t]he measure at issue is section 129(c)(1) of the URAA (19 USC §3538(c)(1))". Document WT/DS221/4 does not "specifically identify" any other measure.[62]

6.3   Throughout these proceedings, Canada never argued that it was making legal claims in respect of a measure or measures other than section 129(c)(1). Indeed, in its very first submission to the Panel, Canada confirmed that "[a]t issue in this dispute is section 129(c)(1) of the *Uruguay Round Agreements Act* [...]".[63]

---

[60]   See, *infra*, paras. 6.23, 6.70 and 6.85.

[61]   WT/DS221/5 (referring to WT/DSB/M/108).

[62]   Appellate Body Report, *Guatemala – Anti-Dumping Investigation Regarding Portland Cement from Mexico* ("*Guatemala – Cement I*"), WT/DS60/AB/R, adopted 25 November 1998, DSR 1998:IX, 3767, para. 86.

[63]   Canada's First Submission, para. 1. We note that, in its request for consultations, Canada stated that "[t]hese consultations concern Section 129(c)(1) of the Uruguay Round Agreements Act (the URAA) and the Statement of Administrative Action accompanying the URAA (at page 1026)". See WT/DS221/1. However, Canada's subsequent panel request does not reference the Statement of Administrative Action as a measure which is being challenged in addition to section 129(c)(1).

6.4   We note that, in the course of these proceedings, Canada made numerous references to the provisions of title VII of the United States Tariff Act of 1930, as amended.[64] However, Canada has not argued that title VII of the Tariff Act of 1930 or any of its sections was itself a measure within this Panel's terms of reference. As a result, we need not examine whether the relationship between title VII of the Tariff Act of 1930 and section 129(c)(1) is such that title VII, or any of its individual sections, could be considered to be "included" in our terms of reference.[65]

6.5   In the light of the above, we conclude that the only measure that is within this Panel's terms of reference is section 129(c)(1). Accordingly, we will examine whether section 129(c)(1), taken alone, is inconsistent with the WTO provisions invoked by Canada.

B.   Claims and Arguments of the Parties and Analytical Approach of the Panel

1.   Arguments of the Parties

6.6   According to **Canada**, section 129(c)(1) provides that a new antidumping or countervailing duty determination made by the Department of Commerce or the ITC to bring a previous antidumping, countervailing duty or injury determination into conformity with an adverse WTO panel or Appellate Body report applies only to imports that enter the United States on or after the date that the USTR directs implementation of the new determination. In Canada's view, section 129(c)(1) implies that imports that entered the United States *prior to* that date, and that are subject to an order imposing potential liability for the payment of antidumping or countervailing duties, remain subject to future administrative review determinations and definitive duty assessment without regard to the new determination made by the Department of Commerce or the ITC and any consequent revocation or amendment of the original order.

6.7   Canada refers to the latter type of imports as *"prior unliquidated entries"*, since those imports entered the United States prior to the date on which the USTR directs implementation of a new determination pursuant to section 129(a)(6) and section 129(b)(4) and remain unliquidated (that is, the definitive duty, if any, to be levied on the imports remains undetermined) on that date. For the purposes of this dispute, Canada is assuming that the USTR directs the Department of Commerce or the ITC to implement an adverse DSB ruling at the

---

[64]   Title VII of the Tariff Act of 1930, codified at 19 U.S.C. §§ 1671 *et seq.*

[65]   We note that there may be circumstances in which a measure that is not specifically identified in a panel request may nevertheless be considered to be "included" in a measure that *is* specifically identified, if such a measure is "subsidiary or closely related" to the measure that is referenced in the panel request. See Panel Report, *Japan – Measures Affecting Consumer Photographic Film and Paper* ("*Japan – Film*"), WT/DS44/R, adopted 22 April 1998, DSR 1998:IV, 1179, para. 10.8. However, as already pointed out, Canada did not assert before us that title VII of the Tariff Act of 1930 or any of its sections should be considered to be "included" in Canada's references, in its panel request and elsewhere, to section 129(c)(1).

end of the reasonable period of time accorded to a Member pursuant to Article 21.3 of the DSU. Canada refers to that date as the "*implementation date*".

6.8   Canada considers that where an order imposing duty liability on imports has been revoked or amended under section 129(c)(1) in response to an adverse WTO ruling, there is no legal basis in the AD Agreement, the SCM Agreement or the GATT 1994 for the United States to conduct administrative reviews and to assess definitive antidumping or countervailing duties with respect to "prior unliquidated entries" without regard to the new determination made by the ITC or the Department of Commerce pursuant to section 129 and the revocation or amendment of the original order. Canada further argues that there is no legal basis in the AD Agreement, the SCM Agreement or the GATT 1994 for the United States to retain cash deposits collected in respect of "prior unliquidated entries" pending the determination of definitive duty liability for those entries, to the extent that these cash deposits were made pursuant to the original order, which has been revoked or amended only with respect to entries that entered the United States on or after the implementation date.

6.9   Canada asserts that section 129(c)(1) requires the Department of Commerce, in determining whether to retain cash deposits previously collected on "prior unliquidated entries" and whether to conduct administrative reviews and assess duties with respect to such entries, to disregard (i) the new determination made by the ITC or the Department of Commerce pursuant to paragraphs (a)(6) and (b)(4) of section 129, and (ii) any revocation or amendment of the original order. Canada submits that where a new determination results in a negative finding of injury, a negative finding of dumping or subsidization, or a reduction in the dumping or subsidization margin, and the Department of Commerce, as a result of section 129(c)(1), subsequently retains cash deposits previously collected in respect of "prior unliquidated entries", conducts an administrative review of "prior unliquidated entries" or assesses definitive antidumping or countervailing duties with respect to such entries without taking into account the new determination and the adverse DSB ruling, the Department of Commerce is acting inconsistently with the obligations of the United States under the AD Agreement, the SCM Agreement or the GATT 1994.

6.10   Specifically, Canada claims that section 129(c)(1) is inconsistent with:

    (a)   Article VI:2, VI:3 and VI:6(a) of the GATT 1994;

    (b)   Articles 1, 9.3, 11.1 and 18.1 of the AD Agreement; and

    (c)   Articles 10, 19.4, 21.1 and 32.1 of the SCM Agreement.

6.11   Canada further submits that, in view of the fact that section 129(c)(1) is inconsistent, in its view, with the aforementioned provisions of the AD Agreement, the SCM Agreement and the GATT 1994, section 129(c)(1) is also inconsistent with Article 18.4 of the AD Agreement, Article 32.5 of the SCM Agreement and Article XVI:4 of the WTO Agreement, because these provisions require that a Member's laws be in conformity with its WTO obligations as of the entry into force of the WTO Agreement.

6.12   Canada considers that, in making the above claims, Canada is not seeking retroactive application of adverse DSB rulings. Whereas Canada considers that the DSU contemplates prospective implementation of adverse DSB rulings, in its view, the principle of prospective implementation does not justify the United States making legal determinations with respect to "prior unliquidated entries" after the implementation date on a WTO-inconsistent basis. Canada submits that the logical outcome of prospective implementation of an adverse DSB ruling in a retrospective duty assessment system is for the United States to apply new determinations implemented under section 129 to "prior unliquidated entries" as well as future entries. Canada emphasizes that it is not seeking to have the United States apply such determinations to entries which were liquidated *before* the implementation date. In Canada's view, to do so would amount to a retroactive application of an adverse DSB ruling.

6.13   The **United States** argues that Canada has failed to establish that section 129(c)(1) is inconsistent with Articles VI:2, VI:3, and VI:6(a) of the GATT 1994, Articles 1, 9.3, 11.1, 18.1 and 18.4 of the AD Agreement, Articles 10, 19.4, 21.1, 32.1 and 32.5 of the SCM Agreement, and Article XVI:4 of the WTO Agreement.

6.14   The United States considers that any discussion of whether section 129(c)(1) is inconsistent with the WTO obligations of the United States must start with an understanding of the obligations that the DSU imposes with respect to implementing adverse WTO reports. The United States submits, in this regard, that the DSU creates an obligation on the part of a Member whose measure has been found to be WTO-inconsistent to bring that measure into conformity in a prospective manner. In the view of the United States, prospective implementation in a case involving an antidumping or countervailing duty measure requires a Member to ensure that a new, WTO-consistent antidumping or countervailing duty determination applies to all merchandise that enters for consumption on or after the date of implementation.

6.15   The United States asserts that there is no requirement to apply a new, WTO-consistent antidumping or countervailing duty determination to "prior unliquidated entries". The United States submits that, pursuant to Article 21 of the DSU, there is no obligation to cease or otherwise suspend a WTO-inconsistent measure with respect to its impact on entries that take place during the reasonable period of time. In the view of the United States, neither the AD Agreement, nor the SCM Agreement or the GATT 1994 addresses the timing of the implementation of adverse WTO reports. The United States adds that, to the extent that those agreements refer to effective dates for any purpose, those effective dates are based on the date of entry. The United States submits that using the date of entry as the basis for implementation is, therefore, consistent with the basic manner in which the AD Agreement and the SCM Agreement operate.

6.16   Regarding section 129(c)(1), the United States argues that that provision specifies that a new, WTO-consistent determination which the USTR directs the Department of Commerce to implement will be effective as to all entries that occur on or after the date of implementation. The United States submits that, with that action, the United States will have met its obligations in respect of the implementation of an adverse WTO report, because all entries occurring on or after the date of implementation would enter and be treated in accordance with the WTO report. The United States considers, therefore, that section 129(c)(1) is not inconsistent with Articles VI:2, VI:3, and VI:6(a) of the GATT 1994, Articles 1, 9.3, 11.1 and 18.1 of the AD Agreement, Articles 10, 19.4, 21.1 and 32.1 of the SCM Agreement.

6.17   The United States contends that Canada can only establish that section 129(c)(1) is inconsistent with Article 18.4 of the AD Agreement, Article 32.5 of the SCM Agreement and Article XVI:4 of the WTO Agreement to the extent that it establishes that section 129(c)(1) is inconsistent with the other WTO obligations relied on by Canada. Since the United States is of the view that section 129(c)(1) does not contravene any of those other WTO obligations, it considers that section 129(c)(1) does not infringe Article 18.4 of the AD Agreement, Article 32.5 of the SCM Agreement or Article XVI:4 of the WTO Agreement.

6.18   The United States further argues that, in any event, Canada must establish that section 129(c)(1) mandates action that is inconsistent with the WTO obligations of the United States or that it precludes action that is consistent with those obligations. The United States submits that if section 129(c)(1) does not mandate or preclude any of the actions identified by Canada, then Canada's claims must fail, regardless of what it means to implement a new antidumping or countervailing duty determination in a WTO-consistent manner.

6.19   According to the United States, section 129(c)(1) only addresses the application of a new, WTO-consistent determination to entries made on or after the date of implementation. In the view of the United States, section 129(c)(1) does not mandate that the Department of Commerce take, or preclude Commerce from taking, any particular action with respect to "prior unliquidated entries" in a separate segment of an antidumping or countervailing duty proceeding, such as in a separate administrative review. The United States submits that Canada has, therefore, failed to demonstrate that section 129(c)(1) mandates WTO-inconsistent action or precludes WTO-consistent action and that, as a consequence, Canada's claims must fail.

2.   *Evaluation by the Panel*

6.20   The **Panel** notes that Canada has made claims of violation under Articles VI:2, VI:3 and VI:6(a) of the GATT 1994; Articles 1, 9.3, 11.1 and 18.1 of the AD Agreement; and Articles 10, 19.4, 21.1 and 32.1 of the SCM Agreement. It has also made claims under Article 18.4 of the AD Agreement, Article 32.5 of the SCM Agreement and Article XVI:4 of the WTO Agreement.[66]

---

[66]   Canada has not pursued its claims under the DSU before the Panel.

6.21   Canada argues that section 129(c)(1) is inconsistent with Article 18.4 of the AD Agreement, Article 32.5 of the SCM Agreement and Article XVI:4 of the WTO Agreement because it is inconsistent with the other WTO provisions invoked by Canada.[67] Accordingly, it is clear from Canada's arguments that the success of these claims depends on that of its first group of claims. For this reason, we will refer to the first group of claims as "principal claims" and to the second as "consequential claims".[68] Our findings will address Canada's principal claims first.

6.22   As concerns Canada's principal claims, we note that Canada in this case is challenging section 129(c)(1) "as such", that is to say independently of a particular application of section 129(c)(1). It is clear to us that a Member may challenge, and a WTO panel rule against, a statutory provision of another Member "as such" (for example, section 129(c)(1)), provided the statutory provision "mandates" the Member either to take action which is inconsistent with its WTO obligations[69] or not take action which is required by its WTO obligations[70]. In accordance with the normal WTO rules on the allocation of the burden of proof, it is up to the complaining Member to demonstrate that a challenged measure mandates another Member to take WTO-inconsistent action or not to take action which is required by its WTO obligations.[71]

6.23   In the light of the foregoing, it will be clear that Canada's principal claims will be sustained only if Canada succeeds in establishing that section 129(c)(1) mandates the United States to take action which is inconsistent with the WTO provisions which form the basis for those claims or mandates the United States not to take action which is required by those WTO provisions. In other words, for Canada to discharge its burden with respect to its principal claims, it must demonstrate both of two elements: *first*, that section 129(c)(1) mandates that the United States take or not take the action identified by Canada, and *second* that this mandated behaviour is inconsistent with the WTO provisions that it has invoked.

---

[67]   Canada's First Submission, paras. 80 and 84; Canada's First Oral Statement, paras. 28-29.

[68]   We note that the explicit characterization of Canada's claims as either "principal" or "consequential" is ours and that Canada has not used these terms.

[69]   Appellate Body Report, *United States – Anti-Dumping Act of 1916 ("US – 1916 Act")*, WT/DS136/AB/R, WT/DS162/AB/R, adopted 26 September 2000, DSR 2000:X, 4793, paras. 88-89. We note that both parties agree that the issue of whether section 129(c)(1) is a mandatory or discretionary provision is relevant to this dispute.

[70]   Both parties agree that a statutory provision may be challenged "as such" not only if it mandates WTO-inconsistent action, but also if it "precludes" action that is required by WTO rules. Canada's Second Oral Statement, para. 17; US Second Submission, para. 7. We understand the parties to this dispute to use the term "preclude" in the sense of "mandate not to". Whereas we are aware that another panel spoke of statutory provisions "precluding WTO-consistency" which could, as such, violate WTO provisions (see Panel Report, *United States – Sections 301-310 of the Trade Act of 1974 ("US – Section 301 Trade Act")*, WT/DS152/R, adopted 27 January 2000, DSR 2000:II, 815, footnote 675), we will, in the interests of clarity, use the expression "mandate not to" rather than "preclude".

[71]   Appellate Body Report, *US – 1916 Act*, *supra*, paras. 96-97; Panel Report, *Brazil – Export Financing Programme for Aircraft – Second Recourse by Canada to Article 21.5 of the DSU ("Brazil – Aircraft (Article 21.5 – Canada II)")*, WT/DS46/RW/2, adopted 23 August 2001, DSR 2000:II, 815, para. 5.50.

6.24   We consider that the issue of whether section 129(c)(1) mandates the United States to take certain action or not to take certain action is distinct from the issue of whether such behaviour would be inconsistent with the WTO provisions relied on by Canada. As a result, those two issues appear to us to be capable of independent examination.

6.25   We think that we need not address both of the aforementioned issues if we find that Canada has failed to meet its burden with respect to either one of them. As for the sequence in which we will address those issues, we find it appropriate, in the circumstances of this case, to analyse first whether section 129(c)(1) mandates the United States to take specified action or not to take specified action.[72]

6.26   With these considerations in mind, we now turn to analyse Canada's principal claims.

C.   Canada's Principal Claims

6.27   In this Section, the **Panel** will address Canada's principal claims in respect of section 129(c)(1), i.e., Canada's claims under Articles VI:2, VI:3 and VI:6(a) of the GATT 1994; Articles 1, 9.3, 11.1 and 18.1 of the AD Agreement; and Articles 10, 19.4, 21.1 and 32.1 of the SCM Agreement.

6.28   As a preliminary matter, we note that an assessment of whether section 129(c)(1) is inconsistent with any of the aforementioned WTO provisions will inevitably involve us in a close examination of the meaning and scope of that section. It should be recalled, in this regard, that panels are entitled (indeed, even obliged) to conduct a detailed examination of the domestic law of a Member, to the extent that doing so is necessary for the purposes of determining the WTO-conformity of that Member's domestic law.[73] For the purposes of such an

---

[72]   We note that the Panel in *United States - Measures Treating Exports Restraints as Subsidies* first considered whether certain action was in conformity with WTO requirements and only then addressed whether the measure at issue mandated such action. See Panel Report, *United States – Measures Treating Export Restraints as Subsidies* ("*US – Export Restraints*"), WT/DS194/R and Corr.2, adopted 23 August 2001, DSR 2001:XI, 5767, para. 8.14. In the circumstances of the case at hand, where there is a major *factual* dispute regarding whether section 129(c)(1) requires and/or precludes certain action, we think that a panel is of most assistance to the DSB if it examines the factual issues first. Moreover, we do not see how addressing first whether certain actions identified by Canada would contravene particular WTO provisions would facilitate our assessment of whether section 129(c)(1) mandates the United States to take certain action or not to take certain action. Finally, we have taken into account the fact that, in the present case, our ultimate conclusions with respect to Canada's claims would not differ depending on the order of analysis we decided to follow.

[73]   Appellate Body Report, *United States – Section 211 Omnibus Appropriations Act of 1998* ("*US – Section 211 Appropriations Act*"), WT/DS176/AB/R, adopted 1 February 2002, para. 105; Appellate Body Report, *United States – Anti-Dumping Measures on Certain Hot-Rolled Steel Products from Japan* ("*US – Hot-Rolled Steel*"), WT/DS184/AB/R, adopted 23 August 2001, 2001:X, 4697, para. 200; Appellate Body Report, *India – Patent Protection for Pharmaceutical and Agricultural Chemical Products* ("*India – Patents (US)*"), WT/DS50/AB/R, adopted 16 January 1998, DSR 1998:I, 9, para. 66; Panel Report, *United States – Anti-Dumping Act of 1916 – Complaint by the European Communities* ("*US – 1916 Act (EC)*"), WT/DS136/R and Corr.1, adopted 26 September 2000, as upheld by the Appellate Body Report, WT/DS136/AB/R, WT/DS162/AB/R, DSR 2000:X, 4593, para. 6.51; *United States –*

---

examination, the meaning and scope of relevant provisions of domestic law are questions of fact.[74]

6.29   Our analysis of Canada's principal claims is structured in accordance with these principles governing a panel's assessment of a Member's domestic law. We first identify the various actions which, in Canada's view, are "required" or "precluded" by section 129(c)(1) and, if taken (in cases where they are required) or not taken (in cases where they are precluded), would result in violations of the WTO provisions invoked by Canada. We will then turn to ascertain the meaning and scope of section 129(c)(1). Next, we will examine, based on our understanding of section 129(c)(1), whether Canada has established, as a matter of US law, that section 129(c)(1) requires and/or precludes any of the actions it has identified. Thereafter, we will proceed to assess whether Canada has established, as a matter of WTO law, that section 129(c)(1) "mandates" the United States to take any of the actions identified by Canada and/or "mandates" the United States not to take any of the actions identified by Canada.[75] Finally, if section 129(c)(1) mandates the United States to take any of the actions identified by Canada and/or mandates the United States not to take any of those actions, we will examine whether the United States would be in breach of the WTO provisions invoked by Canada if it were to take any of those actions (in cases where it is mandated to do so) or were not to take any of them (in cases where it is mandated not to do so).

1.   Actions Identified by Canada as Required and/or Precluded by Section 129(c)(1)

6.30   As noted, the **Panel** begins its analysis of Canada's principal claims by identifying first the actions which Canada alleges are "required" or "precluded" by section 129(c)(1) and which, in its view, would give rise to violations of the WTO provisions it has identified.

6.31   First of all, Canada asserts that section 129(c)(1) "requires", or has the effect of "requiring", the Department of Commerce:

(a)   to *conduct administrative reviews* with respect to "prior unliquidated entries"[76] after the implementation date pursuant to an anti-

---

Anti-Dumping Act of 1916 – Complaint by Japan ("US – 1916 Act (Japan)"), WT/DS162/R and Add.1, adopted 26 September 2000, as upheld by the Appellate Body Report, WT/DS136/AB/R, WT/DS162/AB/R, DSR 2000:X, 4831, para. 6.50.

[74]   Panel Report, *US - Section 301 Trade Act, supra*, para. 7.18.

[75]   We consider, in the circumstances of this case, that if Canada does not succeed in demonstrating, as a factual matter, that section 129(c)(1) "requires" (or has the effect of requiring) or "precludes" (or has the effect of precluding) any of the actions identified by it, Canada will not have established, as a matter of WTO law, that section 129(c)(1) "mandates" the United States to take any of those actions or "mandates" the United States not to take any of those actions.

[76]   Here and hereafter, we will use the term "prior unliquidated entries" in the sense ascribed to it by Canada. See, *supra*, para. 6.7. Unlike Canada, however, we will put the term in inverted commas to reflect the fact that it is not used in relevant US laws or regulations. See US replies to Panel Questions 5 and 20.

dumping or countervailing duty order found by the DSB to be WTO-inconsistent[77];

(b)   to *make administrative review determinations regarding dumping or subsidization* with respect to "prior unliquidated entries" after the implementation date pursuant to an antidumping or counter-vailing duty order found by the DSB to be WTO-inconsistent[78];

(c)   to *assess definitive antidumping or countervailing duties* with re-spect to "prior unliquidated entries" after the implementation date pursuant to an antidumping or countervailing duty order found by the DSB to be WTO-inconsistent[79]; and

(d)   to *retain cash deposits* in respect of "prior unliquidated entries" af-ter the implementation date at a level found by the DSB to be WTO-inconsistent.[80]

6.32   Canada alleges, furthermore, that section 129(c)(1), by "precluding" par-ticular actions, infringes the WTO provisions identified by Canada. Specifically, Canada asserts that section 129(c)(1) "precludes", or has the effect of "preclud-ing", the Department of Commerce from:

(a)   *making administrative review determinations regarding dumping or subsidization* with respect to "prior unliquidated entries" after the implementation date in a manner that is consistent with an ad-verse DSB ruling[81];

---

[77]   E.g., Canada's reply to Panel Question 74(b); Canada's Second Oral Statement, paras. 35 and 53; Canada's Second Submission, para. 32; Canada's reply to Panel Question 31. Canada considers that, after the implementation date, administrative reviews for "prior unliquidated entries" are, under WTO law, either: (i) not to be conducted in cases in which the ITC or the Department of Commerce makes a section 129 determination which results in the revocation of the original antidumping or counter-vailing duty order, or (ii) to be conducted on the basis of a section 129 determination by the Depart-ment of Commerce in cases in which such a determination does not result in the revocation of the original antidumping or countervailing duty order but may result in a lower definitive antidumping or countervailing duty being assessed on "prior unliquidated entries".

[78]   E.g., Canada's First Submission, paras. 33, 42 and 54.

[79]   E.g., Canada's First Submission, paras. 33, 42 and 54. We note that Canada also asserts that section 129(c)(1) requires the Department of Commerce to "make definitive duty determinations" with respect to "prior unliquidated entries". See Canada's Second Submission, para. 4. It appears to us that Canada's reference to the "making of definitive duty determinations" is a reference to the levying or assessment of definitive antidumping or countervailing duties. See Canada's reply to Panel Ques-tion 7. We further note that Canada has used, but not explained, the expression "definitive legal de-terminations of duty liability". See Canada's Second Submission, paras. 42 and 44. In the absence of any elaboration by Canada, we will not assume that the expression "definitive legal determinations of duty liability" covers any aspect of section 129(c)(1) that would not already be covered by Canada's broad reference to the actions identified in subparagraphs 6.31(b) and (c) above.

[80]   E.g., Canada's reply to Panel Question 74(a); Canada's Second Oral Statement, para. 35; Can-ada's Second Submission, para. 32. In Canada's view, the retention, after the implementation date, of cash deposits collected on "prior unliquidated entries" is not justified in whole or in part in cases in which: (i) the ITC or the Department of Commerce makes a section 129 determination which results in the revocation of the original antidumping or countervailing duty order, or (ii) the Department of Commerce makes a section 129 determination which may result in a lower definitive antidumping or countervailing duty being assessed on "prior unliquidated entries".

[81]   E.g., Canada's Second Oral Statement, para. 34; Canada's First Oral Statement, paras. 20-21.

(b)   *assessing definitive antidumping or countervailing duties* with respect to "prior unliquidated entries" after the implementation date in a manner that is consistent with an adverse DSB ruling[82]; and

(c)   *refunding*, after the implementation date, *cash deposits* collected on "prior unliquidated entries" pursuant to an antidumping or countervailing duty order found by the DSB to be WTO-inconsistent.[83]

6.33   Having identified the actions which Canada alleges are either required or precluded by section 129(c)(1), we can now proceed to examine whether section 129(c)(1) in fact requires (or has the effect of requiring) and/or precludes (or has the effect of precluding) any of those actions.[84]

2.   *Meaning and Scope of Section 129(c)(1)*

6.34   In order to determine whether section 129(c)(1) requires (or has the effect of requiring) and/or precludes (or has the effect of precluding) any of the actions specified by Canada, the **Panel** must first make a detailed examination of the meaning and scope of section 129(c)(1).

(a)   Examination of the URAA

6.35   Consistently with the parties' submissions, our examination of section 129(c)(1) will address both the text of section 129(c)(1) and relevant portions of the Statement of Administrative Action (the "SAA") accompanying the URAA.[85]

---

[82]   E.g., Canada's Second Oral Statement, paras. 34-35; Canada's Second Submission, paras. 8 and 14; Canada's First Oral Statement, paras. 20-21.

[83]   E.g., Canada's replies to Panel Questions 71 and 80. According to Canada, after the implementation date, cash deposits collected on "prior unliquidated entries" must be refunded in whole or in part in cases in which: (i) the ITC or the Department of Commerce makes a section 129 determination which results in the revocation of the original antidumping or countervailing duty order, or (ii) the Department of Commerce makes a section 129 determination which may result in a lower definitive antidumping or countervailing duty being assessed on "prior unliquidated entries".

[84]   We note that the United States has argued, in response to a question from the Panel, that the issue of the conduct, after the implementation date, of administrative reviews concerning "prior unliquidated entries" and the issue of the retention, after the implementation date, of cash deposits collected on such entries are not within the Panel's terms of reference. In support of this view, the United States states that section 129(c)(1) does not address either of these issues and that Canada's misunderstanding of what section 129(c)(1) allegedly requires cannot bring within the Panel's terms of reference measures which Canada did not identify in its panel request. See US reply to Panel Question 74. We do not consider that the issues in question are outside our terms of reference. Canada's assertions regarding the conduct of administrative reviews and the retention of cash deposits are clearly related to section 129(c)(1), i.e., the measure at issue in this case. In such circumstances, we do not think that the mere fact that Canada may be mistaken in its understanding of what action section 129(c)(1) requires bars us from addressing Canada's assertions.

[85]   We note that, in addition to being consistent with the parties' submissions, our approach to examining US statutory law is consistent with that of previous panels. See Panel Reports on *US – 1916 Act (EC)*, *supra*, para. 6.101; *US – 1916 Act (Japan)*, *supra*, para. 6.112; *US - Export Restraints*, *supra*, paras. 8.88 *et seq.*; *US - Section 301 Trade Act*, *supra*, paras. 7.31 and 7.98.

6.36   With respect to the relationship between section 129(c)(1) and the SAA, we note Canada's statement that:

> The SAA sets forth the authoritative interpretation of the URAA and the US Administration's obligations in implementing the URAA, as agreed between the US Administration and the US Congress. Congress approved the SAA in section 101 of the URAA and provided, in section 102 of the URAA, that "[t]he statement of administrative action approved by the Congress under section 101(a) shall be regarded as an authoritative expression by the United States concerning the interpretation and application of the Uruguay Round Agreements and this Act in any judicial proceeding in which a question arises concerning such interpretation or application".[86]

6.37   The United States has raised no objections to Canada's statement on the relationship between the SAA and the URAA.[87] We therefore adopt it for the purposes of our analysis in this case.[88]

6.38   Accordingly, in our examination of section 129(c)(1), we must be mindful of the legal status of the SAA in US law and take account of its content. This said, two caveats should be noted. *First*, it should be remembered that section 129(c)(1) is to be interpreted in the light of the SAA, and not the other way round.[89] *Second*, it should be recalled that, even though the SAA is intended to shed light on the meaning of the various provisions of the URAA, the statements contained in the SAA may, themselves, be open to interpretation.

> (b)   Examination of Section 129(c)(1) as Interpreted by the SAA

6.39   Section 129(c)(1) reads:

> (1)   EFFECTS OF DETERMINATIONS.— Determinations concerning title VII of the Tariff Act of 1930 that are implemented under this section shall apply with respect to unliquidated entries of the subject merchandise (as defined in section 771 of that Act) that are entered, or withdrawn from warehouse, for consumption on or after—
>
> > (A) in the case of a determination by the Commission under subsection (a)(4), the date on which the Trade Representative directs the administering authority under

---

[86]   Uruguay Round Agreements Act, Pub. L. No. 103-465, sections 101 and 102, 108 Stat. 4814-4819.

[87]   US reply to Panel Question 45.

[88]   Canada's statement on the legal status of the SAA is consistent with the findings of the Panel in *US - Export Restraints*. See Panel Report, *US - Export Restraints, supra*, paras. 8.93-8.100.

[89]   The Panel in *US - Export Restraints* found that the SAA has no operational life or status independently of the statute. See Panel Report, *US - Export Restraints, supra*, para. 8.99.

subsection (a)(6) to revoke an order pursuant to that determination, and

(B) in the case of a determination by the administering authority under subsection (b)(2), the date on which the Trade Representative directs the administering authority under subsection (b)(4) to implement that determination.

6.40   The SAA, in the first paragraph of section B.1.c.(3), contains the following statement regarding section 129(c)(1):

Consistent with the principle that GATT panel recommendations apply only prospectively, subsection 129(c)(1) provides that where determinations by the ITC or Commerce are implemented under subsections (a) or (b), such determinations have prospective effect only. That is, they apply to unliquidated entries of merchandise entered, or withdrawn from warehouse, for consumption on or after the date on which the Trade Representative directs implementation. Thus, relief available under subsection 129(c)(1) is distinguishable from relief available in an action brought before a court or a NAFTA binational panel, where, depending on the circumstances of the case, retroactive relief may be available. Under 129(c)(1), if implementation of a WTO report should result in the revocation of an antidumping or countervailing duty order, entries made prior to the date of Trade Representative's direction would remain subject to potential duty liability.[90]

(i)   Arguments of the Parties

6.41   **Canada** argues that, pursuant to section 129(c)(1), the Department of Commerce can only apply a new WTO-consistent determination made by the Department under section 129(b)(4) or the ITC under section 129(a)(6) to imports that enter the United States after the Implementation date. Canada considers that the words of section 129(c)(1) that limit application of a new, WTO-consistent determination to future entries, have the effect of precluding such application to "prior unliquidated entries". According to Canada, the use of the word "after" in section 129(c)(1) excludes any interpretation that would allow the Department of Commerce to apply the new determination to "prior unliquidated entries". Thus, in Canada's view, section 129(c)(1) directs itself to "prior unliquidated entries" by negative implication.

6.42   The **United States** points out that section 129(c)(1) does not contain any language addressing what Canada terms "prior unliquidated entries". The United States argues that section 129(c)(1) only addresses the treatment of entries that take place on or after the date of implementation, and even then, only addresses the application of the particular determination issued under section 129 to those entries. The United States states that the consequence of this is that the treatment

---

[90]   SAA, section B.1.c.(3), first paragraph, p. 1026.

of "prior unliquidated entries" would not be determined in a section 129 determination. Rather, the United States argues, the treatment of "prior unliquidated entries" would be determined in a separate proceeding.

(ii)   Evaluation by the Panel

6.43   The **Panel** recalls that section 129(c)(1) provides that "[d]eterminations concerning title VII of the Tariff Act of 1930" that are "implemented" under "this section" "shall apply with respect to unliquidated entries of the subject merchandise [...] that are entered [...] on or after" the date on which the USTR (i) directs revocation of an antidumping or countervailing duty order pursuant to such determinations or (ii) directs implementation of such determinations in cases where those determinations result in the setting of a new cash deposit rate.

6.44   We begin our examination of section 129(c)(1) by considering the phrase "[d]eterminations concerning title VII of the Tariff Act of 1930 that are implemented under this section". First of all, like the parties, we understand the term "this section" as used in the aforementioned phrase to refer to section 129 as a whole. The context of section 129(c)(1) supports this reading. As Canada points out, when a reference in section 129 is not to the section as a whole, but to a section within section 129, the terms "subsection" or "paragraph" are normally used.[91]

6.45   As concerns the term "[d]eterminations concerning title VII of the Tariff Act of 1930", we concur with the parties that it limits the scope of section 129(c)(1) to determinations which are made under section 129 and pertain to dumping, subsidization and injury. As an initial matter, we note that title VII of the Tariff Act of 1930 contains the antidumping and countervailing duty provisions of US law. Further, it appears to us that the qualifying words "concerning title VII of the Tariff Act of 1930" are used in section 129(c)(1) in order to make it clear that section 129(c)(1) applies to antidumping and countervailing duty determinations, but not to safeguards determinations, which are contemplated in subsection 129(a). Since the issuance of antidumping and countervailing duty determinations is dealt with in subsections 129(a)(4) and 129(b)(2), we consider that the term "[d]eterminations concerning title VII of the Tariff Act of 1930" as it appears in section 129(c)(1) should be understood to refer to antidumping and countervailing duty determinations which have been made under those subsections.

6.46   Finally, with respect to the term "implemented", we agree with the parties that this term limits the application of section 129(c)(1) to those determinations which are given legal effect. As the United States has explained, in instances where a new determination under section 129 would not change the antidumping or countervailing duty measure in place, it may not be necessary to give a new determination legal effect. Subsections 129(a)(6) and 129(b)(4) would appear to

---

[91]   E.g., section 129(c)(1)(A) ("subsection") and section 129(a)(2) ("paragraph").

confirm that the USTR has the authority, but is not obligated to implement determinations made under section 129.[92]

6.47   In the light of the above, we find that the phrase "[d]eterminations concerning title VII of the Tariff Act of 1930 that are implemented under this section" refers to antidumping and countervailing duty determinations made under subsections 129(a)(4) and 129(b)(2) (hereafter "section 129 determinations") and implemented under subsections 129(a)(6) and 129(b)(4). With this in mind, we now turn to examine the remainder of section 129(c)(1).

6.48   Pursuant to section 129(c)(1), a section 129 determination that is implemented "shall apply with respect to unliquidated entries of the subject merchandise [...] that are entered [...] on or after" the date on which the USTR directs revocation of an antidumping or countervailing duty order pursuant to the section 129 determination (as contemplated in section 129(c)(1)(A)) or directs implementation of the section 129 determination (as contemplated in section 129(c)(1)(B)). Thus, it is clear to us that whenever a section 129 determination is implemented, it applies to entries[93] that take place *on or after* the date of implementation.[94]

6.49   We further find, and the parties agree, that the language of section 129(c)(1) - "shall apply to [...] entries [...] that are entered [...] *on or after* [the date of implementation]" (emphasis added) - necessarily implies that a section 129 determination that is implemented does not apply to entries that took place *before* the date of implementation, i.e., to what Canada terms "prior unliquidated entries".[95]

6.50   Our reading of the text of section 129(c)(1) is not contradicted by either the context or purpose of section 129(c)(1). As regards the context of section 129(c)(1), we are not aware of anything in the provisions of section 129 as a

---

[92]   We find confirmation for our reading of the term "implemented" in the first paragraph of section B.1.c.(2) of the SAA ("The Trade Representative may decline to request implementation of [a section 129] determination.") and section B.1.c.(5) of the SAA ("Section 129 determinations that are not implemented will not be subject to judicial or binational panel review [...]"). See SAA, *supra*, pp. 1025 and 1026.

[93]   Here and hereafter, we employ the term "entries" as a shorthand expression for "entries of the subject merchandise", as stated in section 129(c)(1). In other words, the term "entries", as used in our findings, refers to entries which are subject to a particular antidumping or countervailing duty order. We understand the term "entries" as it appears in Canada's term "prior unliquidated entries" in the same sense.

[94]   Under the terms of section 129(c)(1), a section 129 determination that is implemented also applies to entries that are "withdrawn from warehouse" for consumption on or after the date on which the USTR directs implementation of that determination. The parties' submissions did not specifically address this aspect of section 129(c)(1). See Canada's First Submission, paras. 5 and 26; US First Submission, para. 14. Consistently with the parties' submissions, in our examination of section 129(c)(1) we will make no further mention of the fact that section 129(c)(1) covers entries that are withdrawn from warehouse on or after the implementation date.

[95]   This is consistent with the first paragraph of section B.1.c.(3) of the SAA ("[Section 129 determinations] have prospective effect only. That is, they apply to unliquidated entries of merchandise entered [...] for consumption on or after the date on which the Trade Representative directs implementation."). See SAA, *supra*, p. 1026.

whole, the URAA or title VII of the Tariff Act of 1930 which would support a different reading of the terms of section 129(c)(1).[96]

6.51   Regarding the purpose of section 129(c)(1), the United States submits, and Canada does not dispute, that section 129(c)(1) has the "purpose of providing the effective date for new, WTO-consistent [Department of] Commerce or ITC determinations that USTR directs [the Department of] Commerce to implement".[97] We agree and note that, on our reading, section 129(c)(1) fully effects that purpose.[98]

6.52   As for the purpose of section 129 as a whole, we share the US view that section 129 as a whole is intended "to provide a basis in domestic law for [the Department of] Commerce and the International Trade Commission to reconsider and revise final determinations so as to be consistent with adverse WTO reports and for USTR to direct implementation of those determinations".[99] It should be recalled, in this regard, that, in the view of the United States, there is no obligation under WTO law to implement adverse DSB rulings with respect to "prior unliquidated entries".[100] Section 129(c)(1), as we understand it, is consis-

---

[96]   Canada has contrasted section 129(c)(1) with section 516a of the Tariff Act of 1930. According to Canada, section 516a provides that in instances where a final decision by a US court or NAFTA Chapter Nineteen Binational Panel overturns a decision of the Department of Commerce or ITC in whole or in part, "prior unliquidated entries" are liquidated in accordance with the court or panel decision. See Canada's reply to Panel Question 3; 19 U.S.C. § 1516a(c)(1) of the Tariff Act of 1930. We see no need to examine section 516a further, as Canada does not argue that, in view of section 516a, section 129(c)(1) should be read in such a way that section 129 determinations would apply also to "prior unliquidated entries". Indeed, the first paragraph of section B.1.c.(3) of the SAA confirms that section 129(c)(1) is intended to provide for a different result from the one envisaged in cases of judicial review by US courts or NAFTA panels ("[Section 129] determinations have prospective effect only. [...] Thus, relief available under subsection 129(c)(1) is distinguishable from relief available in an action brought before a court or a NAFTA binational panel, where, depending on the circumstances of the case, retroactive relief may be available."). See SAA, *supra*, p. 1026.

[97]   US reply to Panel Question 7.

[98]   We find support for the United States' view in the title of section 129(c)(1) ("Effects of Determinations") as well as the second paragraph of section B.1.c.(3) of the SAA, which talks about the "effective date of an implemented [section 129] determination". See SAA, *supra*, p. 1025.

[99]   US reply to Panel Question 4. We note that Canada has stated along very similar lines that "[s]ection 129 provides for the issuance of a new antidumping or countervailing duty determination by the Department of Commerce or a new injury determination by the ITC to ensure that the new determination is 'not inconsistent with' the United States' obligations under the AD Agreement or the SCM Agreement". See Canada's First Submission, para. 4. We further note that these statements are supported by the provisions of subsections (a)(1), (a)(4), (a)(6), (b)(1), (b)(2) and (b)(4) of section 129. Finally, we note that the first paragraph of section B.1.c. of the SAA confirms our understanding of the purpose of section 129 ("Section 129 [...] establishes a procedure by which the Administration may obtain advice it requires to determine its response to an adverse WTO panel or Appellate Body report concerning U.S. obligations under the Agreement on Safeguards, Antidumping, or Subsidies and Countervailing Measures. Section 129 also establishes a mechanism that permits the agencies concerned [...] to issue a second determination, where such action is appropriate, to respond to the recommendations in a WTO panel or Appellate Body report."). See SAA, *supra*, p. 1022.

[100]   We have no reason to doubt that the United States adhered to the same interpretation of WTO law when section 129 was enacted. The first paragraph of section B.1.c.(3) of the SAA in fact confirms that the United States did not consider that it was obligated to implement with respect to "prior unliquidated entries" ("Consistent with the principle that GATT panel recommendations apply only

---

tent with this view, inasmuch as it does not provide for the application of section 129 determinations to "prior unliquidated entries". In that sense, we think that our reading of section 129(c)(1) is not contradicted by the purpose of section 129 as a whole.

6.53   Based on the foregoing considerations, we conclude that only determinations made and implemented under section 129 are within the scope of section 129(c)(1) and that such determinations are not applicable to "prior unliquidated entries".

3.   Whether Section 129(c)(1) Requires and/or Precludes any of the Actions Identified by Canada

6.54   The **Panel** will now proceed to assess whether section 129(c)(1), as understood by the Panel, supports Canada's assertions that, with respect to "prior unliquidated entries", section 129(c)(1) "requires" the United States to take the actions listed in para. 6.31 and that it "precludes" the United States from taking the actions listed in para. 6.32.

6.55   We recall, in this regard, that section 129(c)(1), on its face, does not address entries that took place *before* the implementation date, i.e., "prior unliquidated entries". Section 129(c)(1) only speaks to entries that take place *on or after* the implementation date. It is clear to us, therefore, that section 129(c)(1) does not, by its express terms, require or preclude any particular action with respect to "prior unliquidated entries". We consider that the above-quoted paragraph of the SAA - i.e., the first paragraph of section B.1.c.(3) - supports our view.[101]

6.56   Therefore, we conclude that Canada has not succeeded in establishing that, with respect to "prior unliquidated entries", the express terms of section 129(c)(1), read in the light of the SAA, require the Department of Commerce to take any of the actions listed in para. 6.31 above or preclude the Department of Commerce from taking any of the actions listed in para. 6.32 above.

4.   Whether Section 129(c)(1) has the Effect of Requiring and/or Precluding any of the Actions Identified by Canada

6.57   The **Panel** next turns to consider Canada's additional assertions that section 129(c)(1) has the *effect* of requiring the Department of Commerce to take

---

prospectively, subsection 129(c)(1) provides that where determinations by the ITC or Commerce are implemented under subsections (a) or (b), such determinations have prospective effect only. That is, they apply to unliquidated merchandise entered [...] for consumption on or after the date on which the [USTR] directs implementation [of a section 129 determination]."). See SAA, *supra*, p. 1025.

[101]   The SAA paragraph in question is reproduced at para. 6.40 above. Since we will provide a detailed analysis of the first paragraph of section B.1.c.(3) of the SAA in Subsection C.4.(b) below, we do not offer any discussion of the relevant SAA paragraph at this point. We further note that the evidence before us relating to the application of section 129(c)(1) to date does not support Canada's view that section 129(c)(1) requires and/or precludes any of the actions which it has identified. See, *infra*, Subsection C.4.(c).

specified actions with respect to "prior unliquidated entries" and that section 129(c)(1) has the *effect* of precluding the Department of Commerce from taking specified actions with respect to such entries.[102]

6.58   We will first examine the arguments of the parties relating to section 129(c)(1) as enacted. After that, we will consider the parties' arguments concerning relevant portions of the SAA. We wish to be clear that we assess these arguments separately for convenience of analysis only. As we have noted, section 129(c)(1) must be read together with the SAA.[103] Accordingly, we will not reach any conclusions regarding Canada's assertions that section 129(c)(1) has the effect of requiring and precluding certain actions until after we have taken into account relevant parts of the SAA. Our conclusions regarding the assertions in question will, as a result, be based on section 129(c)(1) as interpreted by the SAA, rather than on section 129(c)(1) read in isolation. Moreover, before reaching any conclusions regarding Canada's assertions, we will also address the application of section 129(c)(1) to date.

(a)   Section 129(c)(1) as Enacted

6.59   As noted above, under this subheading, the **Panel** will describe and analyse the arguments of the parties which relate to section 129(c)(1) as enacted. For the reasons set forth in the previous paragraph, our findings under this subheading will be provisional.

(i)   Arguments of the Parties

6.60   **Canada** considers that the effect of section 129(c)(1) is broader than just the immediate determinations made under section 129. Canada submits that a US court would find that the language of section 129(c)(1) has the effect of precluding the Department of Commerce from applying a new, WTO-consistent determination to "prior unliquidated entries" because otherwise the express limitation to future entries contained in section 129(c)(1) would be meaningless. Canada argues that the wording in section 129(c)(1) would be materially undermined if section 129(c)(1) were interpreted to allow the Department of Commerce to take action to comply with an adverse DSB ruling with respect to "prior unliquidated entries".

6.61   The **United States** argues that section 129(c)(1) does not address what actions the Department of Commerce may or may not take in a *separate* determination in a *separate* "segment" of the same proceeding (e.g., any separate administrative review of the same antidumping or countervailing duty order).[104]

---

[102]   For a description of the actions specified by Canada see, *supra*, paras. 6.31 and 6.32.

[103]   See, *supra*, para. 6.38.

[104]   The United States notes that section 351.102 of the regulations of the Department of Commerce defines a "segment" of a proceeding as follows:

> (1) *In general.* An antidumping or countervailing duty proceeding consists of one or more segments. "Segment of a proceeding" or "segment of the proceeding" refers to a portion of the proceeding that is reviewable under section 516A of the Act.

According to the United States, a determination made in a distinct segment of the same proceeding would not, therefore, be subject to section 129(c)(1).

6.62   This can be illustrated, in the view of the United States, by considering two scenarios identified by Canada in the course of the proceedings. Under the *first scenario* (which concerns what Canada terms "*methodology cases*"), the challenged determination is a final dumping determination in an investigation. The United States notes that if the challenge were successful, the Department of Commerce may be able to implement the adverse DSB ruling by making changes in its methodologies and issue a new, WTO-consistent determination under section 129. That determination would be applied to all entries that took place on or after the implementation date. The United States further notes that, if a company subsequently requested an administrative review of "prior unliqui-dated entries", the Department of Commerce would conduct the administrative review of those entries and issue a determination in that segment of the proceed-ing. According to the United States, because the administrative review determi-nation would not be the determination implemented under section 129, nothing in section 129(c)(1) would preclude Commerce from applying a WTO-consistent methodology developed in the section 129 determination in that administrative review (i.e., in another segment of the same proceeding). [105]

6.63   The *second scenario* addressed by the United States involves what Can-ada describes as a "*revocation case*", i.e., a situation where a WTO challenge results in the revocation of an antidumping or countervailing duty order because the new, WTO-consistent determination issued under section 129 results in a finding of no injury, no dumping or no subsidization. The United States notes that, under the terms of section 129(c)(1), the revocation would apply to all en-tries taking place on or after the date of implementation. With respect to the treatment of "prior unliquidated entries" in such a situation, the United States notes that it is not clear which of a number of options the Department of Com-merce would pursue, as the Department has not faced such a situation to date. The United States submits, however, that section 129(c)(1) would not mandate any particular treatment of "prior unliquidated entries" in such situations. The United States points out, in particular, that section 129(c)(1) does not require the United States to apply duties to those entries, does not limit the discretion of the Department of Commerce in deciding how to interpret and apply the antidump-

---

(2) *Examples.* An antidumping or countervailing duty investigation or a review of an order or suspended investigation, or a scope inquiry under § 351.225, each would constitute a segment of a proceeding. (19 C.F.R. 351.102 (2000))

[105]   The United States points out, in this regard, that, in the administrative review pursuant to section 751 of the Tariff Act of 1930, the Department of Commerce would have the legal authority to alter its statutory interpretation or methodology from one announced prior to the implementation of the DSB ruling, provided that it gives a reasonable explanation for doing so. In support of this contention, the United States refers to *INS v. Yang*, 519 U.S. 26, 32 (1996); *Atchison, Topeka & Santa Fe Ry v. Wichita Board of Trade*, 412 U.S. 800, 808 (1973); *British Steel, PLC v. United States*, 127 F.3d 1471, 1475 (Fed. Cir. 1997). According to the United States, the so-called *Charming Betsy* doctrine could be relied on by the Department of Commerce as a reasonable explanation for its change in interpretation or methodology in the administrative review determination.

ing and countervailing duty laws in separate segments of the proceedings with respect to those entries, does not limit judicial review of the results of those separate proceedings, and does not limit the obligation of the Department of Commerce to implement the results of any such judicial proceedings.

6.64   **Canada** submits that the US assertion that, in *methodology cases*, the Department of Commerce could "circumvent" the limitation in section 129(c)(1) with respect to "prior unliquidated entries" in cases where implementation of a DSB ruling requires the Department of Commerce to change its interpretation of the law or its methodology is untested in the administrative practice of the Department of Commerce or in US courts. Canada further argues that the US assertion goes against US principles of statutory construction. Canada notes, in this respect, that the US assertion implies that section 129(c)(1) would have no effect other than to prevent the refund of unjustifiable cash deposits on "prior unliquidated entries" while leaving the Department of Commerce free to make definitive duty determinations for such entries in administrative reviews in a WTO-consistent manner. Canada considers it unlikely that the US Congress would have created the limitation in section 129(c)(1) merely to permit temporary retention of excessive cash deposits that would be returned at the end of the administrative reviews. Canada points out, in this regard, that US jurisprudence establishes that a court "cannot presume that Congress intended [one result] with one hand, while reducing it to a veritable nullity with the other".[106]

6.65   Regarding *revocation cases*, Canada argues that, at least with respect to cases in which an antidumping or countervailing duty order was revoked as a result of a new no-injury determination by the ITC, the Department of Commerce, because of section 129(c)(1), would have to retain cash deposits on "prior unliquidated entries", conduct an administrative review and levy definitive duties with regard to such entries. In Canada's view, the Department of Commerce would have no legal authority or administrative discretion to decline to assess definitive duties on such entries, as it could not disregard the original injury finding, which would remain in effect as a matter of US law with respect to "prior unliquidated entries" notwithstanding the new no-injury determination by the ITC.[107] For Canada it is clear that it is because of section 129(c)(1) that the Department of Commerce would retain cash deposits, conduct administrative reviews and assess definitive duties in such situations. Canada submits, in this respect, that if there were no section 129(c)(1), then a negative injury finding by the ITC and the revocation of an antidumping or countervailing duty order under section 129 would apply to all unliquidated entries, including "prior unliquidated entries". Canada notes that, in such circumstances, cash deposits would be re-

---

[106] Canada's quotation is taken from *Katie John* v. *United States*, 247 F.3d 1032, 1038 (9th Cir. 2001) citing *Johnson* v. *United States R.R. Retirement Board*, 969 F.2d 1082, 1089 (D.C. Cir. 1992), which found that it was "unreasonable to conclude that Congress meant to create an entitlement with one hand and snatch it away with the other". Canada further references *American Tobacco Co.* v. *Patterson*, 456 U.S. 63, 71 (April 5, 1982) which stated that "[s]tatutes should be interpreted to avoid untenable distinctions and unreasonable results whenever possible".

[107] Canada notes that it could be different only where a decision by a US court resulted in the revocation of the original antidumping or countervailing duty order for reasons of US law.

turned to importers, and the Department of Commerce would neither conduct an administrative review nor assess definitive duties.

(ii)   Evaluation by the Panel

6.66   Since the parties have discussed the issue of whether section 129(c)(1) has the effect of requiring and/or precluding certain actions with respect to "prior unliquidated entries" on the basis of two scenarios identified by Canada, the **Panel**, too, will conduct its analysis on that basis. For ease of reference, we will adopt Canada's terminology and refer to those scenarios as the "methodology cases" and the "revocation cases", respectively.[108]

Methodology Cases

6.67   We first consider the operation of section 129(c)(1) in methodology cases. Methodology cases are cases in which the section 129 determination does not result in the revocation of the original antidumping or countervailing duty order, but instead results in a new margin of dumping or a new countervailable subsidy rate. Such an outcome may be due, for instance, to the application of a new, WTO-consistent methodology or a new, WTO-consistent interpretation of US antidumping or countervailing duty laws.[109] If the USTR directs implementation of a section 129 determination of the aforementioned type, that determination would be applied, pursuant to section 129(c)(1), to all entries that take place on or after the implementation date.[110] As a practical matter, the section 129 determination would be applied by setting a new cash deposit rate for such entries.[111]

6.68   Turning now to Canada's assertions regarding the "effect" of section 129(c)(1) *vis-à-vis* "prior unliquidated entries", we begin our analysis by considering what would be the impact on "prior unliquidated entries" of a section 129 determination which establishes a new dumping margin or a new countervailable subsidy rate. As we understand it, since a section 129 determination of this type would not be applicable to "prior unliquidated entries", that determination, as such, would not have an impact on such entries. In other words, we think it can be inferred from the fact that a section 129 determination which establishes a new dumping margin or a new countervailable subsidy rate is inapplicable to "prior unliquidated entries" that the Department of Commerce would *not* be required, because of section 129(c)(1), to refund excessive cash deposits previously collected on "prior unliquidated entries" or to make determinations regarding dumping or subsidization and assess definitive antidumping or countervailing duties with respect to such entries on the basis of the new, WTO-consistent methodology.

---

[108]   Canada's Second Oral Statement, para. 19; Canada's reply to Panel Question 81(a).

[109]   In their argumentation, the parties have primarily discussed cases in which a section 129 determination is based on a new methodology rather than on a revised statutory interpretation. Accordingly, our analysis similarly focuses on methodology cases.

[110]   We recall that we have found at para. 6.53, *supra*, that, pursuant to section 129(c)(1), section 129 determinations do not apply to "prior unliquidated entries".

[111]   US Second Submission, para. 17.

6.69   Conversely, we think it can *not* be inferred from the mere fact that a section 129 determination which establishes a new dumping margin or a new countervailable subsidy rate is inapplicable to "prior unliquidated entries" that the Department of Commerce would be required to retain excessive cash deposits collected on such entries or would be precluded from refunding such cash deposits. Nor does it follow from the fact that a section 129 determination does not apply to "prior unliquidated entries" that the Department of Commerce would be required to make administrative review determinations regarding dumping or subsidization and assess definitive antidumping or countervailing duties with respect to "prior unliquidated entries" on the basis of the previous, WTO-inconsistent methodology, or would be precluded from making such determinations and assessing definitive duties with respect to such entries on the basis of the new, WTO-consistent methodology.[112]

6.70   Canada nevertheless seeks to convince us that section 129(c)(1), by itself, has the effect, in methodology cases, of requiring or precluding the above-mentioned actions with respect to "prior unliquidated entries". Canada's arguments in support of its position on this point are explained most clearly in response to an assertion made by the United States. Accordingly, our analysis of Canada's arguments will focus on the evidence and arguments presented by Canada in response to the US assertion.[113] The assertion in question is to the effect that, notwithstanding section 129(c)(1), the Department of Commerce would have the legal authority, in methodology cases, to make determinations regarding dumping or subsidization and assess definitive antidumping or countervailing duties with respect to "prior unliquidated entries" in an administrative review on the basis of a new, WTO-consistent methodology developed in a section 129 determination.[114]

6.71   Canada argues, first of all, that if the Department of Commerce were to make definitive duty determinations with respect to "prior unliquidated entries" in an administrative review on the basis of a new, WTO-consistent methodology,

---

[112]   It might of course be the case that, because section 129(c)(1) limits the application of section 129 determinations to entries that take place on or after the implementation date, "prior unliquidated entries" would remain subject to other provisions of US antidumping or countervailing duty laws which might, for instance, *require* the Department of Commerce to assess definitive antidumping or countervailing duties with respect to "prior unliquidated entries" on the basis of the old, WTO-inconsistent methodology or might *preclude* the Department of Commerce from assessing such duties with respect to such entries on the basis of the new, WTO-consistent methodology. However, in such instances, it would not be because of section 129(c)(1) that the Department of Commerce would be required to take, or be precluded from taking, such action with respect to "prior unliquidated entries", but because of those other provisions of US law. Since the only measure before us is section 129(c)(1), we are not called on to make findings regarding whether any other provisions of US law would require the United States to take any of the actions which Canada has identified and considers contrary to WTO law.

[113]   This should not be construed to mean that the Panel has not carefully considered all arguments presented by Canada in the course of these proceedings.

[114]   Consistently with our terms of reference, we refrain from making findings regarding whether the United States is correct in asserting that the Department of Commerce would, as a matter of US law, have the legal authority to make administrative review determinations with respect to "prior unliquidated entries" on the basis of a new, WTO-consistent methodology.

it would "circumvent" the limitation in section 129(c)(1) or "materially undermine" the effect of the wording in section 129(c)(1). We are not persuaded by this argument. As we have stated above, by its terms, section 129(c)(1) only addresses the application of section 129 determinations. Section 129(c)(1) does not speak to the application to "prior unliquidated entries" of *separate determinations* made in *separate segments* of the same proceeding[115] and *under separate provisions* of US antidumping or countervailing duty laws, such as administrative review determinations. Accordingly, we see no basis for concluding that the language used in section 129(c)(1), by itself, has the effect of precluding the Department of Commerce from making definitive duty determinations in an administrative review with respect to "prior unliquidated entries" on the basis of a methodology developed in a section 129 determination.

6.72   What is more, we find convincing the argument of the United States that a distinction is to be drawn between the section 129 determination, which, e.g., establishes a particular dumping margin or countervailable subsidy rate, and the methodologies developed and applied in a section 129 determination.[116] As we understand the terms of section 129(c)(1), they limit the application of section 129 determinations to entries that take place on or after the implementation date. We see nothing in section 129(c)(1) which would similarly limit the use of methodologies developed and applied in a section 129 determination to such entries. Thus, section 129(c)(1) does not have the effect of precluding the application of methodologies developed in a section 129 determination in administrative reviews of "prior unliquidated entries".

6.73   Finally, we note that, in the hypothetical circumstances under consideration, what the Department of Commerce would be applying in an administrative review of "prior unliquidated entries" is a methodology developed in a section 129 determination, and not the section 129 determination *itself*. As a consequence, we are not convinced that, in such a situation, the Department of Commerce would be considered by a US court to be applying a section 129 determination to "prior unliquidated entries" in circumvention of the provisions of section 129(c)(1). Nor do we think that the Department of Commerce could be said to be applying a section 129 determination *in effect*. As the United States has pointed out, the Department of Commerce would be applying the section 129 methodology to the facts established in the administrative review proceedings. It would not be applying the section 129 methodology to the facts developed in the original segment of the proceedings which was challenged at the WTO.[117] We are not persuaded, therefore, that section 129(c)(1) has the effect of precluding the Department of Commerce from utilizing a methodology adopted in a section 129 determination in a separate segment of the proceeding, i.e., in an administrative review concerning "prior unliquidated entries".

---

[115]   For an explanation of the concept of "segment", see, *supra*, footnote 104.
[116]   US reply to Panel Question 92(b).
[117]   US reply to Panel Question 92(c).

6.74   Canada further argues that section 129(c)(1) has the effect of precluding the Department of Commerce from making definitive duty determinations with respect to "prior unliquidated entries" in an administrative review on the basis of a WTO-consistent methodology, because, under US principles of statutory construction, it must not be presumed that the US Congress intended for the results which it sought to achieve to be reduced to a veritable nullity.[118] More specifically, Canada submits that it is unlikely that the US Congress enacted the limitation in section 129(c)(1) merely to permit the Department of Commerce to retain excessive cash deposits collected on "prior unliquidated entries" and to return them at the end of the administrative review proceedings concerning those entries.

6.75   We do not find this argument on statutory construction convincing. Section 129(c)(1) fulfils its limited purpose of providing an effective date for the application of section 129 determinations that are implemented regardless of whether a methodology developed in a section 129 determination is used in an administrative review of "prior unliquidated entries". Moreover, regardless of whether a methodology developed in a section 129 determination is used in an administrative review of "prior unliquidated entries", section 129(c)(1) ensures that section 129 determinations are only applied to entries that occur on or after the implementation date. We are, therefore, not persuaded that a US court would interpret section 129(c)(1) to preclude the Department of Commerce from using a methodology developed in a section 129 determination in an administrative review of "prior unliquidated entries" on the grounds that, on any other interpretation, it would become meaningless and devoid of any useful effect.

6.76   As regards Canada's reliance on the likely intent of the US Congress, it would seem to be reasonable to assume, as Canada does, that the US Congress did *not* enact section 129(c)(1) "to permit temporary retention of excessive cash deposits" collected on "prior unliquidated entries". In our view, the US Congress enacted section 129(c)(1) to ensure compliance with adverse DSB rulings only with respect to entries that take place *on or after* the implementation date. It did so apparently in the belief that there was no requirement under WTO law to implement an adverse DSB ruling with respect to "prior unliquidated entries". Contrary to what Canada's argument suggests, however, the fact that the US Congress sought to ensure compliance only with respect to post-implementation entries does not necessarily imply that the US Congress sought to *preclude* compliance with respect to "prior unliquidated entries". Indeed, such an assumption strikes us as rather implausible. We think it more likely that the US Congress simply did not seek to *ensure* compliance with respect to "prior unliquidated entries". In any event, we note that, other than the SAA (which, as we will see below, does not support Canada's position), Canada has provided no evidence regarding the legislative history of section 129. For these reasons, we do not consider that a US court would interpret section 129(c)(1) to preclude the Depart-

---

[118]   For Canada's references to relevant US jurisprudence, see, *supra*, footnote 106.

ment of Commerce from making administrative review determinations with respect to "prior unliquidated entries" consistently with an adverse DSB ruling.

6.77   In the light of the above considerations, we provisionally find that Canada has not succeeded in establishing that, in methodology cases, section 129(c)(1), by itself, has the effect of precluding the Department of Commerce from making administrative review determinations regarding dumping or subsidization and assessing definitive antidumping or countervailing duties with respect to "prior unliquidated entries" on the basis of a new, WTO-consistent methodology developed in a section 129 determination. Based also on the above considerations, we provisionally find that the evidence and arguments presented by Canada are, likewise, insufficient to establish that, in methodology cases, section 129(c)(1), by itself, has the effect of requiring the Department of Commerce to make administrative review determinations regarding dumping or subsidization and assess definitive antidumping or countervailing duties with respect to "prior unliquidated entries" on the basis of a methodology found by the DSB to be WTO-inconsistent.[119]

6.78   We consider, next, whether Canada has succeeded in establishing any of its other assertions regarding the effect of section 129(c)(1) in methodology cases, i.e., Canada's assertion that section 129(c)(1), by itself, has the effect (i) of requiring the Department of Commerce to retain excessive cash deposits collected on "prior unliquidated entries", (ii) of precluding the Department of Commerce from returning such cash deposits and (iii) of requiring the Department of Commerce to conduct administrative reviews with respect to such entries on the basis of a methodology found by the DSB to be WTO-inconsistent.

6.79   In support of these assertions, Canada has not offered evidence or arguments different from, or additional to, the evidence and arguments adduced by it in connection with its assertions regarding administrative review determinations. We have found the evidence and arguments adduced by Canada in connection with its assertions regarding administrative review determinations to be insufficient to sustain those assertions. In our assessment, the evidence and arguments in question are also insufficient to sustain Canada's assertions in respect of cash deposits and the conduct of administrative reviews.

6.80   In particular, we do not think that if the Department of Commerce did *not* retain excessive cash deposits collected on "prior unliquidated entries" or did *not* conduct administrative reviews with respect to such entries on the basis of the methodology found by the DSB to be WTO-inconsistent, it would be "circumventing" the limitation in section 129(c)(1) or "materially undermining" the ef-

---

[119]   We note Canada's assertion that, in cases where a section 129 determination is based on a revised statutory interpretation rather than a new methodology, section 129(c)(1) constrains the discretion the Department of Commerce would otherwise have to interpret the law in a manner consistent with an adverse DSB ruling. We do not find this assertion persuasive. There is no need to address this issue at length, as our findings regarding "methodology cases" and the reasoning supporting them are applicable, *mutatis mutandis*, also to "interpretation cases". We refer, in particular, to paras. 6.69 and 6.71-6.76 above.

fect of the wording in section 129(c)(1).[120] As we have pointed out above, section 129(c)(1) only addresses the application of section 129 determinations. It does not require or preclude any particular actions with respect to "prior unliquidated entries" in a separate segment of the same proceeding. Nor do we consider that if the Department of Commerce did *not* retain excessive cash deposits collected on "prior unliquidated entries" or did *not* conduct administrative reviews with respect to such entries based on the WTO-inconsistent methodology, it would render section 129(c)(1) ineffective or would be acting inconsistently with the likely intent of the US Congress. The return of excessive cash deposits collected on "prior unliquidated entries" or the conduct of administrative reviews with respect to such entries on the basis of a WTO-consistent methodology developed in a section 129 determination would not make the provisions of section 129(c)(1) meaningless. Moreover, such actions would not, in our view, be inconsistent with the likely intent of the US Congress in enacting section 129(c)(1), *viz.*, to ensure implementation of an adverse DSB ruling only with respect to post-implementation entries.

6.81   Accordingly, we provisionally find that Canada has failed to demonstrate that section 129(c)(1), by itself, has the effect, in methodology cases, of requiring the Department of Commerce to retain excessive cash deposits collected on "prior unliquidated entries" or of precluding the Department of Commerce from returning such cash deposits, or of requiring the Department of Commerce to conduct administrative reviews for "prior unliquidated entries" on the basis of a methodology found by the DSB to be WTO-inconsistent.

Revocation Cases

6.82   As stated above, as part of our assessment of Canada's reading of section 129(c)(1), we also need to consider the other cases specifically addressed by Canada, i.e., revocation cases. Revocation cases are cases in which the section 129 determination results in the revocation of the original antidumping or countervailing duty order. An antidumping or countervailing duty order would be revoked if a section 129 determination established that there was no dumping, no subsidization or no injury. Pursuant to section 129(c)(1), the revocation of a WTO-inconsistent antidumping or countervailing duty order would apply to all entries that take place on or after the implementation date.[121] We are led to understand that, in practice, this would mean that, as of the implementation date, cash deposits would no longer be required on new entries.[122]

---

[120]   It should be recalled here that we are not called on, in this case, to make findings regarding whether provisions of US law other than section 129(c)(1) would preclude the Department of Commerce from returning excessive cash deposits collected on "prior unliquidated entries" or require it to conduct administrative reviews with respect to such entries on a basis found by the DSB to be WTO-inconsistent.

[121]   We note that it is not in dispute that a revocation would not apply to "prior unliquidated entries". See Canada's Second Oral Statement, para. 26; US Second Submission, para. 19; US reply to Panel Question 46.

[122]   US Second Submission, para. 19.

6.83   Turning now to Canada's assertions regarding the "effect" of section 129(c)(1) *vis-à-vis* "prior unliquidated entries", we begin our analysis by considering what would be the impact on "prior unliquidated entries" of a section 129 determination which results in the revocation of an antidumping or countervailing duty order. As we see it, since, pursuant to section 129(c)(1), a section 129 determination of this type would not be applicable to "prior unliquidated entries", that determination, as such, would not have an impact on "prior unliquidated entries". In other words, we think it can be inferred from the fact that a revocation of an antidumping or countervailing duty order would apply only with respect to post-implementation entries that the Department of Commerce would *not* be required, because of section 129(c)(1), to refund cash deposits previously collected on "prior unliquidated entries" on the basis of the WTO-inconsistent antidumping or countervailing duty order, to decline to conduct administrative reviews for such entries, to decline to make determinations regarding dumping or subsidization with respect such entries on the basis of the WTO-inconsistent antidumping or countervailing duty order or to decline to assess definitive antidumping or countervailing duties with respect to such entries on the basis of the WTO-inconsistent antidumping or countervailing duty order.

6.84   Conversely, we think it can *not* be inferred from the mere fact that a revocation is inapplicable to "prior unliquidated entries" that the Department of Commerce would be required to retain cash deposits collected on such entries on the basis of the WTO-inconsistent antidumping or countervailing duty order or would be precluded from refunding such cash deposits. Nor does it follow from the fact that a revocation does not apply to "prior unliquidated entries" that the Department of Commerce would be required to conduct administrative reviews for such entries. Nor does the non-application of a revocation to "prior unliquidated entries" necessarily imply that the Department of Commerce would be required to make administrative review determinations regarding dumping or subsidization and assess definitive antidumping or countervailing duties with respect to "prior unliquidated entries" on the basis of the WTO-inconsistent antidumping or countervailing duty order, or would be precluded from making such determinations and assessing definitive duties with respect to such entries in a manner consistent with WTO requirements.[123]

---

[123]   As we have noted above with respect to methodology cases, it might be the case that, because section 129(c)(1) limits the application of a revocation to entries that take place after the implementation date, "prior unliquidated entries" would remain subject to other provisions of US antidumping or countervailing duty laws which might, for instance, *require* the Department of Commerce to assess definitive antidumping or countervailing duties with respect to "prior unliquidated entries" on the basis of the old, WTO-inconsistent antidumping or countervailing duty order or might *preclude* the Department of Commerce from declining to assess such duties with respect to such entries. However, in such instances, it would not be because of section 129(c)(1) that the Department of Commerce would be required to take, or be precluded from taking, such action with respect to "prior unliquidated entries", but because of those other provisions of US law. Since the measure before us is section 129(c)(1), we are not called on to make findings regarding whether any other provisions of US law would require the United States to take any of the actions which Canada has identified and considers contrary to WTO law.

6.85   Canada nevertheless seeks to convince us that section 129(c)(1), by itself, has the effect, in revocation cases, of precluding the Department of Commerce from (i) returning cash deposits collected on "prior unliquidated entries" on the basis of the WTO-inconsistent antidumping or countervailing duty order, (ii) declining to conduct an administrative review for such entries and (iii) declining to make administrative review determinations with respect to such entries on the basis of the WTO-inconsistent antidumping or countervailing duty order. In support of this assertion, Canada argues that, but for the existence of section 129(c)(1), the revocation of an antidumping or countervailing duty order would apply not only to entries that occur on or after the implementation date, but also to "prior unliquidated entries". According to Canada, the Department of Commerce would then be required to return cash deposits collected on "prior unliquidated entries" on the basis of the WTO-inconsistent order, and could neither conduct administrative reviews for such entries nor assess duties on such entries.

6.86   The premise of Canada's argument, as we understand it, is that, if there were no section 129(c)(1), a section 129 determination which was implemented, including one which results in the revocation of an antidumping or countervailing duty order, would apply to all unliquidated entries, i.e., "prior unliquidated entries" and future entries.[124] We are not convinced of the validity and relevance of Canada's premise. Indeed, if there were no section 129(c)(1), there would be no effective date for the application of section 129 determinations which the USTR directs to implement. In this regard, it seems to us that the very existence of section 129(c)(1) suggests that it may be necessary, for the purposes of US law, to provide for an effective date for the application of section 129 determinations. In fact, the United States has specifically stated that, in the absence of section 129(c)(1), it would be necessary to establish an effective date for determinations implemented under section 129.[125] Canada has offered nothing in rebuttal of this argument.

6.87   Even disregarding the issue of the effective date and accepting that, in the absence of section 129(c)(1), a revocation would apply to "prior unliquidated entries" as well, we fail to see how this would demonstrate that section 129(c)(1) has the effect of precluding the Department of Commerce from returning cash deposits on "prior unliquidated entries", declining to hold administrative reviews for such entries and declining to assess duties with respect to such entries.

6.88   Indeed, if there were no section 129(c)(1) and a provision like section 129(c)(1) was subsequently enacted, the consequence of this would be that section 129 determinations would not apply to "prior unliquidated entries". As we have said, this would mean that the Department of Commerce would then not be required, as a matter of US law, to return cash deposits collected on such entries based on the WTO-inconsistent antidumping or countervailing duty order, to decline to hold administrative reviews for such entries and to decline to assess

---

[124]   Canada's reply to Panel Question 6.
[125]   US reply to Panel Question 6.

duties with respect to such entries on the basis of the WTO-inconsistent order. Moreover, as we have also observed, it would not follow from the fact that a revocation would then be inapplicable to "prior unliquidated entries" that the Department of Commerce could not return cash deposits collected on "prior unliquidated entries", could not decline to hold administrative reviews with respect to such entries and could not decline to assess duties with respect to such entries.

6.89   Other than the evidence and arguments we have previously considered in the context of methodology cases, Canada has offered no specific arguments or evidence in support of its assertion that the enactment of section 129(c)(1) would nevertheless have the effect, in revocation cases, of precluding any of the actions mentioned in the previous paragraph. Whilst we consider that the evidence and arguments adduced by Canada in the context of methodology cases are applicable, *mutatis mutandis*, in the context of revocation cases as well, it should be recalled that we have found the evidence and arguments in question to be insufficient to sustain Canada's assertions in the context of methodology cases. We see no basis for considering that, notwithstanding this finding, the same evidence and arguments support Canada's assertions in the context of revocation cases.

6.90   In particular, if the Department of Commerce, in revocation cases, did *not* retain cash deposits collected on "prior unliquidated entries" on the basis of the WTO-inconsistent antidumping or countervailing duty order, did *not* conduct administrative reviews with respect to such entries or did *not* assess definitive antidumping or countervailing duties with respect to such entries, it would not, in our view, be "circumventing" the limitation in section 129(c)(1) or "materially undermining" the effect of the wording in section 129(c)(1).[126] Section 129(c)(1) only addresses the application of section 129 determinations. It does not require or preclude any particular actions with respect to "prior unliquidated entries" in a separate segment of the same proceeding. Nor do we consider that if the Department of Commerce did *not* retain cash deposits collected on "prior unliquidated entries" on the basis of the WTO-inconsistent order, did *not* conduct administrative reviews with respect to such entries or did *not* assess duties with respect to such entries, it would render section 129(c)(1) ineffective or meaningless. Furthermore, the return of cash deposits collected on "prior unliquidated entries", the absence of administrative reviews with respect to such entries or the non-assessment of definitive duties with respect to such entries would not, in our view, be inconsistent with the likely intent of the US Congress in enacting section 129(c)(1), *viz.*, to ensure implementation of an adverse DSB ruling only with respect to post-implementation entries.

---

[126]   We once again note that we are not called on, in this case, to make findings regarding whether provisions of US law other than section 129(c)(1) would preclude the Department of Commerce from returning cash deposits collected on "prior unliquidated entries" on the basis of the WTO-inconsistent antidumping or countervailing duty order, from declining to conduct administrative reviews with respect to such entries or from declining to assess duties with respect to such entries on the basis of the WTO-inconsistent order.

6.91   In the light of the foregoing considerations, we provisionally find that Canada has failed to establish that, in revocation cases, section 129(c)(1), by itself, has the effect of precluding the Department of Commerce from returning cash deposits collected on "prior unliquidated entries" based on the WTO-inconsistent antidumping or countervailing duty order, declining to hold administrative reviews for such entries or declining to assess duties with respect to such entries. Based also on the above considerations, we provisionally find that the evidence and arguments presented by Canada are, likewise, insufficient to establish that, in revocation cases, section 129(c)(1) has the effect of requiring the Department of Commerce to retain cash deposits collected on "prior unliquidated entries" based on the WTO-inconsistent antidumping or countervailing duty order, conduct an administrative review for such entries or make administrative review determinations with respect to such entries on the basis of the WTO-inconsistent order.

Conclusion

6.92   As we have noted at para. 6.59, our findings at this stage of our examination are provisional. As a result, we do not, at this point, offer any conclusions regarding whether Canada has succeeded in demonstrating that, with respect to "prior unliquidated entries", section 129(c)(1) has the effect of requiring and/or precluding any of the actions identified by Canada.

6.93   With the above provisional findings in mind, we can proceed to consider whether the SAA supports Canada's assertions regarding the "effects" of section 129(c)(1).

(b)   Statement of Administrative Action

6.94   For the purposes of examining whether the SAA supports Canada's assertions regarding the "effects" of section 129(c)(1), it is well once again to set out in full the portion of the SAA which both parties consider to be relevant to the Panel's examination of section 129(c)(1). The portion in question - the first paragraph of section B.1.c.(3) of the SAA - reads as follows:

> Consistent with the principle that GATT panel recommendations apply only prospectively, subsection 129(c)(1) provides that where determinations by the ITC or Commerce are implemented under subsections (a) or (b), such determinations have prospective effect only. That is, they apply to unliquidated entries of merchandise entered, or withdrawn from warehouse, for consumption on or after the date on which the Trade Representative directs implementation. Thus, relief available under subsection 129(c)(1) is distinguishable from relief available in an action brought before a court or a NAFTA binational panel, where, depending on the circumstances of the case, retroactive relief may be available. Under 129(c)(1), if implementation of a WTO report should result in the revocation of an antidumping or countervailing duty order, entries

made prior to the date of Trade Representative's direction would remain subject to potential duty liability.[127]

(i) Arguments of the Parties

6.95   **Canada** submits that this statement confirms its interpretation of section 129(c)(1). Canada notes that the SAA specifically addresses the situation where an antidumping or countervailing duty order is revoked based on a new determination by the Department of Commerce or the ITC. Canada recalls that the SAA specifically states that, in such situations, "[unliquidated] entries made prior to the date of [USTR's] direction [to implement] would remain subject to potential duty liability". Canada further recalls that, in the US duty assessment system, definitive duty liability for imports subject to an antidumping or countervailing duty order is determined in an administrative review proceeding. In Canada's view, the aforementioned sentence therefore confirms that (1) the administrative review procedure for "prior unliquidated entries" will continue pursuant to an order that was found to be WTO-inconsistent and (2) the definitive duty liability for such entries will be determined by the Department of Commerce without regard to the new, WTO-consistent determination.

6.96   Canada also argues that it is clear from the SAA that implementation of an adverse DSB ruling is contemplated exclusively with respect to entries after the Implementation date. Canada recalls that the referenced passage of the SAA specifically states that determinations to implement DSB rulings apply to "unliquidated entries of merchandise entered, or withdrawn from warehouse, for consumption on or after the date on which the Trade Representative directs implementation". Canada further points out that the SAA, in the portion at issue, states that "relief available under subsection 129(c)(1) is distinguishable from relief available in an action brought before a court or a NAFTA binational panel, where, depending on the circumstances of the case, retroactive relief may be available". Canada notes, in this regard, that there is no mention in the SAA that such "retroactive relief" would be available in conjunction with administrative review determinations. Indeed, according to Canada, it would be inconsistent with the SAA if the Department of Commerce were to implement an adverse DSB ruling in respect of "prior unliquidated entries" in subsequent administrative reviews. In Canada's view, section 129(c)(1) is, therefore, intended to have legal effect in administrative reviews of "prior unliquidated entries".

6.97   The **United States** disagrees with Canada regarding its interpretation of the language in the SAA to the effect that "prior unliquidated entries" would "remain subject to potential duty liability" in cases where an antidumping or countervailing duty order is revoked based on a new section 129 determination. The United States does not consider that this language supports Canada's assertion that section 129(c)(1) mandates WTO-inconsistent action. The United States argues that section 129(c)(1) does not mandate or preclude any particular treatment of "prior unliquidated entries". According to the United States, the afore-

---

[127]   SAA, section B.1.c.(3), first paragraph, p. 1026.

mentioned language in the SAA does not change this fact. The United States considers that the language in question simply reflects the fact that a section 129 determination itself would not resolve whether "prior unliquidated entries" would be subject to definitive duty liability. Moreover, the United States notes that, in any event, all that the SAA states is that "prior unliquidated entries" would "remain subject to potential duty liability". The United States points out that the SAA does not say that the Department of Commerce is required to apply duties to such entries.

6.98   With respect to Canada's argument that it would be inconsistent with the SAA if the Department of Commerce were to implement a DSB ruling in respect of "prior unliquidated entries" in subsequent administrative reviews, the United States notes that the SAA does not say, as Canada suggests, that a DSB ruling will not be implemented with regard to "prior unliquidated entries". Rather, the United States argues, what the SAA actually states is that a *section 129 determination* will have prospective effect only. In the view of the United States, the SAA is therefore consistent with the language of section 129(c)(1) itself. The United States further submits that the SAA says nothing about the treatment to be accorded to "prior unliquidated entries" in any other segment of the proceeding. Therefore, the United States does not agree with Canada that the SAA supports the view that section 129(c)(1) is intended to have legal effect in administrative reviews of "prior unliquidated entries". The United States adds, in this respect, that this view is, in any event, contradicted by the text of section 129(c)(1) itself.

(ii)   Evaluation by the Panel

6.99   The **Panel** considers that, for the purposes of analysis, the first paragraph of section B.1.c.(3) of the SAA can usefully be broken up into three parts. The Panel will discuss those in turn, conscious that it is dealing with one single paragraph.

6.100 The *first* part which we single out for separate analysis reads:

> Consistent with the principle that GATT panel recommendations apply only prospectively, subsection 129(c)(1) provides that where determinations by the ITC or Commerce are implemented under subsections (a) or (b), such determinations have prospective effect only. That is, they apply to unliquidated entries of merchandise entered, or withdrawn from warehouse, for consumption on or after the date on which the Trade Representative directs implementation.

6.101 We understand the logic and structure of these two sentences to be as follows: In the first sentence, the assertion is made that GATT panel recommendations have prospective effect and that, therefore, section 129(c)(1) provides that section 129 determinations, too, "have prospective effect only". The second sentence then explains what is meant by the statement that section 129 determinations "have prospective effect only". That explanation is provided in terms of the language actually used in section 129(c)(1) itself. Although it is not explicitly stated, it is implied in the two sentences that if a section 129 determination were applied to "prior unliquidated entries", this would, in the terminology of the SAA, be viewed as a "retroactive" application.

6.102 We think that our understanding of the effect of section 129(c)(1) is consistent with these two sentences. The first sentence makes it quite clear that it is "such determinations", i.e., section 129 determinations, that have prospective effect only. There is no reference in the two sentences to anything other than section 129 determinations. Specifically, nothing in these sentences indicates that section 129(c)(1) is intended to have the effect of precluding the Department of Commerce from making administrative review determinations with respect to "prior unliquidated entries" on the basis of a WTO-consistent methodology developed in a section 129 determination.[128] We do not, therefore, agree with Canada that it would be inconsistent with the SAA if the Department of Commerce were to make such administrative review determinations.

6.103 Moving on, then, to the *second* part of the relevant passage of the SAA, we note that that part consists of only one sentence, which provides:

> Thus, relief available under subsection 129(c)(1) is distinguishable from relief available in an action brought before a court or a NAFTA binational panel, where, depending on the circumstances of the case, retroactive relief may be available.

6.104 This sentence contrasts relief available under section 129(c)(1), which it characterizes as "prospective", with relief available in an action brought before a US court or a NAFTA binational panel, which it characterizes as (potentially) "retroactive". Canada has stated, in this regard, that if the US Court of International Trade or a NAFTA Chapter Nineteen panel finds that a determination of the Department of Commerce or the ITC is inconsistent with US domestic law, all entries of the subject merchandise would be liquidated in accordance with the adverse decision, including unliquidated entries that took place before the adverse decision.[129]

6.105 As we read it, the above-quoted sentence simply confirms that relief available *under section 129(c)(1)* is different from relief available under certain other provisions of US law and that *section 129(c)(1)*, unlike those other provisions of US law, is intended to provide relief only for post-implementation entries. The sentence does not state, explicitly or by implication, that section 129(c)(1) is intended to have the effect of precluding the Department of Commerce from providing relief for "prior unliquidated entries" through a mechanism other than the section 129 mechanism. More specifically, the sen-

---

[128] In our view, the fact that there is no mention in the two sentences, or elsewhere in the portion in question, of the possibility of making administrative review determinations with respect to "prior unliquidated entries" on the basis of a WTO-consistent methodology developed in a section 129 determination does not, in itself, support the conclusion that section 129(c)(1) is intended to preclude that possibility.

[129] In support of its statement, Canada refers to 19 U.S.C. § 1516a(c)(1) and (e) (1994). The United States has not contested Canada's statement.

tence does not say that section 129(c)(1) is intended to have the effect of precluding the Department of Commerce from making administrative review determinations with respect to "prior unliquidated entries" on the basis of a WTO-consistent methodology developed in a section 129 determination.

6.106 We would agree with Canada that the sentence at issue tends to support the view that implementation of an adverse DSB ruling was "contemplated exclusively with respect to entries after the Implementation date".[130] However, as we have stated above, we consider that the fact that the United States may have sought, via section 129(c)(1), to ensure implementation only with respect to post-implementation entries does not mean that it intended to *preclude* implementation with respect to "prior unliquidated entries".[131] In any event, the sentence in question does not suggest to us that section 129(c)(1) was intended to have that effect.

6.107 Finally, we need to examine the *third* part of the relevant passage of the SAA, which, again, consists of only one sentence. It reads:

> Under 129(c)(1), if implementation of a WTO report should result
> in the revocation of an antidumping or countervailing duty order,
> entries made prior to the date of Trade Representative's direction
> would remain subject to potential duty liability.

6.108 The first thing that should be noted regarding this sentence is that it directs itself exclusively to situations where a section 129 determination results in the revocation of an antidumping or countervailing duty order. This noted, we understand the sentence to provide confirmation that if, pursuant to section 129(c)(1), an antidumping or countervailing duty order is revoked, the revocation would apply only to post-implementation entries and that, as a result, the relevant antidumping or countervailing duty order would continue to apply to "prior unliquidated entries". The statement in the above-quoted sentence to the effect that "prior unliquidated entries" "would remain subject to potential duty liability" supports our understanding. Indeed, as Canada itself has stated, a final antidumping or countervailing duty order "imposes potential duty liability on entries subject to that order".[132] Thus, in our understanding, the sentence is intended to indicate that, notwithstanding the fact that an antidumping or countervailing duty order may have been revoked, under section 129(c)(1), with respect to post-implementation entries, the relevant order would continue to apply to "prior unliquidated entries".

6.109 In Canada's view, the sentence in question confirms that, *because of section 129(c)(1)*, the administrative review process "will" continue with respect to "prior unliquidated entries" and administrative review determinations "will" be made with respect to such entries without regard to the fact that the order has been found to be WTO-inconsistent. We are not persuaded by Canada's reading

---

[130] Canada's reply to Panel Question 79(b).
[131] As we have said, the intention of the US Congress may simply have been not to take any *particular* steps to ensure implementation with respect to "prior unliquidated entries".
[132] Canada's Second Submission, footnote 13.

of the sentence in question. As we have said, the sentence at issue simply clarifies that a revocation determination that is implemented under section 129 would not have any impact on "prior unliquidated entries".

6.110 To be sure, the above-quoted sentence affirmatively states that "prior unliquidated entries" would remain subject to potential duty liability. It is conceivable, therefore, that administrative reviews would be conducted with respect to "prior unliquidated entries" and that administrative review determinations would be made with respect to such entries on the basis of a WTO-inconsistent antidumping or countervailing duty order. However, it is clear to us that such actions, if taken, would not be taken because they were required by section 129(c)(1), but because they were required or allowed under other provisions of US law. At any rate, we see nothing in the above-quoted sentence which would suggest that section 129(c)(1) is intended to have the effect of requiring such actions.

6.111 Having regard to the foregoing considerations, we find that our reading of section 129(c)(1) is fully consistent with the first paragraph of section B.1.c.(3) of the SAA. Based on the same considerations, we further find that Canada has failed to establish that, in view of section B.1.c.(3) of the SAA, a US court would interpret section 129(c)(1) as having the effect of requiring and/or precluding any particular treatment of "prior unliquidated entries" after the implementation date.[133]

6.112 We note that Canada has also referred us to the third paragraph of section B.1.c.(5) of the SAA, which states:

> Since implemented determinations under section 129 may be appealed, it is possible that Commerce or the ITC may be in a position of simultaneously defending determinations in which the agency reached different conclusions. In such situations, the Administration expects that courts and [NAFTA] binational panels will be sensitive to the fact that under the applicable standard of review, as set forth in statute and case law, multiple permissible interpretations of the law and the facts may be legally permissible in any particular case, and the issuance of a different determination under section 129 does not signify that the initial determination was unlawful.

6.113 According to Canada, this paragraph makes clear that more than one interpretation of US antidumping or countervailing duty laws may be permissible and that multiple permissible interpretations would, in fact, be expected in the light of section 129(c)(1). Canada appears to infer from this that section 129(c)(1) must be read to preclude the Department of Commerce from making administrative review determinations with respect to "prior unliquidated en-

---

[133] We recall that section 129(c)(1) implies that a section 129 determination can only be applied to post-implementation entries.

tries" consistently with a WTO-consistent interpretation or methodology adopted in a section 129 determination.[134]

6.114 Canada has not explained to our satisfaction how the above-quoted paragraph of the SAA supports its reading of section 129(c)(1). Even assuming that the paragraph in question established, as Canada seems to suggest, that, because of the operation of section 129(c)(1), the Department of Commerce could apply one interpretation of US laws to post-implementation entries and, at the same time, apply another to "prior unliquidated entries", we do not think that it would necessarily follow from this that the Department of Commerce could not apply a uniform interpretation to all entries. Even if at the time the SAA was agreed multiple statutory interpretations were expected in the light of section 129, as Canada appears to argue, this does not, in our view, support the conclusion that section 129(c)(1) is intended to have the effect of precluding the Department of Commerce from making administrative review determinations with respect to "prior unliquidated entries" on the basis of interpretations developed in a section 129 determination. We are, therefore, not persuaded that, in view of the third paragraph of section B.1.c.(5) of the SAA, we should adopt a different reading of section 129(c)(1).

(c)   Application of Section 129(c)(1) to Date

6.115 As the **Panel** has noted above, before reaching any conclusions on Canada's assertions regarding the "effect" of section 129(c)(1), it will briefly consider the application of section 129(c)(1) to date, thus taking due account of the evidence submitted on this point by the United States.

(i)   Arguments of the Parties

6.116 The **United States** recalls that in the six years since section 129(c)(1) entered into force, it has been applied to two antidumping or countervailing duty investigations. The United States points out that both instances involved the DSB ruling in *United States – Antidumping Measures on Stainless Steel Plate in Coils and Stainless Steel Sheet and Strip from Korea*[135]. In that case, the Department of Commerce made new, WTO-consistent final determinations for the two investigations covered by the DSB ruling. Those determinations were then implemented with respect to all entries taking place on or after the date of implementation. According to the United States, the Department of Commerce has since completed the first administrative reviews of the antidumping orders covering the products in question. The United States notes that some of the issues raised in the WTO dispute were no longer relevant in the administrative reviews. The United States points out, however, that as far as currency conversions are concerned, the Department of Commerce examined the same types of transactions

---

[134] Canada's reply to Panel Question 68(b).

[135] Panel Report, *United States – Anti-Dumping Measures on Stainless Steel Plate in Coils and Stainless Steel Sheet and Strip from Korea* (*"US – Stainless Steel"*), WT/DS179/R, adopted 1 February 2001, DSR 2001:IV, 1295.

that were at issue in the WTO dispute. The United States asserts that, with respect to the issue of currency conversions, the Department of Commerce acted consistently with the DSB ruling.

6.117 **Canada** did not specifically discuss the application of section 129(c)(1).

(ii)   Evaluation by the Panel

6.118 The **Panel** begins by noting that it is not aware, and has not been made aware, of any judicial interpretations of section 129(c)(1).

6.119 As for administrative practice under section 129(c)(1), the Panel notes that it is not in dispute that, to date, the Department of Commerce has applied section 129(c)(1) on only two occasions, both involving implementation of the DSB ruling in *US – Stainless Steel*.

6.120 In this context, it seems that, in a recent administrative review of the US antidumping order on stainless steel plate in coils from Korea, the Department of Commerce made administrative review determinations with respect to "prior unliquidated entries" after the implementation date.[136] According to the United States, the issues addressed in the DSB ruling were either not relevant to the administrative review in question or else were resolved in a manner consistent with the DSB ruling. Canada has not contested the US statement regarding compliance with the DSB ruling in *US –Stainless Steel*.

6.121 In view of the foregoing, we find that the evidence before us relating to the application of section 129(c)(1) to date does not support Canada's view that section 129(c)(1) has the effect of requiring and/or precluding any of the actions which it has identified.

(d)   Conclusion

6.122 The **Panel** recalls that it has considered relevant portions of the SAA and the evidence relating to the application of section 129(c)(1) to date and that it has found that both elements support its provisional findings at paras. 6.67-6.91 regarding the "effects" of section 129(c)(1) as enacted.

6.123 Thus, having regard to its detailed examination of section 129(c)(1) as enacted, of relevant portions of the SAA and of the application of section 129(c)(1) to date, the Panel concludes that Canada has failed to establish that section 129(c)(1), read in the light of the SAA:

    (a)   has the effect of requiring the Department of Commerce:

        (i)   to conduct administrative reviews with respect to "prior unliquidated entries" after the implementation date pursuant to an antidumping or countervailing duty order found by the DSB to be WTO-inconsistent;

---

[136] *Stainless Steel Plate in Coils From the Republic of Korea: Final Results of Antidumping Duty Administrative Review*, 66 Fed. Reg. 64017 (Dec. 11, 2001) (exhibit US-10)

(ii) to make administrative review determinations regarding dumping or subsidization with respect to "prior unliquidated entries" after the implementation date pursuant to an antidumping or countervailing duty order found by the DSB to be WTO-inconsistent;

(iii) to assess definitive antidumping or countervailing duties with respect to "prior unliquidated entries" after the implementation date pursuant to an antidumping or countervailing duty order found by the DSB to be WTO-inconsistent; or

(iv) to retain cash deposits in respect of "prior unliquidated entries" after the implementation date at a level found by the DSB to be WTO-inconsistent; or

(b) has the effect of precluding the Department of Commerce from:

(i) making administrative review determinations regarding dumping or subsidization with respect to "prior unliquidated entries" after the implementation date in a manner that is consistent with an adverse DSB ruling;

(ii) assessing definitive antidumping or countervailing duties with respect to "prior unliquidated entries" after the implementation date in a manner that is consistent with an adverse DSB ruling; or

(iii) refunding, after the implementation date, cash deposits collected on "prior unliquidated entries" pursuant to an antidumping or countervailing duty order found by the DSB to be WTO-inconsistent.

5. *Whether Section 129(c)(1) Mandates the United States to Take Any of the Actions and/or not to Take any of the Actions Identified by Canada*

6.124 The **Panel** has concluded in Subsections C.3 and C.4 above that, as a matter of US law, section 129(c)(1) does not require (or have the effect of requiring) or preclude (or have the effect of precluding) any of the actions identified by Canada.[137] On the basis of these factual conclusions, we must now assess whether Canada has established that, as a matter of WTO law, section 129(c)(1) mandates the United States to take any of the actions identified by Canada and/or mandates the United States not to take any of the actions identified by Canada.

6.125 We have previously stated that, in the circumstances of this case, if Canada does not succeed in demonstrating, as a matter of US law, that section 129(c)(1) requires (or has the effect of requiring) or precludes (or has the effect of precluding) any of the actions identified by Canada, it will not have

---

[137] For a description of the actions identified by Canada see, *supra*, paras. 6.31 and 6.32.

established, as a matter of WTO law, that section 129(c)(1) "mandates" the United States to take any of those actions or "mandates" the United States not to take any of those actions.[138]

6.126 Accordingly, since we have concluded that Canada has failed to demonstrate that, as a factual matter, section 129(c)(1) requires (or has the effect of requiring) or precludes (or has the effect of precluding) any of the actions identified by it, we further conclude that Canada has failed to establish that, as a matter of WTO law, section 129(c)(1) mandates the United States to take any of those actions or mandates the United States not to take any of those actions.

6. Whether the Actions Identified by Canada, if Taken or not Taken, Would Infringe the WTO Provisions that it has Invoked

6.127 Since the **Panel** has concluded in Subsection C.5 that Canada has not succeeded in establishing that section 129(c)(1) mandates the United States to take any of the actions specified by Canada and/or mandates the United States not to take any of the actions specified by Canada, the Panel, consistently with its analytical approach outlined in Section B, considers it unnecessary to proceed with its analysis of Canada's principal claims.

6.128 As a consequence, we do not assess whether Canada's principal claims are based on a correct interpretation of the WTO provisions which Canada invokes in support of those claims.[139] Nor do we assess whether Canada has met its burden of establishing that the actions which Canada alleges the United States, under section 129(c)(1), is mandated to take or mandated not to take are inconsistent with the relevant WTO provisions.

7. Overall Conclusion with Respect to Canada's Principal Claims

6.129 In the light of all its findings and conclusions in Section C, the **Panel** concludes that Canada has failed to establish that section 129(c)(1) is inconsistent with Articles VI:2, VI:3 and VI:6(a) of the GATT 1994; Articles 1, 9.3, 11.1 and 18.1 of the AD Agreement; or Articles 10, 19.4, 21.1 and 32.1 of the SCM Agreement.

6.130 In reaching this conclusion, we note that Canada has requested us to make a specific finding in response to a statement made by the United States. Canada's request stems from the US statement that the Department of Commerce has the

---

[138] See *supra*, footnote 75.

[139] We realize that our decision to examine first whether section 129(c)(1) mandates the United States to take any of the actions identified by Canada and/or mandates the United States not to take any of the actions identified by Canada could be construed to imply acceptance of Canada's premise that such actions, if taken or not taken, would be contrary to the WTO provisions invoked by Canada. However, no conclusions should be drawn from the structure and sequence of our findings as to whether we agree or disagree with Canada's premise.

legal authority to implement an adverse DSB ruling with respect to "prior unliquidated entries" by applying a WTO-consistent methodology to such entries in the context of an administrative review which concludes after the implementation date.[140] Canada requests that if the Panel accepts that such action is consistent with section 129(c)(1), it find that the relevant statement of the United States (i) expresses the official position of the United States in a manner that can be relied on by all Members, and (ii) is an undertaking that the United States will interpret its domestic laws and regulations to apply an adverse DSB ruling to "prior unliquidated entries".[141]

6.131 We understand the United States to have made the statement in question by way of an argument in the alternative, to be considered in the event that we find that the United States is obligated, as a matter of WTO law, to implement adverse DSB rulings with respect to "prior unliquidated entries".[142] As noted in Subsection C.6 above, we do not, in this case, make any findings on this issue. Consequently, we cannot address Canada's request for an additional finding.

D. Canada's Consequential Claims

6.132 The **Panel** recalls that Canada has made consequential claims under Article 18.4 of the AD Agreement, Article 32.5 of the SCM Agreement and Article XVI:4 of the WTO Agreement.

6.133 As we have observed in Section B above, Canada argues that section 129(c)(1) is inconsistent with Article 18.4 of the AD Agreement, Article 32.5 of the SCM Agreement and Article XVI:4 of the WTO Agreement because it is inconsistent with the WTO provisions invoked by Canada in support of its principal claims. Since we have concluded in Section C that Canada has not succeeded in demonstrating that section 129(c)(1) contravenes any of the WTO provisions relied on by Canada, we must, therefore, find that Canada has not succeeded in establishing its consequential claims under Article 18.4 of the AD Agreement, Article 32.5 of the SCM Agreement and Article XVI:4 of the WTO Agreement.

6.134 In the light of this, we conclude that Canada has failed to establish that section 129(c)(1) is inconsistent with Article 18.4 of the AD Agreement, Article 32.5 of the SCM Agreement or Article XVI:4 of the WTO Agreement.

---

[140] Canada's request is based on the US reply to Panel Question 84(a). We see nothing in that reply which would indicate that the United States "will" act in a particular way. To the contrary, the United States simply states what it "might" do in hypothetical circumstances. Moreover, we note that the US reply to Panel Question 84(a) addresses a situation where section 129(c)(1) would not be implicated. This said, it is correct that the United States has stated that the Department of Commerce has the legal authority to implement an adverse DSB ruling with respect to "prior unliquidated entries" by applying a WTO-consistent methodology to such entries in the context of an administrative review which concludes after the implementation date. See US reply to Panel Question 91.

[141] Canada's comments on the US reply to Panel Question 84.

[142] US Second Submission, para. 10; US Second Oral Statement, para. 9; US Second Closing Statement, para. 4.

VII.   CONCLUSION

7.1   For the reasons set forth in this report, the **Panel** concludes that Canada has failed to establish that section 129(c)(1) of the Uruguay Round Agreements Act is inconsistent with:

(a)   Article VI:2, VI:3 and VI:6(a) of the GATT 1994;

(b)   Articles 1, 9.3, 11.1 and 18.1 and 18.4 of the AD Agreement;

(c)   Articles 10, 19.4, 21.1, 32.1 and 32.5 of the SCM Agreement; and

(d)   Article XVI:4 of the WTO Agreement.

7.2   In the light of its conclusion, the Panel makes no recommendations under Article 19.1 of the DSU.

EGYPT – DEFINITIVE ANTI-DUMPING MEASURES ON STEEL REBAR FROM TURKEY

Report of the Panel
WT/DS211/R

*Adopted by the Dispute Settlement Body
on 1 October 2002*

TABLE OF CONTENTS

			Page
I.	INTRODUCTION		2671
	A.	Complaint of Turkey	2671
	B.	Establishment and Composition of the Panel	2671
	C.	Panel Proceedings	2672
II.	FACTUAL ASPECTS		2672
III.	PARTIES' REQUESTS FOR FINDINGS AND RECOMMENDATIONS		2673
	A.	Turkey	2673
	B.	Egypt	2673
IV.	ARGUMENTS OF THE PARTIES		2673
V.	ARGUMENTS OF THE THIRD PARTIES		2673
VI.	INTERIM REVIEW		2673
	A.	Request of Turkey	2674
		1. Claim under Annex II, Paragraph 7	2674
		2. Claim under Article 2.4	2674
		3. Claim under Articles 2.2.1.1 and 2.2.2	2674
		Request of Egypt	2674
VII.	FINDINGS		2675
	A.	Introduction	2675
	B.	Preliminary Objections	2676
		1. Alleged Failure of Turkey to Present a prima facie Case	2676
		2. Alleged Request by Turkey for a de novo Review	2677
		3. Introduction of Evidence that was not before the Investigating Authority	2678

			Page
	4.	Request for Dismissal of Certain Claims	2681
C.		Claims Relating to Injury and Causation	2685
	1.	Claims under Article 3.4 of the AD Agreement	2685
		(a) Alleged Failure to Examine Factors Specifically Listed in Article 3.4	2685
		(b) Alleged Failure to Examine "all relevant economic factors and indices having a bearing on the state of the industry"	2693
	2.	Claim under Articles 3.1 and 3.2 – Alleged Failure to Base the Finding of Price Undercutting on Positive Evidence	2696
	3.	Claim under Articles 6.1 and 6.2 – Alleged Violation Due to "change" in the "scope" of the Injury Investigation from Threat to Present Material Injury	2699
	4.	Claim under Articles 3.5 and 3.1 – Alleged Failure to Develop Specific Evidence Linking Imports to Adverse Volume and Price Effects upon the Domestic Industry, and Consequent Failure to Base the Finding of a Causal Link on Positive Evidence	2705
	5.	Claim under Article 3.5 – Alleged Failure to Take Account of, and Attribution to Dumped Imports of, the Effects of other "known factors" Injuring the Domestic Industry	2707
	6.	Claim under Articles 3.5 and 3.1 – Alleged Failure to Demonstrate that the Imports Caused Injury "through the Effects of Dumping"	2714
D.		Claims Relating to the Dumping Investigation – "facts available"	2715
	1.	Factual Background	2715
	2.	Claim under Article 17.6(I)	2716
	3.	Claim under Article 6.8 and Annex II, Paragraphs 5 and 6 - Resort to "facts available"	2719
		(a) Article 6.8 and Annex II	2720
		(b) Was the Cost Information Requested by the IA on 19 August and 23 September 1999 "necessary information"?	2741

Page

(c)   Did the Respondents "refuse access to" or "otherwise fail to provide" "necessary information"?.. 2747

4.   Claim under Article 2.2.1.1, 2.2.2 and 2.4 Due to Alleged Unjustified Resort to Facts Available........... 2756

5.   Claim under Article 6.1.1, Annex II, Paragraph 6, and Article 6.2 – Dead-Line for Response to 19 August 1999 Request.. 2757

    (a)   Claim under Article 6.1.1 2758

    (b)   Alternative Claim under Annex II, Paragraph 6 and Article 6.2 2759

6.   Claim under Article 6.1.1, Annex II, Paragraph 6, and Article 6.2 - Deadline for the Responses of Habas, Diler and Colakoglu to the 23 September Letter of the IA 2760

7.   Claim under Annex II, Paragraph 7 Due to the Addition of 5 per cent for Inflation to Habas' Highest Reported Monthly Costs.............................. 2763

8.   Claim under Annex II, Paragraphs 3 and 7 Due to Failure to Use Icdas' September – October 1998 Scrap Costs 2766

9.   Claim under Annex II, Paragraphs 3 and 7 Due to Calculation of the Highest Monthly Interest Cost for IDC... 2767

E.   Other Claims Relating to the Dumping Investigation 2768

1.   Claim under Annex II, Paragraph 1; Annex II, Paragraph 6; and Article 6.7, Annex I, Paragraph 7 – Alleged Failure to Verify the Cost Data During the "on-the-spot" Verification, and Conduct of "mail order" Verification Instead............................. 2768

2.   Claim under Article 2.4 – Request for Detailed Cost Information Late in the Investigation Allegedly Imposed an Unreasonable Burden of Proof on the Respondents 2770

3.   Claim under Article 6.2 and Annex II, Paragraph 6 – Alleged Denial of Requests for Meetings 2773

4.   Claim under Article 2.4 – Alleged Failure to Make an Adjustment to Normal Value for Differences in Terms of Sale.. 2776

    (a)   Factual Background 2778

			Page
	(b)	Assessment by the Panel	2787
5.	Claim under of Articles 2.2.1.1 and 2.2.2 – Interest Income Offset		2791
	(a)	Factual Background	2793
	(b)	Assessment by the Panel	2800
F.	Claim under Article X:3 of GATT 1994		2803
VIII.	CONCLUSIONS		2803
IX.	RECOMMENDATION		2806

LIST OF ANNEXES

Annex 1   First written submissions of Turkey and Egypt – Executive summaries

Annex 2   First oral statements of Turkey and Egypt – Executive summaries

Annex 3   Restatement by Turkey of its claims in response to a request from the Panel

Annex 4   Turkey's and Egypt's responses to questions posed in the context of the first substantive meeting of the Panel

Annex 5   Rebuttal submissions of Turkey and Egypt – Executive summaries

Annex 6   Second oral statements of Egypt and Turkey – Executive summaries

Annex 7   Concluding oral remarks of Turkey and Egypt

Annex 8   Turkey's and Egypt's responses to questions posed in the context of the second substantive meeting of the Panel

Annex 9   Third party oral statement of Chile

Annex 10   Third party written submission, oral statement and responses to questions of the European Communities

Annex 11   Third party written submission and responses to questions of Japan

Annex 12   Third party written submission, oral statement and responses to questions of the United States

Annex 13   Supplemental working procedures of the Panel concerning certain business confidential information

I.   INTRODUCTION

A.   Complaint of Turkey

1.1   On 6 November 2000, Turkey requested consultations with Egypt pursuant to Article 4 of the Understanding on Rules and Procedures Governing the Settlement of Disputes ("the DSU"), Article XXIII of the General Agreement on Tariffs and Trade 1994 ("GATT 1994"), and Article 17.3 of the Agreement on Implementation of Article VI of the GATT 1994 ("the Anti-Dumping Agreement" or "the AD Agreement"), with regard to the definitive anti-dumping measures imposed by Egypt on imports of concrete steel reinforcing bar ("rebar") from Turkey[1].

1.2   On 3-5 December 2000 and 3-4 January 2001, Turkey and Egypt held the requested consultations, but failed to reach a mutually satisfactory resolution of the matter.

1.3   On 3 May 2001, Turkey requested the establishment of a panel to examine the matter[2].

B.   Establishment and Composition of the Panel

1.4   At its meeting of 20 June 2001, the Dispute Settlement Body ("the DSB") established a panel in accordance with the request made by Turkey in document WT/DS/211/2 and Corr. 1, and in accordance with Article 6 of the DSU.

1.5   At that meeting, the parties to the dispute also agreed that the Panel should have standard terms of reference. The terms of reference therefore are the following:

> "To examine, in the light of the relevant provisions of the covered agreements cited by Turkey in document WT/DS211/2 and Corr.1, the matter referred to the DSB by Turkey in that document, and to make such findings as will assist the DSB in making the recommendations or in giving the rulings provided for in those agreements."

1.6   On 18 July 2001, the parties agreed to the following composition of the Panel:

Chairman: Mr. Peter Palecka

Members: Mr. Daniel Moulis

Mr. Virachai Plasai

---

[1]   WT/DS/211/1.
[2]   WT/DS/211/2 and Corr.1.

1.7   Chile, the European Communities, Japan and the United States reserved their rights to participate in the panel proceedings as third parties.

C.   Panel Proceedings

1.8   The Panel met with the parties on 27-28 November 2001 and 25-26 February 2002. The Panel met with third parties on 27 November 2001.

1.9   On 21 May 2002, the Panel provided its interim report to the parties (*See* Section VI, *infra*).

II.   FACTUAL ASPECTS

2.1   This dispute concerns the imposition of a definitive anti-dumping measure by Egypt on imports of rebar from Turkey, imported under heading 72.14.00.00, and its subheadings, of the Harmonized Tariff Schedule of Egypt.

2.2   On 23 and 26 December 1998, two applications were filed, by Ezz Steel Company ("Al Ezz") and Alexandria National Iron and Steel Company ("Alexandria National") with Egypt's International Trade Policy Department ("the ITPD"), the Egyptian Investigating Authority ("IA"). The applicants alleged that imports of rebar originating in Turkey were being dumped in Egypt and threatened to cause material injury to the domestic industry since the second half of 1998. On 6 February 1999, a notice of initiation of an anti-dumping investigation was published in the Official Gazette of Egypt.

2.3   On 21 October 1999, Egypt published in the Official Gazette a notice concerning the imposition of definitive anti-dumping duties on imports of steel rebar originating in or exported from Turkey. The anti-dumping duties imposed were as follows:

Manufacturer/Exporter	Duty (%)
Habas	22.63
Diler	27
Colakoglu	45
ICDAS	30
IDC	61
Ekinciler	61
Others*	61

*Egypt's published notice states that the "Others" rate was calculated according to the highest rate, and that according to Article 37.3 of the Regulation of Law No 161/1998 Concerning the Protection of the National Economy From the Effect of Injurious Practices in International Trade, should a company wish to commence exporting, the applicable rate would be the highest rate. [3]

III. PARTIES' REQUESTS FOR FINDINGS AND RECOMMENDATIONS

A. Turkey

3.1 Turkey requests the Panel to find that Egypt's anti-dumping duty investigation and final anti-dumping determination was inconsistent with Article X:3 of the GATT 1994 and with Articles 2.2, 2.4, 3.1, 3.2, 3.4, 3.5, 6.1, 6.2, 6.6, 6.7, and 6.8, and Annex II, paragraphs 1, 3, 5, 6, and 7, and Annex I, paragraph 7 of the Anti-Dumping Agreement, and that as a result the measures nullify and impair the benefits accruing to Turkey under the GATT 1994 and the Anti-Dumping Agreement.

B. Egypt

3.2 Egypt requests the Panel (1)to find that Egypt's anti-dumping measures on imports of rebar from Turkey are in compliance with Egypt's obligations under the GATT 1994 and the Anti-Dumping Agreement, and (2) thus to reject the claims as put forward by Turkey.

IV. ARGUMENTS OF THE PARTIES

4.1 The arguments of the parties are set out in their submissions to the Panel. The parties' executive summaries of their submissions are attached to this Report as Annexes (*See* List of Annexes, page 2670). Also attached as Annexes are the full texts of the parties' responses to questions posed by the Panel and by the other party.

V. ARGUMENTS OF THE THIRD PARTIES

5.1 The arguments of the third parties, Chile, the European Communities, Japan and the United States, are set out in their submissions to the Panel, the full texts of which are attached to this Report as Annexes 9, 10, 11 and 12, respectively (*See* List of Annexes, page 2670).

VI. INTERIM REVIEW

6.1 On 21 May 2002, we submitted our interim report to the parties. Both parties submitted written requests for review of precise aspects of the interim

---

[3] Exh. TUR-17, p.4.

report. Neither party requested an interim review meeting, and neither party submitted written comments on the other party's request for interim review.

A.   Request of Turkey

1.   Claim under Annex II, Paragraph 7

6.2   In its request for interim review, Turkey stated that paragraph 7.300 mischaracterized the claim addressed therein as raising only the issue of the estimated rate of inflation in Turkey during the relevant period. Turkey maintains that this claim also raises the issue of arbitrary adjustments to submitted cost data in the context of facts available.

6.3   We have modified paragraph 7.300 to indicate that the estimated rate of inflation is the main issue raised by the claim. We note that the second aspect identified by Turkey, is addressed in paragraph 7.303, which we have not modified. Finally, we have modified paragraph 7.305 to take into account the second aspect of Turkey's claim.

2.   Claim under Article 2.4

6.4   In its request for interim review, Turkey questioned our characterization in paragraph 7.384 of the significance of references in certain companies' antidumping questionnaire responses to the treatment of credit costs in their cost accounting records.

6.5   We have modified paragraph 7.384 to remove the characterization referred to by Turkey.

3.   Claim under Articles 2.2.1.1 and 2.2.2

6.6   In its request for interim review, Turkey questioned the accuracy of the characterization in paragraph 7.423 of the IA's request for information concerning the issue of interest income offset, and of the responses of certain companies to that request. We have modified the punctuation of the sentence in question, and added a footnote, to clarify the nature of the information request referred to in that paragraph. We also have modified paragraph 7.426 to refer to the point in the investigation at which the question of the relationship to production of interest income arose and how it was addressed by the respondent companies.

Request of Egypt

6.7   In its request for interim review, Egypt identified certain erroneous references, in paragraphs 7.250 through 7.252 to two of the companies that were respondents in the anti-dumping investigation. We have modified these paragraphs to correct these errors.

VII. FINDINGS

A.   Introduction

7.1   Throughout these proceedings we have found ourselves confronted by having to address the relationship between, on the one hand, what an investigating authority is obligated by the provisions of the Anti-Dumping Agreement to do when conducting an anti-dumping investigation and making the required determinations, and on the other hand, what interested parties should themselves contribute to the process of the investigation, in the way of evidence or argumentation, for issues of concern to them to be considered and taken into account during the course of the investigation and in the determinations made by the relevant authorities.

7.2   We note in this respect that the AD Agreement appears to impose two types of procedural obligations on an investigating authority, namely, on the one hand, those that are stipulated explicitly and in detail, and which have to be performed in a particular way in every investigation, and, on the other hand, those that establish certain due process or procedural principles, but leave to the discretion of the investigating authority exactly how they will be performed. In our view, the first type of obligation must be performed by the investigating authority on its own initiative, and exactly as specified in the AD Agreement. There is no need for and no obligation on interested parties to raise these issues and obligations during the course of an investigation in order to protect their rights under the AD Agreement.

7.3   In respect of the second type of obligation, however, the actions of an interested party during the course of an investigation are critical to *its* protection of its rights under the AD Agreement. As the Appellate Body observed in *US – Hot-Rolled Steel*[4], "in order to complete their investigations, investigating authorities are entitled to expect a very significant degree of effort to the best of their abilities from investigated exporters".[5] The Appellate Body went on to state that "cooperation is indeed a two-way process involving joint effort".[6] In the context of this two-way process of developing the information on which determinations ultimately are based, where an investigating authority has an obligation to "provide opportunities" to interested parties to present evidence and/or arguments on a given issue, and the interested parties themselves have made no effort during the investigation to present such evidence and/or arguments, there may be no factual basis in the record on which a panel could judge whether or not an "opportunity" either was not "provided" or was denied. Similarly, where a given point is left by the AD Agreement to the judgement and discretion of the investigating authority to resolve on the basis of the record before it, and where opportunities have been provided by the authority for interested parties to submit

---

[4]   Appellate Body Report, *United States – Anti-Dumping Measures on Certain Hot-Rolled Steel Products from Japan("US – Hot-Rolled Steel")*, WT/DS184/AB/R, adopted 23 August 2001, DSR 2001:X, 4769.

[5]   *Ibid*, para.102.

[6]   *Ibid*, para.104.

into the record information and arguments on that point, the decision by an interested party not to make such submissions is its own responsibility, and not that of the investigating authority, and cannot later be reversed by a WTO dispute settlement panel[7].

B. Preliminary Objections

7.4   Egypt raised three issues as preliminary objections, but did not request us to rule on these issues on a preliminary basis. Egypt's preliminary objections are (i) that Turkey has failed to present a *prima facie* case of a violation of the relevant Articles of GATT 1994 and of the AD Agreement, (ii) that Turkey is trying to lead us to conduct a *de novo* review of the evidence submitted to the Egyptian IA and to act contrary to the required standard of review as set out in Article 17.6(i) of the AD Agreement[8], and (iii), that Turkey has introduced certain new evidence in the context of these proceedings which was not before the IA during the course of the investigation.[9] Egypt also requested us to dismiss certain claims as being outside our terms of reference.

1.   Alleged Failure of Turkey to Present a prima facie Case

7.5   Regarding Egypt's assertion that Turkey has failed to establish a *prima facie* case of violation, it is clear to us that whether a party raises the issue or not, in any WTO dispute the burden of proof is on the complaining party to make a *prima facie* case. We recall in this regard that in *EC - Hormones* the Appellate Body stated:

> "The initial burden lies on the complaining party, which must establish a *prima facie* case of inconsistency with a particular provision of the SPS Agreement on the part of the defending party, or more precisely, of its SPS measure or measures complained about. When that *prima facie* case is made, the burden of proof moves to the defending party, which must in turn counter or refute the claimed inconsistency."[10]

7.6   The Appellate Body furthermore stated in *Korea - Dairy*:

> "We find no provision in the DSU or in the *Agreement on Safeguards* that requires a panel to make an explicit ruling on whether

---

[7]   As the panel noted in, *United States – Anti-Dumping Measures on Certain Hot-Rolled Steel From Japan("US – Hot-Rolled Steel")*, "errors made during the investigation cannot be rectified in subsequent submissions before a WTO panel". (Panel Report, WT/DS184/R, adopted 23 August 2001 as modified by the Appellate Body, WT/DS184/AB/R, DSR 2001:X, 4769, para.7.246.). Although this quotation was in respect of the investigating authority in that case, we find the principle involved to be relevant here.

[8]   First Written Submission of Egypt, p.16-18.

[9]   *Ibid*, p.73.

[10]   Appellate Body Report, *European Communities - Measures Concerning Meat and Meat Products (Hormones)("EC – Hormones")*, WT/DS26/AB/R, WT/DS48/AB/R, adopted 13 February 1998, DSR 1998: I, 135, para.98.

the complainant has established a *prima facie* case of violation before a panel may proceed to examine the respondent's defence and evidence."[11]

7.7   We agree with the Appellate Body, and as we could find no such a provision in the AD Agreement either, we will refrain from making a ruling at this stage on whether Turkey has made a *prima facie* case or not, but will proceed by reviewing the substantive elements of Turkey's case before us.

2.   *Alleged Request by Turkey for a de novo Review*

7.8   Concerning Egypt's assertion that Turkey is seeking a *de novo* review by the Panel of the evidence submitted to the IA, it is clear that in any dispute under the AD Agreement, a panel must adhere to the standard of review set forth in Article 17.6(i) of that agreement, which precludes a *de novo* review by a panel.

7.9   Article 17.6(i) of the AD Agreement provides:

7.10   "In examining the matter referred to in paragraph 5:

> (i) in its assessment of the facts of the matter, the panel shall determine whether the authorities' establishment of the facts was proper and whether their evaluation of those facts was unbiased and objective. If the establishment of the facts was proper and the evaluation was unbiased and objective, even though the panel might have reached a different conclusion, the evaluation shall not be overturned;"

7.11   Although Article 17.6(i) of the AD Agreement specifically addresses this point, we also find guidance on this issue in the Appellate Body's comments on the provisions of Article 11 of the DSU in *EC – Hormones,* with reference to the "objective assessment" of the facts to be made by a panel:

> "So far as fact-finding by panels is concerned, their activities are always constrained by the mandate of Article 11 of the DSU: the applicable standard is neither *de novo* review as such, nor "total deference", but rather the "objective assessment of the facts". Many panels have in the past refused to undertake *de novo* review, wisely, since under current practice and systems, they are in any case poorly suited to engage in such a review. On the other hand, "total deference to the findings of the national authorities", it has been well said, "could not ensure an 'objective assessment' as foreseen by Article 11 of the DSU."[12]

---

[11]   Appellate Body Report, *Definitive Safeguard Measure on Imports of Certain Dairy Products ("Korea – Dairy")*, WT/DS98/AB/R, adopted 12 January 2000, DSR 2000:I, 3, para.145.
[12]   *Ibid*, para.117.

7.12   We also note the ruling by the Appellate Body in *US – Lamb* where it is stated[13]:

> "We wish to emphasize that, although panels are not entitled to conduct a *de novo* review of evidence, nor to *substitute* their own conclusions for those of the competent authorities, this does *not* mean that panels must simply *accept* the conclusions of the competent authorities."

7.13   This was confirmed in an anti-dumping context by the panel in *Guatemala – Cement II*, in which the panel stated:

> "We consider that it is not our role to perform a *de novo* review of the evidence which was before the investigating authority in this case. Rather, Article 17 makes it clear that our task is to review the determination of the investigating authorities. Specifically, we must determine whether its establishment of the facts was proper and the evaluation of those facts was unbiased and objective."[14]

7.14   In light of the above, we are therefore conscious that we should not involve ourselves in a *denovo* review of the facts as submitted to the competent Egyptian authorities. Rather, our task is to review the determinations made by those authorities, in the light of the evidence of record that they had before them. As will become apparent, in the light of the facts of this case, we deem it necessary to undertake a detailed review of the evidence submitted to the IA to be able to determine whether an objective and unbiased investigating authority could have reached the determinations that Turkey challenges in this dispute.

3.   Introduction of Evidence that was not before the Investigating Authority

7.15   The third issue is Egypt's claim that evidence that was submitted by Turkey during this proceeding in an effort to demonstrate that the IA made errors in its analysis and determinations during the rebar anti-dumping investigation, which evidence was not before the investigation authority in that investigation, may not be examined by us.[15] Egypt, relying on Article 17.5(ii) of the AD

---

[13]   Appellate Body Report, *United States – Safeguard Measures on Imports of Fresh, Chilled or Frozen Lamb Meat from New Zealand and Australia("US – Lamb")*, WT/DS177/AB/R, WT/DS178/AB/R, adopted 16 May 2001, DSR 2001:IX, 4051, para.106.

[14]   Panel Report, *Guatemala – Definitive Anti-Dumping Measures on Grey Portland Cement from Mexico("Guatemala Cement II")*, WT/DS156/R, adopted 17 November 2000, DSR 2000:XI, 5295, para.8.19.

[15]   First Written Submission of Egypt, p.18 and 73. On page 73 the following documents are identified by Egypt: *AMM Weekly Steel Scrap Price Composite for 1998* – submitted by Turkey as Exh. TUR-13, and *Metal Bulletin – 1998 European Iron Steel Scrap Prices for 1998*, submitted by Turkey as Exh. TUR-14. In the Oral Presentation of Egypt to the Panel on 27 November 2001, Egypt further identifies the following documents as "new evidence" submitted by Turkey: An article from *The Dow Jones Commodity Service* – Report of 11 September 1997, titled "NKK Singapore to Build Steel Bar Mill for Egypt Steelmaker" and an article from *The Middle East Economic Digest* – Report of 6 March 1998, titled "Egypt: Alexandria National Iron and Steel Company (Both of these articles are referred to by Turkey in its First Written Submission under Claim C.2, but were not submitted by

Agreement, argues that we should reject this evidence as it was not made available to the Investigating Authority in the course of the investigation itself.

7.16   Article 17.5(ii) provides:

"The DSB shall, at the request of the complaining party, establish a panel to examine the matter based upon:

(ii) the facts made available in conformity with appropriate domestic procedures to the authorities of the importing Member."

7.17   As Turkey has confirmed that the mentioned evidence was not made available to the Investigating Authority in conformity with the appropriate domestic procedures, but was submitted for the first time in the context of the proceedings before us, Egypt argues that we should disregard it. Egypt finds support for its contention in the finding of the panel in *US – Hot-Rolled Steel*[16] where it was held that:

"It seems clear to us that, under [Article 17.5(ii) of the AD Agreement], a Panel may not, when examining a claim of violation of the AD Agreement in a particular determination, consider facts or evidence presented to it by a party in an attempt to demonstrate error in the determination concerning questions that were investigated and decided by the authorities, unless they had been made available in conformity with the appropriate domestic procedures to the authorities of the investigating country during the investigation."

7.18   Turkey argues, in response to a written question posed by us during the First Substantive Meeting of the Panel with the Parties,[17] regarding the status of the evidence in question and the legal basis on which we should take these documents into consideration, that the reason that this evidence was not submitted during the course of the investigation was that the Turkish exporters were under the impression that the injury investigation conducted by the Investigating Authority was with regard to "threat" of material injury and not "actual" material injury.[18]

7.19   Turkey also argues that if we should decide, in terms of Article 17.5(ii), that the record that we can take into account should ordinarily be limited to the facts made available to the Investigating Authority during the course of the in-

---

Turkey as exhibits.); the *Birmingham Steel Corporation, Securities and Exchange Commission (SEC)* "Form 10-Q", submitted by Turkey as Exh. TUR-19, and the *EFG-Hermes Study*, submitted by Turkey as Exh. TUR-32.

[16]   Panel Report, *US – Hot-Rolled Steel*, para.7.6.

[17]   In Question 4 to Turkey of the *Written Questions by the Panel*, dated 28 November 2001, we asked Turkey: "Could Turkey please clarify the status of Exhibits TUR-13, TUR-14, TUR-19 and TUR-32, and also of the documents listed in footnote 16 and 17 of its First Written Submission, that is, were these documents submitted to the Egyptian Investigating Authority, and if so, when? If not, please provide legal argumentation regarding the basis on which the Panel could take these documents into consideration" – Annex 4-1.

[18]   This aspect is addressed in Section VII.C.3, *infra*.

vestigation, we nevertheless should adopt the legal principle of taking "judicial notice" of certain other facts.[19] We are not aware of a principle of "judicial notice" at the WTO level. Certainly, we as Panelists have an awareness of matters pertaining to life, nature and society. But the question is not what we as Panelists know or ought to accept as being known by the IA. The question is what the IA did and was expected to do under the AD Agreement at the time of the investigation.

7.20   We note that, as the evidence proffered by Turkey and disputed by Egypt relates exclusively to the injury determination by the IA and the causal link between the injury and dumped imports, Article 3.5 of the AD Agreement also contains specific language addressing the issue of evidence. This article provides, in relevant part:

> "The demonstration of a causal relationship between the dumped imports and the injury to the domestic industry shall be based on an examination of all relevant evidence *before the authorities*." (emphasis added)Furthermore, we agree with the statement by the panel in *US - Hot-Rolled Steel*[20], that:

> "The conclusion that we will not consider new evidence with respect to claims under the AD Agreement flows not only from Article 17.5(ii), but also from the fact that a panel is not to perform a *de novo* review of the issues considered and decided by the investigating authorities."

7.21   It is clear to us (and indeed, there is no disagreement on this point between the parties) that the evidence in question, which was proffered by Turkey in the dispute to challenge determinations made by the IA during the antidumping investigation, was not made available to the Investigating Authority in conformity with the appropriate domestic procedures during the investigation, as required by Article 17.5.(ii), and it is clear as well that consideration of new evidence of this sort can be construed as a *de novo* review, which is not permissible. We thus will not take this evidence into consideration when reviewing the measures of the determinations and actions of the Egyptian Investigating Authority.

---

[19]   On page 3 of its response of 7 December 2001 to Question 4 to Turkey of the *Written Questions by the Panel*, dated 28 November 2001, Turkey responded: "Both at the English and American common law, most proof in a court of law is presented by means of testimonial evidence or by the offering of real evidence. But there is an exception to the requirement that a party who relies on a certain proposition must prove it, and that exception is facts that can be 'judicially noticed'. In the United States, there is a federal rule of evidence permitting both trial courts and appellate courts to take 'judicial notice' of facts that are not subject to reasonable dispute because they are either (1) generally known; or (2) capable of accurate and ready determination by resort to sources whose accuracy cannot be reasonably questioned. ... The first type of fact of which judicial notice may be taken is a fact that is 'so well known that it would be a waste of judicial resources to require proof; reasonably informed people simply could not differ as to the fact.' The second type of fact is 'one that is capable of ready verification through sources whose reliability cannot reasonably be questioned'." – Annex 4-1.
[20]   Panel Report, *US – Hot-Rolled Steel*, para.7.

4. Request for Dismissal of Certain Claims

7.22   In addition to the above preliminary objections, Egypt also requests us to reject certain claims submitted by Turkey as Egypt asserts that these claims are not within the terms of reference of the Panel and are therefore not properly before us.[21]

7.23   As there seemed to be some differences between Turkey's claims, as reflected in its Request for Establishment of a Panel[22], and its claims and legal argumentation in its First Written Submission, we requested Turkey during the First Substantive Meeting of the Panel with the Parties on 28 November 2001 to "set out in summary format its legal argumentation in support of each of its claims, i.e., listing the respective provisions of the Anti-Dumping Agreement and GATT 1994, and explaining briefly in the light of the Vienna Convention on the Law of Treaties how the cited factual circumstances constitute violations of those provisions".[23] Egypt, in its Rebuttal Submission, asserted that Turkey had "in its response of 7 December 2001 to the Panel's Questions, taken this opportunity to (1) introduce new claims; and (2) modify existing claims as regards injury and dumping that were not mentioned in the request for establishment of a Panel".[24]

7.24   In particular, Egypt objects to the following claims as set out in Turkey's response to our question:

(a)   That the IA did not consider factors affecting domestic prices under Article 3.4.

(b)   That Egypt violated paragraph 6 of Annex II of the AD Agreement by sending the letter of 19 August 1999 to the Turkish respondents.

(c)   That the IA violated Article 17.6(i) of the AD Agreement.

(d)   That the IA violated paragraph 3 of Annex II of the AD Agreement and Article X:3 of GATT 1994 in its selection of facts as facts available.[25]

7.25   In reviewing Turkey's Request for Establishment of a Panel[26] and its response to our Question 1, it is clear to us that, with the exception of Article 17.6(i), Turkey has explicitly cited in its Request for Establishment of a Panel all of the above-cited provisions allegedly violated by Egypt. However, it is also clear to us that the way in which some of the provisions are cited in Turkey's "restatement" of its claims[27] does not correspond to the same claims as set out in

---

[21]   Written Rebuttal of Egypt, dated 19 December 2001, p.14.
[22]   WT/DS211/2 of 11 May 2001.
[23]   Question 1 to Turkey of the *Written Questions by the Panel*, dated 28 November 2001 Annex 4.1.
[24]   Written Rebuttal of Egypt, p.1.
[25]   *Ibid.*
[26]   WT/DS211/2, as amended.
[27]   Written Response of Turkey, dated 7 December 2001, to Question 1 of *Questions by the Panel*, of 28 November 2001 – Annex 4.1.

its Request for Establishment of a Panel. In light of this, we requested Egypt to provide us, in respect of each claim that it requests us to dismiss, the two-part analysis referred to in *Korea – Dairy*[28] and *EC – Bed Linen*[29], that is, the asserted lack of clarity in the Request for Establishment of a Panel, and evidence of any resulting prejudice to Egypt's ability to defend its interest in this dispute due to such lack of clarity.[30]

7.26　In its response to our question, Egypt asserts that it was prejudiced with regard to the following claims:[31,32]

(a)　Claims under Article 3.4 as regards "factors affecting domestic prices"

Egypt contends that Turkey presents the same arguments in relation to Article 3.4 and 3.5 and alleges a violation under Article 3.4 *or* 3.5 and that Turkey's claims in relation to these two provisions as stated in its Request for Establishment of a Panel at Claim 3 and 4 were not clarified in Turkey's First Submission, or subsequently. Egypt is of the view that Article 3.4 and 3.5 establish multiple obligations and if any violation with respect thereunder is not presented with sufficient clarity, the burden on the respondent becomes too onerous and both the Panel and the respondent are at risk of being misled as to which claims are in fact being asserted against the respondent. Egypt asserts that it was unclear as to which provision under Article 3 Turkey was presenting its argumentation with respect to "factors affecting domestic prices" and that Egypt was prejudiced as regards the preparation of its defence with respect to those particular factors.[33]

(b)　Paragraph 6 of Annex II

Egypt contends that in its Request for Establishment of a Panel, Turkey claimed a violation of Annex II, paragraph 6, with respect to the deadline granted to the respondents to reply to the letter of 19 August 1999[34], but that Turkey, in its restatement of claims[35], additionally claimed that the sheer fact of sending the letter of 19

---

[28]　Appellate Body Report, *Korea - Dairy*, para.6.

[29]　Panel Report, *European Communities – Anti-Dumping Duties on Imports of Cotton-Type Bed Linen from India ("EC – Bed Linen")*, WT/DS141/R, adopted 12 March 2001, as modified by the Appellate Body Report, WT/DS141/AB/R, DSR 2001:VI, 2077, para.6.26.

[30]　Question 6 to Egypt of the *Written Questions by the Panel*, dated 27 February 2002 – Annex 4-2.

[31]　Response of Egypt, dated 13 March 2002, to Question 6 of the *Written Questions by the* Panel, of 27 February 2002 – Annex 8-2..

[32]　As these claims are the only ones addressed by Egypt in response to our question, we assume that these are the only issues which Egypt would like to pursue in this context and we therefore limit our analysis to these issues as well.

[33]　Written Response of Egypt, dated 13 March 2002, to Question 6 to Egypt of the *Written Questions by the Panel*, of 27 February 2002 - Annex 8-2.

[34]　Exh. TUR-11.

[35]　Written Response, dated 7 December 2001, of Turkey to Question 1 to Turkey of the *Written Questions by the Panel*, of 28 November 2001 - Annex. 8-1.

August 1999 also constituted a violation of paragraph 6. As paragraph 6 provides that an investigating authority should grant a party an opportunity to provide further explanations within a reasonable period as to why its information should not be rejected, Egypt fails to understand the basis for Turkey's claim as it provided no further explanation or clarification. As a result of the absence of any explanation of the claim, Egypt contends that its ability to defend its interest was severely prejudiced.[36]

(c)   Paragraph 3 of Annex II and Article X:3 of GATT 1994

Regarding the alleged violation of Annex II, paragraph 3, Egypt contends that Turkey failed to identify the obligation contained in that provision that the IA would have violated in its selection of "facts available", therefore preventing Egypt from presenting a meaningful defence, as paragraph 3 relates to the circumstances in which the data submitted by respondents must be accepted or can be rejected. Egypt argues that this provision does not address the *selection* of facts available once it has been decided to reject the data submitted by the respondents. As the legal basis for this claim is not clear to Egypt, and as Turkey did not provide any clarification, Egypt contends that its was severely prejudiced in respect to defending its rights.[37]

Regarding the alleged violation of Article X:3 of GATT 1994 is concerned, Egypt contends that the allegations of a violation were vague and unsubstantiated and that it is therefore not in a position to defend its interests.[38]

(d)   Failure to refer to the relevant treaty article in the Request for Establishment of a Panel

(i)   Whether the Final Report contains findings or conclusions sufficient to satisfy the requirements of Article 12.2

Egypt contends that an Article 12.2 claim is not before us as it was not referred to in the Request for Establishment of a Panel, and through a reference to the finding of the panel in *EC – Bed Linen*, para. 6.15, asserts that if a treaty article is not mentioned in the request for establishment of a panel, such a claim is not before a panel. Egypt states that as a result, it did not prepare any defence on this claim.[39]

(ii)   Whether the Panel can disregard evidence under Article 6.4

---

[36]   Written Response of Egypt, dated 13 March 2002, to Question 6 to Egypt of the *Written Questions by the Panel*, of 27 February 2002 – Annex 8-2.

[37]   *Ibid.*

[38]   *Ibid.*

[39]   *Ibid.*

Egypt contends that although Turkey claims in its Rebuttal Submission that we should not consider evidence that was not provided to interested parties during the course of the investigation, such as the report on *Other Causes of Injury*[40], a violation of Article 6.4 was not claimed by Turkey and is therefore not before us.[41]

(iii)   Article 17.6(i) of the AD Agreement

Although Turkey alleges a violation of Article 17.6(i) of the AD Agreement, Egypt contends that this provision governs the standard of review to be applied by a panel when considering whether an investigating authority's establishment of the facts was proper and the evaluation unbiased and objective – it does not govern the rights and obligations of Members under the AD Agreement. Furthermore, Egypt asserts that Article 17.6(i) was not cited in the Request for Establishment of a Panel and is therefore not before us.[42]

7.27   We address the issues raised by Egypt in relation to (a) and (d)(iii) above in Sections VII.C.1 and VII.D.2, *infra*.

7.28   Concerning the issues raised in (d)(i) and (d)(ii), we do not believe that Turkey has attempted to raise claims under Article 12.2 or under Article 6.4, and therefore we neither address nor dismiss such purported "claims".

7.29   With regard to the issues relating to paragraph 6 and paragraph 3 of Annex II under (b) and (c), we are of the view that the relevant issues addressed by these two provisions are so interrelated that Egypt could not have been prejudiced in the preparation of its defence in the way in which Turkey presented its claims in this regard.

7.30   With regard to Egypt's objection regarding Article X:3 of GATT 1994, we consider that Turkey effectively abandoned its claim (set forth in paragraph 9 of its Request for Establishment of a Panel) that the IA's decision to resort to facts available violated Article X:3. In particular, Turkey made no arguments in this respect in any of its submissions to us. Furthermore, in response to a specific question on this point, Turkey indicated that its Article X:3 claim in the context of facts available concerns the selection of particular facts as "facts available", a point addressed in paragraph 11 of its Request for Establishment of a Panel. Paragraph 11 of the Request does not refer, however, to Article X:3.

7.31   Given Turkey's apparent abandonment of its claim that Egypt violated Article X:3 by reason of the IA's decision to resort to facts available[43], we do not consider this claim further. As for Turkey's claim that the selection of particular facts as "facts available" violated Article X:3, it is clear that the Request for Es-

---

[40]   Exh. EGT-6.

[41]   *Ibid.*

[42]   *Ibid.*

[43]   Written Response of Turkey, dated 7 December 2002, to Question 1 of the *Written Questions by the Panel*, of 28 November 2001 – Annex 4-1.

tablishment of a Panel makes no reference to this provision in this context. We consider significant here that, unlike paragraphs 3 and 6 of Annex II (items (b) and (c) above), Article X:3 is not related in any self-evident way to any of the other provisions cited by Turkey in paragraph 11 of its Request for Establishment of a Panel. Nor is this claim of violation of Article X:3 related in any way to Turkey's other claims of violation of this provision. We find that this claim is simply not specified in Turkey's Request for Establishment of a Panel, and that the specifications and justifications for its validity as a claim as presented by Turkey during the course of the dispute have not been clear or convincing. We therefore dismiss this claim and do not consider it further.

7.32   As for Turkey's claim of violation of Article X:3 due to the IA's alleged refusal to schedule a meeting with certain respondents, we address this claim in Section VII.F, *infra*.

C.   Claims Relating to Injury and Causation

1.   Claims under Article 3.4 of the AD Agreement

(a)   Alleged Failure to Examine Factors Specifically Listed in Article 3.4

7.33   Turkey claims that Egypt violated Article 3.4 by failing to examine all of the factors listed in Article 3.4 of the AD Agreement.[44] In particular, Turkey asserts that Egypt did not evaluate productivity, actual and potential negative effects on cash flow, employment, wages, growth and ability to raise capital or investments. Turkey also argues that the public versions of the Essential Facts and Conclusions Report and of the Final Report provide no evidence that there was a sufficient examination or evaluation of capacity utilisation or return on investment.

7.34   Egypt argues that the record of the investigation makes clear that all of the factors listed in Article 3.4 were considered by the IA. In its response to a question from the Panel[45] in the context of the First Substantive Meeting with the Parties[46], Egypt presents a table indicating specific references in the Essential Facts and Conclusions Report and in the Final Report to the following factors listed in Article 3.4: sales, profits, output, market share, return on investments, capacity utilisation, prices, dumping margin and inventories. In its Rebuttal Submission[47], Egypt further states that "growth" (one of the factors alleged by Turkey not to have been addressed at all by the IA) was addressed by the information on "sales volume" and "market share", while "ability to raise capital" (another factor identified in Turkey's claim) is addressed by pre-tax profit as a

---

[44]   Statement by Turkey during the First Substantive Meeting of the Panel with the Parties, 27 November 2001, p.12, and Written Response of Turkey, dated 7 December 2001, to Question 1 of the *Written Questions by the Panel* of 28 November 2001 – Annex 4-1.

[45]   Question 5 of Egypt of the *Written Questions by the Panel*, of 28 November 2001 – Annex 4-2.

[46]   Written Response by Egypt, dated 7 December 2001, to Question 5 of the *Written Questions by the Panel*, of 28 November 2001 – Annex 4-2.

[47]   Written Rebuttal of Egypt, dated 19 December 2001, Section III.A.1.

percentage of shareholders' funds. Concerning the remaining factors alleged by Turkey not to have been considered at all, Egypt refers to the *Confidential Injury Analysis*, a submission containing Business Confidential Information which was provided to the Panel and to Turkey in accordance with the Supplemental Procedures Concerning Business Confidential Information that were adopted by the Panel.[48] According to Egypt, this *Analysis* forms part of the Final Determination in the rebar investigation, which must be distinguished from the Final Report. In particular, Egypt states that the *Confidential Injury Analysis* makes evident that the IA's analysis indeed covered "all of the factors listed in Article 3.4".[49]

7.35   Article 3.4 of the AD Agreement reads as follows:

"The examination of the impact of the dumped imports on the domestic industry concerned shall include an evaluation of all relevant economic factors and indices having a bearing on the state of the industry, including actual and potential decline in sales, profits, output, market share, productivity, return on investments, or utilization of capacity; factors affecting domestic prices; the magnitude of the margin of dumping; actual and potential negative effects on cash flow, inventories, employment, wages, growth, ability to raise capital or investments. This list is not exhaustive, nor can one or several of these factors necessarily give decisive guidance."

7.36   In evaluating this claim, we take note of and agree with the findings of previous panels[50] and the Appellate Body[51] that *all* of the factors listed in Article 3.4 must be addressed in every investigation. Egypt does not argue to the contrary. Rather, the issue raised by this claim is the nature of the consideration performed, as reflected in the Essential Facts and Conclusions Report, in the Final Report, and in the *Confidential Injury Analysis*, taken collectively. Two questions are raised in this regard: first, as a threshold matter, whether the IA addressed each of the listed factors at all; and second, if so, whether the evidence provided by Egypt to the Panel establishes that the consideration of those factors substantively satisfies the requirements of Article 3.4.

7.37   Turning first to the threshold question, i.e., whether each factor is addressed in some way in at least one of these documents, we find in the affirmative. We take note of the references in the *Essential Facts and Conclusions Re-*

---

[48]   Attached hereto as Annex 13.

[49]   Statement by Egypt during the Second Substantive Meeting of the Panel with the Parties, 25 February 2002, p.13.

[50]   *See* e.g., Panel Report, *European Communities – Anti-Dumping Duties on Imports of Cotton-Type Bed Linen from India ("EC – Bed Linen")*, WT/DS141/R, adopted 12 March 2001, as modified by the Appellate Body Report, WT/DS141/AB/R, DSR 2001:VI, 2077, para.6.159, and the Panel Report, *Mexico – Anti-Dumping Investigation of High Fructose Corn Syrup (HFCS) from the United States ("Mexico – Corn Syrup")*, WT/DS132/R and Corr.1, adopted 24 February 2000, DSR 2000:III, 1345, par.7.128.

[51]   *See,* e.g., Appellate Body Report, *Thailand – Anti-Dumping Duties on Angles, Shapes and Sections of Iron or Non-Alloy Steel and H-Beams from Poland ("Thailand – H-Beams")*, WT/DS122/AB/R, adopted 5 April 2001, DSR 2001:VII, 2701, para.128.

port[52] and *Final Report*[53] to sales, profits, output, market share, return on investments, capacity utilisation, prices, dumping margin, and inventories. There is no doubt that these factors were explicitly addressed by the IA. Similarly, we are satisfied that by addressing in the *Essential Facts and Conclusions Report* and the *Final Report* sales volume and market share, the IA addressed "growth", as Egypt argues in its Rebuttal Submission.[54] We therefore do not consider further the factor "growth" in the context of this claim. Thus, the focus of this claim is whether the remaining factors identified by Turkey *are* reflected in the *Confidential Injury Analysis*, and if so, whether their treatment in that document is sufficient to satisfy the requirements of Article 3.4. Concerning the *Confidential Injury Analysis*, we are mindful of the findings of the Appellate Body in *Thailand – H-Beams* that confidential information relied upon by an IA, even if not shared with respondents, should be taken into account by a panel when assessing compliance with Article 3.4.[55].

7.38   Turning to its content, we note that the *Confidential Injury Analysis* contains data on, *inter alia*, cash flow, employment, wages, and productivity. Moreover, we accept, as argued by Egypt[56], that by addressing in the *Confidential Injury Analysis* pre-tax profit as a percentage of shareholders' funds for Alexandria National and Al Ezz, the IA addressed in that *Analysis* "ability to raise capital". Thus, taken together, the *Essential Facts and Conclusions Report*, the *Final Report*, and the *Confidential Injury Analysis* demonstrate that the IA addressed, at least in some way, all of the factors listed in Article 3.4.

7.39   As noted above, however, this is only the threshold issue for our determination of whether the IA complied with the requirement of Article 3.4 in respect of the "examination" of all of the listed factors. Here, we recall the specific wording of the relevant part of that provision:

> "The examination of the impact of the dumped imports on the domestic industry concerned shall include *an evaluation* of all relevant economic factors and indices..." (emphasis added)

Thus, in taking up the second issue raised by this claim, this language compels us to consider whether the IA's "examination" included an "evaluation" in the sense of Article 3.4 of each of the listed Article 3.4 factors that appear only in the *Confidential Injury Analysis*.

7.40   We note Egypt's basic argument that the *Confidential Injury Analysis* is proof that the IA "examined" all of the factors listed in Article 3.4 that are not reflected in the *Essential Facts and Conclusions Report* and in the *Final Report*, and that the IA thus satisfied the requirements of that Article. To recall, Turkey alleges that Egypt failed to "examine" productivity, actual and potential negative effects on cash flow, employment, wages, growth and ability to raise capital or

---

[52]   Exh. TUR-15, *Essential Facts and Conclusions Report*, October 1999, p.29-32..
[53]   Exh. TUR-16, *Final Report*, October 1999, p.35-39.
[54]   Written Rebuttal Submission of Egypt, Section III.A.1.
[55]   Appellate Body Report, *Thailand – H-Beams*, para.107 and 118.
[56]   Written Rebuttal Submission of Egypt, Section III.A.1.

investments, because these factors are not referred to in the *Essential Facts and Conclusions Report* or the *Final Report*. Turkey further argues that to the extent that data are included on some of these factors in the *Confidential Injury Analysis*, this "*Analysis*" consists of data only, and thus is not sufficient to constitute an "evaluation" in the sense of Article 3.4.

7.41   In this regard, we posed two very similar questions to Egypt concerning where in the record of the investigation the IA's consideration could be found or discerned of the factors identified by Turkey and which are not addressed in the *Essential Facts and Conclusions Report* and/or in the *Final Report* (actual and potential negative effects on cash flow, employment, wages, productivity, and ability to raise capital or investment)[57], [58]. Both times, Egypt referred us exclusively to the *Confidential Injury Analysis*.[59]. We emphasize that while (as we have found above) the *Confidential Injury Analysis* refers to and contains data on all of the factors listed in Article 3.4 (including those that are the subject of this claim), it contains no narrative, but rather consists only of tables of data concerning the various factors, for the domestic industry as a whole, and individually, for the two domestic producers (Al Ezz and Alexandria National)[60]. Egypt could not, or did not, provide any document of record other than the *Confidential Injury Analysis* in respect of the factors identified by Turkey. We therefore assume that these tables of data are the only documents of record reflecting or representing the IA's consideration of these factors.

7.42   The question before us, in respect of productivity, actual and potential negative effects on cash flow, employment, wages, and ability to raise capital or investments, therefore, is whether the mere presentation of tables of data, without more, constitutes an "evaluation" in the sense of Article 3.4.

---

[57]   Question 9 to Egypt and Question 3 to Both Parties of the *Written Questions by the Panel*, dated 27 February 2002 – Annex 8-2.

[58]   As noted, we already have concluded above that "growth" effectively was addressed in the *Essential Facts and Conclusions Report* and the *Final Report*, and we thus do not consider that factor further here.

[59]   Written Response of Egypt to Question 9 to Egypt and Question 3 to Both Parties of the *Written Questions by the Panel*, dated 27 February 2002 – Annex 8-2..

[60]   The factors for which data are presented in the *Confidential Injury Analysis*, for the industry as a whole and for Alexandria National and Al Ezz individually, are sales volume, sales revenue, cost of production, gross profit, selling and administrative expenses, cost of sales, profit before interest expenses, finance cost, and net profit, on a total basis and on a per ton basis, as well as cost of production, gross profit, selling and administrative expenses, cost of sales, total cost and net profit as a per cent of revenue, as well as number of employees and per cent change thereof, wages, production capacity, production volume, and capacity utilisation, number of shareholders and per cent change thereof, value of total assets and percent change thereof, volume of finished goods inventory and per cent change thereof, cash flow, and worker productivity. In addition, for the industry as a whole, the *Analysis* contains tables on return on investment, volume of total domestic sales, of dumped imports, of other imports and total domestic market, as well as per cent market shares of the domestic industry, the dumped imports and the other imports, "undercutting" (i.e., domestic industry price, Turkish imports' price, and percentage difference), price depression (domestic industry prices between 1996 and first quarter 1999), price suppression (total cost, domestic industry price, and total cost as a percentage of price, between 1996 and first quarter 1999), and output volume and sales value, and per cent changes, between 1996 and first quarter 1999.

7.43 We first consider the ordinary meaning of the word "evaluation". The Oxford English Dictionary defines "evaluation" as follows:

"(1) The action of appraising or valuing (goods, etc.); a calculation or statement of value. (2) The action of evaluating or determining the value of (a mathematical expression, a physical quantity, etc.), or of estimating the force of (probabilities, *evidence*)."[61](emphasis added)

The Merriam-Webster's Collegiate Dictionary defines "evaluation" as follows:

"(1) To determine or fix the value of. (2) To determine the significance, worth, or condition of *usually by careful appraisal or study.*"[62](emphasis added)

The Merriam-Webster's Thesaurus lists as synonyms for "evaluation" the following:

"(1) appraisal, appraisement, assessment, estimation, valuation (with related words: interpreting; judging, rating); (2) appraisal, appraisement, assessment, estimate, judgement, stock (with related words: appreciation; interpretation; decision)."[63]

7.44 We find significant that all of these definitions and synonyms connote, particularly in the context of "evaluation" of evidence, the act of analysis, judgement, or assessment. That is, the first definition recited above refers to "estimating the force of" evidence, evoking a process of weighing evidence and reaching conclusions thereon. The second definition recited above - to determine the significance, worth, or condition of, usually by careful appraisal or study - confirms this meaning. Thus, for an investigating authority to "evaluate" evidence concerning a given factor in the sense of Article 3.4, it must not only gather data, but it must analyze and interpret those data.

7.45 We nevertheless do recognize that, in addition to the dictionary meanings of "evaluation" that we have cited, the definitions set forth above also refer to a purely quantitative process (i.e., calculating, stating, determining or fixing the value of something). If this were the definition applicable to the word "evaluation" as used in Article 3.4, arguably mere compilation of data on the listed factors, without any narrative explanation or analysis, might suffice to satisfy the requirements of Article 3.4. We find, however, contextual support in Article 17.6(i) of the AD Agreement for our reading that "evaluation" is something different from, and more than, simple compilation of tables of data. We recognize that Article 17.6(i) does not apply directly to investigating authorities, and that instead, it is part of the standard of review to be applied by panels in reviewing determinations of investigating authorities. However, Article 17.6(i) identifies as the object of a panel's review two basic components of a determination: first, the investigating authority's "establishment of the facts", and second, the investigat-

---

[61] Oxford English Dictionary Online: http://dictionary.oed.com.
[62] Merriam-Webster's Collegiate Dictionary online: http://www.m-w.com.
[63] Merriam-Webster's Thesaurus online: http://www.m-w.com.

ing authority's "evaluation of those facts". Thus, Article 17.6(i)'s characterization of the essential components of a determination juxtaposes "establishment of the facts" with the "evaluation of those facts". That panels are instructed to determine whether an investigating authority's "establishment of the facts" was proper connotes an assessment by the panel of the means by which the data before the investigating authority were gathered and compiled. By contrast, the fact that panels are instructed to determine whether an investigating authority's "evaluation of those facts" was objective and unbiased, provides further support for our view that the "evaluation" to which Article 3.4 refers is the process of analysis and interpretation of the facts established in relation to each listed factor.

7.46   Our interpretation of the requirement of Article 3.4 to "evaluate" the factors and indices is consistent with that of panels in a number of past disputes. The panel in *Thailand – H-Beams* found in regard to the examination of the factors listed in Article 3.4 that:

> "Article 3.4 requires the authorities properly to establish whether a factual basis exists to support a well-reasoned and meaningful analysis of the state of the industry and a finding of injury. This analysis does not derive from a mere characterization of the degree of "relevance or irrelevance" of each and every individual factor, but rather must be based on a thorough evaluation of the state of the industry and, in light of the last sentence of Article 3.4 [footnote omitted], must contain a persuasive explanation as to how the evaluation of relevant factors led to the determination of injury."[64]

7.47   In *U S – Hot-Rolled Steel*, the issue was whether the US investigating authority had violated Article 3.4 by failing to explicitly discuss, in its determination, certain factors for each year of the period of investigation. In that case, according to the panel, the authority had discussed each of the factors for the final two years of the three-year period of investigation, and only some of them for the first year of that period. The panel found that the determination explained the particular relevance of the second and third years of the period, and that the authority's failure to explicitly address each factor in its discussion of the first year of the period did not constitute a violation of Article 3.4[65]. That is, the panel found, *inter alia*, that each of the listed Article 3.4 factors was explicitly *discussed* in the authority's determination, and given the explanations provided in that determination for the particular emphasis on a part of the period of investigation, the *evaluation* of the facts was deemed adequate by the panel.

7.48   This contrasts sharply with the situation in the present case, where the Egyptian Investigating Authority appears to have gathered data on all of the listed Article 3.4 factors, as reflected in various documents of record (including the *Essential Facts and Conclusions Report*, the *Final Report* and the *Confidential Injury Analysis*). Egypt has been unable, however, to adduce sufficient evi-

---

[64]   Panel Report, *Thailand – H-Beams*, para.7.236.
[65]   Panel Report, *US – Hot-Rolled Steel*, paras.7.235-7.236.

dence to the Panel, in response to our specific requests, of the IA's evaluation of all of those factors in its written analyses. [66]

7.49   Here we must emphasize that in the context of an anti-dumping investigation, which is by definition subject to multilateral rules and multilateral review, a Member is placed in a difficult position in rebutting a *prima facie* case that an evaluation has *not* taken place if it is unable to direct the attention of a panel to some contemporaneous written record of that process. If there is no such written record - whether in the disclosure documents, in the published determination, or in other internal documents - of how certain factors have been interpreted or appreciated by an investigating authority during the course of the investigation, there is no basis on which a Member can rebut a *prima facie* case that its "evaluation" under Article 3.4 was inadequate or did not take place at all. In particular, without a written record of the analytical process undertaken by the investigating authority, a panel would be forced to embark on a *post hoc* speculation about the thought process by which an investigating authority arrived at its ultimate conclusions as to the impact of the dumped imports on the domestic industry. A speculative exercise by a panel is something that the special standard of review in Article 17.6 is intended to prevent. Thus, while Egypt attempts to derive support from the panel report in the *US – Hot-Rolled Steel* dispute for its position that Article 3.4 does not require an explicit written analysis of all of the factors listed therein[67], to us, the findings in that dispute confirms our interpretation, in that what was at issue, was the substantive adequacy of the authority's written analysis of *each* of those factors.

7.50   Nor do we consider, as suggested by Egypt[68], that the requirement of a written analysis of the Article 3.4 factors is exclusively governed by Article 12 of the AD Agreement (public notice and explanation of determinations). While Article 12 contains a requirement to *publish*, and to make available to the interested parties in the investigation, some form of a report on the investigating authority's determination, this is, as the Appellate Body has noted, a procedural requirement having to do with due process[69], rather than with the relevant sub-

---

[66]   *See* para.7.41, *supra*.

[67]   Written Response, dated 13 March 2002, of Egypt to Question 9 to Egypt and Question 3 to Both Parties of the *Written Questions of the Panel*, of 27 February 2002 – Annex 8-2. Egypt contends in its response that "[t]he *Confidential Injury Analysis* therefore constitutes an evaluation of the factors that it covers in the sense of Article 3.4" and that this approach is consistent with the findings of the panel in *US – Hot-Rolled Steel*. However, the facts in the *US – Hot-Rolled Steel* dispute differ significantly from those in this dispute. In this dispute the allegation is that the IA did not properly evaluated all of the factors listed in Article 3.4 of the AD Agreement, whereas in the *US – Hot-Rolled Steel* case, all Article 3.4 factors were evaluated, but Japan claimed that the discussion did not sufficiently evaluate certain factors by failing to discuss date for all three years which comprised the period of investigation for the determination of injury – paras. 7.231-7.236 of the Panel Report, *ibid.*

[68]   *Ibid*, response to Question 6 and 9 to Egypt.

[69]   In the Appellate Body Report in *Thailand – H-Beams*, para.110, the Appellate Body stated that "... Article 12 establishes a framework of procedural and due process obligations concerning, notably, the contents of a *final determination*". We note that what is at issue before us is not the adequacy of the *final determination* or any other published document, as such, but rather, the adequacy of the *substance* of the analysis performed by the Egyptian investigating authority, in whatever document such analysis might be found. Moreover, the basic issue before the Appellate Body in *Thailand – H-*

stantive analytical requirements (which in the context of this claim are found in Article 3.4).

7.51   On the basis of the above considerations, we find that while it gathered data on all of the factors listed in Article 3.4, the Egyptian investigating authority failed to *evaluate* productivity, actual and potential negative effects on cash flow, employment, wages, and ability to raise capital or investments. We therefore find that Egypt acted inconsistently with Article 3.4.

7.52   We turn finally to Turkey's argument that Article 3.4 was further violated because the IA's evaluation of "capacity utilisation" and of "return on investment" was inadequate. In respect of capacity utilisation, the IA's *Final Report* indicates, in sections 4.3.1 (sales), and 4.3.2 (production), respectively, that sales increased because domestic prices were reduced to compete with dumped imports, and that domestic production also increased, as the companies "attempt[ed] to increase production in order to reduce costs to be able to compete with the low-priced Turkish imports". The report also notes that the IA "concluded that the increase in production is attributed partly to starting new production lines in steel mills". Then, in Section 4.3.6 (production capacity), the *Final Report* states that "[n]o effect on industry capacity utilisation has been found". This statement that capacity utilisation was unaffected, although short, is consistent with the above-quoted statements that sales and production had increased, along with capacity. Given this context, we do not find that the IA failed to adequately evaluate capacity utilisation, and thus we do not find that Egypt violated Article 3.4 in this respect.

7.53   Concerning return on investment, the IA's *Final Report* notes in section 4.3.7 (return on investment) that there was "a decline in return on investment during the period of investigation". We note that this finding, although brief, is consistent with the longer discussion concerning net profits and losses in section 4.3.5 (profits). Given this context, we do not find that the IA failed to adequately evaluate return on investment, and thus we do not find that Egypt violated Article 3.4 in this respect.

Beams was very different from that before us. In that appeal, the issue raised was whether the panel was limited by the language of Articles 3.1 and 17.6 to reviewing the Thai investigating authority's injury determination exclusively on the basis of facts and analysis discernible in documents that had been published or otherwise made available to the respondents in the investigation or their counsel, or whether in addition, the panel could and should take into account internal analysis memoranda and similar documents prepared by and for the exclusive use of the authority during the investigation, the contents of which were not discernible in any documents available to the respondents. Thus, the issue there was essentially about how a panel should address confidential information, an issue not before us in this dispute. Thus, while Egypt cites *Thailand – H-Beams* as support for its position in the present dispute, in our view that dispute pertains to a different issue entirely. To the extent that it may touch upon issues before us, it does not detract in any way from our interpretation of the substantive requirements of Article 3.4 – paras.98 *et al* of the Appellate Body Report.

(b)   Alleged Failure to Examine "all relevant economic factors and indices having a bearing on the state of the industry"

7.54   Turkey claims a further violation of Article 3.4 by reason of the alleged failure by the Investigating Authority to examine "all relevant economic factors and indices having a bearing on the state of the industry", including, in particular, various factors allegedly affecting domestic prices and affecting profits.[70]

7.55   The factors identified by Turkey in this regard are:

(a)   "The dramatic capacity expansion at the two major Egyptian rebar producers and its likely temporary effects on their cost structures";

(b)   "The effects of the capacity expansions, which started production at the end of 1998, on competition between the Egyptian producers as they attempted to fill newly expanded order books";

(c)   "Sharpening competition between Al Ezz and Alexandria National as Al Ezz sought to increase market share by capitalizing on its cost advantages over Alexandria National";

(d)   "Falling prices for steel scrap, the primary raw material input at Al Ezz";

(e)   "A sharp contraction in demand in January 1999, the very month in which prices for rebar fell";

(f)   "The effect of comparably priced, fairly traded imports".[71]

7.56   According to Turkey, factor (a) has a bearing on cost of production and is therefore a "relevant factor" to the state of the industry. Factors (b)-(e) are, in Turkey's view, factors "affecting domestic prices" which either were not mentioned, or their effects on prices were not examined, or were not given any weight, in the investigating authority's analysis of why prices fell. Factor (f), Turkey states, may or may not have had an effect on prices, but Turkey argues that there was no support for a finding that dumped imports had a materially different effect on domestic prices than did other imports. In other words, Turkey claims that these are factors *other than dumped imports* that caused any injury

---

[70]   Written Response of Turkey, dated 7 December 2001, to Question 1 to Turkey of the *Written Questions by the Panel*, of 28 November 2002 – Annex 4-1.

[71]   *Ibid*, p.21-22. We note that in respect of this claim, Turkey's Request for Establishment of a Panel refers to some, but not all of the factors listed above. In particular, the Request for Establishment of a Panel states in this context that: "Such factors include, but are not limited to, a large-scale capacity expansion by the Egyptian rebar producers during the period of review, the effects of non-subject imports from third countries, falling world-wide prices for steel scrap and a sudden contraction in domestic demand in January 1999, when the [IA] found its first evidence of falling domestic prices". Egypt raised no objection to Turkey's reference in its arguments in respect of this claim to factors that were not explicitly referred to in the request for establishment. We posed a question to both parties on this point (Question 1 to Both Parties of the *Written Questions by the Panel*, of 27 February 2002.), and in response, Egypt indicated that where a request for establishment uses an inclusive expression in respect of the specific grounds for a claim, the complaining party can allege additional grounds in its arguments, so long as the party complained against has the opportunity to offer rebuttal arguments.

experienced by the domestic industry[72]. In response to a question, Turkey clarified that factors (b) and (c) are subsumed in factor (a), in that they were alleged adverse effects of the capacity expansion, and that arguably, factor (d) was so subsumed as well.

7.57   Egypt argues that this claim by Turkey is misplaced and thus should be rejected, as in Egypt's view, it raises arguments concerning causation, and in particular has to do with the requirement not to attribute to dumped imports injury caused by other factors. According to Egypt, causation is exclusively regulated by Article 3.5, while Article 3.4 has to do exclusively with the *existence* of injury and not with its causes. Furthermore, Egypt argues, the investigating authority did examine a range of "other factors" in its investigation, but concluded that there were "'no other causes of injury' sufficient to break the causal relationship between the dumped imports and the injury to the domestic industry"[73]. In addition, Egypt argues that Turkey did not, either in the Request for Establishment of a Panel, its first oral submission or its first written submission, refer to "factors affecting domestic prices", and asks us to dismiss this aspect of this claim. Egypt further argues that, in any case, the IA considered as "factors affecting domestic prices", demand and raw material costs.

7.58   We consider first Egypt's request that we dismiss Turkey's claim as to "factors affecting domestic prices" on the grounds that this was not mentioned in the Request for Establishment of a Panel or in Turkey's initial submissions. We find no merit in this request for dismissal, and therefore reject it. First, we view this issue as an argument in support of a claim, not as a claim in itself. Second, as a factual matter, the Request for Establishment of a Panel refers, in the context of Turkey's Article 3.4 claim, to the "effect...of other, neutral factors that caused prices to fall". We see no difference in substance between this reference and the language "factors affecting domestic prices", and no possible basis on which Egypt could have been confused by Turkey's references to and arguments about, "factors affecting domestic prices". This issue is pursued as well in Turkey's submissions.

7.59   Turning to the substance of this claim, we note the text of the relevant part of Article 3.4:

> "The examination of the impact of the dumped imports on the domestic industry concerned shall include an evaluation of all relevant economic factors and indices having a bearing on the state of the industry, including ... *profits*, ...; *factors affecting domestic prices*, ..." (emphasis added)

7.60   We recall that Turkey's claim is that Egypt violated Article 3.4 because the IA did not examine *all factors affecting profits*, and did not examine *all factors affecting domestic prices*. The above text indicates to us, however, a different requirement on an investigating authority. In particular, the text is straightforward in that the requirement is to examine all relevant factors and indices *hav-*

---

[72]   *Ibid*, p.22.
[73]   First Written Submission of Egypt, Section III.B.2.

ing a bearing on the state of the industry. The text then lists a variety of such factors and indices that are presumptively relevant to the investigation and must be examined, one of which is "profits". The text does not say, as argued by Turkey, "all factors affecting profits". To us, this text means that in its evaluation of the state of the industry, an investigating authority must include an analysis of the domestic industry's profits. Turkey has raised no claim that the IA failed to conduct such an analysis in the rebar investigation.

7.61   Another listed element is "factors affecting domestic prices". Here again, we note that contrary to Turkey's argument, the text does not read "all factors affecting domestic prices". Rather, what is required is that there be *an* evaluation of factors affecting domestic prices. This requirement is clearly linked to the requirements of Articles 3.1 and 3.2 for an "objective examination" of "the effect of dumped imports on prices in the domestic market for like products", which must involve a consideration of:

> "whether there has been a significant price undercutting by the dumped imports when compared with the price of a like product of the importing Member, or whether the effect of such imports is otherwise to depress prices to a significant degree or prevent price increases, which otherwise would have occurred, to a significant degree."[74]

In our view, this means that in its evaluation of the state of the industry, an investigating authority must in every case include a price analysis of the type required by Articles 3.1 and 3.2. Turkey has raised no claim that the IA failed to conduct such an analysis in the rebar investigation. In addition, in our view, an investigating authority must consider generally the question of "factors affecting domestic prices". In this regard, we note that in the rebar investigation, the IA considered the potential price effects of imports from third countries[75], and noted as well that the market for rebar was price-driven, rather than technology- or specification-driven[76].

7.62   Turkey's argument that Article 3.4 requires a full "non-attribution" analysis appears to stem from its reading of the term "having a bearing on" as having to do exclusively with causation, (i.e., as meaning factors *having an effect on* the state of the industry). There is another meaning of this term which we find more pertinent in the overall context of Article 3.4, however. In particular, the term "having a bearing on" can mean *relevant to* or *having to do with* the state of the industry[77], and this meaning is consistent with the fact that many of the factors listed in Article 3.4 are descriptors or indicators *of* the state of the industry,

---

[74]   Article 3.2 of the AD Agreement.
[75]   Document on Public File: *Report on Other Causes of Injury for the document no 296 on 5/9/99, Case of Rebar Originating or Exported from Turkey,* non-official translation. Submitted by Egypt as Exh. EGT-6.
[76]   Exh. TUR-16, *Final Report*, para.4.3.5.3.
[77]   For example, *Webster's New World Dictionary*, 2nd College Edition, 1986, at p.123, includes as a definition of "bearing": "relevant meaning, appreciation, relation [the evidence had no bearing on the case]".

rather than being factors *having an effect* thereon. For example, sales levels, profits, output, etc. are not in themselves *causes* of an industry's condition. They are, rather, among the factual indicators by which that condition can be judged and assessed as injured or not. Put another way, taken as a whole, these factors are more in the nature of *effects* than *causes*.

7.63   This reading of "having a bearing on" finds contextual support in the wording of the last group of factors in Article 3.4, namely "actual and potential negative *effects on* cash flow, inventories, ..." (emphasis added). Further contextual support is found in the cross-reference to Article 3.4 contained in the first sentence of Article 3.5: "... the *effects* of dumping as set forth in paragraph[] 4 [of Article 3]".(emphasis added)

7.64   We note in addition that if Turkey were correct that the full causation analysis, including non-attribution, were required by Article 3.4, this would effectively render redundant Article 3.5, which explicitly addresses causation, including non-attribution. Such an outcome would not be in keeping with the relevant principles of international treaty law interpretation, or with consistent practice in WTO dispute settlement.[78]

7.65   Moreover, even if we were to assume, *arguendo,* that Article 3.4 does require a causation and non-attribution analysis, the question would remain whether the IA was legally obligated to evaluate the particular "factors affecting profits" and "factors affecting domestic prices" referred to by Turkey before the Panel. Here we note simply that there is no such specific requirement in the text of Article 3.4. Whilst "factors affecting domestic prices" must be evaluated, there is no requirement to evaluate "all" such factors. Whether or not an evaluation of such factors was sufficient from the causal view point in any given case depends upon a consideration under Article 17.6 of the investigating authority's compliance with Article 3.5. We address causation issues generally, and the specific factors (a)-(f) asserted by Turkey, in Sections VII.C.4, VII.C.5 and VII.C.60, *infra*, which address Turkey's claims under Article 3.5.

7.66   For the foregoing reasons, we find that the IA was not required under Article 3.4 to examine and evaluate factors (a)-(f) listed above, and that Egypt thus did not act inconsistently with Article 3.4 on that basis.

2.   *Claim under Articles 3.1 and 3.2 – Alleged Failure to Base the Finding of Price Undercutting on Positive Evidence*

7.67   Turkey claims that the IA's finding of price undercutting was not based on positive evidence as required by Article 3.1, because the IA failed to make a

---

[78]   Appellate Body Report, *United States – Standards for Reformulated and Conventional Gasoline ("US – Gasoline"),* WT/DS2/AB/R, adopted 20 May 1996, DSR 1996:I,3. On page 23 of the Appellate Body Report it is stated: "... One of the corollaries of the 'general rule of interpretation' in the *Vienna Convention* is that interpretation must give meaning and effect to all the terms of the treaty. An interpreter is not free to adopt a reading that would result in reducing whole clauses or paragraphs of a treaty to redundancy or inutility."

proper determination of price undercutting in accordance with Article 3.2. On price undercutting, Turkey's argument is that Egypt failed to accurately determine whether there was price undercutting by imports of rebar from Turkey because the Investigating Authority failed to make price comparisons on delivered-to-the-customer basis. Turkey elaborates that the *Essential Facts and Conclusions Report* does not reveal the channels of distribution for the domestic and imported product or where in the chain of distribution any actual price competition between those products takes place. Without knowing these facts, according to Turkey, it is impossible to ascertain whether the IA measured the price competition at the correct level of trade, thus violating the Article 3.2 requirement that an investigating authority "consider whether there has been a significant price undercutting by the dumped imports as compared with the price of a like product in the importing country ...".

7.68   Turkey further argues, on the basis of its examination of the *Confidential Injury Analysis*, that the price undercutting analysis is further flawed by the fact that the prices used for the domestic side were the weighted-average revenue per unit of domestic rebar producers, and for the import side, were the weighted-average unit customs entered value. According to Turkey, in addition to being flawed due to the level of trade at which it was made, this comparison was flawed, because the IA did not look at "prices" or ensure that it was comparing prices for the same product. According to Turkey, rebar prices vary by size, with thinner rebar commanding a higher price per unit due to higher production cost. Given this, comparing one weighted average "basket" to another, without knowing whether the composition of each basket is the same, cannot, according to Turkey, yield an accurate assessment of price undercutting.

7.69   Egypt responds[79] that contrary to Turkey's claim, the *Essential Facts and Conclusions Report* makes clear that the price comparison was made at the same level of trade (ex-factory for domestic goods, and ex-importer's store for the dumped imports). Egypt states that Turkey would prefer that the comparison be done at a different level of trade (delivered to the customer), but that there is no such legal requirement. Egypt further argues that such a comparison would ignore the fact that importers and exporters do not sell on a delivered basis. Thus, according to Egypt, the undercutting analysis was performed properly and on the basis of positive evidence, such that Egypt complied with Articles 3.1 and 3.2.

7.70   We understand the legal basis of Turkey's claim to be that, to satisfy the requirements of Article 3.2, a price undercutting analysis must be made on a delivered-to-the-customer basis, as it is only at that level that any such undercutting can influence customers' purchasing decisions, and that in addition, and in any case, for such an analysis to be based on positive evidence as required by Article 3.1, an investigating authority must justify its choice of the basis for the price comparison it makes. In Turkey's view, the IA used the wrong basis for price comparison, and did not adequately explain and justify its choice of that basis in

---

[79]   First Written Submission of Egypt, p.39.

the *Essential Facts and Conclusions Report*[80], in violation of Articles 3.1 and 3.2. Turkey finds further support for its claim that the price undercutting finding violated Article 3.1 in the fact that the average unit customs value of imports was compared with the unit revenue of domestic rebar sales.

7.71   We recall that Article 3.1 provides in relevant part that:

> "A determination of injury ... shall be based on positive evidence and involve an objective examination of ... the effect of the dumped imports on prices in the domestic market for like products, ..."

7.72   Article 3.2 provides in relevant part that:

> "With regard to the effect of the dumped imports on prices, the investigating authorities shall consider whether there has been a significant price undercutting by the dumped imports as compared with the price of a like product of the importing Member, or whether the effect of such imports is otherwise to depress prices to a significant degree or prevent price increases, which otherwise would have occurred, to a significant degree ... ."

7.73   On the basis of the plain text of Article 3.2, we find no requirement that the price undercutting analysis must be conducted in any particular way, that is, at any particular level of trade. Therefore, we find that Turkey has not established that there was a legal obligation on the IA to perform the price undercutting analysis in the way asserted by Turkey. Rather, we find that an objective and unbiased investigating authority could have performed an undercutting analysis on the basis used by the IA. We therefore find that the IA's price undercutting finding is not inconsistent with Article 3.2.

7.74   In respect of the claim of violation of Article 3.1, we take note of the following passage in the *Essential Facts and Conclusions Report*[81] (repeated verbatim in the *Final Report*[82]):

> "In considering price undercutting, the Investigating Authority will normally seek to compare prices at the same level of trade (the ex-factory and ex-importers' store levels), to ensure that differences in distribution costs and margins do not confuse the impact of dumping. Accordingly, the Investigating Authority's position is generally to compare importers' prices, which involve similar cost elements to those in the Egyptian manufacturer's ex-factory price, but do not include cost elements relating to the distribution of goods.
>
> With regard to price undercutting, the Investigating Authority compared prices at the same level of trade. ... ."

---

[80]   We note that the price undercutting discussion in the *Final Report* is identical to that in the *Essential Facts and Conclusions Report*.

[81]   Exh. TUR-15, *Essential Facts and Conclusions Report*, para.4.2.1.

[82]   Exh. TUR-16, *Final Report*, para. 4.2.1.

7.75   While we need not, and do not, opine on the exact nature of the "positive evidence" requirement of Article 3.1, we note that even if we accept, *arguendo,* Turkey's interpretation thereof, the above-quoted passage from the *Essential Facts and Conclusions Report* makes clear that the IA's reports are not, as Turkey implies, devoid of any explanation for the choice of the level of trade at which prices were compared. Moreover, we note that there are any number of bases on which a price undercutting analysis could be performed, and we do not find the IA's justification of the basis that it used to be illogical on its face or not objective, nor do we see in it any evidence of bias. Concerning the undercutting-related information in the *Confidential Injury Analysis,* Turkey has pointed to no record evidence to substantiate its arguments concerning the existence or nature of any product differentiation of rebar generally or as between imports and the domestic product, or any effect thereof on prices. Indeed we note in this regard the statement by three of the respondents in their 28 September 1999 letter to the IA that "as the [IA] well knows, respondents do not break out costs by diameter"[83], suggesting that diameter differences had an immaterial effect on costs.

7.76   On the basis of the foregoing considerations, we find that Turkey has not established that an objective and unbiased investigating authority could not have found price undercutting on the basis of the evidence of record. We therefore find that Turkey has not established that the IA's price undercutting finding was not based on "positive evidence" in violation of Article 3.1.

3.   *Claim under Articles 6.1 and 6.2 – Alleged Violation Due to "change" in the "scope" of the Injury Investigation from Threat to Present Material Injury*

7.77   Turkey alleges that Egypt changed the "scope" of the injury investigation from threat of material to present material injury, without informing Turkey and after the deadline for submitting factual information in the investigation. Turkey claims that by doing so, Egypt violated Article 6.1 by failing to give Turkey notice of the information required by the IA, and Article 6.2 by failing to give Turkey a full opportunity to defend its interests.[84]

7.78   Turkey asserts, in particular, that the *Initiation Report* referred exclusively to threat of injury, and did not mention present material injury. Turkey argues that on that basis, Turkish companies provided evidence and arguments only in respect of the question of threat (i.e., the factors and considerations referred to in AD Article 3.7). Turkey argues that the IA then changed the scope of the injury investigation, after the deadline for submitting factual information and arguments had passed, meaning that the Turkish companies did not have an adequate opportunity to submit information and comment on the question of present material injury, in violation of Articles 6.1 and 6.2.

---

[83]   Exh EGT-3, p.2b.
[84]   Written Response, dated 7 December 2002, of Turkey to Question 1 to Turkey of the *Written Questions by the Panel,* of 28 November 2001, p.25 – Annex 4.1.

7.79   Egypt responds[85] that the IA presented in sufficient detail in the *Essential Facts and Conclusions Report* its findings and conclusions with respect to material injury, but that this is not the issue raised by this claim. Rather, according to Egypt, the issue is whether the IA was under an obligation to inform the Turkish respondents that it had changed the scope of the injury investigation from threat to present material injury during the course of the investigation. Egypt cites the panel report in *Guatemala – Cement II* in support of the proposition that no such obligation exists. According to Egypt, the issue raised by Turkey's claim is nearly identical to that addressed in *Guatemala – Cement II*. Egypt argues that in that case, Mexico claimed that Guatemala had violated Articles 6.1, 6.2 and 6.9 of the AD Agreement by changing the basis of the injury determination from a preliminary determination of threat of material injury to a final determination of present material injury without informing the respondents. Egypt notes that the panel found that "[n]o provision of the AD Agreement requires an investigating authority to inform interested parties, during the course of the investigation, that it has changed the legal basis for its injury determination."[86]

7.80   Egypt also argues that the *Notice of Initiation*,[87] which was published in Egypt's Official Gazette, referred to evidence of material injury starting to occur as of that time, and that in addition, the fact that the investigation covered present material injury was reflected in a facsimile dated 17 July 1999 from the IA to counsel for three of the respondents.[88]

7.81   Article 6.1 provides in relevant part:

"All interested parties in an anti-dumping investigation shall be given notice of the information which the authorities require and ample opportunity to present in writing all evidence which they consider relevant in respect of the investigation in question."

7.82   Article 6.2 provides in relevant part:

"Throughout the anti-dumping investigation all interested parties shall have a full opportunity for the defence of their interests."

7.83   As we understand Turkey's claim, the alleged violation of the Article 6.2 obligation to provide interested parties with a full opportunity for the defence of their interests is at least partially dependent on its claim that Article 6.1 was violated. That is, the alleged failure to be given notice of the information required by the authorities meant, according to Turkey, that the respondents did not have a full opportunity for the defence of their interests.

7.84   We start therefore by considering whether, as a factual matter, it is clear that the scope of the investigation was limited to threat of injury initially, but was thereafter changed, as alleged by Turkey, to an investigation relating to present material injury. We note in this regard first that the published *Notice of Initia-*

---

[85]   First Written Submission of Egypt, p.41.
[86]   First Written Submission of Egypt, Section III.B.8, quoting *Guatemala – Cement II*, para.8.237.
[87]   Exh. EGT-7.3.
[88]   Exh. EGT-8.

tion[89] states that as of the time of initiation, there was evidence that injury was occurring. Furthermore, the (foreign) manufacturers' and exporters' question-naires[90], which were sent by the IA shortly after the investigation was initiated, state explicitly that "the investigation of injury will cover the period from 1996 to 1998. As for the threat of injury, it will cover the period from 1999 to 2000". While these questionnaires then went on to pose specific questions to the foreign manufactures and to the exporters concerning some of the factors and issues addressed by Article 3.7, this is not in itself determinative. Indeed, it is logical, given that these factors have primarily to do with the likelihood of further increases in dumped imports, which is information in the hands of the foreign producers and exporters, that the requests for data on these factors would be directed to those foreign producers and exporters. By the same token, it is logical that requests for data on the Article 3.4 factors, information which is in the hands of the domestic industry, would be directed at the domestic producers, rather than the foreign producers and exporters.[91] The IA's *Final Report* alludes to this point as well, quoting from the fax sent to counsel for three of the respondents on 17 July 1999[92] in connection with the scope of the injury investigation which stated:

> "At initiation, it is normal practice to cover both whether injury has commenced or whether it is threatened through the imports. Because of the requirements on threat of injury, it is also normal practice to include questions on this matter in the questionnaire sent to overseas exporters or producers."[93]

7.85   Thus it is clear to us that a possible determination based on present material injury was, from the outset, within the scope of the investigation. For all of the foregoing reasons, we do not find that Turkey has established as a factual matter that the scope of the investigation was changed.

7.86   Nor do we find that Turkey has established as a factual matter that the IA failed to inform the Turkish respondents of the information required of them, or denied them the opportunity for the full defence of their interests. As noted, the questionnaires sent to the foreign producers and the exporters indicated that the injury investigation covered both present material injury and threat thereof, and identified the particular injury-related information requested of those interested parties by the IA. Three of the respondents then subsequently, and in addition, submitted a written brief, *after* the due date for responses to questionnaires,

---

[89]   *Ibid*, par.4, p.2.
[90]   Exhs. TUR-3 and TUR-2, Sections 1.8 and 1.5, respectively.
[91]   Here it should be emphasized that requests for *data* and *information* by an investigating authority in an investigation are simply that. It is perfectly understandable that an investigating authority would request the various pieces of information that it must consider in an anti-dumping investigation from the interested parties having possession of that information. In our view, such information requests are not the same as the opportunities for interested parties to present arguments in respect of the legal and factual issues in an investigation.
[92]   Exh. EGT-8.
[93]   Exh. TUR-16, *Final Report*, para.4.5.7.

which presented various legal and factual arguments concerning injury issues.[94] There is no evidence to suggest, nor does Turkey claim, that the IA refused to consider this submission or objected to it in any way. To the contrary, the IA appears to have accepted this submission without objection or difficulty.[95]

7.87   Furthermore, while counsel for these same respondents complained in comments on the *Essential Facts and Conclusions Report* about the alleged change in the scope of the investigation, implying that the respondents had learned only in that report that present material injury was at issue, ("For ITPD to assert, *now, long after the Notice of Initiation was issued*, that this case concerns injury rather than threat is to move the goalposts while the game is underway"[96] (emphasis added)), in fact these respondents were explicitly informed by the IA in the fax dated 17 July 1999[97], in response to an inquiry that had been made at verification, that the injury investigation covered both present material injury and threat.[98] These respondents implicitly confirmed their awareness of this fact in their 15 September 1999 submission on cost[99], in which they stated that "…[g]iven the clear fact that the Egyptian industry *is not materially injured* by Turkish exports, coupled with our earlier evidence concerning threat…we urge the ITPD to terminate these proceedings with a negative determination of *material injury or threat thereof*" (emphasis added). We note that this assertion that the industry was not materially injured was accompanied by no argumentation or evidence, however. Nor had these respondents made any attempt, upon receiving on 17 July 1999 explicit confirmation that the injury investigation covered present material injury as well as threat, to submit any such pertinent argumentation or evidence. We find significant that these respondents did not themselves take the initiative to try to protect their interests by requesting an opportunity to submit argumentation and evidence, or by simply presenting a submission, as they had done, apparently successfully, in respect of threat of material injury.[100] In short, we find no evidence that the respondents were "denied" the opportunity to

---

[94]   Exh. TUR-18. This submission was made by respondents Habas, Diler and Colakoglu on 21 May 1999. The responses to the manufacturer's and exporter's questionnaires were due on or about 7 April 1999 (the day that most of them were submitted), i.e., 37 days after having been sent to them.

[95]   Moreover, the document identified by Egypt as being from the Public File of the investigation (Exh. EGT-6) addresses some of the arguments presented in that written brief, indicating that the IA took it into account in its injury analysis.

[96]   Exh. TUR-20, p.17.

[97]   Exh. EGT-8.

[98]   The 17 July 1999 fax states in this regard: "At the recent meeting in Turkey with the investigation team, you raised the question about the dumping investigation ... whether this investigation concerned material injury arising from the importation of allegedly dumped goods from Turkey or threat of material injury arising from the same cause ... ."

[99]   Exh. TUR-34A, -34B and -34C, cover letter, p.2, footnote 1.

[100]   The threat of injury submission was made on 21 May 1999, one day after the IA had informed these respondents that the deadline for any further questionnaire responses on the subject of threat of injury had been the due date for the questionnaires (Exh. TUR-31, p.2), a date already in the past. In presenting the threat submission, these respondents stated that it was not a response to the questionnaire, but was an "independent evidentiary submission" as foreseen in AD Article 6.1. There is no evidence that this submission was rejected. To the contrary, the document from the Public File (Exh. EGT-6) addresses certain arguments made in that submission.

present pertinent arguments on present material injury, nor that they ever attempted to do so.

7.88   Here, we emphasize that the language of the provision at issue creates an obligation on the IA to *provide opportunities* for interested parties to defend their interests. In the situation that is the subject of this claim, there is no evidence that such an opportunity was not *provided*. Rather, the evidence shows that the respondents did not in fact intervene (or even attempt to do so) on this issue. Failure by respondents to take the initiative to defend their own interests in an investigation cannot be equated, through WTO dispute settlement, with failure by an investigating authority to provide opportunities for interested parties to defend their interests.

7.89   We must stress that the foregoing factual analysis of the record evidence concerning the scope of the injury investigation accepts, *arguendo*, Turkey's implicit interpretation of AD Article 3.7. In particular, Turkey's legal premise appears to be that where an injury investigation is limited to threat of material injury, the factors and considerations referred to in AD Article 3.7 are the *only* ones that must be examined by the IA.

7.90   Article 3.7 of the Anti-Dumping Agreement provides as follows:

"A determination of a threat of material injury shall be based on facts and not merely on allegation, conjecture or remote possibility. The change in circumstances which would create a situation in which the dumping would cause injury must be clearly foreseen and imminent. [footnote omitted.] In making a determination regarding the existence of a threat of material injury, the authorities should consider, *inter alia*, such factors as:

(i)   a significant rate of increase of dumped imports into the domestic market indicating the likelihood of substantially increased importation;

(ii)   sufficient freely disposable, or an imminent, substantial increase in, capacity of the exporter indicating the likelihood of substantially increased dumped exports to the importing Member's market, taking into account the availability of other export markets to absorb any additional exports;

(iii)   whether imports are entering at prices that will have a significant depressing or suppressing effect on domestic prices, and would likely increase demand for further imports; and

(iv)   inventories of the product being investigated.

No one of these factors by itself can necessarily give decisive guidance but the totality of the factors considered must lead to the conclusion that further dumped exports are imminent and that, unless protective action is taken, material injury would occur."

7.91   Thus, the text of this provision makes explicit that in a threat of injury investigation, the central question is whether there will be a "change in circumstances" that would cause the dumping to begin to injure the domestic industry. Solely as a matter of logic, it would seem necessary, in order to assess the likelihood that a particular change in circumstances would cause an industry to begin experiencing present material injury, to know about the condition of the domestic industry at the outset. For example, if an industry is increasing its production, sales, employment, etc., and is earning a record level of profits, even if dumped imports are increasing rapidly, presumably it would be more difficult for an investigating authority to conclude that it is threatened with imminent injury than if its production, sales, employment, profits and other indicators are low and/or declining.

7.92   This logic-based conclusion finds explicit support in the plain text of the AD Agreement. In particular, the title of Article 3, "Determination of Injury", carries footnote 9 which provides that:

> "Under this Agreement, the term 'injury' shall, unless otherwise specified, be taken to mean material injury to a domestic industry, threat of material injury to a domestic industry, or material retardation of the establishment of such an industry and shall be interpreted in accordance with the provisions of this Article." (emphasis added)

In other words, where the unmodified term "injury" appears in the AD Agreement, it encompasses all forms of injury – present and threatened material injury as well as material retardation of the establishment of an industry.

7.93   Applying this definition to Article 3.1, it is clear that *any* injury investigation, whether the question is present material injury, threat thereof, or material retardation, must "involve an objective examination of both (a) the volume of the dumped imports and the effect of the dumped imports on prices in the domestic market for like products, *and* (b) the consequent impact of these imports on domestic producers of such products" (emphasis added). It is in turn Article 3.4 which governs "the examination of the impact of the dumped imports on the domestic industry". Thus, in short, the Article 3.4 factors must be examined in *every* investigation, no matter which particular manifestation or form of injury is at issue in a given investigation.

7.94   This indeed is the reasoning applied and the conclusion reached by the panel in *Mexico – Corn Syrup*.[101] There, the allegation by the United States was that the Mexican investigating authority considered the Article 3.7 factors to the exclusion or near exclusion of the Article 3.4 factors. The panel found that:

> "The text of the AD Agreement requires consideration of the Article 3.4 factors in a threat determination. Article 3.7 sets out *additional* factors that must be considered in a threat case, but does not

---

[101]   Panel Report, *Mexico – Anti-Dumping Investigation of High Fructose Corn Syrup (HFCS) from the United States ("Mexico – Corn Syrup")*, WT/DS132/R and Corr.1, adopted 24 February 2000, DSR 2000:III, 1345, paras.7.111-7.143.

eliminate the obligation to consider the impact of dumped imports on the domestic industry in accordance with the requirements of Article 3.4" (emphasis added)."[102]

7.95   Thus, no matter what the initial or final scope of the injury investigation is, the Article 3.4 factors would need to have been examined in either a case of present material injury or of threat of material injury. The only difference would have been that the information and argumentation relating to the Article 3.7 factors would have become less relevant or non-relevant if the basis for the injury investigation was changed from threat to present material injury.

7.96   It may indeed be the case that an investigating authority so clearly misleads interested parties on the relevance to its investigation of the issues of present material injury and threat, or denies them opportunities to address these issues, as to provides the basis for a claim of violation of Articles 6.1 and 6.2. The circumstances of this case fall short of that possibility. On the basis of the foregoing considerations, we find that Turkey has not established that Egypt violated Articles 6.1 and 6.2, in respect of the scope of the injury investigation and the notice thereof provided to the Turkish respondents.

4.   *Claim under Articles 3.5 and 3.1 – Alleged Failure to Develop Specific Evidence Linking Imports to Adverse Volume and Price Effects upon the Domestic Industry, and Consequent Failure to Base the Finding of a Causal Link on Positive Evidence*

7.97   Turkey argues that the principal indicator of injury relied upon by Egypt in its affirmative injury determination was falling prices and profitability in 1998 and 1999, and that the price decline was attributed to price underselling by imports from Turkey. According to Turkey, however, the IA failed to develop "positive evidence" that dumped imports had an effect on domestic prices, or any impact on the domestic industry. According to Turkey, this constituted a violation of the "positive evidence" requirement of Article 3.1, which in turn meant that Egypt also violated the requirement of Article 3.5 to demonstrate that the dumped imports were, through the effects of dumping, causing injury within the meaning of the AD Agreement.[103]

7.98   Turkey argues that the specific positive evidence that imports caused domestic prices to fall would include evidence that purchasers considered Turkish imports to be the price leaders in the market, evidence of specific sales lost by the domestic industry to Turkish imports, or evidence that domestic producers dropped their prices, or had to retract planned price increases, because customers cited, in price negotiations with the domestic producers, availability of rebar from Turkey at lower prices. According to Turkey, the mere existence of in-

---

[102]   *Ibid*, para.7.137.
[103]   Written Response, dated 7 December 2001, to Question 1 to Turkey, of the *Written Questions by the Panel*, of 28 November 2001, p.20 – Annex 4-1.

creases in the volume of dumped imports is insufficient evidence of an injurious impact on the domestic industry, as is the existence of some price underselling, where the domestic industry is increasing its sales volume and market share.

7.99 Egypt argues that on the basis of the data and information available, the IA determined that the volume of dumped imports increased over the period and that this had a significant effect on the price of the domestic rebar, and that the IA also examined the consequent impact on the domestic producers and found *inter alia* that because the industry is sensitive to volume changes, it had to lower prices to meet the competition from the dumped imports and to retain sales. Egypt further argues that there is no requirement in any provision of the AD Agreement that the particular kinds of evidence referred to by Turkey be gathered and analyzed.

7.100 To recall, Article 3.1 provides as follows:

> "A determination of injury for purposes of Article VI of GATT 1994 shall be based on positive evidence and involve an objective examination of both (a) the volume of the dumped imports and the effect of the dumped imports on prices in the domestic market for like products, and (b) the consequent impact of these imports on domestic producers of such products."

7.101 Article 3.5 provides in relevant part as follows:

> "It must be demonstrated that the dumped imports are, through the effects of dumping, *as set forth in paragraphs 2* and 4, causing injury within the meaning of this Agreement. The demonstration of a causal relationship between the dumped imports and the injury to the domestic industry shall be based on an examination of all relevant evidence before the authorities. ... ." (emphasis added)

7.102 We note that neither of the provisions cited above refers to any of the particular kinds of evidence that Turkey argues should have been gathered and examined, or indeed to any kind or type of evidence at all. It is clear that Article 3.1 provides overarching general guidance as to the nature of the injury investigation and analysis that must be conducted by an investigating authority. Article 3.5 makes clear, through its cross-references, that Articles 3.2 and 3.4 are the provisions containing the specific guidance of the AD Agreement on the examination of the volume and price effects of the dumped imports, and of the consequent impact of the imports on the domestic industry, respectively. Thus, any reference in the AD Agreement to the particular kinds of evidence referred to by Turkey in respect of the volume and price effects of the dumped imports presumably would be found, if anywhere, in Article 3.2. This provision contains no such reference, which may explain why Turkey does not also allege a violation of Article 3.2 in respect of this claim.

7.103 In this connection, while Turkey objects to the nature of the price undercutting analysis performed by the IA[104], Turkey does not claim that the IA failed

---

[104] Section VII.C.2, *supra.*

entirely to consider whether there had been price undercutting. Similarly, while Turkey questions the accuracy of some of the data concerning the volume of imports that was relied upon by the IA[105], Turkey does not challenge the IA's basic finding that the imports of rebar from Turkey increased in volume.

7.104 Nor is there any indication in the record (and again Turkey makes no such argument before us) that, during the course of the investigation, the Turkish respondents made any argument that the IA should consider the sorts of evidence that form the subject of this claim, or themselves offered any such evidence. Thus, it is undisputed both that the IA gathered and analyzed the kinds of information that *are* specifically required by the plain language of the AD Agreement, and that the respondents made no attempt during the course of the investigation to complement or expand that information with additional sorts of evidence that are not specifically referred to by the AD Agreement, but which Turkey now asserts in this dispute settlement proceeding that the IA was obligated to consider.

7.105 In short, we do not believe that there is a basis for us to find a violation of the AD Agreement in respect of a kind of evidence or analysis not explicitly required or even mentioned by the AD Agreement, where there is *no* evidence in the record of the investigation to suggest that such an analysis was necessary, or that any interested party pursued the issue during the investigation. Here again, this is a situation where the respondents made decisions during the investigation (which they apparently now regret) *not* to raise specific arguments in defence of their interests in the context of the mandatory price effects analysis, the particular details of which are left by the AD Agreement to the discretion of the investigating authority. It is not within our mandate to reverse through the dispute settlement process the consequences of those respondents' decisions made during the course of the investigation as to which arguments they would present.

7.106 On the basis of the foregoing considerations, we find that Turkey has not established that Egypt violated the "positive evidence" requirement of Article 3.1 by virtue of the IA's not developing certain specific kinds of evidence, nor has Turkey established that, as a consequence, Egypt violated the requirement of Article 3.5 to demonstrate a causal relationship between the dumped imports and the injury to the domestic industry.

> 5. *Claim under Article 3.5 – Alleged Failure to Take Account of, and Attribution to Dumped Imports of, the Effects of Other "known factors" Injuring the Domestic Industry*

7.107 Turkey claims that Egypt violated Article 3.5 by failing to take account of, and by attributing to dumped imports, the effects of other "known factors" that were at the same time injuring the domestic industry.

---

[105] Written Rebuttal of Turkey, p.8-9.

7.108 The particular "known factors" identified by Turkey are the same as those identified in connection with its claim under Article 3.4[106]), namely:

(a)   "The dramatic capacity expansion at the two major Egyptian rebar producers and its likely temporary effects on their cost structures";

(b)   "The effects of the capacity expansions, which started production at the end of 1998, on competition between the Egyptian producers as they attempted to fill newly expanded order books";

(c)   "Sharpening competition between Al Ezz and Alexandria National as Al Ezz sought to increase market share by capitalizing on its cost advantages over Alexandria National";

(d)   "Falling prices for steel scrap, the primary raw material input at Al Ezz";

(e)   "A sharp contraction in demand in January 1999, the very month in which prices for rebar fell";

(f)   "The effect of comparably priced, fairly traded imports".

We recall, as noted above, Turkey's clarification that factors (b), (c) and arguably (d) are subsumed in (a) as adverse effects of capacity expansion.[107]

7.109 Egypt argues that throughout the course of the investigation, the IA examined all evidence that was provided by interested parties, including evidence concerning capacity expansion, competition between domestic producers, falling prices for raw materials, domestic demand, and the effect of non-dumped imports. On the basis of this examination, Egypt argues, the IA found that there were "no other causes of injury" sufficient to break the causal relationship between the dumped imports and the injury to the domestic industry.[108]

7.110 Before turning to the substance of this claim, we note that in response to a request from the Panel for certain documents, Egypt submitted a document which it identified as being part of the public file of the investigation, and which, according to Egypt, contains some of the detailed analysis performed by the IA in respect of a number of the "other factors" that it considered during the investigation. According to Egypt, this document was available for inspection upon request during the investigation (27 January 1999-21 October 1999).[109] The document contains sections on "shrinkage of demand", "non-dumped imports", "costs and administrative expenses", and "competition", in addition to several others.[110]

7.111 This document was not given to Turkey during the course of the investigation[111], (although Egypt claims that it was in the Public File to which Turkey

---

[106]   Section VII.C.1(b), *supra.*

[107]   Para.7.50, *supra.*

[108]   First Written Submission of Egypt, p.28.

[109]   Exh. EGT-6 and cover note to List of Exhibits attached to the Written Response of Egypt to Questions of the Panel, dated 12 December 2001.

[110]   *Ibid*, p.1-4 and 6.

[111]   Written Rebuttal Submission of Turkey, p.1.

could have had access during that period), and Turkey states that it did request information from the Public File during the consultations that began this dispute, but was informed that as the investigation was closed, no further access to the Public File was possible.[112]

7.112 It is not within our terms of reference to consider issues that arose in the context of dispute settlement consultations, and therefore we do not pursue that question further. We do take note, however, that the published *Notice of Initiation*[113] specifically refers to the public file to which all interested parties could have access, and we further note that Turkey does not assert that any Turkish respondents ever sought access to that file during the investigation and was denied such access.

7.113 Turkey considers that the Panel should not rely on the public file document as evidence of the IA's consideration of certain other factors possibly causing injury. While Turkey acknowledges, in the light of the Appellate Body ruling in *Thailand – H-Beams* that Egypt can rely on evidence not referred to in the IA's published reports, it nevertheless maintains that Egypt can rely only on documents that were shared with or otherwise made available to the respondents[114]. It is not clear to us what distinction Turkey is making here, as our reading is that *Thailand – H-Beams* addresses and resolves both of these issues, to the effect that we can take into account the public file document.

7.114 Turning to the substance of the issue raised by this claim, we first recall the relevant language of Article 3.5:

> "The authorities shall also examine any known factors other than the dumped imports which at the same time are injuring the domestic industry, and the injuries caused by these other factors must not be attributed to the dumped imports. Factors which may be relevant in this respect include, *inter alia*, the volume and prices of imports not sold at dumping prices, contraction in demand or changes in the patterns of consumption, trade-restrictive practices of and competition between the foreign and domestic producers, developments in technology and the export performance and productivity of the domestic industry."

7.115 As this provision makes clear, while it is mandatory to consider "known" factors other than the dumped imports which at the same time are injuring the domestic industry and to ensure that any such injury is not attributed to those imports, it also is clear that the particular list of factors contained in Article 3.5 is illustrative only. This is indicated by the language preceding this list: "Factors which may be relevant in this respect *include, inter alia, ...*" (emphasis added). Nor does Turkey argue to the contrary. Rather, Turkey argues that the particular

---

[112] Oral Statement by Turkey during the Second Substantive Meeting of the Panel with the Parties on 25 February 2002.

[113] Exh. EGT-7.3, Section 12.

[114] Statement by Turkey during the Second Substantive Meeting of the Panel with the Parties on 25 February 2002, Section I.B.

factors that it refers to in this dispute were wholly responsible for any injury suffered by the Egyptian domestic industry, that these factors were or should have been "known" to the IA, and that the IA in making its affirmative injury and causation determination improperly attributed the injury caused by the other factors to the dumped imports.

7.116 We start by considering whether, as a factual matter, Turkey is correct that the IA failed to examine the "other" factors identified by Turkey in this dispute. Turning to the first of these factors, capacity expansion, we note that both the IA's *Essential Facts and Conclusions Report*[115] and the *Final Report*[116] mention the fact of the industry's capacity expansion, although not its magnitude, and states that the industry did not reduce production to meet import competition, but rather reduced its prices to maintain capacity utilisation, and to try to cover its costs. The reports then conclude that there was "no effect" on capacity utilisation (i.e., that there was no change in capacity utilisation). Thus, it appears that the IA found the industry's capacity expansion to be a neutral factor in its injury and causation analysis. Moreover, we note that while the issue of the industry's capacity expansion was raised by certain respondents during the investigation, the only detailed arguments that were presented in this regard, which were in the submission on threat of material injury of Habas, Diler and Colakoglu, were to the effect that even after the industry's capacity expansion, the industry had *insufficient* capacity to meet domestic demand.[117] The only other reference by any respondent to the capacity expansion, which can be found in the Turkish Government's comments on the *Essential Facts and Conclusions Report*, consists of a simple assertion to the effect that the new investments made by the Egyptian producers were largely responsible for the decline in those producers' profits and return on investment.[118]

7.117 Concerning Turkey's argument that the capacity expansion would have had a large effect on the industry's costs of production, which should have been pursued by the IA during the investigation, we note that the data on the industry's costs, as contained in the *Confidential Injury Analysis*, the source for the data referred to in the IA's *Essential Facts and Conclusions Report* and its *Final Report*, shows in fact that unit costs of production declined consistently over the period of investigation. Thus, the record evidence does not seem to bear out factually the hypothesis posed by Turkey.[119]

---

[115] *Ibid,* Section 4.3.2.4 and 4.5.4.

[116] *Ibid,* Section 4.3.2.2, 4.3.2.3 and 4.6.

[117] Exh. TUR-20, p. 9. The submission refers to, and attaches, secondary source documents reporting that demand for steel in Egypt was growing rapidly due to a boom in the construction industry, and that the Egyptian market was "growing ahead of supply", such that imports were filling an "otherwise-unfilled demand".

[118] Exh. TUR-30, Section 4.

[119] Upon receiving the *Confidential Injury Analysis*, Turkey raised the further argument that the industry's financing cost had increased at the time of the capacity expansion, and that this increase was what was responsible for the industry's loss of profits - *See* Written Rebuttal of Turkey, p23-24. As noted in the discussion of scrap prices in paragraphs, *infra*, however, unit revenues declined significantly between 1997 and first quarter 1999, particularly between 1998 and first quarter 1999,

7.118 In respect of the decline in scrap prices, in its *Final Report*, the IA acknowledges the arguments made on this point during the investigation, but implies that one comment is illogical and notes that the other is not supported by the evidence. In particular, the Government of Turkey stated in its comments to the IA on the *Essential Facts and Conclusions Report* that the IA had failed to comply with the requirement to properly analyze known factors other than imports because it did not:

> " ... take into consideration decreasing international market prices of scrap in 1998, while establishing a causal relationship between the domestic market prices in Egypt and the export prices of goods originating in Turkey. In fact, as the prices of scrap – which establishes the majority of the rebar costs – decreased so did the prices of rebars in the Egyptian market, as in most of other countries.
>
> The decline in domestic producers' profits and return on investment cannot be related to Turkish exports, either. *Other than the decrease of scrap prices*, this decline can only be associated with the new investments made by the Egyptian producer in the recent years, which ITPD mentioned in paragraph 4.3.2.4 of the Report."[120] (emphasis added)

7.119 Similarly, Habas, Diler and Colakoglu argue in their comments on the *Essential Facts and Conclusions Report* that scrap prices were declining and the pricing in Egypt for rebar simply reflected the drop in input prices.

7.120 In the *Final Report*, the IA notes the first comment that "loss of profits were due to the decrease in scrap prices", and notes that:

> "Normally, a decrease in the price of a raw material would increase profits. However, in this case, the domestic producers necessarily had to reduce prices so as to meet import competition. Thus, the loss of profits were found to be cause [sic] by meeting the price competition rather than due to the reduction in scrap prices Further, the amount of decrease in prices was greater than the amount of decrease of scrap prices."[121]

7.121 We note that the data on the industry's unit costs and unit revenues contained in the *Confidential Injury Analysis* – which was the source for the data reflected in the *Essential Facts and Conclusions Report* and the *Final Report* – show the pattern alluded to by the IA in the above passage. In particular, unit revenues and unit costs declined over the period of investigation, particularly at the end thereof, but the decline in unit revenues outpaced that in unit costs, resulting in a reduction in gross profits. Selling and administrative costs also declined, but not enough to offset the reduction in gross profit, meaning that profit

---

indeed by more than the increase in financing costs. Thus, we believe that an objective and unbiased investigating authority could have reached the conclusion reached by the Egyptian IA in respect of these trends.

[120] Exh. TUR-30, Section 4.
[121] Exh. TUR-16, *Final Report*, para.4.3.5.3.

before interest expense also declined. Thus, the IA's description in its reports of the trends in costs versus rebar prices is consistent with the financial data on the industry.

7.122 Concerning the effects of intra-industry competition, Turkey's argument appears to be somewhat inconsistent, in that Turkey seems to be arguing both that the new capacity would have brought about cost increases at both domestic producers that would have increased their price competition with each other, and that Al Ezz was the lower-cost producer and thus was simply out-competing Alexandria National. While this factor does not seem to be explicitly referred to in the IA published reports, it is mentioned in the document identified as being from the Public File of the investigation, and in that context the IA notes that there was virtually no difference in the prices charged by the two companies. Moreover, it is not clear to us which data in the *Confidential Injury Analysis* would necessarily signify "the effects of intra-industry competition" as such. Indeed, as noted above, overall the industry's costs declined steadily over the period of investigation, and yet industry profits declined as unit revenues declined. Here we recall that, pursuant to the AD Agreement, the IA must evaluate the condition of the domestic industry overall. [122]

7.123 Concerning the alleged sharp contraction in demand in January 1999, which according to Turkey exactly coincided with falling rebar prices, we note that the IA considered the first calendar quarter of 1999 as a whole, rather than month-by-month. There is no requirement the AD Agreement concerning how the time periods within a period of investigation should be broken out analytically. Given that economic data frequently are prone to short-term fluctuations, in our view it could be imprudent for investigating authorities to base significant aspects of their findings and conclusions on data for extremely short periods. Indeed, this seems to have been the point of view, during the investigation, of the respondents that made a separate threat of injury submission. In particular, in that submission's discussion of "other economic factors", in respect of domestic rebar sales data, these respondents restated published government data on a "three-month rolling average basis (to smooth out some of the seasonal fluctuation, such as the annual dip in December) ..."[123]. In addition, as noted above, these respondents' general argument, made in their submission of 20 May 1999 (i.e., four months after the asserted decline in demand) was that rebar demand in Egypt was "booming". The data in the *Confidential Injury Analysis* show that demand in the first quarter of 1999 was running at a level comparable to that in 1998, and considerably higher than that in 1996 and 1997, and that at the same time imports from Turkey and domestic sales were increasing. Furthermore, the document from the Public File shows that the IA did examine whether there had been a contraction in demand during the period of investigation and concluded on the basis of the record evidence that there had not been. Thus, in our view, an unbiased and objective investigating authority could have reached the conclusion

---

[122] Article 3 of the AD Agreement.
[123] Exh. TUR-18, p.8.

that was reached by the IA in the rebar investigation on the basis of the facts of record on this issue.

7.124 Finally, concerning the effects of "comparably-priced, fairly-traded imports", Turkey argues that the imports from Saudi Arabia and Libya were similar in volume, and comparable in price, to the imports from Turkey. Turkey asserts that given this situation, there was no basis for the IA to conclude that the imports from Turkey were causing injury while those from Saudi Arabia and Libya were not. The relevant passage from the *Final Report* states:

> "Market share of the domestic rebar industry declined in 1998 and increased in the first quarter of 1999 due to reduction in the price to combat dumped prices. All of this had a negative impact on the profitability of the domestic producers. The market share of third country imports declined and Turkish rebar imports replaced the market share of third country imports."[124]

The import data contained in the IA's published reports appear to be consistent with the above description. In particular, the volume of imports from third countries, taken as a whole, declined from roughly 700,000 tons per year in 1996-1998 to 43,400 tons in the first quarter of 1999 (extrapolated to an annual level of roughly 174,000 tons), while the imports from Turkey, which had dropped from 145,000 tons in 1996 to zero in 1997, rebounded to 210,000 tons in 1998 and stood at 73,600 tons in the first quarter of 1999, an annual extrapolated rate of 294,000 tons. Thus, by the end of the period of investigation, the volume of dumped imports was considerably greater than the total volume of imports from all other sources. Given these statistics, and in particular the fact that as of the end of the period of investigation, the imports from Turkey had risen to a significantly higher level than the imports from all other countries combined, which were sharply declining, the factual basis for Turkey's argument is not clear to us. Furthermore, the document from the Public File indicates that the IA did consider, and rejected, the more detailed arguments concerning the alleged effects of the imports from Saudi Arabia and Libya that had been raised by the three respondents in their threat of injury submission.[125]

7.125 To summarize, we have taken careful note of the factors asserted by Turkey to have been "other known factors" in the sense of Article 3.5. We also have taken note of the discussions of those factors by the IA in the investigation in its published reports and in the document from the public file, and compared those discussions with the related underlying data of record. As a factual matter, as discussed above, we find that the IA did in fact explicitly discuss in its published reports most of the "other factors" identified by Turkey, a number of which are identified by Turkey as being essentially the same, and covered the remainder of these factors (namely possible effects of intra-industry competition and of any contraction in demand) in the document from the Public File. On the basis of the

---

[124] *Ibid,* Section 4.3.4.5.
[125] Exh. TUR-18.

data of record, we find no evidence that the IA's consideration of those factors, including its conclusions about them, were biased or not objective.

7.126 It is clear that Turkey has reached different conclusions than the IA concerning certain evidence of record, and Turkey invites us to do the same. We recall, however, that we are bound by the requirements of Articles 17.5 and 17.6 of the AD Agreement to consider, on the basis of the evidence that was before the investigating authority during the investigation, whether the establishment of the facts in respect of any factor was improper, and whether the evaluation of any factor was biased or non-objective. That is, we are precluded from basing our findings on our own *de novo* review of the record evidence, and our own conclusions about each factor and the existence of injury and causation overall. We are, rather, to consider whether the conclusions reached in the investigation *could* have been reached by an objective and unbiased investigating authority on the basis of its analysis of the evidence of record at the time of the determination. For the reasons discussed above, we find that this standard has been met, and thus that Turkey has not established that the IA's evaluation of the possible causation of injury by factors other than the dumped imports was inconsistent with Article 3.5.

6. *Claim under Articles 3.5 and 3.1 – Alleged Failure to Demonstrate that the Imports Caused Injury "through the effects of dumping"*

7.127 Turkey claims that because the period of investigation (POI) for dumping ended on 31 December 1998, and most of the injury found by the IA occurred in the first quarter of 1999, the IA failed to demonstrate that dumping and injury occurred at the same point in time such that there was a link between the imports that were specifically found to be dumped and the injury found, violating Articles 3.5 and 3.1.[126] In particular, according to Turkey the largest price and profitability declines occurred in first quarter 1999, but the IA made no finding that imports were sold at less than normal value during that period, nor is there any evidence linking the effect of the dumped imports on prices in the domestic market for like product, or linking these imports to the effects on domestic producers. Turkey further argues that by failing to link the imports in 1998 to the injury in 1999, the IA failed to demonstrate "that the dumped imports are, through the effects of dumping, ... causing injury within the meaning of this Agreement"[127], in violation of Article 3.5.

7.128 We turn first to the factual basis for this claim by Turkey. In particular, Turkey's argument seems largely to rest on its view that there was a differentiation or demarcation as to the nature or extent of the injury found by the IA to exist in 1998 (the period of investigation for the dumping investigation) as compared to first quarter 1999 (the final portion of the period of investigation for the

---

[126] Written Response, dated 7 December 2001, of Turkey to Question 1 to Turkey of the *Written Questions by the Panel*, of 28 November 2001, p.24 – Annex 4-1.
[127] *Ibid*, p.24.

injury investigation). Our review of the *Final Report*, however, shows no hint of such a differentiation. Rather, the Report refers to declines in various indicators in both 1998 and 1999 without reference to any particular qualitative change or shift from the one period to the next. We note that the IA found present material injury during the period of investigation on the basis of those declines. Therefore, there is substantial simultaneity in the period of investigation for dumping and the period during which injury was found.[128]

7.129 Moreover, Turkey's approach rests on the quite artificial assumption that the market instantly absorbs, and reacts to, imports the moment they enter the territory of the importing country. Such an assumption implicitly rests on the existence of so-called "perfect information" in the market (i.e., that all actors in the market are instantly aware of all market signals). Turkey did not establish a *prima facie* case that such a condition existed in the Egyptian market for rebar during the period covered by the investigation.

7.130 In addition, neither of the articles cited in this claim, nor any other provision of the AD Agreement, contains any specific rule as to the time periods to be covered by the injury or dumping investigations, or any overlap of those time periods.

7.131 In fact, the only provisions that provide guidance as to how the price effects and effects on the domestic industry of the dumped imports are to be gauged are (as cross-referenced in Article 3.5), Articles 3.2 (volume and price effects of dumped imports), and Article 3.4 (impact of the dumped imports on the domestic industry). Neither of these provisions specifies particular time periods for these analyses. (We note that Turkey's specific claims in respect of the price effects analysis and the analysis of the effects of the dumped imports on the domestic industry are addressed in Sections VII.C.4 and VII.C.5, *supra*.)

7.132 For the foregoing reasons, we find that Turkey has not established that the IA was obligated by Articles 3.1 and 3.5 to perform an analysis and make a finding of the type asserted by Turkey in respect of whether the imports caused injury "through the effects of dumping". We thus find that Turkey has not established that Egypt violated Articles 3.5 and 3.1 in this respect.

D. Claims Relating to the Dumping Investigation – "facts available"

1. Factual Background

7.133 The dumping-related claims in this dispute all turn on one key event in the dumping investigation, namely a request sent by the IA to all respondents on 19 August 1999[129] ("the 19 August request") for certain cost-related information. The chronology of events was that in its questionnaires sent to foreign manufacturers and exporters in late January or early February 1999, the IA requested

---

[128] See *Recommendation Concerning the Periods of Data Collection for Anti-Dumping Investigations*, G/ADP/6, adopted 5 May 2000 by the Committee on Anti-Dumping Practices.
[129] Exh. TUR-11.

certain information pertaining to the cost of producing rebar.[130] In June 1999, subsequent to receiving the questionnaire responses, the IA conducted on-the-spot verifications at the respondents' premises in Turkey. The verifications covered only the price data, and not the cost data, reported in those responses. Then on 19 August 1999, the IA sent each of the respondents that had submitted a questionnaire response[131] a letter indicating that the IA had certain concerns about the accuracy of the cost data reported in the questionnaire responses, in particular about whether the cost data fully reflected the effects of the hyperinflation then prevailing in Turkey. The IA informed the respondents that it therefore intended to adjust the reported costs to reflect the monthly rate of inflation, and to perform the profitability test on the basis of the adjusted costs, unless the respondents provided, by 1 September 1999 (i.e., 13 days later), certain specified additional cost-related information and explanations. The respondents all requested extensions of time, of varying lengths, to respond. In response to these requests, the IA extended the deadline for all of the respondents by 14 days, i.e., to 15 September 1999. No follow-up or other requests for further extensions were made by any respondent.

2. Claim under Article 17.6(1)

7.134 Turkey claims that the IA's determination of the facts in the rebar investigation was not "proper", nor was its evaluation of the facts "objective" and "unbiased" within the meaning of Article 17.6(i).

7.135 We recall that the full text of Article 17.6(i) of the AD Agreement provides:

> "[I]n its assessment of the facts of the matter, the panel shall determine whether the authorities' establishment of the facts was proper and whether their evaluation of those facts was unbiased and objective. If the establishment of the facts was proper and the evaluation was unbiased and objective, even though the panel might have reached a different conclusion, the evaluation shall not be overturned."

7.136 Turkey's specific claim in this context is that the IA's findings that the respondents' cost of production did not include the effects of hyperinflation in Turkey, which was put by the IA at 5 per cent per month, were speculative and contrary to all the facts on the record.[132] Turkey asserts that:

> "The only support for the Investigation Authority's supposition in this regard is the undisputed fact that Turkey's economy was experiencing high inflation during the period of investigation. However, hyperinflation in the economy as a whole certainly does not

---

[130] Exh. TUR-3.

[131] One Turkish respondent, Ekinciler, did not respond to the questionnaire and thus did not receive a cost-related letter from the IA on 19 August 1999.

[132] Written Response, dated 7 December 2001, of Turkey to Question 1 to Turkey of the *Written Questions by the Panel*, of 28 November 2001, p.30 – Annex 4-1.

mean that each sector and product group is experiencing inflation at the same rate. This is particularly true of industries, like the Turkish rebar industry, that import most of their raw materials and where the raw material input is a commodity product subject to significant swings in price.

...

The Investigating Authority's findings that respondents' costs did not include the effects of inflation, which the Investigating Authority put at 5 % per month, were contrary to all of the facts on the record. For this reason, the Investigating Authority's determination of the fact was not "proper," nor was its evaluation of the facts "objective" and "unbiased" within the meaning of Article 17.6(i)."[133]

7.137 Egypt contends that Article 17.6(i) of the AD Agreement governs the standard of review to be applied by a panel when considering whether the Investigating Authority's establishment of the facts was proper and the evaluation unbiased and objective. Egypt further asserts that Article 17.6(i) does not govern the rights and obligations of Members under the AD Agreement. Egypt also contends that this claim was not cited in the Request for Establishment of a Panel[134] and as a consequence, this claim is not within the terms of reference of the Panel and must be rejected.[135]

7.138 Turkey contests Egypt's view by referring to the Appellate Body finding in *US – Hot-Rolled Steel* where it states that Article 17.6(i) imposes certain substantive obligations upon investigating authorities:

"Article 17.6(i) of the Anti-Dumping Agreement also states that the panel is to determine, first, whether the investigating authorities' "establishment of the facts was proper" and, second, whether the authorities' " evaluation of the facts was unbiased and objective." Although the text of Article 17.6(i) is couched in terms of an obligation on panels – panels "shall" make these determinations – the provision, at the same time, in effect defines when investigating authorities can be considered to have acted consistently with the Anti-Dumping Agreement in the course of their "establishment" and "evaluation" of the relevant facts. In other words, Article 17.6(i) sets forth the appropriate standard to be applied by panels in examining the WTO consistency of the investigating authorities' establishment and evaluation of the facts under other provisions of the Anti-Dumping Agreement."[136]

7.139 Turkey also refers to Claim 1 in its Request for Establishment of a Panel where it stated that "the Egyptian investigative authority ... rendered determina-

---

[133]   *Ibid*, p.31.
[134]   WT/DS211/2, as amended.
[135]   Second Written Submission of Egypt, p.14.
[136]   Statement by Turkey at the Second Substantive Meeting of the Panel with the Parties, p.12.

tions of injury and dumping in its investigation without *proper establishment of the facts* and based on an evaluation of the facts that was neither *unbiased nor objective*" and to Claim 9 where it stated that "[t]he factual basis cited by the [Investigating Authority] for seeking large amounts of supplemental cost information late in the anti-dumping proceeding were unfounded ... . The [Investigating Authority's] subsequent decision to rely on 'facts available' was based on *an improper determination of the facts* in the investigation and on an evaluation of the facts that was neither *unbiased nor objective*. Thus, Turkey asserts that contrary to Egypt's views, Turkey put a violation of Article 17.6(i) squarely in issue in its request for this Panel"[137] and that the claim is properly before us.

7.140 Turkey further argues that:

> "It is not clear, under the Agreement, that Turkey must allege violation of a separate substantive obligation under the Agreement in order to make this claim. Turkey believes there is a violation of the Agreement if, in reaching its final determination on any issue, the investigating authorities' establishment of the facts is improper or its evaluation of the facts fails to meet the test of objectivity and lack of bias.
>
> However, to the extent that the panel considers that it may only review a violation of Article 17.6(i) in the context of a separate substantive claim, we note that in Section II.D of the restatement of our claims, where reference to Article 17.6(i) is made, Turkey's claim is that Egypt's decision to apply "facts available" was a violation of both Article 6.8 and Article 17.6(i) of the Agreement because that decision was based on an improper determination of the facts and upon an evaluation of the facts that was neither unbiased nor objective. Thus to the extent that the Panel considers that Article 17.6(i) merely sets forth a standard of review for Panel consideration of other substantive violations, then we invite the Panel to consider this claim in connection with our claimed violation of Article 6.8."[138]

7.141 Turning first to whether a claim of violation of Article 17.6(i) is properly before us, we note first that Article 17.6(i) is not listed in Turkey's Request for the Establishment of a Panel[139], either in the list of Articles allegedly violated, or in Claims 1 or 9, as referred to by Turkey[140], as an article of the AD Agreement which was alleged by Turkey to be violated by Egypt. While certain language similar to that in Article 17.6(i) is contained in certain paragraphs of the Request for Establishment of a Panel, that provision is never mentioned. It is well-established that in WTO dispute settlement, it is always necessary, at a mini-

---

[137] *Ibid*, p.13.
[138] Response of Turkey to Question 2 to Turkey of the *Written Questions by the Panel*, dated 14 March 2002 – Annex 8-1.
[139] WT/DS211/2, as amended.
[140] Written Response, dated 7 December 2001, to Question 1 to Turkey of the *Written Questions by the Panel*, of 28 November 2002 – Annex 4-1.

mum, for the particular Articles of an agreement which are the subject of any claim to be cited explicitly in the request for establishment of a panel.[141] Given the absence of any such explicit citation, we dismiss this claim as being outside our terms of reference.

7.142 Furthermore, while, given our dismissal of this claim on procedural grounds, we need not rule on whether a violation of Article 17.6(i) can be the subject of a claim by a party in a dispute, we have considerable doubts in this regard. What is clear nevertheless, and in any case, is that Article 17.6(i) lays down the standard which a *panel* has to apply in examining the matter referred to it in terms of Article 17.5 of the AD Agreement. As such, we are of course bound by it in our consideration of the claims in this dispute.

3.   Claim under Article 6.8 and Annex II, Paragraphs 5 and 6 - Resort to "facts available"

7.143 Turkey claims that "[b]ecause the basis for initially questioning and then rejecting Turkish respondents' costs was unfounded", the IA's resort to facts available was unjustified. According to Turkey, the Turkish respondents provided all 'necessary information' and certainly did not 'impede' the investigation".[142] Turkey argues that the rationale for requesting the additional cost data – namely that the originally-reported data did not appear to reflect the high inflation the prevailing in Turkey – was purely speculative, in that hyperinflation in an economy does not necessarily mean that each sector or group experiences inflation at the same rate, in particular industries like the rebar industry which import most of their raw materials and where those materials are commodity products subject to significant swings in price. According to Turkey, the respondents demonstrated in their responses to the IA's 19 August request for cost information that there was nothing "missing" from the respondents' reported costs. Moreover, Turkey states, the Government of Turkey had provided official inflation statistics that showed that inflation did not increase by 5 per cent per month in 1998, but that in a number of months, inflation did not exceed 2.5 per cent. Thus, according to Turkey, because the basis for requesting and then rejecting the cost data was factually unfounded, the IA's resort to "facts available" was unjustified under Article 6.8. Turkey further claims that resort to "facts available" was inconsistent with Annex II, paragraphs 5 and 6, in that the respondents had acted to the best of their ability, in that the IA had failed to inform certain

---

[141] *See*, Appellate Body Report, *European Communities – Regime for the Importation, Sale and Distribution of Bananas ("EC – Bananas* III")*, WT/DS27/AB/R, adopted 25 September 1997, DSR 1997:II, 591, para.143, Appellate Body Report, *Korea – Definitive Safeguard Measure on Imports of Certain Dairy products ("Korea – Dairy")*, WT/DS98/AB/R, adopted 12 January 2000, DSR 2000:I, 3, para.124, and *European Communities – Anti-Dumping Duties on Imports of Cotton-Type Bed Linen from India ("EC – Bed Linen")*, WT//DS141/R, adopted 12 March 2001, as modified by the Appellate Body, DSR 2001:V, 2049, p.9-10.

[142] Turkey's Written response of Turkey, dated 7 December 2001, to Question 1 of the *Written Questions by the Panel*, of 28 November 2001, p.31 – Annex 4-1.

respondents that their information was being rejected, and had failed to give them an opportunity to provide further explanations.[143]

7.144 Egypt argues, first, that Turkey is requesting the Panel to perform a *de novo* review of the evidence that was before the IA, in that, according to Egypt, Turkey's arguments essentially reproduce those made by the respondents during the investigation in respect of cost of production and hyperinflation. Egypt states that the standard of review set forth in Article 17.6(i) does not allow panels to engage in such *de novo* review. According to Egypt, the Panel must limit its review of the decision to rely in part on "facts available" to whether the facts were properly established and whether the conclusions reached were unbiased and objective. Further, Egypt argues, the decision to partially use "facts available" was in compliance with Article 6.8 and Annex II of the AD Agreement. In this regard, Egypt argues that the cost data as originally reported were incomplete and unusable, and that the respondents failed to submit the additional information, in particular supporting evidence and reconciliation sheets, requested by the IA on 19 August, and that in addition, three of them subsequently refused to submit any further information when they were informed that their responses to the 19 August request were deficient. Finally, Egypt argues, the data and allegations presented by the respondents concerning costs were contradicted by the evidence on the record.

(a)   Article 6.8 and Annex II

7.145 Article 6.8 of the AD Agreement governs the use of "facts available" by an investigating authority and provides:

> "In cases in which any interested party refuses access to, or otherwise does not provide, necessary information within a reasonable period or significantly impedes the investigation, preliminary and final determinations, affirmative or negative, may be made on the basis of the facts available. The provisions of Annex II shall be observed in the application of this paragraph."

7.146 Article 6.8 therefore addresses the dilemma in which investigating authorities might find themselves - they must base their calculations of normal value and export price on some data, but the necessary information may not have been submitted. Article 6.8 identifies the circumstances in which an IA may overcome this lack of necessary information by relying on facts which are otherwise available to the investigating authority.

---

[143] Turkey also claims that the IA's resort to facts available was inconsistent with Articles 2.4, 2.2.1.1, and 2.2.2 of the Anti-Dumping Agreement, and with Article X:3 of the GATT. These claims are addressed separately, in Sections VII.D.4 and VII.B.4. In its Request for Establishment of a Panel, Turkey also refers to alleged violations of paragraphs 3 and 7 of Annex II in the context of the IA's resort to facts available. Turkey's arguments in its submissions indicate, however, that the allegations of violation of these provisions are in connection with the information used as facts available, and not with the resort to "facts available" as such. These claims are addressed in Sections VII.D.7-VII.D.9. *infra*.

7.147 It is clear to us that according to the wording of Article 6.8, an investigating authority may disregard the primary source of information and resort to the facts available only under the specific conditions of Article 6.8. An IA may therefore resort to "facts available" *only* where a party: (i) refuses access to necessary information; (ii) otherwise does not provide necessary information within a reasonable period; or (iii) significantly impedes the investigation.

7.148 Egypt does not assert, nor do we find an indication in the record, that the IA considered that any of the Turkish respondents "significantly impede[d]" the investigation. In fact, Egypt states that its reasons for resort to facts available in respect of Habas, Diler and Colakoglu were that these companies "refused access to necessary information" and "failed to provide necessary information", and that in respect of Icdas and IDC, the reason was that these companies "otherwise failed to provide necessary information".[144] We will thus have to consider whether, as indicated by Egypt, the Turkish respondents refused access to necessary information, and/or failed to provide necessary information.

7.149 The IA explained its decision to resort to facts available in paragraph 1.6.5 of the *Final Report*, as follows:

> "Because parties did not provide all the data required, the Investigating Authority decided to proceed with the investigation procedures and calculate margins of dumping in accordance with Article 6.8 of the Anti-dumping Agreement which provides that:
>
> [quotation of Article 6.8 omitted]
>
> Article 27 of the [Egyptian Anti-Dumping] Regulation provides that:
>
> 'In case of absence of the data required, failure to submit data within the time-limit or non-cooperation with the Investigating Authority, the Investigating Authority may proceed in the investigation procedures and come to conclusions according to the best information available ...'
>
> And Article 35 of the Regulation states that:
>
> 'In cases where there is no sufficient data to determine the export price or the normal value, the Investigating Authority may determine them on the basis of the best information available'."[145]

7.150 These statements appear to confirm that the IA based its decision to resort to "facts available" in terms of Article 6.8 on respondents' "not provid[ing] ... necessary" information. We therefore start our analysis by examining the concept of "necessary information" in the sense of Article 6.8, and then consider whether necessary information in that sense was requested by the IA, but not provided by the respondents.

---

[144] Written Response, dated 7 December 2001, to Question 9 to Egypt of the *Written Questions by the Panel*, of 28 November 2001 – Annex 4-2.
[145] Exh. TUR-16, *Final Report*, para.1.6.5.

7.151 Article 6.8 refers to "necessary" information, and not to "required" or "requested" information. As this provision itself does not define the concept of "necessary" information, we consider whether there is guidance on this point anywhere else in the AD Agreement, in particular in Annex II, given Article 6.8's explicit cross-reference to it.

7.152 In this regard, we find significant the specific wording of that cross-reference: "[t]he provisions of Annex II *shall* be observed in the application *of this paragraph*" (emphasis added). In other words, the reference to "this paragraph" indicates that Annex II applies to Article 6.8 in its entirety, and thus contains certain substantive parameters for the application of the individual elements of that article. The phrase "shall be observed" indicates that these parameters, which address both when facts available can be used, and what information can be used as facts available, must be followed.

7.153 Our view of the relationship of Annex II to Article 6.8 is consistent with that of the Appellate Body in *United States – Hot-Rolled Steel*. In that case, the Appellate Body stated that Annex II is "incorporated by reference" into Article 6.8,[146] i.e., that it forms part of Article 6.8. In similar vein, the Appellate Body also referred to the "collective requirements" of Article 6.8 and certain provisions of Annex II.[147] The panel in *Argentina – Ceramic Tiles* came to a similar conclusion.[148]

7.154 It is clear that the provisions of Annex II that address what information can be used as facts available (which, along with the other provisions of Annex II, "shall be observed") have to do with ensuring the reliability of the information used by the investigating authority. This view may further be confirmed, as foreseen in Article 32 of the Vienna Convention on the Law of Treaties[149], by the negotiating history of Annex II. In particular, this Annex was originally developed by the Tokyo Round Committee on Anti-Dumping Practices, which adopted it on 8 May 1984 as a "Recommendation Concerning Best Information Available in Terms of Article 6:8".[150] During the Uruguay Round negotiations, the substantive provisions of the original recommendation were incorporated with almost no changes as Annex II to the AD Agreement. A preambular paragraph to the original recommendation, which was not retained when Annex II

---

[146] Appellate Body Report, *US – Hot-Rolled Steel*, para. 75.

[147] *Ibid*, para. 82.

[148] Panel Report, *Argentina – Definitive Anti-Dumping Measures on Imports of Ceramic Floor Tiles from Italy ("Argentina – Ceramic Tiles")*, WT/DS189/R, adopted 5 November 2001, DSR 2001:XII, 6241.

[149] Art. 32 of the Vienna Convention of the Law of Treaties provides:
"Recourse may be had to supplementary means of interpretation, including the preparatory work of the treaty and the circumstances of its conclusion, in order to confirm the meaning resulting from the application of article 31, or to determine the meaning when the interpretation according to article 31:
(a) leaves the meaning ambiguous or obscure; or
(b) leads to a result which is manifestly absurd or unreasonable".

[150] ADP/21.

was created, in our view, provides some insight into the intentions of the drafters concerning its application. This paragraph reads as follows:

> "The authorities of the importing country have a right and an obligation to make decisions on the basis of the best information available during the investigation from whatever source, even where evidence has been supplied by the interested party. The Anti-Dumping Code recognizes the right of the importing country to base findings on the facts available when any interested party refuses access to or does not provide the necessary information within a reasonable period, or significantly impedes the investigation (Article 6:8). However, all reasonable steps should be taken by the authorities of the importing countries to avoid the use of information from unreliable sources."

To us, this preambular language conveys that the *full* package of provisions in the recommendation, applicable in implementing Article 6:8 of the Tokyo Round Anti-Dumping Code, was intended, *inter alia,* to ensure that in using facts available (i.e, in applying Article 6:8), information from unreliable sources would be avoided.

7.155 On the question of the "necessary" information, reading Article 6.8 in conjunction with Annex II, paragraph 1, it is apparent that it is left to the discretion of an investigating authority, in the first instance, to determine what information it deems necessary for the conduct of its investigation (for calculations, analysis, etc.), as the authority is charged by paragraph 1 to "specify ... the information required from any interested party". This paragraph also sets forth rules to be followed by the authority, in particular that it must specify the required information "in detail", "as soon as possible after the initiation of the investigation", and that it also must specify "the manner in which that information should be structured by the interested party in its response". Thus, there is a clear burden on the authority to be both prompt and precise in identifying the information that it needs from a given interested party. In addition, paragraph 1 refers to a "reasonable" time-period for providing requested information. We note that in this dispute, we have resolved in connection with other claims Turkey's allegations that the IA's requests for cost information were not sufficiently prompt or precise, and that insufficient time was allowed for responding.[151] Thus, we do not consider these issues further here.

7.156 Having concluded that, subject to the requirements of Annex II, paragraph 1, it is left to the discretion of the investigating authority to specify what information is "necessary" in the sense of Article 6.8, we now consider what provisions of Annex II are relevant in respect of determinations that an interested party has "refused access to" or "otherwise has failed to provide" such information. In terms of the issues raised in the present claim, we find that two of the key such provisions are paragraphs 3 and 5 of Annex II.

---

[151] *See*, Sections VII.D.5, VII.D.6 and VII.E.1, *infra.*

7.157 Annex II, paragraph 3 provides:

> "All information which is verifiable, which is appropriately submitted so that it can be used in the investigation without undue difficulties, which is supplied in a timely fashion, and, where applicable, which is supplied in a medium or computer language requested by the authorities, should be taken into account when determinations are made. If a party does not respond in the preferred medium or computer language but the authorities find that the circumstances set out in paragraph 2 have been satisfied, the failure to respond in the preferred medium or computer language should not be considered to significantly impede the investigation."

7.158 Annex II, paragraph 5 provides:

> "Even though the information provided may not be ideal in all respects, this should not justify the authorities from disregarding it, provided the interested party has acted to the best of its ability."

7.159 These two paragraphs together thus provide key elements of the substantive basis for an IA to determine whether it can justify rejecting respondents' information and resorting to facts available in respect of some item, or items, of information, or whether instead, it must rely on the information submitted by respondents "when determinations are made". Some of the elements referred to in these paragraphs have to do with the inherent quality of the information itself, and some have to do with the nature and quality of the interested party's participation in the IA's information-gathering process. Where all of the mentioned elements are satisfied, resort to facts available is not justified under Article 6.8.

7.160 We consider that in the present dispute, the determining factor in the IA's decision to resort to facts available, and thus the central aspect of Turkey's claim in respect of this decision, is the "verifiability", in the sense of paragraph 3, of the cost information submitted by the respondents, and note in this regard Turkey's objection to what it sees as the IA's conducting a "mail-order verification".[152] That is, there seems to be no issue in respect of appropriateness of the manner in which the information was submitted or whether thereby using it would involve undue difficulties, nor is there an issue in respect of the medium or computer language. We note that, in regard to the quality of the information, paragraph 5 provides that information that may not be "ideal in all respects" nevertheless should be used provided the submitter has acted to the best of its ability. We address Turkey's claim in respect of the language "to the best of its ability" in paras. 7.239, et seq., infra, and focus here rather on the relationship of the phrase "not ... ideal in all respects" to the concept of "verifiability" in paragraph 3.

7.161 As we have noted, paragraphs 3 and 5, in addition to some of the other provisions of Annex II, have to do with assessing whether the information submitted by interested parties must be used. Thus, paragraph 5 is a complement to

---

[152] *See*, e.g., Section VII.E.1.

paragraph 3 and the two must be read together in considering the IA's obligations in respect of submitted information. In particular, we believe that under the pertinent phrases in these two paragraphs taken together, information that is of a very high quality, although not perfect, must not be considered unverifiable solely because of its minor flaws, so long as the submitter has acted to the best of its ability. That is, so long as the level of good faith cooperation by the interested party is high, slightly imperfect information should not be dismissed as unverifiable.[153]

7.162   In the context of this dispute, we find the provisions of paragraph 1 also to be relevant as to the "verifiability" of the information ultimately submitted by each respondent. In particular, the factual issue that culminated in the IA's resort to facts available began with the IA's doubts as to the accuracy of the cost data as originally submitted, and its 19 August request for "source data and [] audited financial data *establishing the accuracy* of the summary data that you supplied".[154] In other words, the IA specified in detail in the 19 August letter what information it considered necessary in order to be able to verify the cost data as reported in the respondents' questionnaire responses.

7.163   In assessing whether Article 6.8 was violated in this case, we also must consider whether the IA complied with paragraph 6 of Annex II. In particular, Turkey claims that the IA failed to notify two of the respondents, IDC and Icdas, that their information was being rejected, and failed to given them an opportunity to provide further explanations, as required by this provision. According to Turkey, for this reason as well, the IA's resort to facts available in respect to these respondents violated Article 6.8.

7.164   In sum, to understand in this dispute whether the IA was justified in relying on facts available for cost of production and constructed normal value, pursuant to Article 6.8, we will need to consider whether the information provided by each of the five respondents concerning their costs of production was "verifiable" in the sense of Annex II, paragraphs 3 and 5, and whether the IA provided the notice and opportunity for explanation required by Annex II, paragraph 6. To determine this, we will consider the following questions. In the first instance, did the IA clearly specify the information that it needed in order to satisfy itself as to the accuracy of the respondents' cost of production data (i.e., did the IA specify what it needed to verify the reported cost data)? Did each respondent provide the information that had been specified? In doing so, what were the nature and extent of any flaws in the information that was provided? Did each respondent, in providing information in response to the requests, act to the best of its ability? Finally, was each respondent informed that its information was being rejected, and given an opportunity to provide further explanations?

---

[153]   We note that there is an interplay between the concepts of acting to the best of one's ability in Annex II, para. 5, and "refusing access to" necessary information or "significantly impeding" an investigation in Article 6.8. That is, the behaviour of the interested party is relevant to the right to use facts available in a given situation.

[154]   Exh. TUR-11.

7.165 We now turn to a detailed review of the facts of the rebar investigation, including the nature of the information submitted by each of the Turkish respondents and the actions of those respondents and the IA. Only by applying the analytical framework that we have set out above to the specific facts of this case can we make a judgement as to whether for each respondent the IA respected the requirements of Article 6.8 in conjunction with the cited paragraphs of Annex II.

(i)   Colakoglu, Diler and Habas

7.166 Colakoglu, Diler and Habas responded to the Manufacturers Questionnaire and on 7 April 1999 submitted to the IA their responses, through the same legal counsel.[155] Their responses to Appendix 2 of the Manufacturer's Questionnaire relating to sales in the domestic market to independent customers during the period 1 January 1998 to 31 December 1998 contained information relating only to those sales that were identical in physical characteristics, closest in time and closest in quantity to the Egyptian sales. Furthermore, these producers also reported in their responses monthly average costs of production of rebar only for the months in which they had sales to Egypt, in response to the information requested in Annex 9 to the Manufacturers Questionnaire.[156]

7.167 On 10 May 1999 counsel for these three producers sent a fax to the IA regarding procedural issues, enquiring, *inter alia*, "[i]f there will be supplemental questions, when such questions would be issued".[157] The IA responded on 20 May 1999 that:

> "Before the visit (verification), each company will be advised of the items which the Egyptian Authority wishes to verify and further information that will be sought. In general, the information which is missing is the supporting documentation on which claims for adjustments are based. It is usual for this type of information and explanations to be provided during the verification visit, where the information in the industry response has been sufficient, as it has in this case. Without the supporting data which is requested in the questionnaire however adjustments are not normally allowed."

7.168 The on-site verification of the information submitted by the three producers in response to the Manufacturer's Questionnaire was conducted in Turkey from 11 to 18 June 1999.[158] In the verification reports relating to these three producers, no discrepancies between the information submitted and the verified information were noted by the IA.[159] It is common cause that the verification was limited to export sales and domestic sales and that the reported data on cost of production were not verified.[160]

---

[155]   First Written Submission of Turkey, p.26.
[156]   *Ibid.*
[157]   Exh. TUR-36.
[158]   First Written Submission of Turkey, p.29.
[159]   Exh. TUR-6(Diler), TUR-7(Colakoglu) and TUR-8(Habas), respectively.
[160]   Verification Reports by the IA, submitted by Turkey as Exh. TUR-4(Icdas), TUR-5(IDC), TUR-6(Diler), TUR-7(Colakoglu) and TUR-9(Habas), respectively.

7.169 On 12 August 1999 the IA sent faxes to all five respondents, including Habas, Diler and Colakoglu, regarding certain adjustments to their export prices and home market prices. These three producers responded to this fax and provided certain requested information and explanations, as well as comments, on 13 August 1999.[161]

7.170 On 19 August 1999 the IA sent letters by fax, the operational parts of which were identical, to all five Turkish producers.[162] In these letters the IA informed the producers that:

"The Investigating Authority has reviewed the cost and sales data that [name of company] has submitted thus far in this proceeding. In reviewing this data, the Investigating Authority has identified a number of concerns that are identified below.

As a threshold matter, the Investigating Authority is aware that during the period of investigation, Turkey was experiencing hyper-inflation on the order of roughly 5 percent per month. The Investigating Authority would , therefore, expect to see in the data submitted by [company name] a substantial increase during the period of investigation both in the home market sales prices and in the cost of production. The Investigating Authority has reviewed the data submitted by [company name], and it appears that the data is not consistent with the inflationary conditions experienced in Turkey during the subject period. [The IA then gives details of cost data of materials, labour, manufacturing overhead and selling, general and administrative costs ("SG&A") as submitted by the three producers and noted that these cost elements all showed a decrease during the subject period, despite the inflationary conditions.] The costs reported included no finance cost, yet the income statement that [company name] supplied indicated significant financing expenses. The costs reported include a deduction for "interest expense", the Investigating Authority would need an explanation for this cost and why it is deducted from cost of production.

...

The above data reported by [company name] indicate that your reported costs do not reflect the inflation in effect. The Investigating Authority, therefore, intends to adjust the cost data reported by [company name] and eliminate those home market sales that are determined to be not in the ordinary course of trade.

In the event you disagree with the proposed course of action, we require that you supply the Investigating Authority with source data and with audited financial data establishing the accuracy of the summary data that you supplied. We also require that you pro-

---

[161] Exh. TUR-25.
[162] Exh. TUR-11.

vide a full and complete explanation regarding the issues set forth above. In addition, you must reconcile the costs that you submitted to the audited financial statement. Attached hereto is a list of the data required by [company name] in the event you propose a modification of the Investigating Authority's approach.

The Investigating Authority intends to conclude this investigation in the near future. Therefore, any response to this letter must be accompanied by the data identified in the attached list and must be received by the Investigating Authority no later than September 1st, 1999. Any response received after that date may be rejected by the Investigating Authority.

List of supplemental materials required accompanying any response to this letter.

1. *Basic Source Documents.*

    [Company's name] audited financial statements, including all footnotes, covering full calendar years 1997 and 1998, and any draft or interim financial statements and footnotes covering [different periods for different companies].

    The annual or semi-annual submissions made to the Turkish tax authorities for full calendar years 1997 and 1998.

    A chart of accounts for full year 1998 and the first half of 1999.

    Cost of production data prepared in accordance with app. 9A for the months [different months for the different companies].

2. *Accounting Practices*

    Provide a written summary of the basic books used in your accounting system. Use a diagram if possible.

    Provide a review of the accounting system using the basic books summary, chart of accounts, and the financial statements. Show how sales and expenses are posted to the various ledgers and statements (*i.e.*, demonstrate the manner in which source documents for sales and expenses flow into the financial statements via accounting vouchers, journals, subsidiary ledgers, and general ledger accounts).

    Provide a complete list of the types of computer reports generated and/or available in the ordinary course of business. Provide samples of each of these reports.

3. *Merchandise*

    Provide a complete list of all products sold during the period of investigation, and a list of the internal accounting codes for these products that were used to record costs, sales, or expenses.

4. *Materials*

A. Provide the material inventory ledgers for the subject merchandise showing the raw materials, work in process, and finished goods inventory showing the balance and activity in the accounts for each month during 1998 and an explanation of whether and how inventory values are adjusted for inflation in [company name] accounting records.

B. Reconcile the total value from the inventory ledgers for the months of [different months for each company] to [company name] general ledger and financial statement.

C. Provide a copy of all material purchase orders placed during the months of [different months for each company]. A copy of the appropriate pages from the payments ledger showing payment for those purchases.

D. A worksheet reconciling the materials costs that you submitted in your summary to the Investigating Authority to the company's audited financial statement.

5. *Labour*

A. Explain whether any adjustments have been made in [company name] accounting records to recognize the inflation that occurred during this time.

B. Explain the basis on which labour was allocated to the subject merchandise.

C. Reconcile the labour costs reported for [different months for each company] to the general ledger and to the financial statement, and provide supporting documents, including bank statements for those months.

6. *Overhead*

A. Explain whether any adjustments have been made to account for the inflation that occurred during this time.

B. Provide a complete list of all expenses included in the category "overhead" which you provided in your summary to the Investigating Authority.

C. Provide a complete list of all depreciation expenses and reconcile those expenses to the summary which you provided to the Investigating Authority for the months of [different months for each company].

D. Specifically explain whether your recorded depreciation expenses take into account the inflation that occurred during this time.

7. *Complete sales listing*

A. Provide the complete sales journal for the subject merchandise for the months of [different months for each company]. Provide a worksheet for [different months for each company] which reconciles the monthly sales total to the financial statement sales total.

B. Using the worksheets developed for the previous step, reconcile the total reported export and home-market sales to sales journal(s), summary entries in the general ledger based on sales journals, and the financial statements for [different months for each company]. Show how the sales listing flows to subsidiary ledgers, the general ledger, and the financial statements for 1998."[163]

7.171 Counsel representing these three producers requested on 23 August 1999 an extension of 51 days, to 22 October 1999, of the time-period of 13 days originally provided for the submission of responses to the IA's letter. The stated reasons for requesting the extensions were that Turkey had suffered a major earthquake on 17 August 1999, with consequent absence of key employees attending to their families or helping with relief efforts, as well as the fact that these companies were scheduled to undergo verifications in EU and Canadian antidumping investigations within the following 35 days.[164] Icdas requested on 26 August 1999 an extension of 40 days, until 11 October 1999, and IDC requested an extension until 15 October 1999. The IA informed all five producers, on 26 August 1999, that an extension had been granted to 15 September 1999, that is, an extension of 14 days.

7.172 On 15 September 1999 the counsel for the three producers, Habas, Diler and Colakoglu, submitted their responses to the 19 August 1999 letter.

7.173 The IA informed these producers by letter dated 23 September 1999 that certain requested information and underlying documents had still not been submitted. In all three cases, for example, concerning material costs, for which the IA in the 19 August letter had requested data and supporting documents (purchase orders, payment ledgers, etc.) regarding raw material *purchases*, the respondents had submitted only information relating to billets, i.e., providing their internal transfer prices of the billets they themselves had produced, rather than the requested information on the raw materials used to make the billets.[165]

7.174 In the 23 September 1999 letters, the IA requested the three producers to address the deficiencies in the responses they had submitted on 15 September 1999.

7.175 Specifically, with respect to **Habas** the IA requested the following:

---

[163] *Ibid.*

[164] First Written Submission of Turkey, p.37.

[165] According to Turkey "the original responses of each producer put the IA on notice that each company was reporting its internal cost of billet as the reported raw material cost. Footnote 91 in Turkey's First Written Submission.

"1.   Basic data:" The IA requested Habas to provide the total monthly quantity of billets/rebars produced during the period of investigation.

"2.   Materials:" According to the IA no information was submitted for auxiliary materials used in the production process in attachment no 4 (to the 15 September response) and the IA requested a complete monthly list of all raw materials used to produce rebars and the percentage each represent of the finished product. The information requested was set out in an annex. According to the annex, the information to be submitted under the heading "materials used" was to be broken down into scrap, graphite, ferro alloys, electrodes etc, and "labour" into sub-headings "From scrap to billet" and "From billet to rebar" and the same with regard to "overhead". The other cost items requested were the same as in the format attached to the original Manufacturer's Questionnaire."

7.176   The IA also requested that supporting documents such as purchase orders, purchase invoices, and production line documents that show the total cost of producing billets as well as rebars, be submitted and that all these documents should also be fully translated.

7.177   The IA requested that the allocation base of material used for each size, should also be submitted.

"3. Labour:" The IA requested that the costs of goods sold (COGS – attachment no. 10 to the response of 15 September) be translated and that supporting documents like sample payroll records or time cards be furnished. These documents should also be translated.

"4. Overhead:" The IA requested that the total amounts of factory overhead (item by item) and how they were allocated to each size, be provided.

"5. SG & A:" The IA requested that the total amount of SG & A (item by item) and the allocation basis of these amounts to each size, be submitted.

"6. Complete sales listing:" The IA requested the total sales quantity for each size.

"7. Interest expense:" The IA requested a list identifying separately interest expense from interest income."

7.178   The IA also informed Habas that:

"Generally speaking, most documents provided were in Turkish. A full translation should be attached to each document, for example, a detailed manufacturing cost and packing cost reconciliation.

Please provide us with a full explanation demonstrating how and where the high inflation rate is already included in all cost elements during the POI.

> The above-mentioned items no. 4,7 should be submitted within 2 days."

7.179 The information other than items 4 and 7 was to be submitted within five working days from 23 September 1999. The IA did not indicate what the consequences would be if these deadlines were not met.

7.180 With respect to **Colakoglu**, the IA requested almost exactly the same information. The only difference was that under the heading "Overhead", Colakoglu was also requested to furnish a translation of documents that it had submitted in Turkish.

7.181 In the case of **Diler**, almost exactly the same information as that requested from Colakoglu, was requested, except that under the heading "Basic data", Diler was requested to provide the total monthly quantity of scrap purchased (domestic listed separately from imported scrap), billets produced, billets sold (domestic listed separately from exported billet) and rebars produced during the period of investigation (by size).

7.182 In response to the IA's requests, counsel to these three producers informed the IA on 28 September 1999 that:

> "The previously submitted responses of Colakoglu, Diler and Habas to the ITPD questionnaire are complete and accurate. ... .
>
> Responses which were entirely complete in April 1999 remain so today.
>
> ....
>
> The documents provided on 13 September in response to the questionnaire of 19 August 1999 are translated in sufficient detail to enable ITPD to ascertain their contents. Many of these documents had been previously given and translated in full; for example, financial statements had been previously given in full translation, so we did not provide duplicative translation. Similarly, the packaging cost reconciliations sought in the 23 September letter were in fact provided during the verification, when ITPD fully verified packing costs and inspected, translated, and copied original documents.
>
> If ITPD remains unable to locate the original translations or to identify the pages of the 15 September response where translations are provide, or if ITPD requires any additional explanations, we will be pleased to come to Cairo to review these documents with ITPD. Such a meeting could be arranged after the third week of November, if desired. Before that time, counsel's time is fully booked, but we would expect ITPD to afford us this scheduling courtesy in view of the events herein since verification was concluded.
>
> With reference to ITPD's request for additional information in the ITPD letter of 23 September, we note that ITPD is requiring re-

sponses to the letter 'within 2 days' for certain items and 'no later than 5 working days' for other items.

International courier service from Turkey to Egypt requires 2 days. Therefore it is physically impossible to provide documentation within 2 days. Furthermore, even a 5-day time-limit is unreasonable; no respondent could possibly provide factual responses in such a period of time. Thus the time limits set for this questionnaire response are unreasonable and impossible to meet, and hence in violation of GATT AD Code [sic], Art 2.4 ('unreasonable burden of proof') and Art 6.1 (respondents shall be given 'ample opportunity to present evidence …').

In particular, with reference to 'Attachment 1' of ITPD's 23 September letter,: ITPD has not previously requested this type of information. It thus amounts to a new cost questionnaire. The question is extremely burdensome; respondents estimate that, if the questions were properly posed(sic), it would take at least a month to provide the answers. ….

….. Colakoglu, Diler and Habas object to what is blatantly a mail order verification. …

If ITPD does not understand any of our submissions or wants more explanation, we are willing to meet with ITPD in Cairo to explain anything about which ITPD has questions.

Colakoglu, Diler and Habas have answered every question of the questionnaire, …

As of the end of the verification, the factual record is complete.

In short, Colakoglu, Diler and Habas stand by their responses and demand a calculation based on their responses as submitted."

7.183 On 28 September 1999, the IA responded to this letter, informing the counsel for the three respondents that "we note that you did not fully respond to the following items: materials, labour, overhead, SG&A, interest expense and detailed cost sheet. Therefore, the ITPD will use other data provided by your clients which were satisfactory, but will use facts available for the above-mentioned items."[166]

7.184 On 28 September 1999, counsel for these three companies responded to the IA's letter of 28 September, informing the IA that they:

"reiterate that they are absolutely entitled to a decision based on their own data. They answered the questionnaire, received no supplemental questions, and successfully underwent verification. Questionnaires subsequent to verification are *ultra vires* and cannot be the basis for facts available. … . Furthermore, respondents' submissions of 15 September fully support and verify the accuracy

---

[166] Exh. EGT-13-6.

of respondents' reported costs. ... Colakoglu, Diler and Habas are therefore entitled to a margin calculation based on their own numbers, as submitted. Any other outcome – in particular, any 'facts available' outcome – would be unlawful."[167]

7.185 In a letter dated 5 October 1999 to counsel for these three producers, the IA referred to that counsel's previous suggestion of a "possible" meeting in Cairo to explain the data submitted by Colakoglu, Diler and Habas and stated that "any further comments or explanations regarding the request of ITPD for supplemental information should have been included in your responses, the deadline for which has passed. We will consider any further information to be untimely. ...."

7.186 Concerning the three respondents as a group, in the IA's Essential Facts and Conclusions Report of October 1999[168] under the heading: "The IA's Request for Supplemental Information", the IA stated that:

"On September 15, 1999, respondents Habas, Diler and Colakoglu responded to the Investigating Authority with some incomplete data and argued that the Investigating Authority's request for additional data was procedurally improper. These respondents argued that the Investigating Authority is prohibited from requesting further data and that, following a verification, the Investigating Authority is required to accept all data submitted by respondents that the Investigating Authority did not find to be inaccurate as a result of the verification. The data provided on September 15 were incomplete and some of them were untranslated, so on September 23, 1999, these respondents were requested to complete the data and translations required. On September 28, 1999, respondents replied that they had previously submitted all data required on September 15, 1999."[169]

7.187 Under the heading "Normal Values" the IA commented as follows:

"The Investigating Authority applied partial facts available to calculate the normal value for Habas, Diler and Colakoglu. These respondents failed to respond completely to the Investigating Authority's requests for information. On this point, each of these respondents submitted responses to the Investigating Authority's initial questionnaire and participated in a verification of those responses. Following these verifications, the Investigating Authority issued follow-up requests for information seeking supplemental cost and sales data. These respondents did not provide complete responses to the Investigating Authority's requests. The Investigating Authority forwarded two additional requests for the respondents to complete the responses; however, the requested information was not provided. ... As part of this investigation, the Investi-

---

[167] Exh. EGT-9.
[168] Exh. TUR-15.
[169] Exh. TUR-15, *Essential Facts and Conclusions Report*, para. 1.6.2.

gating Authority requested that respondents supply source documents supporting certain of its claims of material, labor and overhead costs. Respondents were also requested to reconcile certain costs to their financial statements covering the investigations period. Respondents declined to provide the necessary data."[170]

7.188 Concerning the three respondents individually, the IA commented as follows in the *Essential Facts and Conclusions Report* with regard to the failure of each to submit the requested information and/or supporting documentation.

7.189 Regarding **Habas**, the IA commented as follows:

"Although the Investigating Authority twice requested full costs of production for the entire POI, the company only provided costs for two selected months, and there is no evidence on the record that these were representative of the period."[171]

7.190 Regarding **Diler**, the IA commented as follows:

"... Diler did not provide sufficient information for the Investigating Authority to confirm the monthly specific costs of materials, labor, or overhead during the period of investigation despite being requested to do so."[172]

7.191 Regarding **Colakoglu**, the IA commented as follows:

"... Colakoglu did not provide sufficient information for the Investigating Authority to confirm the monthly specific costs of materials, labor, or overhead during the period of investigation despite being requested to do so."[173]

7.192 In comments on the *Essential Facts and Conclusions Report*, counsel for these three producers asserted that "... respondents have submitted complete sales and cost databases which were verified or reconciled to financial statements", "... the respondents' post-verification submissions were fully responsive to ITPD's inquiries – even though those inquiries were, themselves, ill-founded in law and in fact – and as such they provide compelling reason for ITPD to correct the manifest error in the use of facts available and, instead, to issue a final determination in accordance with respondents' databases as submitted and without change", and with reference to the information submitted on 15 September 1999, that "[i]ndeed, the submission was in many respects more than what ITPD had requested, and there were adequate translations for each and every single document".[174] Counsel did not address the specific issues raised by the IA regarding incomplete information.

7.193 In the *Final Report*, issued in October 1999, the IA stated, under the heading "Complete or Incomplete Sales/Cost Responses":

---

[170] *Ibid*, para.3.2.1.1.
[171] *Ibid*, para.3.2.2.1.
[172] *Ibid*, para.3.2.3.1.
[173] *Ibid*, para.3.2.4.1.
[174] Exh. TUR-20.

"We note that these three respondents' [referring to Colakoglu, Diler and Habas] repeated assertion that they 'have submitted complete sales and cost databases which were verified or reconciled to financial statements' is simply incorrect. The sales databases were verified. As for the cost databases being reconciled to financial statements, we requested their trail balances and, when the respondents provided them on September 15, 1999, along with a claim that '[t]rial balances do not contain quantity (tonnage) data, so they will not reveal any information concerning unit costs. Moreover, trial balances are company-wide, and will generally not reveal anything of particular relevance concerning rebar production'. We subsequently requested English translations but never received them. However, in their October 15, 1999 comments respondents assert that they 'clearly and unequivocally reconciled their monthly conversion – labor and overhead – to their trial balances, and thence to the general ledger'. This latter statement is somewhat disingenuous in light of the September 15 statement, regardless, since we never received the requested translations, this information was not usable. Thus, it is simply incorrect that the cost databases were reconciled to financial statements.

....

The Department points out that all cost information was requested for the entire 12-month period in the original questionnaire, but only selected costs were provided; one firm provided detailed cost data for only 4 months, corresponding to the 4 months of Egyptian sales, and a second firm provided detailed cost data for only 2 months of the period. Although the three firms provided 12 months of material, labor and overhead costs, for all three firms these responses were unusable for various reasons: they were limited to materials, labor, and overhead, there was no supporting evidence, no clarifications, and no narrative or further explanations, there were no detailed breakouts of these cost elements such as overhead, and various documents were not translated into English, all of which the Department had requested. Although in response to supplemental requests for information to cure these deficiencies the respondents provided various additional supporting evidence and further arguments about previously furnished data, they failed to provide much of the above necessary information, clarifications, supporting evidence and translations. In sum, the responses remained deficient in many respects; the Department used respondents' data whenever it was sufficient, and only used partial facts available for data that were missing, deficient, or inadequate. "

7.194 Under the heading "Normal Values", with reference to Colakoglu, Habas and Diler, the IA commented as follows:

"These respondents did not provide complete responses to the Investigating Authority's requests. .... As part of this investigation, the Investigating Authority requested that respondents supply source documents supporting certain of their claims of material, labor and overhead costs. Respondents were also requested to reconcile certain costs to their financial statements covering the investigation period. Respondents declined to provide the necessary data.

...

These respondents have argued that the data that they submitted was sufficient and those facts (sic) available should not be applied. However, the submissions of these respondents are deficient in several respects. For example, the Investigating Authority requested copies of invoices and purchase orders for purchases of scrap made by respondents during the investigation period. The Investigating Authority considers these source documents important to determine the reliability of the submitted data. These three respondents refused to provide any such evidence of the cost of scrap, or, in fact, of any other materials. ...

As another example the Investigating Authority requested that the respondents reconcile reported labor costs with the companies' financial statements. None of these respondents supplied the requested reconciliation or explained why such reconciliation could not be provided. Similarly, the Investigating Authority requested that the respondents reconcile monthly sales amounts to the companies' financial statements. Once again, neither the data nor an adequate explanation was provided by these companies. Further, the Investigating Authority requested that translations be provided for the materials submitted by respondents, however, several of the documents were provided with no such translations."[175]

7.195 In its *Final Report* the IA did not add to its comments in the *Essential Facts and Conclusions Report* relating to the individual producers.

(ii)   Icdas and IDC

7.196 As indicated in paragraph 7.170, *supra*, these two companies received basically the same letter, dated 19 August 1999, as Colakoglu, Diler and Habas, from the IA. The contents of the letter are set forth in that paragraph.

7.197 Both of these companies also received, on request, an extension from the IA for the submission of their responses to the 19 August 1999 request, from 1 September 1999 to 15 September 1999.[176]

---

[175]   Exh. TUR-16, *Final Report*, para.3.2.1.1. to 3.2.1.5.
[176]   *See* para. 7.171, *supra*.

Icdas

7.198 On 15 September 1999 Icdas submitted to the IA its response to the 15 August 1999 request.

7.199 The IA responded to Icdas's 15 September submission on 23 September 1999, by stating that:

"1. Attachment 8 has not been received

2. Attachment 9 is unclear, please provide us depreciation expenses for Sep., Oct. and Nov. 1998 translated into English.

The above-mentioned items should be submitted within five working days."

7.200 Attachment 8 (which concerned labour costs) and the depreciation expenses breakdown, translated into English, were faxed by Icdas to the IA on 27 September 1999 and sent by courier on 28 September 1999.[177] According to Turkey, Icdas "responded fully to this information request in a timely manner and received no other indication from the IA that its response on September 15, 1999 was otherwise incomplete or unusable".[178]

7.201 In its *Essential Facts and Conclusions Report* of October 1999, the IA stated:

"Icdas ... provided incomplete data and most of the data submitted were not supported by evidence."[179]

7.202 The IA further stated, under the heading "Comparison of the Net Home Market Price to the Cost of Production":

'... Icdas did not provide sufficient information for the Investigating Authority to confirm the monthly specific costs of materials, labor, or overhead during the period of investigation despite being requested to do so.'

7.203 In response to these statements in the *Essential Facts and Conclusions Report*, Icdas stated in its 14 October 1999 comments thereon that:

"Icdas timely responded to the Department's additional request for information dated August 19, 1999 and provided all the necessary information to the Department. In its letter No. 629 dated September 23, 1999, the Department listed outstanding issues in Icdas' responses dated September 15, 1999 and this remaining items are timely submitted to the department. If there would have been any other missing information, the Department should have notified Icdas to provide this missing or incomplete information in its letter No. 629. In the Report the department does not clearly state what information is found missing or incomplete."[180]

---

[177] Exh.TUR-40.
[178] First Written Submission of Turkey, p.68.
[179] Exh.TUR-15, para.1.6.2.
[180] Exh. TUR-26, p.3.

7.204 In its *Final Report* the IA stated that "Icdas and IDC provided incomplete data and most of the data submitted were not supported by evidence".[181] Although, as recounted above, the IA addressed in detail in the *Final Report* the failure of Colakoglu, Diler and Habas to submit certain requested information, no such detail was included in respect of Icdas or IDC.[182]

7.205 Instead, concerning Icdas' compliance with the 19 August request, the *Final Report* states:

> "On September 23, 1999, the Department requested a missing document and *several* documents to be translated into English. …[183] (emphasis added)
>
> …
>
> As for Icdas' claim that it 'provided all the necessary information' in response to the Department's August 19, 1999 request and that the 'remaining items are[sic] timely submitted' in response to the Department's September 23, 1999 request, that is incorrect. In fact, the firm did not furnish (1) the requested breakdown of labour and overhead costs, (2) the requested supporting documents for labour and overhead costs, (3) the requested allocations and allocation methodologies for materials, overhead, and SG&A, and (4) the requested reconciliations of submitted data to its financial statement. In addition, its explanation of how inflation was reflected/included in its costs was inadequate and unsupported."[184]

IDC

7.206 In response to IDC's submission of the information requested in the 19 August 1999 letter, on 23 September, the IA requested IDC to:

> "… provide the following within five working days:
>
> 1.Interest expense: Furnish a list identifying separately interest expenses from interest income.
>
> 2.In worksheet 2 (factory cost and profit for domestic sales per ton) it is unclear whether the materials listed are scrap or billets, please specify.
>
> 3. Fill in the enclosed cost of production sheet for Aug., Sep., and Oct. 1998.
>
> Item 1 should be submitted within 2 days."[185] [186]

---

[181] Exh.TUR-16, para.1.6.2.
[182] *Ibid*, p.12-15.
[183] *Ibid*, para.3.1.7.10.
[184] *Ibid*, para.3.1.7.15.
[185] Exh. EGT–13-1-2.
[186] The cost of production sheet referred to, is identical to Attachment No 1 to the 23 September letters to Colakoglu, Diler and Habas.

7.207 IDC faxed information on interest expense to the IA on 25 September, the due date. When informed by the IA that the fax had not been received, IDC re-sent it on 29 September 1999.[187]

7.208 On 28 September 1999, IDC faxed the information on the cost of produc-tion for the months of August, September and October 1998 to the IA. In the fax IDC also noted that the "production costs given in Worksheet 2 are calculated from scrap to rebar basis" and that "[m]aterials listed are the same as the cost of production sheets attached for item 3 (Cost of production sheets)".[188]

7.209 On 28 September 1999 the IA requested IDC to submit a list identifying separately interest expenses from interest income showing the difference be-tween both interest expense and interest income per ton during 1998 on a monthly basis, with a note "[y]our effort will be appreciated if we receive the above-mentioned immediately". According to Turkey, IDC faxed the requested information to the IA on 29 September 1999.[189]

7.210 As noted above, the IA issued its *Essential Facts and Conclusions Report* on 5 October 1999, applying "facts available" to IDC. In that report, as indicated above, the IA stated that "Icdas and IDC provided incomplete data and most of the data submitted were not supported by evidence". The IA also stated that:

> "For materials, labor and overhead, since the company did not adequately demonstrate or support its claim that inflation was in-cluded, as facts available, since these costs varied significantly during the period, we used the highest cost for each element during the period to reflect the inclusion of inflation costs."[190]

7.211 The IA did not identify in the *Essential facts and Conclusions Report* any particular document or other information that had been requested by the IA, but not submitted by IDC.

7.212 On 15 October 1999 IDC commented regarding the *Essential Facts and Conclusions Report* that:

> "Up to today, IDC has always become(sic) cooperative with your Authority and have always given all information and supporting documents you requested. Therefore, facts available clause should not have been used. As you know, IDC has never refused your any request of any information. We have given all correct information and documents to you on time and informed you to contact us any-time you need more clarification and explanations."[191]

7.213 IDC attached to this letter "Worksheet 1: Cost of Production (From Billet to Rebar) for 1998", "Worksheet 2: Calculation of Financial Expenses for Con-structed Normal Value Table and Constructed Normal Value table for IDC".

---

187 First Written Submission of Turkey, p.44.
188 Exh. TUR-41.
189 *Ibid.*
190 Exh. TUR-15, para.3.2.6.1.
191 Exh.TUR-27.

Worksheet 1 contains the cost of production from billet to rebar for the months of August, September and October 1998 and is the same information that was faxed to the IA on 28 September 1999, except that in this document ex-factory sales prices and profits were added. Worksheet 2 contains information relating to interest expense (but not interest income), a list of productions items subject to interest expense, and a constructed normal value for IDC for the three months of August, September and October 1998.

7.214 In its *Final Report* the IA repeated that:

"Icdas and IDC provided incomplete data and most of the data submitted were not supported by evidence."[192]

7.215 Turkey takes strong issue with this characterization, alleging that all of the information requested by the IA, most importantly that provided on 15 September in response to the IA's 19 August request, as well as the further information provided in response to the IA's 23 September request, was submitted within the time-periods set by the IA.

7.216 The IA did not refer in the *Final Report* to any specific requested document or information not submitted by IDC. However, the IA stated that:

"With its comments on the Essential Facts Report Izmir (IDC) attached information which the Department, because it determines that this is new information untimely submitted, will not consider in this investigation."[193]

(b) Was the Cost Information Requested by the IA on 19 August and 23 September 1999 "necessary information"?

7.217 We recall that the parties have submitted extensive arguments regarding the validity of the IA's rationale for seeking the detailed cost information. Turkey claims that "because the basis for initially questioning and then rejecting Turkish respondents' costs was unfounded, resort to facts available was unjustified under Article 6.8 of the Agreement". On the other hand, we note that the IA justified its request for the cost data as necessary to enable it to determine whether the respondents had made sales of comparison merchandise in the home market at prices that were below the cost of production, in accordance with Article 34 of the Egyptian Regulations. This provision, which essentially mirrors the provisions of Article 2.2 and 2.2.1 of the Anti-Dumping Agreement, allows investigating authorities to construct a normal value if sales of the like product in the domestic market of the exporting country are below costs of production plus SG&A. Egypt argues that the IA was not in a position to make this determination because the required information to enable it to make the determination was not submitted by the respondents in their responses to the initial questionnaire. On its face, this justification for seeking the detailed cost information appears plausible

---

[192] Exh.TUR-16, para.1.6.2.
[193] Exh.TUR-16, p.30.

to us, given, as noted, that a below-cost test is explicitly provided for in Articles 2.2 and 2.2.1 of the AD Agreement. Thus, the requested information would seem to be "necessary" in the sense of Article 6.8.

7.218 As to the specific basis for the IA's 19 August request, the IA stated in that request that it was seeking the additional, detailed cost data because it was aware that Turkey was a country with a hyperinflationary economy, with inflation averaging "roughly 5 per cent per month". The IA indicated that it would have expected to see the effect of this hyperinflation reflected in the different cost elements reported by the respondents in the original questionnaire responses. The IA maintained this position throughout the process.

7.219 The parties are in agreement that the cost figures reported by the respondents did not reflect the increases one would normally have expected in a hyperinflationary economy. However, in their responses to the 19 August and 23 September information requests, the respondents provided a number of explanations for this in respect of scrap, labour and depreciation, the main cost elements questioned by the IA as not reflecting hyperinflation. According to the respondents, the international price of steel scrap (accounting for 60 per cent of the cost of producing rebar), fixed in US dollar terms, declined substantially during the POI; labour rates were fixed once a year after negotiations with trade unions; and the revaluation of assets for purposes of depreciation was also done once a year through the application of "uplift factors" published by the Turkish Government. The respondents insisted that the cost data that they submitted were their actual figures, reflecting their actual costs of production during the POI. These arguments by the respondents were repeated in their respective comments on the *Essential Facts and Conclusions Report*[194], as well as by the Government of Turkey in its comments.[195]

7.220 Turning first to scrap cost, the IA rejected the data and explanation on world steel scrap prices submitted by the three respondents, stating:

> "... [r]espondents' information on world scrap prices was expressed in annual terms (prices at the end of a year were lower than prices at the beginning of the year), it was not useful in determining price movements during the investigation period (calendar 1998). When the Department examined monthly domestic rebar and purchased scrap prices throughout the period (another respondent in this investigation submitted monthly scrap prices), a very different picture emerged. ... The sharp decline, which respondents implied was sustained throughout the period, was in fact, limited to 3 out of 12 months of the investigation period, ...
>
> Thus, the Department had a reasonable basis for its concern whether domestic costs fully reflected the high inflation."[196]

---

[194] Exh. TUR-20 and TUR-27.
[195] Exh. TUR-30.
[196] Exh. TUR-16, p.12-13.

7.221 As it was not clear to us to which company "another respondent in this investigation" referred, we requested Egypt during the Second Substantive Meeting of the Panel with the Parties to clarify the matter.[197] Egypt indicated that this "other respondent" was Alexandria National Steel, which had submitted the information in response to a telephonic request made by the IA "in order to verify the veracity" of the claim by the Turkish respondents that scrap prices had collapsed throughout the period of investigation.[198]. At our request Egypt provided the scrap cost information as submitted by Alexandria National Steel.[199] The document consists of two parts: one part sourced, from the *Metal Bulletin* of March 1999, which reflects iron and steel scrap prices, fob Rotterdam, for three categories of scrap - "HMS 1"[200], "HMS 1&2" and "shredded" on specific dates covering the period January to December 1998, excluding March and June 1998. The price information gives a minimum and a maximum price per date and per category. The second part of the document consists of prices computed by Alexandria National Steel from the underlying *Metal Bulletin* data. According to Egypt, the IA's "assessment of the evolution of scrap prices was based on the 'source reference' in the second page of EX-EGT-12, and not on the prices mentioned on the cover page of the Alexandria National".

7.222 Egypt asserts before us that the evidence submitted by Alexandria National Steel reveals that the Turkish respondents' claim that scrap prices declined throughout the investigation period was factually wrong.[201] Egypt states:

"Indeed, as explained in the *Final Report*, scrap prices were found to be fairly constant for the first seven months of the investigation period. During the next three months, prices collapsed. Then, prices started to recover in the last two months on the investigation period. In other words, the 'sharp decline' was in fact limited to three out of twelve months."

7.223 Turkey commented on Egypt's response on our questions and states that:

"As the panel can clearly see by a review of ... the second page of EX-EGT-12, HMS1&2 scrap prices declined steeply between January 1998 ($114 – 116 per ton) and April 1998 ($96 - $97 per ton) and continued their decline into July 1998 (to $92 -$94 per ton). This is an overall decline of 19%, hardly evidence of scrap price stability during the first seven months of the year. Scrap prices for HMS 1 show similar declines – from $123 - $124 per ton in January 1998 to $105 - $107 per ton in April 1998 and $98 – $ 99 in July (an overall decline of 20%). Prices then dropped from

---

[197] Question 2 to Egypt of the *Written Questions by the Panel,* dated 27 February 2002 – Annex 8-2.
[198] Written Response of Egypt to the *Two Follow-Up Written Questions by the Panel* of 3 April 2002 – Annex 8-3.
[199] Exh. EGT-12.
[200] Our understanding is that "HMS" refers to "heavy melting scrap".
[201] Written Response of Egypt to the *Two Follow-Up Written Questions by the Panel* of 3 April 2002 – Annex 8-3..

August to October ($70 - $72 per ton) or a further decline of 23% from January levels. ..."[202]

7.224 We have a slightly different reading from that of Turkey of the scrap price data submitted by Alexandria National. In particular, we note that for each of the categories "HMS1" and HMS1&2", prices declined from January through end-February, then were essentially stable from March through mid-July, then declined again from mid-July through end-September, then rose from October through December. Prices in December 1998 were nevertheless considerably lower than in January 1998 in all categories. The IA's characterization that the trend in scrap prices as reported by Alexandria National Steel showed "sharp declines" in only three out of the twelve months of 1998, was essentially borne out by the data. Nevertheless, it is somewhat incomplete given the large end-point-to-end-point decline that took place over the period.

7.225 Turning to the evidence on scrap prices that was submitted by the Turkish respondents in questionnaire responses and other submissions, we note that in general these data also show considerable declines from the beginning to the end of the period of investigation, although again with a certain amount of fluctuation during that period. For example, the data reported by Icdas show that there was a sustained decrease in the scrap prices during the POI, with the month of August the only exception. The scrap price paid by Icdas for locally sourced and imported scrap decreased from US$129.44 in January 1998, to US$85.81 in November 1998.[203] In particular, the price dropped between January and March, was relatively steady in April through July, then rose slightly in August, and dropped again in September through November. The prices of scrap reported by IDC (sourced in Turkey) also reflect a decrease from US$134 in January 1998, to US$85 in December 1998[204]. However, these data show a substantial decrease in April, some recovery in May, June and July, and then a monthly decrease to December 1998.[205] The scrap cost data "sourced from Colakoglu"[206] also reflect a decrease in scrap prices in Turkish Lire over the POI, although with increases in different months compared with the data reported by Icdas and IDC. The overall trend is the same, however, namely that the price of scrap decreased from the beginning to the end of the POI.

7.226 Turning to the questions of labour costs and depreciation, the IA stated here again that the expected effects of hyperinflation were not evident, causing it to doubt the accuracy of these costs as reported in the responses to the original questionnaire, and leading it to seek additional information and supporting documentation in respect of these costs.

7.227 Turkey argues that the three respondents, Colakoglu, Diler and Habas "explained" in their 15 September submissions and elsewhere that labour con-

---

[202] Written Comments by Turkey on Egypt's Response to Certain *Questions Posed by the Panel*, dated 9 April 2002, Annex 8-3 – Annex 8-3.
[203] Exh. EGT-7.1.
[204] *Ibid.*
[205] *Ibid.*
[206] *Ibid.*

tracts are renegotiated once per year, and that depreciation expenses are adjusted at year-end for inflation, meaning that inflation would not be expected to cause these costs to vary from one month to another. According to Turkey, this "factual" information further undermines the IA's rationale for requesting the detailed cost information, as it "proves" that the effects of inflation on the three respondents' costs were not as presumed by the IA.

7.228 The parties also have divergent views concerning the general Turkish inflation rate during the POI. Throughout the process, the IA referred to an estimated inflation rate of 5 per cent per month in Turkey during that period,[207] which it said was derived from statistics sourced from the Turkish State Institute of Statistics.[208] In its comments on the *Essential Facts and Conclusions Report*, the Turkish Government objected to the use of an inflation rate of 5 per cent per month and submitted evidence (also from the Turkish State Institute of Statistics) showing that the inflation rate was less than 5 per cent per month during the POI.[209] The IA rejected the evidence and argument put forward by the Turkish Government, stating that: "[s]ince the referenced exhibit constitutes new, untimely information, the Department will not consider it in this investigation." Nevertheless, it should be noted that Turkey did not at the time and does not now contest the fact that the Turkish economy was "hyperinflationary" during the POI. Thus, there seems to be no disagreement between the parties that the actual monthly rate of inflation during the POI, whatever its exact level, was high. We thus see no basis on which to conclude, as contended by Turkey, that the factual evidence submitted by the Government of Turkey, even if it had been accepted, would have "disproved" the IA's hyperinflation premise for seeking the detailed cost data.

7.229 Further, in reference to inflation, the parties have submitted arguments concerning the significance of the fact that the Turkish respondents do not prepare their financial statements in accordance with International Accounting Standards 29 ("IAS 29"), applicable to economies with hyperinflation. This issue was not raised by Egypt during the investigation, although the audited financial statements of Habas, Diler and Colakoglu, which indicate that they do not apply IAS 29, were submitted by those companies in their 15 September submissions.[210] No direct reference to IAS 29 relating to Icdas and IDC could be found in the documents of record submitted to us.[211] Egypt argues that the auditors' reports support the view of the IA that the data submitted by the respondents did

---

[207] Letter of 19 August 1999 to the respondents, p.21 and 23 of the *Essential Facts and Conclusions Report*, and p.16 of the *Final Report*.
[208] Exh. EGT 7-7.
[209] Exh. TUR 30.
[210] Exh. TUR-34A, TUR-43B and TUR-34C, respectively.
[211] On page 56 of its First Written Submission, Egypt states that Icdas did not submit its audited accounts, although the IA did not request Icdas to submit its audited financial statements in its request of 19 August 1999, or in any subsequent requests. We could therefore not find any reference to IAS 29 with regard to Icdas in the record. In the case of IDC, we could not find any reference to IAS 29 in the translated sections of its audited financial statements, which were submitted by Egypt as Exh. EGT-15.

not reflect the effects of inflation[212]. However, the auditors' reports make clear in all instances that there was not consensus in Turkey on the use of IAS 29. The auditors' notes to the financial statements of two of the companies indicate that the accounts were prepared in US dollars which, being a stable currency, obviated the need to prepare the financial statements according to IAS 29. In any case, it seems to us that the main rationale behind IAS 29 (which requires presentation of three years of figures, together with certain indexes), is to give the reader a clear picture of the financial status of the company, *compared* to *previous* periods, undistorted by hyperinflation. It therefore seems that IAS 29 is primarily useful for comparison purposes.[213]

7.230 We are therefore of the view that the application, or non-application, of IAS 29 by the Turkish respondents in preparing their financial statements is not relevant for our review of the measures taken by the IA. That said, it seems to us that the reference to IAS 29 is a *post hoc* justification by Egypt in respect of the IA's request for cost data, a justification which is in any case not required by Article 2.2 and Article 2.2.1.

7.231 While, as is evident from the above, the parties have argued extensively before us concerning the IA's rationale for seeking the detailed cost data, in our view this question is essentially irrelevant under Article 6.8, because that provision simply does not cover this question. Rather, as noted above, the relevant provisions are Articles 2.2 and 2.2.1 These provisions establish no preconditions for requesting cost data. Indeed, in this case, cost data were requested as a normal, integral part of the initial questionnaire, and Turkey raises no challenge in this regard before us. Rather, Turkey objects to the rationale for requesting additional details and supporting documentation that would allow the originally-reported data to be checked and verified. Given that the IA's overall concern about how the effects of hyperinflation were treated in the five respondents' accounting records was not unsubstantiated (in that there was no disagreement that Turkey was experiencing hyperinflation), and in view of the fact that cost data is a normal part of an anti-dumping investigation, there is in our view no basis in Article 6.8 or for that matter in any other provision of the AD Agreement, for a finding of any violation in respect of the IA's request for the detailed information. In this sense, we confirm our finding above that the requested information was "necessary" in the sense of Article 6.8.

---

[212] In its Rebuttal Submission (at p. 29), Turkey objects to Egypt's arguments regarding IAS 29 as being a *post hoc* rationalisation by Egypt of the anti-dumping determination, and requests the Panel to disregard it, as "errors made during the investigation cannot be rectified in subsequent submission before a WTO panel". As the relevance of IAS 29 to this dispute is at best dubious, there would seem to be no need for the Panel to further address this point. (In any case, the information regarding IAS 29 was submitted by the respondents themselves and is used by Egypt only as confirmation of the IA's view that the cost data of the respondents did not reflect hyperinflation and is only an argument in support of its position. That said, Turkey does appear to be correct factually that IAS 29 did not figure in the IA's reasoning as set forth in its reports.)

[213] We posed a question to Egypt on this point (Question 3 for Egypt of the *Written Questions by the Panel*, dated 27 February 2002). Egypt, while confirming that IAS 29 is useful for comparison purposes, also indicated that it requires restatement of the current year figures adjusted for inflation, and thus is useful for reflecting inflation in a single year as well – Annex 8-2.

(c)   Did the Respondents "refuse access to" or "otherwise fail to provide" "necessary information"?

7.232 We now consider whether the facts of record indicate, as asserted by Egypt that the Turkish respondents Habas, Colakoglu and Diler "'refused access to'" the necessary information and "'failed to provide'" such information, and that the other two respondents (Icdas and IDC) "'otherwise failed to provide'" the necessary information.[214] Turkey asserts that it does not claim that the five respondents "submitted all of the information and documents requested by the Investigating Authority after the original questionnaire responses were filed". In fact, Turkey admits that these companies did not submit all the requested information and/or reconciliations.[215] However, Turkey asserts they acted "to the best of their ability" in providing the information.[216] With regard to Icdas and IDC, Turkey claims that "the Investigating Authority itself found little fault with the responses filed by the respondents, requesting only a few follow-up documents and clarifications, which were promptly provided".

7.233 In light of the facts as set out above, it is clear that a distinction can be made between the information, in terms of both amount and quality, submitted by Colakoglu, Diler and Habas, on the one hand, and Icdas and IDC on the other. We thus conduct our factual analysis on this basis.

(i)   Colakoglu, Diler and Habas

7.234 In reviewing the documentation submitted by Turkey as Exhibits TUR-34A, TUR-34B and TUR-34C, containing the full response of Diler, Colakoglu and Habas, respectively, to the IA's 19 August 1999 request for information, it is clear to us that a great deal of the requested information was not submitted. From the documents submitted by these three respondents, it appears that rather than submitting, or even attempting to submit, all of the information and documents requested by the IA, only selected information was submitted. In the case of Colakoglu and Habas, for example, Appendix 9A – Factory Cost and Profit for Domestic Sales, the sales price ex-factory and profit/loss before tax were not provided. In the case of Diler, only information on direct material, direct labor and factory overhead, but not the breakdown, as requested, was submitted. Of particular note, and emphasized by the IA in its reports, these companies did not submit underlying source documents (purchase orders, invoices, etc.).

7.235 Furthermore, very few of the headings of the submitted documents were translated and no reconciliation of the different cost elements to the audited financial statements were submitted. To clarify the exact situation concerning the requested reconciliations, we posed the following written question to Turkey:

---

[214] Written Response, dated 7 December 2001, to Question 9 to Egypt of the *Written Questions by the Panel*, of 28 November 2001 – Annex 4-2.
[215] *Ibid.*
[216] Written Response of Turkey, dated 14 March 2002, to Question 1 of the *Written Questions by the Pane*, of 27 February 2002 – Annex 8-1.

> "Turkey asserts that the respondents submitted all the requested information and documents, including the requested reconciliations of data to the financial statements. Could Turkey indicate for each of the respondent companies (Habas, Diler, Colakoglu, IDC and Icdas) where in the record these reconciliation could be found and for each one explain exactly, in a step-by-step fashion, how the reconciliations were done?"[217]

7.236 In response to this question, Turkey submitted a detailed step-by-step explanation of how the reconciliations *could* be done for each of the producers[218]. However, Turkey failed to indicate *where in the record* any such reconciliations could be found in the case of Colakoglu, Diler and Habas. It is thus clear that the reconciliations were not submitted to the IA.

7.237 Instead, the three Turkish producers submitted the raw data as is, without any explanatory narrative or translations, in spite of the IA's clear request. We are of the view that the request to translate the documents did not put an unreasonable burden on the exporters, as the narrative parts of the documents were quite limited. Furthermore, the translations could have been provided in handwritten form on the documents themselves without extraordinary effort.

7.238 The extent of the deficiencies of the responses of these three producers is evident from the follow-up requests sent by the IA to Colakoglu, Diler and Habas on 23 September 1999.[219] Then, in response to the IA's request of 23 September 1999, the three respondents made no attempt to provide the information identified as missing. Instead they claimed that that information constituted a "new" request (not previously made) to provide a break-down of the companies' billet costs into a number of separate components.[220] However, a close reading of the requests of 19 August and 23 September 1999 shows that the request of 23 September 1999, which attached a list of the cost components for which information was required, was a follow-up request to the 15 September submissions of these respondents, requesting for a second time the details underlying the originally reported costs, including documentation of raw material *purchases*. The fact that this list was attached only to the 23 September 1999 request does not detract from the fact that the very same information, albeit in a less explicit manner, had already been requested in the 19 August letter.

7.239 We next consider Turkey's claim that although these three respondents did not submit all of the information requested by the IA, they "acted to the best of their ability" in the sense of Annex II, paragraph 5, and that therefore the IA's resort to facts available was not justified. Turkey thus appears to argue that the fact of acting to the best of one's ability should override any substantive flaws in

---

[217] Question 1 to Turkey of the *Written Questions by the Panel*, dated 27 February 2002 – Annex 8-1.

[218] Written Response to Question 1 to Turkey, dated 14 March 2002, of the *Written Questions by the Panel*, of 27 February 2002 – Annex 8-1.

[219] Exh. TUR-13.

[220] First Written Submission of Turkey, p.68.

the information submitted, in determining whether resort to facts available is justified under Article 6.8.

7.240 Egypt argues that these respondents did not supply the requested information and did not act to the "best of their ability". Therefore, Egypt argues, the IA's resort to facts available in respect of these respondents was fully justified. In particular, Egypt states, these exporters explicitly informed the Investigating Authority that they refused to submit the information requested in the Investigating Authority's letter of 23 September 1999 which requested them to fill the gaps of their previous submission, thus effectively terminating their co-operation with the IA on that date. It is clear to Egypt that those respondents cannot therefore be considered to have acted to the best of their ability since they declined to submit information which was readily available to them. Egypt states in this regard that the evidence which Diler, Habas and Colakoglu refused to submit was provided by the two other respondents within the time-limit set by the Investigating Authority, confirming that the requested documentation could have been submitted by Diler, Habas and Colakoglu had they agreed to do so. In consequence, Egypt considers, the IA was fully entitled to make use of the provisions of Article 6.8 of the AD Agreement with respect to these respondents as they refused to provide necessary information and, as a consequence, significantly impeded the investigation.

7.241 Paragraph 5 of Annex II provides, in relevant part:

> "[E]ven though information provided may not be ideal in all respects, this should not justify the authorities from disregarding it, *provided the interested party has acted to the best of its ability.*" (emphasis added)

7.242 We recall that our finding above that the provisions of Annex II, paragraph 5 form part of the substantive basis for interpreting Article 6.8. That is, we found that this paragraph *in conjunction with* other paragraphs of Annex II provides certain substantive parameters that must be followed by an investigating authority in making its assessment of whether, in a particular case, resort to "facts available" pursuant to Article 6.8, in respect of certain elements of information, is justified. In other words, paragraph 5 does not exist in isolation, either from other paragraphs of Annex II, or from Article 6.8 itself. Nor, *a fortiori*, does the phrase "acted to the best of its ability". In particular, even if, with the best possible intentions, an interested party has acted to the very best of its ability in seeking to comply with an investigating authority's requests for information, that fact, by itself, would not preclude the investigating authority from resorting to facts available in respect of the requested information. This is because an interested party's level of effort to submit certain information does not necessarily have anything to do with the substantive *quality* of the information submitted, and in any case is not the *only* determinant thereof. We recall that the Appellate Body, in *US – Hot-Rolled Steel*, recognized this principle (although in a slightly different context), stating that "parties may very well 'cooperate' to a high degree, even though the requested information is, ultimately, not obtained.

This is because the fact of 'cooperating' is in itself not determinative of the end result of the cooperation".[221]

7.243 Furthermore, even if, *arguendo,* acting to the best of one's ability by itself were sufficient to preclude an investigating authority from resorting to facts available in respect of certain information, we do not find that Turkey has established as a *factual* matter that the three respondents – Habas, Diler, and Colakoglu – did act to *the best* of their abilities in responding to the IA's requests for cost-related information in the rebar investigation. We recall that the Appellate Body stated that the phrase "to the best of its ability" suggests a *high* degree of cooperation by interested parties[222], and we agree.

7.244 Considering in more detail the concrete meaning of the phrase to the "best" of an interested party's ability, we note that the *Concise Oxford Dictionary* defines the expression "to the best of one's ability" as "to the *highest level* of one's *capacity* to do something"[223] (emphasis added). In similar vein, the *Shorter Oxford Dictionary* defines this phrase as "to the *furthest extent* of one's *ability*; so far as one can do". We note that in a legal context, the concept of "best endeavours", is often juxtaposed with the concept of "reasonable endeavours" in defining the degree of effort a party is expected to exert. In that context, "best endeavours" connotes efforts going beyond those that would be considered "reasonable" in the circumstances. We are of the opinion that the phrase the "best" of a party's ability in paragraph 5 connotes a similarly high level of effort. [224]

7.245 In applying this test to the actions of Diler, Habas and Colakoglu in responding to the IA's requests for cost information in the rebar investigation, in our view an unbiased and objective investigating authority could find that it *was* within the capacity of these respondents to submit the requested information (particularly the supporting documentation substantiating the reported costs, and the reconciliations of those costs to financial statements). The information undeniably was at their disposal, and they never argued, or submitted, that it was not, or that for some other reason it would be impossible to provide it, or even that it would cause them some hardship to do so. The fact that other respondents provided most, if not all, of the requested information (particularly concerning scrap costs) also indicates that provision of such information was within the three respondents' ability.

7.246 Indeed, these points were made by the IA in the *Final Report.* For example, concerning scrap, the IA stated:

---

[221] Appellate Body Report, *US – Hot-Rolled Steel,* para.99.

[222] *Ibid,* para.100. The Appellate Body further noted in this paragraph that "investigating authorities are entitled to expect a very significant degree of effort – to the 'best of their abilities' – from investigated exporters.

[223] Pages 3 and 128 of *The Concise Oxford Dictionary* (10th ed).

[224] Black's Law Dictionary, Revised 4th Edition, defines "best" as, inter alia: "of the highest quality", and states further that "[w]here one covenants to use his 'best endeavours,' there is no breach if he is prevented by causes wholly beyond his control and without any default on his part [reference omitted]". "Reasonable" is defined, *inter alia,* as "ordinary or usual".

"[t]hese three respondents refused to provide any such evidence of the cost of scrap, or, in fact, of any other materials. *The fact that other respondents supplied such information indicates that the materials are readily available; indeed, these respondents do not contend otherwise.*"[225]

Similarly, concerning labour cost, the IA stated:

"As another example, the Investigating Authority requested that the respondents reconcile reported labor costs with the companies' financial statements. None of these respondents supplied the requested *reconciliation or explained why such reconciliation could not be provided.* Similarly, the Investigating Authority requested that the respondents reconcile monthly sales amounts to the companies' financial statements. Once again, neither the *data nor an adequate explanation was provided by these companies.*"[226]

7.247 To summarize, we are of the view that the nature and extent of the deficiencies identified in the IA's 23 September letter, none of which any of the three respondents attempted to rectify, were such that the IA was justified in considering that information "necessary" to make an analysis of whether domestic sales were made below cost, as provided for in Article 2.2 and 2.2.1 of the AD Agreement, had not been provided. That is, the information submitted was substantially incomplete, lacking in particular underlying documentation and reconciliations to audited financial statements which the IA had identified as the information required to render "verifiable" the respondents' reported cost data. Moreover, in addition to the substantive flaws in the information, we do not find that these companies acted to the best of their ability in responding to the IA's requests of 19 August and 23 September, 1999.

7.248 For the foregoing reasons, we find that an unbiased and objective investigating authority could have found that Habas, Diler and Colakoglu failed to provide necessary information in the sense of Article 6.8. As a consequence, we find that Egypt did not violate Article 6.8 or paragraph 5 of Annex II in resorting to facts available in respect of these respondents' cost of production calculations.

(ii)   Icdas and IDC

7.249 In the case of Icdas and IDC it is clear from the record that these companies submitted almost all, if not all, of the requested information. Nor did the IA clearly indicate in the Essential Facts and Conclusions Report which specific information these companies had failed to provide, which in turn formed the basis of the IA's decision to resort to facts available in respect of those companies. Indeed, in respect of IDC, neither the *Essential Facts and Conclusions Report* nor the *Final Report* identifies any single piece of requested information that was not submitted.

---

[225] Exh. TUR-16, para.3.2.1.4 (emphasis added).
[226] Exh. TUR-16, para.3.2.1.5 (emphasis added).

7.250 To clarify this issue in respect of Icdas, we posed the following written question to Egypt:

> "… . Could Egypt please precisely identify the documents containing the IA's requests for the information referred to in the Final Report as not having been submitted. Please describe the documents that were provided by Icdas on these points and indicate how, in the light of those documents, the IA was satisfied that AD Article 6.8 could be applied".[227]

7.251 Although Egypt pointed out certain deficiencies in the information submitted by Icdas in response to our question, Egypt failed to identify the documents containing the IA's requests for the information referred to in the Final Report as not having been submitted.[228] In other words, the IA apparently never requested of Icdas the documents referred to in the Final Report as missing.

7.252 Moreover, looking at the evidence overall as submitted by Icdas and IDC, it is clear to us that these two producers responded quite comprehensively to the IA's 19 August 1999 request. It is also clear from the record that after receipt of these companies' responses, the IA on 23 September requested from each of them only two or three items of a minor nature, and identified no fundamental problems with, or deficiencies in, the information that they had submitted. These respondents complied with these follow-up requests within the time specified by the IA. In respect of IDC, neither of the IA's published reports identifies any single requested document or piece of information that IDC failed to submit. In respect of Icdas, while the published reports refer to a few documents purportedly not submitted by Icdas, that company was never so informed by the IA.

7.253 This brings us to a further related element of Turkey's claims in respect of the use of facts available for Icdas and IDC, namely, that in resorting to facts available, Egypt violated Annex II, paragraph 6, in that the IA failed to inform these companies that their cost information submitted in response to the 19 August and 23 September requests was not accepted, and that the IA in addition failed to give them the opportunity to provide further explanations.

7.254 To recall the facts, on 23 September 1999, the IA sent letters to respondents IDC and Icdas identifying for each company a few items which according to the IA had not been submitted in these companies' responses to the 19 August questionnaire. According to Turkey, these companies submitted the requested information within the time allowed. Neither company received any further communication from the IA. These respondents' cost data as submitted were rejected by the IA, and certain "facts available" were used instead.

7.255 Egypt argues that in their responses to the 19 August request, these respondents had indicated that their costs of materials were not adjusted for inflation, and that IDC's response did not indicate that the financial statements had

---

[227] *Written Questions by the Panel* to the Parties, 27 February 2002, Question 8 to Egypt – Annex 8-2.

[228] Written Response of Egypt, dated 13 March 2002, to Question 8 of the *Written Questions by the Panel,* of 27 February 2002 – Annex 8-2.

been prepared in accordance with International Accounting Standard 29 dealing with the effects of hyperinflation. According to Egypt, it was therefore clear to the IA that the reported costs did not reflect the hyperinflation and could therefore not be used to determine the costs of production and sale of rebar, and given this, it was not necessary to further investigate this matter. According to Egypt, the IA gave IDC and Icdas ample opportunity to present their views in writing, and the IA therefore acted in full compliance with Annex II, paragraph 6.

7.256 Annex II, paragraph 6 provides as follows:

> "If evidence or information is not accepted, the supplying party should be informed forthwith of the reasons therefor, and should have an opportunity to provide further explanations within a reasonable period, due account being taken of the time-limits of the investigation. If the explanations are considered by the authorities as not being satisfactory, the reasons for the rejection of such evidence or information should be given in any published determinations."

7.257 At issue is first, whether the IA was under an obligation to inform IDC and Icdas that their evidence and information submitted in response to the 19 August request was being rejected and to give them an opportunity to provide further explanations, and second, if so, whether the IA did so.

7.258 Turning to the first aspect, we note that the applicability of this obligation to the responses to the 19 August request is somewhat ambiguous. In particular, it is clear on its face that the 19 August request itself is a communication of the type referred to in Annex II, paragraph 6, at least in so far as the original questionnaire responses on cost were concerned. That is, in that letter as sent to each respondent, the IA identified various problems that it perceived in the cost data originally reported by that respondent in its questionnaire response, indicated that the IA intended to adjust those data for hyperinflation, and then gave the respondent the chance to provide further information on cost of production if it wished to avoid the IA's performing the mentioned inflation adjustment. Thus, the 19 August request informed the respondents that their information was being rejected and provided them an opportunity to submit further explanations, as well as certain additional information.

7.259 The question is then whether the IA, having in the 19 August request informed respondents of its intention to reject their previously-submitted cost information and provided an opportunity for, *inter alia,* further explanations in respect of that information, was under a new obligation to take these steps again in respect of the responses to the 19 August letter. Put another way, was it sufficient at that point for the IA to simply explain in the *Final Report*, in accordance with the last sentence of Annex II, paragraph 6, why Icdas' and IDC's responses to the 19 August request were rejected?

7.260 Here again we believe that this issue can only be decided in the light of the particular situation at the time. While we have concluded in Section VII.D.5, *infra,* that the 19 August request was not a questionnaire in the sense of Article

6.1.1, there is nevertheless no doubt that it was a request *by the IA* for the provision of a great deal of detailed information. The responses to it by IDC and Icdas were quite lengthy, and contained many pages of accounting and other documentation. The IA's 23 September letters following up on these responses identified no fundamental problems in them, but rather identified a few apparently minor missing items that were to be (and were) submitted within two to five days.

7.261 Given the nature of the 19 August communication and of these companies' responses thereto, in our view the IA continued to be bound by the obligation to inform the respondents that their information submitted in response to the 19 August request was being rejected and to give them a final opportunity to explain. For us, the determinative factor in this regard is that the 19 August letter not only gave respondents the opportunity to provide *explanations* concerning their originally-submitted cost data, it also requested them to submit extensive further *information*, which they in fact did. Because the 19 August request was a request for "information" as referred to in Annex II, paragraph 6 (and not just an opportunity for explanation), and because IDC and Icdas provided extensive "information" in response to it, the IA was bound by the first sentence of Annex II, paragraph 6 in respect of that "information". Thus, these companies should have been informed that their responses to the 19 August request were being rejected, and given an opportunity to "provide further explanations". This did not happen. On 23 September, these companies were simply requested to provide a few missing pieces of information, and thus certainly were left with the impression that their responses to the 19 August requests had been accepted by the IA.

7.262 We must emphasize in this connection that it was the IA itself that requested the information at issue (i.e., the information submitted in response to the 19 August letters). As we have found above, it is within the discretion of an investigating authority to determine, subject to the requirements of Annex II, paragraph 1, what information it needs from interested parties. Furthermore, there is nothing in the AD Agreement that precludes an investigating authority from requesting information during the course of an investigation, including after the questionnaire responses have been received.[229] The fact that an investigating authority may request information in several tranches during an investigation cannot, however, relieve of it of its Annex II, paragraph 6 obligations in respect of the second and later tranches, as that requirement applies to "information and evidence" without temporal qualification.[230]

7.263 We note that, at least in respect of Habas, Diler and Colakoglu, the IA itself apparently considered that it had the obligation to explicitly indicate that

---

[229] *See* para. 7.320, *infra*.

[230] We do not mean to imply here that an interested party can impose on an investigating authority an Annex II, para. 6 requirement simply by submitting new information *sua sponte* during an investigation. Rather, the role of para. 6 of Annex II, namely that it forms part of the basis for an eventual decision pursuant to Article 6.8 whether or not to use facts available, makes it clear that its requirements to inform interested parties that information is being rejected and to give them an opportunity to provide explanations, pertain to "necessary" information in the sense of Article 6.8. As discussed above, "necessary" information is left to the discretion of the investigating authority to specify, subject to certain requirements, notably those in Annex II, para. 1.

the information submitted in response to the 19 August request was being rejected. In particular, the 23 September letters identify, as discussed above, a number of very serious inadequacies in the responses of these companies and contain long lists of missing items that would need to be submitted within two to five days. Given these companies' reactions to the 23 September letter, in their own letter of 28 September to the IA, it is evident that they were in no doubt that the IA intended to reject the cost information they had submitted. Nevertheless, the IA sent these three companies one final letter, dated 28 September 1999[231], informing them that they had not fully responded in respect of six items[232], and that therefore the IA "will use other data provided by your clients which were satisfactory, but will use facts available for the above-mentioned items". No similar communication was ever sent to IDC or Icdas.

7.264 Finally, the IA gave no indication in the *Essential Facts and Conclusions Report* or in the *Final Report* that either Icdas and IDC had at any point failed to act to the best of its ability. To the contrary, the record shows that these companies responded on time and comprehensively to the 19 August request, and did so once again in response to the IA's 23 September follow-up requests.

7.265 To summarize in respect of Icdas and IDC, we have found that the IA in the 19 August request not only informed these respondents of problems with their originally-submitted cost data, but informed them of what information would be needed for their costs to be verifiable. Thus, in the 19 August letter, the IA established the standard for verifiability of the respondents' cost data. Icdas and IDC responded in a timely manner, and as evidenced by the narrow scope of the 23 September follow-up requests that they received, their responses also were largely complete. Furthermore, they supplied the further information requested on 23 September within the deadlines set by the IA. Thus, the record evidence indicates that as of their responses to the 23 September requests, these two respondents had submitted all of the information that the IA itself had defined as what was necessary to render their cost information "verifiable". There is no indication whatsoever that the IA considered either of these companies to have failed to act to the best of its ability. Nevertheless, the IA rejected the submitted cost information on the grounds that the IA still was not convinced that the cost data reflected hyperinflation – that is, in effect, it simply did not believe the costs reported by these companies, although the information they submitted complied fully with what the IA itself had defined as necessary to verify those costs. The IA failed to inform these companies that it was rejecting the information submitted in response to the 19 August and 23 September requests, and failed to give them an opportunity to provide further explanations.

7.266 For the foregoing reasons, we find that Egypt violated Article 6.8 and Annex II, paragraph 6, in respect of IDC and Icdas, because the IA, having identified to these respondents the information "necessary" to verify their cost data, and having received that information, nevertheless found that they had failed to

---

[231] Exh. EGT-13.6.
[232] Materials, labour, overhead, SG&A, interest expense, and detailed cost sheet.

provide "necessary information"; and further, did not inform these companies of this finding and did not give them an opportunity to provide further explanations.

4. Claim under Article 2.2.1.1, 2.2.2 and 2.4 Due to Alleged Unjustified Resort to Facts Available

7.267 Under this claim, Turkey cites Articles 2.2.1.1, 2.2.2 and 2.4 as being violated "because the IA was not justified in resorting to facts available". Article 2.2.1.1 requires that costs shall normally be calculated on the basis of records kept by the exporter or producer under investigation, provided such records are kept in accordance with generally accepted accounting principles of that country, and reasonably reflect the relevant costs. Article 2.2.2 deals with calculations of general, selling and administrative costs, and profits, and how these calculations should be done in the case of a constructed normal value. Turkey alleges that the methodologies set forth in those provisions were not followed by the IA. In response to a question from the Panel, Turkey clarified that this was an "alternative" claim to that under Article 6.8 and Annex II. In particular, Turkey stated that this claim was intended to avoid a situation where the Panel might find that even if resort to facts available had not been technically justified, the particular facts that were used could have been used, i.e., that only a harmless error had been committed.

7.268 Given Turkey's characterization and explanation of the rationale for this claim, we understand the claimed violations of Article 2.2.1.1 and Article 2.2.2 to be entirely subsidiary to the claimed Article 6.8 violation. In this regard, we recall that we have found that the IA was justified in resorting to facts available in respect of Habas, Diler and Colakoglu. This can only mean that the IA was justified to use facts *other than* those as submitted by the respondents, i.e, that Articles 2.2.1.1 and 2.2.2 do not apply. We also recall that we have found that the IA was not justified in resorting to facts available, in violation of Article 6.8 and Annex II, paragraph 6, as regards IDC and Icdas. For these two companies, we need not and do not reach the issue of which particular information of the respondents was not used. We therefore exercise judicial economy in respect of the claimed violations of Articles 2.2.1.1 and 2.2.2 in respect of all of the respondents.

7.269 Concerning its Article 2.4 claim in this context, Turkey argues that "[e]ven if there were some basis to conclude that respondents did not respond fully to the IA's 19 August or 23 September information requests, the respondents provided a full explanation of how their submitted costs and prices reflected inflation in Turkey and [ ] the IA's rejection of those well-founded reasons imposed an unreasonable burden of proof in violation of Article 2.4". As discussed in Section VII.E.2, *infra*, Article 2.4 has to do with the *comparison* of export price to normal value, and does not create a generally applicable rule as to burden of proof, and we thus find that Article 2.4 is not applicable to the IA's decision to resort to facts available. Furthermore, even if this provision were applicable, we have found elsewhere[233] that there is no basis in the evidence of record on which to conclude that the information requirements imposed by the IA in respect of costs were unreasonable. We therefore find that Turkey has not established that there is a violation of Article 2.4 under this claim.

5. *Claim under Article 6.1.1, Annex II, Paragraph 6, and Article 6.2 – Deadline for Response to 19 August 1999 Request*

7.270 Turkey argues that Article 6.1.1 requires that a party must be given 37 days to reply "after receiving a questionnaire used in an anti-dumping investigation[]" and that "due consideration" must then be given to any request for an extension of the original period for a response. According to Turkey, Egypt violated these provisions by first setting a 13-day rather than a 37-day deadline, and then by granting an inadequately short extension.

7.271 Turkey claims in the alternative that Egypt violated Annex II, paragraph 6, which provides that parties receiving supplemental request for information should be given "an opportunity to provide further explanations within a reasonable period ...", and Article 6.2 which provides that "[t]hroughout an anti-dumping investigation all interested parties shall have a full opportunity for the defence of their interests". In particular, Turkey argues that the original 13-day deadline was plainly inadequate given the nature and magnitude of the 19 August request, and was more so in light of the earthquake that had occurred in Turkey on 18 August. Turkey argues that the "denial" of the respondents' requests for extensions to 11 and 22 October thus violated Annex II, paragraph 6 and Article 6.2.

7.272 Egypt responds that the 19 August requests did not constitute "new questionnaires", in that they were, in the first place, not "new". Rather, according to Egypt, they re-requested information that already had been requested in the foreign manufacturers' and exporters' questionnaires, which normally should have been readily available to the respondents. Nor, Egypt argues, were they "questionnaires" in the sense of Article 6.1.1, meaning that they were not subject to the minimum response time requirements of that provision. Rather, they were intended to provide an additional opportunity for respondents to report cost data for the full period of investigation, and to clarify whether and to what extent the reported costs reflected the effects of hyperinflation. Egypt further argues that the respondents were given a reasonable period of time in which to respond, noting in particular the 14-day extension that was granted by the IA, a more than doubling of the initial 13-day period.

(a) Claim under Article 6.1.1

7.273 We consider first Turkey's allegation of violation of Article 6.1.1. Article 6.1.1 provides as follows:

---

[233] Section VII.E.2, *infra*.

"Exporters or foreign producers receiving questionnaires used in an anti-dumping investigation shall be given at least 30 days for reply. [15] Due consideration should be given to any request for an extension of the 30-day period and, upon cause shown, such an extension should be granted whenever practicable.

---

[15] As a general rule, the time-limit for exporters shall be counted from the date of receipt of the questionnaire, which for this purpose shall be deemed to have been received one week from the date on which it was sent to the respondent or transmitted to the appropriate diplomatic representative of the exporting Member or, in the case of a separate customs territory Member of the WTO, an official representative of the exporting territory."

7.274 We note first, as a point of clarification, that the time-limit requirement specified in Article 6.1.1 is 30 days, not 37 days. Moreover, footnote 15 provides that (only) in the case of questionnaires sent to exporters is it necessary to count the time-limit from date of receipt, which in turn is deemed (only) for exporters to be seven days from transmittal. In effect, therefore, Turkey's statement that Article 6.1.1 requires a minimum time-limit of 37 days from date of receipt, is not entirely accurate.

7.275 This, however, is not the central issue in this claim. Rather, this claim turns on whether the 19 August requests were "questionnaires" in the sense of Article 6.1.1, because only if so would any specific minimum time-limit (whether 30 or 37 days) apply. Put another way, the question is whether "questionnaires" as referred to in Article 6.1.1 are only the original questionnaires in an investigation, or whether this term also includes all other requests for information, or certain types of requests, including requests in addition and subsequent to original questionnaires.

7.276 The term "questionnaire" as used in Article 6.1.1 is not defined in the AD Agreement, and in fact, this term only appears in Article 6.1.1, and in paragraphs 6 and 7 of Annex I. In our view, the references in Annex I, paragraphs 6 and 7 provide strong contextual support for interpreting the term "questionnaires" in Article 6.1.1 as referring only to the original questionnaires sent to interested parties at the outset of an investigation. In particular, both of these provisions refer to "the questionnaire" in the singular, implying that there is only one document that constitutes a "questionnaire" in a dumping investigation, namely the initial questionnaire, at least as far as the foreign companies (producers and exporters) that might be visited are concerned. Paragraph 6 refers to visits by an investigating authority to the territory of an exporting Member "to explain *the questionnaire*". Paragraph 7 provides that "on-the-spot investigation ... should be carried out after the response to *the questionnaire* has been received..."

7.277 If any requests for information other than the initial questionnaire were to be considered "questionnaires" in the sense of Article 6.1.1, a number of operational and logistical problems would arise in respect of other obligations under the AD Agreement. First, there is no basis in the AD Agreement on which to determine that some, but not all, information requests other than the initial questionnaire also would constitute "questionnaires". Thus, even if an investigating authority was not obligated to provide the minimum time-period in Article 6.1.1 in respect of every request for information, it would not be able to determine from the Agreement which of its requests were and were not subject to that time-period. On the other hand, if all requests for information in an investigation were "questionnaires" in the sense of Article 6.1.1, this could make it impossible for an investigation to be completed within the maximum one year (or exceptionally, 18 months) allowed by the AD Agreement in Article 5.10. Moreover, a 30- or 37-day deadline for requests for information made in the context of an on-the-spot verification - i.e., the "obtain[ing of] further details" explicitly referred to in Article 6.7 to as one of the purposes of such verifications - obviously would be completely illogical as well as unworkable. Finally, such an interpretation would render superfluous the requirement in Annex II, paragraph 6 to allow a "reasonable period ..." for the provision of any explanations concerning identified deficiencies in submitted information.

7.278 Considering the substance of the 19 August requests, particularly in comparison to the original questionnaires, further persuades us that the 19 August requests did not constitute new "questionnaires" in the sense of Article 6.1.1. In particular, as we have noted[234], *supra*, while the questions posed are rather detailed, they are in the nature of follow-up questions to the original questionnaire responses, in that they request cost data for the months for which such data were not originally provided by certain respondents, and they request underlying documentation, reconciliations and explanations of the originally submitted cost data and of the additional cost data being requested.

7.279 For the foregoing reasons, we conclude that the 19 August requests did not constitute questionnaires in the sense of Article 6.1.1, and that therefore the deadline imposed for responses to those requests was not inconsistent with that Article.

(b)   Alternative Claim under Annex II, Paragraph 6 and Article 6.2

7.280 We now turn to Turkey's alternative claim in respect of the deadline for responses to the 19 August requests, that the time allowed did not constitute a "reasonable period", in violation of Annex II, paragraph 6, and that therefore the IA failed to provide the Turkish respondents a "full opportunity for the defence of [their] interests", in violation of Article 6.2.

7.281 Because the claimed violation of Article 6.2 is entirely dependent on the claimed violation of Annex II, paragraph 6, we turn first to Annex II, paragraph 6. We note that the relevant part of this provision reads as follows:

"If evidence or information is not accepted, the supplying party should be informed forthwith of the reasons therefor, and should

---

[234]   *See* para. 7.238, *supra.*

have an opportunity to provide further explanations within a reasonable period, *due account being taken of the time-limits of the investigation ... ."* (emphasis added)

7.282 This text makes clear that the obligation for an investigating authority to provide a reasonable period for the provision of further explanations is not open-ended or absolute. Rather, this obligation exists within the overall time constraints of the investigation. Thus, in determining a "reasonable period" an investigating authority must balance the need to provide an adequate period for the provision of the explanations referred to against the time constraints applicable to the various phases of the investigation and to the investigation as a whole.

7.283 We recall that in the rebar investigation, the IA initially set a 13-day deadline for any responses to the 19 August requests. After receiving the requests for extensions from the respondents, the IA extended by 14 days the time-period that was allowed for the responses.[235] After the IA informed the respondents of the extended deadline, no respondent came back with any additional request for more time, nor did any respondent argue that the new deadline was unreasonable or otherwise object to it. All of the respondents in fact made lengthy submissions in response to the 19 August request on or before the deadline.

7.284 On the basis of the foregoing considerations, we do not find that, as a factual matter, the deadline for responses to the 19 August request was unreasonable. We note that this claim concerns in part Annex II, paragraph 6 outside the context of Article 6.8. Given our finding that the deadline established was not unreasonable, i.e., that the factual basis for this claim does not exist, we need not and do not rule on whether Annex II, paragraph 6 can be invoked outside the context of Article 6.8. As a consequence, we also do not find that in establishing a 27-day deadline for the provision of these responses, the IA failed to provide the respondents with a full opportunity for the defence of their interests, and we thus find no violation of Article 6.2 in this respect.

6. *Claim under Article 6.1.1, Annex II, Paragraph 6, and Article 6.2 - Deadline for the Responses of Habas, Diler and Colakoglu to the 23 September Letter of the IA*

7.285 On 23 September, i.e., approximately one week after receiving the responses to the 19 August request, the IA sent letters to each respondent identifying information and documentation which, according to the IA, that particular respondent had "not yet furnished" in response to the 19 August request. The IA gave all of the respondents the same time-frame in which to furnish the identified information, namely 2 days for some of the listed items and 5 days for the rest.

7.286 Turkey claims that in the 23 September letter to Habas, Diler and Colakoglu, the IA for the first time required these companies to provide a monthly

---

[235] Exh. EGT-14.1(Icdas), EGT-14.2(IDC) and EGT-14.3(Diler, Colakoglu and Habas), respectively.

breakdown of all costs to produce billet, and also demanded that the companies translate each page of the hundreds of pages of documentation that they had been required to provide in their responses to the 19 August request. According to Turkey the two-to-five days allowed these three companies to respond to the 23 September letter was manifestly inadequate, and was contrary to Articles 6.1.1, 6.2 and Annex II, paragraph 6.

7.287 For the same reasons set forth in respect of the preceding claim, we do not find that the 23 September letters constituted "questionnaires" in the sense of Article 6.1.1, and thus we find no violation of that provision.

7.288 As for the claim of violation of the requirement in Annex II, paragraph 6 to provide a "reasonable period", we recall that this provision forms part of the required procedural and substantive basis for a decision as to whether resort to facts available pursuant to Article 6.8. We further recall that we have found, *supra*[236], that the IA's decision to resort to facts available in respect of Habas', Diler's and Colakoglu's costs of production and constructed normal values did not violate Article 6.8, based on considerations under Annex II, paragraphs 3 and 5. Thus, we would not necessarily need to address this aspect of this claim for its own sake. Nonetheless, a full analysis of Annex II, paragraph 6 as it pertains to the factual basis of this claim, appears necessary to evaluate the merits of the claimed violation of Article 6.2 resulting from the deadline for responses to the 23 September requests. In performing this analysis, however, we note that we again do not here take a position on whether Annex II, paragraph 6 can be invoked separately from Article 6.8. We would need to do so only if we find that as a factual matter, the deadline in question was unreasonable.

7.289 We thus turn first to this factual question, i.e., whether the two-to-five day deadline as it applied to Habas, Diler and Colakoglu was unreasonable. We believe that this issue must be judged on the basis of the overall factual situation that existed at the time. Here, it appears that the key element raised by Turkey is whether the information requested was "new" information that was being requested for the first time. In this regard, Turkey complains in particular about the IA's request for a monthly breakdown of costs to produce steel billet (the feedstock used in rebar production).

7.290 In considering whether this was an entirely new information request, we note that item 4 of the "list of supplemental materials" in the 19 August letters requested detailed listings of raw material "purchases" as well as copies of payment ledgers showing payments for those purchases, and copies of the underlying purchase orders. The main information provided by these companies in response to the request for data on raw material costs was their internal transfer price data for billet, a product they make themselves, rather than purchasing it as a raw material. Thus, the 23 September request for a monthly breakdown of the costs to produce steel billet, rather than constituting a new request for previously-unrequested information, in fact, was in essence a restatement of the request in the 19 August letters for data and documentation on raw material *pur-*

---

[236] Para. 7.248.

chases. The other items listed in the 23 September letter similarly were items previously requested. Thus we conclude that the 23 September request was a follow-up to the responses to the 19 August request rather than a new request.

7.291 A further consideration concerning the "reasonableness" of the 23 September request is whether any of the other respondents received a longer period in which to respond to the letters they received from the IA on 23 September. Here the answer is "no"; all respondents were given the same amount of time to respond to those letters. The fact that more information was requested in the letter to Habas, Diler and Colakoglu than in the letters to the other two respondents, IDC and Icdas, is a reflection of the fact that, according to the record, the latter two companies' responses to the 19 August request were much more complete than those of the first three companies. For the IA to have given Habas, Diler and Colakoglu more time than IDC and Icdas to respond to the 23 September follow-up request arguably would have been less than fair, and indeed would have rewarded precisely the companies whose responses to the 19 August request were the least adequate.

7.292 In this context it must be remembered that all five respondents received essentially equivalent information requests on 19 August, and were given an identical period in which to respond. All five respondents then again were given an identical period in which to respond to the 23 September follow-up (deficiency) requests. Thus, for equivalent requests for information, the five respondents received, in total, equivalent (and considerable) time-periods to respond. Thus, the two-to-five-day deadline for responses to the 23 September simply forms part of the overall time granted for responses to the basic request for cost information that was sent on 19 August. The three respondents mentioned in this claim chose to use their initial 27-day response period in a different way from the other two respondents. It was these decisions by the two groups of respondents (not by the IA) that fundamentally gave rise to the different scopes of the 23 September follow-ups that they respectively received.

7.293 We note further that in any case, Habas, Diler and Colakoglu never even attempted to submit any of the information identified in the 23 September letters or sought any extension of the deadline for responding. To the contrary, they made it clear in their response to the IA[237] that they had no intention of submitting further information.

7.294 The factual situation thus was: (1) that the 23 September letter was essentially a restatement of previous requests that had not been responded to in full, rather than a new request, (2) that all five respondents, including Habas, Diler and Colakoglu, received overall the same amount of time to provide the cost data specified in the 19 August request, and (3) that unlike Icdas and IDC, which had used the initial 27 day period to full advantage, these three respondents stated explicitly that they would not provide the information referred to in the 23 September request, (i.e., they made no attempt to comply with the request nor did they request an extension of the two-to-five day period).

---

[237] Exh. EGT-2.

7.295 As a consequence, we do not find that Turkey has established that the two-to-five day period provided to Habas, Diler and Colakoglu for responding to the 23 September request was unreasonable, and thus we do not find that Turkey has established the factual basis for a possible violation of Annex II, paragraph 6 in that regard. As a result, we also do not find that the IA failed to provide Habas, Diler and Colakoglu with a full opportunity for the defence of their interests, and thus find no violation of Article 6.2 in this respect.

7.	*Claim under Annex II, Paragraph 7 Due to the Addition of 5 per cent for Inflation to Habas' Highest Reported Monthly Costs*

7.296 Turkey claims that the Investigating Authority violated Annex II, paragraph 7 by adding an arbitrary 5 per cent to Habas' reported costs when constructing Habas' normal value. Habas submitted cost data for only two of the 12 months of the period of investigation. As a proxy for the effects of hyperinflation, the IA constructed Habas' normal value by using the highest (of the two reported) monthly costs for each cost element as submitted by Habas, and then added to these 5 per cent, the monthly rate of inflation considered by the Investigating Authority as reflecting the ruling rate of inflation during the period of investigation. Turkey claims that in doing this, Egypt violated Annex II, paragraph 7, as this amount which was based on a "secondary source", was wholly arbitrary, was contradicted by data supplied to Egypt by the Government of Turkey, was not corroborated by any other data on the record, and thus was an inappropriate basis for facts available under the AD Agreement.

7.297 Egypt argues that it determined the "facts available" in such a manner that the respondents would still benefit from their own data, by taking the highest monthly cost of production reported by the respondents during the investigation period. In the case of Habas, because Habas had provided costs for two selected months only, and had failed to submit satisfactory evidence that these two months were representative of the period of investigation or had been adjusted for inflation, the IA added 5 per cent to each cost element except interest to account for inflation. For interest, no adjustment was made to the data reported by Habas, as it was found that Habas's interest cost was determined in the marketplace and therefore would reflect inflation. According to Egypt, the IA would have been entitled to reject entirely the reported cost data, and base its determinations on information from secondary sources, as explicitly contemplated by Annex II, paragraph 7, but instead it decided to use the respondents' submitted data to the extent possible.

7.298 Paragraph 7 of Annex II states, in relevant part:

"If the authorities have to base their findings, including those with respect to normal value, on information from a secondary source, including the information supplied in the application for the initiation of the investigation, they should do so with special circumspection. In such cases, the authorities should, where practicable,

check the information from other independent sources at their disposal, such as published price lists, official import statistics and
customs returns and from the information obtained from other interested parties during the investigation. ... ."

7.299 Concerning the "facts available" used in the case of Habas, the IA stated
in its *Final Report*:[238]

"The Investigating Authority first attempted to compare the net
home market to the cost of production. Although the Investigating
Authority twice requested full costs of production for the entire
POI, the company only provided costs for two selected months,
and there is no evidence on the record that these were representative of the period. Therefore, as facts available for the COP, the
Investigating Authority used for each cost element (except interest) the highest of the company's submitted costs and added 5 per
cent to account for inflation during the period of each month."

7.300 We understand that the main issue raised by this claim is the factual validity and accuracy of the estimated 5 per cent for inflation that was used in the cost
of production and constructed value calculations for Habas. In particular, Turkey
argues that the official statistics published by the Government of Turkey show a
lower monthly average rate of inflation, in that in only two months of 1998 did
inflation exceed 5 per cent, fluctuating in the other months between 1.6 and 4.6
per cent.[239] This issue was raised during the investigation, namely in the comments of the Government of Turkey on the *Essential Facts and Conclusions Report*. Along with these comments, the Turkish Government, provided wholesale
price index data published by the Turkish State Institute of Statistics. In its *Final
Report*, the IA indicated that it had rejected the inflation information submitted
by the Turkish Government as "new" and "untimely"[240], and stated that it was
continuing to apply the estimated 5 per cent inflation rate on the basis that it had
other information at its disposal that showed an even higher monthly rate.

7.301 We requested Egypt to submit to us the information on inflation the IA
had referred to in the *Final Report*,[241] and to explain how the IA had arrived at
the 5 per cent figure based on the data at its disposal.[242] Egypt replied that it had
used the same data source as that submitted by the Turkish Government (i.e., the
price indices published by the Turkish State Institute of Statistics), but that the
5 per cent rate was the average of the official wholesale and consumer price indices during the period of investigation, whereas the Turkish Government had referred in its comments only to the wholesale price index.

---

[238] Exh.TUR-16, para.3.2.2.1.
[239] Written Response, dated 15 October 1999, of the Government of Turkey on the *Essential Facts
and Conclusions Report*, submitted by Turkey as Exh. TUR-30, p.2.
[240] Exh. TUR-16, *Final Report*, p.21.
[241] Question 10 to Egypt of the *Written Questions by the Panel*, dated 28 November 2001 – Annex
4-2.
[242] Question 4 to Egypt of *the Written Questions by the Panel*, dated 27 February 2002 - Annex.8-2.

7.302 We recall that the claim before the Panel is that the addition of 5 per cent to Habas' costs was arbitrary, finds no support anywhere in the record and, as information from a "secondary source", should have been used with "special circumspection", and in particular, should have been "check[ed] ... from other independent sources at [the IA's] disposal". Turkey also argues that under the AD Agreement, if data from a company cannot be used, they must be replaced with data from a secondary source. According to Turkey, there is no authority in the AD Agreement to make purely arbitrary adjustments to a respondent's costs. Turkey cites no provision of the AD Agreement in this context, however.

7.303 In considering this claim, we note that the 5 per cent figure was derived from a secondary source, in fact the same secondary source as was proffered by the Government of Turkey during the investigation. Thus, the source of the information as such is not at issue. Given this, there was no need for the IA to check the validity of that source. Rather, the only issue is whether the 5 per cent figure that was derived from that source was calculated and used with "special circumspection". In this regard, the relevant fact is that the 5 per cent figure represents an average of the 1998 wholesale and consumer price indices for Turkey.

7.304 Turkey asserted during this dispute that a consumer price index is "irrelevant" to rebar.[243] Turkey offered no specific argumentation or information in support of this point, however. We note that in its communications with respondents during the investigation concerning the effects on the respondents of hyperinflation in Turkey, the IA appears to have been referring to the general, economy-wide rate of inflation. It is not illogical that such a broad measure of inflation should reflect both wholesale and consumer prices. Nor is it illogical that a company's cost to produce a product would be influenced by both consumer and wholesale prices. In short, to us it is not evident on its face that consumer prices would be wholly irrelevant to a company's production costs. Nor has Turkey advanced any argumentation or evidence to demonstrate that this is so, either as a matter of general principle or in respect of the companies that were respondents in the rebar investigation.

7.305 For these reasons, we do not find that the IA failed to use "special circumspection" in estimating inflation in Turkey at 5 per cent per month, and in applying this figure to Habas. We thus do not find that Egypt violated Annex II, paragraph 7 in this regard. We find, rather, that on the basis of the evidence of record, an objective and unbiased investigating authority could have reached the conclusion that 5 per cent was the approximate average monthly inflation rate in Turkey during the period of investigation. In this regard, it should be emphasized that applying "special circumspection" does not mean that only one outcome is possible on a given point in an investigation. Rather, even while using special circumspection, an investigating authority may have a number of equally credible options in respect of a given question. In our view, when no bias or lack of

---

[243] Written Comments, dated 14 March 2002, by Turkey on Question 4 to Egypt of the *Written Questions by the Panel*, of 27 February 2002 – Annex 8-1.

objectivity is identified in respect of the option selected by an investigating authority, the option preferred by the complaining Member cannot be preferred by a panel.

8.   *Claim under Annex II, Paragraphs 3 and 7 Due to Failure to Use Icdas' September-October 1998 Scrap Costs*

7.306 Turkey claims that in constructing Icdas normal value on the basis of facts available, the IA declined to use the scrap costs as reported by Icdas for September-October 1998 (the months in which it exported to Egypt), and instead used Icdas' January 1998 scrap cost (the highest in the period of investigation). Because, according to Turkey, Icdas had provided all of the requested data and documentation concerning its scrap costs in a timely manner and these data were "verified" (clarified by Turkey to mean "verifiable"[244]), the IA should have used those scrap costs as submitted. Its failure to do so, Turkey argues, was a violation of Annex II, paragraph 3. In addition, Turkey argues that the IA violated the spirit, if not the letter, of paragraph 7 of Annex II, in that a comparison with the "verified" data submitted by Icdas shows that the scrap cost data used by the IA in its calculations were "grossly distorted".

7.307 Egypt argues that Turkey's invocation of Annex II, paragraph 3 is misplaced. In Egypt's view, this provision is only concerned with the circumstances in which the data submitted by the respondents have to be accepted or can be rejected, and says nothing about the selection of appropriate facts available once the data submitted by respondents has been rejected.

7.308 Paragraph 3 of Annex II states, in relevant part:

> "All information which is verifiable, which is appropriately submitted so that it can be used in the investigation without undue difficulties, ..., should be taken into account when determinations are made. ... ."

7.309 We recall that in our assessment of Turkey's claim that Egypt violated Article 6.8 in resorting to the use of "facts available", we found that the provisions of Annex II, paragraph 3 form part of the substantive parameters for the interpretation of Article 6.8. That is, we found that this paragraph *in conjunction with* other paragraphs of Annex II must be followed by an investigating authority in making its assessment of whether, in a particular case and in respect of certain elements of information, it is justified in resorting to "facts available" pursuant to Article 6.8. In other words, paragraph 3 applies to an IA's decision to use "facts available" in respect of certain elements of information. It does not have to do with determining which particular facts available will be used for those elements of information once that decision has been made. Thus, we find that this provision does not apply to the situation that is the subject of this claim. This said, we

---

[244] Written Response, dated 14 March 2002, to Question 4 to Turkey of the *Written Questions by the Panel*, of 27 February 2002 – Annex 8-1.

recall that we have found, *supra*, in part based on an analysis of Annex II, paragraph 3, that the IA was not justified in resorting to facts available in respect of Icdas. We thus do not need to address this claim further.

7.310 Turning to Turkey's claim of violation of Annex II, paragraph 7, given that we have found, in the context of Turkey's Article 6.8 claim, that the IA's resort to "facts available" in respect of Icdas was not justified, we do not need to address this claim, which concerns the selection of particular facts available.

9.   Claim under Annex II, Paragraphs 3 and 7 Due to Calculation of the Highest Monthly Interest Cost for IDC

7.311 Turkey claims that the IA violated Annex II, paragraph 3 in calculating the amount of interest expense to use as facts available in constructing IDC's normal value. In particular, according to Turkey, the IA calculated the interest expense by dividing IDC's total interest expense by rebar production in April 1998. Turkey states that because IDC produces and sells on the market other products (namely billets), and because the April rebar production figures were abnormally low, the result was a distorted, very high, interest component, which overstated the constructed normal value. Turkey argues that the IA should have divided total interest cost by total sales during the period of investigation, based on the audited financial statement, instead of choosing the month with the highest interest cost and dividing that cost by that month's rebar production, which was abnormally low. According to Turkey, IDC's audited financial statement shows that its interest expense expressed as a percentage of the total cost of manufacturing would be much lower. Because the IA failed to use verifiable information (the interest expense as reflected in the audited financial statement), in Turkey's view, the IA violated Annex II, paragraph 3.[245]

7.312 Egypt responds that there are no requirements in the AD Agreement for any particular methodology for calculating interest expense for a constructed value, and that therefore, provided that the methodology used is not partial or biased, the IA's calculation should be upheld. Moreover, Egypt disagrees with the calculation methodology proposed by Turkey, which in Egypt's view would have been totally inappropriate in the context of the rebar investigation, as IDC's reported costs had been found to be unreliable.[246] Egypt argues, having selected April as the appropriate month for calculation of interest expense, it had to use the production for that month as the denominator, as any other choice for allocation would have been arbitrary.

7.313 Concerning Turkey's claim of violation of Annex II, paragraph 3, we find, for the same reasons as stated in Section VII.D.8, *supra*, that this provision does not apply to the situation that is the subject of this claim, and we similarly recall our findings, *supra*, in part based on an analysis of Annex II, paragraph 3, that

---

[245] First Written Submission of Turkey, p.74-76 and Second Written Submission of Turkey, p.77-82.
[246] First Written Submission of Egypt, p.87-88.

the IA was not justified in resorting to facts available in respect of IDC. We thus do not consider this claim further.

7.314 Concerning Turkey's claim of violation of Annex II, paragraph 7, as was the case in respect of the claim concerning Icdas discussed in Section VII.D.8, *supra*, Turkey's exact claim is that Egypt violated the "considerations underlying Annex II, paragraph 7", i.e., once again, that this provision was violated "in spirit". In our view, the factual situation about which Turkey complains in respect of IDC is precisely analogous to that raised in respect of Icdas under the same provision. Our basic reasoning and conclusions therefore are the same.

7.315 In particular, given that we have found, in the context of Turkey's Article 6.8 claim, that the IA's resort to "facts available" in respect of IDC was not justified, we do not need to address this claim, which concerns the selection of particular facts available.

E. Other Claims Relating to the Dumping Investigation

1. Claim under Annex II, Paragraph 1; Annex II, Paragraph 6; and Article 6.7, Annex I, Paragraph 7 – Alleged Failure to Verify the Cost Data During the "on-the-spot" Verification, and Conduct of "mail order" Verification Instead

7.316 Turkey claims that by failing to request the basic cost data identified in its 19 August letter in its original questionnaire, the IA violated Annex II, paragraph 1. Turkey further claims that by waiting until after the verification to raise these issues and then insisting that respondents provide full "mail order" verification of previously-submitted cost responses and the information requested on 19 August, Egypt violated Annex I, paragraph 7 and Article 6.7. According to Turkey, by taking these steps, Egypt also seriously prejudiced the rights of respondents and impaired their "opportunity to provide further explanations" in violation of Annex II, paragraph 6.

7.317 Egypt argues that the AD Agreement permits, but does not require, on-the-spot verification. Egypt further argues that the IA did request cost data from the outset, in the questionnaires, that the additional data was requested by the IA on 19 August due to possible problems in the cost data as originally reported by the Turkish respondents, and that nothing in the AD Agreement prevents an investigating authority from seeking information during the course of an investigation.

7.318 Turning first to the claim of violation of Annex II, paragraph 1, we note that the relevant text of this provision reads as follows:

> "As soon as possible after the initiation of the investigation the investigating authorities should specify in detail the information required from any interested party, and the manner in which that information should be structured by the interested party in its response."

7.319 We recall that in the context of Article 6.8, we found that the various provisions of Annex II contain substantive parameters for the application of Article 6.8.

7.320 In the rebar investigation, the IA sent questionnaires to the Turkish respondents shortly after initiating the investigation, and these questionnaires did request cost information. Furthermore, the import of the 19 August letter was to request certain supplemental cost information as well as explanations concerning certain of the cost information originally submitted in response to the questionnaires. We find no basis on which to conclude that an investigating authority is precluded by paragraph 1 of Annex II or by any other provision from seeking additional information during the course of an investigation.

7.321 We note that this claim concerns in part Annex II, paragraph 1 outside the context of Article 6.8. Given our finding that Annex II, paragraph 1 does not contain the obligation asserted by Turkey, we need not and do not rule on whether Annex II, paragraph 1, can be invoked separately from Article 6.8.

7.322 We turn next to Turkey's claim that Egypt violated Article 6.7 and Annex I, paragraph 7 by waiting until after the on-the-spot verification to raise the cost issues in the 19 August letters, and then by attempting to conduct what Turkey refers to as a "mail order" verification. In evaluating this claim we note that it depends on an interpretation of Article 6.7 and Annex I, paragraph 7 as *requiring* an on-the-spot verification. We thus consider these provisions in detail to determine whether they contain any such requirements.

7.323 Article 6.7 reads in relevant part as follows:

> "In order to verify information provided or to obtain further details, the authorities *may* carry out investigations in the territory of other Members. ... ." (emphasis added)

7.324 Annex I, paragraph 7 provides in relevant part:

> "As the main purpose of the on-the-spot investigation is to verify information provided or to obtain further details, it should be carried out after the response to the questionnaire has been received unless the firm agrees to the contrary and the government of the exporting Member is informed by the investigating authorities of the anticipated visit and does not object to it; ... ."

7.325 Concerning the relationship of Annex I to Article 6.7, we come to the same conclusion as in respect of Annex II and Article 6.8.[247] In particular, we note Article 6.7's explicit cross-reference to Annex I: "[T]he procedures described in Annex I shall apply to investigations carried out in the territory of other Members". This language thus establishes that the specific parameters that must be respected in carrying out foreign verifications in compliance with Article 6.7 are found in Annex I. Thus, we must analyze the relevant provisions of Article 6.7 and Annex I together to determine if the requirement claimed by Turkey exists.

---

[247] *See* paras. 7.152-7.154.

7.326 Considering Article 6.7, we find determinative the use of the word "may" (that is, that authorities "may" carry out investigations in the territory of other Members). This language makes clear that on-the-spot verifications in the territory of other Members are permitted, but not required, by Article 6.7.

7.327 The relevant portion of Annex I, paragraph 7 deals with the *timing* of a foreign verification visit, *if* one is made (i.e., "after the response to the questionnaire has been received"). This provision thus cannot be construed as containing a requirement to conduct such a visit *per se*. We note that our reading of these provisions is consistent with the findings of the panel in *Argentina – Ceramic Tiles*, which stated that the AD Agreement contains no requirement to conduct foreign verifications, but rather that Article 6.7 merely provides for this possibility, and that such on-site visits are neither the only way nor even the preferred way for investigating authorities to meet their obligation under Article 6.6 to "satisfy themselves as to the accuracy of the information supplied by interested parties upon which their findings are based".[248]

7.328 For the foregoing reasons, we find that Turkey has not established that Egypt violated Annex II, paragraph 1, Article 6.7, or Annex I, paragraph 7, as these provisions do not contain the obligations asserted by Turkey.

7.329 This brings us to Turkey's final allegation of a violation in connection with this claim, of Annex II, paragraph 6, regarding the alleged impairment of the respondents' "opportunity to provide further explanations". We note that this alleged violation is entirely dependent on and derivative from the other alleged violations raised by Turkey in connection with this claim. Given that we have found no violation of these provisions, we conclude in this instance as well that Turkey has not established the factual basis for the alleged violation by Egypt of violated Annex II, paragraph 6 in respect of the factual situation that is the subject of this claim.[249]

2. *Claim under Article 2.4 – Request for Detailed Cost Information Late in the Investigation Allegedly Imposed an Unreasonable Burden of Proof on the Respondents*

7.330 Turkey claims that by waiting until late in the investigation to raise issues requiring the submission of new factual information and then imposing an unduly burdensome "mail order" verification requirement on the respondents, the IA imposed an "unreasonable burden of proof" upon respondents in violation of Article 2.4 of the AD Agreement.

7.331 Egypt argues that Article 2.4 pertains exclusively to the requirement to make a fair comparison between export price and normal value, and that its requirement not to impose an unreasonable burden of proof applies to the collection of information concerning allowances required to ensure a fair comparison.

---

[248] Panel Report, *Argentina – Ceramic Tiles,* footnote 65.
[249] Because of this, we again do not opine on whether it is possible to invoke Annex II, para. 6 outside the context of Article 6.8.

Egypt argues in the alternative that should the Panel consider that Article 2.4 must be interpreted as being of general application to data collection in the course of an investigation, the claim of violation is factually incorrect and that the burden of proof imposed upon the respondents did not exceed the limits of reasonableness.

7.332 We start with the text of Article 2.4, which reads as follows:

> "A fair comparison shall be made between the export price and the normal value. This comparison shall be made at the same level of trade, normally at the ex-factory level, and in respect of sales made at as nearly as possible the same time. Due allowance shall be made in each case, on its merits, for differences which affect price comparability, including differences in conditions and terms of sale, taxation, levels of trade, quantities, physical characteristics, and any other differences which are also demonstrated to affect price comparability.[7] In the cases referred to in paragraph 3, allowances for costs, including duties and taxes, incurred between importation and resale, and for profits accruing, should also be made. If in these cases price comparability has been affected, the authorities shall establish the normal value at a level of trade equivalent to the level of trade of the constructed export price, or shall make due allowance as warranted under this paragraph. The authorities shall indicate to the parties in question what information is necessary to ensure a fair comparison and shall not impose an unreasonable burden of proof on those parties."

---

[7] It is understood that some of the above factors may overlap, and authorities shall ensure that they do not duplicate adjustments that have been already made under this provision.

7.333 Article 2.4, on its face, refers to the *comparison* of export price and normal value, i.e., the calculation of the dumping margin, and in particular, requires that such a comparison shall be "fair". A straightforward consideration of the ordinary meaning of this provision confirms that it has to do not with the basis for and basic establishment of the export price and normal value (which are addressed in detail in other provisions)[250], but with the nature of the comparison of export price and normal value. First, the emphasis in the first sentence is on the *fairness* of the *comparison*. The next sentence, which starts with the words "[t]his comparison", clearly refers back to the "fair comparison" that is the subject of the first sentence. The second sentence elaborates on considerations pertaining to the "comparison", namely level of trade and timing of sales on both the normal value and export price sides of the dumping margin equation. The third

---

[250] In this regard, we note that earlier provisions in Article 2, namely Article 2.2 including all of its sub-paragraphs, and Article 2.3, have to do exclusively and in some detail with the establishment of normal value and export price, and in addition that Article 2.1 has to do in part with the establishment of the export price.

sentence has to do with allowances for "differences which affect *price comparability*", and provides an illustrative list of possible such differences. The next two sentences have to do with ensuring "price comparability" in the particular case where a constructed export price has been used. The final sentence, where the reference to burden of proof at issue appears, also has to do with "ensur[ing] a fair comparison". In particular, the sentence provides that when collecting from the parties the particular information necessary to ensure a fair comparison, the authorities shall not impose an unreasonable burden of proof on the parties.

7.334 The immediate context of this provision, namely Articles 2.4.1 and 2.4.2 confirms that Article 2.4 and in particular its burden of proof requirement, applies to the comparison of export price and normal value, that is, the calculation of the dumping margin. Article 2.4.1 contains the relevant provisions for the situation where "the *comparison* under paragraph 4 requires a conversion of currencies" (emphasis added). Article 2.4.2 specifically refers to Article 2.4 as "the provisions governing fair comparison", and then goes on to establish certain rules for the method by which that comparison is made (i.e., the calculation of dumping margins on a weighted-average to weighted-average or other basis).

7.335 In short, Article 2.4 in its entirety, including its burden of proof requirement, has to do with ensuring a fair comparison, through various adjustments as appropriate, of export price and normal value. Thus, we find that it does not apply to the investigating authority's establishment of normal value as such, which was the main (if not only) purpose of the Egyptian IA's 19 August request for certain cost-related information.

7.336 Moreover, even if the burden of proof requirement in Article 2.4 were considered to apply to requests for information for the establishment of normal value, and even if some of the information contained in the IA's 19 August request potentially could have been relevant to the fair comparison exercise that is the subject of Article 2.4, we do not find that Turkey has established that that request imposed an unreasonable burden of proof on the respondents. That is, we agree with Egypt that the factual basis for a claim of violation does not exist. In particular, we note that the request concerned the amplification or clarification of cost information provided or meant to have been provided in the questionnaire responses, and no respondent argued at the time that it received the 19 August request that it was unreasonably burdensome. Moreover, while all of the respondents requested (and received)[251] extensions of the original deadline for responses, and then on or before the deadline submitted responses including relatively voluminous documentation, in no case did any respondent indicate that more time was needed, or otherwise argue or attempt to justify that it simply did not find it possible to comply with the request. While respondents Habas, Diler and Colakoglu did present certain argumentation in their responses to the 19 August request, that argumentation had to do with the alleged illegality of the request under WTO rules, rather than with its burdensomeness.

---

[251] The extensions granted were, however, shorter than those requested.

7.337 For the foregoing reasons, we find that Turkey has not established that the IA's 19 August request for certain cost information imposed an unreasonable burden of proof in violation of Article 2.4.

3.   *Claim under Article 6.2 and Annex II, Paragraph 6 – Alleged Denial of Requests for Meetings*

7.338 Turkey submits that the three respondents Habas, Diler and Colakoglu requested a meeting with the IA after receiving the IA's letter of 23 September 1999, during which "they could explain how the information submitted in their 15 September responses [to the 19 August request] replied to the Investigating Authority's information requests"[252]. Turkey further argues that IDC stated that it was available for a further verification of its cost data if the IA so desired.[253] According to Turkey, the denial of these requests violated Article 6.2, which Turkey quotes as "provid[ing], *inter alia*, that '[i]nterested parties shall ... have the right ... to present ... information orally'"[254]. In addition, Turkey claims, the denial of these requests violated Annex II, paragraph 6 by denying the Turkish respondents the basic right, where "evidence or information is not accepted", to be "informed forthwith of the reasons therefor, and ... given an opportunity to provide further explanations within a reasonable period ... ."

7.339 Egypt counters that the IA was under no obligation to organize a meeting with Habas, Diler and Colakoglu at that stage of the investigation in the absence of any valid justification, in accordance with the last sentence of Article 6.2. Egypt further states that the meeting was requested after those respondents had informed the IA that they would not submit the information requested in the 23 September letter. Egypt argues that according to those respondents, the purpose of such a meeting would have been to explain the information in their responses to the 19 August request, but in Egypt's view that information was largely deficient, meaning that such a meeting was not justified. Egypt states that the IA indicated to those respondents that the explanation of the data submitted in response to the 19 August request should have been provided by submitting a written response to the 23 September letter, which the respondents had explicitly refused to do. Egypt notes that in any event, even if a meeting had been held, these respondents would not thereby have been excused from submitting in writing the explanations proffered orally. during such a meeting, due to Article 6.3's requirement that "[o]ral information provided under [Article 6.2] shall be taken into account by the authorities only in so far as it is subsequently reproduced in

---

[252] Written Response, dated 7 December 2001, to Question 1 to Turkey of *the Written Questions by the Panel*, of 28 November 2001 – Annex 4-1.

[253] Turkey also initially argued that Icdas had requested a hearing as soon as it had reviewed the *Essential Facts and Conclusions Report*. In response to a question from the Panel as to where in the record that request was found, Turkey informed the Panel that Icdas had not in fact made such a request. (*See* Written Response, dated 14 March 2002, to Question 4 to Turkey of the *Written Questions by the Panel, of 27 February 2002.*)

[254] Written Response, dated 7 December 2001, to Question 1 to Turkey of the *Written Questions by the Panel*, of 28 November 2001 – Annex 4-1.

writing ... ." Concerning IDC, Egypt argues that the IA's denial to conduct a verification visit at that company's premises cannot be examined under Article 6.2 of the AD Agreement, as that provision is not concerned with verification visits. Finally, Egypt argues that Annex II, paragraph 6 is inapplicable to the organizing of hearings, and that Egypt had demonstrated in connection with other claims that the IA had acted in full compliance with the obligations in that provision.

7.340 Turning first to the claim of violation of Article 6.2, we note that the full text of the relevant part of that provision, namely the last sentence, reads as follows:

> "Interested parties shall also have the right, on *justification*, to present other information orally." (emphasis added)

7.341 We note that the words "also" and "other" in this sentence refer to other provisions of Article 6.2 concerning the right of interested parties to meet with opposing parties to present views and rebuttal arguments. Thus, with respect to the claim before us, the operative part of this sentence is the nature of the "right" of interested parties to "present information orally" outside the setting of an adversarial hearing. In this regard, while the partial quotation set forth by Turkey would imply that the right in question is open-ended and absolute, the full text of the provision makes clear that the right exists only upon "justification". It is perhaps axiomatic that an interested party seeking to invoke its Article 6.2 right must attempt to exercise that right before it can claim that it has been denied.

7.342 Thus, the first question that must be addressed is whether the respondents in question in fact requested meetings, and if so, whether any such requests were substantiated (i.e., whether justification was presented). Turning first to Habas, Diler and Colakoglu, their reference to a meeting was contained in their 28 September 1999 letter in which they indicated that they would not provide the additional information requested in the 23 September letter. The relevant passage concerning the possibility of a meeting is as follows:

> "If ITPD remains unable to locate the original translations or to identify the pages of the 15 September response where translations are provided, or it ITPD requires any additional explanations, we will be pleased to come to Cairo to review these documents with ITPD. Such a meeting could be arranged after the third week of November, if desired. Before that time, counsel's time is fully booked, but we would expect the ITPD to afford us this scheduling courtesy in view of the events herein since verification was concluded."[255]

7.343 We do not consider that the above passage can be viewed as an attempt by these interested parties concerned to exercise their Article 6.2 rights to a meeting. Nor does it deal adequately, or at all, with the justification for such a meeting, upon which the right to have such a meeting is conditioned. Rather, it seems plainly to be an *offer* to travel to Cairo to participate in a meeting should

---

[255] Exh EGT-2, p.3.

the IA decide that such a meeting would be useful. Indeed, that this was an offer, rather than a request, was explicitly confirmed by these three respondents in their 15 October 1999 comments on the *Essential Facts and Conclusions Report*, in which they state that it was to provide the IA with an understanding of the "meanings and linkages" of the documents that they had submitted that their "counsel *offered* to come to Cairo to assist in the explanation of documents. That *offer* still stands"(emphasis added).[256] Moreover, we question the seriousness of the offer that was made, given that the proposed earliest possible date for such a meeting, due to the stated unavailability of the companies' counsel, was fully two months later. Nor, even if a meeting was requested, do we find that these companies provided any justification for such a meeting. Indeed, while the express purpose of the last sentence of Article 6.2 is the oral provision of *information*, we note that these respondents raised the possibility of a meeting in the context of their informing the IA that they intended to provide *no* further information. Rather they were prepared only to assist the IA in locating any original translations that had been previously submitted or identify where additional translations had been provided, and to furnish any explanations that the IA might need. The IA in fact made these points in its response to these respondents' 28 September letter, as follows:

> "In your letter dated 28 September, 1999, you referred to a possible meeting in Cairo to explain the data submitted by Habas, Diler and Colakoglu. Please note that any further comments or explanations regarding the request of ITPD for supplemental information should have been included in your responses, the deadline for which has passed. We will consider any further information to be untimely. Regarding your concern that ITPD may not understand the submission, the ITPD understands the data that has been submitted. The fact is your clients did not completely respond to the requests for supplemental information, which required the ITPD's use of facts available for portions of the submission."[257]

7.344 Concerning IDC, we note that here again, IDC did not in fact request a meeting with the IA. Rather, it informed the IA that it was available for a further verification at its premises if the IA so wished. In particular, the relevant passage from IDC's 15 October 1999 letter commenting on the *Essential Facts and Conclusions Report* reads as follows:

> "Finally, we kindly request, the Authority to contact us anytime they wish and kindly note that all our files, reports, general ledgers are ready for verification by your authorised investigators."[258]

Here again, this passage cannot in any way be construed as containing a request for a meeting, nor a justification for any such request.

---

[256] Exh. TUR-20, p.10.
[257] Exh. EGT-10.
[258] Exh. TUR-27, p.3.

7.345 For the foregoing reasons, we do not find that the IA denied requests of respondents Habas, Diler, Colakoglu, and IDC for meetings, and thus did not act inconsistently with the last sentence of Article 6.2.

7.346 In view of our findings in the preceding paragraph, in respect of the claim under the last sentence of Article 6.2, that the IA did not reject requests for meetings, we also do not that Turkey has established the factual basis for a possible violation of Annex II, paragraph 6 resulting from the alleged rejection of such requests.[259]

4.   *Claim under Article 2.4 – Alleged Failure to Make an Adjustment to Normal Value for Differences in Terms of Sale*

7.347 Turkey claims that Egypt violated Article 2.4 in that the IA failed to make a credit cost adjustment to normal value for differences in payment terms between home market sales and exports sales to Egypt. According to Turkey, an imputed credit cost adjustment was claimed by the respondents to adjust export prices and home market prices with deferred payment terms to a common sight price basis in order to ensure an "apples-to-apples" comparison. Turkey argues that such a credit cost adjustment is normally granted by the United States, the European Communities, Canada, Chile and Australia. According to Turkey, the Third Party Submission of the European Communities states that it is EC policy to make such an adjustment where constructed normal value is used because that constructed normal value "will typically include an element for costs relating to the granting of credit terms". Turkey argues in this respect that the interest expense that is included in the Turkish companies' administrative, selling and general costs includes interest expenses related to the financing of outstanding receivables, and therefore that a credit cost adjustment should have been made to normal value, as was done to the respondents' export prices to Egypt. Turkey considers that by making a credit cost adjustment to the export price, but not to normal value, Egypt produced a distorted comparison in violation of Article 2.4.

7.348 Egypt argues that the absence of an adjustment for credit expenses to the normal value is based on a permissible interpretation of the AD Agreement. In particular, Egypt notes, due allowances should be made for differences that affect price comparability, and with respect to terms and conditions of sale, in Egypt's view an allowance is normally warranted when normal value is based on actual domestic sales prices, as only then would the prices be affected by contractual conditions and terms of sales. By contrast, constructed normal value is based on cost of production, i.e., items which cannot be influenced by conditions and terms of sale. According to Egypt, this is particularly true with respect to credit terms, as when negotiating a price, the buyer and seller will in principle take into account the credit period granted for deferred payment compared with payment in cash. Thus, according to Egypt, by comparing export price net of

---

[259] Once again, we need not and do not opine on whether it is possible to invoke Annex II, para. 6 outside the context of Article 6.8.

credit costs and a constructed normal value without an adjustment for credit costs, the IA compared prices on a comparable basis. Furthermore, Egypt argues, should the Panel consider that Article 2.4 requires that constructed normal value be adjusted for credit costs, all Turkish domestic rebar sales were made at a loss and therefore there were no domestic sales with relevant credit terms in the ordinary course of trade that the IA could have used to determine the credit cost adjustment. Lastly, for Egypt, the fact that some other jurisdictions may deduct credit costs from constructed normal values does not render Egypt's practice inconsistent with Article 2.4.

7.349 We view both parties as arguing that this issue can be resolved purely as a matter of legal interpretation. That is, Turkey argues, in essence, that in *all* cases, constructed normal value should be adjusted for credit costs. By contrast, Egypt argues in essence that it is permissible as a matter of policy *never* to adjust constructed normal value for credit costs.

7.350 We recall that Article 2.4 provides as follows:

> "A fair comparison shall be made between the export price and the normal value. This comparison shall be made at the same level of trade, normally at the ex-factory level, and in respect of sales made at as nearly as possible the same time. Due allowance shall be made in each case, on its merits, for differences which affect price comparability, including differences in conditions and terms of sale, taxation, levels of trade, quantities, physical characteristics, and any other differences which are also demonstrated to affect price comparability [footnote omitted]. In the cases referred to in paragraph 3, allowances for costs, including duties and taxes, incurred between importation and resale, and for profits accruing, should also be made. If in these cases price comparability has been affected, the authorities shall establish the normal value at a level of trade equivalent to the level of trade of the constructed export price, or shall make due allowance as warranted under this paragraph. The authorities shall indicate to the parties in question what information is necessary to ensure a fair comparison and shall not impose an unreasonable burden of proof on those parties."

7.351 In considering this claim, we note the parties' arguments that Article 2.4 *always* requires on the one hand, or permits a policy of *never* making, on the other hand, a credit cost adjustment to constructed normal value. To us, reading Article 2.4 in this way is not possible, i.e., this claim cannot be resolved on the basis of a judgement as to whether a given legal interpretation of that provision is permissible, in the abstract, and without considering the specific facts of an individual case.

7.352 To the contrary, we read Article 2.4 as explicitly requiring a fact-based, case-by-case analysis of differences that affect price comparability. In this regard, we take note in particular of the requirement in Article 2.4 that "[d]ue allowance shall be made *in each case, on its merits,* for differences which affect price comparability" (emphasis added). We note as well that in addition to an illustrative list of possible such differences, Article 2.4 also requires allowances for "any other differences which are also *demonstrated* to affect price comparability" (emphasis added). Finally, we note the affirmative information-gathering burden on the investigating authority in this context, that it "shall indicate to the parties in question *what information is necessary* to ensure a fair comparison and shall not impose an unreasonable burden of proof on those parties" (emphasis added). In short, where it is demonstrated by one or another party in a particular case, or by the data itself that a given difference affects price comparability, an adjustment must be made. In identifying to the parties the data that it considers would be necessary to make such a demonstration, the investigating authority is not to impose an unreasonable burden of proof on the parties. Thus, the process of determining what kind or types of adjustments need to be made to one or both sides of the dumping margin equation to ensure a fair comparison, is something of a dialogue between interested parties and the investigating authority, and must be done on a case-by-case basis, grounded in factual evidence.

7.353 Our analysis of this claim thus focuses on whether the IA met its burden under Article 2.4 in the process that ultimately resulted in its decision not to adjust constructed normal values for credit costs, i.e., whether that decision was justified on the basis of the evidence of record, and whether, including in the light of the respondents' actions and submissions concerning the issue of credit costs, the IA fulfilled its obligations in developing that evidence. We start by considering the chronology of relevant events during the investigation, beginning with the questionnaires that were sent to the foreign manufacturers and the exporters. Here we note that both of these questionnaires contain questions concerning possible allowances for certain differences that might affect price comparability, including credit costs. In the manufacturer's questionnaire, the question of terms of trade, including credit, is raised in sections 4.3 and 4.4 (domestic sales) and 5.2 and 5.3 (exports to Egypt). In the exporter's questionnaire, the same questions are contained in sections 3.6 and 3.7 (domestic sales) and 4.4 and 4.5 (exports to Egypt). Thus, the IA invited the Turkish respondents' input on the issue of credit at the outset of the investigation, and each respondent included in its questionnaire response certain information and argumentation concerning how a credit cost adjustment should be calculated and applied.[260] The issue of credit costs also was addressed in the verification reports, and was further referred to in letters dated 12 August 1999 from the IA concerning certain problems identified by the IA after verification, and in the 13 August 1999 response on behalf of three respondents to those letters.

(a)   Factual Background

7.354 A chronology of the references to imputed credit costs from all of these documents is set forth below for each respondent separately.

---

[260]   In response to a request from the Panel, Turkey provided certain excerpts from the respondents' questionnaire responses (Exh. TUR-42) which according to Turkey reflect the requests made by the respondents for a credit cost adjustment to normal value.

(i)   Icdas

Questionnaire response

7.355   The relevant portion of Icdas' questionnaire response reads as follows:

"Payments of domestic sales of reinforcing bars are usually received at a later date then [sic] the date on the invoice. The duration between the date of invoice and the date of the receipt of the payment usually varies between 7 and 90 days.

While deciding on the price, the date the customer will make the payment are taken into account and an additional charge is included in the price to offset the depreciation of Turkish Lira. (All sales in domestic market are made in Turkish Lira).

Exact date receipt of payment can not be determined in the recording procedure of Icdas since the accounts receivable are followed by customer basis rather than invoice basis. Therefore we based our calculations on average number of days outstanding.

For calculation of average number of days outstanding for the six months reported, we obtained the accounts receivable balance of and total sales to each customer on a monthly basis. Then we indexed these figures to the end of period of investigation i.e. to December 1998. (Republic of Turkey State Institute of Statistics Wholesale Price Indexes and calculated indexation figures to end of period of investigation are provided as Attachment 2.

After indexation of these figures to the end of period of investigation we added up monthly indexed figures and finally by dividing the total indexed monthly accounts receivable to total indexed sales, we determined an average number of days outstanding for the reported period. For calculation of these figures please see Table 4.

To get a unit interest expense by transaction basis, we used actual short term TL borrowing rate of Icdas. During the reported period Icdas used only one short term loan. Copies of the documents showing the usage of this loan are provided in Attachment 3.

With this interest rate by using the following equation we calculated the unit cost of credit computed at the actual cost of short-term debt borrowed:

(Average number of days outstanding x Average interest rate x Gross unit price)/360)."[261]

---

[261]   Exh. TUR-42, p.4-5.

Verification report

7.356 The verification report for Icdas contains the following text concerning credit cost in respect of home market sales:

"Cost of Credit

The accounts for sales in Turkey can be received later than the date of the invoice. ... The period between due date of settlement of the account and the actual date of payment was established from the accounts outstanding ledger. The average days outstanding per ton was calculated and an adjustment made. The interest used was established from the company records of short term loans."[262]

12 August 1999 letter from the IA

7.357 In its 12 August letter to Icdas, the IA stated in respect of credit cost:

"With regard to the cost of credit for normal values, the investigating authority decided not to adjust this cost for lack of reliable evidence concerning this adjustment."[263]

Response to the 12 August 1999 letter

7.358 Turkey states that on 17 August 1999, Icdas submitted a response to the IA's 12 August, challenging, among other things, the IA's stated intention not to make a credit cost adjustment. Although in its first written submission Turkey quoted what it indicated were excerpts from that letter, it did not submit that letter to the Panel, either as an exhibit to that submission or otherwise. Thus, we have not seen the 17 August letter in original. According to Turkey, Icdas argued that the proposed denial of a credit cost adjustment was contrary to Article 2.4 of the AD Agreement, and noted that all of its home market sales were on "'deferred payment terms'", such that not making a credit cost adjustment to home market prices would "'seriously deteriorate the fair comparison between the export and domestic prices'".[264]

19 August request; 15 September response to the 19 August request; 23 September follow-up request from the IA; 28 September letter from the IA; *Essential Facts and Conclusions Report*; 15 October comments on *Essential Facts and Conclusions Report*; and *Final Report*

7.359 There is no reference to the issue of a credit cost adjustment in any of the above-captioned documents. That is, once the cost and constructed value issue arose (as reflected in the 19 August request), this issue was not mentioned further, either by Icdas or by the IA.

---

[262] Exh. TUR-4, p.6.
[263] Exh. TUR-10.
[264] First Written Submission of Turkey, Section IV.A, para.20-23.

(ii) IDC

Questionnaire response

7.360 The relevant portion of IDC's questionnaire response reads as follows:

"Other (credit) expenses: As explained in response to 4.3 which is credit expenses due to deferred payments in home market sales. IDC used the following equation to calculate home market credit expenses:

$$\frac{No.\ of\ days \times Interest\ Rate \times (Gross\ Invoice\ Value - 1.5\%\ Discount)}{360}$$

IDC calculated the weighted average number of days between invoice date and payment date for sales of rebar for each month. Based on the monthly calculations, IDC calculated the average number of days between invoice date and payment date during the investigation period. A worksheet summarizing the results of these calculations is attached in Exhibit B-1. Weighted-average short-term in the home market interest rate is shown in the worksheets attached to Exhibit B-1".[265]

7.361 We note that in IDC's Appendix 9A concerning cost of production of rebar, IDC reported no data for the line item entitled "Financing Costs".[266] Other documents of record clarify that this was because IDC reported no interest cost component of cost of production. We note Turkey's explanation that IDC was indicating thereby that it had no net financial expense after the application of interest income.[267]

Verification report

7.362 The verification report contains the following passage concerning IDC's credit cost on home market sales:

"Cost of Credit

Izmir has stated that its terms of sale are ex-works. The invoice is issued the same day as the goods are picked up from the mill. The company provided details of the credit period for the sales under review in Turkey. The verification team verified the days credit outstanding from the company records. The interest rate applying was verified from a bank document. The [illegible] used in the calculation was clarified and an adjustment for the cost of credit on local sales was made."[268]

---

[265] Exh. TUR-42. p.7-10.
[266] Exh. TUR-42, p.29.
[267] *See* para. 7.399, *infra*.
[268] Exh. TUR-5, Section 4.3.

12 August letter

7.363 In its 12 August letter to IDC, the IA stated in respect of credit cost:

> "With regard to the cost of credit for normal values, the investigating authority decided not to adjust this cost for lack of reliable evidence concerning this adjustment."[269]

Response to the 12 August letter

7.364 Turkey states that on 13 August 1999, IDC submitted a faxed response to the IA's 12 August letter, expressing "surprise" at the IA's stated decision not to grant a credit cost adjustment to normal value, and indicating that " 'on your verification report (sent to us on 17.07.1999) you have already verified the cost of credit and your verification team confirmed [the adjustment at the verification]' ".[270] Although Turkey's first written submission presents these passages as verbatim excerpts from IDC's 13 August fax to the IA, Turkey did not submit that fax to the Panel, either as an exhibit to that submission or otherwise. Thus, we have not seen the 13 August fax in original.

19 August request; 15 September response to the 19 August request; 23 September follow-up request from the IA; 28 September letter from the IA; *Essential Facts and Conclusions Report*; 15 October comments on *Essential Facts and Conclusions Report*; and *Final Report*

7.365 There is no reference to the issue of a credit cost adjustment in any of the above-captioned documents. That is, once the cost and constructed value issue arose (as reflected in the 19 August request), this issue was not mentioned further, either by IDC or by the IA.

(iii)   Diler

Questionnaire response

7.366 The relevant portion of Diler's questionnaire response concerning imputed credit reads as follows:

> "We add a field (column M) in which we calculate the imputed interest expense according to the formula:
>
> $$(T1-T2)/360 \times INT \times UNIT\ PRICE$$
>
> where T1 is the date of invoice, T2 is the date of receipt of payment, INT is the short-term commercial interest rate in Turkey (80% per annum), and UNIT PRICE is the unit price on the invoice. This field, then, is the unit imputed interest expense for the given line item in the database, and it should be subtracted from the domestic market selling price.

---

[269] Exh. TUR-10.
[270] First Written Submission of Turkey, Section IV.A, para.24.

We add a field showing the net price for the cost test (column N). This field reports the gross unit price minus movement charges (i.e., minus inland freight). Under usual antidumping methodologies, the administering authority tests whether the home market sale is above cost of production. To do this, one uses the ex-factory price exclusive of the imputed interest expense. Imputed interest is excluded from price for purposes of the cost test because a company's financial statement and cost accounts do not contain any entry for imputed expenses, and so the sales price for cost test purposes should also be without imputed interest."[271]

7.367 In another section of its questionnaire response, Diler further elaborates on selling expenses, general and administrative expenses, and interest expense, as follows:

"Selling expenses is the total indirect selling expenses incurred in the sale of rebar in the stated months of 1998, divided by the total cost of goods sold for rebar for the stated months of 1998. We have subtracted direct selling expenses from total selling expenses, since the direct expenses (freight, handling charges and the like) are reported in Apps. 3B and 5 as adjustments to price. Keeping the direct expenses in the cost would result in comparison of a selling-expense-included cost with a selling-expense-excluded price, which would be inappropriate.

General and administrative expenses are the Diler G&A for the full year 1998, divided by total COGS for 1998. We report this on an annual basis because G&A expenses are 'period' costs, i.e., costs which vary greatly in particular months and therefore must be analyzed on an annual basis.

Interest expense is reported in a manner similar to G&A expense, i.e., on an annual basis, since it is also a period cost. Interest expenses is on a consolidated basis (Group interest expense, offset by Group interest income), as this is the practice in antidumping investigations, because of the fungibility of money."[272]

Verification report

7.368 The passage from the verification report on Diler contains the following passage concerning credit cost on home market sales:

"Cost of Credit

The company provided details of the credit period for the sales under review in Turkey. The team verified the difference between the date of sale and the date of payment from accounting records. Because the company has no short-term loan finance on its books the

---

[271] Exh. TUR-42, p.12-13.
[272] Exh. TUR-42, p.21.

short-term loan interest rate from the Economist was taken as an independent source, and used for the applicable interest rate. The result of the calculation using this data gave the cost of credit for local sales. An adjustment for the cost of credit on local sales was made."[273]

12 August letter from the IA

7.369 In its 12 August 1999 letter to Diler, Habas and Colakoglu, the IA stated concerning credit cost:

"With regard to the cost of credit for normal values for the three companies (Habas, Diler and Colakoglu) the investigating authority decided not to adjust this cost for Habas and Colakoglu for lack of evidence concerning this adjustment. The purchase order provided by Diler as an evidence for credit period is unreliable."[274]

Response to 12 August letter

7.370 On 13 August 1999, counsel for the three respondents (Diler, Habas and Colakoglu) responded to the IA's 12 August letter.[275] Concerning the IA's indication that it was rejecting the claimed credit cost adjustment for each of the companies, these companies complained that such a rejection was unjustifiable given that the credit cost figures had been verified. In particular, they argued that the verification reports' indications that adjustments for credit costs had been made constituted legally binding findings of fact by the IA. They noted further that the stated reason for rejecting the adjustment was lack of evidence, and they argued that the evidence had been fully verified as to the number of days credit granted by each company on its home market sales and as to the prevailing interest rate.[276]

19 August request; 15 September response to the 19 August request; 23 September follow-up request from the IA; 28 September letter from the IA; *Essential Facts and Conclusions Report*; 15 October comments on *Essential Facts and Conclusions Report*; and *Final Report*

7.371 There is no reference to the issue of a credit cost adjustment in any of the above-captioned documents. That is, once the cost and constructed value issue arose (as reflected in the 19 August request), there was no further mention of this issue, either by Diler or by the IA.

---

[273] Exh. TUR-6, p.7.
[274] Exh. TUR-10.
[275] Exh. TUR-25.
[276] *Ibid*, p.14-16.

(iv)   Colakoglu

Questionnaire response

7.372 The relevant portion of Colakoglu's questionnaire response reads as follows:

"We add a field in which we calculate the net interest expense according to the formula:

$$(T1-T2)/360 \times INT \times UNIT\ PRICE$$

where T1 is the date of invoice, T2 is the date of receipt of payment, INT is the short term commercial interest rate in Turkey (equal to 80% per annum – see Exhibit 4 hereto), and UNIT PRICE is the unit price on the invoice. This field, then, is the unit imputed interest expense for the given line item in the database. Under typical antidumping practice, the imputed credit should be subtracted from unit price for purposes of making price-to-price comparisons between domestic price and export price (since both such prices have, or can have, imputed credit). However, imputed credit should *not* be subtracted from unit price in determining whether a sale is above cost, since there is not imputed credit component of cost of production, and both sides of the comparison should be viewed *in pari materia.*"[277]

Verification report

7.373 The verification report concerning Colakoglu contains the following passage concerning credit cost:

"Cost of Credit

The credit cost for the sales in Turkey during the period of export (April-August 1998) has been calculated for the domestic sales sold on deferred payment. The deferred payment refers to the waiting time for payment the company has before the post-dated cheque can be presented for payment. The investigating team obtained the details of the maturity date for individual sales over the period thus establishing the period of credit from the firm's records. The interest rate was established from the published rate found in the Economist for the period. The company had no short-term borrowing during the period".[278]

12 August letter from the IA, and Response to the 12 August letter

7.374 The passages from the 12 August letter from the IA, and the response thereto, pertaining to Colakoglu are as reflected, *supra,* in respect of Diler.

---

[277] Exh. TUR-42, p.15-16.
[278] Exh. TUR-7, p.6.

19 August request; 15 September response to the 19 August request; 23 September follow-up request from the IA; 28 September letter from the IA; *Essential Facts and Conclusions Report*; **15 October comments on** *Essential Facts and Conclusions Report*; **and** *Final Report*

7.375 There is no reference to the issue of a credit cost adjustment in any of the above-captioned documents. That is, once the cost and constructed value issue arose (as reflected in the 19 August request), there was no further mention of this issue, either by Colakoglu or by the IA.

(v)   Habas

Questionnaire response

7.376 The relevant portion of Habas' questionnaire response reads as follows:

"We add a field for the interest component of the invoice price, since, as explained above, the interest component depends on the terms of payment and is a material part of the price.

We add a field showing the number of days from invoice to payment (the time-period for imputed interest expense).

We add a field in which we calculate the net interest expense (credit expense, column M) according to the formula:

N/360 x INT x UNIT PRICE

where N is the imputed credit period, INT is the short-term commercial interest rate in Turkey (80%), and UNIT PRICE is the unit price on the invoice. This field, then, is the unit imputed interest expense for the given line item in the database, and it should be subtracted from the domestic market selling price.

We add a field for comparing price with cost of production, namely, column J. This is the invoice value without imputed credit. This is the appropriate figure to use for the cost test, since cost data are also exclusive of imputed credit."[279]

7.377 Habas' questionnaire also contains the following passage concerning selling, general and administrative expenses:

"Selling expenses is the total indirect selling expenses incurred in the sale of rebar in November and December 1998, divided by the cost of goods sold for rebar for November and December 1998. We have subtracted directed selling expenses from total selling expenses, since the direct expenses (freight, handling charges and the like) are reported in Apps. 3B and 5 as adjustments to price. Keeping the direct expenses in the cost would result in a compari-

---

[279]   Exh. TUR-42, p.18-19.

son of a selling-expense-included cost with a selling-expense-excluded price, which would be inappropriate.

General and administrative expenses are the G&A of the Iron and Steel plant for the full year 1998, divided by total COGS for 1998. We report on this on an annual basis because G&A expenses are 'period' costs, i.e., costs which vary greatly in particular months and therefore must be analyzed on an annual basis.

Interest expense is reported in a manner similar to G&A expense, i.e., on an annual basis, since it is also a period cost. Interest expense is on a consolidated basis (Group interest expense, offset by Group interest income)."[280]

Verification report

7.378 The verification report for Habas contains the following passage concerning credit cost:

"Cost of Credit

The credit cost for the sales in Turkey during the period of export (Nov-Dec 1998) was verified from the company's records. The method of calculation using the formula, N/360 x interest rate x unit price, was accepted. As the company had no short-term borrowings, the short-term borrowing rate published in the *Economist* was accepted as the interest rate used. An adjustment for the cost of credit on local sales was made".[281]

12 August letter from the IA, and Response to the 12 August letter

7.379 The passages from the 12 August letter from the IA, and the response thereto, pertaining to Habas are as reflected, *supra,* in respect of Diler.

19 August request; 15 September response to the 19 August request; 23 September follow-up request from the IA; 28 September letter from the IA; *Essential Facts and Conclusions Report*; 15 October comments on *Essential Facts and Conclusions Report*; and *Final Report*

7.380 There is no reference to the issue of a credit cost adjustment in respect of Habas in any of the above-captioned documents. That is, once the cost and constructed value issue arose (as reflected in the 19 August request), there was no further mention of this issue, either by Habas or by the IA.

(b) Assessment by the Panel

7.381 We recall that this claim can only be resolved on the basis of the facts of record as to whether, during the course of the investigation, the respondents

---

[280] Exh. TUR-42, p.26.
[281] Exh. TUR-8, p.7.

demonstrated on the merits (subject to the requirement that the IA not impose an unreasonable burden of proof in respect of such an adjustment) that constructed normal value needed to be adjusted for credit costs to ensure a fair comparison of normal value and export price. Here, we take note that at the outset of the investigation, the IA invited respondents to identify in their questionnaire responses any adjustments which they felt the IA should make to the reported domestic and export prices and to provide information concerning such adjustments including explicitly for credit costs. We also note that all of the respondents asserted in their questionnaire responses that a credit cost adjustment should be made to domestic selling prices to account for the number of days of delay in receiving payment after invoices were issued. All of them provided formulas by which such credit cost could be calculated, and information on the values of certain of the variables in those formulas. That information was discussed in the verification reports, and then, when informed that ultimately it had been rejected, at least three of the respondents submitted comments complaining about that course of action. All of these exchanges of information and correspondence between the respondents and the IA took place in the context of the examination of normal value based on domestic selling prices in Turkey.

7.382 Once the focus of the dumping investigation shifted to constructed value, however, no further reference was made to the question of a credit cost adjustment to normal value, either by any respondent or by the IA. Thus, in the context of the constructed value phase of the investigation, it is clear that no explicit request for or claim of such an adjustment was made by any respondent. The question for us thus becomes whether, in the light of the information of record concerning this issue from the earlier phase of the investigation, the respondents had demonstrated that such an adjustment should apply regardless of whether normal value was determined based on price or based on constructed value.

7.383 Here we recall that the IA on 12 August informed the respondents that their claims of credit cost adjustment (to domestic selling prices) would be rejected essentially for lack of evidence, and we also recall that the three respondents who shared the same counsel (Diler, Colakoglu and Habas) protested this decision of the IA, insisting that their credit cost information had been verified, and that the IA was legally bound by the verification findings. We note as well Turkey's representation that Icdas and IDC also submitted written responses to the 12 August letters that they received from the IA in which they argued that a credit cost adjustment should be made to their domestic selling prices, as such an adjustment had been verified.

7.384 Considering further the credit cost information submitted by Diler, Colakoglu and Habas, we note the references to this issue in their original questionnaire responses concerning the cost of production information to be used for the below-cost sales test (which they refer to as the "cost test"). They indicated that there was no credit cost included, and that therefore cost of production should be compared with a domestic selling price unadjusted for credit expense, to ensure a correct comparison. In particular, Diler stated:

"Imputed interest is excluded from price for purposes of the cost test because a company's financial statement and cost accounts *do not contain* any entry for imputed expenses, and so the sales price for cost test purposes should also be without imputed interest." (emphasis added)[282]

Colakoglu stated:

"However, imputed credit should *not* be subtracted from unit price in determining whether a sale is above cost, *since there is not imputed credit component of cost of production*, and both sides of the comparison should be viewed *in pari materia.*" (underline emphasis added; italic emphasis in original)[283]

Habas stated:

"We add a field for comparing price with cost of production, namely, column J. This is the invoice value without imputed credit. This is the appropriate figure to use for the cost test, since cost data are also *exclusive of* imputed credit." (emphasis added)[284]

7.385 The way in which the question of determining normal value in this case evolved had the potential to cause the IA to consider a number of important technical issues about the differences between the normal value assessed on the basis of domestic selling prices and the constructed normal values arrived at, and the need for any adjustment as between the constructed normal value and the export price. As it turned out, the consideration undertaken by the IA appears to have been limited to the context of credit cost adjustment to domestic selling prices, in which context the credit term information submitted by the respondents was rejected, because it was (in the view of the IA) insufficient and/or unreliable. The Turkish respondents objected to this in communications to the IA. No further consideration of the question of a credit cost adjustment after this point in time in the investigation appears in any document of record provided to the Panel, whether submitted by the respondents or created by the IA. The IA appears not to have considered whether an adjustment for credit cost should be made to the constructed normal values at all. In this dispute, the parties did not provide us with evidence of the consideration of that issue as it might relate to constructed normal values, and we thus must proceed on the basis that the final interchange on the issue was notification to the respondents of rejection of the claim for an adjustment to the domestic selling price-based normal values, and their complaints which then followed.

7.386 Beyond this factual analysis of what actually happened in the investigation, the parties have engaged in a debate about adjustments to constructed normal values, and whether Article 2.4 applies to require such adjustments to be made. Comparative precedent from various jurisdictions has been presented to the Panel, and arguments about economic rationale and the correct appreciation

---

[282] Exh. TUR-42, p.12.
[283] *Ibid*, p.15.
[284] *Ibid*, p.18.

of what a constructed normal value should be taken to represent have been made. It seems to us that these issues are being raised for the first time by the parties before us: they were not dealt with before the IA. The Panel is not the IA, nor does it stand in the shoes of the IA. In this regard we recall our discussion about the relationship between what an investigating authority is obligated by the AD Agreement to do with regard to procedural issues in an anti-dumping investigation, and what interested parties must themselves contribute, in the way of evidence and argumentation, for issues of concern to them to be considered and taken into account in the authority's determinations.[285] In this case, when confronted with the *Essential Facts and Conclusions Report*, which clearly identified that a constructed normal value had been applied without any adjustment for credit terms, the respondents did not take any action to protect their interests.

7.387 This claim by Turkey is an example of the difficulty which is presented for a complaining Member where it comes before a Panel and claims that an investigating authority committed a breach of a merits-based matter, but the merits were not addressed with the investigating authority. The facts and circumstances of each case will vary. Here we find that certain information concerning the respondents' imputed credit costs, and how those costs should be treated, was before the IA. This information was requested in the Exporter's Questionnaire, no doubt for consideration as a possible adjustment to be taken into account at some point in the investigation. However, the issue of an adjustment was then dealt with between the parties in relation to a normal value based on domestic selling prices. When the IA's normal value assessments shifted to a constructed approach, and this was communicated to the respondents, nothing more was said by either the respondents or the IA about the question of whether a credit cost adjustment to the constructed value was necessary, and if so, how it should be calculated. On balance, we consider that the respondents should have raised their concerns at that point in time. In the absence of such a claim and, we reiterate, within the confines of the facts of this case, we do not think that a *prima facie* violation of its obligations by the IA has been made out by Turkey.

7.388 Having said that, and in deference to the efforts of the parties in researching and presenting their respective arguments to the Panel on this point, we would add that we do not think that the construction of a normal value under Article 2.2 precludes consideration of the making of various adjustments as between that normal value and the export price with which it is to be compared. A constructed normal value is, in effect, a notional price, "built up" by adding costs of production, administrative, selling and other costs, and a profit. In any given case, such a built-up price might or might not reflect credit costs. Thus, what might be necessary to take into account by way of due allowance in a particular investigation in order to comply with the obligation to ensure a fair comparison under Article 2.4 cannot be limited by the simplistic characterisation of a normal value as being one arrived at by way of a construction under Article 2.2.

---

[285] Section VII.A, *supra*.

5. *Claim under of Articles 2.2.1.1 and 2.2.2 – Interest Income Offset*

7.389 Turkey claims that by failing to deduct short-term interest earnings from interest expense in computing the net interest expense which it included in the cost of production and constructed normal value, the IA violated Article 2.1.1.1, which provides that "'costs shall normally be calculated on the basis of records kept by the exporter or producer under investigation, provided that such records are in accordance with the generally accepted accounting principles of the exporting country and reasonably reflect the costs associated with production and sale of the product under consideration' ". Turkey claims in addition that the IA's failure to deduct short-term interest expense also violated Article 2.2.2, which provides that " 'amounts for administrative, selling and general costs ... shall be based on actual data pertaining to the production and sales in the ordinary course of trade by the exporter or producer under investigation' ". According to Turkey, the respondents' financial statements were prepared in accordance with generally accepted accounting practices in Turkey, and these statements separate operating and non-operating income, classifying short-term interest income as operating income. Turkey argues that this classification means that this income is related to the companies' core operations involving production and sale of rebar. Furthermore, Turkey argues, short-term interest income is offset against interest expense and other expenses in arriving at the companies' net income, meaning that to arrive at an accurate picture of the fully distributed cost of production, this income must be deducted. Finally Turkey argues that such an interest income offset is given in other jurisdictions because companies commonly maintain a working capital reserve in interest-bearing accounts in order to meet daily case and working capital requirements. Turkey states in this regard that a NAFTA panel reviewing a decision by Revenue Canada instructed Revenue Canada to offset interest expense with short-term interest income, explaining that under generally accepted accounting rules, short-term interest income is considered part of the current operating cycle. Turkey also argues that a US court decision also supports Turkey's point of view.

7.390 Egypt contends that the IA's decision to disallow interest income in the calculation of cost of production, because these revenues were found not to be sufficiently related to the respondents' costs of production was consistent with Articles 2.2.1.1 and 2.2.2 of the AD Agreement, and that Turkey's claims are both legally incorrect and based on a misunderstanding of the practice of other jurisdictions. Egypt notes that the text of Article 2.2.1.1 refers to "costs associated with the production and sale of the product concerned", and that the text of Article 2.2.2 instructs investigating authorities to use, when determining the amounts of administrative, selling and general costs, and profits, "data pertaining to production and sales". Egypt notes that Article 2.2.1.1 also authorises investigating authorities to adjust cost of production for non-recurring items during the period of investigation. For Egypt, the cited provisions confirm that an authority must determine the cost of production normally incurred, and must disregard exceptional items. For Egypt, the exclusion from the cost calculation of expenses that are not related to the production or sale of the product, but which pertain to the financial activities of a company as a whole is based on a permissible interpretation of the provisions at issue and therefore is consistent with the AD Agreement. Furthermore, Egypt argues, other jurisdictions (namely the United States, the EC and Canada) allow an offset for short-term interest income only when it is demonstrated that it is related to production or sale of the product concerned.

7.391 The full text of Article 2.2.1.1 reads as follows:

"For the purpose of paragraph 2, costs shall normally be calculated on the basis of records kept by the exporter or producer under investigation, provided that such records are in accordance with the generally accepted accounting principles of the exporting country and reasonably reflect the costs associated with the production and sale of the product under consideration. Authorities shall consider all available evidence on the proper allocation of costs, including that which is made available by the exporter or producer in the course of the investigation provided that such allocations have been historically utilized by the exporter or producer, in particular in relation to establishing appropriate amortization and depreciation periods and allowances for capital expenditures and other development costs. Unless already reflected in the cost allocations under this sub-paragraph, costs shall be adjusted appropriately for those non-recurring items of cost which benefit future and/or current production, or for circumstances in which costs during the period of investigation are affected by start-up operations." (footnote omitted)

7.392 The relevant part of Article 2.2.2 reads as follows:

"For the purpose of paragraph 2, the amounts for administrative, selling and general costs and for profits shall be based on actual data pertaining to production and sales in the ordinary course of trade of the like product by the exporter or producer under investigation ... ."

7.393 We note that both of these provisions emphasize two elements, first, that cost of production is to be calculated based on the actual books and records maintained by the company in question so long as these are in keeping with generally accepted accounting principles but that second, the costs to be included are those that reasonably reflect the costs *associated with* the production and sale of the product under consideration. While Egypt argues in the first instance that the IA's decision not to offset interest expense with interest income was based on a permissible interpretation of the relevant provisions, we do not believe that the issue raised by this claim can be resolved on this basis. Rather, here again, we believe that the provision itself makes clear that the calculation of costs in any given investigation must be determined based on the merits, in the light of the particular facts of that investigation. This determination in turn hinges on whether a particular cost element does or does not pertain, in that investigation, to the production and sale of the product in question *in that case*. Thus, in particular, we must consider the details of the evidence of record in order to reach a conclusion as to whether, in the rebar investigation, there was evidence in the record that the short-term interest income was "reasonably" related to the cost of producing and selling rebar, and that the IA thus should have included it in the cost of production calculation.

(a) Factual Background

(i) Icdas

Questionnaire response

7.394 The relevant part of Icdas' questionnaire response reads as follows:

"Interest revenue

For late payments Icdas usually charges a new invoice. This invoices are collected under account numbers 602 7000003 and 602 7000004 in the recording procedure of Icdas. This late payment invoices cannot be tied to invoices therefore we distributed this total figures on a monthly basis. Total monthly figure is distributed to all transactions in a given month respecting the quantity. For calculation and allocation of these expenses please see Table 5".

7.395 This particular passage is not referred to in any of the other documents of record that have been submitted to us, and thus it is not clear to what it refers specifically, and how if at all it relates to this claim.

19 August request; response to 19 August request; 23 September follow-up request, reply to 23 September follow-up request

7.396 There is no reference, in any of the above-captioned documents that were sent to or submitted by Icdas, to the issue of interest income.

Essential Facts and Conclusions Report

7.397 The *Essential Facts and Conclusions Report* contains the following text in respect of Icdas' interest expense:

"To the above costs the Investigating Authority added an amount for interest expense. The Investigating Authority did not offset this amount by interest revenue, as the Investigating Authority does not consider interest revenue as sufficiently related to production to be includable in the calculation of constructed value."[286]

---

[286] Exh. TUR-15, p.23(para.3.2.5.2).

Final Report

7.398 The text in the *Final Report* concerning Icdas' interest expense[287] is identical to that in the *Essential Facts and Conclusions Report*.

(ii)   IDC

Questionnaire response

7.399 Turkey has provided no narrative excerpt from IDC's questionnaire response referring to interest income, so we must presume that no such narrative was included in that response. Turkey has simply provided IDC's Appendix 9A to its questionnaire response, which contains no entries whatsoever for the line item entitled "Financing Costs". According to Turkey, this indicates that IDC thereby was indicating that it had no net financial expense after the application of interest income. Turkey notes in this regard that the income statement attached to IDC's 9 September 1999 response to the 19 August request shows that interest revenues offset virtually all of the company's interest expense.[288]

23 September follow-up request

7.400 In its 23 September 1999 request based on IDC's response to the 19 August request, the IA made the following request in respect of interest expense:

"1 – Interest Expense:

Furnish a list identifying separately interest expenses from interest income."[289]

28 September follow-up request

7.401 In its 28 September 1999 letter to IDC following up on IDC's response to the IA's 23 September request, the IA requested the following in respect to interest:

"Please furnish a list identifying separately interest expenses from interest income showing the difference between both interest and interest income per ton during 1998 on monthly basis."[290]

Essential Facts and Conclusions Report

7.402 Concerning IDC, the *Essential Facts and Conclusions Report* states as follows in respect to interest expense, in paragraph 3.2.5.2:

"To the above costs the Investigating Authority added an amount for interest expense. The Investigating Authority did not offset this amount by interest revenue, as the Investigating Authority does not

---

[287] Exh. TUR-16, p.29.
[288] Written Response, dated 14 March 2002, to Question 10 to Turkey of the *Written Questions by the Panel*, of 27 February 2002 – Annex 8-1.
[289] Exh. EGT-13.1.2.
[290] Exh. EGT-13.1.3.

consider interest revenue as sufficiently related to production to be includable in the calculation of constructed value ... ."[291]

IDC's comments on the Essential Facts and Conclusions Report

7.403 In its 15 October comments on the *Essential Facts and Conclusions Report*, IDC makes the following statement concerning the IA's treatment of IDC's interest expense and income[292]:

> "3 – We disagree with you that the Authority does not consider interest revenue as sufficiently related to production.
>
> Even if, we suppose that this argument is correct, the Authority should not have taken the figure out of the period of investigation and long term interest expenses.
>
> As you requested, we separated all our interest expenses at the worksheet given to you on 29th September 1999. As seen from the worksheet, our long term interest expenses are related to ship procurement of which bank documents for both ships "IDC-1" and "IDC-2" are attached. (Attachment 1)
>
> Most importantly, as you know interest expenses must be related to all products which can be sold, such as plain bars, deformed bars, billets, non-quality products, products in short length, scrap products and miss rolled products. Additionally, interest expenses can not be related to deformed bars only, this can not be understood.
>
> The Authority should have considered the months of the period of investigation.
>
> Also, the Authority has taken *the profit figure* from our income statement. This figure includes our *financial profits* which was not taken into consideration by the Authority in the cost of production. This is also contradictory and not understandable."

Final Report

7.404 In the *Final Report*, the text concerning IDC's interest expense is identical to that in the *Essential Facts and Conclusions Report*.[293]

(iii)   Diler

Questionnaire response

7.405 Diler's questionnaire contains the following text concerning interest expense in the section pertaining to cost of production:

---

[291]   Exh. TUR-15, p.23.
[292]   Exh. TUR-27, p.2-3.
[293]   Exh. TUR-16, p.29.

"Interest expense is reported in a manner similar to G&A expense, i.e., on an annual basis, since it is also a period cost. Interest expense is on a consolidated basis (Group interest expense, offset by Group interest income), as is the practice in antidumping investigations, because of the fungibility of money."[294]

Diler's Appendix 9A to its questionnaire response[295] contains a column for "Interest Expense (revenue)" which contains negative numbers (i.e., indicating net revenue) for all of the months for which data are provided.

19 August request

7.406 The 19 August request sent to Diler contains the following passage pertaining to interest income and expense:

"The costs reported included no finance cost, yet the income statement that Diler supplied indicated significant financing expenses. The costs reported include a deduction for 'interest expense', the Investigating Authority would need an explanation for this cost and why it is deducted from cost of production."[296]

15 September response to 19 August request

7.407 Diler replied on 15 September to the 19 August request. This response included a joint cover letter on behalf of Diler, Habas and Colakoglu. That letter contained the following statement in respect of the negative interest expense that these companies had reported in their questionnaire responses:

"Regarding the issue of negative interest expense, the fact is that interest income exceeded interest expense. Companies regularly invest their working capital in very short-term interest income instruments, such as overnight ("repo") loans, on which the interest income can be as high as 120% per year.[297]

....

Regarding respondents' interest expense factors, each respondent has provided its financial statements in the file "mfr income stmt" included in Exhibit 2 of the questionnaire response (the data base submissions). [footnote omitted.] From these income statements, as well as worksheets embedded in the cost submissions (dlsapp9A), it is apparent that sort-term interest income exceeded total interest expense. This is the reason respondents' interest expense for purposes of cost of production is a net negative figure.

As for ITPD's question of why respondents deduct short-term interest income from the interest expense component of cost of production, the answer is simply that, in any reasonable measure of

---

[294] Exh. TUR-42, p.21.
[295] *Ibid*, p.22.
[296] Exh. TUR-11.
[297] Exh. TUR-34 A, B and C, cover letter at p.2.

cost, interest income is netted against interest expense. This is true in dumping cases as well as in any other accounting exercise. If a company pays out $100 in interest expense and earns $120 in interest income, then the company obviously has a net interest expense of -$20, that is, net interest income of +$20. Just as a positive interest expense is an element of cost, so a negative interest expense is an element of cost. The former increases cost, and the later [sic] reduces cost, but there is no reason in accounting or in law why an adjustment to cost may be only made on the upward side. Indeed, scrap revenue is always deducted from material cost, in the same way interest revenue is deducted from interest cost.

...

Indeed, we point out that Colakoglu, Diler and Habas have each submitted not only complete cost databases on a monthly basis – exceeding the requirements of the questionnaire – but they have also provided their financial statements and detailed analyses of their selling, general and administrative, and interest expenses to enable ITPD to evaluate each of these elements. See each company's Exhibit 2 of the questionnaire response, containing tables of financial statements and detailed SGA expense tables."[298]

23 September follow-up request from the IA

7.408 In its 23 September 1999 follow-up request to Diler's response to the 19 August request, the IA made the following request in respect of interest expense:

"7. Interest Expense:

Please, furnish a list identifying separately interest expenses from interest income."[299]

28 September letter from the IA

7.409 In its letter to Diler, Habas and Colakoglu dated 28 September, the IA indicated the following:

"With reference to your fax messages of 15th and 28th September 1999, we note that you did not fully respond to the following items:

...

- Interest expense, and
..."[300]

Essential Facts and Conclusions Report

7.410 At section 3.2.1.6, the *Essential Facts and Conclusions Report* states:

---

[298] *Ibid*, p.7 and 8.
[299] Exh. TUR-12.
[300] Exh. EGT-13.6.

"In addition, these respondents [Diler, Habas and Colakoglu] have asserted that the COP should be reduced in an amount by which investment income exceed finance expenses. The Investigating Authority believes that such an adjustment would not be appropriate. Decisions by respondents to invest funds in interest-bearing accounts do not, in the Investigating Authority's view, bear a sufficiently close relationship to the company's cost of producing the subject products. As such, the Investigating Authority disregarded such income in the calculation of COP."[301]

7.411 For each of the three respondents the *Essential Facts and Conclusions Report* indicates that an amount for interest expense was included in cost of production, and that no offset was made for interest income, for the same reason as outlined in section 3.2.1.6, quoted above. These statements appear at sections 3.2.2.1 and 3.2.2.2 (Habas)[302], 3.2.3.2 (Diler)[303], and 3.2.4.2 (Colakoglu) of the *Final Report.*[304]

15 October comments on the Essential Facts and Conclusions Report

7.412 In their joint comments on the *Essential Facts and Conclusions Report*[305], Diler, Habas and Colakoglu state:

"Regarding §3.2.1.6 and cognate paragraphs, Colakoglu, Diler and Habas reject as a matter of law the Report's statement that interest income should not offset interest expense for cost purposes. This is a universal practice; see, for example, the US *Rebar* case cited above. The Report states that a company's purchase of short-term instruments does not 'bear a sufficiently close relationship to the cost of the company's producing the subject products' to warrant the offset. This test, namely, a 'sufficiently close relationship to the cost of the company's producing the subject merchandise', is not the appropriate test. If the respondent's interest *expense* were unrelated to production, ITPD would surely consider the expense to be an expense for purposes of antidumping cost accounting. In other words, ITPD would not use a linkage-to-production test mathematically, and there is no reason to apply to interest income a test different from the test applied to interest expense. In sum, ITPD's exclusion of interest income from the calculation of net interest expense violates precedents in other GATT countries, is contrary to accounting practices, and is without justification on any normative ground."[306]

---

301 Exh. TUR-15, p.20.
302 *Ibid*, p.21.
303 *Ibid.*
304 *Ibid*, p.22.
305 Exh. TUR-20.
306 *Ibid*, p.15 and 16.

Final Report

7.413 The statements in the *Final Report* on this issue are identical to those in the Essential Facts and Conclusions Report.

(iv)   Colakoglu

Questionnaire response

7.414 Turkey has provided no narrative excerpt from Colakoglu's questionnaire response referring to interest income, so we must presume that no such narrative was included in that response. Turkey has simply provided Colakoglu's Appendix 9A to its questionnaire response, which contains one column entitled "Interest Expense", in which positive numbers are reported, and another column entitled "Short-term interest income", in which (larger) negative numbers are reported.[307]

19 August request

7.415 The 19 August request sent to Colakoglu contains the following passage pertaining to interest income and expense:

> "The costs reported included interest expenses that does not reflect the inflation rate. The costs reported include a deduction for 'short term interest income', the Investigating Authority would need an explanation for this cost and why it is deducted from cost of production."[308]

15 September response to the 19 August request; 23 September follow-up request from the IA; 28 September letter from the IA; *Essential Facts and Conclusions Report*; 15 October comments on the *Essential Facts and Conclusions Report*; and *Final Report*

7.416 The relevant passages concerning Colakoglu in the 15 September response to the 19 August request, the 23 September follow-up request from the IA, the 28 September letter from the IA, the *Essential Facts and Conclusions Report*, the 15 October comments on the *Essential Facts and Conclusions Report*, and the *Final Report*, are identical to those set forth above in respect of Diler.[309]

(v)   Habas

Questionnaire response

7.417 Habas' questionnaire response contains the following text pertaining to interest expense in the section pertaining to cost of production:

---

[307] *Ibid*, p.24.
[308] Exh. TUR-11.
[309] *See* paras. 7.407, *et seq., supra*.

"Interest expense is reported in a manner similar to G&A expense, i.e., on an annual basis, since it is also a period cost. Interest expense is on a consolidated basis (Group interest expense, offset by Group interest income)."[310]

7.418 Habas's Appendix 9A contains a column entitled "Interest Expense", in which negative numbers are reported.

19 August request

7.419 The 19 August request sent to Habas contains the following passage pertaining to interest income and expense:

"The costs reported included no finance cost, yet the income statement that Habas supplied indicated significant financing expenses. The costs reported include a deduction for 'interest expense', the Investigating Authority would need an explanation for this cost and why it is deducted from cost of production."[311]

23 September follow-up request

7.420 In its 23 September 1999 follow-up request to the Habas's response to the 19 August request, the IA made the following request concerning interest expense:

"Interest Expense:

Please furnish a list identifying separately interest expense from interest income."[312]

15 September response to the 19 August request; 23 September follow-up request from the IA; 28 September letter from the IA; *Essential Facts and Conclusions Report*; 15 October comments on the *Essential Facts and Conclusions Report*; and *Final Report*

7.421 The relevant passages concerning Habas in the 15 September response to the 19 August request, the 23 September follow-up request from the IA, the 28 September letter from the IA; the *Essential Facts and Conclusions Report*, the 15 October comments on the *Essential Facts and Conclusions Report*, and the *Final Report*, are identical to those set forth above in respect of Diler.[313]

(b)   Assessment by the Panel

7.422 We recall that to resolve this claim, we must consider whether the evidence of record indicates that the short-term interest income is related to the production and sale of rebar in the Turkish home market. In this regard, we note that it was the respondents who initially advocated (at least implicitly) for an interest

---

[310] Exh. TUR-42, p.26.
[311] Exh. TUR-11.
[312] Exh. TUR-12.
[313] *See* paras. 7.407, *et seq., supra.*

income offset, by reporting in their questionnaire responses on cost their net interest expense figures, which ranged from zero to negative numbers (the latter indicating net interest income). With two exceptions - Diler and Habas - the respondents simply reported the net figures without indicating how they were arrived at or what their components were. Diler and Habas, for their part, indicated that their reported interest figures were "consolidated" item reflecting "Group" interest expense offset by "Group" interest income (suggesting that it was broader than the companies or operations producing rebar), but did not offer further explanations or breakdowns.

7.423 Concerning Diler, Habas and Colakoglu, the IA requested in its 19 August requests explanations of why interest expense was reported as a negative number. These companies provided the narrative explanations noted above[314], (which does not address the relationship of the interest income to production and sale of rebar)[315]. Rather, this narrative simply explains, in some detail, the mathematical reason for interest having been reported by each company as a negative figure, i.e., that interest income exceeded interest expense. The narrative then asserts that just as a positive interest expenses is an element of cost, so too is a negative interest expense, and that there is no accounting or legal reason why an adjustment to cost can be made only on the upward side. The IA then requested in its 23 September follow-up requests that these companies provide lists separately identifying the interest income and expense items. As discussed above, these companies provided no information on any item in response to the 23 September requests. Then, in their comments on the relevant portion of the *Essential Facts and Conclusions Report* that indicates that no interest income offset was allowed because that income was not sufficiently closely related to the companies' costs to produce rebar, these companies made no attempt to demonstrate, or even to argue, that the IA was factually incorrect and that indeed the interest income was related to the cost of producing rebar. To the contrary, they argued that the "'sufficiently close relationship to the cost of the company's producing the subject merchandise' is *not* the appropriate test" (emphasis added).[316] We note however, that the "relationship" test is precisely the test articulated by the relevant provisions of the AD Agreement.

7.424 Concerning IDC, the IA requested in the 19 August request that IDC requested a list separately identifying interest income and interest expense, and in its 28 September letter to IDC, the IA requested a list separately identifying interest income and interest expense showing the difference on a per ton basis monthly for 1998. IDC, in commenting on the indication in the *Essential Facts and Conclusions Report* that no interest income offset would be made due to the insufficient relationship to cost of producing rebar, noted that long-term interest expense should not have been used, that IDC had provided the breakout that the IA had requested on 28 September, which showed that long-term interest expenses were related to ship procurement, and that interest expenses were related

---

[314] *Ibid.*
[315] We note that this issue was raised by the IA later in the investigation (*See para.* 7.426).
[316] *Ibid.*

to all products of the company, not just rebar. In addition, IDC argued that the profit figure that was used by the IA in constructed value included the company's financial profits, but had not been included in the cost of production, which according to IDC was "contradictory". These comments thus clearly are aimed at demonstrating the weakness or absence of any relationship to production of the interest *expense* that was used in the constructed value calculation, rather than at demonstrating any relationship of interest *income* to production.

7.425 Concerning Icdas, other than a passage in its original questionnaire response entitled "Interest Revenue" (having to do with invoices for late payments), to which there is no further reference in the record before us, there is no indication that Icdas asserted any particular approach to or data regarding an interest income offset. Nor did the IA pose any specific questions to Icdas in this regard. While the IA noted briefly in the *Essential Facts and Conclusions Report* that no such offset was made in the constructed value calculation, Icdas made no comment on this point. We see, moreover, no evidence in the record otherwise that appears relevant to the existence of a relationship, if any, between interest income and the cost of producing and selling rebar. We note in this regard that when we asked Turkey to identify any such evidence, Turkey replied:

> "Specific information was not requested by the Investigating Authority on the nature of the interest income at issue. If the Investigating Authority had any doubt as to the validity of the offset in question, it was incumbent upon the Investigating Authority to request additional information. The Investigating Authority cannot justify the denial of an adjustment based on the failure to provide clarifications or supporting evidence that it itself did not seek. We note that the Investigating Authority never cited any evidence that the interest income was not related to production, nor has Egypt produced such evidence to the Panel".[317]

7.426 We note in this regard that three of the respondents simply refused to provide even a breakout of interest income from interest expense, when such a breakout was specifically requested by the IA. Then, in their comments on the *Essential Facts and Conclusions Report* they advanced an incorrect legal argument concerning the relationship-to-production test applied by the IA in deciding not to make an interest income offset, rather than trying to establish factually that their accounting records of the interest income reasonably reflected costs associated with the production and sale of rebar, and not some other aspect of the respondent's operations. The IA thus explicitly identified this issue during the course of the investigation, and provided the respondents with an opportunity to address it, which these companies chose to do in a certain way. The other respondent that commented on this aspect of the *Essential Facts and Conclusions Report* tried to *disprove* the relationship between interest *expense* and the cost of producing rebar, rather than trying to *prove* the existence of a relationship be-

---

[317] Written Response, dated 14 March 2002, to Question 10 to Turkey of the *Written Questions by the Panel*, of 27 February 2002.

tween interest *income* and cost of production. The fifth respondent made no comments or arguments at all on this issue at any point during the investigation (other than the somewhat ambiguous paragraph in its questionnaire response concerning "Interest Revenue"). In short, Turkey has not identified, and we have not found, evidence of record that would demonstrate any relationship of short-term interest income to the cost of producing rebar, nor any indication that any respondent attempted to submit such evidence or advance such an argument during the course of the investigation, in spite of the IA's providing them the opportunity to do so. We therefore find that Turkey has not established a *prima facie* case that the IA violated Article 2.2.1.1 or 2.2.2 in deciding not to make an interest income offset in calculating cost of production and constructed normal value.

F.   Claim under Article X:3 of GATT 1994

7.427 Turkey claims a violation of Article X:3 of GATT 1994 in "connection with Egypt's refusal to schedule a meeting with the Turkish respondents to discuss the adequacy of their responses on September 15, 1999.[318] Turkey contends that this decision was "administrative" in nature and based directly on a substantive law or rule.[319]

7.428 Article X:3 of GATT 1994 provides:

> "(a)   Each contracting party shall administer in a uniform, impartial and reasonable manner all its laws, regulations, decisions and rulings of the kind described in paragraph 1 of this Article."

7.429 We recall that in the present dispute, we have found that Turkey has not established that the respondents "requested" a meeting with the IA, but rather that they offered to travel to Cairo if the IA would find it useful. We see nothing non-uniform, non-impartial or unreasonable in the IA's decision not to accept this offer of the respondents. Accordingly, we find that Turkey has not established that Egypt violated Article X:3.

VIII. CONCLUSIONS

8.1   In light of the foregoing findings, we conclude that Egypt did not act inconsistently with its obligations under:

(a)   Article 3.4 of the AD Agreement, as Turkey has not established that the Egyptian Investigating Authority was required to examine and evaluate the particular factors identified by Turkey as "relevant factors and indices having a bearing on the state of the domestic industry";

(b)   Article 3.2 of the AD Agreement, as Turkey has not established that there was a legal obligation on the Egyptian Investigating Au-

---

[318] First Written Submission of Turkey, Section IV.D.2.
[319] Written Response, dated 7 December 2001, to Question 2 to Turkey of *the Written Questions by the Panel*, of 28 November 2001.

thority to perform the price undercutting analysis in the way as-serted by Turkey;

(c)   Article 3.1 of the AD Agreement, as Turkey has not established that the Egyptian Investigating Authority's price undercutting find-ing was not based on positive evidence;

(d)   Articles 6.1 and 6.2 of the AD Agreement in respect of the alleged change in scope of the injury investigation from threat of material injury to present material injury and notice thereof to the Turkish exporters;

(e)   Articles 3.1 and 3.5 of the AD Agreement, as Turkey has not es-tablished that the Egyptian Investigating Authority violated the positive evidence requirement of Article 3.1 by virtue of the Inves-tigating Authority not developing certain specific kinds of evi-dence, nor has Turkey established that, as a consequence, Egypt violated the requirement of Article 3.5 to demonstrate a causal re-lationship between the dumped imports and the injury to the do-mestic industry;

(f)   Article 3.5 of the AD Agreement, as Turkey has not established that the Egyptian Investigating Authority's evaluation of the possi-ble causation of injury by factors other than the dumped imports was inconsistent with Article 3.5;

(g)   Article 3.1 and 3.5 of the AD Agreement, as Turkey has not estab-lished that the Egyptian Investigating Authority was obligated by Articles 3.1 and 3.5 to perform an analysis and make a finding of the type asserted by Turkey in respect of whether the imports caused injury "through the effects of dumping";

(h)   Article 6.8 of the AD Agreement and paragraph 5 of Annex II thereto, with regard to three of the Turkish exporters, as an unbi-ased and objective investigating authority could have found that these three exporters failed to provide necessary information and that resort to facts available was therefore justified in calculating the cost of production in respect of these three exporters;

(i)   Article 6.1.1 of the AD Agreement, as the request for information at issue was not a "questionnaire" in the sense of this provision, and the minimum time-period provided for in Article 6.1.1 was therefore not applicable to this request for information;

(j)   Article 6.2 of the AD Agreement, or paragraph 6 of Annex II thereto, with regard to the 19 August 1999 request for information, as Turkey has not established that the time-period allowed by the Egyptian Investigating Authority for submission of the requested information was unreasonable or, as a consequence, that the Egyp-tian Investigating Authority failed to provide the Turkish exporters with a full opportunity for the defence of their interests;

(k)   Article 6.2 of the AD Agreement, or paragraph 6 of Annex II thereto, with regard to the 23 September 1999 request for information, as Turkey has not established that the time-period allowed by the Egyptian Investigating Authority for the submission of the requested information was unreasonable or, as a consequence, that the Egyptian Investigating Authority failed to provide the Turkish exporters with a full opportunity for the defence of their interests;

(l)   Paragraph 3 of Annex II to the AD Agreement, as this provision does not apply to the selection of particular information as "facts available";

(m)   Paragraph 7 of Annex II to the AD Agreement, as Turkey has not established that the Egyptian Investigating Authority failed to use "special circumspection" in estimating the prevailing inflation rate in Turkey, which was applied to the data reported by one respondent, at 5 per cent per month;

(n)   Article 6.7 of the AD Agreement, paragraph 7 of Annex I thereto, and paragraphs 1 and 6 of Annex II thereto, as Turkey has not established that these provisions contain the obligations asserted by Turkey, i.e., Turkey has not established that it is mandatory for investigating authorities to conduct "on-the-spot" verification of information submitted, that investigating authorities are precluded from requesting additional information during the course of the investigation, that the rights of the Turkish exporters were seriously prejudiced, or that the actions of the Egyptian Investigating Authority impaired their "opportunity to provide further explanations";

(o)   Article 2.4 of the AD Agreement, as Turkey has not established that the burden of proof requirement of that provision is applicable to the request for certain cost information by the Egyptian Investigating Authority in its letter of 19 August 1999, nor, even if that requirement were applicable, that the request imposed an unreasonable burden of proof on the Turkish respondents;

(p)   Article 6.2 of the AD Agreement and paragraph 6 of Annex II thereto, as Turkey has not established that the Egyptian Investigating Authority denied requests of Turkish exporters for meetings;

(q)   Article 2.4 of the AD Agreement, as Turkey has not made a *prima facie* case that the Egyptian Investigating Authority violated this provision in failing to make an adjustment to normal value for differences in terms of sale;

(r)   Articles 2.2.1.1 and 2.2.2 of the AD Agreement, as Turkey has not made a *prima facie* case that the Egyptian Investigating Authority violated these provisions in deciding not to make an interest income offset in calculating cost of production and constructed normal value; and

    (s)   Article X:3 of GATT 1994 as Turkey has not established that Egypt administered its relevant laws, regulations, decisions or rulings in a non-uniform, non-impartial or unreasonable manner in deciding not to accept an offer of certain respondents to travel to Cairo for a meeting with the Investigating Authority.

8.2   In the light of the foregoing findings, we conclude that Egypt acted inconsistently with its obligations under:

    (t)   Article 3.4 of the AD Agreement, in that while it gathered data on all of the factors listed in Article 3.4, the Egyptian Investigating Authority failed to evaluate all of the factors listed in Article 3.4 as it did not evaluate productivity, actual and potential negative effects on cash flow, employment, wages, and ability to raise capital or investments; and

    (u)   Article 6.8 of the AD Agreement, and paragraph 6 of Annex II thereto, with regard to two of the Turkish exporters, as the Egyptian Investigating Authority, having received the information that it had identified to these two respondents as being necessary, nevertheless found that they had failed to provide the necessary information, and further, did not inform these two exporters of this finding and did not give them the required opportunity to provide further explanations before resorting to facts available.

8.3   With respect to those of Turkey's claims not addressed above, we have:

    (v)   concluded that the claim was not within our terms of reference (claim under AD Article 17.6(i), claim under Article X:3 of GATT 1994 in respect of selection of particular facts available), or was abandoned by Turkey (claim under Article X:3 in respect of resort to facts available); or

    (w)   concluded that, in the light of considerations of judicial economy, it is neither necessary nor appropriate to make findings.

8.4   Under Article 3.8 of the DSU, in cases where there is infringement of the obligations assumed under a covered agreement, the action is considered *prima facie* to constitute a case of nullification or impairment of benefits under that Agreement. Accordingly, we conclude that to the extent Egypt has acted inconsistently with the provisions of the AD Agreement, it has nullified or impaired benefits accruing to Turkey under that Agreement.

IX.   RECOMMENDATION

9.1   In accordance with Article 19.1 of the DSU, we recommend that Egypt brings its definitive anti-dumping measures on imports of steel rebar from Turkey into conformity with the relevant provisions of the AD Agreement.

ANNEXES

Content		Page
Annex 1-1	First Written Submission of Turkey – Executive Summary	2809
Annex 1-2	First Written Submission of Egypt – Executive Summary	2813
Annex 2-1	First Oral Statement of Turkey – Executive Summary	2824
Annex 2-2	First Oral Statement of Egypt – Executive Summary	2830
Annex 3	Restatement by Turkey of its Claims in Response to a Request from the Panel	2837
Annex 4-1	Responses of Turkey to Questions Posed in the Context of the First Substantive Meeting of the Panel	2854
Annex 4-2	Responses of Egypt to Questions Posed in the Context of the First Substantive Meeting of the Panel	2878
Annex 5-1	Rebuttal Submission of Turkey – Executive Summary	2892
Annex 5-2	Rebuttal Submission of Egypt – Executive Summary	2901
Annex 6-1	Second Oral Statement of Egypt – Executive Summary	2909
Annex 6-2	Second Oral Statement of Turkey – Executive Summary	2915
Annex 7-1	Concluding Statement of Turkey at the Second Substantive Meeting of the Panel	2920
Annex 7-2	Closing Statement of Egypt at the Second Substantive Meeting of the Panel	2923
Annex 8-1	Responses of Turkey to Questions Posed in the Context of the Second Substantive Meeting of the Panel	2927
Annex 8-2	Responses of Egypt to Questions Posed in the	2955

	Context of the Second Substantive Meeting of the Panel	
Annex 8-3	Response of Egypt to Follow-Up Questions Posed by the Panel, and comments by Turkey on Egypt's Response	2977
Annex 9	Third Party Oral Statement of Chile	2980
Annex 10-1	Third Party Written Submission of the European Communities	2981
Annex 10-2	Third Party Oral Statement of the European Communities	2989
Annex 10-3	Third Party Responses to Questions from the Panel of the European Communities	2995
Annex 11-1	Third Party Written Submission of Japan	2998
Annex 11-2	Third Party Oral Responses of Japan to Questions from the Panel	3008
Annex 12-1	Third Party Written Submission of the United States	3012
Annex 12-2	Third Party Oral Statement of the United States	3021
Annex 12-3	Third Party Responses of the United States to Questions from the Panel	3028
Annex 13	Supplemental Working Procedures of the Panel Concerning Certain Business Confidential Information	3033

ANNEX 1-1

FIRST WRITTEN SUBMISSION OF TURKEY
EXECUTIVE SUMMARY

1.   Based on a petition filed by Al Ezz Rebars Co. and Alexandria National Iron and Steel Co., the Egyptian Ministry of Trade and Supply, International Trade Policy Department ("Investigating Authority" or "IA") commenced an anti-dumping duty investigation with respect to imports of concrete steel reinforcing bar ("rebar") from Turkey in February 1999.[1] The investigation was completed by the same office, then within the Ministry of Economy and Foreign Trade, in October 1999. As a result of the investigation, anti-dumping duties were imposed, ranging from 22.63 per cent - 61.00 per cent *ad valorem*.[2]

2.   It is the view of the Government of Turkey that Egypt's anti-dumping duty investigation and final anti-dumping determination was inconsistent with Articles VI and X:3 of the General Agreement on Tariffs and Trade 1994 ("GATT 1994") and with several provisions of the Agreement on Implementation of Article VI of the GATT 1994 (the "Anti-Dumping Agreement" or the Agreement"), including Articles 2.2, 2.4, 3.1, 3.2, 3.4, 3.5, 6.1, 6.2, 6.6, 6.7 and 6.8 and Annex II, Paragraphs 1, 3, 5, 6 and 7 and Annex I, paragraph 7.

3.   In summary, Turkey's claims are as follows:

(a)   Egypt made determinations of injury and dumping in the rebar investigation without a proper establishment of the facts and based on an evaluation of the facts that was neither unbiased nor objective.

(b)   During the investigation of material injury, Egypt failed to develop "positive evidence" linking imports from Turkey to the adverse trends that it found within the Egyptian rebar industry. Egypt did not investigate whether there were any specific sales lost by the domestic industry to imports from Turkey, or whether in specific transactions involving head-to-head competition the domestic producers were forced to lower their prices to meet Turkish import competition. Nor did Egypt investigate whether domestic purchasers considered imports from Turkey, imports from some other source, or domestic companies themselves as the price leaders in

---

[1]   *See* Arab Republic of Egypt, Ministry of Trade and Supply, International Policy Department, *Initiation Report – Steel Reinforcing Bars from Turkey* (Feb. 1999) ("Initiation Report")(reproduced in Ex. TUR-1).

[2]   *See* Arab Republic of Egypt, Ministry of Economy and Foreign Trade, Foreign Trade Sector, International Trade Policies Department, Anti-Dumping, Subsidy and Safeguards Department, Rebar from Turkey – Final Report – Dumping Investigation (Oct. 1999) ("Final Report")(reproduced in Ex. TUR-16) and Notice No. (6) 1999, Imposition of Definitive Anti-dumping Duties on the Dumped Imports of Steel Rebars Originating in or Exported From Turkey, Official Gazette No. (238)(Supplemental), Oct. 21, 1999(reproduced in Ex. TUR-17).

the market. Egypt did not investigate whether or not there was a temporary supply disturbance in the fast-growing Egyptian market, such that imports from Turkey were needed to meet demand. Indeed, there is no evidence on the public record of head-to-head competition between imports and the domestic producers other than the bare, conclusory allegations submitted by the domestic industry in their application for anti-dumping measures. Egypt's imposition of definitive anti-dumping measures despite its failure to develop "positive evidence" specifically linking the adverse trends in the domestic industry to imports from Turkey is inconsistent with Articles 3.1 and 3.5 of the Agreement.

(c) Moreover, Egypt failed to investigate or to take account of the effect of several factors - other than imports from Turkey - that had a substantial adverse effect on the Egyptian industry. Egypt also failed to take account of other, neutral factors that caused prices for rebar to fall. These factors included the effects of a large capacity expansion within the domestic industry during the period of investigation on the industry's cost structure and on price competition between the Egyptian producers; the effect of falling steel scrap input prices on the worldwide and domestic price of rebar; the effect of a sudden contraction in domestic demand in January 1999 just when domestic prices fell; and the effect of a larger volume of comparably priced, non-dumped imports from third countries. The effect of these factors was either ignored, or improperly discounted, or improperly attributed to imports from Turkey in Egypt's final anti-dumping determination in violation of Articles 3.1, 3.4 and 3.5 of the Agreement.

(d) The public record of the injury investigation indicates that Egypt failed to compare the prices of domestic products and the prices of imports on a comparable, delivered basis to the customers who had to choose between imports and domestic rebar to meet their requirements. Egypt therefore failed to establish properly whether there was price undercutting by imports as required by Articles 3.1 and 3.2 of the Agreement.

(e) Egypt changed the scope of its injury investigation without giving adequate notice to the Turkish respondents, and without giving them an opportunity to submit evidence on the present material injury issue, in contravention of Articles 6.1 and 6.2 of the Agreement.

(f) Egypt relied on evidence of injury for its affirmative injury determination which was taken from a period that was subsequent to, and therefore did not coincide with, its finding that there were sales at less than normal value. In so doing, Egypt failed to establish, consistent with the requirements of Article 3.5 of the Agreement, that the dumped imports were, "through the effects of the dumping", causing injury to a domestic industry within the meaning of the Agreement.

(g)   During the sales-at-less-than-normal-value investigation, Egypt's request for substantial new cost information, and substantiation of the accuracy of respondent's prior responses, late in the anti-dumping duty proceeding, after the time for issuing questionnaires and well after the verification, severely prejudiced respondents. Furthermore, this action was inconsistent with Annex II, paragraph 1, Annex I, paragraph 7 and Articles 2.4, 6.1, 6.6 and 6.7 of the Agreement.

(h)   The deadlines imposed for responses to Egypt's supplemental requests for information were unreasonably short, resulting in an improper determination to resort to "facts available", in violation of Articles 6.1.1 and 6.2 and Annex II, paragraph 6 of the Agreement.

(i)   The factual basis cited by Egypt for seeking large amounts of supplemental cost information late in the anti-dumping duty proceeding was speculative and unfounded, as shown in subsequent submissions by the respondents. Given the explanations provided by respondents on this score, Egypt's decision to rely on "facts available" was based on an improper determination of the facts and on an evaluation of the facts that was biased or lacked objectivity. In addition, that determination was inconsistent with Article X:3 of the GATT 1994 and Articles 2.4, 2.2.1.1, 2.2.2, and 6.8 and Annex II, paragraphs 3, 5, 6 and 7 of the Agreement.

(j)   Egypt's refusal to schedule a meeting during which respondents could explain their responses to the supplemental questionnaires was inconsistent with Article X:3 of the GATT 1994, as well as Article 6.2 and Annex II, paragraph 6 of the Agreement.

(k)   Egypt's selection of particular data as "facts available" in the case of each respondent was also improper and lacked objectivity. The costs employed were, in most cases, much higher than the actual contemporaneous costs experienced by the respondents, as shown by other, reliable data developed during the investigation. As a result, the costs selected as "facts available" produced an unfair and unreasonable comparison between normal value and the export price in violation of Articles 2.4, 2.2.1.1, 2.2.2 and 6.8 and Annex II, paragraphs 5 and 7 of the Agreement.

(l)   Egypt's refusal to offset interest expenses with short-term interest income in determining cost of production was inconsistent with Articles 2.2.1, 2.2.1.1 and 2.2.2 of the Agreement.

(m)   And finally, Egypt's failure to make an adjustment to the normal value for imputed credit expenses between the date of shipment and the date of payment was inconsistent with Article 2.4 of the Agreement.

4.	Consultations were held between the Governments of Turkey and Egypt in Cairo, Egypt on 3-5 December 2000 and again in Ankara, Turkey on 3-4 January 2001, but no resolution to this dispute could be reached. Subsequently, on 11 June 2001, following Turkey's request for the establishment of a panel, the Governments of Turkey and Egypt again held consultations with a view to settlement of the dispute, again to no avail.

5.	The panel is respectfully requested to find that Egypt's anti-dumping duty investigation and final determination were inconsistent with the GATT 1994 and with the Anti-Dumping Agreement. Egypt should either revoke the definitive anti-dumping measure imposed on imports of rebar from Turkey or suspend the application of that measure pending a reopening of its investigation for the purpose of addressing the deficiencies identified above.

ANNEX 1-2

FIRST WRITTEN SUBMISSION OF EGYPT
EXECUTIVE SUMMARY

I.   BACKGROUND

1.   On 6 November 2000, the Government of Turkey requested consultations at the WTO with the Government of Egypt regarding definitive anti-dumping measures imposed by Egypt on steel rebar from Turkey.[1] Consultations were held in Cairo and Ankara on 3-5 December 2000 and 3-4 January 2001 respectively. The consultations did not lead to a mutually satisfactory resolution of the matter and Turkey requested that the establishment of a Panel be placed on the agenda of the DSB meeting of 16 May 2001.[2] Egypt opposed the request for the establishment of a Panel at the DSB meeting of 16 May 2001 in order to permit further consultations between the parties, which took place on 11 June 2001. However, consultations again failed to resolve the dispute. Accordingly, a Panel was established at the DSB meeting of 20 June 2001 in which the United States, Japan, the European Communities and Chile reserved their third party rights.

2.   In its request for the Establishment of a Panel, Turkey considers that the measures imposed by Egypt on steel rebar from Turkey are inconsistent with Article X:3 of the General Agreement on Tariffs and Trade 1994 (GATT 1994); Articles 2.2, 2.4, 3.1, 3.2[3], 3.4, 3.5, 6.1, 6.2, 6.6, 6.7, 6.8 and Annex II, paragraphs 1, 3, 5, 6 and 7 and Annex I, paragraph 7 of the Agreement on Implementation of Article VI of the General Agreement on Tariffs and Trade (the "AD Agreement" or "Agreement"). As a result, Turkey considers that the measures nullify and impair the benefits accruing to it under the GATT 1994 and the Anti-Dumping Agreement.

3.   The claims submitted by Turkey are individually addressed below, together with an analysis of Egypt's rights and obligations under the relevant provisions of the AD Agreement and the GATT 1994. An examination of the relevant provisions will demonstrate that Egypt applied the measures in question only pursuant to an investigation that was initiated and conducted in accordance with Egypt's rights and obligations as provided for in Article VI of GATT 1994 and the Anti-Dumping Agreement.

---

[1]   WTO Doc. WT/DS211/1.
[2]   *Ibid.*, at p. 2.
[3]   This provision was inserted at a later date via a corrigendum (WTO Doc. WT/DS211/2/Corr.1).

II. INJURY AND CAUSAL LINK

A. Opening Statement

4.   Steel is, by its very nature, a commodity product. When imports of this kind arrive in the marketplace in very substantial volumes and at very low prices, the domestic industry is bound to suffer injury. As demonstrated below, Egypt was careful to distinguish and to separate other factors than the dumped imports that may have contributed to the injury.

> 1.   *Turkey has not demonstrated that the Investigating Authority failed to establish by "positive evidence" a causal link between imports from Turkey and injury to the domestic industry*

5.   Turkey alleges that Egypt failed to establish by "positive evidence" that there was a causal link between imports from Turkey and declining prices in the domestic market. The "positive evidence" to which Turkey refers is "that consumers purchased imported rebar supplied by the domestic manufacturers for price reasons". Turkey therefore alleges that Egypt's imposition of definitive anti-dumping measures was inconsistent with Articles 3.1 and 3.5 of the Agreement.

6.   Contrary to Turkey's allegation, the Investigating Authority determined on the basis of the data and information available that the volume of dumped imports increased over the period considered and that this had a significant effect on prices of locally produced rebar as required under *Article 3.1(a)*. The Investigating Authority also examined the consequent impact of the dumped imports on the domestic producers as required under *Article 3.1(b)* and found, *inter alia*, that because the industry is sensitive to volume changes, it had to lower prices to meet the competition from the dumped imports and in order to retain sales.

7.   With regard to the establishment of a causal link, the Investigating Authority considered all evidence that was provided by interested parties and found that there were "no other causes of injury" sufficient to break the causal relationship between the dumped imports and the injury to the domestic industry. Moreover, at the time of the investigation, the Investigating Authority was not aware of any "known factors", other than those that it did consider, which would be likely to cause injury to the domestic industry.

8.   *Article 3.5* of the AD Agreement clearly states that factors listed therein "*may be relevant*" in the establishment of a causal link. Accordingly, unlike *Article 3.4*, which mandates that "[t]he examination of the impact of the dumped imports *shall* include an evaluation of all relevant economic factors", it is clear from the wording of Article 3.5 that consideration of the factors listed therein is *not* mandatory.

9.   It follows that Egypt is under no obligation to investigate whether domestic manufacturers lowered their prices *specifically* in response to competing of-

fers by suppliers of Turkish rebar or whether *specific* sales were lost by the domestic industry to imports from Turkey. In addition, the AD Agreement does not require that the Investigating Authority investigate whether the dumped imports are the price leaders in the market, as such is not relevant to the establishment of a causal link. As to contraction in demand or changes in the patterns of consumption, these factors were examined during the course of the investigation and found to be irrelevant to the Investigating Authority's determination of a causal relationship.

10.   Turkey incorrectly alleges that the Investigating Authority failed to take account of the effect of other factors that had a substantial adverse effect on the Egyptian industry

11.   Turkey alleges that the Investigating Authority failed to take account of, and improperly attributed to rebar imports from Turkey, the effect of other factors that had a substantial adverse effect on the Egyptian industry as well as of other neutral factors that caused the price of rebar in Egypt to fall.

12.   It is clear that the above allegation relates to **causation**. The relevant provision of the AD Agreement is Article 3.5. Turkey's claim under Article 3.4 should therefore be **rejected**, as it is not relevant to the issue under consideration.

13.   Turkey has not established that the Investigating Authority failed to take account of the effect of other factors that had a substantial adverse effect on the Egyptian industry in violation of *Article 3.5* of the AD Agreement. Throughout the course of the investigation, the Investigating Authority examined all evidence that was provided by interested parties. To this end, the Investigating Authority examined capacity expansion, competition between domestic producers, falling prices for raw materials, domestic demand and the effect of non-dumped imports. On the basis of this examination, the Investigating Authority found that there were "no other causes of injury" *sufficient* to break the causal relationship between the dumped imports and the injury to the domestic industry.

> 3.   *Turkey's argument with regard to capacity expansion and the establishment of a causal link is fundamentally flawed*

14.   Turkey's argument with regard to the capacity expansion of the Egyptian rebar industry in the establishment of a causal link is fundamentally flawed in a number of respects. First, the Panel should reject all new evidence that was not before the Investigating Authority during the course of the investigation. Second, contrary to Turkey's allegation, the Investigating Authority did consider the capacity expansion of the domestic industry as required under the AD Agreement. Third, the capacity expansion of the Egyptian industry was invoked during the investigation by the Turkish exporters as an economic factor indicating the *absence of injury*, rather than a factor that was *known* to be contributing to the injury incurred by the domestic industry.

4. Turkey has failed to demonstrate that Egypt's application of Article 3.5 of the AD Agreement was incorrect

15.   Turkey is concerned that Egypt improperly attributed to imports from Turkey the decline in prices that took place in 1999. In particular, Turkey alleges that by attributing falling prices caused by declining demand, increased domestic competition and falling raw material costs to imports, the Investigating Authority violated Articles 3.4 and 3.5 of the AD Agreement.

16.   It is evident that the issue raised here is yet again one of *causation*. Turkey is not alleging that Egypt failed to examine the impact of the dumped imports on the domestic industry as required under *Article 3.4*. To this end, Turkey has not provided any legal argumentation to support this claim. The invocation of Article 3.4 in this manner is thus without legal foundation and should therefore be dismissed by the Panel.

17.   With regard to *Article 3.5* of the AD Agreement, the Panel must ask whether the Investigating Authority considered the effect upon price, factors such as declining demand, increased domestic competition and falling raw material costs.

18.   During the investigation, the Investigating Authority found no evidence to prove the existence of a contraction of demand of the product concerned. To the contrary, demand increased. Moreover, there was insufficient evidence before the Investigating Authority to conclude that capacity expansion could have been a factor contributing to the injury. However, the Investigating Authority did examine whether there was any increased competition as a result thereof. As to declining cost of raw materials, the Investigating Authority found that the alleged decline in the price on steel was not a sufficient factor to break the causal link between the dumped imports and the injury to the domestic industry.

5. Turkey's analysis and establishment of the facts as regards the comparison of imports from non-dumped sources is flawed

19.   Turkey's analysis and establishment of the facts concerning the comparison of imports from non-dumped sources is flawed in two respects. First, Turkey implies that the AD Agreement requires that the Investigating Authority determine whether the dumped imports were the price leaders in the market in the establishment of a causal relationship under Article 3.5. Second, Turkey falsely accuses the Investigating Authority of failing to investigate the effects of non-dumped imports from third countries when reaching its determination that the dumped imports were, through the effects of dumping, causing injury to the domestic rebar industry.

20.   While the prices of non-dumped imports from third countries *may* be relevant in the establishment of a causal link under *Article 3.5*, nowhere in the Agreement is there the requirement that Egypt consider whether the Turkish imports were acting as the price leaders in the market. What is relevant in this re-

gard is that the Investigating Authority investigate *known* factors which at the same time are injuring the industry. To this end, Turkey has not presented a *prima facie* case that non-dumped imports from third countries were a factor that was known to the Investigating Authority to be simultaneously causing injury to the domestic industry.

21.   Nonetheless, the Investigating Authority was careful to consider any potential effects of third country imports, both in terms of volume and of price, upon the domestic industry. There is no particular method prescribed by the AD Agreement that Egypt must employ to separate and distinguish the injurious effects of dumped imports from the injurious effects of other causal factors. Thus, the Investigating Authority examined *all* sources of non-dumped imports and found that the fall in domestic prices was caused by the dumped imports rather than imports from other sources.

22.   With respect to Saudi Arabia and Libya, the examination of the import volumes from these countries in Q1-1998 and Q1-1999 demonstrated that their individual import volumes were declining sharply. This is in contrast to the dumped imports from Turkey, which increased significantly during the same period. Moreover, the Investigating Authority reviewed the prices of imports from both Saudi Arabia and Libya and found them to be much higher than the prices of Turkish imports. As a result, the Investigating Authority concluded that other sources of imports were not the cause of injury suffered by the domestic industry.

6.   *Turkey incorrectly asserts that the Investigating Authority's finding of price undercutting was based on a flawed price comparison*

23.   Turkey alleges that by comparing domestic prices and imported prices on a basis that was neither truly comparable nor at the appropriate level of trade, the Investigating Authority's finding of price undercutting was based on a flawed price comparison in violation of Articles 3.1, 3.2 and 3.5 of the Agreement.

24.   It is clear that the Investigating Authority's comparison of import price with domestic price was indeed made at the same level of trade (i.e. the exfactory price for the local industry and ex-importer's store levels for the dumped imports). Turkey, on the other hand, would prefer that the comparison take place on a delivered-price basis. There is, however, no legal foundation to require the Investigating Authority to confine its analysis in this manner.

> 7.   *The task of the Panel is not to conduct a* de novo *review of the Investigating Authority's determination with respect to domestic sales, but to determine whether the Investigating Authority's establishment of the facts was unbiased and objective*

25.   Turkey alleges that the Investigating Authority misinterpreted certain data. In particular, Turkey alleges that the Investigating Authority sought to blame the increase in domestic sales on imports from Turkey and that the Investigating Authority concluded that this increase was the result of reducing domestic prices significantly to compete with the dumped product and to retain market share.

26.   By alleging that the Investigating Authority misinterpreted certain data, Turkey is in fact challenging the Investigating Authority's determination with respect to that data. *Article 17.6(i)* of the AD Agreement, however, makes it very clear that the task of the Panel is solely to assess whether the Investigating Authority's establishment of the facts was proper and the evaluation thereof unbiased and objective. If affirmative, the evaluation shall not be overturned even if it the Panel might have reached a different conclusion. In any event, *Turkey has not alleged any particular violation of the AD Agreement and thus there is no legal basis to support this claim.*

> 8.   *The AD Agreement does not require an Investigating Authority to inform interested parties that it has changed the legal basis for its injury determination during the course of the investigation*

27.   Turkey claims that by failing to give notice of the change in the scope of the investigation from threat of material to present material injury, the Investigating Authority violated Articles 6.1 and 6.2 of the AD Agreement. Egypt is not, however, under any obligation under the AD Agreement to inform the respondents that it had changed the legal basis for its injury determination during the course of the investigation.

> 9.   *Turkey has not shown that the Investigating Authority failed to demonstrate that the imports caused injury to the Egyptian Industry "through the effects of dumping found"*

28.   Turkey is of the opinion that because the only dumping occurred in 1998 and the injury found by the Investigating Authority occurred in 1999, the Investigating Authority failed to show that the imports were, through the effects of the dumping, causing injury to the domestic industry. According to Turkey, "the resulting determination is, therefore, inconsistent with Articles 3.1 and 3.5".

29.   Two points will be addressed. The first is that the AD Agreement does not require that any specific period of time be established for the purpose of data

collection with regard to the investigations of dumping and of injury. Second, the Investigating Authority found that the injury that occurred in Q1-1999 confirmed the injury that took place in 1998 as a result of the dumped imports. Thus, in setting the periods of data collection for both dumping and injury, the Investigating Authority included the first quarter of 1999 for injury in order give adequate consideration to the effects of the dumping that primarily took place, in terms of volume, in 1998. Moreover, the period of data collection for injury included the full period of data collection established by the Investigating Authority for dumping.

B.   Dumping Determination

1.   Opening Statement

30.   The Investigating Authority made numerous attempts to obtain the requisite information from the respondents, but was met with insufficient co-operation and unreliable data. As a consequence, the Investigating Authority had no other alternative but to base its determinations on the information at its disposal. In determining the appropriate facts available, the Investigating Authority primarily used the data submitted by each respondent, thereby giving respondents the benefit of their own data to the extent possible.

2.   The requests for additional information were made in full compliance with the relevant provisions of the AD agreement

31.   Turkey claims that the request for cost information sent to the respondents on 19 August and 23 September 1999 violated Articles 6.1, 6.1.1, 6.2, 6.6 and 6.7 as well as paragraph 7 of Annex I and paragraphs 1 and 6 of Annex II of the AD Agreement. Lastly, Turkey alleges that these requests also contravene Article 2.4 of the AD Agreement dealing with the comparison between normal value and export price. Those claims are without merit.

32.   Contrary to Turkey's allegations, the letters of 19 August 1999 did not constitute "a long, supplemental cost questionnaire that was, in fact, an entirely new cost questionnaire". The Investigating Authority's requests for additional information on cost of production of rebar were sent as a result of two undisputed facts:

(a)   All respondents with the exception of IDC had submitted incomplete and partial replies to the section of the Manufacturers' Questionnaire concerning cost of production. Contrary to the explicit requirements of the Manufacturers' Questionnaire, they reported monthly costs data only for those months during which they had export sales of rebar to Egypt. Since this limited information was largely insufficient to verify whether domestic sales were made in the ordinary course of trade, the respondents were requested to provide cost data for the entire investigation period.

     (b)   During the investigation period, Turkey experienced hyperinflation at an average rate of 5 per cent per month. Since this factor was likely to have a major impact on cost of production, the Investigating Authority asked the respondents to explain whether their cost of production had been adjusted to reflect inflation and to provide supporting evidence, pursuant to paragraph 1 of Annex II and Article 2.2.1.1 of the AD Agreement.

33.   In Egypt's view, this course of action is in accordance with the provisions of Articles 2.4, 6.1, 6.1.1, 6.2, 6.6 and 6.7 as well as with paragraph 7 of Annex I and paragraphs 1 and 6 of Annex II of the AD Agreement.

34.   The Investigating Authority complied with *paragraph 1 of Annex II* when it sent to each respondent in February 1999 a Manufacturers' Questionnaire specifying the information required and the manner in which the information should be structured. The Questionnaire also drew the attention of the respondents to the fact that the Investigating Authority could make determinations on the basis of facts available if the required information was not supplied in a reasonable period of time. As demonstrated in this submission, the same level of assistance was provided in all subsequent requests for additional information.

35.   The compliance with *Article 6.1* is evident since the purpose of the requests for additional information was precisely to give notice to the interested parties of the information which the Investigating Authority required to make its determinations.

36.   The Investigating Authority did not contravene *Article 6.2*. This Article is irrelevant to the requests for additional information since it only concerns the submission of oral information. Furthermore, Egypt considers that the Investigating Authority was under no obligation to accede to the request for a meeting which was presented at a late stage of the investigation and at a time when it had already been established that the costs data submitted by the respondents were not reliable.

37.   As explained in this submission, the requests for additional information were sent in accordance with *Article 6.6* which entitles, and in fact obliges, the Investigating Authority to satisfy itself as to the accuracy of the information used as a basis for its determinations.

38.   The Investigating Authority furthermore informed the respondents of the reasons why the information submitted on costs of production could not be accepted, and granted them ample opportunity to present in writing the evidence required, in accordance with *Article 6.1* and *paragraph 6 of Annex II*. In Egypt's view however, the provisions of *Article 6.1.1* are inapplicable to requests for additional information and clarifications such as those sent by the Investigating Authority in the rebar investigation. Indeed, Article 6.1.1 concerns only the deadline to be granted for the response to questionnaires, which clearly the requests for additional information were not.

39.   With respect to the claim under *Article 6.7* and *paragraph 7 of Annex I*, Egypt considers that, contrary to Turkey's allegations, the AD Agreement does

not suggest that the Investigating Authority must verify information solely through on-the-spot verification visits nor that verification visits should be preferred over other means of verification. Furthermore, the AD Agreement does not prevent the Investigating Authority from requesting the submission of additional information and documentary evidence after having carried out verification visits.

40.   Lastly, the claim of violation of *Article 2.4* is ill-founded since this Article, and the burden of proof requirement contained therein, only concern the issue of fair comparison between export price and normal value. In any case, it is submitted that the Investigating Authority never imposed an unreasonable burden of proof on the respondents since the data requested consisted of readily available accounting records and the clarifications required were essentially descriptive.

> 3.   *The decision to use partially facts available was fully justified by the respondents' failure to submit reliable costs data*

41.   Contrary to Turkey's allegations, the decision to use facts available is in full compliance with Egypt's obligations under the provisions of the AD Agreement and, in particular, of the provisions of *Article 6.8* and *Annex II* of the AD Agreement. As demonstrated in this submission, the costs data submitted by the respondents were incomplete, unsubstantiated by sufficient supporting evidence and did not demonstrate that they duly reflected the costs associated with the production and sale of rebar, in accordance with *Article 2.2.1.1* of the AD Agreement. In consequence, the Investigating Authority was entitled to make its determinations on facts available in accordance with *Article 6.8* and paragraph 5 of Annex II. Pursuant to *paragraph 6 of Annex II*, the Investigating Authority informed the respondents of the reasons why their costs data could not be accepted and gave them ample opportunity to provide further explanations. The Investigating Authority furthermore stated in the Final Report the reasons why the explanations and the information provided were not satisfactory, therefore justifying the use of facts available.

42.   As explained in this submission, the claims of violation of *Articles 2.2.1.1, 2.2.2 and 2.4* are redundant since they rely on the assumption that the Investigating Authority was not entitled to use facts available. They are furthermore based on the wrong premise that the Investigating Authority calculated monthly cost production and constructed normal value, whereas they were calculated for the entire investigation period. They are lastly without merit as a matter of law and would lead to absurd results in the circumstances of this case.

> 4.   *The investigating authority used data submitted by the respondents as appropriate facts available*

43.   The circumstances briefly described in points 1 and 2 above would have entitled the Investigating Authority to disregard the reported costs data altogether

and to make full use of facts available for the determination of the normal value. Instead, the Investigating Authority decided to use the data submitted by the respondents as appropriate facts available. This methodology is considered to be reasonable and fair since, in spite of the poor quality of the reported costs data, the respondents were given the benefit of their own data. This is furthermore fully in line with the relevant provisions of the AD Agreement.

44.   The cost of production and constructed normal value of the respondents were calculated in accordance with the above methodology. Turkey contends that the Investigating Authority violated various provisions of the AD Agreement in the reconstruction of the cost of production and normal value of Icdas, Habas, IDC and Diler. No claim is presented concerning the calculations pertaining to Colakoglu. It is explained in this submission that those claims are without any merit and must, therefore, be rejected.

> 5.   *The disallowance of interest revenue in the reconstruction of the cost production and normal value is in line with the AD Agreement*

45.   The relevant provisions of the AD Agreement make it clear that the cost of production must correspond to the costs associated to the production and sale of the product concerned, to the exclusion of any other cost item which bears no relationship to production or sale. In consequence, Egypt considers that interest income, which is generated by the financial activities of the respondents, should not be included in the computation of the cost of production. This is in line with the provisions of *Article 2.2* of the AD Agreement as well as with the usual practice of other jurisdictions, such as, for instance, the United States and the European Communities.

> 6.   *The absence of a credit cost adjustment to the reconstructed normal value does not violate the AD Agreement*

46.   Turkey alleges that the Investigating Authority's denial of an adjustment for credit costs to the reconstructed normal value while such adjustment was made to the export price contravenes *Article 2.4* of the AD Agreement. This claim has no merit as a matter of law. Egypt considers that, unlike actual selling prices that are negotiated between seller and buyer on the basis of, among other things, the conditions and terms surrounding the sale, the construction of the normal value produces a notional price, the level of which cannot be influenced by any conditions and terms of the relevant sales. In consequence, Egypt considers that the constructed normal value does not need to be adjusted for differences in credit terms, since such normal value is not affected by any credit terms. In any case, since all domestic sales were made at a loss, the Investigating Authority could not use any credit terms granted in the ordinary course of trade to calculate the adjustment. For the foregoing reasons, Egypt considers that the absence of an adjustment for credit costs to a reconstructed normal value is based

on a permissible interpretation of Article 2.4 of the AD Agreement and should therefore be upheld by the Panel.

7. Egypt did not contravene Article X:3 of GATT 1994 in the conduct of the rebar anti-dumping investigation

47.   Lastly, Turkey alleges that some of the actions of the Investigating Authority violated *Article X:3* of GATT 1994. This claim is redundant and without any merit.

48.   In Egypt's view, actions taken by an Investigating Authority in one single anti-dumping case should only be reviewed under the obligations of Article X:3 if such actions had a significant impact on the overall administration of the law, and not simply on the outcome of the single case in question. Furthermore, a conclusion that Article X:3 is violated could in any case not be reached where the actions in question are found to be consistent with more specific obligations of the applicable WTO Agreement.

ANNEX 2-1

FIRST ORAL STATEMENT OF TURKEY
EXECUTIVE SUMMARY

1.   The Government of Turkey considers that the imposition of definitive anti-dumping measures in this case is inconsistent with Articles VI and X:3 of the GATT 1994 and with Articles 2.2, 2.4, 3.1, 3.2, 3.4, 3.5, 6.1, 6.2, 6.6, 6.7 and 6.8 of the Agreement, as well as Annex I, Paragraph 7 and Annex II paragraphs 1, 3, 5, 6 and 7.

I.   INJURY CLAIMS

2.   During the injury investigation in the Turkish rebar case, the Investigating Authority found that both domestic production and sales within Egypt *increased* during the period of investigation, capacity utilization either remained constant or increased, and the domestic industry was able *to increase* its market share. In particular, domestic sales volume increased by 46 per cent in 1997 and by 19.5 per cent in 1998. Domestic market share increased by 5.7 per cent in 1998 and by 22.9 per cent in the first quarter of 1999, as compared to 1996 levels. The principal *indicia* of injury cited in the Final Report were evidence of falling prices, significant declines in domestic industry profitability in both 1998, and the first quarter of 1999, and rising inventories.

3.   It is the view of the Government of Turkey that the Investigating Authority improperly attributed the declining prices, declining profitability, and rising inventories to the effects of imports from Turkey. In this regard, the Final Report found evidence of price underselling by imports from Turkey and attributed a price decline of 1.6 per cent in 1998 and 10.8 per cent in the first quarter of 1999 to such price underselling. However, there is no "positive evidence" linking imports from Turkey to these effects. Increases in the volume of imports cannot be injurious when the domestic industry is itself increasing the volume of its sales, maintaining capacity utilization, and increasing its domestic market share. The existence of some price underselling is also insufficient positive evidence of injury causation. Positive evidence of injury causation would include evidence that purchasers considered Turkish imports to be the price leaders in the market, evidence of lost sales, or evidence that the domestic industry dropped its prices or was unable to raise prices in specific response to the prices of imports from Turkey. None of this evidence is on the record. Where there is no specific, "positive evidence" that imports caused prices to fall, the price declines could just as well have been caused by other factors, as has been claimed elsewhere by Turkey. Because Egypt failed to establish, by "positive evidence," that imports from Turkey caused the price and profitability declines experienced by the Egyptian rebar

industry, the imposition of definitive anti-dumping measures in this case was contrary to Articles 3.1 and 3.5 of the Agreement.

4.   Turkey considers that the Investigating Authority failed to examine all relevant economic factors and indices having a bearing on the state of the industry in violation of Article 3.4 and that it improperly attributed to imports from Turkey the effects of other factors and conditions of competition in violation of Article 3.5. Specifically, the Investigating Authority failed to consider the adverse effects on domestic profitability and pricing produced by five factors: (a) the dramatic capacity expansion at the two major Egyptian rebar producers and its likely, temporary effects on the producers' cost structure, as well as its effects on competition between the Egyptian producers to fill newly expanded order books; (b) sharpening competition between Al Ezz and Alexandria National as Al Ezz sought to increase market share by capitalizing on its cost advantages over Alexandria National; (c) falling prices for steel scrap, the primary raw material input into finished rebar produced by Al Ezz; (d) a sharp contraction in domestic demand in January 1999, when prices for rebar fell; and (e) the effect of comparably priced, fairly traded imports.

5.   Turkey also notes that the Investigating Authority did not evaluate all of the mandatory factors identified in Article 3.4. These factors include productivity, actual and potential negative effects on cash flow, employment, wages, growth, and ability to raise capital or investments. Furthermore, the public version of the Essential Facts and Conclusions Report provides no evidence that there was sufficient examination or evaluation of capacity, capacity utilization, or return on investment.

6.   Turkey considers that Egypt failed to determine accurately whether there was price undercutting by imports of rebar from Turkey because the Investigating Authority failed to make price comparisons on a delivered-price-to-the-customer basis. The Essential Facts and Conclusions Report does not reveal the channels of distribution for domestic and imported product or where in the chain of distribution any actual price competition between imported product and domestic product takes place. Without knowing these facts, it is impossible to ascertain whether the Investigating Authority measured price competition between imported and domestic products at the correct level of trade. The Investigating Authority's findings in this regard are contrary to Articles 3.1, 3.2 and 3.5.

7.   Turkey considers that the Investigating Authority violated Article 6.1 and 6.2 of the Agreement by changing the scope of its injury investigation – from an investigation solely concentrated on threat of injury to an investigation of present material injury – after the deadline for submission of factual information and comment and without adequate notice to the Turkish respondents. Failure to give this notice deprived the Turkish interested parties of their right to submit relevant information and comment on the present material injury question.

8.   By investigating the existence of dumping during calendar year 1998 and relying on evidence of injury taken from the first quarter of 1999, the Investigating Authority violated Article 3.5, which requires a showing that "imports are, through the effects of the dumping, ... causing injury with the meaning of [the]

Agreement." No linkage was shown to exist between dumping in 1998 and injury in 1999.

II.   DETERMINATION OF DUMPING

9.   Egypt turned the normal sequence of events in an anti-dumping duty investigation on its head, and in so doing seriously prejudiced the rights and interests of the Turkish respondents. Normally, it is anticipated that the anti-dumping duty questionnaire will contain all basic questions setting forth the format in which home market sales and costs of production will be reported as well as requesting all basic documentary support for such costs that must be submitted outside of the on-the-spot investigation. Furthermore, such questionnaires must be sent out as soon as possible after initiation of the investigation.

10.   In the Egyptian rebar investigation, more than a month after the verification took place, more than four months after the questionnaire responses were filed, and when, in the Investigating Authority's own words, the end of its investigation was "near", the Investigating Authority suddenly issued a long, supplemental cost questionnaire that was, in fact, an entirely new and much more complex cost questionnaire. Much of the data requested was basic preliminary data that should have been requested either in the original questionnaire or at verification. Moreover, the Investigating Authority required that the respondents provide substantial new cost information. And then, instead of extending its investigation in order to conduct a new cost verification, the Investigating authority asked respondents to do the impossible – to respond to a substantially expanded and more complex cost questionnaire than was contained in its original questionnaire and to submit tables and charts tying each aspect of cost and sales responses to their books and records, together with adequate source documentation to verify each and every sales price and cost. All of the source documentation was, of course, supposed to be fully translated, organized, explained and tied together in English so that the Egyptian authorities could follow the trace from the response to the books. Literally thousands of pages would have had to have been translated, organized and explained in order to respond fully to the questionnaire.

11.   As explained by three of the Turkish respondents at the time, this attempt at a "long-range" or "mail order" verification was doomed to failure from the start. In fact, given the tone, content and deadline set by the 19 August letter, the fact that nearly identical letters were sent to each of the five respondents notwithstanding the absence of evidence that they had coordinated their responses, the timing of this letter just 24 hours after a major earthquake hit Turkey and the absurd deadline imposed for a response, it seems that Egypt hoped and expected that respondents would be unable to respond providing a pretext for a final determination with margins based on "facts available".

12.   By failing to request the basic cost data identified in its 19 August letter in its original questionnaire, the Egyptian Authorities violated Paragraph 1 of Annex II of the Agreement. By waiting until after the verification to raise these issues and then insisting that respondents provide full "mail order" verification of

their previously submitted cost responses and the new information that the Investigating Authority for the first time requested on August 19, Egypt seriously prejudiced the rights of respondents and their ability to provide the data required in violation of Paragraph 6 of Annex II. Egypt also imposed "an unreasonable burden of proof" on respondents in violation of Article 2.4 of the Agreement.

13.   This prejudice was compounded by the absurd deadlines imposed for responses to the Investigating Authority's 19 August 1999 and 23 September 1999 questionnaires. The deadline of 13 days in which to respond to the 19 August questionnaire was plainly inadequate in the best of circumstances in light of the expansive new requests for information and for self-verification that that questionnaire contained. It was utterly devoid of consideration for the actual circumstances respondents faced in light of the massive earthquake that hit Istanbul the day before.

14.   Respondents reasonably requested extensions to 11 October 1999 and 22 October 1999 in which to respond to this questionnaire. But the Investigating Authority granted an extension only to 15 September 1999, just 27 days after the questionnaire was issued. Failure to provide a full 37 days in which to respond to this questionnaire, and failure to grant respondents' reasonable requests for extension of the initial 37-day deadline violated Article 6.1.1. In the alternative, these actions violated Article 6.2 and Annex II, paragraph 6.

15.   On 23 September 1999, the Investigating Authority, for the first time, required of these companies a break-down of all costs to produce billet, supplied on a monthly basis. The Investigating Authority also demanded that these three companies translate each and every page of the hundreds of pages of documentation that they were required to provide in their 15 September responses. The period given for a response to this questionnaire, just two to five days, was manifestly inadequate and contrary to Articles 6.1.1 and 6.2 of the Agreement, as well as Annex II, paragraph 6.

16.   After receiving the Investigating Authority's letter of 23 September 1999, Colakoglu, Diler and Habas requested a hearing during which they could explain how the information submitted in their 15 September 1999 responses replied to the Investigating Authority's information requests. The denial of this request violated Article 6.2, which provides, *inter alia*, that "[i]nterested parties shall ... have the right ... to present ... information orally." Icdas requested a hearing as soon as it reviewed the Essential Facts and Conclusions Report. The denial of this request also violated Article 6.2.

17.   The Investigating Authority's rationale for requesting additional cost data after the verification was that respondents' costs and prices for rebar did not increase as the Investigating Authority had anticipated given high inflation in Turkey. However, this reasoning was purely speculative. The only support for the Investigating Authority's supposition in this regard is the undisputed fact that Turkey's economy was experiencing high inflation during the period of investigation. However, hyperinflation in the economy as whole certainly does not mean that each sector and product group is experiencing inflation at the same rate. This is particularly true of industries, like the Turkish rebar industry, that

import most of their raw materials and where the raw material input is a commodity product subject to significant swings in price.

18.   Respondents showed in their responses, filed on 15 September 1999, that the Investigating Authority was incorrect in assuming that constant, slightly declining or slightly increasing costs meant that there was something missing from respondents' reported costs of production. Specifically, respondents showed that their scrap prices declined by 30 per cent-40 per cent in dollar terms during 1998. The TL was also devaluing against the dollar during this period. However, where the constant currency cost declines by this much, the cost in TL could decline as well, or stay stable, or rise only a bit, but by much less than inflation.

19.   Moreover, respondents explained that labour contracts are renegotiated once per year, such that one would not expect changes in the unit labour cost throughout the year all other things being equal. What causes unit labour costs to rise and fall in these circumstances are changes in the volume of production. Similarly, in the case of depreciation expenses, respondents showed that the expense is adjusted at year-end for inflation. Some companies used the year-end total depreciation to calculate their monthly depreciation costs. Other companies used their monthly values but explained that annual inflation is predicted at the beginning of the year and included in the monthly depreciation expenses in the companies' books. Therefore, while 1998 depreciation costs were certainly higher than 1997's, all other things being equal, the unit depreciation expense would not vary from month to month during 1998. Finally, the Government of Turkey provided official import statistics showing that inflation did not increase at 5 per cent month as had been assumed by the Investigating Authority. During many months, including the May-August 1998 period, inflation did not exceed 2.5 per cent *per annum*. Thus, in the context of this industry, it is not at all surprising that neither costs nor home market prices increased at 5 per cent per month.

20.   The Investigating Authority's findings that respondents' costs did not include the effects of inflation, which the Investigating Authority put at 5 per cent per month, were contrary to all of the facts on the record. For this reason, the Investigating Authority's determination of the facts was not "proper," nor was its evaluation of the facts objective and unbiased. (See Article 17.6 (i)). Furthermore, resort to facts available was unjustified under Article 6.8 and 2.4 of the Agreement.

21.   The Investigating Authority sought to characterize the Colakoglu's, Habas's and Diler's responses to the 19 August and 23 September letters as a "refusal" to provide necessary information. However, given the enormous amounts of information and analysis requested and the limited amount of time provided for a response, the voluminous responses provided, and the respondents' expressed willingness to come to Cairo to explain the information submitted, this panel should conclude that each respondent, at a minimum, "acted to the best of its ability". Accordingly, resort to facts available violated paragraph 5 of Annex II. Furthermore, if the responses received by the Investigating Authority from IDC and Icdas were considered inadequate, it was incumbent upon the Investi-

gating Authority to notify these companies that additional information or explanations were required. No such notice was ever provided. See Annex II, paragraph 6.

22.   As noted in our submission at page 69, because the Investigating Authority's resort to Facts Available was not justified, the final determination was not compliant with Articles 2.2.1.1, 2.2.2 or 2.4.

23.   The facts available used to calculate respondents' costs were severely distorted and inconsistent with other reliable information in the record in violation of Annex II, paragraph 3.

24.   The failure to deduct short-term interest income from interest expense violates Articles 2.2.1.1 and 2.2.2 of the agreement. Turkish respondents' financial statements were prepared in accordance with generally accepted accounting practices in Turkey. There is a separation in respondents' financial statements between operating income and non-operating income. Operating expense and income is expense and income that relates directly to the companies' core operations involving the production and sale of rebar. Short-term interest income is fungible and it is classified as operating income in the companies' financial statements. Therefore, as a matter of generally accepted accounting principles, such income is related to the production and sale of the product under investigation.

25.   The failure to make an adjustment to normal value for differences in credit terms violates Article 2.4 of the Agreement. The credit cost adjustment claimed by respondents is normally granted by the United States, EU, Canada, Chile and Australia. Such adjustments are made both to the normal value and the constructed normal value.

ANNEX 2-2

FIRST ORAL STATEMENT OF EGYPT
EXECUTIVE SUMMARY

I.   INTRODUCTION & SCOPE OF REVIEW

1.   A number of claims have been raised by Turkey under Articles 2, 3, 6, and Annexes I & II of the AD Agreement, together with Article X:3 of GATT 1994. In response, Egypt submits that it applied the definitive measures on rebar from Turkey pursuant to an investigation that was initiated and conducted in accordance with Egypt's rights and obligations as required under the relevant provisions of the Anti-dumping Agreement and the GATT 1994.

2.   Most of Turkey's claims rely on a different interpretation of the factual circumstances of the rebar investigation; however, this is not sufficient to demonstrate the existence of a violation under the AD Agreement. Facts may be evaluated in different ways. What matters under Article 17.6 of the AD Agreement is whether the establishment of the facts by the Investigating Authority was unbiased and objective and whether its determinations are based on a permissible interpretation of the applicable provisions of the AD Agreement. Also of key importance under Article 17.5(ii) is that when reviewing the Investigating Authority's determinations, the Panel must only consider facts *made available* to the Investigating Authority during the course of the investigation.

II.   INJURY

A.   *Causation*

3.   Turkey has failed to demonstrate that Egypt's application of Article 3.5 of the AD Agreement was incorrect. Turkey's case appears to be based upon a fundamental misconception under the AD Agreement that dumping must be the *sole* cause of injury. Since the conclusion of the Tokyo Round, however, it is not even required that dumping be the *principle* cause of injury.

4.   During the course of the investigation, Egypt was careful to distinguish and to separate factors other than the dumped imports that may have contributed to the injury experienced by the domestic industry. The Investigating Authority considered *all* evidence that was provided by interested parties, including any "known factors" other than the dumped imports likely to cause injury to the domestic industry. On the basis of this examination, the Investigating Authority found that there were "no other causes of injury" sufficient to break the causal relationship between the dumped imports and the injury to the domestic industry. To the contrary, the Investigating Authority found that the volume and price of

dumped imports had a direct impact upon the domestic rebar industry in terms of price, profitability and inventories.

5.   There is no express requirement in Article 3.5 that investigating authorities seek out and examine in each case on their own initiative the effects of all possible factors other than imports that may be causing injury (*Thailand – Steel*, Panel at 7.273). The Agreement does not require that Egypt examine whether specific sales were lost by the domestic industry to imports from Turkey or whether domestic manufacturers lowered their prices specifically in response to competing offers by suppliers of Turkish rebar. While consideration of the prices of non-dumped imports from third countries *may* be relevant in the establishment of a causal link under Article 3.5, nowhere in the Agreement is there the requirement to consider whether the Turkish imports were acting as the price leaders in the market. In any event, as detailed in Egypt's First Submission, the Investigating Authority was careful to consider the effects of third country imports, including those of Saudi Arabia and Libya, both in terms of volume and price, upon the domestic industry.

6.   Consideration of contraction in demand or changes in the patterns of consumption is not mandatory under Article 3.5 unless relevant to the Investigating Authority's determination of a causal relationship. Article 3.5 of the AD Agreement therefore does not, as alleged by Turkey, impose any obligation on the Investigating Authority to investigate "whether there was a supply-demand gap that could not be filled by domestic production". The Panel should note, however, that (a) demand in the Egyptian market was considered by the Investigating Authority and found to have increased; and (b) the injury incurred to the domestic industry was not in the form of lost sales. Indeed, in the *Submission of Turkish Respondents Concerning Threat of Injury* (attached as TUR – 18), the respondents point to the fact that demand is, in fact, increasing.

7.   As to the declining cost of raw materials, the Investigating Authority considered the evidence and found that it did not prevent the domestic industry from suffering losses. Given that the injury to the domestic industry included a decline of profit, the falling cost of raw materials is even more poignant to the establishment of the causal relationship between the dumping and the injury that occurred to the domestic industry.

8.   Turkey alleges that the Investigating Authority failed to investigate the capacity expansion of domestic rebar producers. This is incorrect: the capacity expansion of the domestic industry *was* considered by the Investigating Authority during the course of the investigation as required under Article 3.4. The Investigating Authority also examined whether there was any increased competition in the domestic industry as a result of capacity expansion any found that it was not a factor that was relevant to the establishment of a causal relationship under Article 3.5. The capacity expansion was not, however, a factor that was known to be contributing to the injury. Indeed, the capacity expansion of the Egyptian industry was presented by the respondents as an economic factor demonstrating the *absence of any injury to the domestic industry.*

9.   As demonstrated in Egypt's First Submission, the invocation by Turkey of Article 3.4 to matters pertaining to the examination of a causal link under Article 3.5, is legally incorrect. Turkey is alleging that Egypt improperly attributed the injury (i.e. falling prices and a decrease in profitability) to imports from Turkey. According to Turkey, the injury was "produced", that is to say that it was *caused*, by factors other than the dumped imports, such as increased domestic capacity and domestic competition, a decline in the price of raw materials and domestic demand, and the effect of non-dumped imports. The examination of injury differs from that of a causal link. The injury analysis under Article 3.4 does not involve an examination of other potential factors contributing to injury, which is the sole prerogative of Article 3.5.

10.   In any event, Turkey has provided neither the legal argumentation nor the evidence to support a claim under Article 3.4. It is not sufficient for Turkey to simply allege, without more, any particular violation under the AD Agreement. Turkey must present a *prima facie* case of inconsistency. To this end, Turkey has failed.

B.   Method and Interpretation of Data

1.   Price undercutting

11.   Turkey alleges that, by comparing domestic prices and imported prices on a basis that would be neither truly comparable nor at the appropriate level of trade, the Investigating Authority's finding of price undercutting was based on a flawed price comparison in violation of Articles 3.1, 3.2 and 3.5 of the Agreement. This is wrong: the level of trade that the Investigating Authority considered appropriate in this context is the ex-factory price for the local industry and ex-importer's store levels for the dumped imports, which are two perfectly comparable prices for the determination of price undercutting. Turkey, on the other hand, would prefer that the comparison take place on a delivered-price basis. There is, however, no legal foundation on which to base this claim. In addition, such a comparison would ignore the fact that importers and exporters do not sell on a delivered basis.

2.   Sales and prices

12.   By alleging that the Investigating Authority misinterpreted certain data with respect to sales and prices, Turkey is in fact challenging the Investigating Authority's evaluation of that data. We will recall that Article 17.6(i) makes it very clear that the task of the Panel is solely to assess whether the Investigating Authority's establishment of the facts was proper and the evaluation thereof unbiased and objective. If affirmative, the evaluation cannot be overturned, even if the Panel might have reached a different conclusion. In any event, Turkey has not alleged any particular violation of the AD Agreement and thus there is no legal basis whatsoever to support this claim.

3.   *Period of time established*

13.   Turkey is of the opinion that, because dumping occurred in 1998, and the injury to the domestic industry in 1999, Egypt failed to show that the imports were, through the effects of dumping, causing injury to the domestic industry in violation of Articles 3.1 and 3.5. Contrary to Turkey's allegation, however, the injury to the domestic industry took place in 1998 *and* Q1-1999. Moreover, the AD Agreement does not require that any specific period of time be established for the purpose of data collection with regard to the investigations of dumping and of injury. As noted in Egypt's First Submission, the period of data collection for dumping and injury is consistent with the *Recommendation of the Committee on Anti-Dumping Practices Concerning the Periods of Data Collection for Anti-Dumping Investigations* adopted 5 May 2000. Indeed, the period of data collection for injury, which examined the period of 1997 to Q1-1999, *included* the full period of data collection established by the Investigating Authority for dumping, which covered 1998.

4.   *Scope of the Investigation*

14.   Turkey claims that, by failing to give notice of the change in the scope of the investigation from threat of material to present material injury, the Investigating Authority violated Articles 6.1 and 6.2 of the AD Agreement. However, no provision of the AD Agreement requires an investigating authority to inform interested parties, during the course of the investigation, that it has changed the legal basis for its injury determination (*Guatemala – Cement II*, Panel at 8.237).

III.   DUMPING

15.   The Investigating Authority made numerous attempts to obtain the requisite information from the respondents, but was met with insufficient co-operation and unreliable data. As a consequence, the Investigating Authority had no other alternative but to base its determinations on the information at its disposal.

A.   *Requests for Additional Information*

16.   Contrary to Turkey's allegations, the letters of 19 August 1999 did not constitute "a long, supplemental cost questionnaire that was, in fact, an entirely new cost questionnaire". The Investigating Authority's requests for additional information on cost of production of rebar were sent as a result of two facts. First, all respondents with the exception of IDC had submitted incomplete and partial replies to the section of the Manufacturers' Questionnaire concerning cost of production, and second, the reported costs data were inconsistent with the hyperinflation experienced by Egypt during the investigation period.

17.   In Egypt's view, the letter of 19 August 1999 is consistent with the provisions of Articles 2.4, 6.1, 6.1.1, 6.2, 6.6 and 6.7 as well as with paragraph 7 of Annex I and paragraphs 1 and 6 of Annex II of the AD Agreement.

18.   The Investigating Authority complied with *paragraph 1 of Annex II* when it sent to each respondent in February 1999 a Manufacturers' Questionnaire specifying the information required and the manner in which the information should be structured. The Questionnaire also drew the attention of the respondents to the fact that the Investigating Authority could make determinations on the basis of facts available if the required information was not supplied in a reasonable period of time. The same level of assistance was provided in all subsequent requests for additional information. Compliance with *Article 6.1* is evident since the purpose of the requests for additional information was precisely to give notice to the interested parties of the information which the Investigating Authority required to make its determinations. The Investigating Authority did not contravene *Article 6.2*. This Article is irrelevant to the requests for additional information since it only concerns the submission of oral information. The requests for additional information were sent in accordance with *Article 6.6* which entitles, and in fact obliges, the Investigating Authority to satisfy itself as to the accuracy of the information used as a basis for its determinations. The Investigating Authority furthermore informed the respondents of the reasons why the information submitted on costs of production could not be accepted, and granted them ample opportunity to present in writing the evidence required, in accordance with *Article 6.1* and *paragraph 6 of Annex II*. In Egypt's view, however, *Article 6.1.1* is not applicable as it relates solely to the deadline to be granted for the response to questionnaires, which clearly the requests for additional information were not. With respect to the claim under *Article 6.7* and *paragraph 7 of Annex I*, Egypt considers that, contrary to Turkey's allegations, the AD Agreement does not suggest that the Investigating Authority must verify information solely through on-the-spot verification visits nor that verification visits should be preferred over other means of verification. Furthermore, the AD Agreement does not prevent the Investigating Authority from requesting the submission of additional information and documentary evidence after having carried out verification visits.

19.   Lastly, the claim of violation of *Article 2.4* is ill-founded since this Article, and the burden of proof requirement contained therein, only concern the issue of fair comparison between export price and normal value.

B.   The Use of Partially Facts Available was Fully Justified

20.   Contrary to Turkey's allegations, the decision to use facts available is in full compliance with Egypt's obligations under the relevant provisions of the AD Agreement. The costs data submitted by the respondents were incomplete, unsubstantiated by sufficient supporting evidence and did not demonstrate that they duly reflected the costs associated with the production and sale of rebar, in accordance with *Article 2.2.1.1* of the AD Agreement. In consequence, the Investigating Authority was entitled to make its determinations on facts available in accordance with *Article 6.8* and *paragraph 5 of Annex II*. Pursuant to *paragraph 6 of Annex II*, the Investigating Authority informed the respondents of the reasons why their costs data could not be accepted and gave them ample opportu-

nity to provide further explanations. The Investigating Authority furthermore stated in the Final Report the reasons why the explanations and the information provided were not satisfactory, therefore justifying the use of facts available. It was furthermore demonstrated that the claims of violation of *Articles 2.2.1.1, 2.2.2 and 2.4* are redundant.

C. *Data Submitted by the Respondents*

21.   The Investigating Authority decided to use the data submitted by the respondents as appropriate facts available. This methodology is considered to be reasonable and fair since, in spite of the poor quality of the reported costs data, the respondents were given the benefit of their own data. The cost of production and constructed normal value of the respondents were calculated in accordance with the above methodology. Turkey contends that the Investigating Authority violated various provisions of the AD Agreement in the reconstruction of the cost of production and normal value of Icdas, Habas, IDC and Diler. No claim is presented concerning the calculations pertaining to Colakoglu. It was explained that those claims are without any merit and must, therefore, be rejected.

D. *Disallowance of Interest Revenue*

22.   Egypt considers that interest income, which is generated by the financial activities of the respondents, should not be included in the computation of the cost of production. This is in line with the provisions of *Article 2.2* of the AD Agreement as well as with the usual practice of other jurisdictions, such as the United States and the European Communities.

E. *Absence of a Credit Cost Adjustment*

23.   Egypt considers that, unlike actual selling prices that are negotiated between seller and buyer on the basis of, among other things, the conditions and terms surrounding the sale, the construction of the normal value produces a notional price, the level of which cannot be influenced by any conditions and terms of the relevant sales. As such, Egypt considers that the constructed normal value does not need to be adjusted for differences in credit terms, since such normal value is not affected by any credit terms. In any case, since all domestic sales were made at a loss, the Investigating Authority could not use any credit terms granted in the ordinary course of trade to calculate the adjustment. For the foregoing reasons, Egypt considers that the absence of an adjustment for credit costs to a reconstructed normal value is based on a permissible interpretation of Article 2.4 of the AD Agreement and should therefore be upheld by the Panel.

F. *Article x:3 of GATT 1994*

24.   In Egypt's view, actions taken by an Investigating Authority in one single anti-dumping case should only be reviewed under the obligations of Article X:3 if such actions had a significant impact on the overall administration of the law,

and not simply on the outcome of the single case in question. Furthermore, a conclusion that Article X:3 is violated could in any case not be reached where the actions in question are found to be consistent with more specific obligations of the applicable WTO Agreement.

ANNEX 3

RESTATEMENT BY TURKEY OF ITS CLAIMS IN RESPONSE
TO A REQUEST FROM THE PANEL

I.   INJURY CLAIMS

A.   Article 3.1

1.   According to the Appellate Body, the phrase "positive evidence", as used in Article 3.1, means "the evidence must be of an affirmative, objective and verifiable character, and that it must be credible".[1]

1.   Failure to Develop Specific Evidence Linking Imports to Adverse Volume and Price Effects Upon the Domestic Industry

2.   As noted in the Executive Summary of the Statement of Turkey at the First Substantive Meeting (paras. 1 & 2), the principal *indicia* of injury relied upon by Egypt for its affirmative injury determination was falling prices and profitability in 1998 and 1999. In this connection, the Final Report attributed the price decline to price underselling by imports from Turkey. Turkey claims that Egypt violated Article 3.1 by failing to develop "positive evidence" that dumped imports had an effect on domestic prices or, indeed, that dumped imports had any impact on the domestic industry.

3.   The mere existence of increases in the volume of allegedly dumped imports is insufficient evidence of an injurious impact on the domestic industry where the domestic industry is substantially increasing the volume of its own sales, and experiencing strong increases in market share. The existence of some price underselling is also insufficient "positive evidence" of injury causation. Without something more, the Investigating Authority "may mistake a coincidence in time for a causal relationship".[2]

4.   "Positive evidence" that imports caused domestic prices to fall would include evidence that purchasers considered Turkish imports to be the "price leaders" in the market, evidence of specific sales lost by the domestic industry to Turkish imports, or evidence that domestic producers dropped their prices, or had to retract planned prices increases, because customers cited, in price negotiations with the domestic producers, the availability of rebar from Turkey at lower prices. None of this evidence was developed by the Investigating Authority. In-

---

[1]   *Hot Rolled Carbon Steel Products from Japan* at 192.
[2]   *United States – Anti-Dumping Measures on Certain Hot-Rolled Steel Products from Japan*, WT/DS184/R, 28 Feb. 2001, DSR 2001:X, 4769, para 7.252.

deed, there is no "positive evidence" on the administrative record that there was any head-to-head competition between imports and the domestic industry.

2. Failure To Make a Proper Determination of Price Undercutting

5. Egypt also failed to make a proper determination of price undercutting. (See Section D below and First Submission of Turkey at III.G.). By failing to establish properly that imports from Turkey were priced below comparable sales prices charged by the domestic industry, the Investigating Authority failed to develop "positive evidence" of, and failed to undertake an "objective examination" of the "effect of the dumped imports on prices in the domestic market" in violation of Article 3.1.

3. Failure To Link the Imports Which Were Specifically Found To Be Dumped to the Injury

6. Egypt failed to demonstrate that dumping and injury occurred at the same point in time such that there was a link between the imports that were specifically found to be dumped and the injury found. This was a violation both of Article 3.5 (see Section C below and First Submission of Turkey at III.J) and of Article 3.1.

7. During its investigation, the Investigating Authority found most of the injury upon which it relied for its affirmative injury determination in the first quarter of 1999. Specifically, the largest price and profitability declines occurred during that period. But the Investigating Authority made no findings that imports were sold at less than normal value during that period and there is no evidence or reasoning that would link the injury found in 1999 to the dumped imports in 1998. By failing to establish such a linkage, the Investigating Authority failed to develop "positive evidence" linking "the effect of the dumped imports on prices in the domestic market for like products". The Investigating Authority also failed to develop "positive evidence" linking the imports which were dumped to the "impact of these imports on domestic producers of such products". In both respects, the Investigating Authority violated Article 3.1.

B. Article 3.4

1. Failure to Examine "All Relevant Economic Factors and Indices Having a Bearing on the State of the Industry," Affecting "Profits" and "Affecting Domestic Prices"

8. The Investigating Authority failed to "evaluate[] ... all relevant economic factors and indices having a bearing on the state of the industry", including all relevant economic factors and indices "affecting domestic prices". Specifically, the Investigating Authority failed to examine, or failed to examine adequately, the following factors which had a direct bearing on the state of the domestic industry:

(a) The dramatic capacity expansion at the two major Egyptian rebar producers and its likely temporary effects on their cost structures;

(b) The effect of the capacity expansions, which started production at the end of 1998, on competition between the Egyptian producers as they attempted to fill newly expanded order books;

(c) Sharpening competition between Al Ezz and Alexandria National as Al Ezz sought to increase market share by capitalizing on its cost advantages over Alexandria National;

(d) Falling prices for steel scrap, the primary raw material input at Al Ezz;

(e) A sharp contraction in demand in January 1999, the very month in which prices for rebar fell; and

(f) The effect of comparably priced, fairly traded imports.[3]

9.   Factor (a) has a bearing on the costs of production experienced by the domestic industry. It is, therefore, a "relevant factor[] or indice[] having a bearing on the state of the industry". It is also a factor that affects the domestic industry's profits. "[P]rofit[]" is a factor specifically mentioned in Article 3.4.

10.   Factors (b)-(e) are factors "affecting domestic prices", yet they were either not mentioned in the Final Report or their effects on domestic prices were not examined by the Investigating Authority or were not given any weight in the Authority's analysis of why prices fell. While the Investigating Authority noted that falling raw material prices should increase profits, rather than vice-versa, the Investigating Authority failed to consider that falling scrap prices affected only Al Ezz, and not Alexandria National, and that the increase in Al Ezz's cost advantages might have allowed it to reduce prices and gain market share from Alexandria National without sacrificing profitability. Al Ezz's growing cost advantages and growing market share must have been evident in the cost data received by the Investigating Authority.

11.   Factor (f) may or may not have had an effect on domestic prices. However, given that there were comparably priced non-subject imports in the market at the same time as imports from Turkey, and there was no support for a finding that imports from Turkey had materially different effects on domestic prices than imports from other sources, the Investigating Authority's finding that imports from Turkey caused price declines, while imports from other sources did not, is inconsistent at least.

2.   Failure to Examine Factors Specifically Listed in Article 3.4

12.   Moreover, the Investigating Authority did not evaluate all of the factors specifically listed in Article 3.4. These factors include productivity, actual and

---

[3]   *See* First Submission of Turkey at III.B, III.C, III.D, III.E.

potential negative effects on cash flow, employment, wages, growth, and ability to raise capital or investments.[4]

13.   As held by the Panel in *European Communities – Anti-dumping duties on Imports of Cotton-Type Bed Linen from India*, the list of factors enumerated in Article 3.4 of the Agreement "must be evaluated by the investigating authorities in each case in examining the impact of the dumped imports on the industry concerned".[5] While the investigating authority may determine that some of the Article 3.4 factors are not relevant in a particular case, it may not disregard those factors, and must explain the lack of relevance such that its objective consideration of all factors is apparent in the final determination.[6] Egypt failed to meet that requirement in this case.

3.   Failure of the Public Final Report to Disclose Adequate Examination of Certain Factors Listed in Article 3.4

14.   The public version of the Essential Facts and Conclusions Report provides no evidence that there was a sufficient examination or evaluation of capacity utilization or return on investment. This also violated Article 3.4 because the record does not permit the Panel to discern an objective and complete consideration of these factors.[7]

C.   Article 3.5

1.   Absence of Positive Evidence That Imports Were Having an Adverse Volume or Price Effect on the Domestic Industry

15.   The absence of any positive evidence that imports were having an adverse volume or price effect on the domestic industry, as discussed in Section I.A above in connection with the violation of Article 3.1, also represents a violation of Article 3.5. By failing to develop "positive evidence" that imports were having a volume or price effect on the domestic industry, the Investigating Authority also failed to demonstrate "a causal relationship between the dumped imports and the injury to the domestic industry" as required in Article 3.5.[8]

---

[4]   Statement by Turkey at the First Substantive Session at 12.
[5]   WT/DS141/R, 30 Oct. 2000, DSR 2001:VI, 2077, para. 6.159.
[6]   *Ibid.* at para 6.162.
[7]   *Ibid.*
[8]   *See* First Submission of Turkey at III.A.

> 2. *Failure to Separate and Distinguish the Effects of Known Factors Other Than Imports Which Were, or May Have Been, Causing Injury to the Domestic Industry*

16.   The factors listed above in Section I.B were "known factors other than the dumped imports which at the same time" were, or may have been, causing injury to the domestic industry. The failure to "appropriately separate[] and distinguish[]" the effects of those factors from the effects of the dumped imports violated Article 3.5.[9] This failure resulted in improper attribution of the effects of those factors to imports from Turkey.[10]

> 3. *Failure to Demonstrate that the Imports Caused Injury to the Domestic Industry "Through the Effects of the Dumping" Found*

17.   As discussed above in connection with Article 3.1, Egypt failed to demonstrate that dumping and injury occurred at the same point in time such that there was a link between the imports that were specifically found to be dumped and the injury found. This was a violation both of Article 3.1 (see Section I.A above and First Submission of Turkey at III.J) and of Article 3.5.

18.   During its investigation, the Investigating Authority found most of the injury upon which it relied for its affirmative injury determination in the first quarter of 1999. Specifically, the largest price and profitability declines occurred during that period. But the Investigating Authority made no findings that imports were sold at less than normal value during that period and there is no evidence or reasoning that would link the injury found in 1999 to the dumped imports in 1998. By failing to establish such a linkage, the Investigating Authority failed to demonstrate "that the dumped imports are, *through the effects of the dumping*, ... causing injury within the meaning of this Agreement", as required by Article 3.5.

19.   Whatever else this clause may mean, it must mean that the injury must be found to have been caused by imports which have been shown to have been dumped, *i.e.*, sold at less than normal value. While there was a finding of dumping with respect to imports from Turkey in 1998, there was no comparable finding with respect to imports in 1999. Nor was there any information or analysis in the Final Determination linking imports in 1998 with the injurious impacts to the domestic industry found in the first quarter of 1999. Therefore, the Investigating Authority failed to meet the requirements of Article 3.5, first sentence.

---

[9]   "In order that the investigating authorities, applying 3.5, are able to ensure that the injurious effects of the other known factors are not 'attributed' to dumped imports, they must appropriately assess the injurious effects of those other factors. Logically, such an assessment must involve separating and distinguishing the injurious effects of other factors from the injurious effects of the dumped imports. If the injurious effects of the dumped imports are not appropriately separated and distinguished from the injurious effects of other factors, the authorities will be unable to conclude that the injury they ascribe to the dumped imports is actually caused by those imports, rather than by other factors." *Hot-Rolled Carbon Steel Products from Japan*, at para. 223.
[10]   *See* First Submission of Turkey at III.B, III.C, III.D, III.E, and III.F.

D.   Article 3.2

20.   Egypt failed to determine accurately whether there was price undercutting by imports of rebar from Turkey because the Investigating Authority failed to make price comparisons on a delivered-to-the-customer basis. The Essential Facts and Conclusions Report does not reveal the channels of distribution for the domestic and imported product or where in the chain of distribution any actual price competition between the imported product and the domestic product takes place. Without knowing these facts, it is impossible to ascertain whether the Investigating Authority measured price competition between the imported and domestic products at the correct level of trade.

21.   If, for example, the manufacturer sells directly to end users and the importers sell to middlemen who then sell to end users, the real competition is at the end user level. The importer's price to the middle man will have no effect on the domestic producer's price if the middleman mark-up is greater than the difference between the importer's price to the middleman and the producer's price to the end-user. Price undercutting, in this situation, must be measured at the end-user level where there is direct competition between the price of the imported rebar and the price of the domestic rebar.

22.   Similarly, if the domestic manufacturer and the importer sell on a delivered basis, comparison of domestic and import prices on an ex-factory basis will mask differences in transportation costs that are included in the price to the customer and that affect price comparability. Because the Final Report does not disclose whether price comparisons were made on an appropriate basis, Egypt failed to make a proper determination that import prices were undercutting domestic prices, in violation of Article 3.2 ("With regard to the effect of the dumped imports on prices, the investigating authorities shall consider whether there has been a significant price undercutting by the dumped imports as compared with the price of a like product in the importing country ...")

E.   Articles 6.1 and 6.2

23.   Article 6.1 of the Agreement provides that "All interested parties in an anti-dumping investigation shall be given notice of the information which the authorities require and ample opportunity to present in writing all evidence which they consider relevant in respect of the investigation in question." Article 6.2 provides: "Throughout the anti-dumping investigation, all interested parties shall have a full opportunity for the defence of their interests."

24.   Turkey considers that Egypt violated Articles 6.1 and 6.2 of the Agreement by changing the scope of its injury investigation – from an investigation solely concentrated on threat of injury to an investigation of present material injury – after the deadline for submission of factual information and comment and without adequate notice to the Turkish respondents. Failure to give this notice deprived the Turkish respondents of their right to submit relevant information and comment on the present material injury question. It also deprived them of their fundamental due process right to know what allegations were being

lodged against them at the time that they were called upon to submit information and comment.

25.   The Investigating Authority clearly indicated in its Initiation Report that the allegations received from the domestic industry were allegations of threatened material injury only. Under "Other Causes of Injury", for example, the Initiation Report states that "[t]he industry indicated that there were no other causes of a threat of injury other than the allegedly dumped imports. Therefore, the Investigating Authority did not consider other factors that are likely to threaten to cause material injury".[11] The Investigating Authority did consider it necessary to mention that there were no causes of current injury, other than the allegedly dumped imports, no doubt because the allegations of injury contained in the domestic industry's application were limited to allegations of threat of injury. In its questionnaires to the Turkish interested parties, the Investigating Authority also stated that "[t]he application by the Egyptian industry for an investigation was based on threat of material injury resulting from importation of the allegedly dumped goods from Turkey. Therefore, the Department must examine whether the Egyptian industry is likely to suffer material injury in the near future if the dumped imports continue."[12]

26.   Later in the investigation, after the time for submitting factual information and argument on the injury question had passed, the Investigating Authority changed the scope of its investigation in order to examine the present material injury question. By failing to give adequate notice of the change in the scope of its investigation and by failing to give the Turkish interested parties an adequate opportunity to submit information and comment on this issue, the Investigating Authority violated Articles 6.1 and 6.2.

II.   CLAIMS REGARDING DETERMINATION OF DUMPING

A.   *Annex II, Paragraph 1; Annex II, Paragraph 6; Article 6.7; Annex 1, Paragraph 7*

27.   Egypt turned the normal sequence of events in an anti-dumping duty investigation on its head in this case, and in so doing seriously prejudiced the rights and interests of the Turkish respondents.

28.   Normally, it is anticipated that the anti-dumping duty questionnaire will contain all basic questions setting forth the format in which home market sales and costs of production will be reported as well as requesting all basic documentary support for such costs that must be submitted outside of the on-the-spot investigation. Furthermore, such questionnaires must be sent out as soon as possible after initiation of the investigation. Thus, paragraph 1 of Annex II to the Anti-Dumping Agreement states:

---

[11]   TUR-1 at 19.
[12]   TUR-2 at 9.

> "As soon as possible after the initiation of the investigation, the investigating authorities should specify in detail the information required from any interested party, *and the way in which that information should be structured by the interested party in its response.*"

29. The Investigating Authority also has an obligation to examine the responses to that questionnaire closely and to inform the respondents promptly if it has rejected any part of that information or if supplemental information is required. Thus, paragraph 6 to Annex II to the Anti-Dumping Agreement states:

> "If evidence or information is not accepted, the supplying party shall be informed forthwith of the reasons thereof and have an opportunity to provide further explanations within a reasonable period ..."

30. Following this step, an on-the-spot verification may be scheduled at respondents' place of business. See Article 6.7 and Annex I. The purpose of the verification is to check the information reported in the responses to the company's books and records in order to determine its accuracy. Once the verification is completed, the factual record of the investigation is ordinarily closed. According to Paragraph 7 of Annex I, "[a]s the main purpose of the on-the-spot verification is to verify the information provided or to obtain further details, it should be carried out after the response to the questionnaire has been received". Further, paragraph 8 of Annex I provides that "[e]nquiries or questions put by the authorities ... and essential to a successful on-the-spot investigation should, whenever possible, be answered before the visit is made".

31. In the Egyptian rebar investigation, the anti-dumping duty questionnaire was issued to each of the six Turkish exporters and each of the exporters, with the exception of Ekinciler's supplier, responded in full to that questionnaire. The cost questionnaire contained in the original questionnaire was a relatively simple one, requesting just one figure for all raw materials costs and failing to specify the period over which costs should be reported. Respondents were directed to report home market sales as near as possible at the same time as their sales to Egypt, and given the hyperinflationary character of the Turkish economy and common practice in other jurisdictions, the Turkish respondents reported their monthly costs of production for the same months in which they reported home market sales.

32. The responses to the original questionnaire filed by Colakoglu, Diler, Habas, Icdas and IDC were found to be complete by the Investigating Authority and no supplemental questionnaire was issued prior to verification. Verification was conducted and it found no discrepancies between the reported information and the companies' books and records. Preliminary margin calculations were made as to each of respondents' export sales to Egypt and they found margins ranging from zero to 4.17 per cent.

33. Then, more than a month after the verification took place, more than four months after the questionnaire responses were filed, and when, in the Investigat-

ing Authority's own words, the end of its investigation was "near", the Investigating Authority suddenly issued a long, supplemental cost questionnaire that was, in fact, an entirely new and much more complex cost questionnaire. Much of the data requested was basic preliminary data that might be used to evaluate a cost response but which should have been requested either in the original questionnaire or at verification.

34.   Moreover, the Investigating Authority required that the respondents provide substantial new basic cost information by requiring that monthly cost data be provided not only for the months during which sales were made to Egypt but for all other months as well. And then, instead of extending its investigation in order to conduct a new cost verification, the Investigating authority asked respondents to do the impossible – to respond to a substantially expanded and more complex cost questionnaire than was contained in its original questionnaire and to submit tables and charts tying each aspect of cost and sales responses to their books and records, together with adequate source documentation to verify each and every sales price and cost. All of the source documentation was, of course, supposed to be fully translated, organized, explained and tied together in English so that the Egyptian authorities could follow the trace from the response to the books. Literally thousands of pages would have had to have been translated, organized and explained in order to respond fully to the questionnaire.

35.   As explained by three of the Turkish respondents at the time, this attempt at a "long-range" or "mail order" verification was doomed to failure from the start. In fact, given the tone, content and deadline set by the August 19 August letter, the fact that nearly identical letters were sent to each of the five respondents notwithstanding the absence of evidence that they had coordinated their responses, the timing of this letter just 24 hours after a major earthquake hit Turkey and the absurd deadline imposed for a response, it seems that Egypt hoped and expected that respondents would be unable to respond providing a pretext for a final determination with margins much higher than preliminarily calculated based on "facts available".

36.   By failing to request the basic cost data identified in its 19 August letter in its original questionnaire, the Egyptian Authorities violated Paragraph 1 of Annex II of the Agreement. The Investigating Authorities failed "as soon as possible after the initiation of the investigation, ... [to] specify in detail the information required from any interested party, and the way in which that information should be structured". Moreover, Egypt had no excuse for waiting until the investigation was nearly over to issue its supplemental request for information. All of the information upon which the Egyptian Authorities based their request for supplemental cost information was contained in the responses filed by respondents on 7 April 1999. If the Egyptian Authorities wished to question aspects of those responses, they should have done so by issuing supplemental questionnaires at that time, given the Turkish respondents time to respond, and then conducted a full verification of both the price and cost issues.

37.   By waiting until after the verification to raise these issues and then insisting that respondents provide full "mail order" verification of their previously

submitted cost responses and the new information that the Investigating Authority for the first time requested on 19 August Egypt violated Annex 1, paragraph 7 and Article 6.7. "In order to verify information", on-site verifications are permitted under the agreement, "mail order" verifications are not authorized. By taking these steps, Egypt also seriously prejudiced the rights of respondents and impaired their "opportunity to provide further explanations" in violation of Paragraph 6 of Annex II.

B. Article 6.1.1, Annex II, Paragraph 6, and Article 6.2

1. Deadline for August 19, 1999 Questionnaire Response

38.   Under Article 6.1.1, a party must be given 37 days to reply after "receiving a questionnaire used in [an] anti-dumping investigation[]." "Due consideration" must then be given to any request for an extension of the original period for a response. Turkey contends that Egypt failed to meet this obligation when it gave only 13 days for a response to the questionnaire issued on 19 August 1999, and when it extended the deadline upon request to no more than 27 days after the questionnaire was issued.

39.   Although the questionnaire issued on 19 August 1999 was not the first questionnaire issued in this proceeding, it amounted to an entirely new cost questionnaire, requesting several new kinds of information, various basic documents that would ordinarily be requested, if at all, in an original cost questionnaire (such as a chart of accounts, income tax returns, a written summary of the company's books and records, a flow-chart of the accounting system, a list of each type of accounting record kept, lists of all products manufactured and their accounting codes, lists of depreciable assets, and an explanation of how inflation is taken into account in the company's accounting system), the reporting of costs of production over a much larger number of months, and the preparation of detailed tables and charts tying each aspect of the cost sales responses to the companies' books and records, together with adequate source documentation to verify each and every sales price and cost.

40.   The document issued on 19 August 1999 was certainly in the form of a "questionnaire" for use in anti-dumping investigations. By the plain terms of Article 6.1.1, therefore, the Investigating Authority was obliged to give the respondents at least 37 days in which to respond and to give "due consideration" to any extensions requested by the respondents.

41.   In the alternative, the Investigating Authority violated Annex II, paragraph 6 and Article 6.2 by failing to give the respondents a reasonable period of time in which to respond to the 19 August 1999 questionnaires. Annex II, paragraph 6 provides that that parties receiving supplemental requests for information should be given "an opportunity to provide further explanations within a reasonable period. . . ". Article 6.2 provides that "[t]hroughout an anti-dumping investigation all interested parties shall have a full opportunity for the defense of their interests".

42.   The initial deadline of just 13 days in which to respond to the 19 August questionnaire was plainly inadequate in the best of circumstances in light of the expansive new requests for Information and for self-verification that that questionnaire contained. It was utterly devoid of consideration for the actual circumstances respondents faced in light of the massive earthquake that hit Istanbul the day before. Respondents reasonably requested extensions to 11 October 1999 and 22 October 1999 in which to respond to the questionnaire in light of its contents, the disruption to normal business operations caused by the earthquake and the fact that, in several instances, competing verification were scheduled in Canadian and European anti-dumping investigations being conducted at the same time. The denial of these requests violated Annex II, paragraph 6 and Article 6.2.

> 2.   *Deadline for September 23, 1999 Questionnaire Response*

43.   On 23 September 1999, the Investigating Authority, for the first time, required of Colakoglu, Habas and Diler to provide a monthly break-down of all costs to produce billet, supplied on a monthly basis. The Investigating Authority also demanded that these three companies translate each and every page of the hundreds of pages of documentation that they were required to provide in their 15 September responses. The period given for a response to this questionnaire, just two to five days, was manifestly inadequate and contrary to Articles 6.1.1 and 6.2 of the Agreement, as well as Annex II, paragraph 6.

> 3.   *Failure to Notify Icdas and IDC of Continuing Deficiencies After Receipt of Their Responses to the 19 August 1999 and 23 September 1999 Follow-Up Questionnaires*

44.   Icdas and IDC provided full and complete responses to the 19 August 1999 questionnaire. The Investigating Authority only had a few, minor follow-up questions, which were answered in a timely fashion. No other communications were received from the Investigating Authority noting any other deficiencies or missing data. The Investigating Authority's subsequent decision to rely for its determination completely on facts available is plainly contrary to Annex II, paragraph 6. If information is "not accepted", that section requires that the supplying party be informed "and have an opportunity to make further explanations". Icdas and IDC were deprived of that right in this case.

> 4.   *Denial of Requests for Meetings*

45.   After receiving the Investigating Authority's letter of 23 September 1999, Colakoglu, Diler and Habas requested a hearing during which they could explain how the information submitted in their 15 September 1999 responses replied to the Investigating Authority's information requests. The denial of this request violated Article 6.2, which provides, *inter alia*, that "[i]nterested parties shall ...

have the right ... to present ... information orally". Icdas requested a hearing as soon as it reviewed the Essential Facts and Conclusions Report. IDC stated that it was available for further verification of its cost data if the Investigating Authority desired one. The denial of these requests also violated Article 6.2.

46.   The denial of these requests also violates paragraph 6 of Annex II, which provides: "If evidence or information is not accepted, the supplying party should be informed forthwith of the reasons therefor, and should be given an opportunity to provide further explanations within a reasonable period ... ." In this case, the Turkish respondents were denied that basic right.

C.   Article X:3

47.   The denial of respondents' requests for meetings at which they could explain how their responses to the Investigating Authority's request for information were complete and accurate and show that their responses could be tied to their books and records was abusive, discriminatory and unfair to respondents in violation of Article X:3 of the GATT.

48.   The calculation of an interest charge for IDC that overstated IDC's interest expenses as a percent of cost of goods manufactured by a factor of eight was also abusive and discriminatory in violation of Article X:3.[13]

D.   Article 6.8 and 17.6 (I)

49.   The Investigating Authority's rationale for requesting additional cost data after the verification was that respondents' costs and prices for rebar did not increase as the Investigating Authority had anticipated given high inflation in Turkey. However, this reasoning was purely speculative. The only support for the Investigating Authority's supposition in this regard is the undisputed fact that Turkey's economy was experiencing high inflation during the period of investigation. However, hyperinflation in the economy as whole certainly does not mean that each sector and product group is experiencing inflation at the same rate. This is particularly true of industries, like the Turkish rebar industry, that import most of their raw materials and where the raw material input is a commodity product subject to significant swings in price.

50.   Respondents showed in their responses, filed on 15 September 1999, that the Investigating Authority was incorrect in assuming that constant, slightly declining or slightly increasing costs meant that there was something missing from respondents' reported costs of production. Specifically, respondents showed that their scrap prices declined by 30 per cent-40 per cent in dollar terms during 1998. The TL was also devaluing against the dollar during this period. However, where the constant currency cost declines by this much, the cost in TL could decline as well, or stay stable, or rise only a bit, but by much less than inflation.

---

[13]   *See* First Submission of Turkey at 74-76.

51.   Moreover, respondents explained that labour contracts are renegotiated once per year, such that one would not expect changes in the unit labour cost throughout the year all other things being equal. What causes unit labour costs to rise and fall in these circumstances are changes in the volume of production. Similarly, in the case of depreciation expenses, respondents showed that the expense is adjusted at year-end for inflation. Some companies used the year-end total depreciation to calculate their monthly depreciation costs. Other companies used their monthly values but explained that annual inflation is predicted at the beginning of the year and included in the monthly depreciation expenses in the companies' books. Therefore, while 1998 depreciation costs were certainly higher than 1997's, all other things being equal, the unit depreciation expense would not vary from month to month during 1998.

52.   Finally, the Government of Turkey provided official import statistics showing that inflation did not increase at 5 per cent month as had been assumed by the Investigating Authority. During many months, including the May-August 1998 period, inflation did not exceed 2.5 per cent *per annum*. Thus, in the context of this industry, it is not at all surprising that neither costs nor home market prices increased at 5 per cent per month.

53.   The Investigating Authority's findings that respondents' costs did not include the effects of inflation, which the Investigating Authority put at 5 per cent per month, were contrary to all of the facts on the record. For this reason, the Investigating Authority's determination of the facts was not "proper", nor was its evaluation of the facts "objective" and "unbiased" within the meaning of Article 17.6(i). Because the basis for initially questioning and then rejecting Turkish respondents' costs was unfounded, resort to facts available was unjustified under Article 6.8 of the Agreement. The Turkish respondents provided all "necessary information" and certainly did not "impede" the investigation.

E.   Annex II, Paragraph 5

54.   Annex II, Paragraph 5 provides that "[e]ven though information provided may not be ideal in all respects, this should not justify the authorities from disregarding it, *provided the interested party has acted to the best of its ability*". The Investigating Authority sought to characterize the Colakoglu's, Habas's and Diler's responses to the 19 August and 23 September letters as a "refusal" to provide necessary information. However, given the enormous amounts of information and analysis requested and the limited amount of time provided for a response, the voluminous responses provided, and the respondents' expressed willingness to come to Cairo to explain the information submitted, this panel should conclude that each respondent, at a minimum, "acted to the best of its ability". Accordingly, resort to facts available violated paragraph 5 of Annex II.

F. *Articles 2.2.1.1, 2.2.2 and 2.4*

1. *Breach of Article 2.4 by Imposing an Unreasonable Burden of Proof on Respondents*

55.   As discussed in Section II.A, the Investigating Authority waited until the last minute to raise issues requiring the submission of new factual information and then imposed an unduly burdensome "mail order" verification requirement upon the respondents. In so doing, it imposed an "unreasonable burden of proof" upon respondents in violation of Article 2.4 of the Agreement.

2. *Breach of 2.2.1.1 and 2.2.2 and 2.4 Due to Unjustified Resort to Facts Available*

56.   As noted in our First Submission at page 69, because the Investigating Authority's resort to facts available was unjustified, its final determination was not compliant with Articles 2.2.1.1 or 2.2.2 or 2.4.

57.   Article 2.2.1.1 states that "costs shall normally be calculated on the basis of records kept by the exporter or producer under investigation". The Investigating failed to meet this requirement reasonably by picking the very highest cost for each cost element from among the monthly costs supplied. Article 2.2.2 provides that "amounts for administrative, selling and general costs and for profits shall be based on actual data pertaining to production and sales in the ordinary course of trade. . . ". The Investigating Authority failed to meet this requirement when it included in constructed normal value interest expenses from months other than the month in which the constructed value was being calculated. Finally, Article 2.4 requires "a fair comparison" "between the export price and the normal value". The Investigating Authority breached this provision by comparing a constructed value based on higher costs incurred in months other than the months in which the sales to Egypt took place, distorting the dumping margin calculation.

3. *Breach of Articles 2.2.1.1 and 2.2.2 Due to Failure to Deduct Short-Term Interest Offset*

58.   The Investigating Authority did not deduct short-term interest earnings from interest expense in computing the net interest expense which it included in the cost of production and constructed normal value. The Investigating Authority claimed that "decisions by respondents to invest funds in interest-bearing accounts do not, in the Investigating Authority's view, bear a sufficiently close relationship to a company's cost of producing the subject products". This finding is inconsistent with generally accepted accounting principles and thus with the Agreement. It also inconsistent with generally accepted dumping practice in other jurisdictions.

59.   Article 2.2.1.1 provides that "costs shall normally be calculated on the basis of records kept by the exporter or producer under investigation, provided that such records are in accordance with the generally accepted accounting principles of the exporting country and reasonably reflect the costs associated with

production and sale of the product under consideration". Article 2.2.2 provides that amounts for administrative, selling and general costs ... shall be based on actual data pertaining to the production and sales in the ordinary course of trade by the exporter or producer under investigation".

60.   In this case, Turkish respondents' financial statements were prepared in accordance with generally accepted accounting practices in Turkey. There is a separation in respondents' financial statements between operating income and non-operating income. Operating expense and income is expense and income that relates directly to the companies' core operations involving the production and sale of rebar. Non-operating expense and income is expense and income that is divorced from the production and sale of the companies' main products.

61.   In each case, short-term interest income is classified as an operating income in the companies' financial statements. Therefore, as a matter of generally accepted accounting principles, such income is related to the production and sale of the product under investigation. Moreover, in each case, in arriving at net income, short-term interest income is offset against interest expense and other expenses. Therefore, in order to arrive at an accurate picture of the fully distributed cost to produce the product under consideration, this income must be deducted.

62.   The United States, the EU and Canada all give such an allowance because companies commonly maintain a working capital reserve in interest-bearing accounts in order to meet daily cash requirements and working capital requirements. A NAFTA panel reviewing a decision by Revenue Canada in this area reversed and remanded with instructions to offset interest expense with short-term interest income. It explained in doing so that, under generally accepted accounting rules, short-term interest income is considered part of the current operating cycle. As a US court has explained, moreover, a company that chooses to invest short-term funds rather than use them to pay off or avoid short-term debt should not be penalized in the calculation of net overhead expenses. It is the net cost (interest income minus interest expense) that represents a company's true interest financing expense.

63.   Because each of the companies' records show that short-term interest income is operating income and because that income is fungible, the Investigating Authority's failure to offset interest expense with interest income violates Article 2.2.1.1 and 2.2.2 of the Agreement.

4.   *Breach of Article 2.4 Due to Failure to Make An Adjustment to Normal Value for Differences in Terms of Sale*

64.   The Investigating Authority also failed to make a credit cost adjustment to the normal value for differential payment terms on home market and export sales to Egypt. The Government of Turkey considers that this inaction violated Article 2.4 of the Agreement.

65.   Article 2.4 provides that the comparison between the export price and the normal value "shall be made at the same level of trade, normally, at the ex-

factory level, and in respect of sales made at as nearly as possible the same time. Due allowance shall be made in each case ... for differences which affect price comparability, including differences in ... terms of sale. ..."

66.   An imputed credit cost adjustment was claimed by the respondents to adjust export prices and home market prices with deferred payment terms to a common sight price basis in order to make an apples-to-apples comparison. Where prices carry different payment terms, a credit cost adjustment is necessary in order to adjust for "differences in terms of sale". The credit cost adjustment claimed by respondents is normally granted by the United States, EU, Canada, Chile and Australia. Such adjustments are made both to the normal value and the constructed normal value. As noted by the Third-Party Submission of the EU, it is EU policy to make such adjustments where the normal value is based on constructed normal value, because the constructed normal value "will typically include an element for costs relating to the grant of credit terms".[14] Specifically, the interest expense that is included in administrative, selling and general costs includes interest expenses related to the financing of receivables. Consequently, in order to make an apples-to-apples comparison, an adjustment should be made and that adjustment should be based on the imputed credit cost computed on contemporaneous identical or similar home market sales.

67.   The Investigating Authority did make a credit cost adjustment to the export sales to Egypt. By making an adjustment to the export price but not to the normal value, Turkey considers that Egypt produced a distorted comparison in violation of Article 2.4 of the Agreement.

G.   Annex II, Paragraphs 3 and 7

68.   The Investigating Authority selected as facts available costs that were highly distorted in several instances and used that data in place of more reliable, verified data. In so doing, the Investigating Authority violated the letter of Annex II, paragraph 3 and the spirit of Annex II, paragraph 7.

69.   Annex II, paragraph 3 provides that "All information which is verifiable ... [and] which is supplied in a timely fashion ... should be taken into account when determinations are made." This provision was violated when the Investigating Authority declined to use Icdas' scrap costs for the period September–October 1999 for purposes of constructing normal value for comparison to that company's sales to Egypt. Icdas provided detailed monthly scrap costs to the Investigating Authority, as well as invoices and purchase orders verifying the accuracy of its submitted scrap costs. Icdas also showed that its scrap cost in September-October 1999 was substantially lower than its scrap cost in January 1999.[15] Because these facts were provided in a timely fashion and were verified, the Investigating Authority's determination to use Icdas' January scrap cost in these circumstances violated Annex II, paragraph 3.

---

[14]   Third-Party Submission of the European Communities, 1 Nov. 2001, at para. 32.
[15]   See TUR-28, First Submission of Turkey at 70-71.

70.   This action also violated the spirit, if not the letter, of Annex II, paragraph 7. That paragraph provides: "If the authorities have to base their findings, including those with respect to normal value, on information from a secondary source, ... they should do so with special circumspection". Although this paragraph refers to data taken from a secondary source, rather than data taken directly from the responses, it expresses the drafters' intent that data used in place of specific data supplied by the respondents for a particular cost be checked for its fundamental fairness and accuracy. In this case, reference to verified data reveals that the data used was grossly distorted. Its use was therefore in conflict with the considerations underlying Annex II, paragraph 7.

71.   A similar error was made in the case of IDC. There, the Investigating Authority managed to compute an interest expense that amounted to [XX] per cent of the company's cost of manufacturing. However, IDC's audited financial statement shows that the company's interest expense should be no more than [XX]% of the company's cost of manufacturing. Once again, the failure to use verified information to calculate this expense violated Annex II, paragraph 3 and the considerations underlying Annex II, paragraph 7.

72.   The interest expense computed for Diler is similarly overstated by comparison to the expenses shown in that company's audited financial statement.[16]

73.   Finally, the addition of an arbitrary 5 per cent to Habas' reported costs finds no support anywhere in the record. This amount was, if anything, based on a "secondary source". Therefore, in making this adjustment, the Investigating Authority violated Annex II, paragraph 7 and made an improper finding of fact.

---

[16]   *See* First Submission of Turkey at 76.

ANNEX 4-1

RESPONSES OF TURKEY TO QUESTIONS POSED IN THE CONTEXT OF THE FIRST SUBSTANTIVE MEETING OF THE PANEL

QUESTIONS POSED BY THE PANEL TO TURKEY

Question 1

Could Turkey set out in summary format its legal argumentation in support of each of its claims, i.e., listing the respective provisions of the Anti-Dumping Agreement and the GATT 1994, and explaining briefly in the light of the Vienna Convention on the Law of Treaties how the cited factual circumstances constitute violations of those provisions. For example, [cites to claims in brief/oral statement]

Response

1.   Please see Appendix (reproduced in Annex 3).

Question 2.1

Claim 2: Failure to take account of, and attribution to dumped imports of, the effect of other factors: In Turkey's Request for Establishment of a Panel (WT/DS211/2 and Corr. 1) at para. 3, and its Executive Summary of its First Submission, (at para. I.3.c) Turkey cites Article 3.1, along with Articles 3.4 and 3.5, in connection with the non-attribution claim, but in the text of the argument on this claim, there is no mention of Article 3.1. Could Turkey please clarify.

Response

2.   We do not rely on Article 3.1 in making this claim.

Question 2.2

Claim 4: Finding of price undercutting based on a flawed price comparison: It is noted that in paragraph 5 of its Request for Establishment of a Panel, Turkey claims a violation of Articles 3.1 and 3.2 with regard to price undercutting. However, in its First Written Submission, Turkey also alleges a violation of Article 3.5 in connection with this claim (see page 21 of Submission).

Should the Panel regard the violation of Article 3.5 as a separate claim, and if so, what is the legal basis for the claim, as a violation of Article 3.5 was not claimed in the context of this specific claim in WT/DS211/2?

Response

3.   Our claim that Egypt has made a flawed finding of price undercutting does not depend on reference to Article 3.5.

4.   We have, however, claimed that the Investigating Authority failed to establish by "positive evidence" a causal link under Article 3.5 between imports from Turkey and injury to the domestic industry in Egypt.[1] The absence of valid evidence of price undercutting, as discussed in Section III.G., could be viewed as further support for this claim.

Question 2.3

Claim 9: Factual basis to seek additional information was unfounded and therefore basis to resort to facts available improper: **In its Request for Establishment of a Panel Turkey cites Article X:3 of GATT 1994, and AD Agreement Articles 2.4, 2.2.1.1, 2.2.2 and 6.8 and Annex II, paragraph 3, 5, 6 and 7. However, in its First Written Submission, Turkey cites only Article 2.2.1.1, 2.2.2, 2.4 and 6.8 and Annex II, paragraph 5 and 6 in connection with this claim.**

Could Turkey confirm that the scope of this claim is as set forth in its First Written Submission, i.e., Articles 2.2.1.1, 2.2.2, 2.4 and 6.8, and Annex II, paragraphs 5 and 6?

Response

5.   We did make claims as to Article X:3, paragraph 3 of Annex II and Annex II, paragraph 7. See Appendix and response to Question 2.4, below.

Question 2.4

Claim 11: Selection of particular data as facts available was not proper, biased and not objective: **In the Request for Establishment of a Panel, Turkey cites Articles 2.4, 2.2.1.1, 2.2.2 and 6.8 and Annex II, paragraphs 5 and 7. However, in its First Written Submission, Turkey cites only Article 2.4 and Annex II, paragraphs 5 and 7, but claims, in addition, a violation of Article X:3(a) of GATT and Annex II, paragraph 3.**

Could Turkey confirm that the scope of this claim is as set forth in its First Written Submission, i.e., Article 2.4 and Annex II, paragraph 5 and 7, and clarify its position regarding the claims relating to a violation of Article X:3(a), and Annex II, paragraph 3, i.e., whether the reference to these two provisions should be regarded as separate claims by the Panel, and if so, what is the legal basis thereof, as they were not cited in the Request for Establishment of a Panel in the context of this specific claim?

---

[1]   *See* Claim 2, Request for Establishment of a Panel by Turkey; Section III.A, First Submission of the Government of the Republic of Turkey ("First Submission of Turkey").

Response

6.   We reference Article X:3, paragraph 3 of Annex II and Annex II, paragraph 7 in claim number 9 which broadly asserts that resort to facts available was a violation of Article X:3 and several provisions of the Agreement. Claim number 9 is integrally related to claim number 11. In particular, we question in claim 11 the selection and use of particular facts available in place of information the accuracy of which should not be in question, *i.e.*, data in audited financial statements and scrap cost data that was supported by invoices, raw material ledgers and other such documentation. The argument that data from audited financial statements or data verified to source documentation should have been used by the Investigating Authority instead of facts available relies on paragraph 3 of Annex II and the considerations underlying paragraph 7 of Annex II. Article X:3 is also cited in claim 9 as having been violated because the selection of facts available in particular circumstances was so distorted as to be abusive and discriminatory.

Question 2.5

Claim under Article VI of GATT 1994: **At page 81, section V, "Conclusion" of its First Submission, and at page 1 of its First Oral Statement, Turkey asks the Panel to find that Egypt's final anti-dumping determination was inconsistent with,** *inter alia*, **Article VI of GATT 1994. There is no reference to a claim under this provision in Turkey's Request for Establishment of a Panel, and there is no other reference to any such claim elsewhere in the First Submission or the Oral Statement. Could Turkey please clarify.**

Response

7.   Our citation to Article VI of GATT 1994 is in recognition of the fact that the Anti-Dumping Agreement interprets the obligations contained in GATT Article VI and that we have made an argument that several provisions of the Anti-dumping Agreement have been violated. Turkey does not purport to set out any separate claim by its reference to Article VI in this context.

Question 2.6

Reference to Annex I, para. 8: At page 27 of its First Oral Statement, Turkey refers to Annex I, paragraph 8. Could Turkey please indicate whether it is claiming a violation of this provision. If so, could Turkey provide the legal basis for this claim, as it is not referred to in Turkey's Request for Establishment of a Panel.

Response

8.   Turkey is not claiming a violation of Annex I, paragraph 8. In Turkey's view this provision sheds light on the normal sequence of events in antidumping investigations, but Turkey does not claim that Annex I, paragraph 8 has been violated in this case.

Question 3

Claim 1: Failure to establish by positive evidence a causal link: Is Turkey claiming that under Articles 3.1 and 3.5, only evidence of the specific kinds that it lists at III.A.4, could "demonstrate" a causal link between imports and injury?

Response

9.   No, there may be other ways to link imports to injury. These examples are illustrative. However, we do think that it was incumbent upon the Investigating Authority to secure this kind of information pursuant to Article 3.5 in order to determine whether or not there was a causal link between dumped imports and injury. The absence of any lost sales or confirmed examples of price reductions due to competing offers from import sources would be "positive evidence" that no such link exists.

10.   The Investigating Authority bears a special burden to collect this data – it is uniquely available from the petitioners in Egypt and cannot be secured through other means by the Turkish respondents.

Question 4

Could Turkey please clarify the status of Exhibits TUR-13, TUR-14, TUR-19 and TUR-32, and also of the documents listed in footnote 16 and 17 of its First Written Submission, that is, were these documents submitted to the Egyptian Investigating Authority ("IA"), and if so, when? If not, please provide legal argumentation regarding the basis on which the Panel could take these documents into consideration.

Response

11.   The documents referenced in this question were not submitted to the Investigating Authority. As discussed in the Additional Comments Made at the First Substantive Meeting by the Turkish Delegation (at 1-2), Turkey believes that these documents should be taken into account in this proceeding.

12.   First, we note Egypt concedes in its submission that nothing in the DSU prevents consideration by the Panel of evidence not presented to the competent authorities at the time of their investigation.[2]

13.   Second, the additional evidence contained in our submission on factors causing present material injury was not presented by Turkish respondents to the Investigating Authority during the course of the investigation because respondents had been advised that the Investigating Authority's investigation was limited to the question of threat of material injury.[3] Moreover, the allegations submitted by the Egyptian industry to the Investigating Authority in their application for the imposition of anti-dumping measures was apparently limited to allega-

---

[2]   *See* First Written Submission of Egypt at 18.
[3]   *See, e.g.*, Initiation Report, TUR-1, at 1-1 and 4-5-7; Manufacturers Questionnaire, at 6, p. 10-11.

tions of threat of future material injury as well.[4] Turkish respondents had no reason to believe that evidence on possible causes of present material injury was relevant to the investigation. This understanding also informed the manner in which respondents presented certain injury information early in the proceeding (e.g., information regarding the capacity expansions at ANSDK and Al Ezz).[5]

14.   It would have been unusual, to the say the least, for the Turkish side to present evidence showing that other factors were causing *present* material injury the domestic industry where there had been no claim by the domestic industry of current material injury and where the Egyptian authorities plainly stated at the outset that their conduct of the investigation was based on allegations of threatened injury only.

15.   Third, if the Panel decides, under Article 17.5(b) (as argued by the EU and the United States), that the record should ordinarily be limited to the facts "made available" to the Investigating Authority during the course of its investigation, then Turkey requests the Panel to adopt the legal principle that the Panel can take "judicial notice" of certain other facts. Both at English and American common law, most proof in a court of law is presented by means of testimonial evidence or by the offering of real evidence. But there is an exception to the requirement that a party who relies on a certain proposition must prove it, and that exception is facts that can be "judicially noticed". In the United States, there is a federal rule of evidence permitting both trial courts and appellate courts to take "judicial notice" of facts that are not subject to reasonable dispute because they are either (1) generally known; or (2) capable of accurate and ready determination by resort to sources whose accuracy cannot be reasonably questioned.[6] Appellate courts may take judicial notice of such facts even though they were not before, or were not considered by, the trial court.[7]

16.   The first type of fact of which judicial notice may be taken is a fact that is "so well known that it would be a waste of judicial resources to require proof; reasonably informed people simply could not differ as to the fact".[8] The second type of fact is "one that is capable of ready verification through sources whose reliability cannot reasonably be questioned".[9] This type of fact is "the one more often relied upon, because a fair argument can be made that most facts are not generally known, but yet that many of these facts can be reliably verified".[10]

17.   The requirement that panels base their review on facts presented to the competent authorities ensures that the competent authorities have the ability to test and pass judgement on the validity of the facts presented. But the same considerations would not preclude a Panel from considering facts that can be judi-

---

[4]   *Ibid.*

[5]   *Compare* TUR-18 at 9-10 *with* TUR- 20 at 18.

[6]   *See* Rule 201, Federal Rules of Evidence – Judicial Notice of Adjudicative Facts.

[7]   *See* Rule 201(f).

[8]   Federal Rules of Evidence Manual, Editorial Explanatory Comment, Rule 201, at 122; *Wooden v. Missouri Pac. R.R.*, 862 F.2d 560 (5th Cir. 1989).

[9]   Fed. R. Ev. Man. at 122.

[10]   *Ibid.; Terrabone v. Blackburn*, 646 F.2d 997 (5th Cir. 1981).

cially noticed – such facts can be reliably and easily verified by reference to public sources.

18.   In our case, the fact that Alexandria National and Al Ezz were engaged in major expansion projects, and the timing and size of those projects, were widely reported in the press. The Turkish respondents supplied some articles on this subject to the Investigating Authority.[11] The Investigating Authority must have received other information directly from the Egyptian industry on these capacity expansions, although none of this information appears directly in the public record. Additional press articles with respect to these expansions are cited in Turkey's first written submission.[12] The Panel should take judicial notice of these articles and the information they contain regarding the expansion projects.

19.   The Panel should also take judicial notice of the Form 10Q filed by Birmingham Steel Corporation with the Securities and Exchange Commission cited in the First Submission of Turkey (at note 20) with reference to start-up problems associated with that company's new melt shop at Memphis, Tennessee. There are severe penalties for making false or misleading statements in such reports to the SEC. Moreover, Birmingham would have had no conceivable motive for mentioning these embarrassing difficulties other than its statutory obligation to disclose all events having a material effect on its operations.

20.   The Panel may also take judicial notice of the decline in scrap prices as presented in the *American Metal Market* and *Metal Bulletin* articles presented in our submission.[13] *American Metal Market* and *Metal Bulletin* are the most widely read periodicals in the steel industry worldwide. Each regularly publishes scrap prices.

21.   The Panel should also take judicial notice of the fact that Al Ezz uses the electric arc furnace technology. (The fact that Alexandria National relies on the DRI technology to make rebar was specifically made known to the Investigating Authority by Turkish respondents.[14]) Once again, the fact in question is readily verifiable from public sources.[15]

22.   Finally, even if the Panel declined to consider information not presented to the Investigating Authority in reviewing this matter, we believe that there is sufficient evidence on the record to support each of our claims. The fact that there was a capacity expansion at Al Ezz and Alexandria National was certainly known to the Investigating Authority and it was mentioned in submissions made by the Turkish respondents.[16]

---

[11]   *See infra.*
[12]   *See* First Submission of Turkey, n. 16, 17, 19.
[13]   *See* TUR-13, 14.
[14]   *See* TUR 18 at Exhibit 4, page 5.
[15]   *See Iron and Steel Works of the World*, Metal Bulletin Books Ltd., 13th Edition (1999) at 104.
[16]   *See* Letter from Law Offices of David Simon to the Investigating Authority, May 21, 1999, (reproduced in TUR-18)(hereafter "TUR-18") at 9, 10 and Exhibit 4 at page 5 ("The Ezz Group, one of the country's fastest growing private conglomerates, manufactures 600,000 tones of long products annually. It plans to increase production to 1.1 million tonnes by the end of 1998 ... "); *id.* at Exhibit 4, pages 7-8 ("Other expansion projects of the steel sector include an increase in output capacity of

23.   The decline in scrap prices was also made known to the Investigating Authority and was documented in respondents' submissions.[17]

24.   The contraction in domestic demand in January 1999 was noted by respondents in their submission of 19 May 1999 and is documented in the exhibits to that submission.[18] The fact that comparably priced non-dumped imports were in the market at greater volumes than imports from Turkey was also specifically brought to the Investigating Authority's attention.[19]

25.   The fact that Al Ezz was increasing its market share at the expense of Alexandria National and had a much lower unit cost of production should have been apparent from the domestic manufacturer responses filed by the two parties with the Investigating Authority.

26.   With respect to TUR-13 and TUR-14, we note that we supplied this information to refute a finding made by the Investigating Authority for the first

1.55 million tons at Alexandria National Iron and Steel Company at the cost of $170 million for a second direct reduction unit and $225 million to expand and upgrade its existing steel plant (MEED, April 1996). In Sadat City, the El Ezz Group is also investing about $130 million in a new steel plant"); Letter from Law Offices of David Simon to Investigating Authority, 15 October 1999 (reproduced in TUR-20)(hereafter "TUR-20") at 18 ("[I]t is evident there has been no consideration of whether petitioners' declining profitability might be due to ... petitioners' capital investment ... . As we have explained, the imports had no volume effect and no price effect, so it is not appropriate to conclude that petitioners' profit picture is the result of imports"); Views and Comments of the Turkish Government on "Essential Facts and Conclusions Report," 15 October 1999 (reproduced as TUR-30)(hereafter "TUR-30") at 4 ("The decline in domestic producers' profits and return on investment can not be related to Turkish exports either. ...[T]his decline can only be associated with the new investments made by the Egyptian producers in recent years, which the ITPD mentioned in paragraph 4.3.2.4 of the Report").

[17]   See TUR-18 at 13 ([F]alling prices are not the result of price suppression, but, rather, flow from the decline in world scrap prices ..."), 11, n. 7, 14 and Exhibit 3, page 3; TUR-20 at 17 ("If scrap goes down, the domestic industry's prices should also go down ... . Hence, to suggest that in March 1999 the Turkish prices suppressed prices in Egypt is an unwarranted conclusion without evidentiary support"), 18 ("Scrap prices were substantially down during Q-1 (see Table on page 4, above), and the pricing in Egypt was simply reflecting the drop in input prices"); TUR-30 at 4 (According to the provisions of the GATT 1994 Anti-Dumping Agreement, the investigating authorities should examine any known factors other than imports in question, which at the same time are injuring the domestic industry, and the injuries caused by these factors must not be attributed to the dumped imports. ITPD fails to comply with these provisions as it does not take into consideration decreasing international market prices for scrap in 1998 ... . In fact, as the prices of scrap - which establishes the majority of the rebar costs – decreased so did the prices of rebars in the Egyptian market, as in most of other countries"). See also Letter from Law Offices of David Simon to IA, 15 September 1999 (TUR-21)("[W]e are submitting data – tallies of Colakoglu, Diler and Habas raw material purchases – which show that the input (scrap) costs for these companies declined from [[$XX/MT to $XX/MT, thence to $XX/MT and thence even to $XX/MT]] during {1998}; First Written Submission of the Government of the Republic of Turkey at 63 (reproducing scrap cost data from 15 September 1999 response of Icdas showing steady decline in scrap costs totaling 33.93 per cent during 1998).

[18]   See TUR-18 at 13 ("Regarding the allegation of price depression, we have three comments. First, the rebar industry is seasonal, as is apparent from the monthly Egyptian sales figures in Exhibit 3 hereto, with a distinct seasonal trough in January. ...") and Exhibit 3, page 3.

[19]   See TUR-18 at 5-6 (Saudi Arabia and Libya characterized by Turkish respondents as the "largest [foreign] suppliers" of rebar to Egypt), 11 ("Egyptian import statistics clearly establish that Turkish imports were at the same price level as other major suppliers to the Egyptian market in 1998, on a duty-paid basis"), and Exhibit 2 (chart showing imports from Saudi Arabia increased in volume by more than imports from Turkey).

time in this proceeding in the Final Report that scrap prices were relatively constant during 1998. In the context in which this finding was explained, the false impression was given that scrap prices in constant currency were relatively constant during this period. This finding is clearly contrary to fact, as can be easily determined by reference to the scrap prices published in *Metal Bulletin* and *American Metal Market*.

27.   In sum, this Panel should consider the additional evidence presented in our briefs on injury because Turkish respondents had no advance warning prior to the deadline for submission of new factual information that the Investigating Authority would change the focus of its investigation and find current material injury. They also had no notice of any allegations that current material injury existed and thus nothing to rebut. In the alternative, the Panel should take "judicial notice" of those facts which are capable of ready verification by reference to public sources and whose accuracy cannot be reliably questioned. The Panel should also take judicial notice of the information contained in TUR-13 and TUR-14 for the same reasons.

28.   Finally, the basic facts and argument with respect to Turkey's claims regarding improper attribution of other causes of injury to imports from Turkey were made available to the Investigating Authority during the investigation itself, contrary to Egypt's claims. Therefore, the Panel should address those claims even if it decides to exclude evidence not available before the Investigating Authority during its original investigation.

Question 5

What in Turkey's view legally falls under the term "any known factors other than the dumped imports which at the same time are injuring the domestic industry"?

Response

29.   Article 3.5 of the Antidumping Agreement provides that "[t]he authorities shall also examine any *known* factors other than the dumped imports which are at the same time injuring the domestic industry, and the injuries caused by these other factors must not be attributed to the dumped imports."

30.   Turkey agrees with the European Communities' position that such factors are, in the first place, factors that are brought to the attention of the investigating authority by the interested parties in the domestic procedure. In addition, Turkey agrees with the European Communities that there are circumstances where an interested party can raise other factors but cannot itself prove conclusively that those factors are causing injury. In such a case, such factors are "known" to the investigating authority and should be examined.[20]

31.   Moreover, Turkey believes that other factors and conditions of competition which are evident in the factual record before the Investigating Authority

---

[20]   *See* Third Party Submission of the European Communities, 1 November 2001, at 3.

and are having a large effect on the domestic industry, are "known" factors that should be examined, regardless of whether or not a specific allegation has been made by an individual party that those factors are injuring the domestic industry.

32.   There is, in Turkey's view, a special burden on the competent authorities to identify other known factors that, at the same time, may be causing present material injury when the competent authorities commence their investigation based on allegations filed by the domestic industry that are confined to threatened future material injury and the authorities subsequently, after the time for notice and comment has expired, discovers evidence of what they consider supports a finding of current material injury. In such a case, the respondents, not having had notice of any allegation of present material injury, cannot be expected to have researched and briefed that theoretical possibility. The protection of the non-attribution requirement in Article 3.5 would lose its force if the Investigating Authority could, in such a situation, decline to investigate any factor other than the subject imports that might at the same time be causing injury to the domestic industry.

33.   The obligation to identify other factors, which at the same time may be causing injury to the domestic industry, also stems from Article 3.4, which, regardless of what is "known" by the investigating authority, requires a full investigation "of all relevant economic factors and indices having a bearing on the state of the industry, including actual and potential decline in sales, profits, ... productivity, return on investments, or utilization of capacity [and] factors affecting domestic prices. ..."

34.   In interpreting a parallel provision in the Agreement on Safeguards, the Appellate Body ruled that:

> [the central role played by interested parties in the investigation] does not mean that the competent authorities may limit their examination of "all relevant factors," under Article 4.2(a) of the Agreement on Safeguards, to the factors which the interested parties have raised as relevant. The competent authorities must, in every case, carry out a full investigation to enable them to conduct a proper evaluation of all the relevant factors expressly mentioned in Article 4(2)(a) of the Agreement on Safeguards. Moreover, Article 4(2)(a) requires the competent authorities - and *not the interested parties* – to evaluate fully the relevance, if any, of "other factors." If the competent authorities consider that a particular "other factor" may be relevant to the situation of the domestic industry, under Article 4(2)(a), their duties of investigation and evaluation preclude them from remaining passive in the face of possible shortcomings in the evidence submitted, and views expressed, by the interested parties. In such cases, if the competent authorities do not have sufficient information before them to evaluate the possible relevance of such an "other factor," they must investigate fully

that "other factor", so that they can fulfill their obligations of evaluation under Article 4(2)(a).[21]

35.   In that case, the Panel had ruled that Article 4.2(a) required an examination of only those factors, other than those enumerated in Article 4.2(a), that were clearly raised as relevant by the interested parties in the domestic investigation.[22] The Appellate Body disagreed, holding that "the investigating authorities must undertake additional investigative steps, when the circumstances so require, in order to fulfill their obligation to evaluate all relevant factors."[23]

36.   The same analysis should apply to the Antidumping Agreement. The competent authorities have an obligation under Article 3.4 to examine "all relevant factors and indices having a bearing on the domestic industry". Therefore, where the record before the competent authorities indicates that a particular factor is having a significant effect on the domestic industry, such as the capacity expansion in this case, increasing market share by a new, low-cost entrant (which should have been evident from Al Ezz's questionnaire responses), falling scrap prices, high volumes of comparably priced non-subject imports, and falling demand coincide with the fall in domestic prices, the Investigating Authority has an obligation under Article 3.4 to investigate that factor fully, regardless of whether or not interested parties have brought those factors specifically to its attention. And where that factor is causing injury to the domestic industry, the Investigating Authority has an obligation under Article 3.5 to isolate the effects of that factor and not to attribute those effects to the subject imports.

Question 6

Turkey lists four important factors which it says are relevant to consider under Article 3.5: (1) a capacity expansion of the domestic industry; (2) non-subject imports; (3) declining scrap prices; and (4) contraction in domestic demand. Is it Turkey's case that these were "known factors" which were before the IA, or is it Turkey's case that they were not factors placed before the IA but should have been "known factors" nevertheless?

Response

37.   As stated above, these factors were "known" to the Investigating Authority during the investigation.

---

[21]   Appellate Body Report, *United States – Definitive Safeguard Measures on Import of Wheat Gluten From the European Communities*, WT/DS166/AB/R, adopted 19 January 2001 (hereafter "*Wheat Gluten*"), DSR 2001:II, 717, para. 55. *Accord* Third Party Submission of the European Communities, at 4. *See also United States – Anti-dumping Measures on Certain Hot-Rolled Carbon Steel Products from Japan*, WT/DS184/AB/R, 24 July 2001 (hereafter "*Hot-Rolled Carbon Steel Products from Japan*"), DSR 2001:X, 4697, para. 230 (causation requirements under Antidumping Agreement and Safeguards Agreement are sufficiently similar that adopted panel and Appellate Body Reports on the injury causation requirements under the Safeguards Agreement can provide guidance in interpreting the language of the Antidumping Agreement).

[22]   *Wheat Gluten* at para. 46.

[23]   *Ibid.* at para. 55.

Question 7

Is Turkey arguing, in respect of third country imports, that the reference at para. 4.3.2 of the Essential Facts and Conclusions Report and para. 4.5.2 of the Final Report is the IA's only reference to such imports. If not, what are Turkey's arguments, especially in the light of the reference to third country imports in para. 4.3.4 of the Essential Facts and Conclusions Report and paras. 4.3.4 and 4.3.5 of the Final Report.

Response

38.   Turkey is not taking the position stated in the first sentence of this question. Paragraph 4.3.2 of the Essential Facts and Conclusions report concerns domestic production and makes no reference to non-subject imports.

39.   First, we note that imports from Latvia, Ukraine and Romania, previously found by the Investigating Authority to be dumped and injurious, remained in the market until 22 June 1998, when antidumping duties were imposed.[24] However, there was no attempt to discern and segregate the effects of these imports in order to assess their effects on prices in 1998. That is, the Investigating Authority found that prices fell in 1998, but did not state whether that price decline occurred in the first half of 1998 when imports from Latvia, Ukraine and Romania were in the market, or the second half of 1998 when Turkish imports were in the market. If it was during the first half of 1998, then it would have been incumbent upon the Investigating Authority to segregate the effects of imports from Latvia, Ukraine and Romania so as not to attribute those effects, already found to be injurious, to imports from Turkey.

40.   With respect to the second half of 1998, we believe that the Investigating Authority should have examined the other import sources which remained in the market after the exit of imports covered by the first round of antidumping cases. These included imports from Saudi Arabia, the largest import source, and imports from Libya. According to published statistics, imports from Saudi Arabia increased in volume in 1998 by 136 per cent of the increase in the volume of imports from Turkey and, on a landed, duty-paid basis, were comparably priced.[25] Imports from Turkey were higher priced than imports from Libya.

41.   Notwithstanding the presence of comparably priced imports of greater volume simultaneously in the market with imports from Turkey just prior to the price decline in the first part of January, 1999, the Investigating Authority "examined other economic factors but concluded that such factors were not causing injury to the domestic industry".[26] Presumably, those other economic factors included non-subject imports. Egypt has also asserted that the Investigating Authority found material injury both in 1998 and in the first quarter of 1999.

42.   As discussed in our First Written Submission (at III.A), the Investigating Authority made no findings that imports from Turkey were causing any specific

---

[24]   See TUR-1 at 10 (4.1.6) and TUR-18 at Exhibit 2-1.
[25]   *See* TUR-18 at 5-6 and Exhibit 2-1.
[26]   TUR-16 at 4.5.1.

injury to the domestic industry or were having different effects than imports from Saudi Arabia and Libya. Because non-subject imports of comparable or even more pronounced volume trends and comparable or lower prices were in the market at the same time as imports from Turkey, in the absence of any more specific information, it must be assumed that they were having comparable effects. The failure of the Investigating Authority to identify and distinguish those effects violated Article 3.5.[27]

43.   While it is true that the market share of imports from Turkey, Saudi Arabia and Libya increased in 1998, the market share of imports from third countries declined by a greater amount. Put another way, the market share of *all* import sources, including Turkey, declined in 1998. Does this mean that imports from Turkey were non-injurious? One could conclude so. What one cannot conclude from this data is that there is any logical basis upon which to distinguish the effects of imports from Turkey in 1998 from imports from Saudi Arabia and Libya in 1998, as was done by the Investigating Authority.

44.   It is unreasonable and unsound to base a determination of current material injury on a period as short as one calendar quarter. However, an objective review of the facts from the first quarter of 1999 discloses, once again, no basis to conclude that imports from Turkey were causing the effects claimed. According to the Investigating Authority, imports from Turkey undersold the domestic product by only 0.3 per cent in March 1999, an insignificant amount.[28] The price effects of imports from Turkey in the first quarter of 1999 were, therefore, negligible. If it is the position of the Investigating Authority that the price decline which took place in January 1999[29] was caused by the volume and pricing of imports in 1998, then it is essential that the Investigating Authority segregate the effects of imports from Turkey from the effects of imports from other, comparably priced sources prior to making that determination.

45.   Furthermore, Saudi Arabia lost its duty-free status in Egypt at the beginning of 1999, possibly explaining its declining shipments in the first quarter of 1999.[30] Imports as a whole in that quarter, including imports from Turkey, stood at 117,000 tons.[31] This converts an annual import level of 468,000 tons. This is a drop of 50 per cent as compared to annual import levels in 1998! Therefore, while imports from Turkey increased in the quarter, they merely replaced a small part of the volume formerly represented by imports from other sources. Using the same trend analysis employed by the Investigating Authority, one should reach the conclusion that imports as a whole were not causing material injury to the domestic industry in the first quarter of 1999. The Investigating Authority's focus on the increase in imports from Turkey and its failure to take into account

---

[27]   *See Hot-Rolled Carbon Steel Products from Japan* at paras. 223 and 226.
[28]   Final Report, TUR-16, at 4.2.1.2.
[29]   We know from the Initiation Report that the price decline in fact took place early in January 1999. See TUR-1 at 4.1.9.
[30]   TUR-32 at 20.
[31]   Final Report, TUR-16, at 4.3.4.1.

the countervailing effect of the decline in imports from other sources underlines the lack of an objective and reasoned analysis by the Investigating Authority.

46.   Finally, domestic market share also increased by 23 per cent in the first quarter of 1999, at the same time that imports from Turkey increased.[32] Thus, imports from Turkey in the first quarter of 1999 did not displace one ton of rebar formerly shipped by the Egyptian industry. Imports of rebar from Turkey cannot be said to have had a significant volume effect upon the domestic industry in the first quarter of 1999.

Question 8

The focus of Turkey's arguments regarding third country imports is on imports from Libya and Saudi Arabia. The IA's references to third country imports seem to cover total imports from third countries. Is Turkey arguing that the IA committed a legal error in not looking separately at imports from Libya and Saudi Arabia? If so, what is the legal basis for such an allegation?

Response

47.   Yes, because these imports were large volume players in the market in the second half of 1998 when the injury allegedly occurred. Also Turkish respondents specifically showed that, according to published statistics, Saudi Arabia's volume increased by more than Turkey's and that Turkish prices were within 2 per cent of Saudi Arabia's and were higher than Libya's.[33] Therefore the price effects of these imports and the volume effects of these imports were comparable to Turkey's and yet the IA found that non-subject imports were not injuring the domestic industry.

48.   We should note at this point that there is an unexplained discrepancy in the import statistics from Turkey that were used by the Investigating Authority for its investigation. The Investigating Authority cites an import figure of 210,000 tons in its Final Report (4.1.1.1). However, according to import statistics published by the Government of Egypt, total imports of rebar from Turkey amounted to only 116,194 tons in 1998.[34] According to the same, published import statistics, imports from Saudi Arabia totaled 239,749 tons in that year, up from 86,227 tons in the prior year.[35] Egypt acknowledged the discrepancy between its official import statistics and the figures used in the investigation during negotiations with Turkey, but claimed that there was an error in the published statistics with respect to imports from Turkey. Egypt further claimed that it had computed total imports from Turkey by reference to actual import documentation, but that documentation has never been provided to respondents. Nor do respondents believe that any comparable effort was made to correct the import database for imports from third countries, such as Saudi Arabia and Libya.

---

[32]   *Ibid.*
[33]   TUR-18 at 5-6.
[34]   TUR-18 at Exhibit 2, page 6.
[35]   *Ibid.*

49.   We are doubtful that the number ultimately stated in the Final Report is accurate, for the following reasons. The figure 210,000 was initially described to the Egyptian Authorities in their initiation report as an "estimate" of total imports from Turkey.[36] This report is dated 26 January 1999. Egyptian Government import statistics would not have been finalized as of that date. The estimated number is, moreover, a very round number – it looks like an estimate by comparison to the published import statistics and the figures published in the Final Report for non-subject imports. The same number, without modification, appeared in the Essential Facts and Conclusions report in October 1999 and in the Final Report that same month. In addition, this figure exceeds the figure shown for total exports by Turkey to Egypt in 1998 and 1997 by more than 5 per cent.[37] There were substantial exports from Turkey in December 1998 and, given shipping times, it is unlikely that all of the exports from Turkey in December were entered into Egypt before the end of the year. Hence, the figure used appears to be significantly overstated and appears to overstate the volume of imports from Turkey as compared to the volume of imports from Saudi Arabia and Libya.

Question 9

Please respond to Egypt's argument that Turkey has not alleged any particular violation in its claim that Egypt misinterpreted certain data on domestic sales (Egypt's First Submission at pp. 39-40, section III.B.7).

Response

50.   This is not a separate claim; it is part of our claims under 3.1, 3.4 and 3.5. This section shows that the finding that Turkish imports caused injury to the domestic industry by causing domestic shipments to rise in 1998 is illogical and improper and thus cannot constitute a separate basis for finding that the Egyptian authority's injury determination was supported by the facts found. This argument should be considered in connection with Turkey's other claims in Section III.B of the First Written Submission.

Question 10

Please identify the factors listed in Article 3.4, if any, that in your view were (1) not evaluated properly; or (2) not evaluated at all.

Response

51.   The Article 3.4 factors not addressed at all in the Final Report are productivity, actual and potential negative effects on cash flow, employment, wages, growth, and ability to raise capital or investments. Furthermore, the public information in the Essential Facts and Conclusions Report and in the Final Report does not reveal whether or not the Investigating Authority conducted a sufficient examination of capacity, capacity utilization or return on investment.

---

[36]   TUR-1 at 17.
[37]   TUR-18 at Exhibit 1.

52. We also maintain, in Section III.B of our First Written Statement, that the following factors were not evaluated at all or were not evaluated adequately:

    1. Capacity expansion at the two major Egyptian rebar producers.

    2. Effects of the capacity expansion on the producers' costs of production.

    3. Effects of the capacity expansion on intra-industry competition.

    4. Falling prices for steel scrap.

    5. Contraction in demand in 1999

    6. Effect of comparably priced, fairly traded imports

53. While these factors, other than contraction in demand, are not specifically listed in Article 3.4, that Article does require "an evaluation of all relevant economic factors and indices having a bearing on the state of the industry", and it is Turkey's position that each of these factors falls into that category. Moreover, it is Turkey's position that Factors 1, 3, 4, 5 and 6 are potential "factors affecting domestic prices", a factor specifically listed in Article 3.4.

54. Factors 1, 4 and 6 were evaluated, but not properly. It would appear from the public record made available to the Government of Turkey that factors 2, 3 and 5 were not evaluated at all.

Question 11

Turkey states in its First Submission that "the two prices [of the domestic goods and the imported goods] must be compared on a delivered basis to a customer who is in a position to choose between purchasing domestic or imported products". Is it Turkey's case that the importers are not actual or prospective customers for the domestic manufacturers?

Response

55. Since the price undercutting was measured by comparing the importer's ex-warehouse price to the domestic manufacturer's price, we presume this not to be the case. If the importer were a customer of the manufacturer, its resale price would not be the appropriate basis for a comparison – the importer's acquisition price would be the appropriate basis for a comparison. However, the facts on the record do not disclose whether the importers also purchased from the manufacturers, so we do not know whether this was the case or not.

Question 12

How broadly does the burden of proof requirement of Article 2.4 apply in anti-dumping investigations. What is your legal reasoning in support of your view, based on a "Vienna Convention" analysis of that provision?

Response

56. Article 31 of the Vienna Convention on the Law of Treaties provides that "[a] treaty shall be interpreted in good faith in accordance with the ordinary

meaning to be given to the terms of the treaty in their context and in light of its object and purpose".

57.   The first sentence of Article 2.4 provides that "a fair comparison shall be made between the export price and the normal value". This is a general obligation imposed upon the parties. The last sentence of Article 2.4 is also general in nature: "The authorities shall indicate to the parties in question the information that is necessary to ensure a fair comparison and shall not impose an unreasonable burden of proof on the parties". Turkey believes that this obligation extends to all aspects of fact finding necessary to determine the export price and the normal value and to ensure a fair comparison between the two. That is, in collecting information with respect to the export price and the normal value or information necessary to adjust these values to a common basis, the authorities are prohibited from "impos[ing] an unreasonable burden of proof".

58.   This is consistent with the Appellate Body's statement in *Hot-Rolled Carbon Steel Products from Japan*, albeit interpreting other sections of the Agreement, that "[t]he Investigating Authorities are not entitled to insist upon absolute standards or impose unreasonable burdens upon . . . exporters".[38]

Question 13

In relation to the issue of the alleged change in the grounds for action to be taken against dumped imports being considered by the IA (from threat of injury to present injury). Could Turkey comment on the Panel report in *Guatemala-Cement II*, which appears to support the proposition that no obligation to notify arose in a similar circumstance? Should this Panel adopt the same view? Is it Turkey's view that the statement in paragraph 1.8 of the Manufacturers' Questionnaires (page 6) (Exh. TUR-3) in any case did not constitute notification that present injury would be investigated?

Response

59.   Turkey disagrees with the *Guatemala-Cement* panel decision on this issue and we urge this Panel to consider the inequity of applying that decision in this case.

60.   Moreover, the specific finding of the panel in *Guatemala-Cement* is that there is no obligation in the Agreement upon investigating authorities to inform interested parties "of the legal basis for its final determination on injury".[39] We are not arguing that Egypt was obliged to inform us in advance that its final determination would be based on a finding of current material injury. Our claim is that, where Egypt initiated its investigation based on alleged threat of material injury and advised respondents in its questionnaires that its injury investigation was limited to consideration of whether there was a threat of material injury, it

---

[38]   *Hot-Rolled Carbon Steel Products from Japan*, at para. 102
[39]   *Guatemala – Antidumping Investigation Regarding Portland Cement from Mexico*, WT.DS 60/AB/RW, 2 Nov. 1998 at para. 8.238.

was incumbent upon Egypt to give the parties notice when it expanded its investigation to consider the question of present material injury. It was also obliged at that time to give the parties an opportunity to submit factual comment and argument on this question. As a matter of fundamental due process, a party accused of engaging in unfair trade practices should know, prior to the due date for its submission of factual information and argument, what the nature of the charges are that have been lodged against it and that are being investigated by the competent authorities. That notice and opportunity to submit information was not provided in this case.

61.   In light of the clearly expressed passages in the Manufacturers Questionnaire and in the Initiation Report, we do not consider the passage in paragraph 1.8 as a clear indication that the IA would investigate present material injury.

Question 14

At page 6 of its First Oral Statement, Turkey argues that capacity expansion by the Egyptian industry would have caused an increase in the industry's per unit cost of production, due to low start-up levels of production. How does this argument reconcile with the statements in the Essential Facts and Conclusions Report and the Final Report that capacity utilization was stable during the period of investigation?

Response

62.   We have no idea how capacity utilization figures were developed or what they show as none of these data have been released to the public. Specifically, we do not know what capacity level was reported by the domestic industry. Was it the level at the beginning of 1998 or end of 1998? It does not appear that monthly data were provided, so which was it? Conceivably, the value reported by the domestic industry was the value at the beginning of the year, in which case the data reported masked what was really going on.

63.   This points up a broader problem with the record that the Panel must examine. So little data has been disclosed that it is impossible to discern whether a proper factual determination was made with respect to the trend in capacity utilization, as required in Article 3.4, and whether the determination noted in the Panel's question is truly inconsistent with our claim.

64.   We know, in the case of Al Ezz, that it took 2-3 months for its rebar expansion project to reach full production.[40] Thus, unit costs must have been affected, if only for a short period of time. We do not have similar information for Alexandria National but it would be truly extraordinary if one day the expansion projects were opened and they immediately achieved full capacity utilization. This simply never happens in real life.

---

[40]   First Submission of Turkey at 14.

Question 15

At page 20 of Turkey's First Oral Statement, Turkey states that the questionnaire provided no direction concerning how to respond to the questionnaire concerning costs of production. Some of the Turkish respondents took the decision to provide certain information on a monthly basis, and only for certain months during the period of investigation. Under the circumstances in which Appendix 9 to the questionnaire did not indicate any particular basis for the provision of the cost of production information, while the questionnaire did specify the period of investigation for the dumping investigation, what justified these respondents in selecting periods less than the full period of investigation for provision of cost data?

Response

65.   Turkey's economy is acknowledged to be hyperinflationary. During 1998, annual inflation exceeded 40 per cent per annum. In such cases, on average, it would be grossly distortive to compare an annual average cost of production to individual sales prices. Assuming constant monthly production and constant cost increases, the use of a single, average annual cost of production would tend to understate, by as much as 20 per cent, the cost to produce goods sold at the end of the period and would overstate, by as much as 20 per cent, the cost to produce goods at the beginning of the period.

66.   It should be noted that the last sentence of Article 2.2.1 of the Anti-Dumping Agreement contemplates separate calculations of costs of production for comparison to sales prices during sub-periods of the period of investigation when costs vary over the investigation period. Thus, that sentence states: "If prices which are below costs of production at the time of sale are above weighted average costs for the period of investigation, such prices shall be considered to provide for recovery of costs within a reasonable period of time." This sentence contemplates different results depending on whether one is comparing sales prices to cost of production "at the time of sale" or sales prices to "average costs of production for the period of investigation". If sales prices are above cost of production "at the time of sale," they may not be treated as "outside the ordinary course of trade," within the meaning of the first sentence of Article 2.2.1.

67.   Because the use of average costs of production for comparison to individual sales prices can be so distortive in a hyperinflationary economy, many jurisdictions, including the United States, the European Communities and Israel, require respondents in hyperinflationary economies to calculate monthly costs of production and then limit cost-to-price comparisons to sales prices on sales transactions in the same month that costs are calculated.[41]

---

[41]   *See, e.g., Certain Steel Wire Ropes and Cables from Turkey*, Regulation No. 230/2001 (2/2/2001), Official Journal of the European Communities, No. L34/4 (3/2/2001) at 11:

In line with the general methodology, it was possible, for some of the product types, to establish normal value on the basis of the domestic price of comparable types in accordance with Article 2(1) of the Basic regulation. Representativeness

68.   The Egyptian questionnaire requested respondents to report only those sales prices in the home market that were contemporaneous with respondents' export sales to Egypt. Respondents complied with this request. Because it would have been distortive to compare an annual average cost of production to these sales, and because the common practice in other jurisdictions is to limit cost comparisons to sales prices and monthly costs in the same month, respondents reported monthly costs only for those months for which they reported sales. If Egypt followed the same practice as these other jurisdictions, it would have no use of costs for the other months because there were no sales reported in those other months.

69.   Respondents were very clear about what they were doing in their April 7, 1999 responses and what they did was reasonable under the circumstances. There was no complaint from the Investigating Authority prior to verification about incompleteness in the responses. Indeed, when, after the responses were filed, counsel for Colakoglu, Habas and Diler inquired of the Investigating Authority regarding the timetable for supplemental questionnaires, the Investigating Authority replied that that the responses filed were "sufficient" and that no supplemental questionnaires would be issued.[42] It seems that early in the investigation, prior to its u-turn in August, the Investigating Authority found respondents' response methodology reasonable as well.

Question 16

Is interest income properly considered as a cost under Article 2.2.2? Assuming that interest income can be part of the cost of production calculation, is the accounting definition of operating and non-operating income a sufficient determinant of whether the cost is associated with or pertaining to the production of the goods?

Response

70.   Interest income must be considered a negative cost or a normal cost offset. There are other kinds of offsets as well, including revenue from sales of by-products. In rebar production there are some very short ends of billets, some very

---

and ordinary course of trade tests for the domestic sales of comparable types were carried out on a monthly basis given the high inflation in Turkey during the IP.

For all other types of the product concerned sold for export to the Community by the cooperating companies, normal value was constructed in accordance with Article 2(3) of the basic Regulation. The companies' own domestic SG&A expenses and the profit margin realised on the domestic market in the ordinary course of trade were added to the manufacturing cost. To account for the high inflation, constructed normal values were calculated for each month of the IP.

See also Notice of Final Results of Anti-Dumping Duty Administrative Review: Certain Welded Carbon Steel Pipe and Tube From Turkey, 62 Fed. Reg. 51,629 (2 Oct. 1997) (Comment 3) (citing *Final Results of Anti-Dumping Duty Administrative Review: Ferrosilicon from Brazil,* 61 Fed. Reg. 59,407, 59,408 (22 November 1996)). The reporting of cost data in this manner "reflects the increases in materials costs from month to month due to inflation." *Notice of Final Results of Antidumping Duty Administrative Review: Certain Welded Carbon Steel Pipe and Tube From Turkey,* 62 Fed. Reg. 51,629 (Oct. 2, 1997) (Comment 3) (emphasis added).

[42]   Facsimile from IA to Law Offices of David Simon, 20 May 1999, TUR-31.

short ends of rebars and some shavings from the rebar in the rolling process. These scraps or byproducts are either returned to the production process and credited to the cost of manufacturing or sold to customers and credited to the cost of manufacturing or reported as other income by the producers. These revenues also must be taken into account in calculating the true net cost of production.

71.   Another example is foreign exchange gain on loans. Foreign exchange loss on loans is normally considered a financing expense, while foreign exchange gain on loans is ordinarily considered an offset to financing costs. It is a common practice in the EU and the United States at least to recognize these offsets. If the agreement were read to include only those items that involve cash outlays, it would have to be read to require calculation of a fully distributed cost of production that was far in excess of the true net cost of production. It is very unlikely that that this was the original intent of the Contracting Parties in drafting the language of Article 2.

72.   The accounting definition of operating income and non-operating income is a sufficient determinant of whether the cost is associated with or pertains to the production of the particular goods in question when the income is a fungible item, like short-term interest income on working capital accounts. There might be non-fungible items of income for which further investigation is required. For example, income from the provision of shipping services on ships that are also used to transport the subject merchandise or which constitute a separate line of business, might be considered not sufficiently related to the production and sale of the subject merchandise to take into account. But interest income on working capital accounts is a fungible item – it cannot be segregated to any particular business line. Therefore, it benefits all production activities of the firm.

Question 17 - Additional Documents To Be Submitted

Could Turkey please submit the following documents:

1.   **Documents referred to in footnote 16 and 17 (except TUR-32).**

2.   **Annexes to letter of 15 September 1999 from the Law Offices of David Simon to IA.**

3.   **Letter of 10 May 1999 from the Law Offices of David Simon to the IA to which the IA responded on 20 May 1999.**

4.   **IDC's comments on the Verification Report.**

5.   **Turkey states on page 43 of its First Written Submission that the Law Offices of David Simon requested an extension to submit information required and to hold a meeting in Cairo. Please submit request and response by the IA.**

6.   **Letter of 23 September 1999 from the IA to IDC.**

Response

73.   Pease see the attachments to this submission.

74.   Please note that we did not state, as implied in Question 17.5, that the Law Offices of David Simon requested a specific period of time as an extension in which to submit the information required by the Investigating Authority in its letter of 23 September 1999. We stated that "Colakoglu, Habas and Ekinciler (*sic* – should be Diler) sent a letter to the IA noting that it would be impossible to respond to the request for additional information sent on 24 September 1999 within the 2-5 day time-frame requested by the Administering Authority".[43] This could be taken as an implicit request for an extension. However, there was no explicit request for a particular period of time.

75.   We further stated: "The IA did not provide an extension of time for Colakoglu, Habas and Diler to respond to the 23 September 1999 letter ... ". There was no letter to this effect. The IA simply did not respond to Mr. Simon's letter dated 28 September 1999.

QUESTIONS POSED BY THE PANEL TO BOTH PARTIES

Question 1

Concerning the period of data collection, what is the legal status and relevance of the recommendation of the Anti-Dumping Committee for the interpretation of the Anti-Dumping Agreement?

Response

76.   Article 31 of the Vienna Convention on the Law of Treaties states:

1.   A treaty shall be interpreted in good faith in accordance with the ordinary meaning to be given to the terms of the treaty in their context and in light of its object and purpose.

2.   The context for the purpose of the interpretation of a treaty shall comprise, in addition to the text, including its preamble and annexes:

(a)   any agreement relating to the treaty which was made between all the parties in connection with conclusion of the treaty;

(b)   any instrument which was made by one or more parties in connection with the conclusion of the treaty and accepted by the other parties as an instrument related to the treaty.

3.   There shall be taken into account, together with the context:

(a)   any subsequent agreement between the parties regarding interpretation of the treaty or the application of its provisions;

(b)   any subsequent practice in the application of the treaty which establishes the agreement of the parties regarding its interpretation;

---

[43]   First Submission of the Government of the Republic of Turkey, at 43.

(c)   any relevant rules of international law applicable in the relations between the parties.

77.   A recommendation by the Antidumping Committee does not qualify as "a subsequent agreement between the parties regarding the interpretation of the treaty or the application of its provisions", nor does it qualify as "a subsequent practice in the application of the treaty". We note in this regard that there was a proposal before the Antidumping Committee at its meeting in April 2001, that the Committee adopt a decision concerning the legal status of adopted recommendations. No consensus could be reached on this proposal. Nor could a consensus be reached at the Committee's meeting in October 2001.[44] It is clear, therefore, that the legal status of the Committee's recommendations remains controversial even among members of the Committee. Consequently, recommendations of the Committee should have no bearing on the Panel's consideration of the legal issues presented in this case.

78.   We further note that Recommendation of the Anti-Dumping Committee does not specifically address the issue that Turkey has raised in this case. The recommendation of the Committee that there be a three-year period of investigation for injury does not endorse findings by Investigating Authorities in violation of the requirement in Article 3.5 that there be a demonstration that "the dumped imports are, through the effects of the dumping, causing injury within the meaning of this Agreement".

Question 2

Could the parties comment on the significance for this dispute, if any, of the ruling of the Panel in the *Argentina – Bovine Hides* dispute on the claims under Article X:3 of the GATT 1994.

Response

79.   We believe that the *Argentina-Bovine Hides* panel decision offers the following guidance to this Panel's consideration of Turkey's claims under Article X:3:

(a)   Article X applies to the *administration* of the laws, regulations, decisions and rulings. It does not apply to inconsistency between the letter of the law and the GATT 1994 or the Anti-Dumping Agreement. (paras. 11.60-11.61)

(b)   There is "no requirement that Article X:3(a) be applied only in situations where it is established that a Member has applied its Customs laws and regulations in an inconsistent manner with respect to the imports of or exports to two or more Members". (para 11.67)

---

[44]   *Report (2001) of the Committee on Antidumping Practices*, G/L/495 (31 October 2001) at Section V, para. 15 (Possible Committee Decision on the Status of Adopted Recommendations).

(c) "A WTO Member may challenge the substance of a measure under Article X. The relevant question is whether the substance of such a measure is administrative in nature or, instead, involves substantive issues more properly dealt with under other provisions of the GATT 1994." (para. 11.70)

(d) Resolutions which do not establish substantive Customs rules for enforcement of export laws are administrative in nature and may be challenged under Article X:3. (para. 11.72)

(e) "It would seem that any rule of "general application" would be deemed a substantive rule by Argentina based on its use of that term elsewhere in its arguments. This would then leave a situation where any rule of general application could not come under Article X because it would involve substantive rules rather than administrative ones. On the other hand an administrative rule, as that would appear to be defined, could not be a rule of general application. This also would render Article X effectively a nullity, which obviously cannot be the case." (para. 11.75)

80. Turkey has alleged violations of Article X:3 in connection with Egypt's refusal to schedule a meeting with Turkish respondents to discuss the adequacy of their responses on 15 September 1999 and in connection with Egypt's calculation of a "highly inflated and distorted interest charge" for IDC.[45] Both of these decisions were clearly "administrative" in nature. Furthermore, neither was based directly on a substantive law or rule. While Egypt may have a rule permitting resort to facts available in cases in which a party fails to respond adequately to a questionnaire, that rule certainly cannot be said to have dictated the selection of facts available in IDC's case. That action was purely administrative in nature. Moreover, the decision not to grant a hearing to various parties was clearly an administrative decision.

81. Egypt seeks to avoid review by this Panel of Turkey's claim under Article X:3, claiming that no review is warranted unless the actions complained of had a significant impact on the overall administration of the law. This interpretation, like Argentina's in *Bovine Hides*, would run the risk of rendering Article X a nullity, because actions which have general application, similar to rules of general application, would likely be reviewable under the other substantive rules of the GATT and thus would not be reviewable under Article X.

82. Article X is focused on administration of the laws and on particular administrative rulings and decisions. It thus covers an area not covered by the formal rules of the Anti-Dumping Agreement – the administration of the anti-dumping rules. Turkey has challenged Egypt's application of its rules in this case in two respects as inherently unreasonable. Turkey maintains that this was precisely the sort of conduct intended to be reached under Article X, as confirmed by the Panel in *Argentina – Bovine Hides*.

---

[45] *See* First Submission of Turkey at IV.D.2 and IV.J.8.

Question 3

In relation to the claim of a breach of Annex II, paragraph 1 by reason of the alleged late request for cost information, what is the relevance of Annex II, paragraph 1 at a time in an investigation prior to the decision to use facts available?

Response

83.   The first sentence of Annex II, paragraph 1 clearly imposes an independent obligation upon the parties. Failure to meet this obligation invalidates the subsequent use of "facts available" under the Agreement.

ANNEX 4-2

RESPONSES OF EGYPT TO QUESTIONS POSED IN THE
CONTEXT OF THE FIRST SUBSTANTIVE MEETING
OF THE PANEL

QUESTIONS POSED BY THE PANEL TO EGYPT

Question 1

Egypt argues at p. 30 of its first submission (section III.B.3.b) that the
IA examined SG&A and COP of the industry as potential sources of injury
to the domestic industry. Where in the Essential Facts and Conclusions Report, the Final Report, and any other documents of record is this examination found?

Response

1.   The information requested by the Panel as regards the Investigating Authority's examination of SG&A and COP is contained in the *Public File*, which is specifically referred to in the Notice of Initiation at paragraph 12 (attached as EX-EGT-7.3) and in the Essential Facts and Conclusions Report (see TUR-15) and the Final Report (see TUR-16) at Section 1.7.

2.   A copy of the relevant report of the public file is provided for the Panel's reference in EX-EGT 6 (see in particular paragraph V).

3.   In the examination of material injury during the investigation period, the SG&A and COP of ANSDK and EZZ were analyzed (1) *individually* on a company basis; and (2) *together* as part of the examination of the total domestic industry.

Question 2

Concerning Egypt's argument that new evidence that was not before
the investigating authority cannot be taken into account by the Panel, what
if anything is the significance of the recent ruling by the Appellate Body in
the *US – Cotton Yarn* dispute (WT/DS192/AB/R at para. 77 et. seq.); and the
ruling of the Panel in *US – Hot-rolled steel* (WT/DS184/R, paras. 7.6-7.7)?
Does Egypt view these rulings as complementary or contradictory? Please
explain. Is the *Cotton Yarn* ruling applicable or relevant in the context of
anti-dumping?

Response

4.   The rulings of the Panel in *US-Hot-rolled Steel* and of the Appellate Body in *US-Cotton Yarn* confirm that the role of the DSB is not to conduct a *de novo* review of the facts of the case. Article 17.5(ii) effectuates this general standard of review in the context the AD Agreement and directs the DSB to disregard

evidence that was not made available to the Investigating Authority during the course of the domestic proceeding.

5.   The findings of the Appellate Body in *Cotton Yarn* concern a panel's review of the authority's determination under Article 6.2 of the ATC Agreement. In particular, the ruling addresses the issue of whether the DSB may consider evidence relating to facts which predate the determination, but which did not exist at the time the determination was made. In other words, the question is whether a panel is entitled to take into account evidence that could not possibly have been examined by that Member when it made that determination. To this, the Appellate Body replied in the negative, emphasizing that in connection with the investigative obligations of Members, "[t]*he exercise of due diligence by a Member cannot imply, however, the examination of evidence that did not exist and that, therefore, could not possibly have been taken into account when the Member made its determination*".[1]

6.   Egypt considers the above rulings to be complementary as they both rely on the basic principle that the Panel is not to conduct a *de novo* review of the facts of the case. In Egypt's view, however, the *Cotton Yarn* ruling is not applicable in the context of anti-dumping for two fundamental reasons.

7.   *First*, unlike anti-dumping investigations, interested parties are not involved in the context of ATC investigations and, in particular, do not normally have the opportunity to actively participate in the data collection exercise carried out by the Investigating Authority. Accordingly, Egypt considers that, in the context of an ATC investigation, the exercise of due diligence by a Member is all the more important in reaching a determination under Article 6 of the ATC.[2].

8.   *Second*, the ATC does not contain a similar provision to Article 17.5(ii) of the AD Agreement, which expressly limits the review of the Panel to the evidence that was made available to the Investigating Authority in conformity with the appropriate domestic procedures. Thus, the standard of review to be applied by a panel in the content of an ATC investigation is higher that that applied under the Anti-Dumping Agreement. The standard of review to be applied by a panel in the context of an ATC investigation is not limited to the evidence as presented to the investigating authority during the course of the investigation. To the contrary, under the ATC Agreement a panel may consider evidence that existed during the investigation, but which was not presented to the Investigating Authority.

Question 3

Egypt also argues at p. 31 of its first submission that no new claims can be raised before the Panel that were not before the IA during the course of the investigation. What are the legal basis and any relevant precedents for this assertion?

---

[1]   WT/DS192/AB/R, DSR 2001:XII, 6027, para. 77.
[2]   WT/DS192/AB/R, DSR 2001:XII, 6027, para. 76.

Response

9.   As stated before the Panel on 28 November 2001, the term "new claims" does not refer to new "legal" claims in the context of this sentence, but to new factual considerations that were not presented to the Investigating Authority during the course of the investigation.

Question 4

Section II.B of Egypt's First Submission deals with the standard of review. Is it correct that an IA can arrive at a decision that is factually incorrect as long as it properly established the facts and evaluated them without bias and objectively? What is the legal test for a panel to determine whether an evaluation of facts by an Investigation Authority was "unbiased and objective" under Article 17.6(i)?

Response

10.   Egypt submits that it is conceivable that an Investigating Authority can arrive at a decision that is factually incorrect even though it properly established the facts and evaluated them without bias and objectively. It must be borne in mind that the Investigating Authority essentially relies on information provided by interested parties. As illustrated in the Rebar case, the quality of such information may be poor and the Investigating Authority's ability to verify the accuracy thereof limited. Moreover, the possibility to resort to facts available in the circumstances contemplated by the AD Agreement is evidently another factor that will affect the factual correctness of the Investigating Authority's decision.

11.   As regards the legal test for a Panel to determine whether an evaluation of facts was "unbiased and objective", Egypt wishes to refer to the findings of in *US-Hot-rolled Coils*, where the Appellate Body held that:[3]

> "Article 17.6(i) of the Anti-Dumping Agreement also states that the panel is to determine, first, whether the investigating authorities' "establishment of the facts was proper " and, second, whether the authorities' "evaluation of those facts was unbiased and objective" (emphasis added). Although the text of Article 17.6(i) is couched in terms of an obligation on panels – panels "shall" make these determinations – the provision, at the same time, in effect defines when investigating authorities can be considered to have acted inconsistently with the Anti-Dumping Agreement in the course of their "establishment" and "evaluation" of the relevant facts. In other words, Article 17.6(i) sets forth the appropriate standard to be applied by panels in examining the WTO-consistency of the investigating authorities' establishment and evaluation of the facts under other provisions of the Anti-Dumping Agreement. Thus, panels must assess if the establishment of the facts by the investigating authorities was proper and if the evaluation of those facts

---

[3]   WT/DS184/AB/R, DSR 2001:X, 4697, para. 56.

by those authorities was unbiased and objective. If these broad standards have not been met, a panel must hold the investigating authorities' establishment or evaluation of the facts to be inconsistent with the Anti-Dumping Agreement."

12.   In consequence, the Panel may only reject the factual findings made by the national authorities in special cases, such as where the conclusions drawn by the authorities are not supported by the evidence examined or where there is a clear indication of bias in their evaluation of the facts. As explained by the Appellate Body in *Thailand – Steel*, "*Article 17.6(i) places a limitation on the panel in the circumstances defined by the Article. The aim of Article 17.6(i) is to prevent a panel from "second-guessing" a determination of a national authority when the establishment of the facts is proper and the evaluation of those facts is unbiased and objective.*"[4]

Question 5

Could Egypt direct the Panel to where in the record of the investigation each of the factors listed in Article 3.4 was examined.

Response

13.   The following table shows the factors that the Investigating Authority considered relevant to the injury determination under Article 3.4, which are referred to in the Essential Facts & Conclusions Report as well as in the Final Report.

Economic Factor	EFCR	FR
Sales	Section 2.4.1 Section 4.3.1 Section 4.5.2 Section 4.5.4	Section 2.4.1 Section 4.3.1 Section 4.6.2 Section 4.6.4
Profits	Section 4.3.5 Section 4.5.2 Section 4.5.4	Section 4.3.5 Section 4.6.2 Section 4.6.4
Output	Section 2.4.2 Section 4.3.2	Section 2.4.2 Section 4.3.2
Market Share	Section 2.4.1 Section 4.3.4 Section 4.5.4	Section 2.4.1 Section 4.3.4 Section 4.6.4
Return on investments	Section 4.3.7 Section 4.5.2	Section 4.3.7 Section 4.6.2
Capacity utilization	Section 4.3.6	Section 4.3.6
Prices	Section 4.2.1.2 Section 4.2.2.1 Section 4.5.1 Section 4.5.2 Section 4.5.3 Section 4.5.4	Section 4.2.1.2 Section 4.2.2.1 Section 4.6.1 Section 4.6.2 Section 4.6.3 Section 4.6.4

---

[4]   WT/DS122/AB/R, DSR 2001:VII, 2701, para. 117.

Economic Factor	EFCR	FR
Dumping margin	Section 3.3	Section 3.3 Section 4.4 Section 4.6.2
Inventories	Section 4.3.3 Section 4.5.2	Section 4.3.3 Section 4.6.2

EFCR = Essential Facts & Conclusions Report

FR = Final Report

14.   The fact that the injury analysis of the Investigating Authority was thorough and indeed covered all the factors listed in Article 3.4 is evident in the *Confidential Injury Analysis* of the Rebar Investigation. A copy of the *Confidential Injury Analysis* is available only for the Panel's review and upon request. If required, a non-confidential summary will be provided for Turkey's review.

Question 6

     The test of causation referred to in the Egyptian submission is to ask whether any "other factor was sufficient to break the causal relationship between the dumped imports and the injury to the domestic industry" (e.g., Section III.B.1, page 24). This (a) assumes that a causal link between the dumped imports and the injury has been found; but then (b) tries to find a cause, or at least a different cause, to replace dumping as a cause. Turkey says that other causes of injury were improperly discounted. First, can Egypt direct the Panel to where the causal link finding is reported by the IA? Second, is the test Egypt has enunciated ("to break the causal relationship") one which is consistent with either the words of the Anti-Dumping Agreement or the way in which it has been interpreted (c.f., *US – Hot-rolled steel* (WT/DS184/AB/R at paras. 226 et. seq.)?

Response

(a)   Causal link finding

15.   The conclusions regarding the causal link between the dumped imports and the material injury to the domestic industry can be found in the Essential Facts & Conclusions Report at Sections 4.4 and 4.5 (see TUR-15) and in the Final Report at Sections 4.5 and 4.6 (see TUR-16). The specific findings upon which these conclusions are based are indicated in the following table.

Causal link factor	EFCR	FR
Volume of dumped imports	Section 2.3.1 Section 4.1.1.1 Section 4.1.1.2 Section 4.1.2.1 Section 4.1.2.2 Section 4.1.2.3	Section 2.3.1 Section 4.1.1.1 Section 4.1.1.2 Section 4.1.2.1 Section 4.1.2.2 Section 4.1.2.3
Price undercutting	Section 4.2.1.2	Section 4.2.1.2

Causal link factor	EFCR	FR
	Section 4.2.1.3 Section 4.2.1.4 Section 4.2.1.5	Section 4.2.1.3 Section 4.2.1.4 Section 4.2.1.5
Price suppression and depression	Section 4.2.2.1 Section 4.2.2.2 Section 4.2.2.3	Section 4.2.2.1 Section 4.2.2.2 Section 4.2.2.3
Sales	Section 4.3.1.1 Section 4.3.1.2	Section 4.3.1.1 Section 4.3.1.2
Production	Section 4.3.2.1 Section 4.3.2.2 Section 4.3.2.3 Section 4.3.2.4	Section 4.3.2.1 Section 4.3.2.2 Section 4.3.2.3 Section 4.3.2.4
Inventory	Section 4.3.3.1 Section 4.3.3.2 Section 4.3.3.3	Section 4.3.3.1 Section 4.3.3.2 Section 4.3.3.3 Section 4.3.3.4
Market share	Section 2.4.1 Section 4.3.4.1 Section 4.3.4.2 Section 4.3.4.3 Section 4.3.4.4	Section 2.4.1 Section 4.3.4.1 Section 4.3.4.2 Section 4.3.4.3 Section 4.3.4.4 Section 4.3.4.5
Price of raw materials		Section 4.3.5.3
Profits	Section 4.3.5.1 Section 4.3.5.2 Section 4.3.5.3	Section 4.3.5.1 Section 4.3.5.2 Section 4.3.5.3 Section 4.3.5.4
Return on investment	Section 4.3.7.1 Section 4.3.7.2	Section 4.3.7.1 Section 4.3.7.2
Margin of dumping	Section 3.3.2	Section 3.3.2 Section 4.4.1 Section 4.4.2 Section 4.4.3

EFCR = Essential Facts & Conclusions Report

FR = Final Report

(b)   Causal link test

16.   The causal link test referred to by Egypt does not imply that the dumped imports as a cause of injury are subsequently replaced by other causes of injury. Indeed, the AD Agreement does not require that dumped imports be the sole or even the principal cause of injury. To the contrary, the purpose of the examination of other factors of injury is to determine whether the impact of other factors on the state of the domestic industry is such that the dumped imports are not contributing to the existence of the injury of the domestic industry. If, conversely, the dumped import remain a cause of material injury in spite of the impact of other factors, the causal link test is positive.

17.   In Egypt's view, this is consistent with Article 3.5 of the AD Agreement and the findings of the Appellate Body in *US-Hot-rolled Steel*.[5] Indeed, under

---

[5]   WT/DS184/AB/R, DSR 2001:X, 4697.

Article 3.5 of the AD Agreement, the Investigating Authority must separate the injuries caused by other factors in order to ensure that they are not attributed to the dumped imports. As noted by the Appellate Body in *US-Hot-rolled Steel*, "[t]his requires a satisfactory explanation of the nature and extent of the injurious effects of other factors, as distinguished from the injurious effects of the dumped imports".[6]

18.   The non-attribution obligation of Article 3.5, in practice, means that the Investigating Authority must determine whether the injury experienced by the domestic industry is caused entirely by other factors, to the exclusion of the dumped imports. In other words, that there is no injury that can be attributed to the dumped imports. Accordingly, the non-attribution obligation should not be interpreted to mean that the injury caused by the dumped imports must be greater than the injury caused by other factors. Indeed, such an interpretation would mean that the injury caused by dumped imports must be the principal or sole cause of the material injury to the domestic industry, which as explained above, the AD Agreement does not require. Indeed, that the dumped imports must be the principal cause of injury was specifically deleted from the Anti-Dumping Code during the *Tokyo Round*.

19.   Egypt's position is furthermore consistent with the Appellate Body's interpretation of Article 4.2(b) of the Agreement on Safeguards in *United States – Definitive Safeguard Measures on Imports of Wheat Gluten from the European Communities*[7] and in *United States – Safeguard Measures on Imports of Fresh, Chilled or Frozen Lamb Meat from New Zealand and Australia.*[8]

20.   In *United States – Wheat Gluten*, the Appellate Body noted that:[9]

> *"The word "link" indicates simply that increased imports have played a part in, or contributed to, bringing about serious injury so that there is a causal "connection" or "nexus" between these two elements. Taking these words together, the term "the causal link" denotes, in our view, a relationship of cause and effect such that increased imports contribute to "bringing about", "producing" or "inducing" the serious injury. Although that contribution must be sufficiently clear as to establish the existence of "the causal link" required, the language in the first sentence of Article 4.2(b) does not suggest that increased imports be the sole cause of the serious injury, or that "other factors" causing injury must be excluded from the determination of serious injury. To the contrary, the language of Article 4.2(b), as a whole, suggests that "the causal link" between increased imports and serious injury may exist, even though other factors are also contributing, "at the same time", to the situation of the domestic industry." (emphasis added)*

---

[6]   WT/DS184/AB/R, DSR 2001:X, 4697, para. 226.
[7]   WT/DS166/AB/R, DSR 2001:II, 717.
[8]   WT/DS178/AB/R, DSR 2001:IX, 4051.
[9]   WT/DS166/AB/R, DSR 2001:II, 717.

21.   Given the considerable similarities between Article 4.2(b) of the Safeguards Agreement and Article 3.5 of the Anti-Dumping Agreement, the Appellate Body's interpretation of Article 4.2(b) is indeed relevant to the interpretation
of the non-attribution language in Article 3.5, as emphasized by the Appellate
Body in *US-Hot-rolled Steel.*[10]

22.   In any event, as a final point Egypt wishes to stress that the non-
attribution obligation is relevant *only* in cases where the Investigating Authority
has found that there were factors other than the dumped imports that caused injury to the domestic industry. If, as in the Rebar case, the Investigating Authority
has found that the other factors alleged to cause injury are in fact not causing
injury to the domestic industry, the non-attribution obligation does not apply. In
such cases, there is no injury that could possibly be mistakenly attributed to the
dumped imports. In this respect, Egypt would like to direct the Panel's attention
to the Appellate Body's finding in *US-Hot-rolled Steel.*[11] The Appellate Body
stated very clearly that:

> *"The non-attribution language in Article 3.5 of the Anti-Dumping
> Agreement applies solely in situations where dumped imports and
> other known factors are causing injury to the domestic industry at
> the same time." (emphasis added)*

Question 7

At pp. 37-38 of its first submission (Section III.B.5.b(i)-(iii)), Egypt
refers to an analysis of the price of non-dumped imports, the volume of non-
dumped imports, and consideration of price and volume over the period of
1996-1998. Where in the Essential Facts Report, the Final Report, and any
other documents of record are these analyses found?

Response

23.   These analyses can be found, *inter alia*, in Section 4.3.4.1 of the Final
Report. See also the Public File, in particular EX-EGT-6 at paragraph III.

Question 8

At page 9 of its First Oral Statement, Egypt states that the IA considered increased domestic competition. Where can this consideration be found
in the Essential Facts and Conclusions Report, the Final Report, and any
other documents of record?

Response

24.   As stated at page 34 of our First Submission, which is based on, *inter
alia*, the conclusions reported in Section 4.3.4 of the Final Report, when examining whether there was any increased competition in the domestic industry, the
Investigating Authority found that the individual market shares of the domestic

---

[10]   WT/DS184/AB/R, DSR 2001:X, para. 229.
[11]   WT/DS184/AB/R, DSR 2001:X, para. 223.

producers from 1996 to Q1-1999 had increased[12], together with an increase of sales.[13] At the same time, the market share of non-subject imports decreased by 80 per cent.[14] Thus, the increase of market share of the domestic industry and sales volume was gained at the expense of the non-subject imports and also as a result of the increase in consumption during that period.[15]

25.   Supporting documentation is contained in the Public File, which is provided for the Panel's reference in EX-EGT-6 at paragraph VIII.

Question 9

Egypt seems to imply in its arguments concerning the use of "partial facts available " that it was not selecting facts so as to arrive at an outcome "less favourable" than would have been the case had the Turkish companies "cooperated" (p. 62, section IV.B.1.e). Rather, Egypt argues (p. 58, section IV.A.13) that the "most appropriate" approach was to choose the highest monthly cost of production reported by the respondents to verify whether there were below-cost sales and to calculate constructed normal values. What was, specifically, the IA's basis under Article 6.8 for the use of partial facts available? That the Turkish companies "refused access to" necessary information, " otherwise failed to provide" such information, or "significantly impeded the investigation"? (For example, at page 22, section D.1, of Egypt's First Oral Statement, reference is made to both insufficient cooperation and to failure to provide information.)

Where is this basis for resort to facts available reflected in the Essential Facts and Conclusions Report, the Final Report, and any other documents of record?

How was it that only the highest monthly costs were found to be "reliable " (see heading of Section IV.A.13)?

In connection with Egypt's argument that the IA used "favourable" facts available by using the data of respondents in spite of insufficient cooperation (p. 62, section IV.B.1.e), where in the text of the AD Agreement is it provided that "adverse facts available" would by definition exclude any and all data provided by investigated companies, no matter how such data were employed in dumping calculations?

What is meant by the expression "facts available" as referred to in Article 6.8 and paragraph 1 of Annex II of the Anti-Dumping Agreement?

Response

26.   Egypt confirms that, when making use of "partial facts available", it was not seeking to arrive at an outcome less favourable than would have been the case had the Turkish companies offered satisfactory cooperation. The Investigat-

---

[12]   See Essential Facts & Conclusions Report and Final Report at Section 4.3.4.
[13]   *Ibid.*, at Section 4.3.1.
[14]   *Ibid.*, at Section 4.3.4.
[15]   *Ibid.*, at Section 2.4.1.

ing Authority resorted to "partial facts available" for the sole purpose of arriving at appropriate and meaningful determinations in view of the lack of or insufficient probative value of the information provided by the Turkish respondents.

(a) Basis under Article 6.8 of the AD Agreement for the use of partial facts available

27.   The basis for the Investigating Authority's use of partial facts available is that three respondents "refused access to necessary information" and "failed to provide necessary information (Habas, Colakoglu and Diler); and that the other two respondents "otherwise failed to provide" the necessary information (IDC and Icdas).

28.   The basis for resort to facts available can be found, *inter alia*, in Section 3.2 of the Essential Facts & Conclusions Report as well as page 15 (General issues, para. 4) and 3.2 of the Final Report.

(b) Use of the highest monthly costs

29.   In its First Submission at Section IV.A.13, Egypt is not suggesting that "only the highest monthly costs were found to be 'reliable'". The heading of Section IV.A.13 explains that, when calculating the margin of dumping of the respondents, the Investigating Authority used the data provided by the respondents to the extent that such data were found to be reliable. Thus, the export sales data and adjustments thereto were found reliable and therefore used in the determination of the export price. For the determination of the normal value, the Investigating Authority had to resort to facts available because the costs data submitted by the respondents were found unreliable. As facts available, the highest monthly costs data was in this respect found to be "the most appropriate approach in the circumstances of the case".

(c) Notion of "favourable" facts available

30.   In connection with the Panel's question concerning the notion of "favourable" facts available, Egypt does not suggest that the use of the party's own data necessarily leads to a good result, e.g. a finding of no dumping or a low margin of dumping. The use of the party's data only ensures that the Investigating Authority's findings will reflect as closely as possible the actual situation of the company. In anti-dumping investigations, the most favourable result to which an investigated company is legitimately entitled is a dumping determination based on the data it submitted. This pre-supposes that the company provided verifiable and reliable data within a reasonable period of time. If the investigated company fails to meet these requirements, the Investigating Authority is entitled to resort to "facts available" in order to rectify the deficiencies of the information provided by the companies concerned.

31.   The AD Agreement does not provide and Egypt did not suggest that " 'adverse facts available' would by definition exclude any and all data provided

by investigated companies, *no matter how such data were employed in dumping calculations*" (emphasis added). It should be noted that the AD Agreement contains no guidance on how data used as "facts available", whatever their origin (the respondent or secondary sources), must be *employed* by the Investigating Authority. It is however conceivable that, when resorting to "facts available", an Investigating Authority decides to use the data provided by the investigated companies in such a way that it intentionally seeks to reach adverse determinations.

32.   This is not the case in the Rebar investigation. In this case, the Investigating Authority used the costs data submitted by each company in order to calculate the cost of production and to construct the normal value of the companies concerned. This ensured that the determinations made with respect to those companies were as close as possible to the findings that would have been reached, had those companies offered sufficient cooperation and provided verifiable and reliable data on cost. This is what Egypt means by "favourable facts available" in this case.

33.   As explained in Egypt's First Submission at Section IV.B.1.e, the decision of Habas, Diler and Colakoglu to terminate their cooperation with the Investigating Authority would have entitled the Investigating Authority to seek to reach adverse results in accordance with paragraph 7 of Annex II.

(d)   Meaning of "facts available" in Article 6.8 and paragraph 1 of Annex II of the AD Agreement

34.   In Egypt's view, the notion of "facts available" covers information that is available to the Investigating Authority and that needs to be used in order to make appropriate determinations in a situation where interested parties do not supply reliable and verifiable information within a reasonable period of time, as requested. Two sets of circumstances are therefore envisioned, namely (1) the investigated parties refuse to provide the requested data, and (2) the investigated companies submit the requisite data, but these data are found unreliable and, therefore, unsuitable to reach meaningful determinations.

Question 10

Additional documents to be submitted:

Could Egypt please submit the following documents:

1.   Information on scrap steel prices on a monthly basis on which the final determination was based.

2.   Cover letter of the Essential Facts and Conclusions Report which was sent to interested parties in October 1999.

3.   The Notice of Initiation of the Investigation.

4.   Letter of 17 July 1999 to Habas, Diler and Colakoglu.

5.   Letter to Law Offices of David Simon on 28 September 1999 to advise of the use of facts available.

6.   Egypt states on page 56 of its First Written Submission that the auditors of the respondents certified that their financial statements were not prepared according to IAS 29. Please submit documentation to substantiate the allegation.

7.   Documentary evidence on which the calculation of the 5 per cent Turkish inflation rate was based, and the other sources of information on inflation in the IA's possession as referred to in the Final Report.

8.   Letter of 21 September 1999 by the IA to the Law Offices of David Simon.

9.   The reply by IDC and Icdas referred to in the second paragraph of section III.E.2 (page 24) of Egypt's First Oral Statement.

Response

35.   A copy of the documents requested by the Panel is attached as EX-EGT-7.

QUESTIONS POSED BY THE PANEL TO BOTH PARTIES

Question 1

Concerning the period of data collection, what is the legal status and relevance of the recommendation of the Anti-Dumping Committee for the interpretation of the Anti-Dumping Agreement?

Response

36.   Egypt agrees with the Panel in *Guatemala – Cement II* that the *Recommendation Concerning the Periods of Data Collection for Anti-Dumping Investigations* adopted by the Committee on 5 May 2000 is non-binding, but constitutes relevant indication of the understanding of WTO Members as to the selection of the appropriate period of data collection for the injury and dumping determinations.[16]

Question 2

Could the parties comment on the significance for this dispute, if any, of the ruling of the Panel in the *Argentina – Bovine Hides* dispute on the claims under Article X:3 of the GATT 1994.

---

[16] Guatemala–Definitive Anti-Dumping Measures on Grey Portland Cement from Mexico, WT/DS156/R, DSR 2000:XI, 5295, at footnote 68.

Response

37.   In Egypt's view, the findings in *Argentina – Bovine Hides*[17] confirm Egypt's position that the Investigating Authority's actions in the context of an anti-dumping investigation should not reviewed under Article X:3 of GATT 1994.

38.   Indeed, the Panel stated:

> *"In our view, Argentina has attempted to stretch the Appellate Body finding that Article X is not applicable when the alleged inconsistency involves the substance of another GATT 1994 provision, to argue that Article X cannot be referred to when challenging the substance of any measure. Of course, a WTO Member may challenge the substance of a measure under Article X. The relevant question is whether the substance of such a measure is administrative in nature or, instead, involves substantive issues more properly dealt with under other provisions of the GATT 1994."(underline added)*

39.   This finding confirms that actions that are covered by other WTO provisions do not fall within the scope of Article X:3(a). In the Rebar case, the actions of the Investigating Authority are evidently covered by Article VI of GATT 1994 and the WTO AD Agreement. Accordingly, Article X:3 does not apply.

Question 3

   In relation to the claim of a breach of Annex II, paragraph 1 by reason of the alleged late request for cost information, what is the relevance of Annex II, paragraph 1 at a time in an investigation prior to the decision to use facts available?

Response

40.   Annex II, paragraph 1 imposes upon the Investigating Authority the obligation to specify in detail the information required from any interested party, and the manner in which that information should be structured, as soon as possible after the initiation of the investigation. The Investigating Authority must furthermore inform the party that, if information is not supplied within a reasonable time, determinations will be made on the basis of facts available.

41.   In Egypt's view, Annex II, paragraph 1 applies only to the issuance of the initial questionnaire, where the information the Investigating Authority requires to base its determinations must be specified. This interpretation is consistent with the requirement that the notification should be made as soon as possible after the initiation of the investigation. Conversely, Annex II, paragraph 1 does not apply to requests for clarification and additional information that the Investigating Authority might send in the course of the investigation. Indeed, such requests will

---

[17]   Argentina – Measures Affecting the Export of Bovine Hides and the Import of Finished Leather, WT/DS155/R and Corr.1, DSR 2001:V, 1779, para. 11.70

be sent after a preliminary review of the information provided in the question-naire responses. Contrary to Turkey's suggestions, it goes without saying that Annex II, paragraph 1 does not prevent the Investigating Authority from request-ing additional information in the course of the investigation, if necessary. To decide otherwise would contradict the possibility for an Investigating Authority to verify the information submitted in response to the initial questionnaire and to seek further details, as explicitly provided in Article 6.7 of the AD Agreement. In any event, assistance was provided for all requests for additional information and/or clarification. The letters of 19 August 1999 and 23 September 1999, for instance, provided detailed guidance to the exporters as to the nature of the in-formation sought and the manner in which that information should be structured.

42.   Egypt considers that requests for clarification and additional information might fall within the scope of Annex II, paragraph 6 of the AD Agreement, which requires the Investigating Authority to inform interested parties of the reasons why the information submitted is not accepted and to give them an op-portunity to provide further explanations within a reasonable period, due account being taken of the time-limits of the investigation. As demonstrated in Egypt's First Submission, the Investigating Authority fully complied with those require-ments in the course of the Rebar investigation.

ANNEX 5-1

REBUTTAL SUBMISSION OF TURKEY
EXECUTIVE SUMMARY

1.   The Panel should not consider evidence, purportedly of a public nature, that was not supplied to all interested parties during the course of Egypt's anti-dumping investigation. The "Report of Other Causes of Injury" in EGT-6 was not supplied to interested parties and was not "available" to Turkish respondents during the investigation. It should therefore be disregarded under Article 6.4 of the Anti-Dumping Agreement.

2.   The Panel should not consider the confidential information on injury, re-ferred to in Egypt's Response to Panel Question #5, if Turkey is denied access to the information in the same form. To do otherwise would involve an impermissi-ble *ex parte* communication.

3.   Turkey is not seeking *de novo* review by the Panel. Turkey is seeking a determination of whether Egypt's "establishment" of the facts was "unbiased" and "objective," as required by Article 17.6(i), and whether its injury findings were based on "positive evidence" under Article 3.1. Article 17.6(i) requires panels to make an assessment of the facts. In order to determine whether an in-jury finding is supported by "positive evidence", a panel must examine the fac-tual basis for the findings to determine whether the Investigating Authority prop-erly identified the appropriate facts, and whether the stated factual basis reasona-bly supported the findings.

4.   The Panel should consider the so-called "new" information supplied in Turkey's First Submission because respondents were deprived of adequate notice that the scope of the investigation had changed from consideration of threat of injury to consideration of present material injury. The respondents would have or could have submitted this information had they had adequate notice that it would be relevant to the Investigating Authority's determination. Alternatively, the Panel should take "judicial notice" of those facts.

5.   The Panel need not accept the Investigating Authority's interpretation of the agreement unless the Panel finds that that interpretation is "permissible". This standard is less deferential than one requiring deference to interpretations that are merely "reasonable".

6.   The only "positive evidence" cited by Egypt as support for its finding that a "causal link" existed between imports from Turkey and injury to the domestic industry is (a) an increase in the volume of imports; and (b) a finding by the In-vestigating Authority of price undercutting by imports. However, increases in the volume of imports cannot be said to be injuring the domestic industry when the domestic industry is, itself, experiencing strong increases in both sales volume and market share. In the first quarter of 1999, when the Investigating Authority claims that most of the injury occurred, the domestic producers increased their

market share by 22 per cent! Moreover, imports overall, including imports from Turkey, declined in volume by 50 per cent in the first quarter of 1999. Contrary to a finding by the Investigating Authority, imports from Turkey did not increase by 40 per cent in the first quarter of 1999 over import levels in the second half of 1998. Rather, the volume of imports from Turkey declined in the first quarter of 1999 as compared to import levels in the second half of 1998.

7.   A finding of price undercutting, standing alone, without other evidence that import prices are having an adverse effect on domestic prices, is not sufficient "positive evidence" that import pricing is having any effect on domestic prices. Because of long lead times for import shipments, uncertainties regarding delivery or the condition of the merchandise when delivered, and difficulties in making returns or quality claims, imports of commodity products must nearly always be priced below domestic prices. But that does not mean that they are having any impact on domestic prices. Where there is no specific "positive evidence" that imports caused prices to fall, the price declines could just as well have been caused by other factors (as Turkey claims has occurred in this case).

8.   Turkey does not claim that imports must be the "sole" cause of injury to the domestic industry. Turkey claims that Egypt has not established that the dumped imports were even a "contributing cause" of the injury found to the domestic industry.

9.   Turkey does not claim that Egypt had to consider and evaluate each and every factor listed in Article 3.5 as Egypt contends, only that Egypt had to consider those factors that were "relevant" to the case before it. Article 3.5 requires a "demonstration of a causal relationship between the dumped imports and injury to the domestic industry". This demonstration must be made based on "an examination of all relevant evidence before the authorities". Injuries caused by "known factors" other than the dumped imports must be "separated" and "distinguished" so that they are not attributed to imports.

10.   Contrary to Egypt's claims, "known factors" does not include solely those factors that the foreign interested parties have brought to the attention of the Investigating Authority. Nor is there an obligation that the foreign interested parties make a *prima facie* case that those factors are injuring the domestic industry. The foreign interested parties may not be in possession of the information necessary to make such a case. Furthermore, "known" factors should include factors that are having a large, and discernible, effect on the conditions of the competition or on the size and shape of the domestic industry. *Wheat Gluten* indicates that the Investigating Authority has an independent obligation to conduct a full investigation in order to identify all factors having a bearing on the state of the domestic industry, including other factors that might be, at the same time, causing injury to the domestic industry. The Investigating Authority bears a special burden to identify such factors where there has been no public allegation that the domestic industry is suffering from current "material" injury, and the final determination is based upon an affirmative finding of present "material" injury.

11.   The Investigating Authority failed to engage in an objective and thorough investigation of causes of injury other than imports. In this case, the other causes

of injury include (1) large capacity expansions at the two major Egyptian producers; (2) the effects of the capacity expansion on the producers' costs of production; (3) the effects of the capacity expansion on intra-industry competition; (4) increasing competition between Al Ezz and Alexandria National; (5) falling prices for steel scrap; (6) a sharp contraction in demand in January 1999; and (7) the effect of comparably priced, fairly traded imports. Each of these other factors was identified by the Turkish interested parties or known to the Investigating Authority.

12.   With respect to the capacity expansions, Egypt alternately claims that it did investigate the expansion, citing a finding in the Final Report with respect to capacity utilization, and that the Investigating Authority did not "know" that the capacity expansions were causing injury. However, this was a factor that was known to the Investigating Authority and it should have been obvious that a change in the size and shape of the domestic industry of this magnitude (700,000 new tons of capacity) could have had an adverse effect upon the domestic cost structure during start-up and on intra-industry competition after start-up. The findings in the Report on Other Causes of Injury, if they are to be considered by this Panel, do not contradict this analysis.

13.   With respect to contraction in demand, the investigating authority noted a demand increase from 1997 to 1998 but ignored a decline in demand of 33 per cent in January 1999, the very month in which domestic prices fell. While demand picked up after January, the demand decline in January coincided with a number of other factors that acted to depress prices, including: (a) the commencement of operations at two capacity expansion projects; (2) falling scrap prices that permitted Al Ezz to reduce prices while maintaining profitability; and (3) sharpening competition between Al Ezz and Alexandria National.

14.   With respect to non-dumped imports, Egypt claimed that (a) imports from Saudi Arabia and Libya declined in the first quarter of 1999, while imports from Turkey increased; (b) prices from Turkey are below those from Saudi Arabia and Libya; and (c) additions should be made to the Saudi and Libyan prices prior to comparison with prices from Turkey. These claims ignore the fact that Saudi Arabia was the largest foreign supplier in 1998, with volume increases exceeding those from Turkey, according to published statistics. In addition, the published data, when corrected for an error in Egypt's brief, show that Turkey's prices were comparable to those of imports from Saudi Arabia and above those for Libya. The published data are reported on a CIF basis, so there is no basis for further adjustment for transportation expenses. And, while the volume of imports from Saudi Arabia fell in the first quarter of 1999, after that country lost duty-free treatment, this meant that imports overall, including those from Turkey, declined substantially in the first quarter of 1999.

15.   With respect to the decline in raw material prices, Egypt noted that, because of a simultaneous decline in profits, that factor cannot explain falling prices. However, this analysis ignores the fact that declining scrap prices affected Al Ezz, but not Alexandria National. Thus Al Ezz could reduce prices without sacrificing profitability, which was strong during the period. Al Ezz had an in-

centive to do so, with the confluence of declining demand in January and the start-up of a new, 400,000-ton facility.

16.   The Investigating Authority failed to examine all of the mandatory factors listed in Article 3.4, including productivity, actual and potential negative effects on cash flow, employment, wages, growth and ability to raise capital. The Investigating Authority also failed to provide a sufficient examination of capacity, capacity utilization and return on investment. In *High Fructose Corn Syrup*, the Panel found that Article 3.4 requires more than the mere recitation of the Article 3.4 factors in the final determination – it requires a meaningful analysis.

17.   Egypt claims that its determination of price undercutting was made by comparing prices at the same level of trade. This is, however, insufficient unless the level of trade at which prices are compared happens to be the level where those prices are in actual competition with each other. There is insufficient information to establish whether that was the case in the rebar investigation.

18.   Egypt argues that Turkey's claim with respect to lack of adequate notice of a change in the scope of the injury investigation was considered and rejected by the Panel in *Guatemala-Cement II*. Turkey considers the decision in *Guatemala-Cement II* to be highly inequitable and, in effect, a denial of fundamental due process. Parties cannot defend themselves adequately if they do not know what allegations are being investigated. Turkey therefore urges this Panel to reach its own determination on the issue.

19.   With respect to Turkey's claim that Egypt violated Article 3.5 by failing to find a linkage between the imports found to be dumped in 1998 and the injury found in 1999, Egypt asserts that the Agreement does not contain any requirements for the period over which data should be collected. But that is not the issue. The issue is the absence of a finding of a link between the imports specifically found to be dumped and the injury to the domestic industry. Egypt also claims that such a finding was made but provides no citation to the Final Report. In fact, there was no such finding.

20.   Egypt contends that the original manufacturers' questionnaire requested cost data for a full twelve-month period. Egypt further contends that the Investigating Authority's letter of 20 May 1999, characterizing the responses filed by Colakoglu, Habas and Diler as "sufficient," such that no supplemental questionnaires or requests for information would be issued, as being confined to the price and sales aspects of respondents' questionnaire responses. This bit of historical revisionism does not match the facts. Respondents were instructed to report only those home market sales that were contemporaneous with their reported sales to Egypt. Costs are ordinarily compared to sales on a transaction-by-transaction basis. Respondents operate in hyperinflationary conditions. Investigating authorities in other jurisdictions limit their price-cost comparisons to sales prices and costs computed in the same month so as to limit the potential distorting effect of inflation. Respondents reasonably reported costs for those months in which they reported sales in Egypt and sales in the home market. The Investigating Authority was initially satisfied with this methodology as indicated in its letter of 20 May 1999. Neither the inquiry to which that letter responded nor the letter

itself was limited to the price and sales aspects of the response. Moreover, the 19 August letter, where cost data was requested for additional months, did not predicate its request on the rationale that this information should have been supplied in response to the initial questionnaire. Rather, the Investigating Authority justified its request for the data on the rationale that respondents' submitted cost data did not appear to reflect mounting inflation in Turkey.

21.   Egypt claims that respondents' limit on the reporting of their costs to the month in which they reported sales transactions was "tantamount to an absence of a response". If so, why did the Investigating Authority wait for four months, until the end of the investigation was, in the Investigating Authority's own words, "near," to notify the respondents of the deficiency? Even if this explanation were accepted, the Investigating Authority's delay in notifying respondents that it considered their responses deficient violated Paragraph 6 of Annex II. By failing to obtain the necessary information in advance of verification, moreover, and then requiring respondents to self-verify all of their submitted costs and prices on paper, the Investigating Authority imposed an "unreasonable burden of proof" in violation of Article 2.4, and violated Annex I, paragraph 7 (verification "should be carried out after the response to the questionnaire has been received") and Article 6.7.

22.   Contrary to Egypt's claims, the calculations attached to the verification reports were clearly tentative dumping calculations. The calculation sheet for Icdas, for example, states at the top "ICDAS DUMPING CALCULATION". While a dumping margin was not calculated in the document itself, it can easily be done with the data shown in the table.

23.   Egypt questions why Turkey would claim it "extraordinary" that the Investigating Authority would question in its 19 August letter whether respondents' costs of production included the effects of inflation. While there are many "extraordinary" elements to that letter, Turkey characterized as "extraordinary" the Investigating Authority' questioning of respondents' sales prices, and whether those prices reflected inflation, when, in fact, the Investigating Authority had just verified those sales prices to respondents' books and records without discrepancy.

24.   Egypt raises, for the very first time in its written submission to the Panel, the claim that respondents' financial statements did not comply with IAS-29, which deals with financial reporting in hyperinflationary economies, as evidence that their submitted costs did not reflect to the effects of inflation. This argument is nothing more than *post-hoc* rationalization of Egypt's anti-dumping determination. "[E]rrors made during the investigation cannot be rectified in subsequent submissions before a WTO Panel." *(Hot-Rolled Carbon Steel Products from Japan* – Report of the Panel.) The Final Report does not mention IAS-29 and it is evident that the Investigating Authority never asked any questions about it. Moreover, the evidence on the record shows that complying with IAS-29 is not required by generally accepted accounting principles in Turkey. None of the respondents comply with IAS-29 and one of the auditors noted that "there is currently no consensus in Turkey on the application of IAS-29". Under Article

2.2.1.1 "costs shall normally be calculated on the basis of records kept by the exporter or producer under investigation, provided that such records are in accordance with generally accepted accounting principles *in the exporting country*". Since respondents costs were kept in accordance with generally accepted accounting principles in Turkey, they should have been used under the Agreement.

25.   Egypt states throughout its written submission that the information submitted by Icdas and IDC did not demonstrate that their costs reflected inflation. But Egypt has not shown that their submitted costs do not reflect the costs shown in their books and records, or that their books and records were not kept in accordance with generally accepted accounting principles in Turkey. Nor has Egypt shown how it complied with the requirements of Annex II, paragraph 6. That paragraph provides that if information is "not accepted", the supplying party must be informed and it must be given "an opportunity to make further explanations". Neither Icdas, nor IDC, were so informed or given such an opportunity.

26.   Egypt claims that there is no "normal sequence of events" contemplated by the Agreement. However, the provisions we have cited, Annex II, paragraph 1, Annex II, paragraph 6, Article 6.7 and Annex I, paragraph 7, certainly appear to contemplate a normal sequence events – i.e., questionnaire, supplemental questionnaire, verification (if there is one), preliminary determination, argument, final determination. This sequence is, in fact, how anti-dumping investigations are conducted throughout the world. The provisions cited also contemplate that, if there is to be a verification, it will be conducted on-site, and if there are further details to be gathered after the questionnaire responses have been filed, they will be collected during the verification. The respondents in this case were severely prejudiced by the Investigating Authority's failure to request the additional cost information it later considered necessary early in the investigation, the Investigating Authority's failure to take advantage of the on-site verification to test the submitted data submitted, and the Investigating Authority's demand that respondents engage in a full "mail order" verification in order to compensate for the Investigating Authority's earlier failures to identify and ask questions at verification about the data with respect to which it had questions or concerns.

27.   Contrary to Egypt's claims, and those of the United States, the obligations stated in the first and last sentence of Article 2.4 (requirement of a "fair comparison" between the export price and the normal value and prohibition against imposing an "unreasonable burden of proof") apply to all of Article 2. The Appellate Body took the position in *Hot-Rolled Carbon Steel Products from Japan* that the first sentence of Article 2.4 ("fair comparison") "informs all of Article 2". The last sentence of Article 2.4 is as general in its language and intended effect as the first sentence and so should be read equally broadly.

28.   Contrary to claims by Egypt, the United States and the EU, the 37-day period established in Article 6.1.1 for responses to "questionnaires used in an anti-dumping investigation" does not apply only to the initial questionnaires issued in those investigations. It applies, by its terms, to any "questionnaire" the response to which is to be "used in an anti-dumping investigation". Nor does the

context of Article 6.1.1 indicate that this provision is intended to be applied only to initial questionnaires. In the absence of an express limitation in the language or an implied limitation in the context in which that language appears, Article 6.1.1 should be given its full effect. It should therefore be read to apply to questionnaires such as the one contained in the 19 August 1999 letter.

29. In the alternative, the deadlines established for a response to the 19 August questionnaire were unreasonable, in violation of Annex II, paragraph 6. "[W]hat constitutes a reasonable period or a reasonable time, under Article 6.8 and Annex II of the Anti-Dumping Agreement, should be defined on a case-by-case basis, in light of the specific circumstances of that investigation". (*Hot-Rolled Carbon Steel Products from Japan* – Report of Appellate Body). In this case, even the extended deadline was clearly insufficient in light of the mass of detail, documentation and analysis required for a response to the 19 August questionnaire. And the specific circumstances facing the respondents – a massive earthquake hitting Istanbul the day before the questionnaire was issued causing widespread devastation and loss of life – made the deadlines even more unreasonable. The deadlines for the 23 September 1999 supplemental information request to Habas, Colakoglu and Diler were also plainly insufficient. It would have been literally impossible to provide the requested data in just 2-5 days.

30. Egypt claims that it properly denied a request by Colakoglu, Habas and Diler for an oral hearing because that request came after respondents supposedly informed the Investigating Authority that they would not submit information in response to the information request of 23 September 1999. Turkey notes, first, that Colakoglu, Habas and Diler did not refuse to answer the supplemental information request of 23 September 1999 – they noted that the deadline for doing so was impossible to meet. Second, those companies' failure to respond to the 23 September information request does not excuse Egypt's decision not to grant an opportunity to "present other information orally". If Egypt wanted to get at the truth – whether or not respondents' submitted costs matched the costs shown in their books and records, and whether and how respondents' booked costs reflected inflation – it would have granted respondents an opportunity to come and explain these issues to it. By refusing that request, and a similar request by Icdas, Egypt violated Article 6.2 of the Agreement.

31. The inflation statistics provided in EGT-7.7 plainly show that inflation was significantly lower than 5 per cent per month in 1998, and that inflation did not exceed 2.5 per cent per month in the June-August period. The Investigating Authority prominently relied on an assumption that inflation was running at 5 per cent per month throughout the investigation period in its determination to resort to facts available. This represented an improper establishment of the facts.

32. The Investigating Authority has also provided Icdas' scrap costs to the Panel as evidence of scrap costs during the investigation period. These scrap costs are the same costs that are discussed in Turkey's First Submission (at 63). They in fact show that the conclusions reached by the Investigating Authority with respect to the movement of the scrap costs were unfounded. Specifically,

the Investigating Authority's finding that scrap costs (in dollar terms) declined in only three months of the period of investigation is unsupported by the facts.

33.   Turkey's claims of violations of Articles 2.2.1.1, 2.2.2 and 2.4 are intended to demonstrate that the normal value calculated in this case is inappropriate in the event that the Panel concludes that resort to facts available was unjustified.

34.   Turkey agrees that if data has been properly rejected because it cannot be verified or is inaccurate, that data need not be used in the Investigating Authority's determination. However, when some data is unverified and other data is verified or otherwise reliable, the verified or reliable data should be used in accordance with Annex II, paragraph 3. Moreover, the Investigating Authority should endeavor, in finding other "gap filling" data, to approximate, as closely as possible, the costs that would have been submitted or verified had the party cooperated completely with the investigating authority. Nothing in the agreement permits an investigating authority to "punish" respondents with adverse "facts available."

35.   Egypt claims that the Investigating Authority was "solely concerned with the reasonableness, neutrality and consistency of its approach" and that the IA was actually acting leniently by using respondents' own data as "facts available". This claim is ludicrous. Egypt could not have constructed a financial expense from secondary information equal to 64 per cent of IDC's cost of manufacture as it did in this case. Nor could it have justified, based on secondary sources, the use of a January 1998 scrap cost to compute the cost of producing rebar sold by Icdas to Egypt in the last half of the year. The Investigating Authority has also not provided a rational basis for arbitrarily increasing Habas' costs by 5 per cent. Why not 10 per cent or 50 per cent?

36.   Egypt incorrectly claims Turkey has conceded that the short-term interest income claimed by Turkey as an offset to interest expense was not related to the production or sale of the subject merchandise. To the contrary, Turkey claims that (a) this income *was* related to the production and sale of rebar; (b) evidence on the record supports such a classification (interest income is classified as "operating income" on the companies' financial statements); and (c) there is no information on the record supporting the Investigating Authority's conclusion that that revenue was *not* related to the production or sale of rebar.

37.   Turkey has argued that Egypt should have made an adjustment to the constructed normal value for differences in imputed credit costs. Egypt argues that the adjustments mandated by Article 2.4 for differences in "conditions and terms of sale" are limited to situations in which the normal value is based on sales prices and does not apply when the normal value is based on costs of production. Turkey notes that the United States, the EU and Canada make these adjustments when the normal value is based on constructed normal value. Moreover, Egypt deducted imputed credit costs from the export price to Egypt. Comparison of a "sight" price to Egypt with a cost of production that includes the full cost of financing receivables in the home market and export market is like comparing apples to oranges. A "fair comparison" requires that the cost of financing receiv-

ables be deducted from the constructed normal value or that an adjustment be made based on the imputed credit costs included in the prices of comparable sales transactions in the home market.

38.   Egypt notes that some Panels have expressed doubt as to whether the actions of an Investigating Authority in the context of one single anti-dumping investigation could be considered a measure of "general application" contemplated in Article X:1 of the GATT 1994. However, Turkey has alleged a violation of Article X:3(a), not Article X:1. Article X:3(a) obliges each contracting party to "administer in a uniform, impartial and reasonable manner all its laws, regulations, decisions and rulings of the kind described in paragraph 1 of this Article". Paragraph 1 includes "laws [and] regulations . . . of a general application ... pertaining to ... rates of duty, taxes or other charges". Turkey's claim in this case is that Egypt was administering its anti-dumping law in manner that violated Article X:3(a). Thus, Turkey needed to show only that the anti-dumping laws of Egypt were laws of "general application" not that the administration complained of was "of general application". Administration of laws of general application normally has a limited application to the case before the investigating authority. No requirement of "general application" should be read into this language.

39.   Turkey agrees with the United States that the Agreement does not require a verification. However, evaluation of Egypt's refusal to conduct a second verification must be examined in the context of the entire case and in consideration of the degree of "cooperation" extended by the respondents.

40.   Turkey agrees with the views expressed by Japan in this proceeding.

ANNEX 5-2

REBUTTAL SUBMISSION OF EGYPT
EXECUTIVE SUMMARY

I.   PRELIMINARY REMARK

1.   Turkey has, in its Response of 7 December 2001 to the Panel's Questions, taken this opportunity to (1) introduce new claims; and (2) modify existing claims as regards injury and dumping that were not mentioned in the Request for Establishment of a Panel. Accordingly, those claims are not within the terms of reference of the Panel and must be rejected. In particular, Turkey alleges that:

- the Investigating Authority did not consider factors affecting domestic prices under Article 3.4;

- the Investigating Authority violated Paragraph 6 of Annex II of the AD Agreement by sending the letter of 19 August 1999 to the Turkish respondents;

- the Investigating Authority violated Article 17.6(i) of the AD Agreement;

- the Investigating Authority violated Paragraph 3 of Annex II and Article X:3 of GATT 1994 in its selection of facts as facts available.

2.   Moreover, the majority of evidence upon which Turkey relies to substantiate its claims, which themselves lack the requisite legal basis under the AD Agreement, have not been presented to the Investigating Authority during the course of the investigation. In fact, what Turkey is attempting is to persuade the Panel to conduct a *de novo* review of the Investigating Authority's determinations. The obligations of the Panel under Article 17.5(ii) and 17.6 are very clear in this respect. Article 17.5(ii) of the AD Agreement expressly limits the review of the Panel to the evidence that was *made available*, and thus made *known* to the Investigating Authority in conformity with the appropriate domestic procedures.

3.   Turkey urges the Panel to ignore these provisions by taking "judicial notice" (a concept which has no foundation in DSB practice) of facts that were not before the Investigating Authority during the course of the proceeding. However, the reference to facts "*made available*" in Article 17.5(ii) is significant as it *precludes* a panel from taking "*judicial notice*" of facts that were not *made available* to the Investigating Authority during the course of the investigation.

II.   INJURY

A.   *Obligations of the Investigating Authority under Article 3.4*

4.   An important distinction must be made. That distinction is between the *final determination* as from the *Final Report* of the Rebar Investigation. Whereas the former reviews all factors listed in Article 3.4 in its examination of the impact of the dumped imports on the domestic industry, the latter focuses on the conclusions central to the Investigating Authority's determination of material injury.

5.   The fact that the injury analysis of the Investigating Authority was thorough and indeed covered all the factors listed in Article 3.4 is apparent in the *Confidential Injury Analysis* of the Rebar Investigation. Thus, in addition to factors specifically referred to in the *Essential Facts & Conclusions Report* and the *Final Report*, the following Article 3.4 factors were explicitly examined by the Investigating Authority during the course of the investigation:

- Sales volume and revenue;
- Cost of production, selling & administrative costs, cost of sales and finance costs;
- Gross profit, pre-tax profit and profit after cost;
- Output (i.e. volume of production);
- Market share (i.e. total sales of all Egyptian producers, including subject and non-subject countries);
- Productivity (i.e. output per employee);
- Return on investments;
- Capacity utilization;
- Cash flow;
- Inventories;
- Employment (i.e. number of employees);
- Wages;
- Domestic prices;
- Growth (i.e. in terms of sales volume and market share);
- Ability to raise capital (i.e. pre-tax profit as a % of shareholders funds)

An analysis of the magnitude of the margin of dumping is clearly evident in Section 3.3 of the *Essential Facts & Conclusions Report* and Sections 3.3, 4.4 and 4.6.2 of the *Final Report*.

6.   Accordingly, Egypt submits that during the investigation of material injury, the Investigating Authority did indeed examine "*all relevant economic factors and indices having a bearing on the state of the industry*" as required under Article 3.4

of the AD Agreement. Turkey's claim is thus without foundation and therefore must be rejected by the Panel in this present dispute.

7.　　　Turkey claims that "*the Panel should disregard evidence not shared with the respondents in assessing the consistency of the Egyptian anti-dumping investigation and findings with the Anti-Dumping Agreement*".[1] In support of this claim Turkey refers to the decisions reached by the panels in *Korean Resins* and *Thailand – H Beams*. The Panel should note, however, that Turkey has failed to mention that the findings of the Panel in *Thailand – H Beams*, upon which Turkey relies, were reversed by the Appellate Body on appeal. Indeed, the Appellate Body in *Thailand – H Beams* stated that there is "*nothing in Article 3.1 which limits an investigating authority to base an injury determination only upon non-confidential information*" (emphasis added).[2] It follows that the findings of the Panel in *Korean Resins*, a pre-WTO claim brought under the GATT 1947, should be reviewed in this light.

B.　　Turkey Confuses the Relevant Obligations of Articles 3.4 and 3.5

8.　　　In Turkey's First Written Submission in Section III.B.5 (page 9) and again in its Oral Presentation at the First meeting of the Panel in Section II.B (page 5), Turkey alleges that:

> "*the Investigating Authority failed to examine all relevant economic factors and indices having a bearing on the state of the industry in violation of Article 3.4. Specifically, that the Investigating Authority failed to consider the adverse effects on domestic profitability and pricing produced by five factors.*" (*emphasis added*)

The five factors specifically referred to by Turkey are (a) capacity expansion of the domestic industry; (b) increased domestic competition; (c) falling prices for raw materials; (d) contraction in domestic demand; and (e) the effect of comparably priced, fairly traded imports.

9.　　　It is clear that Turkey is alleging that Egypt improperly attributed the injury (i.e. falling prices and a decrease in profitability) to imports from Turkey. According to Turkey, the injury was "produced", that is to say that it was *caused*, by factors other than the dumped imports, such as increased domestic capacity and domestic competition, a decline in the price of raw materials and domestic demand, and the effect of non-dumped imports. Accordingly, Egypt maintains that the issue is one of causation and attribution, in which the relevant provision is Article 3.5.

---

[1]　　See page 7 of Turkey's Oral Presentation at the First Meeting of the Panel.

[2]　　*Thailand – Anti-Dumping Duties on Angles Shapes and Sections of Iron or Non-Alloy Steel and H-Beams from Poland* WT/DS122/R, Appellate Body Report WT/DS122/AB/R, DSR 2001:VII, 2741, para. 107, adopted 5 April 2001.

10.   Attention should be called to the fact that nowhere in the Request for the Establishment of a Panel, nor in Turkey's First Written Submission or in its Oral Presentation at the First Meeting of the Panel, has Turkey alleged that the Investigating Authority failed to investigate "*factors affecting domestic prices*" under Article 3.4. Turkey should not be permitted, at this late stage, to modify its allegations of inconsistency. Should the Panel rule on this claim, Egypt submits that there is no prescribed method under the AD Agreement by which the Investigating Authority must consider "*factors affecting domestic prices*".

11.   Thus, contrary to what Turkey alleges, an examination of "*factors affecting domestic prices*" under Article 3.4 does not necessarily require that the Investigating Authority consider capacity expansion and its effects on intra-industry competition, falling prices of raw materials, contraction in demand and the effect of non-dumped imports. In any event, as demonstrated above, Egypt considers that an examination of domestic competition, contraction in demand and the effect of non-dumped imports are factors which may be relevant in the Investigating Authority's examination of "*any known factors other than the dumped imports*" under Article 3.5. As for the other alleged factors affecting domestic prices, the capacity expansion of the domestic industry was indeed examined by the Investigating Authority in addition to demand and the price of raw materials.

12.   Turkey is of the opinion that it is *incumbent upon the Investigating Authority to secure certain kinds of information pursuant to Article 3.5 in order to determine whether or not there was a causal link between the dumped imports and injury.* Thus, according to Turkey, the Investigating Authority is under an obligation to develop "positive evidence" that:

- consumers purchased imported rebar from Turkey in place of rebar supplied by the domestic manufacturers for price reasons;

- specific sales were lost by the domestic industry to imports from Turkey;

- domestic manufacturers lowered their prices specifically in response to competing offers by suppliers of Turkish rebar;

- Turkey was considered by purchasers in Egypt as the price leader in the market.

13.   Egypt would like to take this opportunity to clarify the obligations of the Investigating Authority with respect to its examination of "*any known factors other than the dumped imports which at the same time are injuring the domestic industry*". What is known to the Investigating Authority clearly includes factors presented to the Investigating Authority during the course of the investigation. We agree with the European Communities "*that an interested party must make a prima facie case that a factor might be relevant in order for a factor to be known in the sense of Article 3.5*" (emphasis in the original).

14.   Unlike Article 3.5 of the AD Agreement, the examination of causality under Article 4.2(b) of the Safeguards Agreement does *not* specifically direct the Investigating Authorities to examine "*known factors*" other than the imports under investigation which might be injuring the domestic industry. Moreover, in-

terested parties are not *as* involved in the context of safeguard investigations and do not actively participate in the data collection exercise carried out by the Investigating Authority. Accordingly, in the context of a Safeguard investigation, the exercise of due diligence by a Member is all the more important in reaching a determination under Article 4.2(b). Finally, the Safeguard Agreement does not contain a similar provision to Article 17.5(ii) of the AD Agreement, which expressly limits the review of the Panel to the evidence that was *made available*, and thus made *known* to the Investigating Authority in conformity with the appropriate domestic procedures.

C. Scope of the Investigation

15.   Turkey claims that the additional evidence on causation that was presented in its First Written Submission was not presented by the Turkish respondents during the course of the investigation because the investigation was initially limited to a threat of material injury. However, in the Notice of Initiation with respect to the *"allegation of threat of injury"* (at paragraph 4), it is clearly stated that "[t]*he applicant alleged and provided supporting evidence that the dumped imports have started to cause material injury to the domestic industry"*. Accordingly, the Turkish respondents, assuming they read the Notice, could not have been unaware that the investigation would include an examination of present material injury. Moreover, attention to this fact was again pointed out by the Investigating Authority in a facsimile dated 17 July 1999 to David Simon, who acted as counsel for the Turkish respondents during the investigation (attached as EX-EGT-8).

16.   In any event, contrary to that submitted by Turkey, it would not be "inequitable" for the current Panel to apply the decision in *Guatemala – Cement II*[3] to the facts of this case. The issue in *Guatemala – Cement II* is nearly identical to that in the current proceeding before the Panel. Indeed, it would be unreasonable to require an Investigating Authority to determine precisely the scope the injury examination at the beginning of the proceeding before it has even had a chance to review the evidence and to evaluate its findings.

III.   DUMPING

A.   Claims not within the Panel's Terms of Reference

17.   Turkey alleges that the Investigating Authority violated Paragraph 6 of Annex II of the AD Agreement by sending the letter of 19 August 1999 to the Turkish respondents[4]. Egypt submits that this claim is not within the Panel's terms of reference. Indeed, in the Request for Establishment of a Panel, a violation of Paragraph 6 of Annex II was invoked solely with respect to the deadline

---

[3]   *Guatemala – Definitive Anti-Dumping Measures on Grey Portland Cement from Mexico* WT/DS156/R, DSR 2000:XI, 5295, Report of the Panel, adopted 17 November 2000.
[4]   See last sentence of Appendix TUR. II.A.

granted to the respondents to reply to the letter of 19 August 1999. Conversely, Turkey did not claim in its Request for Establishment of a Panel that the sheer fact of sending the letter of 19 August 1999 constituted a violation of Paragraph 6 of Annex II. Accordingly, this claim must be rejected as it is not within the Panel's terms of reference.

18.   Turkey also alleges a violation of Article 17.6(i) of the AD Agreement in Section II.D. However, that provision governs the standard of review to be applied by a panel when considering whether the Investigating Authority's establishment of the facts was proper and the evaluation unbiased and objective. It does not govern the rights and obligations of Members under the AD Agreement. In any event, it was not cited in the Request for Establishment of a Panel. As a consequence, this claim is not within the terms of reference of the Panel and must be rejected.

19.   Turkey also contends that the Investigating Authority violated Paragraph 3 of Annex II and Article X:3 of GATT 1994 in its selection of facts as facts available. As noted by the Panel, those provisions were not cited in support of Claim 11 of the Request for Establishment of a Panel. Accordingly, the alleged violation of Paragraph 3 of Annex II and Article X:3 of GATT 1994 must be rejected as not being within the terms of reference of the Panel in the context of Claim 11.

B.   Failure to Submit Costs Data for the Entire Investigation Period

20.   Turkey attempts to justify the failure of all respondents except IDC to submit costs data for the entire investigation period by referring to the practice of other jurisdictions. The practice of other jurisdictions is not at issue in this case nor should this practice have been considered by the respondents to determine the format in which they needed to submit their costs data in the Rebar investigation conducted by the Egyptian Investigating Authority. The Questionnaire sent to the respondents made it clear that data needed to be provided for the entire investigation period, and not for selected parts of such period.

C.   Requests for Additional Information did not Constitute a New Questionnaire

21.   Turkey suggested at the First Substantive Meeting and repeated in its replies to the Panel's Questions that the requests for additional information contained in the letter of 19 August 1999 constituted a new questionnaire because the letter contained a larger number of questions and raised more complex issues on costs than the initial Questionnaire. This is irrelevant. The original questionnaire requested the respondents to provide their costs of production for the entire investigation period. Four of the five respondents did not comply with that request. In fact, they provided costs data for a maximum period of four months. As thoroughly explained in Egypt's First Submission, the purpose of the letter of 19 August was therefore twofold:

- first, to provide an additional opportunity to the respondents to report their costs data for the entire investigation period;

- second, to seek to clarify whether and, if so, to what extent the respondents' costs data duly reflected the hyperinflation that Turkey was experiencing during the investigation period.

D.   Data Submitted did not Reflect Costs Associated with Production and Sale

22.   Turkey claims that the costs of production of the Turkish respondents were prepared in accordance with the generally accounting principles of Turkey and should therefore have been used by the Investigating Authority pursuant to Article 2.2.1.1 of the AD Agreement. In Egypt's view, it is clear that records that are not prepared in order to reflect hyperinflation cannot be considered to reflect the costs associated with the production and sale of the product under consideration, even though they would follow the generally accepted accounting principles of the exporting country.

23.   Egypt considers that the fact that the respondents did not apply IAS 29 is not disputed by Turkey. Furthermore, Egypt disagrees with Turkey that the Panel could not consider the fact that IAS 29 was not followed by the respondents. Indeed, this fact is explicitly mentioned in the Auditors' notes to the Audited Accounts of the respondents, which were submitted to the Investigating Authority by the respondents themselves.

24.   Turkey further alleges that there was no need to adjust raw material costs for hyperinflation since the prices of raw materials in USD were converted into Turkish Lira at the exchange rate of the day of purchase; however, the fact that Turkish respondents used the exchange rate of the date of purchase of raw materials cannot cope with the effect of hyperinflation on the value of raw materials that are not immediately used in the production.

E.   Interest Income was not Related to Production or Sale

25.   Turkey alleges in its reply to Question 16 that interest income on working capital is sufficiently related to production and sale of rebars because it is a fungible item that cannot be segregated to any particular business line and therefore benefits all production activities of the firm. It is precisely because this cost item is not associated to any business line that it must be excluded from the calculation of the cost of production of the product concerned.

F.   The Letter of 28 September 1999

26.   Turkey states that the Investigating Authority did not reply to the letter of 28 September 1999. This is factually wrong. A reply was sent on the same day to the legal counsel of the three Turkish respondents concerned informing them that the Investigating Authority would resort to facts available in view of the absence of reply on several issues (see EX-EGT-7.5). David Simon acknowledged receipt

of this letter on the same day (see EX-EGT-9). The offer for a meeting in Cairo was subsequently addressed by the Investigating Authority in a letter of 5 October 1999 to David Simon (See EX-EGT-10). As a consequence, contrary to Turkey's erroneous allegations, the Turkish respondents were timely and appropriately informed of the legal consequences of their failure to submit the information requested in the letter of 23 September 1999.

ANNEX 6-1

SECOND ORAL STATEMENT OF EGYPT
EXECUTIVE SUMMARY

I.   PRELIMINARY REMARK

1.   Turkey has not challenged Egypt's arguments from a legal standpoint. To the contrary, Turkey has treated its Rebuttal Submission as yet another opportunity to establish a *prima facie* case of the alleged inconsistencies and, even at this late stage, it is attempting to introduce new claims that were not included in the Request for the Establishment of a Panel.

2.   Throughout the various stages of this proceeding, Turkey is attempting to persuade the Panel to correct the deficiencies of the Turkish respondents' participation in the rebar investigation. It was, however, the responsibility of the Turkish respondents to cooperate and to present all the requisite information and evidence pertinent to their defence during the investigation. The Panel cannot now correct that deficiency.

3.   It has been noted that the majority of evidence upon which Turkey relies to substantiate its claims was not presented to the Investigating Authority during the course of the investigation. By introducing new information before the Panel, Turkey hopes to persuade the Panel that the Investigating Authority's establishment of the facts was not based on positive evidence. Moreover, Turkey has also exerted a considerable effort to reconstruct the facts that were before the Investigating Authority in an attempt to persuade the Panel that the Investigating Authority's establishment of the facts was improper and that its examination with respect thereto was biased and not objective. In essence, by introducing new evidence and reconstructing the facts, Turkey is in fact attempting to persuade the Panel to *reconsider* the Investigating Authority's determination in light of the existing evidence together with new facts; in other words, to conduct a *de novo review* of the Investigating Authority's determinations.

4.   As previously noted, the obligations of the Panel under Article 17 of the AD Agreement are very clear in this respect: paragraph 6(i) directs the Panel to consider whether the authorities' *establishment of the facts was proper* in light of *the facts that were made available* as specified under paragraph 5(ii). Still, Turkey urges the Panel to ignore these provisions by taking "*judicial notice*" of facts that were not before the Investigating Authority during the course of the proceeding.

II.   INJURY

5.   Turkey has failed to demonstrate that the Investigating Authority's determination of injury under Article 3 of the Anti-Dumping Agreement was incon-

sistent with respect to Egypt's obligations thereunder. In particular, Turkey alleges that the Investigating Authority failed to examine the mandatory factors listed in Article 3.4. Turkey also alleges that the Investigating Authority failed to establish, by positive evidence, a causal link between the dumped imports and the injury to the domestic industry under Article 3.5.

A.   The Examination under Article 3.4

6.   It is apparent in the *Confidential Injury Analysis* that the Investigating Authority's final determination with respect to material injury was based on positive evidence and that it involved an objective examination of all the elements as required under Article 3, paragraphs 2 and 4 of the Anti-Dumping Agreement. A copy of the *Confidential Injury Analysis* was presented to Turkey, as requested by the Panel. A non-confidential version of the *Analysis* would have been provided to the Turkish respondents had a request been made to review the public file during the course of the investigation. Indeed, the respondents must have been aware of the existence of the public file, as reference to its availability was specifically made in the *Notice of Initiation*, the *Essential Facts & Conclusions Report* and the *Final Report.*[1]

7.   The very first time a request was made to review the public file was by the Turkish Government in a letter dated 12 July 2000 to the Investigating Authority. Egypt responded to that request at a meeting in Cairo on 6 August 2000. As the investigation had been closed for almost one year, access to the public file was accordingly denied. Nonetheless, Turkey alleges that the Panel should disregard evidence that was not previously made available to the Turkish respondents or to the Turkish Government.[2]

8.   In view of the findings of the Appellate Body in *Thailand – H Beams*[3], it is clear that the Panel cannot disregard the *Confidential Injury Analysis* simply because it was not shared with the respondents during the course of the investigation. In *Thailand – H Beams*, the Appellate Body confirmed that there is "*nothing in Article 3.1 which limits an investigating authority to base an injury determination only upon non-confidential information*".[4] Accordingly, in its review of whether the Investigating Authority's examination of the factors listed in Article 3.4 was complete, the Panel must consider the information contained in the *Confidential Injury Analysis*.

9.   Turkey also claims in its Rebuttal that the Panel should disregard consideration of certain Article 3.4 factors mentioned in the working papers of the Investigating Authority when evaluating whether the *Final Report* contains findings or

---

[1]   See Ex-EGT-7.3 (*Notice of Initiation*), Ex-TUR-15 (*Essential Facts & Conclusions Report*) and Ex-TUR-16 (*Final Report*).

[2]   See the Rebuttal Submission of Turkey of 2 January 2002 at Claim II.A, page 1.

[3]   *Thailand – Anti-Dumping Duties on Angles Shapes and Sections of Iron or Non-Alloy Steel and H-Beams from Poland* WT/DS122/R, DSR 2001:VII, 2741, Appellate Body Report WT/DS122/AB/R, DSR 2001:VII, 2701, adopted 5 April 2001.

[4]   *Ibid.*, at para. 107.

conclusions sufficient to satisfy the requirements of Article 12.2, with respect to each of the Article 3.4 factors.[5] *Egypt wishes to stress that whether all of the Investigating Authority's conclusions on material injury are reproduced in the Final Report, however, is not an issue that is before the Panel. A claim under Article 12.2 was not introduced in the Request for the Establishment of a Panel and accordingly, is not within the Panel's Terms of Reference.*

B.   The Examination under Article 3.5

10.   Turkey has raised a number of claims in connection with the Investigating Authority's examination of the causal relationship under Article 3.5. In particular, Turkey alleges that the Investigating Authority failed to demonstrate that the dumped imports caused injury "*through the effects of dumping*" found and that the Investigating Authority failed to establish by positive evidence a causal link by not thoroughly investigating other potential causes of injury.

11.   As previously submitted, the Investigating Authority's investigation of injury was based on positive evidence and involved an objective examination of the volume of the dumped imports, both in absolute terms and relative to consumption, and the effect of those imports on prices in the domestic market. Indeed, the Investigating Authority found significant price undercutting resulting in price depression and suppression.

12.   Turkey, however, suggests that because the dumping occurred in 1998 and the injury in 1999, the Investigating Authority failed to show that the dumped imports caused injury to the domestic industry. As previously submitted, the Investigating Authority found that the injury in 1999 confirmed the effects of the dumping that took place in 1998. Moreover, it was demonstrated in our First Written Submission that the periods for data collection for both injury and dumping as established by the Investigating Authority are in line with the Recommendations of the Anti-Dumping Committee.

13.   Turkey also claims that because the Investigating Authority allegedly failed to secure very "*specific*" positive evidence with regard to other potential causes of injury, Egypt failed to meet its obligations under Article 3.5. To this end, Turkey presents new evidence to the Panel that was not submitted to the Investigating Authority during the course of the investigation, which it alleges should have been taken into account. However, Article 3.5 only requires that the Investigating Authority examine known factors that are simultaneously injuring the domestic industry. Article 17.5(ii) of the Anti-Dumping Agreement expressly limits the review of the Panel to the evidence that was *made available*, and was thus *known* to the Investigating Authority. Article 3.5 does not require that the Investigating Authority secure, for example, information pertaining to consumers' perceptions as to whether the dumped imports were price leaders in the market.

---

[5]   See the Rebuttal Submission of Turkey of 2 January 2002 at Claim III.H, page 31.

14.   Turkey also places a great deal of emphasis in its Rebuttal Submission that the Investigating Authority did not separate and distinguish the injurious effects of these allegedly known factors that were contributing to the injury. Turkey in fact assumes that the injury was caused by a multitude of factors. However, the report on *Other Causes of Injury* demonstrates that the examination of the causal relationship included an inquiry into a number of other potential causes of injury. On the basis of this review, the Investigating Authority found that *there were no other causes of injury*. Accordingly, there was no need to separate and distinguish the injurious effects of factors other than the dumped imports that were simultaneously injuring the domestic industry.

15.   Turkey has failed to demonstrate that the Investigating Authority's examination of a causal relationship under Article 3.5 was inconsistent with Egypt's obligations thereunder. In view of the evidence *before the Investigating Authority*, Turkey has failed to present a *prima facie* case that there were other known factors that were contributing to the injury. The report on *Other Causes of Injury was available for review* in the public file of the Investigation. The Turkish respondents therefore had the opportunity to review and to comment upon the report and to present refuting evidence. Egypt cannot be held accountable for the fact that the respondents did not avail themselves of that opportunity.

III.   DUMPING

A.   The Use of Facts Available

16.   With respect to the dumping determinations, the principal feature of this case is the fact that Turkish respondents offered very poor cooperation from the very beginning of the investigation onwards. The Anti-Dumping Agreement foresees and wisely provides for the circumstances in which an interested party refuses access to, or otherwise does not provide necessary information within a reasonable period or significantly impedes the investigation. In such instances, the Investigating Authority may resort to the use of "the facts available" as provided under Article 6.8.

17.   It must be emphasised, however, that the use of facts available in the rebar investigation was *not* intended to be punitive. Egypt was not seeking to arrive at an outcome less favourable than would have been the case had the Turkish companies offered satisfactory cooperation. In that respect, Egypt disagrees with Turkey's interpretation of the Appellate Body's findings in *United States – Hot-Rolled Steel from Japan*.[6] Turkey's understanding of the case is that the US Administration did not have the grounds to resort to the use of facts available. To the contrary, the use of facts available in the specific circumstances of the case was held to be permissible by the DSB.[7] What was found incompatible with the

---

[6]   *United States – Anti-Dumping Measures on Certain Hot-Rolled Steel Products from Japan* WT/DS184/R, Appellate Body Report WT/DS184/AB/R, DSR 2001:X, 4697, adopted 23 August 2001.
[7]   *Ibid.*, Report of the Panel at para. 7.69.

Anti-Dumping Agreement was the fact that the US Administration sought to reach an unfavourable determination through the deliberate selection of certain "adverse facts" available.[8]

B.   Claims that are not within the Panel's Terms of Reference

18.   Turkey alleges that the Investigating Authority violated Paragraph 6 of Annex II of the Anti-Dumping Agreement by sending the letter of 19 August 1999 to the Turkish respondents.[9] In the Request for the Establishment of a Panel, however, a violation of Paragraph 6 of Annex II was invoked solely with respect to the deadline granted to the respondents to reply to the letter of 19 August 1999. Conversely, Turkey did not claim in its Request for Establishment of a Panel that the sheer fact of sending the letter of 19 August 1999 constituted a violation of Paragraph 6 of Annex II. Accordingly, this claim must be rejected.

19.   Turkey also claims that the Investigating Authority violated Paragraph 3 of Annex II and Article X:3 of GATT 1994 in its selection of particular data as facts available.[10] As previously noted by the Panel, those provisions were not cited in Claim 11 of the Request for the Establishment of a Panel. Accordingly, the alleged violation of Paragraph 3 of Annex II and Article X:3 of GATT 1994 cannot be considered in this regard.

C.   The Dumping Determinations were in Compliance with the AD Agreement

20.   All the issues raised in Turkey's Rebuttal Submission consist essentially of a mere repetition of the arguments developed in Turkey's First Submission and other statements. They were all thoroughly addressed in Egypt's previous Submissions to the Panel, in particular:

- All respondents except IDC failed to submit costs data for the entire investigation period, despite the fact the Questionnaire sent to the respondents made clear that data needed to be provided for the entire investigation period;

- The requests for additional information contained in the Investigating Authority's letter of 19 August 1999 provided *an additional opportunity* to the respondents to report their costs data for the entire investigation period and to *clarify* whether and, if so, to what extent *the respondents' costs data duly reflected hyperinflation*;

- The respondents' records failed to reasonably reflect the costs associated with the production and sale of the product under consid-

---

[8]   *Ibid.*, at para. 7.70.
[9]   See Response of Turkey to Questions of the Panel of 7 December 2001, Appendix TUR.II.A (last sentence).
[10]   *Ibid.*, at Sections II.C and II.G.

eration by not taking into account the hyperinflation of the Turkish economy;

- The 5 per cent monthly hyperinflation rate was determined on the basis of reliable data and was also used to adjust the costs of production of Habas;

- The computation of a weighted average cost of production for the entire investigation period was fully justified by the circumstances of the case and was in compliance with the AD Agreement.

ANNEX 6-2

SECOND ORAL STATEMENT OF TURKEY
EXECUTIVE SUMMARY

I.   RESPONSE TO EGYPTIAN REBUTTAL BRIEF

1.   I would like to use this opportunity to address specifically the claims made by Egypt in its Rebuttal Brief and to make some comments on the information provided in the confidential injury analysis provided to us on 2 February 2002.

A.   *Failure to Examine all of the Article 3.4 Factors*

2.   Turkey has claimed that Egypt failed to examine all of the mandatory factors identified in Article 3.4 in its final determination. Specifically, Turkey has pointed out that the Essential Facts and Conclusions Report and the Final Report contain no discussion of productivity, actual or potential effects on cash flow, employment, wages, growth and ability to raise capital or investments. Turkey also noted that there is an insufficient examination and evaluation of capacity utilization or return on investment in the Final Report.

B.   *Confidential Evidence to which Respondents did not have Access*

3.   We agree with Egypt and withdraw our claim that Egypt may support its final determination only upon information placed in the public record. However, this does not relieve the Egyptian Authority of the requirement that it provide a meaningful analysis of all of the Article 3.4 factors in its Final Report. Nor does it mean that, in supporting its determination before this Panel, Egypt may rely on documents purportedly in the Public Record that were not shared with, or otherwise made available to, the Government of Turkey and the Turkish private respondents.

C.   *Article 3.4 and 3.5*

4.   Egypt attempts to re-characterize all of Turkey's claims under Articles 3.4 and 3.5 as claims under Article 3.5 in an attempt to avoid Panel review of the Egyptian determination under Article 3.4. Articles 3.4 and 3.5 operate hand-in-hand. First, the Investigating Authority must identify what factors and indices are affecting the domestic industry under Article 3.4, including all relevant factors and indices having a bearing on domestic prices and profitability. Then, under Article 3.5, the Investigating Authority must ensure that it does not attribute effects of factors, other than imports, that are injuring the domestic industry to the dumped imports.

D. Factors Affecting Domestic Prices

5.   Egypt claims that Turkey did not include a claim in its request for Panel review or in its First Written Submission that the Investigating Authority failed to examine "factors affecting domestic prices" under Article 3.4. This claim is incorrect. (See Turkey's request for Panel consideration at paragraph 3).

E. The Obligation to Consider any Known Factors under Article 3.5

6.   With respect to the obligation in Article 3.5 Egypt argues that respondents must make *a prima facie* case that other factors are causing injury to the domestic industry before any obligation is imposed on the Investigating Authority to examine those factors.

7.   We have extensively addressed this issue previously. (See, our reply to Panel Question Number 5 and Section III.C-D of our rebuttal brief).

F. The Scope of the Injury Investigation

8.   Turkey has claimed that additional evidence on causation of present material injury was not submitted during the original investigation because respondents were led to believe that investigation was limited to threat of injury issues. In the only Notice of Initiation made available to the Turkish respondents during the course of the investigation (See TUR-1), it is states that "the domestic industry alleges that the significant and continuing increase of dumped imports of rebars from Turkey in 1998 and the expected increase of imports ... *will threaten to cause* material injury to the domestic industry. Aspects of threat of injury were detected in the second half of 1998".

G. Turkey has not Introduced any New Claims not within the Panel's Terms of Reference

9.   Turkey claims that the Investigating Authority violated Annex II, paragraph 6 of the Anti-Dumping Agreement by waiting until after the verification to raise the cost issues identified in the August 19 letter. (See Response to Panel Question #1, at II.A.)

10.   Egypt now asserts that this claim is not within the terms of reference for the Panel. This claim is incorrect. Turkey raised this issue in Claims 8 and 9.

11.   Turkey has also alleged a violation of Article 17.6(i) of the AD Agreement. Egypt has claimed that this provision concerns the standard of review and does not govern the rights and obligations of the Members under the Agreement. Egypt has also asserted that this particular claim was not contained in Turkey's request for the Panel.

12.   Turkey disagrees on both points. As indicated in our Rebuttal Brief at pages 3-4, the Appellate Body specifically found *in Hot-Rolled Carbon Steel*

Products from Japan that Article 17.6(i) imposes certain procedural obligations upon Investigating Authorities.

H. *Failure to Submit Cost Data for the Entire Investigation Period in the Original Response*

13.   Egypt claims that there was no justification for Turkish respondents to submit cost data in their original responses that was limited to the months in which export sales and home market sales were reported. Contrary to Egypt's claims, the original anti-dumping duty questionnaire did not clearly define the period over which costs should be reported. The questionnaire required the reporting of all sales to Egypt during the period of investigation, but it also directed respondents to limit their reporting of home market sales to those sales that were contemporaneous with sales that were made to Egypt. Since home market and Egyptian sales were reported only in a few months, it is only logical that costs of production should be reported for those months as well. This conclusion was particularly appropriate in the context of a hyperinflationary economy.

I. *The Requests for Additional Information did Constitute a New Questionnaire*

14.   Egypt claims that the 19 August 1999 letter did not constitute a new questionnaire. Regardless of whether or not monthly costs were requested in the original questionnaire, there were a substantial number of additional questions and demonstrations required in response to the 19 August 1999 letter that were in the nature of a questionnaire.

J. *The Data Submitted Reflected Costs Associated with the Production and Sale of the Product Concerned*

15.   Egypt claims that because no company in Turkey applies IAS-29, it should be free to apply facts available. The fact that respondents did not apply IAS – 29 was never investigated by the Investigating Authority or mentioned in the Authority's Final Report. Second, if Egypt was unsatisfied with the costs generated by the respondents' internal accounting systems, even though organized in accordance with generally accepted accounting principles in Turkey, then it was incumbent upon Egypt to advise respondents how to revise their costs in order to meet Egypt's requirements.

K. *Reply to Mr. Simon's Letter of 28 September 1999*

16.   Egypt claims that Habas, Diler and Colakoglu did not request an extension of time in which to respond to the 23 September 1999 supplemental questionnaire issued by the Investigating Authority. While it is true that there was no request for a specific period of additional time in which to respond to that questionnaire, counsel to Habas, Diler and Colakoglu noted, in his letter of 28 Sep-

tember 1999, that it would be impossible to respond to Egypt's request for additional information within the 2-5 day period allowed for a response by the Investigating Authority. This, in Turkey's view, constituted an implicit request for an extension of time.

II. THE "CONFIDENTIAL INJURY ANALYSIS" RECENTLY PROVIDED BY EGYPT SUBSTANTIATES MANY OF THE CLAIMS MADE BY TURKEY EARLIER IN THIS PROCEEDING

A. There was an Enormous Capacity Expansion during the Period of Investigation

17.   The "Confidential Injury Analysis" first supplied by Egypt to the Panel on 31 January 2002 establishes that there was a very large capacity expansion during the period of review. Between 1996 and 1998, domestic capacity to produce rebar increased by [[XX]] tons, or [[XX]] per cent. Between the end of 1998 and the first quarter of 1999, capacity increased by another [[XX]] tons, or [[XX]] per cent as compared to 1996.

B. An Increase in Finance Expenses Attributable to the Capacity Expansion Adversely Affected Profitability

18.   The Confidential Injury Analysis shows that [[XX]] decline in profitability in 1998 is attributable to an increase in finance costs per unit. Profits per ton declined from 1997 to 1998 by [[XX]] Egyptian lira per ton. Finance costs per unit increased in that year by [[XX]] Egyptian lira per ton. Had finance costs per unit not increased, industry profits would have increased in 1998.

C. It Appears that the Capacity Expansion had a Temporary, Adverse Effect on al EZZ'S Profitability in 1998

19.   Al Ezz uses steel scrap as a raw material input for making rebar. Scrap accounts for 60-70 per cent of the cost of a finished rebar and steel scrap prices declined by 34 per cent during 1998. That should have translated into a 20-24 per cent decline in the cost of finished goods sold between the beginning and end of 1998. However, Al Ezz's cost of goods sold declined in 1998 by only [XX] per cent as compared to 1997. Accordingly, it appears that temporary disruptions caused by the capacity expansion acted to keep Al Ezz's costs higher than they would otherwise have been in 1998, adversely affecting the company's profitability.

D. [[XX]]

20.   Al Ezz's expansion project came fully on stream at the end of 1998 its cost of goods sold [[XX]].

21.   This [[XX]].

E.   [[XX]]

22.   [[XX]]

F.   Imports Took a Declining Share of the Domestic Market in 1999

23.   The confidential injury analysis supports our claims in previous submissions that total import market share declined dramatically in the first quarter of 1999. Thus, total import market share declined from [[XX]] per cent of the market in 1998 to just [[XX]] per cent of the market in the first quarter of 1999, a decline of nearly [[XX]] per cent. The domestic industry also increased its market share, from [[XX]] per cent of the market in 1998 to [[XX]] per cent of the market in the first quarter of 1999. While Turkey took an increasing share of the market in 1999, it did so at the expense of other imports, including fairly traded imports from Saudi Arabia and Libya, it did not replace one ton of rebar formerly sold by the domestic industry, nor did it increase its market share at the expense of domestic market share.

G.   The Investigating Authority's Determination of Price Undercutting was Flawed in Violation of Article 3.1

24.   It was not clear from the Final Report or the Essential Facts and Conclusions Report how the Investigating Authority made its determination of price undercutting – that is what prices were used and at what level of trade prices were compared. The Investigating Authority did not actually look at "prices" or make a proper comparison between prices charged for the same product. Prices for different rebar products when sold in the domestic market normally vary with the size and grade of the product sold.

III.   CORRECTIONS TO REBUTTAL BRIEF

25.   In Rebuttal Brief, footnote 55 on page 23 should make reference to our response to Panel Question # 4, rather than to Panel Question #16. Footnote 107 on page 42 should have been omitted. Footnote 106 should be read as appearing in the spot where footnote 107 is currently located.

IV.   CONCLUSION

26.   This statement must be read in combination with what we have said in our First Written Submission, responses to the Panel's questions, and Rebuttal Submission in order to appreciate our position on each of the issues.

27.   For the reasons stated here, and in those prior submissions, we respectfully request the Panel to render a decision that the Egyptian Anti-Dumping investigation was not in accordance with the provisions of the Anti-Dumping Agreement that we have cited or with Article X:3 of the GATT.

ANNEX 7-1

CONCLUDING STATEMENT OF TURKEY AT THE SECOND
SUBSTANTIVE MEETING OF THE PANEL

1.   This Panel is reviewing an anti-dumping investigation by Egypt that took a very curious turn in the middle of the case, just after the first draft anti-dumping margins were calculated by the Investigating Authority. Up to that point in time, the Investigating Authority's informational demands and treatment of the respondents was very proper and correct. The Investigating Authority was satisfied with the content and coverage of the initial responses and it verified the price and sales responses at each of the respondents without discrepancy. Communications between the Investigating Authority and the respondents were quite cordial.

2.   However, something happened in a short period of time after the tentative anti-dumping margins, ranging from zero to just over 4 per cent, were calculated by the Investigating Authority staff. Suddenly, the Investigating Authority began to adopt a very hostile attitude toward the Turkish respondents, sending threatening letters alleging various errors and omissions in the responses, even those aspects of the responses that had been fully verified without discrepancy, and announcing the Investigating Authority's intention to apply "facts available" if additional information and explanations were not provided within impossible deadlines. We submit that the Investigating Authority came under strong political pressure after the preliminary margins were calculated to come up with a margin that would prevent further imports of rebar from Turkey, and that this explains the subsequent series of events.

3.   It explains why, four three weeks later, the Investigating Authority sent nearly identical letters to each of the five respondents alleging that they had misreported or not reported various price adjustments, when in fact, the Investigating Authority had already verified that those price adjustments were not included in the price or were reported under an expense with a different label. It explains why the Investigating Authority sought to heap a huge new and burdensome cost reporting requirement and self-verification requirement on the respondents and then initially provided only 13 days for a response. It explains why the Investigating Authority denied the respondents a reasonable extension of the original deadline for a response to the 19 August questionnaire. It explains why the Investigating Authority persisted in its conclusion that each and every respondent had failed to include inflation in its costs when the respondents had adequately explained why their costs did not rise with inflation. It explains why the Investigating Authority persisted in using an inaccurate inflation figure after having been shown authoritatively that costs did not rise by 5 per cent per month. It explains why the Investigating Authority applied "facts available" to IDC and Icdas notwithstanding the fact that it found those companies' responses to all question-

naires to be complete. It explains why, after securing what it considered to be an adequate pretext for the application of facts available, the Investigating Authority refused to grant respondents an opportunity for a hearing in Cairo to explain how their cost systems worked and why their costs did not increase by 5 per cent per month as the Investigating Authority had anticipated. And it explains the particular selection of facts available in each case – a selection that was plainly designed to secure the highest possible dumping margin for each company.

4.   Turkey considers that this investigation was not carried out in an objective and unbiased manner and it urges the Panel to so find.

5.   Egypt's injury investigation was also severely flawed. Egypt never gave the respondents adequate notice that the focus of its investigation had shifted from threat of injury to material injury. Nor were any allegations or information concerning current material injury made available to respondents prior to their deadline to submit information and argument on the injury issues. Egypt failed to develop any "positive evidence" linking the dumped imports to the injury that it found to the domestic industry, which consisted solely of a loss of industry profitability and a price decline in the first quarter of 1998. Egypt's conclusion that import prices were undercutting domestic prices was fundamentally flawed. It remains unclear whether the import price used by Egypt in its calculation was a price that was in direct competition with the prices being charged by the domestic industry; that is, whether the price selected for comparison was a price to a purchaser who had to make a choice between the domestic and imported product.

6.   Moreover, it is clear now that Egypt never obtained any actual pricing data from the domestic industry. Rather, it compared the average revenue per unit for the industry as a whole for an entire year to average import prices for that year. This comparison fails to recognize that rebar is a commodity product and that prices change over time with changing raw material costs. Most of the Turkish material entered Egypt in the second half of 1998 when raw material costs were lower than they were during the first half of the year. Moreover, it fails to account for different prices being charged for different products. An accurate determination of price undercutting requires a comparison of prices in competition with each other for a product of the same dimensions and grade.

7.   Egypt failed to investigate adequately and failed to separate and distinguish the effects of the very large capacity expansion that took place over the investigation period and, more particularly, during 1998 and the first quarter of 1999. As we showed yesterday, that capacity expansion certainly had negative effects on industry profitability in 1998 and 1999, yet those effects were never "separated and distinguished" from the effects of dumped imports in assessing industry profitability. Indeed, the increase in finance expenses per unit in 1998 explains the [[XX]] decline in industry profitability. If those finance expenses had remained at 1997 levels, industry profitability in the first quarter of 1999 would have been comparable to industry profitability in 1996, the first year of the investigation. And, it is clear that at Al Ezz, at least, manufacturing costs such as labour and probably depreciation were adversely affected by the expansion.

8.   As we showed yesterday, there was a confluence of two events that had a dramatic effect on the domestic market at the same time. As confirmed by the "Confidential Injury Analysis", [[XX]] tons of new capacity came on stream at the end of 1998. At the same time demand dropped in January 1999 by one-third as compared to the prior month. It is textbook economics that an increase in supply, all other things being equal, will cause a drop in the market price. This particular increase in supply was a very large one – it was a [[XX]] increase in total domestic supply as compared to the prior year. It is also textbook economics that a decline in demand will produce a decline in the marketplace. Yet the effects of neither of these two factors was fully examined or quantified by the Investigating Authority. Instead the entire decline in price and profitability experienced by the domestic industry was attributed to dumped imports, notwithstanding the fact that the market share of imports as a whole declined in the first quarter of 1999 by [[XX]] per cent. The failure to investigate fully the effects of these factors on domestic pricing and profitability violated Article 3.4 of the Agreement. The failure to separate and distinguish the effects of these other factors violated Article 3.5.

9.   In sum, neither Egypt's injury determination, nor its anti-dumping determination, was in compliance with the Anti-Dumping Agreement and we ask the Panel to so find.

10.   I would like to take this opportunity to thank the Panel for all of its time and attention to this matter.

ANNEX 7-2

CLOSING STATEMENT OF EGYPT AT THE
SECOND SUBSTANTIVE MEETING OF THE PANEL

1.   We would like to conclude our presentation with the following comments on Turkey's oral presentation:

I.   THE FINAL DETERMINATION

2.   Turkey is confusing the *Confidential Injury Analysis*, which is a single set of documents, with the "*final determination*" of the Investigating Authority in the rebar investigation. For the record, we wish to stress that the "*final determination*" is not a document and has never been presented as such by Egypt. *The "final determination" is rather the complete overview of all the findings (injury and dumping) of the Investigating Authority*, including the information contained in the record of the rebar investigation (e.g. statistics, questionnaire responses, internal notes, memos and analysis, etc.). The *Confidential Injury Analysis*, on the other hand, comprises part of the set of findings which form part of the "*final determination*" of the Investigating Authority with respect to injury. The *Final Report* is a document that reflects the central points of these findings.

II.   ARTICLE 3.4 AND ARTICLE 3.5

3.   We notice that once again, Turkey is confused as to the respective objectives of Article 3.4 and Article 3.5. Turkey is attempting to extend the mandatory nature of the obligations of the Investigating Authority under Article 3.4 to the factors that may be relevant with respect to the examination of a causal relationship under Article 3.5. The questions before the Panel are simple:

(a)   Did the Investigating Authority examine all the factors under Article 3.4? We submit that the Investigating Authority did.

(b)   Did the Investigating Authority examine all the known factors that might have contributed to the injury? Again, we submit that the Investigating Authority did.

4.   *These two issues are separate*. One given factor cannot be an indicator of injury and the cause thereof. Take the example of a pedestrian who is hit by a car. The injury is the broken leg and the cause of the injury is the car accident.

III.   *PRIMA FACIE* EVIDENCE IN SUPPORT OF A CLAIM UNDER ARTICLE 3.5

5.   An anti-dumping investigation is initiated at the request of a domestic industry, which must submit *prima facie* evidence of the allegations of injurious dumping. Likewise, Egypt considers that the other interested parties, including the exporting producers concerned, should play an active role in the rebuttal of the allegations made in the complaint. It is not sufficient to make unsubstantiated claims without providing any supporting evidence. There must be enough documentation to give an indication that the examination of any given cause of injury is warranted.

IV.   THE NOTICE OF INITIATION

6.   There is only one single *Notice of Initiation*, which is the one submitted to the Panel in Ex-EGT-7.3, together with a non-official English translation.

7.   The *Notice of Initiation* should not be confused with the *Initiation Report* (see Ex-TUR-1), which is a document summarizing the complaint and recommending the initiation of the investigation. Since the *Initiation Report* was not published, a non-confidential version thereof was sent to the interested parties.

8.   The *Notice of Initiation*, on the other hand, was published in the *Official Gazette*. Unfortunately, the non-official English translation submitted to the Panel as Ex-EGT-7.3 was mistakenly stamped "*confidential*" by a clerk of the Investigating Authority when compiling the documentation for the purposes of this DSB proceeding. The official Arabic version, however, which was also submitted to the Panel in Ex-EGT-7.3, is stamped "*public file*".

V.   COSTS DATA FOR THE INVESTIGATION PERIOD

9.   There is no inconsistency in requesting the costs of production data for the entire investigation period while requesting information on domestic sales for months during which export sales were made. Indeed, the Investigating Authority has a legitimate interest in making sure that no cost incurred during the relevant period was allocated to certain months only, thus distorting the true cost picture in any given month.

VI.   MANIPULATION OF THE FACTS

10.   Turkey continues to set great store on capacity expansion as a cause of injury. By interpreting the data contained in the *Confidential Injury Analysis*, Turkey is again trying to extrapolate the facts in an attempt to present a different scenario than that which was before the Investigating Authority during the rebar investigation.

11.　　It is difficult to conceive that an increase in the production capacity, even of the magnitude suggested by Turkey, is likely to be a cause of injury *if this capacity increase was not met by a corresponding reduction in capacity utilization.* On the contrary, the *Confidential Injury Analysis* shows quite clearly that the capacity utilization increased between 1996 and 1998. Furthermore, *the corresponding increase in the production volume did not translate into a disproportionate increase in inventory levels.* Indeed, *the ratio of inventory compared to production remained relatively stable between 1996 and 1999.*

12.　　In order to address Turkey's comments on this issue, Egypt wishes to stress that it is not suggesting that injury was not felt, among other factors, through increased inventory levels, but rather that the capacity expansion did not have an injurious effect on those inventory levels.

13.　　Likewise, the increase in finance costs should be examined not in absolute terms, but with reference to the evolution of production quantities. In this respect, it is necessary to evaluate the profitability on the basis of unit values, which is why a table on unit values was included in the *Confidential Injury Analysis.* Indeed, it makes no sense to compare absolute profit values between one year and another without taking into consideration variations in total turnover. Moreover, the finance costs did not affect the profit before interest expenses. As a matter of fact, the weighted average unit profit before interest expenses declined by over 30 per cent in 1999 (86) compared to 1998 (127). This simple comparison shows that the decline in the weighted average price had a direct impact on profitability.

14.　　Last but not least, Turkey appears to focus on the figures of Al Ezz in particular. Egypt wishes to stress that Al Ezz alone does not constitute the entire domestic industry.

VII.　THE INVESTIGATING AUTHORITY DID NOT DISREGARD THE COSTS OF PRODUCTION OF THE RESPONDENTS

15.　　Once again, Turkey alleges that the Investigating Authority "disregarded" the costs data submitted by the respondents. As explained on many occasions, this allegation is incorrect. All the costs data were taken on board by the Investigating Authority, where possible and were only adjusted in order to reflect the monthly hyperinflation rate of 5 per cent that the respondents failed to take into account in the computation of their costs data.

VIII.　OBJECTION BY EGYPT TO THE ALLEGATIONS THAT THE INVESTIGATING AUTHORITY ACTED UNDER POLITICAL PRESSURE

16.　　Turkey states that from the beginning, everything was going smoothly in the rebar investigation and that after the verification, the Investigating Authority suddenly became "*hostile*" to the Turkish respondents, allegedly as a result of political pressure.

17.   For the record, *Egypt would like to state its very strong objection to the allegation that the Investigating Authority acted under political pressure*. To the contrary, as previously demonstrated, what occurred during the course of the investigation was that it became clear to the Investigating Authority that the costs data submitted by the Turkish respondents seemingly did not reflect the hyperinflation experienced by Turkey during the period under consideration. Quite naturally, as any other anti-dumping administration would have done in a similar situation, the Investigating Authority simply requested that the respondents supply additional information and an explanation as to how hyperinflation was taken into account in their costs data.

18.   Thus, contrary to Turkey's insinuations, there was no element of political pressure that influenced the Investigating Authority's determinations in the Turkish rebar investigation.

ANNEX 8-1

RESPONSES OF TURKEY TO QUESTIONS POSED IN THE CONTEXT OF THE SECOND SUBSTANTIVE MEETING OF THE PANEL

QUESTIONS POSED BY THE PANEL TO TURKEY

Q1. Turkey asserts that the respondents submitted all the requested information and documents, including the requested reconciliations of data to the financial statements. Could Turkey indicate for each of the respondent companies (Habas, Diler, Colakoglu, IDC and Icdas) where in the record these reconciliations could be found and for each one explain exactly, in a step-by-step fashion, how the reconciliations were done?

Reply

1. Turkey does not believe that it ever claimed that respondents submitted all of the information and documents requested by the Investigating Authority after the original questionnaire responses were filed. In fact, what Turkey has claimed is that it was impossible, or unreasonable to expect respondents, to provide all of the information requested within the deadlines imposed and that, in light of those deadlines, the respondents "acted to the best of their ability". Restatement of Claims at Sections II.B and E.

2. Moreover, Turkey has not claimed that all of the reconciliations requested in the 19 August 1999 letter were provided by each respondent. It has claimed, with respect to Icdas and IDC, that the Investigating Authority itself found little fault with the responses filed by the respondents, requesting only a few follow-up documents and clarifications, which were promptly provided. The failure to notify Icdas and IDC of continuing deficiencies after receipt of their responses violated Annex II, paragraph 6 of the Anti-Dumping Agreement. Restatement of Claims, Section II.B.3.

3. That said, the respondents individually provided many, and in some cases all, of the reconciliations requested in the 19 August letter. Each respondent traced its materials, labour and overhead costs to internal invoices, books and ledgers, proving the accuracy of those costs. One of the respondents, IDC, provided a comprehensive trace of its extended reported costs through to its annual financial statement. Another, Colakoglu, provided a comprehensive trace for its reported costs in two months for which it had sales to Egypt, April and August, to its cost of goods sold and quarterly financial statements. A third respondent, Habas, provided records establishing that its extended costs reconcile to its annual cost of goods sold with only a minor difference. Diler and Icdas also reconciled their reported costs to internal books and records.

4.   We review each respondents' response to the 19 August 1999 questionnaire in turn below.

1.   Colakoglu

5.   The 19 August 1999 questionnaire (Question 4B) requested Colakoglu to reconcile its raw material inventory ledgers to its general ledger and financial statement. In Exhibit 9 to Colakoglu's 15 September 1999 response (Exhibit TUR-34B), the company provided the raw material inventory ledger as at 31/12/98 and reconciled that ledger to its financial statement. The first page of the Exhibit is a reconciling item. The second page of the Exhibit is Colakoglu's balance sheet at 31/12/98. The remainder of the Exhibit is Colakoglu's internal inventory movement record for each month of the POR and each type of inventory (first billet, then rebar, then scrap). The balance sheet shows that raw material inventory totaled [XX] thousand TL at 31/12/98. The last page of the Exhibit shows a raw material inventory total of [XX] thousand TL. The difference between these two figures is shown on the first page of the exhibit and is attributable to material purchased, but not yet imported.

6.   Questions 4D, 5C and 6C of the 19 August 1999 questionnaire requested worksheets reconciling materials, labour and overhead costs that were submitted to the Investigating Authority for certain months to the company's audited financial statement. Colakoglu provided in its response, at Exhibit 4, a summary of its costs of production by month for the twelve months of 1998. As indicated in previous submissions to the Panel, Colakoglu, Habas and Diler submitted their billet costs as the raw material cost, since billet is the material that enters the rebar rolling mill. This information was submitted both in their original cost responses and in the 15 September 1999 response. (The Investigating Authority subsequently requested on 23 September 1999 that these respondents break down their billet costs into component raw material, labour and overhead costs, but provided only 2-5 days for the companies to do so. See Exhibit TUR-12.) Therefore, Colakoglu understood Question 4D as requiring it to reconcile the cost of billet to its internal books and records. This reconciliation, as well as the reconciliation of labour and overhead expenses, is provided in Exhibit 10 to Colakoglu's 15 September 1999 response. See Exhibit TUR-34B.

7.   For example, for August 1998, Colakoglu reported a material cost of [XX] TL/ton, a labour cost of [XX] TL/MT, and a factory overhead expense of [XX] TL /ton. See Exhibit 4. The first page of Exhibit 10 is an internal document (Rolling Mill Production Cost List (TL)) prepared in the ordinary course of business that computes the monthly cost of production for rebar and provides a cost breakdown for the month of August (*Agustos*) 1999.

8.   The total cost of direct material per ton of rebar in the month is shown as [XX] TL per ton. See line item 1510301 Total (*Toplami*), far right column (TL/ton). This is the same amount that Colakoglu reported in its response. It reflects the sum of scrap (1510301001), scrap loss (*hurda firesi*), electricity (1510301011), gas (1510301021), and other costs (1510301031 – 81). Labour

cost, [XX] TL per ton, is shown on line 1510302001. This is also the same amount that Colakoglu reported in its response. Overhead is shown just below line 1510303. It also matches the amount reported in the response, after an adjustment to exclude packing costs (ambalaj), which are separately reported on the cost listings. The overhead includes depreciation (*amortisman*).

9.   The total monthly cost of rebar production from this page, [XX] TL, is shown in the August trial balance on the next page opposite an item referencing total cost of rebar (*neverulu ve cubuk*). The difference between this amount and the total cost shown on the August trial balance four lines down is the value of scrap by-product produced (*haddehane* (2) *hurda*). Entries in the general ledger (*kebir defteri*) in August total the same amount. See Page 4 of Exhibit 10 (part of TUR-34B). The Subsidiary Ledger (on page 7) shows the derivation of August cost of goods sold as the beginning balance for finished goods inventory on 1 August 1998 (item 33), plus cost of goods manufactured in August (item 35 = total costs shown on page one; i.e., the costs that Colakoglu reconciled previously to its submission cost), less cost of finished goods remaining in inventory on 31 August 1998. The cost of goods sold for the month is [XX] TL. (Item 41). This matches the figure on page 9, cost of goods sold detail for August in the Subsidiary Ledger.

10.   On page 11, marked Subsidiary Ledger - COGS Rebar, the cost of rebar goods sold in August is added to the cost of rebar goods sold for January–July and September to arrive at a cost for the first nine months of the year ([XX]). On page 13, marked September Trial Balance, this figure is shown being added to the cost of goods sold for other products to arrive at a nine-month cumulative cost of manufactured goods sold of [XX] TL. On page 14, this figure is shown on Colakoglu's cumulative income statement for the first nine months of the year as the cost of manufactured goods sold.

11.   Thus, Colakoglu comprehensively tied its reported raw material cost, reported labour cost and reported overhead cost in August to its financial statement.

12.   A demonstration for April 1998 is also provided. Although the first page of the April demonstration (Rolling Mill Production Cost List (TL) for April) is difficult to read because of the darkness of the copy, one can make out the total billet cost at line 1510301 Total as [XX] TL/ton, the amount reported for total raw material cost by Colakoglu on Exhibit 4. One can also make out a labour cost of [XX] TL/ton (line 1510302001) and an overhead cost, less packing, of [XX] TL/ton, the amounts reported. The total cost of manufacture of rebar on the page before deduction of scrap is [XX] TL. After the scrap deduction, the cost of manufacture is [XX] TL.

13.   Colakoglu reconciles these figures to its trial balance, general ledger and monthly cost of goods sold on the following pages. Specifically, on the page marked Subsidiary Ledger, Colakoglu calculates its cost of goods sold in the month by adding beginning inventory to cost of manufacture in the month ([XX]) and deducting ending inventory to arrive at a total of [XX] TL. This figure is then shown being added on a Subsidiary Ledger to the cost of goods sold

of rebar in other months for the first half of 1998 to a cumulative total of [XX] for the first six months. The cumulative total for rebar is then added on the next page to the cumulative totals for other products to arrive at a cumulative total cost of goods sold for all finished products of [XX]. This figure is shown on the next page, on Colakoglu's cumulative income statement for the first half of 1998, as cost of manufactured goods sold.

14.   Thus, Colakoglu comprehensively tied its reported raw material costs, overhead expenses and labour costs in April to the cost of goods sold on its half-yearly financial statement as well.

15.   Colakoglu was separately asked to reconcile its reported depreciation expenses. We note that it did so in reconciling its total reported costs, including overhead (which, in turn, included a separate element for depreciation expenses), to the cost of goods sold reported in its financial statement.

2.   Habas

16.   Habas was also asked to provide a reconciliation of its raw material costs, labour costs and overhead costs to its internal books and financial statements.

17.   In Exhibit 4 to its September 15, 1999 response (Exhibit TUR-34C), Habas provided monthly costs of production for 1998. Like Colakoglu, Habas reported its cost of billet as the raw material entering the rebar rolling mill. For December 1998, Habas reported a raw material cost of [XX] TL/ton, a direct labour cost of [XX] TL/ton and a factory overhead expense of [XX] TL/ton. See Exhibit 4 (attached to Exhibit TUR-34C).

18.   On Exhibit 4, Habas grossed up its total material costs by multiplying the quantity produced by the reported raw material cost per unit in each month and then summing the costs for all of the months. Thus, the total cost of direct material in December is [XX] (TL/ton) * [XX] (total tons produced) = [XX] TL (total material cost of manufacture in the month). The total material cost of manufacture for all months of 1998 is [XX] TL. *See* Exhibit 4. Page 11 of Exhibit 10 (marked page one on the page itself), reconciles this amount to the cumulative cost of billet incurred for the year. The item at the top of the page reports the total cost of billet (*kutuk*) for the year at [XX] TL. (Note that this cost relates to [XX] kg of billet. See same line under the heading *Aciklama*.) The difference between the TL amount shown on this line and the reported amount is shown on the bottom of the page and is accounted for by scrap that was recycled into the production process. The scrap cost is listed on the same report with the letter "b" beside it. It is normal to claim a byproduct credit for scrap produced that can be reused in production as long as the cost of that scrap is included in the new production cost. Page 10 of Exhibit 10 (marked page 2) also shows the yearly cost of billet (*hammade*).

19.   Page 8 of the Exhibit (marked page 4) is a trial balance showing the booking of labour costs in December 1998, and the derivation of the per unit charge (dividing by total monthly production). Page 9 of the Exhibit (marked page 3) is a monthly trial balance showing the booking and derivation of the labour cost per

unit reported in November 1998. There is a slight adjustment in the books, reflecting a year-end adjustment.

20. Page 4 of the Exhibit (marked page 8) shows total yearly overhead expenses in the rolling mill. These, with an adjustment for tolling charges, equal the extended total amount of overhead reported in Habas response for the twelve month period. *Compare* Exhibit 4. We note in this regard that factory overhead includes depreciation (*yili ayirlan amortisman*).

21. Habas also provided data that shows that its reported costs reconcile to its monthly and annual cost of goods sold:

Reported Raw material costs	27,584,102,609[1]
Scrap Offset	214,338,288[2]
Direct Labour	328,764,580[3]
Overhead Expenses	1,241,196,036[4]
Adjusting Entries for Overhead	*456,383,862*[5]
Total Cost of Manufacture	29,368,401,513
Total Cost of Manufacture Per Subsidiary Ledger:	*29,608,110,717*[6]
Difference	239,709,204
%	0.8%

22. Habas reconciled its cost of manufacture for rebar for the year, [XX], to its cost of goods sold for rebar for the year, [XX] on Exhibit 10, page 2. This figure was then reconciled to its overall cost of manufactured goods sold ([XX]) on page one of the Exhibit. Compare Exhibit 2, third page from the end, item D.1 (cost of goods manufactured [XX]) (difference of less than half of one per cent apparently due to auditor adjustments).[7]

23. Thus, Habas reconciled its total submission costs to its financial statements with a minor difference.

24. Habas was separately asked to reconcile its reported depreciation expenses to its financial expenses. It already did so, however, by reconciling its reported overhead expenses (which included depreciation expenses) and its total reported expenses to its annual cost of goods sold.

---

[1]   See Exhibit 10, page 11. Compare Exhibit 4.
[2]   *See* Exhibit 10, page 11.
[3]   See Exhibit 4; Exhibit 10, page 8.
[4]   See Exhibit 4; Exhibit 10, page 4.
[5]   See Exhibit 10, pages 3-4.
[6]   See Exhibit 10, page 2, second item.
[7]   The difference between the amount shown on this income statement in Turkish and the audited statement appears to be due in large part to reclassifications between SG&A expenses and cost of goods sold, because the net profit is approximately the same.

3. Diler

25. Diler was also requested to provide reconciliations of its monthly reported raw material, labour and overhead expenses to its internal books and records and financial statements.

26. Diler provided its monthly costs of production in Exhibit 4 to its 15 September 1999 response. *See* Exhibit TUR-34A. For December 1998, Diler reported a raw material cost of [XX] TL/ton, a labour cost of [XX] TL per ton and an overhead expense of [XX] TL/ton. See Exhibit 4. Diler has two affiliated companies that each produce rebar in Turkey, Yazici Demir Celik and Diler Demir Celik (described as Yazici or YDC and Diler or DDC). In Exhibit 10, page one, is a worksheet on which Diler showed how it weight-averaged the direct material, labour and scrap costs between these two companies. Subsequent pages and other Exhibits show how these costs reconcile to the companies' books and records.

27. Page 2 of the Exhibit is an internal cost calculation by Yazici in December (*Aralik*), prepared in the ordinary course of business. The costs on the left-hand side of the chart are total costs for all sections of the mill. *Malzeme* is materials, *Genel Uretim* is factory overhead, *Iscilik* is labour – as indicated on the Exhibit in English. The costs under *Celikhane* are costs in the electric arc furnace for steelmaking. The costs under *Haddehane* are for the rolling mill.

28. The total materials cost for all sections in the mill is [XX] TL for the month of December. This total cost is reconciled to the company's internal books on page 4 of the Exhibit (*Sark Cekislari* means withdrawal from inventory for consumption).

29. The total labour cost in the month is [XX] TL. *See* Exhibit 10, page 2. This cost is shown entering the company's trial balance subsidiary journal on page 12 of the Exhibit. The overhead cost is shown entering the trial balance subsidiary ledger on page 13 of the Exhibit. We note that this expense includes depreciation (*amortisman giderleri*).

30. *Haddehane* is the rolling mill. The total cost of billet (*kutuk*) consumed in production in the rolling mill December is shown as [XX] TL on page 2 of the Exhibit, the internal monthly cost calculation. This is the figure that appears under Material Cost opposite YDC (Yazici) on page one of the Exhibit where the weight-averaging occurs. Total production in the rolling mill (*Uretim* Kg) is shown as [XX] Kgs. Compare page one of the Exhibit. As shown on page one of the Exhibit, the raw material cost is equal to the billet entering production less recycled scrap. The total cost of recycled scrap is the sum of edges (*ucbas*) ([XX]) plus defective bar (*hadde bozu*)([XX]), or [XX]. Compare pages one and two of the Exhibit.

31. Total labour cost in the rolling mill (*Iscili*) is [XX]. Total factory overhead (*malezeme* plus *genel yo*) is [XX] TL ([XX] in *malzeme* plus [XX] in *genel yo*). Compare page one of the Exhibit. We note in this regard that factory overhead includes depreciation.

32. Thus, Diler reconciled its total raw material costs, labour costs and factory overhead expenses to its trial balance for the month and showed the allocation of expenses between the different sections of the mill based on a record generated monthly in the ordinary course of business.

33. A similar demonstration is then provided for Diler.

4. Icdas

34. Icdas was also asked to provide a reconciliation of its submitted materials, labour and overhead expenses to its internal books and records and financial statements.

35. Icdas presented its monthly costs in Attachments 2 and 11 (part 2) to its 15 September response. *See* Exhibit TUR-39. Attachment 2 reports the costs in dollars per ton on a monthly basis; Attachment 11, part two shows total costs in TL, the exchange rate for each month and the production quantity in the month. Icdas divided the total TL cost by the production quantity to arrive at a TL cost per ton and by the exchange rate to derive a cost per ton in US dollars. Thus, in January 1998, the total scrap cost was [XX] TL and total billet production was [XX] metric tons. The cost per ton was [XX] TL/ton. The exchange rate for the month is 212,830 TL/$. Hence, the dollar cost of scrap is [XX] $/ton. Compare Attachment 11, part two, page one with Attachment 11, part two, page two and Attachment 2, page 3.

36. Note that there are also two affiliated mills producing rebar at Icdas – Icdas Celik Enerji Tersane ve Ulasim San. and Demir Sanayi Demir ve Celik Ticaret ve Sanayi A.S., hence the separate cost charts for each. We shall refer to the first as Icdas and the second as Demir Sanayi.

37. Raw materials costs (all items marked with a single * on Attachment 11, part two, page one) are reconciled to the company's books and records in Attachment 11, part one. Page one of this attachment shows the average cost of scrap in TL/Kg for each month. The figure shown for January, [XX] per kg, is the same figure derived above ([XX] per ton/1,000 kgs per ton). The pages following the first page of this attachment are used to reconcile the production quantities shown on the first page to company internal production control records. The circled figures are the monthly production amounts in kilograms.

38. The next page is a worksheet showing the monthly consumption of electrodes and the monthly consumption of ferroalloys, together with the average inventory value, for each month of 1998. The TL per ton amount reconciles to page one. The next set of pages are records kept in the ordinary course of business by the Inventory Control Department showing withdrawals of these items from inventory, quantity and value for each month of the period of investigation. The figures on these chart reconcile to the monthly summary described earlier and to the submission costs. A report on other materials and refractories follows.

39. Following that are documents referencing purchases of scrap. The page marked 1998/05/01 – 1998/05/31 Hurda Fiyat Ortalamasi is a document pro-

duced in the ordinary course of business showing the total quantity and value of different types of scrap purchased in May 1998, and the unit value of the purchases. Similar information is provided for other months of 1998. Note that the cost of scrap used by Icdas for May, [XX] TL per kilogram, exceeds the average cost of scrap purchased in the month, because the reported cost was based on the average inventory cost of scrap taken out of inventory to put into production in the month. The cost of scrap purchased in the month of May, in constant currency terms, was lower than the average value of scrap in inventory. This proves, as we have claimed throughout this proceeding, that use of a replacement cost would have produced a lower reported cost than use of the company's actual costing system.

40.   Attachment 6 provides purchase documentation relating to Icdas' purchases of scrap during the period of investigation, including a material purchase contract in May for delivery in September–October showing scrap prices of $[XX] per ton, several invoices showing the same price, a purchase contract in November for delivery in November showing a price of $[XX] per ton, an invoice in the same amount, a contract in October for delivery in November 1998 showing a price of $[XX] per ton, a numerous other similar documents for scrap purchased in August through November.

41.   Icdas reconciled its reported labour cost to its books and records in Attachment 8. The figures on pages two and three of that attachment reconcile to the total labour cost shown in the rolling mill for the months of February and March 1998. *Compare* Attachment 8, pages two and three with Attachment 11, part two, page two. These are the figures for Section 1 (rolling mill). There are also monthly pages for Section 2 (transport) and Section 3 (steelmaking). The figure for January for Section 1 ([XX]) and the figure for January for Section 3 ([XX]) seem to have been inadvertently switched. The sum of the figures for sections two and three in February reconcile to the total labour cost shown for the electric arc furnace on Attachment 11, part two, page two ([XX]) and the figures for January match two if those for Section 1 and Section 3 are switched.

42.   Attachment 11, part two, page six, shows the monthly trial balance in January 1998 regarding financing expense (*kredi faizleri*). The amount shown, [XX] TL, reconciles to the item marked "A" on page one of that attachment. Copies of the trial balance for each month of 1998 are provided showing the booking of this expense. Financing revenue (marked "B") on page one of the attachment is shown on the succeeding pages (you must add item 642 and item 646). On the monthly trial balance page labelled "Other", the amounts incurred in January for electricity, natural gas in the electric arc furnace, oxygen, natural gas in the rolling mill, other overheads in the meltshop (Item marked A plus item marked B, plus item marked C, less items 5,6,7 = [XX]) and other overheads in the rolling mill (Item D less item 8 = [XX]) are shown as booked into the trial balance.

43.   In Attachment 4, Icdas provided its inventory ledgers as at 31/12/98. Attachment 5 reconciles those inventory ledgers to the trial balance. Attachment 10

provides a complete listing of all sales in the domestic and export markets and reconciles those figures to Icdas' income statement.

5. IDC

44.   IDC was also asked to reconcile its raw material costs, labour and overhead expenses to its internal books and records.

45.   In Worksheet 2, attached to IDC's 9 September 1999 response, the company reconciled the costs it reported on a monthly basis to the annual cost of goods sold shown on its income statement.[8] The income statement provided as an attachment to IDC's original response (and one in Attachment 1 – see detailed income statement in English) shows a total cost of goods sold for 1998 of [XX] TL. That is the figure that appears at the bottom right-hand corner of Worksheet 2.

46.   Worksheet two shows both the gross materials, labour and factory overhead costs of goods sold in each month and the unit costs, after division by the number of units sold. The total materials cost shown for January on Worksheet 2, [XX], divided by the total production of rebar, [XX], yields the reported materials cost of [XX] TL/ton. This is the amount that Icdas reported as its materials cost in its original response. Labour cost and manufacturing overheads per ton were similarly calculated. The sum of the raw materials, labour, and factory overhead shown in each month for the calendar year is [XX]. *See* Worksheet 2, far hand side bottom. This is the cost of goods sold for rebar during the year.

47.   To this figure, some adjustments must be made to arrive at the cost of goods sold in the financial statement. First, the cost of products manufactured by IDC other than rebar is added. Also added is depreciation on the meltshop and the rolling mill, service costs, and the cost of commercial goods purchased and resold. *See* Worksheet 2, far right. Worksheet 5 shows how depreciation expenses should be allocated to the product. Service costs, the costs of products other than rebar and the cost of commercial goods purchased and sold are not costs of production of the subject merchandise and so were appropriately excluded from the submitted costs. The cost of other products includes the cost of round bar that is not deformed.

48.   Page 2 of Worksheet 2 shows the detailed trial balance at 31/12/98. The detailed trial balance confirms the amount of the reconciling items. Thus, it shows the total cost of service sales at item 62200, the total cost of other sales (spares) at item 62300, and the total cost of bar sales at line 62001 that were reported on Worksheet 2. The total cost of bar sales, [XX] TL (item 620), plus an adjusting item (item 621), is equal to the cost of rebar, the cost of other products and the cost of depreciation shown on Table 2. Thus, IDC showed that it incorporated all of the cost of goods sold in its income statement, with the exception

---

[8]   This document will, we understand, be submitted as an Exhibit by Egypt in response to a Panel Question. Counsel for Turkey first obtained this document from the company on Monday, 11 March 2002.

of the adjusting items, in the costs of production that it reported to the Investigating Authority. And, as noted, other than depreciation, which was quantified and separately reported in IDC's 15 September 1999 response, none of the adjusting items should have been included in IDC's cost.

49.   Worksheet 3 reconciles the reported labour cost to the books. It shows total labour cost consumed in the meltshop in January of [XX] TL and total labour consumed in the rolling mill of [XX] TL. The rebar labour cost per ton is [XX], calculated by dividing total labour cost by total production. This is the labour cost included in the cost of manufacture in the month. Since IDC reported the average labour cost in cost of goods sold, some adjustments were required.

50.   The labour cost per ton of material in inventory was [XX] TL/ton. The labour cost per ton for product produced and sold in January, as calculated above ([XX] TL/ton), was averaged with labour cost per ton for product sold from inventory in the same month to arrive at a weighted average labour cost of goods sold of [XX] TL/ton. This amount, multiplied by the quantity sold in the month, yields the total labour cost in cost of goods sold for the month, [XX] TL. Compare Worksheet 2, page one. Similar worksheets are provided for December, August, September and October. The following pages are extracts from the detailed trial balance showing the booking of each of the detailed entries on the worksheets. For example, the first figure on the labour cost worksheet for January under item number 72101100, [XX] TL, is the first item on the detailed Trial Balance extract for January. Thus, for labour cost, IDC has traced from its detailed trial balance, through a worksheet, to the figures reported in the response, and from there to the cost of goods sold reported on the income statement.

51.   Worksheet 4 is a similar exercise for manufacturing overhead expenses. It operates in just the same way.

52.   Worksheet 5 shows calculation of the unit cost of depreciation. Since this is based on the year-end total depreciation amount, divided by total production, it is a fixed amount that should be added to the production cost in each month. The following pages reconcile the amounts on the worksheet to the subledger (*muavin defter*).

53.   Worksheet 1 reconciles IDC's inventory movement records to the company's internal inventory records. There are separate charts for scrap, billet and rebar. The figures on the scrap inventory movement are tied to the stock records. Thus, the beginning balance for scrap on January 1, 1998, [XX] TL, is tied to the first figure on the page entitled *ILK MADDE VE MALZEME STOKLARI* (stock record). A similar reconciliation is provided for billet and rebar.

54.   Attachment 4, part one, provides substantial documentation with respect to IDC's purchase invoices and payment ledgers for ferroalloys and scrap. For example, in the October scrap section, IDC has provided a payment ledger listing individual payments for scrap in October 1998. IDC has coded the ledger with numbers that relate the detail to the scrap invoices paid by the company in that month. The first set of invoices are from domestic suppliers, and show the quantity (*miktari*), unit price (*fiyati*) and total invoice amount (*tutar*). The second set

of invoices are related to imports and are all in English, showing prices denominated in dollars, ranging from $[XX] per ton to $[XX] per ton. Full documentation is provided for four months. Invoices and payment ledgers for other materials and factory overhead items are provided in Attachment 4, part two.

55.   IDC provided a complete sales ledger in Attachment 6 and reconciled that sales ledger into its internal ledgers and financial statement in Attachment 7.

Q2.   Could Turkey comment on the legal basis of a claim of a violation of Article 17.6(i) by a Member, in light of the fact that Article 17.6(i) seemingly sets the standard of review which the Panel needs to follow when reviewing the measures in question in a dispute. That is, can a party to a dispute bring a legal claim of violation by an investigating authority of the provision? If so, what would be the legal basis for such a claim?

Reply

56.   This issue is addressed at pages 12-13 of Turkey's Oral Statement at the Second Substantive Session, 25 February 2002. We further elaborate on that response below.

57.   As confirmed by the Appellate Body in *Hot-Rolled Carbon Steel Products from Japan*, Article 17.6(i) imposes an obligation upon investigating authorities with respect to their establishment and evaluation of the facts in an anti-dumping duty proceeding – their establishment of the facts in the context of an anti-dumping duty proceeding must be "proper" and their "evaluation" of the facts must be "unbiased and objective".[9] In this case, Turkey claims that the investigating authorities "establishment of the facts" was improper and their "evaluation of the facts" was neither unbiased nor objective. It is not clear, under the Agreement, that Turkey must allege violation of a separate substantive obligation under the Agreement in order to make this claim. Turkey believes there is a violation of the Agreement if, in reaching its final determination on any issue, the investigating authorities' establishment of the facts is improper or its evaluation of the facts fails to meet the test of objectivity and lack of bias.

58.   However, to the extent that the panel considers that it may only review a violation of Article 17.6(i) in the context of a separate substantive claim, we note that in Section II.D of the restatement of our claims, where reference to Article 17.6(i) is made, Turkey's claim is that Egypt's decision to apply "facts available" was a violation of both Article 6.8 and Article 17.6(i) of the Agreement because that decision was based on an improper determination of the facts and upon an evaluation of the facts that was neither unbiased nor objective. Thus, to the extent that the Panel considers that Article 17.6(i) merely sets forth a standard of review for Panel consideration of other substantive violations, then we invite the Panel to consider this claim in connection with our claimed violation of Article 6.8.

---

[9]   *United States – Anti-Dumping Measures on Certain Hot-Rolled Steel Products from Japan*, WT/DS 184/AB/R, DSR 2001:X, 4697, 24 July 2001, paras. 55-56.

Q3.   Turkey asserts that all Icdas' scrap cost data were "verified" (7 December 2001 response to questions posed by the Panel, Appendix at Section G, page 34). Could Turkey explain what is meant by the term "verified" as used in this context.

Reply

59.   Icdas verified its scrap costs in the sense that it provided invoices and other internal documentation establishing that the scrap costs it reported were based on actual purchases of scrap in the month in question. This documentation was provided in Icdas' response to the 19 August 1999 letter-questionnaire. (See Response to Question # 1, above.)

Q4.   On page 58 of Turkey's First Written Submission it is asserted that Icdas requested "a hearing as soon as it had an opportunity to review the Essential Facts and Conclusions Report", Exhibit TUR-26 is cited as reference. However, it seems as if the referenced exhibit does not mention such a request. Could Turkey please clarify.

Reply

60.   It seems that Icdas did not, in fact, make such a request in its comments on the Essential Facts and Conclusions report. We apologize to the Panel for our error.

Q5.   In its 7 December 2001 response to the Panel's question 2.3, Turkey did not indicate whether it has dropped its allegations of violation of Articles 2.2.1.1, 2.2.2, and 6.8 in connection with its claim in paragraph 11 of the Request for Establishment of the Panel. Could Turkey please clarify whether these allegations are maintained.

Reply

61.   Turkey has not dropped its allegations of violation of Articles 2.2.1.1, 2.2.2 or 6.8 in connection with its claims in Paragraph 11 of the Request for Establishment of the Panel. These claims are set forth in our restatement of claims at Section II.F.2, II.F.3 and II.D. *See* Response of Turkey to the Questions Posed by the Panel, 7 December 2001 at Appendix – Restatement of Claims in Response to Question 1.

62.   As we indicated previously, we would not object to a finding by the Panel that our claims in Section II.F.2 are rendered moot if the Panel considers that Egypt was unjustified in resorting to "facts available" and if the Panel then concluded that a re-determination was necessary. *See United States –Definitive Safeguards Measures on Imports of Circular Welded Carbon Quality Line Pipe from Korea*, WT/DS 202/AB/R (February 4, 2001), para. 199.

63.   Our claims in Section II.F.2 were intended to address and argue against any counter-argument by Egypt that its determination of normal value was correct, even if it was not justified in applying "facts available". To the extent that

Egypt's position can be understood to make this counter-argument, we stand by our claim in Section II.F.2.

Q6. **Turkey argues that the Investigating Authority "declined" to adjust constructed normal value for credit costs. Turkey indicates that such an adjustment was requested by "respondents" during the course of the investigation. Could Turkey please indicate where in the record those requests and the relevant data can be found? How does Turkey interpret the reference in Article 2.4 to due allowance being made "on its merits" for differences which affect price comparability, both in the context of Article 2.4 itself, and in the context of the review by a panel pursuant to Article 17.6(i)?**

Reply

64.   This claim was made in the initial responses and on the original sales listings. *See* Exhibit TUR - 42.[10]

65.   We note further that the verification report for Icdas states:

"Cost of Credit

The accounts for sales in Turkey can be received later than the date of the invoice. [XX.] The period between the date of settlement of the account and the actual date of payment was established from the accounts outstanding ledger. The average days per ton was calculated and an adjustment was made. The interest used was established from the company records of short-term loans".

66.   *See* Exhibit TUR-4 at 6. The "Cost of Credit" for each sale is shown on the second page of the dumping calculation attached to the verification report. *See* Exhibit TUR-4, ICDAS DUMPING CALCULATION (field Y).

67.   A similar statement and calculation appears in the report for IDC (Exhibit TUR-5 at 4.3 "Adjustments to Normal Value" and dumping calculation, page 1, "Cost of Credit"), Diler (Exhibit TUR-6 at 7 "Cost of Credit" and dumping calculation, page 2, "Cost of Credit"), Colakoglu (Exhibit TUR-7 at 6 and dumping calculation, page 2, "Cost of Credit"), and Habas (Exhibit TUR-8 at 7 "Cost of Credit" and dumping calculation page 4 "Cost of Credit"). Thus, in each case, the imputed credit cost calculations were verified as accurate by the Investigating Authority, including both the number of days from shipment to payment and the interest rate used to calculate the adjustment.

68.   Turkey believes "on the merits" means, in this context, whether or not the facts supporting the claim are verified and whether an adjustment is necessary in order to achieve price comparability. The verification reports show that each of the underlying facts claimed by the respondents were verified, including the number of days the invoice was outstanding prior to payment and the applicable interest rate. Clearly, where there is a different payment term in the export and the domestic market, or where the interest rates applicable to sales in local cur-

---

[10]   *See also* Exhibit TUR-25 at 14-16 (Letter from Law Offices of David Simon, 13 August 1999, objecting to tentative decision not to adjust normal value for imputed credit costs).

rency and in foreign currency are different, as here, an adjustment must be made for different payment periods in order to ensure price comparability. Therefore, respondents are entitled to this adjustment both as a matter of the express obligation in the Anti-Dumping Agreement and on the facts of the case.

Q7.   In the Appendix to its 7 December 2001 responses to the Panel's questions, Turkey does not refer to a claim under Article 6.1 in the context of its dumping-related claims. Could Turkey please clarify whether this allegation is maintained. If so could Turkey please identify in its submissions and statements to the Panel its arguments in support of this allegation.

Reply

69.   Turkey cited Article 6.1 in Section II.B of its First Written Submission in support of its claims of violation of other provisions of the Agreement in connection with the request, late in the proceeding, for substantial new cost information. However, Turkey did not claim there, or in its Restatement of Claims, that this Article was specifically violated in that regard and it does not maintain such a claim.

70.   We note, as did the European Union, that Turkey could have cited this provision in support of its claims in Section II. B.

Q8.   In the annexes to Exhs. TUR-34A-C, Turkey includes a series of tables preceded by a cover sheet entitled "[company] databases". Could Turkey please explain whether these tables were part of the 15 September submissions by Habas, Diler and Colakoglu. Could Turkey also please explain what these tables are, whether they form part of the record of the investigation, and what they are intended to show.

Reply

71.   These documents are the databases originally submitted in the response to the original foreign manufacturers' questionnaire (Total Sales of Steel Reinforcing Bars – Appendix 1; Sales in the Domestic Market – Appendix 2; Sales Price Structure – Appendix 3, and so forth), as revised on 11 June 1999 (see First Written Submission at II.A.9) and at verification. *Compare* Manufacturers Questionnaire, Exhibit TUR-3 at Appendices 1-9. [11]The revised databases were pro-

---

[11]   More specifically, in the case of Colakoglu, the first table (Appendix A) reports the value and volume of sales during the period of investigation. The second table (Appendix 2) is a listing of home market sales transactions made at the same time as, and of the same product and type as, the products sold in Egypt during the period of investigation, together with transaction specific prices and price adjustment information. The "Interest" column is the imputed credit cost adjustment. The third table (App. 3) is a listing of the domestic prices and price changes during the period of investigation for products also sold in Egypt. The fourth table (Appendix 3B) is the sales price structure in the domestic market. The fifth table (Appendix 4) is a listing of sales to Egypt during the period of investigation, together with price adjustment information. The sixth table (App. 5) is the sales price structure for export sales to Egypt. The seventh table (App. 9A) is respondent's costs of production for the domestic sales. The eighth table (App. 9A) is respondent's cost of production for sales in Egypt and the last table is the income statement.

vided to the Egyptian verification team during the verification together with the explanatory boxes that appear on the charts to explain how the data fits together.

72.   The file of documents submitted by the Turkish respondents to the IA, as forwarded to us by the Law Offices of David Simon, indicates that these documents were also attached to the companies' 15 September 1999 response. However, Mr. Simon has indicated to us that he has no specific recollection concerning this matter and so we were not able to independently confirm this fact. Nevertheless, Mr. Simon has confirmed that this data was submitted to the IA in exactly the same form as it appears in TUR-34 A-C during the verification.

Q9.   Did any of the Turkish respondents submit any documents to the Investigating Authority regarding how inflation is to be taken into account in accordance with Turkish generally accepted accounting principles? If so, did any such documents support the proposition that non-application of IAS 29 is in accordance with Turkish GAAP? Please explain, and indicate where in the record the relevant documents can be found. If not already submitted, please furnish copies of those documents.

Reply

73.   We note, first, that the Investigating Authority never addressed a question to respondents with respect to the non-application of IAS-29 and thus respondents never addressed this issue in their responses.

74.   With respect to the more general issue, IDC explained in its response of 9 September 1999 (Exhibit TUR-29) that:

> "Izmir Demir Celik Sanayi A.S. has agreed (*sic*) that Turkey is experiencing high inflation during the period of investigation, but disagree[s] with the statement of "The reported costs do not reflect inflation in effect." Because in our accounting system all costs are already indexed and further indexations to account for inflation is unnecessary (*sic*).
>
> Material costs; these costs have not been indexed for inflation because they reflect the cost of procurement of materials used in production. Approximately 75% of the total cost of manufacturing of deformed steel bars is coming from the imported materials procurement and costs were converted from "foreign currency" to "Turkish lira" at the current exchange rate of the Turkish Central Bank, in which the inflation rate has been already taken into consideration.
>
> Labour costs and overhead; these costs depend on production, not on sales. The increase in production results in a decrease in labour cost per ton, an increase in manufacturing overhead per ton. . .
>
> SG&A expenses reported to you was based on the fixed expenses of total SG&A expenses. . . Therefore, the total yearly fixed SG&A expenses were divided by the total yearly export quantity and reported to you. There is no need for an inflation adjustment.

Because the fixed portion of SG&A expenses had already covered
the effect of the inflation, such as salary increases etc."

75.   IDC is explaining here that the TL devalues against stable foreign currencies at approximately the rate of inflation in Turkey in order to maintain constant
purchasing power parity between the currencies. The devaluations occur on a
weekly and often daily basis. Therefore, a $100 raw material cost in January will
translate into 10,000 TL (at a rate of 100 TL/$) and into 15,000 TL in December
(at a rate of 150 TL/$), reflecting an annual inflation/devaluation rate of 50 per
cent. Furthermore, because labour costs are adjusted for inflation once per year,
and the size of the labour force does not change with changes in the production
quantity, labour cost is essentially a fixed cost and it already reflects inflation in
the economy – certainly it reflects what is actually being paid out in wages and
benefits on a monthly basis. SG&A expense was calculated by IDC on an annual
basis (reflecting full inflation over the entire year) and divided by total quantity.

76.   Icdas provided a similar explanation in its response to the 19 August 1999
letter. *See* Exhibit TUR-28 (discussion of materials, labour and overhead). Habas and Diler provided a similar explanation in their response of 15 September
1999. *See* Exhibit TUR-21.

77.   Habas' audited financial statement notes that company maintains its books
of account and prepares its statutory financial statement in accordance with accounting policies based on the Turkish Tax Laws and the Turkish Commercial
Code. *See* Exhibit TUR-34C at note 2.1. Moreover, "transactions in foreign currencies during the year have been translated at rates ruling at the dates of the
transactions." *Id.,* at note 2.7. Finally, the financial statement notes, under the
rubric "Inflation Accounting".

"IAS 29, which deals with the effects of inflation in the financial
statements has become applicable for the first time to financial
statements covering the periods as from 1 January 1990. This standard requires financial statements prepared in accordance with IAS
be stated in terms of the measuring unit current at the balance
sheet data and corresponding figures for previous periods be restated in the same terms. * * *

The Group has not reflected the results of this standard in the accompanying financial statements as restatement of financial statements in terms of the measuring unit current at the balance sheet
date by applying a general price index is neither envisaged nor required by Turkish Commercial practice and tax legislation except
for the revaluation of fixed assets referred to in note 2.4 above. As
there is currently no consensus in Turkey on the application of IAS
29, the Management of the Group believes that the necessary restatement would be confusing and inappropriate at the present time
until such consensus is reached in particular since it would prevent
comparison with financial statements of other companies or groups
in Turkey".

Id., at note 2.10.

78.   Colakoglu's financial statement is prepared in dollars. See EGT 7.6; TUR-34B at Appendix 1. As noted in the auditor's opinion letter: "[T] provisions of International Accounting Standard 29 – Financial Reporting in Hyperinflationary Economies ("IAS 29") ... have not been applied since we believe that they are not applicable to financial statements reported in a stable currency. The effects of inflation on the financial statement have been dealt with by selecting the US$ (a stable currency) as the reporting currency and recording TL denominated trans-actions and balances in US$". *See* Exhibit TUR 34-B at Appendix 1, audit opin-ion letter, page 2.

Q10   Concerning Turkey's claim that the interest income offset was related to production such that it ought to be accepted as an element in the cost of production of the subject goods, did any of the Turkish respondents explain to the Investigating Authority, in detail or otherwise, and/or furnish evi-dence to document, the exact nature of the income offset or offsets con-cerned, how they were generated, and their relationship to the production of the subject goods? If so, please indicate where in the record such submis-sions can be found, and furnish copies of the relevant documents.

Reply

79.   Specific information was not requested by the Investigating Authority on the nature of the interest income at issue. If the Investigating Authority had any doubt as to the validity of the offset in question, it was incumbent upon the In-vestigating Authority to request additional information. The Investigating Au-thority cannot justify the denial of an adjustment based on the failure to provide clarifications or supporting evidence that it itself did not seek. We note that the Investigating Authority never cited any evidence that the interest income was not related to production, nor has Egypt produced such evidence to the Panel.

80.   In Diler's original response (at 14), the company noted that "[i]nterest expense is reported on a consolidated basis (Group interest expense, offset by Group interest income) as is the practice in anti-dumping investigations, because of the fungibility of money". *See* Exhibit TUR-42. A separate field appears on its App. 9A – Cost (TL/MT) (Domestic Merchandise) for Interest Expense (Reve-nue). *Id.* This field is a negative reflecting net interest revenue. The audited fi-nancial statement for Diler (at note 21), attached as Exhibit 1 to TUR-34-A, indi-cates that most of the interest income for Diler was comprised of "Bank Interest (Repo and TL Accounts)" – all of which are short-term working capital accounts.

81.   In the combined letter covering the responses of Colakoglu, Diler and Habas, dated 15 September 1999, it was explained:

> "Regarding the issue of negative interest expenses, the fact is that interest income exceeded interest expense. Companies regularly invest their working capital in very short-term income instruments, such as overnight ("repo") loans, on which interest income can be as high as 120% per year".

See Exhibit TUR-34-A at 2.

Moreover,

> "Regarding respondents' interest expense factors, each respondent has provided its financial statements in the file "mfr income stmt" included in Exhibit 2 of the questionnaire response (the database submissions). From these income statements, as well as the work-sheets embedded in the cost submissions (disapp 9A), it is apparent that short-term interest income exceeded total interest expense. This is the reason that the respondents' interest expense for purposes of cost of production is a negative figure.

> As for the ITPD's question of why respondents deduct short-term interest income from the interest expense component of cost of production, the answer is simply that, in any reasonable measure of cost, interest income is netted against interest expenses".

> *Id.*, at 7-8.

82.   As in the case of Diler, for Colakoglu, the original response at App 9A – Cost of Production contained a field for short-term interest income as an offset to cost of production. *See* Exhibit TUR-42. Attachment 1 to the 15 September response is a financial statement audited by Pricewaterhouse Coopers. The income statement prepared by PriceWaterhouse Coopers shows net financial income for 1998. See Exhibit TUR-34B.

83.   Habas' original response notes that "[i]nterest expense is on a consolidated basis (Group interest expense, offset by Group interest income)." App 9A – Cost (TL/MT) – Domestic Market shows a net negative interest expense; *i.e.*, that interest revenue exceeds interest income. *See* Exhibit TUR-42. This is confirmed by Habas' financial statement, audited by Grant Thornton. *See* Exhibit TUR-34-C, Attachment 1, at Income Statement. Habas' financial statement also shows that the company had [XX] billion TL in cash at banks at 31/12/98. *See id.* at note 3. Ordinarily, as indicated above, these funds would be in interest bearing deposits to avoid loss of value in a highly inflationary economy, accounting for the interest income.

84   In its original response in Appendix 9A – Factory Cost and Profit for Domestic Sales, IDC listed no amount under financing costs, meaning that it had no net financial expense after the application of interest income. See Exhibit TUR-42. The income statement attached to its 9 September 1999 response shows that interest revenues offset [XX] of the company's interest expenses.

Q11. Could Turkey please provide the following documents:

-     **Annexes to Icdas 15 September 1999 submission (Exh. TUR-28);**

-     **Responses of Icdas and IDC to the 23 September 1999 letters from the Investigating Authority.**

Reply

85.   *See* Exhibits TUR-39, TUR-40, and TUR-41 attached to this response. Please note that Attachment 9 to Icdas' 15 September 1999 response is missing from our files. The Investigating Authority subsequently requested another copy of Attachment 9 on 23 September 1999 and it is our belief that it became separated from the file when a copy of the Attachment was made and sent to the Investigating Authority on 27 September 1999.

* * *

QUESTIONS POSED BY THE PANEL TO EGYPT – RESPONSES OF TURKEY

86.   Turkey would like to take this opportunity to comment on a few of the questions addressed to Egypt as well.

Q2.   In the Final Report at page 13, the IA refers to the scrap cost data provided by "another respondent" and describes the trends in those data. In Egypt's oral response to this question at the 26 February 2002 meeting with the Panel, Egypt clarified that the "respondent" referred to was Alexandria National. Could Egypt please confirm this, and provide the scrap cost data referred to and copies of the supporting documents from which those data were drawn.

Reply

87.   Egypt gave a very surprising tentative answer to this question during the Second Substantive Meeting. It stated that Alexandria National was the source of the scrap data referenced in the Final Report as having been provided by "another respondent". This response seems dubious in light of the context in which that statement was made in the Final Report.

88.   First, as noted by Chairman Palecka, Alexandria National was not a "respondent" in this proceeding; it was an applicant or petitioner for anti-dumping relief. Everywhere else in the Final Report where the term "respondent" or "respondents" is used, that term refers to the Turkish producers and exporters. Thus, for example, in Section 1.5, the report states: "Review of the cost and sales data provided by the respondents raised significant questions regarding the accuracy of the data." In Section 1.6.3, the report states: "The Investigating Authority disagrees with respondents regarding the requests for supplemental information". When the domestic producers are referred to in the Final Report, they are invariably referred to by name or as "the domestic industry" or as the "Egyptian industry". *See* Exhibit TUR-16.

89.   The particular reference and surrounding text also suggests that the source of this scrap data was one of the Turkish respondents:

"Diler, Habas and Colakoglu claim that they "have proved in a number of different ways that the sharp decline in such world scrap prices gave the respondents' constant currency declining costs, which in a hyperinflationary economy appear in local currency as steady costs even though the macroeconomy is hyperinflationary * * *

Respondents then "tabulated the rebar pricing data from each respondents' verified sales database, and the result showed a steep decline in Turkish rebar prices during 1998." Thus, they claim, Turkey's domestic rebar prices collapsed in 1998. They conclude that prices fell because scrap cost fell. * * *

The Department disagrees for several reasons. First, since respondents' information on world scrap prices was expressed in annual terms (prices at the end of the year were lower than prices at the beginning of the year), it was not useful in determining price movements during the investigation period (calendar 1998). When the Department examined *monthly domestic rebar and purchased scrap prices throughout the period (another respondent in this investigation submitted monthly scrap prices)*, a very different picture emerged. For the first 7 months of the period, both were fairly constant and did not decline to any noticeable extent. For the next three months scrap prices declined sharply, and in the last 2 months, they began a noticeable recovery. The sharp decline, which respondents implied was sustained throughout the period, was, in fact, limited to 3 out of 12 months of the investigation period, *despite a high inflation rate throughout the period*. Thus, the Department had a reasonable basis for its concern whether domestic costs fully reflected inflation".

Exhibit TUR-16 at 12-13 (emphasis added).

90.   In this context, the term "domestic rebar and purchased scrap prices" clearly refers to domestic rebar prices in Turkey (as opposed to export prices to Egypt) and purchased scrap prices in Turkey. Turkey is the relevant market to examine in evaluating the accuracy of respondents' cost information. It is very unlikely that this language would have been drafted as it was if rebar prices were based on prices in Turkey and the scrap prices were those in Egypt. The IA would then have had to explain this fact and that use of Egyptian scrap prices made sense in comparison to rebar prices submitted by the Turkish respondents. Moreover, the sentence – "The sharp decline, which respondents implied was sustained throughout the period, was, in fact, limited to 3 out of 12 months of the investigation period, *despite a high inflation rate throughout the period*" – makes sense only if the scrap prices were provided by a Turkish respondent – given the explicit reference to the high inflation rate in Turkey during the period.

91.   In addition, it is not entirely clear why Alexandria National would have provided this information to the Investigating Authority. Ordinarily, cost data obtained from a domestic industry is not broken down to this level of detail be-

cause such information is not needed to analyze the question of whether the domestic industry has been materially injured by reason of imports. Moreover, the confidential injury analysis, submitted by Egypt, does not provide cost data at this level of detail.

92.   Finally, in Panel Question #10, addressed to Egypt on 28 November 2001, the Panel requested that Egypt supply to the panel "[i]nformation on scrap steel prices on a monthly basis on which the final determination was based". This was an obvious reference to page 12 of the Final Report. That Egypt took it as a reference to page 12 of the Final Report and not as a request for all scrap data upon which the final determination of normal value was based is evident in the fact that, in its response, Egypt provided scrap costs from only three of the five respondents – Icdas, IDC and Colakoglu. Colakoglu was one of the companies whose costs were specifically being questioned at page 12 of the Final Report and Icdas and IDC were the two other respondents whose costs were not being specifically questioned in that section of the report. By submitting this data, the Investigating Authority tacitly admitted that it was relying either on data submitted by Icdas or data submitted by IDC in questioning the declining scrap cost data submitted by Colakolgu, Habas and Diler. Certainly, all of the scrap costs provided in that exhibit were those of Turkish respondents.

93.   We noted in our rebuttal brief that the data presented for Icdas supports the claims we have made challenging the factual findings in the Final Report and observing that the Investigating Authority seems to have been quite confused about the interplay of inflation, devaluation and costs reported in constant and nominal currencies. *See* Rebuttal Brief of Turkey at 68-69. Indeed, we initially made this claim in our First Written Submission. *See* First Submission of Turkey at II.E.11. At no time prior to its response to this Panel question at the Second Substantive Session did Egypt take the position that Turkey was incorrect in concluding that the Final Report was referring to scrap data supplied by Icdas. It had an obvious opportunity to do so both in its Rebuttal Brief and in its response to the Panel's First Set of Questions, but did not.

Q4.   Could Egypt please indicate exactly which inflation data contained in Exhibit EGT 7.7 it used as the basis for its conclusion that the average monthly inflation rate in Turkey was 5 per cent. In this regard, the Panel notes that the exhibit contains, *inter alia*, the same data from the Turkish State Institute of Statistics (submitted by the Turkish Government in its response of 15 October 1999 to the Essential Facts and Conclusions Report (Exhibit TUR-30)) on which the Turkish Government relied to indicate that the inflation rate was much lower during 1998.

Reply

94.   In its tentative response, Egypt states that it used a simple average of the wholesale price index and the consumer price index in 1998. We note that the wholesale price index rose by only 40.2 per cent in 1998, which, on a monthly basis, converts to an inflation rate of 3.4 per cent per month. Moreover, in its letters of 19 August 1999, the Investigating Authority cited comparisons between

costs in September, October and November (Icdas), August-December (Diler), April and August (Colakoglu), and November and December (Habas). *See* Exhibit TUR-11. However, the inflation rate was less than 3 per cent on average in those months.

95.   The Consumer Price Index is irrelevant to the issue before the Investigating Authority. The Consumer Price Index refers to a market basket of goods purchased by individual consumers, not purchases of raw materials by large manufacturing enterprises. As claimed by the Government of Turkey in the Egyptian investigation, the relevant price index is the Wholesale Price Index.

Q5.   Egypt has requested the Panel to dismiss a number of Turkey's claims on the grounds that they are outside the Panel's terms of reference. In respect of each claim that Egypt has requested be dismissed, could Egypt please provide the two-part analysis referred to e.g. in *EC – Bed Linen*, i.e., the asserted lack of clarity in the Request for Establishment of the Panel, and evidence of any prejudice to Egypt's ability to defend its interests in this dispute due to such lack of clarity.

Reply

96.   Turkey notes that it would like the opportunity to respond to any claims made by Egypt in this regard. Turkey believes that its Request for Establishment of the Panel contained all of the claims that it has asserted before the Panel. *See, e.g.,* Response of Turkey to the Questions Posed by the Panel, 7 December 2001 at 1-2; Statement of Turkey at the Second Substantive Meeting at 12-14. Moreover, Egypt has had a more than adequate opportunity to respond to each of those claims and has in fact responded to each of the claims. Therefore, under the test enunciated in *EC-Bed Linens*, Egypt suffered no prejudice to its ability to defend its interests.

Q8.   Concerning Icdas, at page 6 of the Final Report, the IA stated that "Icdas ... provided incomplete data and most of the data submitted were not supported by evidence". Further concerning Icdas, at page 22 of the Final Report, the IA stated that "[o]n 23 September 1999, the Department requested a missing document and several documents to be translated into English". At page 23 of the Final Report, the IA stated, "[a]s for Icdas's claim that it 'provided all the necessary information' in response to the Department's 19 August 1999 request, and that the 'remaining items are [*sic*] timely submitted' in response to the Department's 23 September 1999 request, that is incorrect. In fact, the firm did not furnish (1) the requested breakdown of labour and overhead costs, (2) the requested supporting documents for labour and overhead costs, (3) the requested allocations and allocation methodologies for materials, overhead, and SG&A, and (4) the requested reconciliations of submitted data to its financial statement. In addition, its explanation of how inflation was reflected/included in its costs was inadequate and unsupported". At page 29 of the Final Report, the IA stated that "as described above, Icdas did not provide sufficient information for the investigating authority to confirm the monthly specific costs of materi-

als, labour, or overhead during the period of investigations, despite being requested to do so". Could Egypt please precisely identify the documents containing the IA's requests for the information referred to in the Final Report as not having been submitted. Please describe the documents that were provided by Icdas on these points and indicate how, in light of those documents, the IA was satisfied that AD Article 6.8 could be applied.

Reply

97.   As indicated in response to Question #1 to Turkey, Icdas did provide this data. Specifically, Icdas provided a breakdown of its labour and overhead costs in the electric arc furnace and in the rolling mill in Attachment 11, part two, page two. It provided supporting documentation for its labour costs in Attachment 8 and supporting documentation for its overhead expenses in Attachment II, part two. Its allocation methodology is obvious from the documents in Attachment II, part two – total costs incurred in the month in the electric arc furnace are divided by total production to arrive at a cost of billet and total production costs incurred in the month in the rolling mill are divided by total production of bar to arrive at a cost of bar processing through the rolling mill. These two costs are added to arrive at a total cost of manufacturing.

QUESTIONS POSED BY THE PANEL TO BOTH PARTIES

Q1.   In paragraph 3 of the Request for Establishment of the Panel, four factors are specified by Turkey as being grounds for a breach of the cited Articles. However, in the submissions made by Turkey, it is arguable that other grounds are added. In the view of the parties, is it permissible:

(a)   to use an inclusive expression when listing grounds for an alleged breach in request for establishment; and

(b)   where a list of grounds is included in a request for establishment, to add another or other grounds in submissions:

(i)   where the list is said to be inclusive; and

(ii)   where the list is not said to be inclusive.

Reply

98.   If Turkey identified all of its grounds for claiming a violation of the Agreement clearly in its Request for Establishment of the Panel, no issue of interpretation arises. Turkey maintains that all of the claims that it asserted in connection with Paragraph 3 are fairly raised in the language of Paragraph 3 itself.

99.   In the alternative, it is Turkey's position that since the Articles of the Anti-Dumping Agreement alleged to be breached were clearly set forth in the Request for Establishment of the Panel, together with a general description of how those Articles were breached and a non-inclusive list of factors that were not evaluated or were not evaluated properly was provided, Egypt was on fair notice as to Turkey's claims. Moreover, all of those claims were set out in Tur-

key's First Written Submission such that Egypt suffered no prejudice to its position if there was any lack of clarity in the Request for Establishment of the Panel.

100. In paragraph 3 of the Request for Establishment of the Panel, Turkey alleged a violation of Articles 3.1, 3.4 and 3.5 of the Anti-Dumping Agreement because the Investigating Authorities "failed to take account of, and improperly attributed to Turkish imports, the effects of other factors that had a substantial adverse effect on the Egyptian industry and of other, neutral factors that caused prices to fall". The claim went on to state: "Such factors include, but are not limited to, a large-scale capacity expansion by the Egyptian rebar producers during the period of review, the effects of non-subject imports from third countries, falling worldwide prices for steel scrap and a sudden contraction in domestic demand in January 1999 ... ."

101. In its rebuttal brief, Turkey listed the following factors that had negative effects on industry profitability and domestic prices:

> Capacity expansions at the two major Egyptian rebar producers;
>
> The effects of the capacity expansion on the producer's costs of production;
>
> The effects of the capacity expansion on the intra-industry competition;
>
> Increasing competition between Al Ezz and Alexandria National as Al Ezz sought to increase market share capitalizing on its cost advantages;
>
> Falling prices for steel scrap;
>
> Contraction in demand in January 1999, and
>
> The effect of comparably priced, fairly traded imports.

See Rebuttal Brief at 21. *See also* First Written Submission of Turkey at II.C. (items 1-2), II.D (items 3 - 6), II.E (item 7).

102. Items 1, 5, 6 and 7 are specifically referenced in paragraph 3 of the Request for Establishment of the Panel. Items 2 and 3 are subsumed in item 1 – they are the "adverse effect[s]" of the capacity expansion alleged in item 1 and in paragraph 3 of the Request for Establishment of the Panel. Turkey clearly alleged in its Request for Establishment of the Panel that the capacity expansion was having an adverse effect on the domestic industry or was a neutral factor causing prices to fall. Items 2 and 3 above merely specify how the capacity expansion had those effects.

103. Arguably, item 4 is subsumed in item 1 as well. [XX]

104. In any event, Turkey put Egypt on notice in paragraph 3 that it was alleging violations of Article 3.1, 3.4 and 3.5 due to the failure to take account of, and improper attribution to Turkish imports of the effects of other factors. Turkey also put Egypt on notice that the enumerated list of factors in that paragraph non-inclusive through use of the words "including, but not limited to". Turkey then spelled out its claims in its First Written Submission and Egypt has had adequate opportunity to respond. Hence, even if the Request for Establishment of the

Panel can be deemed to lack clarity, there has certainly been no prejudice to Egypt's position.

Q2.   Could the parties please comment, in the light of Article 31 of the Vienna Convention on the Law of Treaties, on the meaning of the phrases:

> **(a)   "special circumspection" in Annex II, paragraph 7; and**
>
> **(b)   "to the best of its ability" in Annex II, paragraph 5.**

Reply

105.   Annex II, paragraph 7 provides: "if the authorities have to base their findings, including those with respect to normal value, on information from a secondary source, ... they should do so with special circumspection. In such cases, the authorities should, where practicable, check the information from other independent sources at their disposal, such as published price lists, official import statistics and customs returns, and from information obtained from other interested parties during the course of the investigation."

106.   "Special circumspection" means, in this context, with extreme care to ensure the accuracy and pertinence of the data relied upon. Whenever it must rely on information from a secondary source as "facts available," the Investigating Authority should endeavour to replicate, as closely as possible, the missing data and should check the data selected to verified data or other reliable public data. This provision also informs an investigating authority's obligations when it uses data provided by respondents, but that data is other than the data that the respondents supplied as costs for the particular sale concerned. *See* Rebuttal Brief of Turkey at 77-79. When this step is taken, the Investigating Authorities must compare the data they have chosen to other verified or reliable data in the record and to published data in order to determine the pertinence and accuracy of the data. The Investigating Authority failed in this obligation in several respects in the Egyptian rebar investigation. *See, e.g.,* Rebuttal Brief of Turkey at 80-82.

107.   Egypt maintained, up to the convening of the commencement of the Second Substantive Session, that it relied solely on the information submitted by the Turkish respondents for its final determination and that, therefore, Article II, paragraph 7 was inapplicable. *See, e.g.,* Oral Presentation of Egypt, 27 November 2001, at 27. We note, however, that during the Second Substantive Session, Egypt claimed, for the first time, that it obtained scrap data from Alexandria National and that it relied upon that data in determining the normal value of respondents. Specifically, Egypt now claims that scrap data obtained from Alexandria National was compared to scrap data supplied by Colakoglu, Habas and Diler and, based on that comparison, it was concluded that the data submitted by Colakoglu, Habas and Diler was incorrect. We note, in this regard, that the Investigating Authority apparently did not follow the requirement of Annex II, paragraph 7 that data from this secondary source be used only with "special circumspection." In particular, it evidently did not compare the data allegedly supplied by Alexandria National to public pricing information published in *American Metal Market* and *Metal Bulletin*, the two most widely read periodicals on the steel industry

worldwide. If it had, it would have seen that the data allegedly provided by Alexandria National do not reflect the worldwide trend in scrap prices, while the scrap price data provided by Colakolgu, Habas and Diler did reflect those trends. *See* First Written Submission of Turkey at II.E.14-15 and TUR 13-14.

108.   Regarding Annex II, paragraph 5, please see our response to joint question #4 below.

Q3.   Do you consider that the BCI submission of Egypt (*Confidential Injury Analysis*), by itself, constitutes an "evaluation" of the factors that it covers, in the sense of Article 3.4? Please cite any relevant legal authority and/or precedent.

Reply

109.   No, we do not. *See* Statement of Turkey at the Second Substantive Session, 1-3.

Q4   Could the parties please comment, in the light of the Vienna Convention on the Law of Treaties, on the Appellate Body's ruling in *United States – Hot-rolled Steel*, (at paragraph 101 and 102)[12] concerning Annex II, paragraphs 2 and 5.

Reply

110.   Annex II, paragraph 2 provides that the authorities may request that the response be put in a particular computer medium (e.g., computer tape). However, "[w]hen such a request is made, the authorities should consider the reasonable ability of the interested party to respond in the preferred medium or computer language, and should not request the company to use for its response a computer system other than that used by the firm". Moreover, "The authorities should not maintain a request for a response in a particular medium or computer language ... if presenting the response as requested would result in an unreasonable extra burden on the interested party, *e.g.,* it would entail unreasonable additional cost and trouble".

111.   In *United States – Hot-Rolled Steel from Japan*, the Appellate Body drew on this language to conclude that

> "investigating authorities [must] strike a balance between the effort they can expect interested parties to make in responding to questionnaires and the practical ability of those interested parties to comply fully with all demands made of them by the investigating authorities. We see this provision as another detailed expression of the principle of good faith, which is, at once, a general principle of law and a principal of general international law, that informs the provisions of the Anti-Dumping Agreement, as well as the covered agreements. This organic principle of good faith, in this particular

---

[12]   WT/DS184/AB/R, DSR 2001:X, 4697.

context, restrains investigating authorities from imposing on exporters burdens which, in the circumstances, are not reasonable".[13]

112.   Annex II, paragraph 5 provides that "[e]ven though information provided may not be ideal in all respects, this should not justify the authorities from disregarding it, provided the interested party has acted to the best of its ability".

113.   Considering both of these provisions in combination, the Appellate Body in *United States – Hot-Rolled Steel from Japan* concluded:

> "We, therefore, see paragraphs 2 and 5 of Annex II of the Anti-Dumping Agreement as reflecting a careful balance between the interests of investigating authorities and exporters. In order to complete their investigations, investigating authorities are entitled to expect a very significant degree of effort – to the "best of their abilities" – from investigated exporters. At the same time, investigating authorities are not entitled to insist upon absolute standards or impose unreasonable burdens upon those exporters".[14]

114.   Turkey agrees with all of these observations. In the Egyptian rebar investigation, the investigating authorities imposed an unreasonable burden on the exporters by requesting all of the new cost information identified in the 19 August 1999 questionnaire, and then insisting upon a "mail order" verification of all of that data and, in addition the cost and pricing data submitted in the original responses too. As discussed elsewhere, this was an impossible task, requiring the review, collation, translation and synthesis of thousands of pages of company books and records. If the investigating authorities desired a verification of the data in question, they should have scheduled a second "cost" verification in Turkey. There was sufficient time, given administrative deadlines, to do so.[15]

---

[13]   *United States – Imposition of Definitive Anti-Dumping Measures on Hot-Rolled Steel Products from Japan,* WT/DS 184/AB/R, July 24, 2001, DSR 2001:X, 4697, para. 101.

[14]   *Ibid.* at para. 102.

[15]   As noted in our Rebuttal Brief, Egyptian law imposes a 12-month deadline for completion of anti-dumping investigations, with the possibility of a six month extension in certain circumstances. Rebuttal Brief of Turkey at note 152 and related text. Thus, in August 1999, the Investigating Authority still had at least five months in which to complete its investigation, and could have sought an extension of its investigation for another six months if necessary.

115.   Moreover, the investigating authorities, according to the interpretation of their rationale offered by Egypt to the Panel in this proceeding, imposed an absolute standard or unreasonable burden on respondents by insisting that their cost data was useless because the companies' cost of inventory was not indexed to inflation – a practice that is not common in Turkey and that was certainly not followed by the companies in their internal book-keeping systems. Annex II, paragraph 2 and Article 2.2.1.1 suggest that the Investigating Authority should accept costs drawn from the companies' own computerized accounting systems. At a minimum, as a matter of "good faith," it was incumbent upon the Investigating Authority, if it felt that the companies' internal book-keeping systems required modification, to advise the respondents how their costs should be modified, and in doing so, not to impose an unreasonable burden upon the respondents.

ANNEX 8-2

RESPONSES OF EGYPT TO QUESTIONS POSED IN THE CONTEXT OF THE SECOND SUBSTANTIVE MEETING OF THE PANEL

QUESTIONS POSED BY THE PANEL TO EGYPT

Q1. In paragraph 3.2.2.1 of the Final Report, the Investigating Authority states with reference to the methodology used to calculate the normal value of Habas that "[t]herefore, as facts available for COP, the Investigating Authority used for each cost element (except interest) the highest of the company's submitted costs and added 5 per cent to account for inflation during the period for each month". It is not exactly clear to the Panel how this was done. Could Egypt please explain in detail how the calculations were done.

Reply

1.   Habas reported cost data for only two months of 1998. The Investigating Authority took the highest monthly value found for each cost element (except interest) and added 5 per cent monthly to account for inflation. This was done as follows. The Investigating Authority used the raw materials, labour and overhead expenses from the month of November 1998. Those costs were adjusted by the monthly inflation rate of 5 per cent according to the following formula.

(a)   Adjustment for inflation rate of November 1998

Submitted Costs of November 1998 X 1.05

(b)   Adjustment for inflation rate of December 1998

Adjusted costs in (a) X 1.05

2.   The interest expenses were calculated as a percentage of costs of goods sold on the basis of the data submitted by Habas. The result (5 per cent) was applied to the costs as adjusted above.

3.   Lastly, a reasonable amount for profit of 5.5 per cent was added. This margin was based on the profit achieved by Habas as shown in the income statement submitted by the company.

4.   We attach the costs data submitted by Habas in EX-EGT-11.1 and the normal value constructed by the Investigating Authority as explained above in EX-EGT-11.2.

Q2. In the Final Report at page 13, the IA refers to the scrap cost data provided by "another respondent" and describes the trends in those data. In Egypt's oral response to this question at the 26 February 2002 meeting with the Panel, Egypt clarified that the "respondent" referred to was Alexandria National. Could Egypt please confirm this, and provide the scrap

cost data referred to and copies of the supporting documents from which those data were drawn.

Reply

5.　　The other "*respondent*" from whom the Investigating Authority obtained information on scrap costs is Alexandria National Steel, one of the complainant respondents. The data submitted by this "respondent" is attached in EX-EGT-12.

Q3.　　The Panel notes the comments made in Annexes 1 to Exhibit TUR-34A, B and C, respectively, by the auditors of the three companies to the effect that there is no consensus in Turkey on the use of IAS 29 and that it seems to be only of value when a comparison is to be made with a previous period (which would not be the case with a POI of one year only). In the light of these comments, could Egypt please explain the relevance of IAS 29 in this dispute.

Reply

6.　　The absence of consensus in Turkey on the application of IAS 29 is irrelevant to the current issue.

7.　　Indeed, as explained in previous submissions, it is not sufficient that costs data be prepared in accordance with the generally accepted accounting principles of the exporting country in order for such data to be used by the Investigating Authority without adjustment. In addition, the records must reasonably reflect the costs associated with the production and sale of the product under consideration. In this respect, Egypt considers that the non-application of IAS 29 can seriously distort the accuracy and reliability of cost records of companies operating in an hyperinflationary economy since such records will underestimate the actual costs incurred by the company in producing and selling the product concerned.

8.　　Furthermore, IAS 29 is not only of value for comparison with previous years but also for the restatement of values of the reporting year.

9.　　IAS 29 is summarized as follows[1]:

"-　　Hyperinflation is indicated if cumulative inflation over three years is 100 per cent or more (among other factors).

-　　In such a circumstance, financial statements should be presented in a measuring unit that is current at the balance sheet date.

-　　Comparative amounts for prior periods are also restated into the measuring unit at the current balance sheet date.

-　　Any gain or loss on the net monetary position arising from the restatement of amounts into the measuring unit current at the balance sheet date should be included in net income and separately disclosed."

---

[1]　*Source*: International Accounting Standard Board

10. While it is correct that IAS 29 seeks to readjust the corresponding amounts of previous periods to reflect hyperinflation when comparing these amounts to the current balance sheet as pointed out in Question 3, the summary of IAS 29 also specifically refers to the effects of hyperinflation on the profit/loss accounts of the reporting year. Accounts that are not restated in accordance with IAS 29 will therefore not reflect the full costs of production during the reporting period.

11. Furthermore, contrary to what Turkey stated in point J of its Oral Statement of 25 February 2002, Egypt did not conclude that the costs of production did not reflect hyperinflation simply because IAS 29 was not applied. The non-application of IAS 29 constitutes only one indication that the reported costs data may not have reflected hyperinflation. However, the Investigating Authority was careful not to rely exclusively on this factor. Indeed, it also relied on the information received from the respondents that the costs were not adjusted to reflect hyperinflation of which the Panel received a copy (audited accounts, admissions by the respondents themselves). This was specifically acknowledged by Turkey in its rebuttal.

Q4. Could Egypt please indicate exactly which inflation data contained in Exhibit EGT 7.7 it used as the basis for its conclusion that the average monthly inflation rate in Turkey was 5 per cent. In this regard, the Panel notes that the exhibit contains, *inter alia*, the same data from the Turkish State Institute of Statistics (submitted by the Turkish Government in its response of 15 October 1999 to the Essential Facts and Conclusions Report (Exhibit TUR-30)) on which the Turkish Government relied to indicate that the inflation rate was much lower during 1998.

Reply

12. Egypt used the average yearly inflation rate for wholesale (54.3 per cent) and for retail (69.7 per cent) expressed on a monthly basis and rounded to 5 per cent. The details of the calculations are as follows:

- $54.3/12 = 4.5\%$
- $69.7/12 = 5.8\%$
- $(4.5 + 5.8)/2 = 5.1\%$, rounded to 5%.

Those data are contained in the *document 1(b) TURKEY UPDATE* in EX-EGT-7.7.

13. In response to Question 2 submitted by Turkey, Egypt wishes to confirm that the above inflation rates relate to the calendar year 1998.

Q5. For each respondent company, please identify the communication or communications that in Egypt's view informed that respondent that its evidence was not being accepted, and giving it an opportunity to provide further explanations within a reasonable period, as referred to in Annex II, paragraph 6.

Reply

14.   The communications by which the respondents were informed that their costs data were not accepted and giving them an opportunity to provide further explanations are as follows:

(1)   Letters of 19 August 1999 to all respondents

15.   On 19 August 1999, the Investigating Authority sent all respondents a letter informing them that it had reasons to believe that the reported costs of production were unreliable and insufficient for the purposes of the dumping investigation and provided an initial period of 13 days to provide clarification and additional data. The deadline was later extended by 14 days. The responses received from the respondents were incomplete.

(2)   Letters of 23 September 1999 to all respondents

16.   On 23 September 1999, after review of the responses to the letter of 19 August 1999, the Investigating Authority sent a second letter to all respondents offering them another opportunity to clarify the matters raised in the letters of 19 August 1999. The Investigating Authority granted a deadline of two to five days.

17.   Since Habas, Diler and Colakoglu informed the Investigating Authority that they would not supply the information requested in the letter of 23 September 1999, the Investigating Authority informed these respondents that it would use facts available by letter of 28 September 1999 to counsel to the said respondents.

18.   As to Icdas and IDC, the information submitted did not show that the costs data duly reflected hyperinflation and, therefore, could not be used as submitted for the determination of the normal value. In consequence, the Investigating Authority had to resort to facts available in order to compensate for the unreliability of the submitted costs data.

19.   The reasons for the use of partial facts available were given in the *Essential Facts & Conclusions Report* and the *Final Report*.

20.   For the Panel's reference, a copy of the above-mentioned communications to the respondents is attached in EX-EGT-13.

Q6.   Egypt has requested the Panel to dismiss a number of Turkey's claims on the grounds that they are outside the Panel's terms of reference. In respect of each claim that Egypt has requested be dismissed, could Egypt please provide the two-part analysis referred to e.g. in *EC – Bed Linen*, i.e., the asserted lack of clarity in the Request for Establishment of the Panel, and evidence of any prejudice to Egypt's ability to defend its interests in this dispute due to such lack of clarity.

Reply

21.   In view of the reasoning of the Panel in *EC – Bed Linen* and the Appellate Body in *Korea – Dairy Safeguards*, Egypt requests that the following claims be dismissed:

(a)   *Claims under Article 3.4 as regards* "factors affecting domestic prices"

22.   Throughout its various submissions, Turkey presents the same arguments in relation to Article 3, paragraphs 4 and 5 and even goes so far as to allege a violation under Article 3.4 or Article 3.5[2] as regards the Investigating Authority's examination of "*factors affecting domestic prices*". Turkey's claims in relation to these two provisions as stated in the Panel Request at Claim 3 or 4 were not in any way clarified in Turkey's First Written Submission. Nor were these claims clarified at the First Meeting of the Panel on 27 November 2001. Indeed, it will be recalled that the very first question of the Panel, dated 28 November 2001, was that Turkey set out in summary format its legal argumentation in support of each of its claims, including those relating to the Investigating Authority's examination of injury under Article 3. Moreover, when requested by the Panel to clarify its position on this issue at the First Meeting of the Panel on 27 November 2001, Turkey stated that it was presenting a claim solely under Article 3.4. The following day, on 28 November 2001, Turkey modified that response and stated that it was presenting a claim under both Articles 3.4 and 3.5.

23.   In applying the approach of the Appellate Body in *Korea – Dairy Safeguards* to the particular facts of this case, Egypt submits that the Panel must look further into the nature of the particular provision at issue – i.e. where the Articles listed establish not one single distinct obligation, but rather multiple obligations. Articles 3.4 and 3.5 establish multiple obligations. If any violation with respect thereunder is not presented with sufficient clarity in the Panel Request, (1) the burden on the respondent becomes too onerous; and (2) both the Panel and the respondent are at risk of being misled at to which claims are in fact being asserted against the respondent.

24.   Article 6.2 of the DSU requires at the very least, that the claims, although not the arguments, must be presented with sufficient clarity in the Panel Request. This was not done in the present case before the Panel. Because it was unclear as to which provision under Article 3 Turkey was presenting its argumentation with respect to "*factors affecting domestic prices*", Egypt was prejudiced as regards the preparation its defense with respect to those particular factors.

(b)   *Paragraph 6 of Annex II*

25.   In the Request for Establishment of a Panel, a violation of Paragraph 6 of Annex II was invoked with respect to the deadline granted to the respondents to

---

[2]   See for example the Rebuttal Submission of Turkey of 2 January 2002 at Claim III.C, page 15.

reply to the letter of 19 August 1999. In its Restatement of Claims, Turkey additionally claimed that the sheer fact of sending the letter of 19 August 1999 constituted a violation of Paragraph 6 of Annex II. However, as the Panel will have noted, Turkey fails to explain its reasoning underlying the claim that the simple fact of sending a letter constitutes by itself a violation of Paragraph 6 of Annex II.

26.   Yet, such an explanation was particularly called for in this case.

27.   Indeed, it will be recalled that Paragraph 6 of Annex II imposes upon the Investigating Authority the obligation to inform a responding party of the reasons why information submitted by such party is not accepted and to grant that party an opportunity to provide further explanations within a reasonable period, due account being taken of the time-limits of the investigation. Since the purpose of the letter of 19 August 1999 was precisely to inform the respondents of the reasons why some of their data were not accepted and to provide them with an opportunity to supply additional information and clarification, the claim of violation presented by Turkey in its Restatement of claims is quite perplexing and should have been given special consideration by Turkey.

28.   As a result of the absence of any explanation of the claim presented by Turkey with respect to Paragraph 6 of Annex II, Egypt's ability to defend its interests in this context was severely prejudiced and, in fact, simply denied.

(c)   Paragraph 3 of Annex II and Article X:3 of GATT 1994

29.   Turkey alleged that the Investigating Authority violated Paragraph 3 of Annex II and Article X:3 of GATT 1994 in its selection of facts as facts available. As noted by the Panel, those provisions were not cited in support of Claim 11 of the Request for Establishment of a Panel addressing the selection of facts available.

30.   For the reasons set out below, Egypt submits that the alleged violation of Paragraph 3 of Annex II and Article X:3 of GATT 1994 must be rejected as not being within the Terms of Reference of the Panel in the context of Claim 11.

(i)   Paragraph 3 of Annex II

31.   As regards the alleged violation of Paragraph 3 of Annex II, Turkey failed to identify the obligations contained in that provision that the Investigating Authority would have violated in its selection of "facts available", therefore preventing Egypt from presenting a meaningful defence. As already noted in Egypt's First Written Submission[3], Paragraph 3 of Annex II concerns the circumstances in which the data submitted by respondents must be accepted or can be rejected. This provision, however, does not address the *selection* of facts available once it has been decided to reject the data submitted by the respondents. The reference to Paragraph 3 of Annex II in this latter context was definitely odd. Accordingly, Egypt would have expected Turkey to be particularly careful and

---

[3]   Section IV.B.8.b).i)

thorough in explaining the legal basis for its claim that the Investigating Authority violated this provision by its selection of facts available. However, although invited to elaborate on this claim by the Panel, Turkey merely restated that the Investigating Authority's selection of facts available was inconsistent with Paragraph 3 of Annex II without any further detail.

32.   In those circumstances, Egypt submits that its rights of defence were severely prejudiced with respect to the alleged violation of Paragraph 3 of Annex II since Turkey never explained the legal basis for the alleged violation.

(ii)   Article X:3 of GATT 1994

33.   The allegations of a violation of Article X:3 of GATT 1994 were equally vague and unsubstantiated. Thus, at page 30 of its Restatement of Claims, Turkey alleges that

> "The denial of respondents' requests for meetings at which they could explain how their responses to the Investigating Authority's request for information were complete and accurate and show that their responses could be tied to their books and records was abusive, discriminatory and unfair to respondents in violation of Article X:3 of the GATT. The calculation of an interest charge for IDC that overstated IDC's interest expenses as a per cent of costs of goods sold manufactured by a factor of eight was also abusive and discriminatory in violation of Article X:3." (emphasis added)

34.   Besides the fact that the language of Article X:3 does not seem to contain the obligations of non-discrimination and unfairness that Turkey considers were violated, it must be stressed that Turkey failed at any point during the proceeding to explain the elements of "abusiveness", "discrimination" and "unfairness" which allegedly would characterize the decisions to refuse a meeting and the calculation of interest expenses. In other words, Turkey has made unsubstantiated and legally-ill allegations of violation to which therefore it is virtually impossible to respond in any meaningful way.

(d)   Failure to refer to the relevant treaty article in the Panel Request

35.   According to the Panel in EC – Bed Linen, a "[f]ailure to even mention in the request for the establishment the treaty Article alleged to have been violated in our view constitutes failure to state a claim at all"[4]. It follows that the following claims must be dismissed.

---

[4]   WT/DS141/R, DSR 2001:VI, 2077, para. 6.15.

(i) Whether the Final Report contains findings or conclusions sufficient to satisfy the requirements of Article 12.2

36.   Turkey claims that the Panel should disregard consideration of certain Article 3.4 factors mentioned in the working papers of the Investigating Authority when evaluating whether the *Final Report* contains findings or conclusions sufficient to satisfy the requirements of Article 12.2, with respect to each of the Article 3.4 factors.

37.   Again, Egypt wishes to stress that whether all of the Investigating Authority's conclusions on material injury are reproduced in the *Final Report* is not an issue that is before the Panel. A claim under Article 12.2 was not introduced in the Request for the Establishment of a Panel and accordingly, is not within the Panel's Terms of Reference. As a result, Egypt did not prepare any defense in this regard.

(ii) Whether the Panel can disregard evidence under Article 6.4

38.   In its Rebuttal Submission, Turkey claims that the Panel should not consider evidence that was not provided to interested parties during the course of the investigation, such as the report on *Other Causes of Injury*. In support of this contention, Turkey refers to Article 6.4 of the Anti-Dumping Agreement.

39.   Apart from the fact that a violation of Article 6.4 was not alleged in the Request for the Establishment of a Panel and accordingly, is not within the Panel's Terms of Reference, it is indeed ironic that Turkey should ask the Panel to dismiss evidence that was not provided to the Turkish respondents, while at the same time claim that the Panel should accept evidence that was not provided to the Investigating Authority during the course of the investigation. This is even more unreasonable in view of the fact that the Turkish respondents did not, at any time during the course of the investigation, request that the Investigating Authority provide non-confidential information to interested parties through its public file system.

(iii) Article 17.6(i) of the AD Agreement

40.   Turkey alleges a violation of Article 17.6(i) of the AD Agreement. However, that provision governs the standard of review to be applied by a panel when considering whether the Investigating Authority's establishment of the facts was proper and the evaluation unbiased and objective. It does not govern the rights and obligations of Members under the AD Agreement. In any event, it was not cited in the Request for Establishment of a Panel. As a consequence, this claim is not within the Terms of Reference of the Panel and must be rejected.

Q7.   At page 6 of the Final Report, the IA stated that "IDC ... provided incomplete data and most of the data submitted were not supported by evidence". At page 29 of the Final Report, the IA stated in respect of IDC that "[f]or materials, labour and overhead, ... the company did not adequately

demonstrate or support its claim that inflation was included...". At para. 3 of page 2 of Egypt's Rebuttal, it is said that it was clear that the records of the respondents were not prepared in order to reflect hyperinflation. However, in TUR-29, IDC submits that "inflation had been taken into account by the procurement price mechanism automatically" (in relation to materials). In your Oral Presentation dated 25 February 2002, it is said that "it cannot be contested that the costs data of the respondents was not adjusted to reflect hyperinflation". It is also said that ample evidence was submitted to establish that, and reference is made to EX-EGT-7.6. There is no document relating to IDC in that Exhibit. Could Egypt please identify how, and on the basis of what specific information in the record, the investigating authority arrived at its above-cited opinions and conclusions about hyperinflation in relation to IDC? Please furnish the documents relied upon by Egypt in reaching these conclusions.

Reply

41.   In EX-EGT-7.6, Egypt submitted a copy of the Auditors' notes to the Financial Statements in which IAS 29 was specifically discussed. Conversely, as explained in Egypt's First Written Submission, the Audited Accounts of IDC seemingly did not contain any indication that the financial statements had been prepared in accordance with the provisions of IAS 29, or were otherwise adjusted to reflect inflation.[5] It should be noted that Turkey admitted on several occasions that no company applies IAS 29.

42.   However, the fact that the costs data of IDC were not duly adjusted for inflation is apparent from other documents submitted by Egypt to the Panel.

43.   Egypt wishes to refer to the documents attached in EX-EGT-7.9. This exhibit contains a copy of the reply of IDC to the Investigating Authority's questions on cost and sales data. In its response, IDC acknowledges that it makes "*no adjustments for inflation in [its] accounting practice*". The "*procurement price mechanism*" for materials mentioned by IDC in point 4 of its reply and reproduced in the Panel's question refers only to the fact that IDC converts the prices of imported materials at the exchange rate "*on the day which the materials were imported*". As explained on many occasions, this is irrelevant since it cannot cope with the effect of hyperinflation on the value of raw materials that are not immediately used in the production. Indeed, as from the moment the value of the raw materials is converted into Turkish Lira, e.g. at the date of purchase, this value is "frozen" and will not be adjusted for inflation during any subsequent months until the raw materials concerned are used.

44.   As regards the other costs items, IDC either failed to provide any explanation on whether hyperinflation was taken into account (labour and overhead) or supplied unconvincing and unsubstantiated explanations (depreciation expenses).

---

[5]   See IV-B.6.b)

45.   Accordingly, the Investigating Authority legitimately came to the conclusion that IDC did not demonstrate that the above-captioned cost items adequately reflected hyperinflation.

Q8.   Concerning Icdas, at page 6 of the Final Report, the IA stated that "Icdas ... provided incomplete data and most of the data submitted were not supported by evidence". Further concerning Icdas, at page 22 of the Final Report, the IA stated that "[o]n 23 September 1999, the Department requested a missing document and several documents to be translated into English". At page 23 of the Final Report, the IA stated, "[a]s for Icdas's claim that it 'provided all the necessary information' in response to the Department's 19 August 1999 request, and that the 'remaining items are [sic] timely submitted' in response to the Department's 23 September 1999 request, that is incorrect. In fact, the firm did not furnish (1) the requested breakdown of labour and overhead costs, (2) the requested supporting documents for labour and overhead costs, (3) the requested allocations and allocation methodologies for materials, overhead, and SG&A, and (4) the requested reconciliations of submitted data to its financial statement. In addition, its explanation of how inflation was reflected/included in its costs was inadequate and unsupported". At page 29 of the Final Report, the IA stated that "as described above, Icdas did not provide sufficient information for the investigating authority to confirm the monthly specific costs of materials, labour, or overhead during the period of investigation, despite being requested to do so". Could Egypt please precisely identify the documents containing the IA's requests for the information referred to in the Final Report as not having been submitted. Please describe the documents that were provided by Icdas on these points and indicate how, in the light of those documents, the IA was satisfied that AD Article 6.8 could be applied.

Reply

46.   The documents and explanations regarding Icdas's costs data were requested in the Investigating Authority's letters to Icdas of 19 August 1999 and 23 September 1999, respectively.

47.   The main purpose of the questions was to give Icdas an opportunity to explain whether, contrary to what the submitted data appeared to reveal, such data duly reflected the hyperinflation experienced by Turkey during the investigation period.

48.   The main questions raised in the letter of 19 August 1999 as well as the responses and documentation submitted by Icdas can be described as follows:

> *(a)   Materials*
> "A.   Provide the material inventory ledgers for the subject merchandise showing the raw materials, work in process, and finished goods inventory showing the balance and activity in the accounts for each month during 1998 and an explanation of whether and

how inventory values are adjusted for inflation in ICDAS's accounting records."

49.   Icdas did not provide the inventory ledgers on a monthly basis as requested, but only at year-end 1998 arguing that monthly inventory ledgers are not prepared within the ordinary course of trade.

50.   Icdas furthermore stated that inventory is not adjusted "*with regard to the inflation*".

"B.   Reconcile the total value from the inventory ledgers for the months of January, September, October, November and December, to ICDAS' general ledger and financial statement."

51.   No monthly reconciliation of inventory values was provided. Icdas only supplied a reconciliation of the year-end stock values to the inventory ledger. It was therefore impossible for the Investigating Authority to reconcile the monthly cost of production to the company's records.

52.   Furthermore, no reconciliation to the Financial Statements was provided.

"C.   Provide a copy of all raw material purchase orders placed during the months of January, September, October, November, and December 1998. Provide a copy of the appropriate pages from the payments ledger showing payment for those purchases."

53.   Icdas provided copies of purchase contracts and invoices together with copies of listings which were presented as "payment documentation" for the purchase invoices.

54.   However, the listings were not translated into English and Icdas failed to explain how the payment of the submitted purchase invoices could be verified on the basis of the listings.

55.   Lastly, no data was submitted for December 1998, as requested.

"D.   [Provide] a worksheet reconciling the materials costs that you submitted in your summary to the Investigating Authority to the company's audited financial statement"

56.   Icdas provided a table showing the monthly production volumes of billet and rebar as well as the monthly unit value in Turkish Lira of scrap, electrodes, ferro-alloys, other materials and refractories. Were appended to this table copies of unidentified documents.

57.   If some of the figures reported in the table could be found in the appended documents such as the production figures of billet, Icdas failed to give any description of the submitted documents and, more importantly, Icdas did not supply any explanation on how these documents should be read and interpreted by the Investigating Authority. As a result, it was impossible for the Investigating Authority to perform any kind of verification of the data submitted.

58.   Furthermore, no reconciliation to the Financial Statements was provided.

(b)   Labour

"A.   Explain whether any adjustments have been made in ICDAS' accounting records to recognize the inflation that occurred during this time"

59.   Icdas replied that wages and salaries were allegedly adjusted for inflation on an annual basis and stated that, with respect to the investigation period (January–December 1998), the adjustment was performed in January 1998.

60.   Besides the fact that Icdas did not provide any detail on the adjustment concerned, it should be noted that an adjustment in January evidently cannot account for the hyperinflation occurring in any subsequent month until the end of the year.

61.   Accordingly, the allegation that labour costs data for the investigation period were adjusted for inflation could not be accepted.

"B.   Explain the basis on which labour was allocated to he subject merchandise"

62.   The explanation was provided as requested.

"C.   Reconcile the labour costs reported for January, September, October, November and December 1998 to the general ledger and to the financial statement, and provide supporting documents, including bank statements for those months"

63.   The reconciliation of labour costs was not submitted in Icdas' response of 15 September 1999. Accordingly, the Investigating Authority requested by letter of 23 September 1999 that such reconciliation be submitted within five working days.

64.   The documents received in response to the letter of 23 September 1999 were presented in the same format as the so-called reconciliation of material costs. Thus, Icdas presented a table showing total monthly labour costs and attached copies of extracts from an unidentified ledger. No data was provided for December 1998.

65.   Once again, Icdas failed to provide any narrative explanation on how these documents should be used in order to reconcile the submitted data.

66.   Furthermore, Icdas only provided copies of the relevant ledger but failed to provide a reconciliation to the financial statements, as requested.

67.   Lastly, Icdas failed to submit the requested supporting documents, such as bank statements.

(c)   Overhead

"A.   Explain whether any adjustments have been made to account for the inflation that occurred during this time"

68.   Icdas failed to explain whether any adjustments for inflation were made to the overhead expenses.

"B.   Provide a complete list of all depreciation expenses and reconcile those expenses to the summary which you provided to the Investigating Authority for the months of January through December, 1998"

69.   Instead of supplying monthly depreciation expenses as requested, Icdas supplied one single amount for the full calendar year 1998 and allocated this amount equally to each month of the investigation period.

"C.   Specifically explain whether your recorded depreciation expenses take into account inflation that occurred during this time"

70.   The explanation provided by Icdas was minimal. Indeed, Icdas limited its response to the general statement that "depreciation expenses are calculated over the revalued rates of the fixed assets according to the revaluation rate which is determined annually by the Ministry of Finance according to the inflation rate". Icdas failed however to give any detail on this alleged revaluation. In particular, Icdas did not indicate whether this revaluation was performed at the end of the year or at the beginning of the year, as for labour costs (see above). As a consequence, the Investigating Authority could not accept the claim.

(d)   Conclusions

71.   As demonstrated above, the minimal explanations and insufficient documentary evidence submitted by Icdas in response to the Investigating Authority's letters of 19 August 1999 and 23 September 1999 could not allow the Investigating Authority to verify the accuracy of the costs data submitted by Icdas. In fact, far from presenting a reconciliation of its costs data as requested, Icdas simply submitted copies of voluminous raw documents without any walk-through instructions which would have allowed the Investigating Authority to perform a meaningful verification of the costs data.

72.   Furthermore, Icdas's responses did not contradict but in fact confirmed that its costs data did not reflect the hyperinflation experienced by Turkey in 1998. Icdas's allegations to the contrary can only be considered as disingenuous or, at best, erroneous.

73.   As a consequence, Egypt submits that the Investigating Authority was entitled to use partial facts available with respect to Icdas pursuant to Article 6.8 of the AD Agreement in order to arrive at meaningful determinations.

Q9.   In Egypt's 7 December 2001 response to Question 5 from the Panel, Egypt highlighted how, in its opinion, the *Confidential Injury Analysis* demonstrates that the injury analysis was thorough and covered all factors listed in Article 3.4. Could Egypt please indicate where the analysis of each factor is reflected in the Essential Facts and Conclusions and/or Final Reports.

Reply

74.   The Panel has asked Egypt to indicate "*where*" in the *Essential Facts & Conclusions Report* and the *Final Report* the analysis of each factor listed under

Article 3.4 is reflected. We would like to refer the Panel to the table provided in Question 5 of Egypt's 7 December 2001 response to the Panel, which has been reproduced for ease of reference below:

Economic Factor/Indices	EFCR	FR
Sales	Section 2.4.1 Section 4.3.1 Section 4.5.2 Section 4.5.4	Section 2.4.1 Section 4.3.1 Section 4.6.2 Section 4.6.4
Profits	Section 4.3.5 Section 4.5.2 Section 4.5.4	Section 4.3.5 Section 4.6.2 Section 4.6.4
Output	Section 2.4.2 Section 4.3.2	Section 2.4.2 Section 4.3.2
Market Share	Section 2.4.1 Section 4.3.4 Section 4.5.4	Section 2.4.1 Section 4.3.4 Section 4.6.4
Return on investments	Section 4.3.7 Section 4.5.2	Section 4.3.7 Section 4.6.2
Capacity utilization	Section 4.3.6	Section 4.3.6
Prices	Section 4.2.1.2 Section 4.2.2.1 Section 4.5.1 Section 4.5.2 Section 4.5.3 Section 4.5.4	Section 4.2.1.2 Section 4.2.2.1 Section 4.6.1 Section 4.6.2 Section 4.6.3 Section 4.6.4
Dumping margin	Section 3.3	Section 3.3 Section 4.4 Section 4.6.2
Inventories	Section 4.3.3 Section 4.5.2	Section 4.3.3 Section 4.6.2

EFCR = Essential Facts & Conclusions Report

FR = Final Report

75. It may be the case that the Panel considers that the *Confidential Injury Analysis* is not fully reflected in the *Essential Facts & Conclusions Report* and/or the *Final Report*. However, we repeat that whether all of the Investigating Authority's conclusions on material injury are reproduced in these reports is not an issue that is before the Panel. A claim under Article 12.2 was not introduced in the Request for the Establishment of a Panel and accordingly, is not within the Panel's Terms of Reference.

76. What is relevant, however, is whether the Investigating Authority's examination under Article 3.4 was complete. Accordingly, we wish to direct the Panel's attention Question 3 of the "Questions to Both Parties" below.

Q10. In respect of each of the five respondents (Habas, Diler, Colakoglu, Icdas and IDC), the Investigating Authority stated in the Final Report that "[t]he Investigating Authority did not offset this interest expense by interest revenue, as the Investigating Authority does not consider interest revenue as sufficiently related to production to be includable in the calculation of con-

structed value". **Where in the record can the basis for this conclusion be found in respect of each of these companies? That is, what information and considerations were relied upon in the Investigating Authority's analysis on this point for each?**

Reply

77.   The determination that interest revenue was not found to be sufficiently related to production was based on the treatment of this income as a non-operating income by the auditors of the companies concerned and/or on the extraordinary nature of this income in comparison to previous years.

(a)   Icdas

78.   First, the interest income was reported after the calculation of the operating profit or loss and could therefore not be considered as related to production or sales activities. Second, it was apparent from the amount of interest income of 1998 that such interest income could not reasonably be related to production or sales activities. Indeed, according to the "Detailed Statement of Income" of Icdas, the amount of interest income for 1998 was as high as 1,022,244 million Turkish Lira for a total turnover of 80,561,205 million Turkish Lira and a total cost of sales of 74,529,114 million Turkish Lira. By contrast, in 1997, interest income amounted to only 13,728 million Lira while the total turnover and costs of sales amounted to 44,072,138 million and 38,722,381 million Turkish Lira, respectively.

79.   The above figures show beyond any doubt that the amount of interest income in 1998 is in no way related to production or sale activities but represents rather an extraordinary income. Should the interest income be related to production or sale, then the ratio between interest income on the one hand and turnover/cost of sales on the other hand would not vary so significantly from one year to the next.

(b)   Habas

80.   The interest income of Habas was reported as a non-operating income in the company's Income Statement and, accordingly, was considered by the Investigating Authority as not being sufficiently related to production or sale activities.

(c)   Colakoglu

81.   The interest income of Colakoglu was also reported as a non-operating income in the Income Statement (i.e. it was reported after the calculation of the operating profit or losses of the company). Furthermore, the absence of any relationship to production and sale was underlined by the fact that the interest income in 1998 was almost 6 times higher than in 1997 while, in the same period of time, gross sales had increased by approximately 50 per cent only.

(d)   Diler

82.   The interest income of Diler was reported as a non-operating income in the Income Statement of the company (i.e. it was reported after the calculation of the operational profit or losses of the company). Accordingly, such income was not considered to be sufficiently related to production activities.

(e)   IDC

83.   The interest income of IDC was reported as a non-operating income in the Income Statement of the company (i.e. it was reported after the calculation of the operating profit or losses of the company). Accordingly, such income was not considered to be sufficiently related to production activities.

* * *

84.   In view of the foregoing considerations, Egypt submits that the Investigating Authority was entitled to reject interest income from the calculation of the construction normal value since the evidence on the record indicated that such income was not sufficiently related to production activities. It should be noted that no respondent provided any evidence to the contrary.

85.   As explained in Egypt's First Written Submission and subsequent submissions, the Investigating Authority's actions in this regard are in line with the practice of other major jurisdictions such as the European Communities and the USA.

Q11.   Could Egypt please provide a copy of the following documents:

-    **letter dated 26 August 1999 from the Investigating Authority to all of the respondents granting the 14-day extension for responses to the letters of 19 August 1999 (the granting of the extension is referred to at page 35 of the First Written Submission of Turkey);**

-    **letter dated 23 September 1999 from the Investigating Authority to Icdas;**

-    **Annexes to IDC's 9 September 1999 submission (Exh TUR-29)**

Reply

(a)   Letter dated 26 August 1999 to all respondents

-    Icdas: EX-EGT-14.1

-    IDC: EX-EGT-14.2

-    Counsel to Diler, Colakoglu and Habas: EX-EGT-14.3

(b)   Letter dated 23 September 1999 from the Investigating Authority to Icdas

-    EX-EGT-13.2.2

(c)   Annexes to IDC's 9 September 1999 submissions

-    EX-EGT-15

QUESTIONS POSED BY THE PANEL TO BOTH PARTIES

Q1. In paragraph 3 of the Request for Establishment of the Panel, four factors are specified by Turkey as being grounds for a breach of the cited Articles. However, in the submissions made by Turkey, it is arguable that other grounds are added. In the view of the parties, is it permissible:

    (a)   to use an inclusive expression when listing grounds for an alleged breach in a request for establishment; and

    (b)   where a list of grounds is included in a request for establishment, to add another or other grounds in submissions:

        (i)   where the list is said to be inclusive; and

        (ii)   where the list is not said to be inclusive?

Reply

(a)   Egypt considers that, while it is permissible to use an inclusive expression when listing grounds for an alleged breach in a request for the establishment of a panel, the list of factors contained therein should be as exhaustive as possible. The DSU does not impose any time limits as to when the request for establishment of a panel must be submitted once consultations are formally initiated. Accordingly, the complainant has ample opportunity to identify the specific measure at issue and the

relevant legal basis of the complaint.

(b.i)   Where the list of grounds is said to be inclusive, Egypt considers that it is permissible to add additional grounds in submissions on the condition that the legal basis of those grounds is clearly identified in connection with each treaty article in the request for the establishment of a panel. Moreover, the complainant must be able to explain why these grounds were not included in the panel request if the information on which the grounds are based is not new to the complainant. Lastly, the respondent must be granted adequate opportunity in which to prepare a defence.

(b.ii)   Where the list of grounds is not said to be inclusive, Egypt considers that it is not permissible to add additional grounds in submissions, unless new facts come to light during the course of the proceeding that were not previously available to the complainant. In this latter situation, Egypt considers that it is permissible to add other grounds to a non-inclusive list, provided that the complainant can demonstrate that these grounds are relevant to the legal basis of its claim and that the respondent is granted adequate opportunity in which to prepare a defence.

Q2. Could the parties please comment, in the light of Article 31 of the Vienna Convention on the Law of Treaties, on the meaning of the phrases:

    (a)   "special circumspection" in Annex II, paragraph 7; and

    (b)   "to the best of its ability" in Annex II, paragraph 5.

Reply

86.   Egypt considers that the following interpretations are in accordance with the ordinary meaning to be given to the terms of the provisions in their context and in light of their object and purpose under the AD Agreement.

(a)   The meaning of "special circumspection"

87.   As a preliminary remark, it should be noted that Annex II, paragraph 7 contemplates circumstances in which the Investigating Authority must use information from a *secondary* source, as opposed to information obtained from the respondents concerned. Accordingly, as explained in Egypt's First Written Submission, this provision does not apply to the rebar investigation since all dumping findings were made on the basis of the data submitted by the respondents, with the sole exception of the hyperinflation rate which was based on official statistics and the data on scrap prices which were obtained from another respondent that furnished supporting evidence (see reply to Question 2 to Egypt).

88.   In Egypt's view, the use of the terms "*special circumspection*" indicates that the Investigating Authority should resort to information from secondary sources *only* to the extent strictly necessary to fill the gaps in the information obtained from the respondents concerned, i.e. from the primary source. The terms also indicate that the Investigating Authority should carefully check the information used as facts available with other information that the Investigating Authority has at its disposal from other sources. In the rebar investigation, the only information coming from a secondary source was the monthly hyperinflation rate of 5 per cent. As explained previously (see, e.g., Egypt's reply to Question 4), this rate was calculated on the basis of the average yearly inflation rate for wholesale and for retail reported by the State Institute of Statistics of the Republic of Turkey.

(b)   The meaning of "to the best of its ability"

89.   Egypt considers that the terms "*to the best of its ability*" in Annex II, paragraph 5, qualifies the level of cooperation that an Investigating Authority may legitimately expect from respondents in an anti-dumping investigation. In particular, the word "best" indicates that the level of cooperation must be very high.

90.   Thus, Egypt considers that respondents are expected to provide within a reasonable period of time all information required by the Investigating Authority which is at the immediate disposal of the respondents concerned or can be obtained by them without undue difficulty.

91.   Thus, a respondent cannot be considered to have acted "*to the best of its ability*" if it does not submit copies of its own records and meaningful explanations on how these records were prepared. On the other hand, Egypt recognizes that a respondent may encounter more difficulties in complying with an Investigating Authority's request if the data requested by the Investigating Authority

have to be obtained from a source upon which the respondent has no or little control. In such case, the Investigating Authority should take into account the specific circumstances of the respondents, without prejudice, however, to its right to resort to "fact available" if meaningful data are not obtained from the respondents in order to reach accurate determinations. The fact that some respondents provide all the documents requested while others do not is already an indication that, all other things being equal, the failing respondents do not act to the best of their ability.

92.   In the rebar investigation, the requests for additional information and explanations exclusively concerned the respondents' own records and data. Accordingly, the Investigating Authority was entitled to expect full and complete answers to its questions. Failure to submit full and complete answers indicates that the respondents concerned did not act to the *best of their ability* within the meaning of Annex II, paragraph 5.

Q3.   Do you consider that the BCI submission of Egypt (*Confidential Injury Analysis*), by itself, constitutes an "evaluation" of the factors that it covers, in the sense of Article 3.4? Please cite any relevant legal authority and/or precedent.

Reply

93.   Egypt considers that the *Confidential Injury Analysis* demonstrates that the injury analysis was thorough and covered all the factors listed in Article 3.4. The *Confidential Injury Analysis* is the set of findings upon which the Investigating Authority based its final determination of injury, the central points of which are reflected in the *Final Report*.

94.   It is clear from the *Confidential Injury Analysis* that a substantial amount of data was requested and collected for the Article 3.4 factors listed therein. The data was compiled individually for each domestic producer and for the entire domestic industry. Each factor was analysed separately for each individual domestic producer and for the entire domestic industry and set in a table format so as to enable the Investigating Authority to compare the trends and review the situation of the domestic industry as a whole from 1996 to Q1 1999. The Investigating Authority was therefore able to examine the data in context, and assess its internal evolution and *vis-à-vis* the other factors examined. Accordingly, the Investigating Authority was able to determine which of the factors had a bearing on the state of the industry. The *Confidential Injury Analysis* therefore constitutes an evaluation of the factors that it covers in the sense of Article 3.4.

95.   Egypt submits that this approach is consistent with the findings of the Panel in *United States – Hot-Rolled Steel from Japan*.[6] In that case, the Investigating Authority analysed all relevant economic factors having a bearing on the state of the industry on the basis of data covering a three-year period and discussed the trends at various instances in its *Final Report*[7], which is similar to the

---

[6]   WT/DS184/4, at para. 7.232.
[7]   *Ibid.*, at paras. 7.226 – 7.227.

approach adopted by the Egyptian Investigating Authority in the rebar investigation.

96.   In *United States – Hot-Rolled Steel*, the question before the Panel was whether the Investigating Authority failed to sufficiently evaluate certain factors by failing to discuss and to compare particular data over a specified period.[8] Similarly, in the present dispute before this Panel, Turkey alleges that the Investigating Authority failed to take into account certain trends in the data and it is on this basis that Turkey concludes that the examination of the IA was not based on positive evidence. However, as noted by the Panel in *United States – Hot-Rolled Steel*, a proper evaluation is dynamic in nature and takes into account changes in the market that determine the current state of the industry – the fact that the Investigating Authority did not explicitly address certain trends should not undermine the adequacy of its evaluation with respect thereto.[9] Accordingly, the evaluation was upheld by the Panel.

97.   Moreover, the Panel in United States – Hot-Rolled Steel made very clear that it is indeed "another question whether the evaluation and the conclusion with regard to these factors is supported by the facts".[10] What is important in this respect is to keep in mind that the Panel is bound in its analysis by the standard of review set forth in Article 17.6 of the AD Agreement.[11]

Q4.   Could the parties please comment, in the light of the Vienna Convention on the Law of Treaties, on the Appellate Body's ruling in *United States – Hot-rolled Steel*, (at paragraphs 101 and 102)[12] concerning Annex II, paragraphs 2 and 5.

Reply

98.   The Appellate Body's ruling in *United States - Hot-rolled Steel* concerning Annex II, paragraphs 2 and 5 was reached in the context of the US Administration's decision to apply "*adverse*" facts available to one of the Japanese respondents, namely KSC, on the grounds that KSC had not sufficiently cooperated with the US Administration in the course of the domestic investigation. The issue before the DSB was whether the quality of cooperation offered by KSC during the investigation entitled the US Administration to seek to arrive at unfavourable results.

99.   The questions that the DSB needed to examine were twofold: (1) the meaning of the term "*cooperation*" and (2) the efforts that an Investigating Authority may legitimately expect from respondents in the course of an investigation.

100.   Thus, the Appellate Body noted that "cooperation is a process, involving joint effort, whereby parties work together towards a common goal. In that re-

---

[8]   *Ibid.*, at paras. 7.228 – 7.231.
[9]   *Ibid.*, at para. 7.234.
[10]   *Ibid.*, at para. 7.235.
[11]   *Ibid.*
[12]   WT/DS184/AB/R, DSR 2001:X, 4697.

spect, we note that parties may very well "cooperate" to a high degree, even though the requested information is, ultimately, not obtained".[13]

101.   Examining the level of cooperation expected from respondents, the Appellate Body noted that the provisions of Annex II, paragraph 5 "*suggest[s] to us that the level of cooperation required of interested parties is a high one – interested parties must act to the "best" of their abilities*"[14], although an Investigating Authority should not impose an "*unreasonable extra burden*" upon the respondents. On this basis the Appellate Body concluded that "[paragraph 2 of Annex II] *requires investigating authorities to strike a balance between the effort that they can expect interested parties to make in responding to questionnaires, and the practical ability of those interested parties to comply fully with all demands made of them by the investigating authorities*". *In order to complete their investigations, investigating authorities are entitled to expect a very significant degree of effort – to the "best of their abilities" – from investigated exporters. At the same time, however, the investigating authorities are not entitled to insist upon absolute standards or impose unreasonable burdens upon those exporters*".[15]

102.   Applying the above principles to the case at hand, the Appellate Body upheld the Panel's findings that KSC had acted to the best of its ability in trying to obtain the data requested by the US Administration and that, therefore, the Investigating Authority was not entitled, when resorting to facts available, to seek to reach intentionally an adverse outcome.

103.   The exact scope of the above ruling must be understood well. Contrary to Turkey's interpretation, it was not held in *United States – Hot-rolled Steel* that the use of facts available is not warranted when a company acts to the best of its ability. To the contrary, the Appellate Body specifically stated that cooperation does not necessarily result in obtaining the information requested. In such case, as held by the Panel, the use of facts available is fully justified. Thus, the Panel stated that "*[i]t is undisputed in this case that KSC did not provide the requested information regarding resale prices and further manufacturing costs with respect to its sales through its affiliate CSI. Thus, it appears that USDOC was justified in deciding to apply facts available with respect to the information not provided by KSC concerning CSI's further manufacturing costs, as this necessary information was not provided within a reasonable period.*"(emphasis added).[16]

104.   Conversely, according to the DSB, the use of "*unfavourable*" facts available is only permissible when the respondent fails in its duty to cooperate within the meaning of the AD Agreement.

105.   In conclusion, *United States – Hot-rolled Steel* confirms that the use of facts available is legitimate also in case of full cooperation by the respondents if the information provided is not sufficient to reach meaningful findings.

---

[13]   WT/DS184/AB/R, DSR 2001:X, 4697, para. 99.
[14]   *Ibid.*, at para. 100 – emphasis added.
[15]   *Ibid.*, at paras. 101-102.
[16]   WT/DS184/R, DSR 2001:X, 4769, para. 7.69.

QUESTIONS POSED BY TURKEY TO EGYPT

Q1. Egypt claims that the "another respondent" who submitted scrap costs that were reviewed by the Investigating Authority as mentioned in the Final Report was Alexandria National. We understand, however, that Alexandria National uses the direct reduction iron (DRI) method of steelmaking, which uses iron pellets as the raw material, and that Alexandria National does not use an electric arc furnace (EAF) to melt steel scrap. Please comment on whether this understanding is correct and, if so, what is the nature and relevance of the scrap price data submitted by Alexandria National?

Reply

106.   Contrary to Turkey's understanding, Alexandria National Steel uses both the DRI method for steelmaking and the electric arc furnace method for melting scrap.

Q2. Please identify the period over which the inflation figures supplied in your oral response to Panel Question Number 4 were calculated.

107.   The period over which the inflation figures were calculated is the calendar year 1998.

ANNEX 8-3

RESPONSE OF EGYPT TO FOLLOW-UP QUESTIONS POSED BY THE PANEL, AND COMMENTS BY TURKEY ON EGYPT'S RESPONSE

B. **RESPONSE OF EGYPT TO PANEL'S FOLLOW-UP QUESTIONS**

Question 1

Could Egypt please explain the context in which Alexandria National provided the scrap price data in its fax to the IA dated 15 September 1999 (Exhibit EGT-12). In particular, was this information provided in response to a request from the IA? If so, please furnish a copy of that request. If not, please explain Alexandria National's having provided the information.

Response

1.   The scrap prices data in Exh. EGT-12 were provided by Alexandria National further to a request made by the Investigating Authority upon receipt of the claim by Turkish respondents that scrap prices would have collapsed throughout the investigation period. In order to verify the veracity of this factual claim, the Investigating Authority asked the Egyptian industry to supply information on the evolution of scrap prices on a monthly basis for 1998. This request was made by telephone.

Question 2

Could Egypt please provide the calculations showing exactly how each of the monthly scrap prices for 1998, shown in the first page of EGT-12, were derived from the "source reference" in the second page of EGT-12, and could Egypt explain why the methodology employed was chosen.

Response

2.   The prices indicated on the first page of Exh. EGT-12 were computed by Alexandria National, and not by the Investigating Authority. This matter is, in any case, irrelevant. Indeed, the Investigating Authority's assessment of the evolution of scrap prices was based on the "source reference" in the second page of Exh. EGT-12, and not on the prices mentioned on the cover page of Alexandria National. The evidence submitted by Alexandria National revealed that the Turkish respondents' claim that scrap prices would have collapsed throughout the investigation period was factually wrong. Indeed, as explained in the *Final Report*, scrap prices were found to be fairly constant for the first seven months of the investigation period. During the next three months, prices collapsed. Then, prices started to recover in the last two months of the investigation period. In

other words, the "sharp decline" was in fact limited to three out of twelve months.

3.   Incidentally, Egypt wishes to stress that the Investigating Authority's assessment of the evolution of scrap prices during the investigation period on the basis of the information provided by Alexandria National is in line with the trends showed in the documents submitted by Turkey in Exh. TUR-13 and Exh. TUR-14. Indeed, those documents, which were submitted for the first time by Turkey in the course of the current dispute, show that the scrap prices were relatively stable during the first seven months of 1998, and then, collapsed for a period of approximately three months.

4.   Lastly, it is important to note that, contrary to Turkey's contentions, the scrap prices submitted by Alexandria National were *not* used to calculate the normal value of the Turkish respondents. This information was used for the *sole* purpose of verifying the accuracy of the claim made by the Turkish respondents regarding the decrease of scrap prices during the investigation period. Conversely, the material costs used for the calculation of the normal value of the Turkish respondents were based *exclusively* on the costs data submitted by each respective respondent.

5.   Egypt considers that the Investigating Authority's actions are in full compliance with the WTO Anti-Dumping Agreement and, in particular, with paragraph 7 of Annex II thereof.

* * *

C.   COMMENTS OF TURKEY ON EGYPT'S RESPONSE TO CERTAIN QUESTIONS POSED BY THE PANEL

1.   Egypt states in its April 5, 2002 response to a panel question that the scrap data it used for its final determination appears on page two of EX-EGT-12. Egypt then states that this data on the "evolution of scrap prices during the investigation period ... is in line with the trends showed in the documents submitted by Turkey in EX-TUR-13 and EX-TUR-14." We agree that the scrap prices on page two of EX-EGT-12 are in line with the data in EX-TUR-13 and EX-TUR-14. In fact, the prices shown on the Egyptian Exhibit in question for HMS 1&2 scrap are precisely the same as the scrap prices provided in EX-TUR-14 – as they should be since they are both from the same source, *Metal Bulletin*.[1]

2.   Where we disagree is with Egypt's statement that "those documents" – a reference to EX-TUR-13 and EX-TUR-14 – "show that the scrap prices were relatively stable in the first seven months of 1998 and, then collapsed for a period of approximately three months." As the panel can plainly see by a review of EX-TUR-13 and EX-TUR-14, as well as the second page of EX-EGT-12, HMS

---

[1]   Since EX-TUR-14 is merely a graphical representation of the data that Egypt acknowledges was presented to the IA during the original investigation, the Panel should not disregard EX-TUR-14 for the reasons that Egypt set forth earlier in this proceeding. Specifically, the Panel is not barred from considering this data under Article 17.5(b) of the Agreement.

1&2 scrap prices declined steeply between January 1998 ($114 – 116 per ton) and April 1998 ($96-$97 per ton) and continued their decline into July 1998 (to $92-94 per ton). This is an overall decline of 19%, hardly evidence of scrap price stability during the first seven months of the year.[2] Certainly, these data, which Egypt now acknowledges the IA had before it when it rendered its Final Determination, do not support the factual finding in the Final Report that "[f]or the first seven months of the period," scrap prices "were fairly constant and did not decline to any noticeable extent." Final Report at 12. That finding is patently incorrect. Moreover, the data on these charts do not support the conclusion that the sharp decline in scrap prices was limited to three months out of the twelve month period. While there was an additional decline between July and October of some $35 per ton, or an additional 30% as compared to January, contrary to the impression given in the Final Report, the decline during the latter three-month period was only 3/5 of the total decline between January and October. There certainly were significant declines that took place earlier in the year.

3.   The significance of these declines must be examined in terms of the issue being considered by the Investigating Authority (IA). The IA was specifically responding to a claim by respondents that the decline in stable currency scrap prices offset the effects of the inflation and devaluation in the Turkish economy such that their costs in Turkish lira were not increasing with the inflation rate. In this context, a decline in constant currency costs of 19-20% for the first seven months of the period of investigation is very significant indeed, and it directly undermines the IA's finding that scrap costs should have increased by 5% per month over this period. In addition, as we pointed out earlier, most sales of rebar to Egypt took place in the second half of 2001 when the scrap price declines had their most significant impact on rebar costs of production. During this period, scrap prices were up to 44% below January 1998 levels, or by more than the intervening inflation rate.

4.   Finally, we never claimed, as Egypt contends, that the scrap price data purportedly submitted by Alexandria National was used by the IA to calculate respondents' cost of production. We acknowledged that the IA used respondents' data; however, we claimed that that data was based, in at least some instances, on scrap costs in January for comparison with selling prices in the second half of 2001, when scrap prices were demonstrably much lower.

---

[2]   Scrap prices for HMS 1 show similar declines – from $123-$124 per ton in January 1998 to $105-$107 per ton in April 1998 and $98-99 in July (an overall decline of 20%). Prices then dropped from August to October ($70-$72 per ton) or a further decline of 23% from January levels. Note that the decline in August to October is not that much greater, in percentage terms, than the decline that took place earlier in the year.

ANNEX 9

THIRD PARTY ORAL STATEMENT OF CHILE

1.   Thank you Mr. Chairman and members of the Panel.

2.   We appreciate your giving us the opportunity to express our views in this dispute. As we stated in our letter on 1 November, we did not present any written submission but we wanted to reserve our rights to raise some points during this hearing.

3.   Chile has no commercial interest in this case but strong systemic concerns, resulting from the alarming increase in the use of anti-dumping measures among WTO members. Especially when these measures are applied in an arbitrary way that, in our view, give grounds to the conclusion that the final intention is to keep out imports and protect uncompetitive local industries.

4.   The way some national laws and practices interpret and apply the provisions of Article VI of GATT 94 and the Anti-Dumping Agreement clearly go beyond the true meaning, scope, spirit and text of those multilateral provisions. These rules provide for remedy in exceptional cases when real and effective injury occurs and when the specific conditions laid down in the AD Agreement are fulfilled.

5.   Therefore, it is the duty of Panels to confirm - by rejecting unfounded interpretations and practices - the principles of transparency and fairness on which the WTO Agreements are based. Guaranteeing that the multilaterally agreed principles and rules will be fully respected and, in particular, that the disciplines of the AD Agreement will be strictly observed.

6.   Thank you.

ANNEX 10-1

THIRD PARTY WRITTEN SUBMISSION
OF THE EUROPEAN COMMUNITIES

I.   INTRODUCTION

1.   The European Communities welcomes this opportunity to present its views in the proceeding brought by Turkey concerning the consistency with Article X of the General Agreement on Tariffs and Trade (hereafter "GATT 1994"), and with Articles 2, 3, 6 and Annexes I and II of the Agreement on Implementation of Article VI of the GATT (hereafter the "Anti-Dumping Agreement") of the definitive anti-dumping duties imposed by Egypt on Steel Rebar originating in Turkey.

2.   The European Communities has decided to intervene as third party in this case because of its systemic interest in the correct interpretation of the Anti-Dumping Agreement. Many of the issues in dispute relate to questions of fact on which the European Communities is not in a position to comment. Accordingly, the European Communities will limit its submission to a number of issues of legal interpretation which are of particular interest to the European Communities. Indeed, given that some of the underlying factual situations remain unclear, the European Communities remains at the Panel's disposition should it be interested in the views of the European Communities on issues which emerge at a later stage and which have not been addressed in the present submission.

3.   The European Communities shall set out below a number of comments on three aspects of the dispute brought before the Panel. In turn, the European Communities will examine 1) the range of evidence which the Panel is entitled to examine; 2) issues relating to the determination of injury and causal link, and 3) issues relating to the determination of dumping.

II.   THE RANGE OF EVIDENCE WHICH THE PANEL IS ENTITLED TO EXAMINE

4.   Egypt has argued that Turkey has placed evidence before the Panel which was not placed before the investigating authority. The European Communities understand that while the specific evidence before the Panel was not brought to the attention of the investigating authority, the underlying arguments on causal link were made before the investigating authority. Turkey argues that Egypt failed to prove, on the basis of positive evidence, the existence of a causal link between dumping and injury.[1] Egypt considers that the Panel should regard as inadmissible all evidence submitted to it which was not made available to the

---

[1]   Turkey – First Written Submission, 27 September 2001, page 6 *et seq.*

Investigating Authority. Egypt bases this argument on Article 17.6(i) of the Agreement and on requirements of "due process".[2]

5.   However, Article 17.6(i) does not direct a Panel to consider inadmissible any evidence which was not before the investigating authority. Rather it directs the Panel to "verify whether the authorities establishment of the facts was proper and whether their evaluation of those facts was unbiased and objective". As the Appellate Body has pointed out:

> [Article 17.6(i)], at the same time, in effect defines when investigating authorities can be considered to have acted inconsistently with the Anti-Dumping Agreement in the course of their "establishment" and "evaluation" of the relevant facts.[3]

6.   It may thus be the case that a panel could be asked whether the exclusion of certain evidence from a domestic procedure was consistent with an investigating authority's obligation to establish the facts in a "proper" manner. In such an event a panel may be confronted with evidence which was not before the investigating authority, and may need to take such evidence into consideration to examine whether the investigating authority has "properly" established the facts.

7.   Article 17.5(ii) is also relevant in this regard. If it is alleged that an investigating authority did not examine a particular issue, through excluding it from the domestic procedure, then the record of "the facts made available in conformity with appropriate domestic procedure" will shed light on the investigating authority's examination of this issue.

8.   However, as already noted, the European Communities understands that Turkey is not alleging that Egypt improperly excluded evidence from the domestic record. Rather, Turkey alleges that by failing to base itself on "positive evidence" in conformity with Article 3.1 Egypt did not properly establish the facts or did not make an unbiased an objective evaluation of those facts. In such an event, Article 17(5)(ii) directs a Panel to consider facts made available in conformity with the appropriate domestic procedures. In so doing the Panel should look to see whether facts made available were not taken into consideration and also whether all appropriate steps have been taken to establish the necessary facts.

III.   THE DETERMINATION OF INURY AND CAUSAL LINK

A.   Article 3.5 of the Agreement

9.   Egypt points out that the list of factors to be examined in the last sentence of Article 3.5 is an illustrative rather than mandatory list. This conclusion has

---

[2]   Egypt – First Written Submission, 24 October 2001, page 28.

[3]   Appellate Body Report, , United States – Anti-Dumping Measures on Certain Hot-Rolled Steel Products from Japan, WT/DS184/AB/R, adopted 23 August 2001, DSR 2001:X, 4697, para. 56.

also been reached by the Panel in *US-Hot Rolled Steel.*[4] The European Communities does not disagree with this interpretation, but notes that Article 3.5 imposes an obligation on the investigating authority to "examine any known factors other than the dumped imports which at the same time are injuring the domestic industry". The list in the final sentence suggests a number of factors which may be relevant in conducting this examination. It is, however, of crucial importance to determine what is understood by "known factors". The European Communities considers, in the first place, that such factors would be those brought to the attention of the investigating authority by the interested parties in the domestic procedure. However, there may be circumstances where an interested party can raise other factors but cannot itself prove conclusively that other factors are causing injury. In such circumstances, the European Communities would consider that that such factors would be "known" to the investigating authority in the sense of Article 3.5, and should therefore be examined. Indeed, the Appellate Body, when considering Article 4(2)(a) of the Agreement on Safeguards (which also deals with the investigation of causal link) has stated:

> *[the central role played by interested parties in the investigation] does not mean that the competent authorities may limit their evaluation of "all relevant factors", under Article 4(2)(a) of the Agreement on Safeguards, to the factors which the interested parties have raised as relevant. The competent authorities must, in every case, carry out a full investigation to enable them to conduct a proper evaluation of all of the relevant factors expressly mentioned in Article 4(2)(a) of the Agreement on Safeguards. Moreover, Article 4(2)(a) requires the competent authorities – and not the interested parties – to evaluate fully the relevance, if any, of "other factors". If the competent authorities consider that a particular "other factor" may be relevant to the situation of the domestic industry, under Article 4(2)(a), their duties of investigation and evaluation preclude them from remaining passive in the face of possible shortcomings in the evidence submitted, and views expressed, by the interested parties. In such cases, where the competent authorities do not have sufficient information before them to evaluate the possible relevance of such an "other factor", they must investigate fully that "other factor", so that they can fulfil their obligations of evaluation under Article 4(2)(a).*[5] *(emphasis in original)*

10.   Thus, the European Communities consider that where the investigating authority knows of the existence of other factors which may be causing injury it

---

[4]   Panel report, *United States – Anti-Dumping Measures on Certain Hot-Rolled Steel Products from Japan*, WT/DS184/R, adopted 23 August 2001, as modified by the Appellate Body Report, WT/DS184/AB/R, DSR 2001:X, 4769, para. 7.247

[5]   Appellate Body Report, United States – Definitive Safeguard Measures on Import of Wheat Gluten from the European Communities ("United States – Wheat Gluten Safeguards"), WT/DS166/AB/R, adopted 19 January 2001, DSR 2001:II, 717, para. 55

is under an obligation to fully investigate any such factor. It cannot fail to react in the face of limitations on the information presented to it by interested parties, where it has the means to investigate further.

B. Determination of the Investigation Period for Dumping and Injury

11.   Turkey has argued that the period of the injury determination must coincide with the period of the dumping determination.[6] The European Communities does not understand Turkey as suggesting that the two periods of investigation should be the same length. The requirements set down in the Anti-Dumping Agreement on injury assessment logically require that the injury investigation period include a substantial period preceding the investigation period for dumping, in order to allow an evaluation of the trends affecting the domestic industry over a number of years. The European Communities rather understands Turkey as suggesting that a difference in the periods of investigation may lead to injury being found where there is no causal link to dumping, and that such a situation would be inconsistent with the Anti-Dumping Agreement.

12.   The European Communities notes first of all that the Anti-Dumping Agreement does not establish any particular period of investigation, either for dumping or for injury. In any particular case, various factual considerations may require a particular investigation period. On the other hand, there can be no doubt that the Agreement sets in place an overarching substantive obligation; *viz.* that anti-dumping duties can only be imposed where a causal link between dumped imports and injury has been established, in accordance with Articles 3.1 and 3.5. It is noted that the Panel in *EC -Bed Linen* found that the injury assessment should be made for all imports originating in a country from which it has been determined that dumping has occurred and that it was not necessary to assess the injurious impact of only those individual imports which had been found to be dumped.[7]

13.   Thus, as a matter of substance, in order to prove a causal link, it is likely that the period of investigation for injury must be broadly contemporaneous with the period of investigation for dumping, and will, in most cases be considerably longer.[8] As the injurious effects of dumping may only be apparent some time

---

[6]   Turkey – First Written Submission. page 24.

[7]   Panel Report, *European Communities – Anti-Dumping Duties on Imports of Cotton-type Bedlinen from India ("European Communities – Bedlinen")*, WT/DS141/R, adopted 12 March 2001, as modified by the Appellate Body Report, WT/DS141/AB/R, DSR 2001:VI, 2077, para. 6.132 to 6.142.

[8]   It is noted that the Committee on Anti-Dumping Practices recommended that the investigation period for injury "should include the entirety of the period of data collection for the dumping investigation". This recommendation has been considered to be non-binding. See Panel Report, *Guatemala – Definitive Anti-Dumping Measures on Portland Cement from Mexico ("Guatemala – Cement II")*, WT/DS156/R, adopted 17 November 2000, DSR 2000:XI, 5295, para. 8.266 and footnote 868 thereof, and Panel report, *United States – Anti-Dumping Measures on Certain Hot-Rolled Steel Products from Japan, ("United States – Hot Rolled Steel")* WT/DS184/R, adopted 23 August 2001,

after the dumping itself has taken place it would be an unwarranted limitation on the investigatory powers of a domestic authority to prevent the period of investigation for injury lasting longer than that for dumping. In any event, irrespective of the length and the extent of overlap of the periods of investigation, it would be inconsistent with Articles 3.1 and 3.3 were a Member to impose anti-dumping duties had it not found, in the respective investigation periods, evidence of dumping, injury and a causal link.

IV. THE DETERMINATION OF DUMPING

A. Applicable Time-Limits for Requests for Further Information

14. Turkey argues that Egypt's requests for further information after the on-the-spot verification were in violation of Turkey's rights under Articles 6.1, 6.1.1 of the Anti-Dumping Agreement and Annex II, paragraphs 1 and 6 thereof.[9] Turkey argues, in particular, that the time limits granted for responses to requests for further information did not allow the exporters "ample opportunity" to present all evidence, in conformity with Article 6.1 and that Egypt had not specified in detail the information it required as it should have done under paragraph 1 of Annex II. Turkey also argues that Egypt should have applied the time limit set down in Article 6.1.1 to its requests for further information.

15. The European Communities takes issue with Turkey's suggestion that the deadlines set down in Article 6.1.1 should apply to requests for further information. Such a suggestion would inhibit the ability of Members to conduct an in-depth investigation consistent with the requirements set out in Article 6.6 and within the time limits for the conduct of investigations set out in Article 5.10.

16. Turkey's suggestion is, moreover, not supported in law. Article 6.1.1 refers to "questionnaires used in an anti-dumping investigation". From its context, it is apparent that this refers to questionnaires issued at the initiation of an investigation. Thus, Article 6.1.3 refers to the obligation to send to known exporters the written application for an investigation. Furthermore, paragraph 7 of Annex I refers to "the questionnaire" in the singular (*"[i]t should be carried out after the response to the questionnaire has been received"*).

17. Indeed, the Anti-Dumping Agreement makes several references to the possibility to obtain "further information" without imposing an express time limit on such a request. For instance, Article 6.7 provides that on-the-spot verifications may be used to "obtain further details". Article 6.6 requires authorities to satisfy themselves as to the accuracy of information supplied, clearly implying that further questions may be posed. Additionally, in a slightly different context, paragraph 6 of Annex II requires an authority to inform an interested party of the reasons for rejecting information and obliges it to give a "a reasonable period"

---

as modified by the Appellate Body Report, WT/DS184/AB/R, DSR 2001:X, 4769, para. 7.226, footnote 152.

[9] Turkey – First Written Submission – page 56.

for such a party to provide explanations. If the party succeeds in providing further satisfactory information, it may be taken account of in any determination. This is thus an opportunity for further information to be provided where the time limit of Article 6.1.1 is not applicable. The European Communities note that the Panel in *Guatemala – Cement II* concluded that there were no applicable time-limits for the presentation of evidence or arguments other than that contained in Article 6.1.1 for the questionnaire response.[10]

18.   In conclusion, while the European Communities believe that the reasonableness of any time limits imposed on requests for further information should be examined under Article 6.1, the European Communities cannot see the justification, as a matter of law or practice, in applying the time limit of Article 6.1.1 to requests for further information.

B.   *Deduction of Short-Term Interest Income from Interest Expenses*

19.   Turkey considers that Egypt's failure to deduct short-term interest income from interest expenses in calculating normal value is in violation of Article 2.2.1, 2.2.1.1 and 2.2.2 of the Agreement.[11] Egypt claims that this was done because the interest earnings did not bear a sufficiently close relationship to the cost of production.[12]

20.   The European Communities considers that it follows from Articles 2.2.1.1 and 2.2.2 of the Agreement that short-term interest income can only be deducted from interest expenses where such income, as a matter of fact, can be linked to the sale or production of the product concerned. Thus, the Panel's attention is drawn to the requirement in Article 2.2.1.1 that costs are to be based on records which "reasonably reflect the costs associated with production and sale of the product under consideration". In addition, Article 2.2.2 states that amounts for the calculation of administrative, selling and general costs shall be "based on actual data pertaining to production and sales in the ordinary course of trade". From this, the European Communities in its practice has concluded that interest income can only be deducted from interest expenses where it has a relationship to the production or sale of the product concerned. It is consequently a matter of fact, to be determined by the investigating authority, whether the interest income in question is sufficiently closely related to the production or sale of the product concerned.

---

[10]   *Guatemala – Cement II op cit.* para. 8.118 - 8.120. Note that this Panel deals with the issue of the submission of evidence and argument in the period between the imposition of provisional measures and the imposition of definitive measures.

[11]   Turkey – First Written Submission – page 77.

[12]   Egypt – First Written Submission – page 89.

C. Adjustments for Credit Costs to Normal Value

21.   Turkey has argued that there is a violation of Article 2.4 of the Agreement since Egypt did not make an adjustment to normal value for credit costs while doing so for the export price.[13] Egypt considers that since the normal value was constructed a possible adjustment for credit costs need not be considered because, according to Article 2.4 due allowance should only be made for differences affecting price comparability.[14] According to Egypt, as the normal value has been constructed on the basis of cost of production it cannot be influenced by conditions and terms of sale.

22.   The practice of the European Communities is to grant adjustments for credit costs to both normal value and export prices where they are justified also in the event that normal value has been constructed. The reason for this is that the constructed normal value will typically include an element for costs relating to the granting of credit terms. Thus, Article 2.2 of the Agreement provides that constructed normal value should be based on the cost of production in the country of origin plus a reasonable amount for administrative, selling and general costs and for profits. Article 2.2.2 provides three possible means of calculating administrative selling and general cost and profits should it be necessary to construct normal value. These costs used to construct normal value may also include credit costs. Thus, if an adjustment were to be made for credit costs on the actual amounts used under Article 2.2.2 as a basis to calculate constructed normal value, the European Communities considers that an adjustment should be permitted to constructed normal value. The European Communities also notes, by analogy, that the fourth sentence of Article 2.4 explicitly refers to the possibility of granting allowances for costs where the export price has been considered to be unreliable and has to be constructed.

V.   CONCLUSION

23.   In conclusion, the European Communities considers:

- •   That the admissibility of evidence which was not before the investigating authority should not be determined on the basis of Article 17.6(i);

- •   That an investigating authority is under an obligation to fully investigate the existence of other known factors which may be causing injury, even in the absence of short-comings in the evidence submitted;

- •   That the investigation period for injury and dumping need not be identical, but should permit the establishment, on the basis of positive evidence, of a causal link between dumped imports and injury suffered by the domestic industry;

---

[13]   Turkey – First Written Submission – page 78.
[14]   Turkey – First Written Submission – page 89.

- That the Anti-Dumping Agreement does not impose deadlines on the submission of responses to requests for further information from investigating authorities, but that any deadlines set must respect Article 6.1 of the Anti-Dumping Agreement;

- That interest income can only be deducted from interest expenses when it is sufficiently closely linked to production or sales of the product concerned; and,

- Credit costs may be deducted from constructed normal value where factually justified.

ANNEX 10-2

THIRD PARTY ORAL STATEMENT OF THE
EUROPEAN COMMUNITIES

I.   INTRODUCTION

1.   Mr. Chairman, distinguished members of the Panel, on behalf of the European Communities, let me express first our appreciation for the opportunity to submit our views in this dispute.

2.   As was noted in our written third party submission, many of the issues before you in this dispute relate to detailed questions of fact which the European Communities is not in a position to comment upon. As such this intervention will concentrate on some of the systemic issues which the European Communities raised in its written third party submission. Our comments will therefore focus on:

- First, the interpretation of Article 3.5 of the Anti-Dumping Agreement;

- Second, the relationship between the investigation period for dumping and injury;

- Third, the time limits applicable to requests for further information in the course of an investigation;

- Fourth, the treatment of interest income in calculating interest expenses; and,

- Finally, adjustments for credit costs to constructed normal value.

II.   INTERPRETATION OF ARTICLE 3.5 OF THE AGREEMENT

3.   The parties to the dispute have disagreed over whether the Egyptian investigating authority carried out an analysis of the existence of a causal link which conformed with Article 3.5 of the Anti-Dumping Agreement. In particular, Egypt has argued that the list of factors to be examined in the last sentence of Article 3.5 is an illustrative rather than mandatory list. The European Communities agrees that Article 3.5 sets out a non-mandatory list, both on the basis of the language of Article 3.5 when compared to Article 3.4, and on the basis of the conclusion of the Panel in *US-Hot Rolled Steel.*[1]

4.   Japan has argued, in its written third party submission, that Article 3.5 requires a detailed examination of other factors injuring the domestic injury and

---

[1]   Panel report, *United States – Anti-Dumping Measures on Certain Hot-Rolled Steel Products from Japan*, WT/DS184/R, adopted 23 August 2001, as modified by the Appellate Body Report, WT/DS184/AB/R, DSR 2001:X, 4769, para. 7.247

a rigorous segregation of those factors from the effects of dumping.[2] The European Communities would agree that a detailed examination must take place. However, the initial focus of Article 3.5 in this respect, and the preliminary issue before this panel, is whether other factors which are to be examined are "known factors". In *Thailand – H Beams* the Panel considered:

> "We consider that other "known" factors would include those causal factors that are clearly raised before the investigating authorities by interested parties in the course of an AD investigation. We are of the view that there is no express requirement in Article 3.5 AD that investigating authorities seek out and examine in each case on their own initiative the effects of all possible factors other than imports that may be causing injury to the domestic industry under investigation".[3]

5.   This statement suggests that the onus lies on the interested parties to raise factors which may be relevant to the causal link before the investigating authorities. It would seem logical that in raising other relevant issues, the interested parties must provide some *prima facie* evidence or argument that a particular factor may be relevant and merits detailed examination by the investigating authority. Otherwise, an interested party would simply list the factors set out in Article 3.5 and an investigating authority would be obliged to fully investigate such factors, hence circumventing the deliberate choice of language of Article 3.5 illustrated in the use of the term "any known factors", by transforming the list of factors into mandatory factors to be examined.

6.   Thus, the European Communities considers that the Panel should first examine whether the Turkish exporters made a *prima facie* case in the domestic investigation that a particular factor might be a cause of the injury suffered by the Egyptian industry. Should this be the case, then the Panel should examine whether the examination made of such factors meets the standards set out in, *inter alia*, Article 3.1 and Article 17.6(i). The relevance of Article 17.6(i) has recently been explained by the Appellate Body in *US – Hot Rolled Steel*:

> "[Article 17.6(i)], at the same time, in effect defines when investigating authorities can be considered to have acted inconsistently with the Anti-Dumping Agreement in the course of their "establishment" and "evaluation" of the relevant facts".[4]

7.   In conclusion, the Panel should determine first, whether the factors which Turkey alleges should have led the investigating authority to conclude that im-

---

[2]   Third party Written Submission of Japan, 1 November 2001, para. 27.

[3]   Panel Report, Thailand – Anti-Dumping Duties on Angles, Shapes and Sections of Iron or Non-Alloy Steel and H-Beams from Poland ("Thailand – H-Beams"), WT/DS122/R, adopted 5 April 2001, as modified by the Appellate Body Report, WT/DS122/AB/R, DSR 2001:VII, 2701, para. 7.273. The European Communities does not understand Turkey as suggesting the existence of factors which the investigating authority should have known about independent of the domestic investigation.

[4]   Appellate Body Report, , United States – Anti-Dumping Measures on Certain Hot-Rolled Steel Products from Japan, WT/DS184/AB/R, adopted 23 August 2001, DSR 2001:X, 4697, para. 56.

ports were not responsible for injury were known to the investigating authority, and second, whether the examination of such factors meets the criteria set down by Article 3.1 and Article 17.6(i) of the Agreement.

III. RELATIONSHIP BETWEEN THE INVESTIGATION PERIOD FOR DUMPING AND INJURY

8.   Turkey has argued that the period of the injury determination must coincide with the period of the dumping determination.[5] The European Communities understands Turkey as suggesting that a difference in the periods of investigation may lead to injury being found where there is no causal link to dumping, and that such a situation would be inconsistent with the Anti-Dumping Agreement.

9.   The European Communities agrees that an investigating authority must always be able to show that dumped imports are the cause of injury to the domestic industry. This does not require, however, that the investigation periods for dumping and injury must end at the same time. In practice, in the case of investigations carried out by the European Communities, investigation periods for dumping and injury do however end at the same time.

10.   The European Communities has already noted in its written submission that the Anti-Dumping Agreement does not establish any particular period of investigation, either for dumping or for injury. According to the recommendation adopted by the Committee on Anti-Dumping Practices (G/ADP/6) the injury investigation period "should include the entirety of the period of data collection for the dumping investigation". The end-points of both the investigation period for dumping and injury will therefore have to be quite close to each other.

11.   In any event, it would be inconsistent with Articles 3.1 and 3.3 if a Member imposed anti-dumping duties without having found, in the respective investigation periods, evidence of dumping, injury and a causal link between the two. It will be for the Panel to evaluate whether such a causal link exists on the basis of the facts before it. To do so, the Panel is not required to make any findings as to the respective lengths of injury and dumping investigation periods.

IV. APPLICABLE TIME-LIMITS FOR REQUESTS FOR FURTHER INFORMATION

12.   The European Communities shares the pre-occupations of the United States with respect to the notion, put forward by Turkey, that the time-limit set down in Article 6.1.1 should apply to requests for further information made after the submission of the initial questionnaire.[6] Such a suggestion is without basis in the Agreement and would inhibit the ability of Members to conduct an in-depth

---

[5]   Turkey – First Written Submission. page 24.
[6]   Third party Submission of the United States, 1 November 2001, part IV, page 9.

investigation consistent with the requirements set out in Article 6.6 and within the time limits for the conduct of investigations set out in Article 5.10.

13.   Article 6.1.1 refers to "questionnaires used in an anti-dumping investigation". From its context, it is apparent that this refers to questionnaires issued at the initiation of an investigation. As the European Communities have already pointed out, paragraph 7 of Annex I refers to "the questionnaire" in the singular (*"[i]t should be carried out after the response to the questionnaire has been received"*).

14.   Several provisions allow investigating authorities to request further information without referring to a specific deadline. For instance, Article 6.7 provides that on-the-spot verifications may be used to "obtain further details". Article 6.6 requires authorities to satisfy themselves as to the accuracy of information supplied, clearly implying that further questions may be posed. Paragraph 6 of Annex II requires an authority to inform an interested party of the reasons for rejecting information and obliges it to give a "a reasonable period" for such a party to provide explanations.

15.   The European Communities moreover note that the Panel in *Guatemala – Cement II* concluded that there were no applicable time-limits for the presentation of evidence or arguments other than that contained in Article 6.1.1 for the questionnaire response[7].

16.   In conclusion, while the European Communities believe that the reasonableness of any time limits imposed on requests for further information should be examined under Article 6.1, the European Communities cannot see the justification, as a matter of law or practice, in applying the time limit of Article 6.1.1 to requests for further information.

V.   DEDUCTION OF SHORT-TERM INTEREST INCOME FROM INTEREST EXPENSES

17.   The parties are also in dispute as to the legality of Egypt's decision not to deduct short-term interest income from interest expenses in calculating normal value. Turkey argues that this is in violation of Article 2.2.1, 2.2.1.1 and 2.2.2 of the Agreement while Egypt claims that this is possible because the interest earnings did not bear a sufficiently close relationship to the cost of production.[8]

18.   The European Communities broadly agrees with Egypt's position as a matter of law. It follows from Articles 2.2.1.1 and 2.2.2 of the Agreement that short-term interest income can only be deducted from interest expenses where such income, as a matter of fact, can be linked to the sale or production of the product concerned. Article 2.2.1.1 requires that costs are to be based on records

---

[7]   Panel Report, *Guatemala – Definitive Anti-Dumping Measures on Portland Cement from Mexico* (*"Guatemala – Cement II"*), WT/DS156/R, adopted 17 November 2000, DSR 2000:XI, 5295, paras 8.118-8.120. Note that this Panel deals with the issue of the submission of evidence and argument in the period between the imposition of provisional measures and the imposition of definitive measures.

[8]   Egypt – First Written Submission – page 89.

which "reasonably reflect the costs associated with production and sale of the product under consideration". In addition, Article 2.2.2 states that amounts for the calculation of administrative, selling and general costs shall be "based on actual data pertaining to production and sales in the ordinary course of trade". The European Communities interpret this as meaning that interest income can only be deducted from interest expenses where it bears a sufficiently close relationship to the production or sale of the product concerned. It is consequently a matter of fact, to be determined by the investigating authority, and subject to review by the Panel in accordance with Article 17.6(i), whether the interest income in question is sufficiently closely related to the production or sale of the product concerned.

VII.   ADJUSTMENTS TO CONSTRUCTED NORMAL VALUE FOR CREDIT COSTS

19.   Turkey has argued that there is a violation of Article 2.4 of the Agreement since Egypt did not make an adjustment to normal value for credit costs while doing so for the export price.[9] Egypt considers that since the normal value was constructed a possible adjustment for credit costs need not be considered because, according to Article 2.4, due allowance should only be made for differences affecting price comparability.[10] According to Egypt, as the normal value has been constructed on the basis of cost of production it cannot be influenced by conditions and terms of sale.

20.   The European Communities typically grants adjustments for credit costs to both normal value and export prices where justified. This also applies to the case where normal value has been constructed. This interpretation is based on the fact that the constructed normal value will typically include an element for costs relating to the granting of credit terms. Article 2.2 of the Agreement provides that constructed normal value should be based on the cost of production in the country of origin plus a reasonable amount for administrative, selling and general costs and for profits. Article 2.2.2 provides three possible means of calculating administrative selling and general cost and profits should it be necessary to construct normal value. These costs used to construct normal value may thus also include credit costs. Therefore, if an adjustment were to be made for credit costs on the actual amounts used under Article 2.2.2 as a basis to calculate constructed normal value, the European Communities considers that an adjustment should be permitted to constructed normal value. The European Communities also notes, by analogy, that the fourth sentence of Article 2.4 explicitly refers to the possibility of granting allowances for costs where the export price has been considered to be unreliable and has to be constructed.

---

[9]   Turkey – First Written Submission – page 78.
[10]   Turkey – First Written Submission – page 89.

VII. CONCLUSION

21. In conclusion, the European Communities asks the Panel to find:

- First, that under Article 3.5 it must first establish whether other factors were known to the investigating authorities, and then review whether the examination of the investigating authority was consistent with the requirements of Article 3.1 and Article 17.6(i);

- Second, that the Agreement does not prescribe a specific investigation period for either injury or dumping. However, any periods chosen must permit the establishment, on the basis of positive evidence, of a causal link between dumped imports and injury suffered by the domestic industry;

- Third, that the Anti-Dumping Agreement does not impose explicit deadlines on requests for further information, but that any deadlines set must respect Article 6.1 of the Anti-Dumping Agreement;

- Fourth, that interest income can only be deducted from interest expenses when it is sufficiently closely linked to production or sales of the product concerned; and,

- Finally, that credit costs may be deducted from constructed normal value where factually justified.

22. Thank you for your attention.

ANNEX 10-3

THIRD PARTY RESPONSES TO QUESTIONS FROM THE PANEL
OF THE EUROPEAN COMMUNITIES

Q1.   What role does the EC foresee for an investigating authority in an anti-dumping investigation establishing the existence of "other known factors" of Article 3.5 and what is the legal basis for the EC's position?

Reply

1.   The European Communities considers that the Anti-Dumping Agreement regulates the role of an investigating authority principally in Article 17.6(i) and, for injury and causal link determinations, in Article 3.1. Article 17.6(i) requires that the establishment of the facts be proper and the evaluation of such facts unbiased and objective. Article 3.1 requires that a determination of causal link shall be based on positive evidence and involve an objective examination.

2.   Article 3.5 requires the investigating authority to "examine any known factors". It obliges an investigating authority to determine whether another known factors are causing injury and not to attribute injury caused by any such factor to dumped imports. This raises the threshold issue of whether a factor is "known" to the investigating authority and then a secondary issue of whether the investigating authority has examined it in accordance with Articles 3.1 and 17.6(i). Evidently, a factor must be "known" to an investigating authority where it is raised in the domestic procedure. However, it cannot be the case that an interested party must simply make an unsubstantiated claim. Were this sufficient for a factor to be "known" to the investigating authority, then the non-mandatory nature of the list in the final sentence of Article 3.5 could easily be circumvented by an interested party simply listing those factors. From this, the European Community deduces that an interested party must make a *prima facie* case that a factor might be relevant in order for a factor to be "known" in the sense of Article 3.5, thus engaging an analysis under Article 3.1 and 17.6(i).

3.   The European Communities has not touched upon, and it does not seem to be an issue in this dispute, whether an investigating authority might be deemed to "know" of the existence of other factors possibly relevant for Article 3.5 when they have not been raised before it by an interested party.[1]

Q2.   In the EC's view, is there a different obligation on an investigating authority in an anti-dumping investigating with regard to establishing "other known factors" in terms of Article 3,5 of the AD Agreement, com-

---

[1]   See, Panel Report, *Thailand – Anti-Dumping Duties on Angles, Shapes and Sections of Iron or Non-Alloy Steel and H-Beams from Poland* ("Thailand – H-Beams"), WT/DS122/R, adopted 5 April 2001, as modified by the Appellate Body Report, WT/DS122/AB/R, DSR 2001:VII, 2701, para. 7.273.

pared with the establishment of "all relevant factors" in terms of Article 4(2)b of the Safeguards Agreement, and if so, what are the different obligations and the legal bases for these obligations?

Reply

4.   Article 4(2)(b) of the Safeguards Agreement, which concerns the establishment of a causal link, uses neither the term "all known factors" (which is found in Article 4(2)(a)) nor "other known factors" (as in Article 3.5 of the Anti-Dumping Agreement). Article 4(2)(b) is indeed silent with respect to the issue of what are the other factors referred to in its second sentence. The reference to "all relevant factors" in Article 4(2)(a) of the Safeguards Agreement can be seen as a parallel to "all relevant economic factors .." in Article 3.4 of the Anti-Dumping Agreement (and, like Article 3.4, prescribes the action to be undertaken by the investigating authority).

5.   When comparing Article 3.5 of the Anti-Dumping Agreement and Article 4(2)(b) of the Safeguard's Agreement several differences can be noted. The first two sentences of Article 3.5, like the first sentence of Article 4(2)(b), set out the requirement for the existence of a causal link. However, Article 3.5 provides examples of other factors which may be causing injury, unlike Article 4(2)(b) (the language on non-attribution is similar). Moreover, there is no list in Article 4(2)(b) comparable to the non-mandatory list of factors in Article 3.5. It can also be noted that the qualifier "known" is not used in Article 4(2)(b). Thus, the European Communities considers that while the underlying general obligation is similar *viz.* to examine other factors which might be causing injury and not to attribute such injury to dumped or increased imports, Article 3.5 provides an illustrative list of other factors which are possibly relevant and it also qualifies the nature of other factors to be examined ("known"), while Article 4(2)(b) is silent thereupon.

6.   For the avoidance of confusion, the European Communities reference to the Appellate Body report in *United States – Wheat Gluten* in its written submission was intended to illustrate by analogy the fact-finding obligations incumbent upon an investigating authority when a factor is "known" to it under Article 3.5, in the event that an interested party is not in a position to conclusively prove the effect of such a factor.

Q3.   Regarding your argument at paragraph 5 of the EC's written submission, that Article 17.6(i) does not direct a panel to consider inadmissible any evidence that was not before the investigating authority, what is the significance of the provision of Article 17,5(ii), that a panel "shall examine the matter based upon ... *the facts made available in conformity with appropriate domestic procedures* to the authorities of the importing Member" (emphasis added)?

Reply

7.   The European Communities commented upon this issue because Egypt had argued that certain evidence was inadmissible on the basis of Article 17.6(i), an argument clearly not borne out by the text of this article. Article 17.6(i) does not control the admissibility of evidence before a panel. It articulates a standard of review for matters of fact, and hence also imposes certain obligations on an investigating authority.[2] Thus a Panel cannot find evidence inadmissible on the basis of Article 17.6(i). Article 17.5(ii), on the other hand, is the only provision of the Anti-Dumping Agreement which regulates the status of evidence on which a Panel should base its examination. Thus, as the Panel's question suggests, Article 17.5(ii) is of significance in this respect. Indeed, the European Communities pointed out the relevance of Article 17.5(ii) in para. 7 of its written submission.[3]

8.   In so doing, the European Communities raised the hypothetical situation of evidence which a Member claimed was improperly excluded from an investigation and pointed out that it may be the case that such evidence should not be excluded from a panel's examination since the domestic record would shed light on the treatment of such evidence. Thus, the absence of the evidence on the record might be of relevance to the sufficiency and objectiveness of an investigating authority's investigation. However, since this issue is not before the Panel, the European Communities will not develop this argument further.[4]

---

[2]   Appellate Body Report, *United States – Anti-Dumping Measures on Certain Hot-Rolled Steel Products from Japan*, WT/DS184/AB/R, adopted 23 August 2001, DSR 2001:X, 4697, para. 56.

[3]   See, Panel report, *United States – Anti-Dumping Measures on Certain Hot-Rolled Steel Products from Japan*, WT/DS184/R, adopted 23 August 2001, as modified by the Appellate Body Report, WT/DS184/AB/R, DSR 2001:X, 4769, para. 7.6, in which the Panel refused to consider evidence which had not been submitted in the domestic procedures.

[4]   See, *Ibid.*, para.7.8, where the Panel also reserved its position on whether evidence improperly excluded could be considered by a panel.

ANNEX 11-1

THIRD PARTY WRITTEN SUBMISSION OF JAPAN

I.   THE INVESTIGATING AUTHORITY HAS FAILED TO COMPLY WITH THE PROCEDURAL REQUIREMENTS FOR ANTI-DUMPING INVESTIGATIONS

1.   It appears that Egypt conducted its anti-dumping investigation of Steel Rebar from Turkey in a manner that is not consistent with the Agreement on Implementation of Article VI of GATT 1947 (the "Agreement"). The Agreement specifies procedural requirements for the conduct of anti-dumping investigations. These requirements serve "the fundamental underlying principle that anti-dumping investigations should be fair".[1]

2.   In this case, Turkey has made certain compelling arguments that the Investigating Authority failed to comply with the minimum procedural requirements of the Agreement. Indeed, extensive and significant irregularities in Egypt's investigation procedures call into question the fairness of the investigation as a whole.

A.   *The Investigating Authority did not Provide Respondents a "reasonable time" to Answer its Questions under the Circumstances*

3.   Turkey claims that, after the Investigating Authority received and verified the respondents' answers to its questions, the Investigating Authority asked the respondents to answer many additional questions. Turkey further claims that the Investigating Authority required the respondents to provide extensive supporting documentation and to translate all those documents into English. These requests were made immediately after Turkey had suffered a devastating earthquake, indeed, at a time when key personnel of the respondents were absent from work to search for relatives and assist relief efforts. Yet, even in those trying circumstances, the Investigating Authority did not afford the respondents a reasonable time to respond. In fact, the Investigating Authority repeatedly set short deadlines – in one case as little as two days.

4.   These deadlines are inconsistent with several provisions of the Agreement, including:

- Article 6.1 which requires, "All interested parties in an anti-dumping investigation shall be given . . . ample opportunity to pre-

---

[1]   *European Communities – Anti-Dumping Duties on Imports of Cotton-Type Bed Linen from India*, WT/DS141/R, DSR 2001:VI, 2077, para. 6.181.

sent in writing all evidence which they consider relevant in respect of the investigation in question."

- Article 6.2, whose *first sentence*, requires, "Throughout the anti-dumping investigation all interested parties shall have a full opportunity for the defense of their interests."

- Article 6.13 which requires, "The authorities shall take due account of any difficulties experienced by interested parties, in particular small companies, in supplying information requested, and shall provide any assistance practicable."

5.   These provisions make clear that Investigating Authorities must afford a reasonable period of time to respondents to answer questions presented. They also make clear, moreover, that Investigating Authorities have a duty to provide additional time when circumstances warrant. In that regard, the Appellate Body recently emphasized that Investigating Authorities must set deadlines "in a manner that allows for account to be taken of the particular circumstances of each case".[2] Among the factors that "investigating authorities should consider" are "the nature and quantity of the information submitted" and "the difficulties encountered by an investigated exporter in obtaining the information".[3] Turkey claims that several important factors warranted additional time in this case, including the number of documents requested, the requirement for translating these documents into English, and the after-effects of the tragic earthquake. After setting short initial deadlines, the Investigating Authority erred in these circumstances by refusing to grant an extension for "cause shown" and by failing to assist the respondents with their "difficulties".

6.   Egypt tries to justify its short deadlines as being "more than adequate".[4] It argues that the time allowed is "somewhat longer than the normal time period granted by other jurisdictions in similar circumstances", *i.e.* the standard response time for supplemental questionnaires.[5] This argument shows that the Investigating Authority set the deadline without taking into account the difficulties that the Turkish respondents would face in the particular circumstances of this case. The conduct of the Investigating Authority is therefore inconsistent with Article 6 of the Agreement.

---

[2]   *United States – Anti-Dumping Measures on Certain Hot-Rolled Steel Products from Japan*, WT/DS184/AB/R, DSR 2001:X, 4697, para. 85 (discussing the factors affecting whether information is submitted within a "reasonable time" even though it is submitted after a deadline set by the Investigating Authority).

[3]   *Ibid.*

[4]   First Written Submission of Egypt (WT/DS211) ("Egypt Submission"), page 55 ("a time period of 13 days was, in Egypt's view, more than reasonable").

[5]   *Ibid.* at 55 n.26 (citing standard EC practice for requesting additional information in ordinary circumstances).

B. The Investigating Authority did not Provide the Respondents an Adequate Opportunity to Explain their Questionnaire Responses

7.   As mentioned, the supplemental questionnaires at issue were sent after the Investigating Authority had verified the respondents' answers to the initial questionnaires through an on-site examination under Article 6.7 of the Agreement. The Investigating Authority requested the respondents to provide extensive supporting documentation – translated into English – so that the Investigating Authority could attempt to verify the answers. Turkey has shown, and Egypt has conceded, that the Investigating Authority chose not to hold a second on-site examination to verify the respondents' answers to the new questionnaires.[6] Respondents then offered to meet the Investigating Authority in Cairo, but that offer was not accepted.[7] When the Investigating Authority had questions about the respondents' answers and documents, apparently for lack of the routine explanations and dialogue that take place at on-site examinations, it rejected the information submitted and used "facts available".

8.   The Investigating Authority's approach to verification is inconsistent with the procedural requirements of the Agreement in at least four respects.[8]

9.   First, the Agreement establishes that questionnaires and supplemental questionnaires ordinarily should precede verification.[9] This is not to say that Investigating Authorities are precluded from ever issuing supplemental questionnaires after verification. But if the Investigating Authority considers that substantial new information is needed after verification, then it is incumbent on the Investigating Authority to obtain such information in a manner that ensures the fundamental fairness of the proceeding. At a minimum, the Investigating Authority must afford the respondent adequate time to respond to the new questions and adequate opportunity to explain its new responses.

10.   Second, the Agreement expressly authorizes on-site verifications; it does not provide for any other type of verification.[10] There are sound reasons for preferring on-site verifications over other possible procedures – such as what Turkey calls "mail order verification" – because they reduce the burdens on the respondent and allow the respondent a full opportunity to explain its documents to the verifiers. Therefore, if an Investigating Authority chooses not to conduct an

---

[6]   *See* Egypt Submission, page 57.
[7]   *See* Egypt Submission, page 72.
[8]   The use of "facts available" is discussed in Part II *infra*.
[9]   "As the main purpose of the on-the-spot investigation is to verify information provided or to obtain further details, it should be carried out after the response to the questionnaire has been received... " Agreement, Annex I, para. 7. "Enquiries or questions put by the authorities . . . should, whenever possible, be answered before the visit is made." *Ibid.*, para. 8.
[10]   Agreement, art. 6.7 ("the authorities *may* carry out investigations") (emphasis added).

on-site verification, it should accept any timely information submitted by the respondents.[11]

11.   Third, the Agreement recognizes the value of face-to-face meetings, providing respondents the right to meet the Investigating Authorities on request.[12] Turkey has shown, and Egypt conceded, that the Investigating Authority chose not to meet with the respondents. Respondents should have been given such opportunity.

12.   Finally, the Agreement prohibits Investigating Authorities from imposing "an unreasonable burden of proof" on respondents.[13] It is clearly unreasonable to require that respondents anticipate every possible question the Investigating Authority might have about a document, and answer each such question in writing. A respondent should only have to answer questions in accordance with its own cost and sales records and data; a respondent should not be required to make any additional adjustments, such as the alleged hyperinflation adjustment, which it would not be required to make in accordance with the GAAP(Generally Accepted Accounting Principle*).* Further, a respondent should have the opportunity to explain its answers orally to the Investigating Authority's satisfaction.

13.   By requiring the respondents to defend by mail their responses to the post-verification questionnaires without giving an opportunity to explain their responses in person, the Investigating Authority violated Article 6 of the Agreement.

II.   THE INVESTIGATING AUTHORITY IMPROPERLY USED "FACTS AVAILABLE"

14.   As mentioned, when the Investigating Authority determined that it could not verify the accuracy of certain questionnaire responses by examining the supporting documents mailed by the respondents, it rejected those responses and used "facts available" to calculate the normal value of respondents' rebar. The decision to use "facts available" and the choice of the "facts" to use are both inconsistent with the Agreement. This improper resort to "facts available" inexorably led to errors in calculation of the normal value and therefore to a failure to make a "fair comparison . . . between the export price and the normal value," as required by Article 2.4.

---

[11]   "All information which is verifiable, which is appropriately submitted so that it can be used in the investigation without undue difficulties, [and] which is supplied in a timely fashion, . . . should be taken into account when determinations are made." Agreement, Annex II, para. 3.

[12]   "Throughout the anti-dumping investigation all interested parties shall have a full opportunity for the defence of their interests. To this end, the authorities shall, on request, provide opportunities for all interested parties to meet those parties with adverse interests, so that opposing views may be presented and rebuttal arguments offered... Interested parties shall also have the right, on justification, to present other information orally." Agreement, art. 6.2.

[13]   Agreement, art. 2.4.

A. The Investigating Authority should not have Used "facts available" in the Circumstances of this Case

15.   Article 6.8 of the Agreement authorizes Investigating Authorities to use "facts available" only where a party (1) "refuses access to, or otherwise does not provide, necessary information within a reasonable period", or (2) "significantly impedes the investigation". Annex II then elaborates on the circumstances in which an Investigating Authority may use "facts available," as follows:

> "1. ... The authorities should also ensure that the party is aware that if information is not supplied within a reasonable time, the authorities will be free to make determinations on the basis of the facts available, including those contained in the application for the initiation of the investigation by the domestic industry.
>
> ...
>
> 3. All information which is verifiable, which is appropriately submitted so that it can be used in the investigation without undue difficulties, [and] which is supplied in a timely fashion, . . . should be taken into account when determinations are made...
>
> ...
>
> 5. Even though the information provided may not be ideal in all respects, this should not justify the authorities from disregarding it, provided the interested party has acted to the best of its ability.
>
> 6. If evidence or information is not accepted, the supplying party should be informed forthwith of the reasons therefor, and should have an opportunity to provide further explanations within a reasonable period, due account being taken of the time-limits of the investigation. If the explanations are considered by the authorities as not being satisfactory, the reasons for the rejection of such evidence or information should be given in any published determinations.
>
> 7. ... [I]f an interested party does not cooperate and this relevant information is being withheld from the authorities, this situation could lead to a result which is less favourable to the party than if the party did cooperate."

16.   The Appellate Body recently had occasion to explain these provisions. It concluded that an Investigating Authority cannot reject information provided within a "reasonable time" by a respondent that "cooperate[s]" and "act[s] to the best of its ability".[14] The Appellate Body expressly noted that a respondent's mere inability to provide all the information requested by an Investigating Authority does not, by itself, warrant use of "facts available". Rather, a respondent may "cooperate" "to the best of its ability" and still not be able to answer every

---

[14]   *United States – Anti-Dumping Measures on Certain Hot-Rolled Steel Products from Japan*, WT/DS184/AB/R, DSR 2001:X, 4697, paras. 99-100.

single question posed by the authorities.[15] Accordingly, an Investigating Authority cannot simply make demands of respondents and then use "facts available" whenever a respondent fails to completely satisfy those demands. Instead, "cooperation" is "a two-way process involving joint effort" by the Investigating Authority and the respondent.[16] In imposing requirements for respondents, therefore, Investigating Authorities must:

> "strike a balance between the effort that they can expect interested parties to make in responding to questionnaires, and the practical ability of those interested parties to comply fully with all demands made of them by the investigating authorities. We see this provision as another detailed expression of the principle of good faith, which is, at once a general principle of law and a principle of general international law, that informs the provisions of the *Anti-Dumping Agreement*, as well as the other covered agreements. This organic principle of good faith, in this particular context, restrains investigating authorities from imposing on exporters burdens which, in the circumstances, are not reasonable".[17]

17.   In this case, the Investigating Authority failed to "strike a balance" between its demands on the respondents and their "practical ability" to comply – especially taking into account the short time afforded the respondents to reply[18] and the dire circumstances then prevailing in Turkey. Turkey claims that the respondents "cooperated" consistently with the Investigating Authority throughout the investigation, and that they "acted to the best of their ability" even after the earthquake. In these circumstances, the decision to reject the information provided by respondents in favour of "facts available" was inconsistent with Article 6.8 and Annex II of the Agreement. If the Investigating Authority concluded that it needed further information to verify the respondents' answers, then it should have specified its concerns and given the respondents an opportunity to address those concerns through either an on-site examination under Article 6.7 or a meeting under Article 6.2.[19]

18.   Finally, it appears that the Investigating Authority decided to reject respondents' answers based not on contrary facts, but on a conflict between the answers and the Investigating Authority's own assumptions. The Investigating Authority assumed that the respondents' costs for steel scrap – the main input for rebar – should have increased during the investigation period due to Turkish hyperinflation at that time. The Investigating Authority rejected respondents' data on their steel scrap costs, based on its finding that the reported costs de-

---

[15]   "[P]arties may very well 'cooperate' to a very high degree, even though the requested information is, ultimately, not obtained. This is because the fact of 'cooperating' is in itself not determinative of the end result of the cooperation." *Ibid.* at 99.

[16]   *Ibid.* at 104 (citing Agreement, art. 6.13).

[17]   *Ibid.* at 101.

[18]   *See* Part I.A *supra. See also* Egypt Submission, page 56 (conceding that Egypt provided only two to five days to respond to its September 23 questionnaire).

[19]   Annex II, para. 6.

creased during the investigation period notwithstanding inflation in the economy as a whole. It may be the case, however, that the cost of a raw material declines even during a hyperinflationary period in the overall economy due to material-specific factors. When a conflict arose between the Investigating Authority's assumption and the actual data, the Investigating Authority should have discarded its own assumption – and not the respondents' data.

B. The Investigating Authority should not have Used, as "facts available," an Inflation Rate at Odds with Official Inflation Data

19.   Turkey claims that, even if this were an appropriate case in which to use "facts available", the facts used by the Investigating Authority do not comport with the Agreement's requirements. Annex II, Paragraph 7 requires Investigating Authorities to use "special circumspection" when resorting to "facts available".[20] In particular, "the authorities should, where practicable, check the information from other independent sources at their disposal... ".[21]

20.   The Investigating Authority did not exercise "special circumspection" in the facts that it chose to use. For example, as Egypt has conceded, the Investigating Authority selected 5 per cent as the monthly inflation rate in Turkey during the investigation period.[22] Egypt, however, did not identify the source of this figure even in its submission in this proceeding, while Turkey claims that the figure does not comport with official inflation data. Turkey called the official data to the Investigating Authority's attention during the investigation, but the Investigating Authority compounded its error by rejecting the Turkish Government's comments as untimely.[23] In this case, it would have been "practicable" for the Investigating Authority to "check" the inflation rate it proposed to use against "independent sources," such as the official publications on Turkey's inflation rates, but the Investigating Authority simply failed to do so. It therefore violated Annex II, Paragraph 7 of the Agreement.

C. The Improper Use of "facts available" Distorted the Calculation of the Dumping Margins

21.   Article 2.4, first sentence, of the Agreement requires, "A fair comparison shall be made between the export price and the normal value." A fair comparison cannot be made, however, when the export price or the normal value is calcu-

---

[20]   Agreement, Annex II, para. 7
[21]   Ibid.
[22]   Egypt Submission, pages 58, 84.
[23]   Article 6.9 of the Agreement provides: "The authorities shall, before a final determination is made, inform all interested parties of the essential facts under consideration which form the basis for the decision whether to apply definitive measures. Such disclosure should take place in sufficient time for the parties to defend their interests." Where an Investigating Authority informs the parties late in an investigation that it has selected a 5 per cent inflation rate as one of the essential facts forming the basis for its decision, the parties (including the respondents' government) must be allowed to "defend their interests" by submitting data that establishes a different inflation rate.

lated improperly. Turkey claims that Investigating Authority's improper resort to "facts available" led to the calculation of a higher normal value than otherwise would have been found. Such an improper calculation in turn prevents a fair comparison of export price to normal value, and leads to the determination of inflated dumping margins and the imposition of excessive anti-dumping measures.

III. THE INJURY INVESTIGATION DOES NOT COMPORT WITH THE AGREEMENT

22. The Investigating Authority Failed To Notify the Respondents of the Information Required for the Injury Investigation Turkey claims that the Investigating Authority stated in its Initiation Report that the investigation concerned an allegation of *threat* of injury (and not of present injury). Likewise, the questionnaires concerned threat of injury. The respondents accordingly focused their responses and arguments on issues pertaining to threat of injury. Ultimately, however, the Investigating Authority found present injury (and not a threat of injury). Egypt concedes that it changed the basis of its injury investigation from threat of injury to actual injury without informing the respondents.[24]

23. The Agreement does not permit Investigating Authorities to act in this manner. Under Article 6, Respondents must be "given notice of the information which the authorities require".[25] They also must be given "ample opportunity to present in writing all evidence which they consider relevant in respect of the investigation in question"[26] and a "full opportunity for the defence of their interests".[27]

24. The basic fairness of an investigation is called into question if the Investigating Authority invites evidence and argument on one issue and then bases its ruling on a different issue. A determination of threat of injury must be based on one legal standard, while a determination of actual injury must be based on a different legal standard. To account for the prospective nature of a threat analysis, and to avoid determinations based "merely on allegation, conjecture or remote possibility," Article 3.7 of the Agreement requires that a determination of threat of injury must be based on a "conclusion that further dumped exports are imminent and that, unless protective action is taken, material injury would occur". Actual injury investigations, by contrast, are not prospective in nature and thus do not require consideration of such forward-looking factors. In light of these significant differences between threat cases and actual injury cases, a respondent cannot present the relevant evidence and defend its interests under Articles 6.1 and 6.2 without knowledge of the issue in question.

---

[24] Egypt Submission, pages 10-11.
[25] Agreement, art. 6.1.
[26] *Ibid.*
[27] Agreement, art. 6.2.

25.　　Should an Investigating Authority consider it necessary to change the basis for its injury investigation after receiving responses to its initial question-naire, then it has a duty to notify the respondent of the change and afford the respondent a full opportunity to address the new issues. Absent such notice and opportunity, the Investigating Authority here violated Article 6 of the Agreement.

B.　The Injury Analysis did not Consider all the Factors and Issues Required by Article 3 of the Agreement

26.　　Under Article 3 of the Agreement, an Investigating Authority must consider in its injury analysis for an anti-dumping investigation "any known factors other than dumped imports which at the same time are injuring the domestic industry". It must not attribute to the dumped imports any injury caused by any other factor.[28]

27.　　The Appellate Body recently addressed the "non-attribution" requirement of Article 3.5. It held that Investigating Authorities must "examine *all* known factors other than imports. . . ".[29] Then they "must ensure" that they do not attribute to dumped imports any injury due to other factors.[30] To satisfy that obligation, they must "separat[e] and distinguish[] the injurious effects of the other factors from the injurious effects of the dumped imports".[31] The Appellate Body highlighted the importance of this requirement in the WTO regime:

> "[I]n the absence of such separation and distinction of the different injurious effects, the investigating authorities would have no rational basis to conclude that the dumped imports are indeed causing the injury which, under the *Anti-Dumping Agreement*, justifies the imposition of anti-dumping duties".[32]

It is clear, therefore, that Article 3.5 requires both a detailed examination of other factors injuring the domestic industry, and a rigorous segregation of the effects of those factors from the effects of dumping. Only then can an Investigating Authority legitimately conclude that dumped imports are *causing* injury to the domestic industry.

28.　　Turkey claims that the Investigating Authority failed to conduct a sufficiently rigorous examination and segregation of the effects of several factors other than dumped imports on the Egyptian rebar industry. The critical factors include production capacity within Egypt, competition among Egyptian producers, contracted demand, input costs, and non-dumped imports.

---

[28]　*Ibid.*
[29]　*United States – Anti-Dumping Measures on Certain Hot-Rolled Steel Products from Japan*, WT/DS184/AB/R, DSR 2001:X, 4697, para. 222 (emphasis in original; internal punctuation omitted).
[30]　*Ibid.*
[31]　*Ibid.* at para. 223.
[32]　*Ibid.*

29.   In response, Egypt argues that "there were no other causes of injury sufficient to break the causal link between the dumped imports and the injury to the
domestic industry".[33] Egypt, however, does not claim that it examined the other
possible causes of injury and concluded that none of them contributed to the injury. Rather, Egypt simply considers that no other single factor has a stronger
causal link to injury to the domestic industry than the dumped imports. That approach misplaces the causation standard. Under Article 3 of the Agreement, as
explained by the Appellate Body, Investigating Authorities have the burden to
separate and distinguish the effects of other factors from the effects of dumped
imports. In the end, therefore, Egypt does not address the "non-attribution" allegations in this case.

30.   As the effects of other factors were not adequately described and segregated from the effects of the Turkish imports, the Investigating Authority has not
met the "non-attribution" obligation of Article 3.5.

IV.   CONCLUSION

31.   Due to the substantive and procedural errors discussed above, the Panel
should conclude that the anti-dumping investigation was conducted in a manner
that breached the Agreement. These violations led to the imposition of improper
and excessive anti-dumping measures on Turkish rebar. The Panel, accordingly,
should recommend that Egypt bring its anti-dumping measures into conformity
with the Agreement.

---

[33]   Egypt Submission, pages 7, 24.

ANNEX 11-2

THIRD PARTY ORAL RESPONSES OF JAPAN
TO QUESTIONS FROM THE PANEL

1.   The Government of Japan respectfully submits the following answers to the questions presented at the First Meeting of the Panel.

Q1.   Japan argues that the deadlines imposed by the investigating authority were inconsistent with AD article 6.13. Given that Turkey has made no claim under this provision, what is its legal relevance to this case?

Reply

2.   Article 31 of the Vienna Convention of the Law of Treaties, which has been recognized to provide rules of construction for the WTO Agreements,[1] provides that the terms of a treaty shall be interpreted "in their context and in the light of [the treaty's] object and purpose". Article 31 further defines the "context" of a treaty to include its "text, including its preamble and annexes". The Appellate Body has accordingly recognized that the entire text of the WTO Agreements is relevant to the construction of any part thereof.[2] More particularly, the Appellate Body has also held that the context for one paragraph of one article of one WTO Agreement includes another paragraph of that same article.[3]

3.   In the present dispute, Turkey claims that Egypt has acted in violation of Articles 6.1 and 6.2 of the WTO Agreement on Implementation of Article VI of GATT 1994 (the "Anti-Dumping Agreement"). Article 6.1 requires in part that an Investigating Authority must provide respondents with "ample opportunity" to submit written evidence. Likewise, Article 6.2 requires in part that an Investigating Authority must provide respondents with "a full opportunity for the defence of their interests".

4.   The meaning of the terms "ample opportunity" and "full opportunity" in Articles 6.1 and 6.2 must be understood in their "context." Article 6.13 forms part of that context. Specifically, Article 6.13 provides:

---

[1]   *See, e.g., Dispute Settlement Understanding*, Art. 3.2; *United States – Standards for Reformulated and Conventional Gasoline*, Report of the Appellate Body, WT/DS2/AB/R, AB-1996-1, DSR 1996, 3, at 16.

[2]   *See Korea – Definitive Safeguard Measure on Imports of Certain Dairy Products*, Report of the Appellate Body, WT/DS98/AB/R, DSR 2000:I, 3, para. 81 ("Article II:2 of the *WTO Agreement* expressly manifests the intention of the Uruguay Round negotiators that the provisions of the *WTO Agreement* and the Multilateral Trade Agreements included in its Annexes 1, 2 and 3 must be read as a whole.").

[3]   *See European Communities – Measures Affecting the Importation of Certain Poultry Products*, WT/DS69/AB/R, DSR 1998:V, 2031, AB-1998-3, page 52 (In considering the context of Article 5.1(b), "We look first to the rest of Article 5.1... Paragraph 5 of Article 5 is also part of the context of Article 5.1(b).").

"The authorities shall take due account of any difficulties experienced by interested parties, in particular small companies, in supplying information requested, and shall provide any assistance
practicable."

5.   Construing Articles 6.1 and 6.2 in this context, Japan considers that a
failure by an Investigating Authority to take due account of difficulties experienced by a respondent and to provide practicable assistance to the respondent
should inform the Panel's decision whether the respondent was afforded the
"ample opportunity" and the "full opportunity" mandated by Articles 6.1 and 6.2.

6.   In this regard, it is noteworthy that the Appellate Body has relied on Article 6.13 when analyzing the reasonableness of the deadlines in another case; the
allegation there, as here, arose under another paragraph of Article 6 and not under paragraph 13 itself.[4] This Appellate Body decision further supports that
evaluation of claims under any part of Article 6 should take place in context,
including Article 6.13.

**Q2.   Japan argues at paragraph 11 of its written submission that parties
have the right to meet investigating authorities upon request. The provision
cited by Japan in this connection, Article 6.2, states that this right exists "on
justification". Please comment.**

Reply

7.   The second sentence of Article 6.2 provides a right to meet "on request".
Specifically, the first two sentences provide:

"Throughout the anti-dumping investigation all interested parties
shall have a full opportunity for the defence of their interests. To
this end, the authorities *shall, on request,* provide opportunities for
all interested parties to meet those parties with adverse interests, so
that opposing views may be presented and rebuttal arguments offered". (emphasis added).

8.   The inclusion of the word "shall" makes clear that this provision obliges
an Investigating Authority to grant requests to meet. Parties in anti-dumping investigations thus have the right to meet the Investigating Authority upon request.

9.   The last sentence of Article 6.2 provides a separate right to present oral
evidence "on justification." Specifically, this sentence provides:

"Interested parties shall *also* have the right, *on justification,* to present other information orally". (emphasis added).

10.   The use of the phrase "shall also have the right" makes clear that this right
to present oral evidence is in addition to the aforementioned right to meet. The

---

[4]   *See United States – Anti-Dumping Measures on Certain Hot-Rolled Steel Products from Japan,*
WT/DS184/AB/R, DSR 2001:X, 4697, AB-2001-2, pages 39-41. Japan raised a "conditional appeal"
under Article 6.13, but the condition was not satisfied and the Appellate Body did not reach that
claim. *Ibid.* at 81.

fact that the latter right is conditioned on "justification" in no way affects the automatic nature of the right to meet. The "justification" language in the last sentence therefore should not be read into the right to meet.

Q3   How does Japan interpret Article 2.4, in this context?

Reply

11.   Article 2.4 is a key provision of the Anti-Dumping Agreement, establishing several crucial rules concerning the calculation of dumping margins. In this context, Japan has commented on two aspects of Article 2.4:

- *First*, the first sentence of Article 2.4 requires, "A fair comparison shall be made between the export price and the normal value." Japan has submitted that the necessary comparison cannot be made fairly if either the export price or the normal value is calculated improperly.[5]

- *Second*, the last sentence of Article 2.4 requires that the Investigating Authorities must tell the parties to an anti-dumping investigation "what information is necessary to ensure a fair comparison" and "shall not impose an unreasonable burden of proof" on those parties. Japan has submitted that this sentence forbids an Investigating Authority from requiring that respondents anticipate every possible question the Investigating Authority might have about a document and answer each such question in writing.[6]

12.   Egypt claims that Article 2.4 does not apply here, asserting that it is "strictly limited" to determining "allowances" for price comparisons.[7] But that claim is incorrect. *First*, it has no basis in the text of the Article. Indeed, it is inconsistent with the text, which requires a "fair comparison" in the first sentence (without the limitation suggested by Egypt) and which expressly refers back to that "fair comparison" in the last sentence when addressing the burden of proof. *Second*, the claim is also inconsistent with the Appellate Body's view of Article 2.4. The Appellate Body held that the "fair comparison" requirement of Article 2.4 is a "general obligation" that goes beyond the Article's "specific obligations" (such as determining "allowances").[8] It further emphasized that the "fair comparison" requirement applies to all aspects of dumping calculations: "This is a general obligation that, in our view, informs all of Article 2... "[9] In the end, therefore, the obligation to conduct a "fair comparison" and the ban against "an unreasonable burden of proof" run throughout the proceeding.

---

[5]   *See Japan's Submission*, para. 21.

[6]   *See Japan's Submission*, para. 12.

[7]   *See Egypt's Submission*, page 67.

[8]   *See Bed Linen, supra* note 4, page 16. That holding is crucial to the Appellate Body's conclusion that a price comparison that uses "zeroing" violates the "fair comparison" requirement of Article 2.4, because the rules on "allowances" are not implicated by the practice of "zeroing."

[9]   *See European Communities – Anti-Dumping Duties on Imports of Cotton-Type Bed Linen from India*, WT/DS141/AB/R, DSR 2001:V, 2049, AB-2000-13, page 18.

13.   Finally, Japan also notes the US view that, "To the extent a comparison has been made in accordance with the [specific] rules of Article 2.4, a fair comparison is established."[10]   This view is inconsistent with the Appellate Body's holding discussed above. It also, moreover, fails to take account of a key difference between Article 2.4 of the Anti-Dumping Agreement and its predecessor in Article 2:6 of the Tokyo Round Anti-Dumping Code (the "Code"). In Article 2:6 of the Code, the "fair comparison" language was limited to an introductory phrase leading into the Article's specific provisions concerning the price comparison: "In order to effect a fair comparison...." That wording "made clear that if the requirements of that Article were met, any comparison thus undertaken was deemed to be 'fair.'"[11]   The current language in Article 2.4 is not so limited. Article 2.4 today begins with a sentence requiring a "fair comparison" separate and apart from the specific provisions in the following sentences. This free-standing sentence establishes requirements independent of the other aspects of Article 2.4. The US view would improperly render the first sentence of Article 2.4 "inutile".[12]

---

[10]   *See US Submission*, para. 8.

[11]   *See European Communities — Imposition of Anti-Dumping Duties on Imports of Cotton Yarn from Brazil*, Report of the Panel, ADP/137, adopted on 30 October 1995, para. 492.

[12]   *See Reformulated Gasoline, supra* note 1, DSR 1996, 3, at 21 ("An interpreter is not free to adopt a reading that would result in reducing whole clauses or paragraphs of a treaty to redundancy or inutility.").

ANNEX 12-1

THIRD PARTY WRITTEN SUBMISSION OF THE
UNITED STATES

I.   INTRODUCTION

1.   The United States makes this third party submission to provide the Panel with its view of the proper legal interpretation of the provisions of the Agreement on Implementation of Article VI of the General Agreement on Tariffs and Trade 1994 (the "AD Agreement") under which this dispute arises. In particular, the United States will address the following issues: (1) the proper understanding of the first sentence of Article 2.4; (2) the proper understanding of Annex I of the AD Agreement; (3) the proper understanding of Article 6.1.1; and (4) the lack of clarity with respect to the Agreement provisions alleged to have been breached. The United States recognizes that many of the issues raised in this dispute are strictly factual. The United States takes no view as to whether, under the facts of this case, the measure at issue is consistent with the Agreement.

II.   EGYPT'S CALCULATION OF THE COST OF PRODUCTION AND THE CONSTRUCTED NORMAL VALUE DOES NOT IMPLICATE ARTICLE 2.4

2.   Turkey has alleged that, in calculating cost of production and the constructed normal value, Egypt did not act in compliance with Articles 2.2.1.1, 2.2.2, and the first sentence of Article 2.4.[1] The United States takes no position with respect to Turkey's claim under Articles 2.2.1.1 and 2.2.2. Article 2.4, however, does not address the calculation of cost of production and the constructed normal value. Turkey's limited argument on this point takes the first sentence of that article entirely out of context. Because detailed rules for making the calculations at issue are set forth in Articles 2.2.1, 2.2.1.1 and 2.2.2, in the view of the United States, the Panel must resolve the issue before it by reference to the specific rules negotiated to address those issues.

3.   Articles 2.2.1, 2.2.1.1 and 2.2.2 relate to the proper establishment of normal value, by permitting the elimination of sales below cost from normal value under certain circumstances, and by providing for the use of constructed normal value as the basis for normal value under certain circumstances. Turkey has made its arguments under those provisions and Egypt has made its replies.[2]

---

[1]   *First Submission of the Government of the Republic of Turkey*, ("*Turkey First Submission*"), section IV-G, para. 4 and section IV-H, para. 1 (pp. 69-70). As discussed further below, it is unclear whether Turkey has actually asserted a breach of Article 2.4 in section IV-H of its brief (p. 70).

[2]   *First Written Submission of Egypt* (25 October 2001) ("*Egypt First Submission*"), section IV.7 (pp. 79-82).

4.   However, Turkey has also asserted an argument under the first sentence of Article 2.4. Although the basis of Turkey's argument is somewhat unclear, in the view of the United States Article 2.4, and in particular the first sentence, is wholly inapposite to the issue Turkey has put before the Panel. Moreover, it is wholly unnecessary for the Panel to address this issue, as the dispute can be resolved by applying the specific rules of Articles 2.2.1.1 and 2.2.2, which Turkey alleges to have been breached.

5.   Article 2.4 addresses the comparisons and adjustments Members must make after identifying the proper basis for normal value and export price and prior to calculating the margins of dumping. Article 2.4 provides, in its entirety:

> "A fair comparison shall be made between the export price and the normal value. This comparison shall be made at the same level of trade, normally at the ex-factory level, and in respect of sales made at as nearly as possible the same time. Due allowance shall be made in each case, on its merits, for differences which affect price comparability, including differences in conditions and terms of sale, taxation, levels of trade, quantities, physical characteristics, and any other differences which are also demonstrated to affect price comparability. In the cases referred to in paragraph 3 of Article 2, allowances for costs, including duties and taxes, incurred between importation and resale, and for profits accruing, should also be made. If in these cases, price comparability has been affected, the authorities shall establish the normal value at a level of trade equivalent to the level of trade of the constructed export price, or make due allowance as warranted under this paragraph. The authorities shall indicate to the parties in question what information is necessary to ensure a fair comparison and shall not impose an unreasonable burden of proof on those parties".

6.   Turkey's arguments in this regard relate to the *identification* of normal value under Article 2.2, 2.2.1, 2.2.1.1 and 2.2.2, and not to its subsequent *comparison* with export price under Article 2.4. As can be seen from the language of this provision quoted above, Article 2.4 presupposes that export price and normal value have already been identified. Specifically, under Article 2.4, once the basis for normal value and export price have been established, the administering authority is required to select the proper sales for comparison (sales at the same level of trade and as nearly as possible the same time), and make appropriate adjustments to those sales (due allowances for differences which affect price comparability). In this way, the Agreement establishes a fair comparison.

7.   Thus, the United States does not agree that an improper calculation of cost of production or constructed normal value can constitute a breach of the first sentence of Article 2.4. The language of Article 2.4, which relates solely to the comparison, should not be taken out of context and applied to other issues related to calculation of dumping margins. Article 31 of the *Vienna Convention on the Law of Treaties* requires that a treaty be interpreted in accordance with "the ordinary meaning to be given to the terms of the treaty *in their context*" (empha-

sis supplied).[3] The Panel should not adopt Turkey's proposed approach to the Agreement of taking the general language of the first sentence of Article 2.4 out of context in order to override the detailed rules negotiated in Articles 2.2, 2.2.1, 2.2.1.1 and 2.2.2.

8.   Moreover, the fair comparison language simply does not apply outside of the context in which it is contained: the rules for making comparisons under the remainder of Article 2.4. The language of the first sentence of Article 2.4, which provides for a fair comparison, must be read in the context of the second sentence which defines how "this comparison" is to be made. To the extent a comparison has been made in accordance with the rules of Article 2.4, a fair comparison is established.[4] Claims that do not relate to obligations under Article 2.4 cannot constitute breaches of the first sentence of Article 2.4.

9.   In addressing the issues of calculation of cost of production and constructed normal value, the Panel should limit its analysis to whether Turkey has established a breach of Articles 2.2.1.1 and 2.2.2. To the extent the Panel is required to address arguments under Article 2.4, the Panel should find that Turkey has failed to satisfy its burden of proof.

III.   ARTICLE 6.7 AND ANNEX I DO NOT REQUIRE VERIFICATION, NOR DO THEY PROHIBIT COLLECTION OF INFORMATION AFTER VERIFICATION

10.   Turkey has argued that certain procedures relating to verification[5] followed by Egypt in the subject anti-dumping investigation were inconsistent, *inter alia*, with Article 6.7 and Annex I of the AD Agreement.[6] Specifically, at several points in its argument Turkey complains that Egypt refused an offer of a second verification, and collected a substantial amount of information after verification.[7] As stated previously, the United States takes no position on the factual issues in this case, nor on whether the facts raised by these issues may establish a claim under another provision of the Agreement, such as Article 6.2. However, the

---

[3]   The rules reflected in the *Vienna Convention on the Law of Treaties* have attained the status of customary rules of international law. See, *United States - Standards for Reformulated and Conventional Gasoline*, WT/DS2/AB/R, adopted 20 May 1996, DSR 1996, 3, at 16; *Japan - Taxes on Alcoholic Beverages*, WT/DS8/AB/R, WT/DS10/AB/R, WT/DS11/AB/R, adopted 1 November 1996, DSR 1996:I, 97, at 106; *Australia - Subsidies Provided to Producers and Exporters of Automotive Leather (WT/DS126) - Recourse to Article 21.5 of the DSU by the United States*, WT/DS126/RW and Corr.1, 14 January 2000, DSR 2000:III, 1189, para. 6.25.

[4]   Further support for this reading of Article 2.4 is found in the first sentence of Article 2.4.2 which refers to "the provisions governing fair comparison in paragraph 4." This clause clarifies that the entirety of Article 2.4, and not just the first sentence, constitutes the provisions which "govern fair comparison".

[5]   Turkey and Egypt have both repeatedly used the term "verification" to refer to the on-the-spot investigations referred to in Article 6.7 and Annex I. Because so many Members use the term "verification" to refer to these investigations, and to avoid confusion, the United States will continue to use this term in this submission.

[6]   *Turkey First Submission*, section IV-B (pp. 52-55).

[7]   *Ibid.*, paras. 5 and 6 (p. 53).

United States wishes to make clear its views on verification and collection of information after verification.

A.   The Agreement does not Prohibit Collection of Information After Verification

11.   First, collection of information after verification is not *per se* prohibited by the Agreement. Although the facts are somewhat unclear at this stage in the dispute, according to Turkey, after the respondents made their initial submissions, and after Egypt conducted verification, Egypt requested additional information. In a nutshell, Turkey asserts that the information requested was so substantial, and the request was made so late in the proceeding, that respondents were severely prejudiced. Thus, Turkey has raised a factual issue relating to the exporters' opportunity to present evidence and defend their interests, which may best be analyzed under the obligations of Article 6, and on which the United States takes no position.

12.   In the course of its arguments, however, Turkey also asserts that "it is not contemplated in the structure of the Agreement that new information will be sought after verification. Such action should be taken only in exceptional circumstances".[8] In fact, the Agreement does not prohibit gathering information after verification, and the "exceptional circumstances" standard advanced by Turkey appears nowhere in the Agreement.

13.   As a preliminary matter, verification is an entirely optional procedure. Article 6.7 states that authorities may conduct verification, but does not require that they do so. The Panel must keep this fact in mind when addressing Turkey's arguments. Given that verification is not required, it would be absurd to interpret the Agreement to prohibit collection of information after an event which may never take place.

14.   This being said, the only provision of the Agreement arguably dealing with collection of information after verification is Annex I, paragraph 7, which states in pertinent part:

> "As the main purpose of the on-the-spot investigation is to verify information provided or to obtain further details, it should be carried out after the response to the questionnaire has been received unless the firm agrees to the contrary and the government of the exporting Member is informed by the investigating authorities of the anticipated visit and does not object to it".

15.   The United States observes that the language of this provision is not mandatory. As such, there is no basis for Turkey's assertion that, barring "exceptional circumstances", investigating authorities are restricted in their ability to seek information after verification. While some Members may limit collection of information after verification out of concern that such information will not be subject to the check on completeness and accuracy which verification provides,

---

[8]   *Ibid.*, para. 4 (p. 53).

there is nothing in the Agreement which restricts the ability to solicit and accept information at that time.

16.   Moreover, Annex I, paragraph 7, is limited on its face to responses to "questionnaires". This limitation is important because not every request for clarification or follow-up question constitutes a "questionnaire". Rather, the Agreement distinguishes between initial "questionnaires," under Article 6.1.1, and supplemental requests for "further explanation" under Annex II, paragraph 6. After the initial request for information under Article 6.1.1 the authorities may identify areas where the response appears to be incomplete or confusing. Rather than rejecting the response, authorities are required, under Annex II, paragraph 6, to present supplemental requests for clarification and other follow-up questions. Because such supplemental requests for further explanation may occur throughout the investigation, Annex I, paragraph 7, must be limited to the initial "questionnaire". It may be for this reason that Turkey emphasizes its view that the information solicited after verification was so extensive that it amounted to a new questionnaire.[9]

17.   Additionally, interpretation of Annex I, paragraph 7, to apply to all information requests, rather than merely "questionnaires" could result in the absurd situation that conduct of verification, the purpose of which is to clarify the issues, would cut off the authority's ability to seek further clarification. Such a rule would work either to discourage authorities from conducting verification or to limit authorities' ability to solicit clarifications. Either situation could result in determinations based upon unclear information, and greater reliance on the facts available under Article 6.8.

18.   Finally, this provision must be read in light of its object and purpose. A careful reading of Annex I reveals two purposes: 1) ensuring that authorities obtain permission before conducting a verification; and 2) ensuring that interested parties and governments are notified of what they need to do to prepare for verification, and that they are given sufficient time to prepare.[10] Thus, paragraph 7 is not aimed at preventing authorities from gathering information after verification; rather, it is aimed at preventing them from conducting verification before the party has even had an opportunity to analyze the initial questionnaire and pro-

---

[9]   See, e.g. *Turkey First Submission*, at Section IV-C, para. 2 (p. 56). Egypt disputes this assertion. *Egypt First Submission*, section IV.A.7 (pp. 51-55).

[10]   This understanding of the purpose of Annex I is reinforced by its history. The United States notes that Annex I began life as, and indeed remains virtually unchanged from, a recommendation adopted in November, 1983 by the Committee on Antidumping Practices under the GATT Antidumping Code. *Recommendation Concerning Procedures for an On-the-Spot Investigation*, adopted 15 November 1983, GATT Doc. ADP/18, *reprinted in* GATT, *BISD* 30th Supp., p. 28 (March 1984). This document begins with the following recitation of the problems which had caused Signatories to develop specific recommendations:

> The Committee is aware that some difficulties have arisen in this area which have been caused mainly by the failure of the investigating authorities to advise the exporting firms of the proposed date of the visit and the purpose of the investigation. It should be borne in mind that the firms will require time to prepare for the visit. There have also been instances where the authorities of the exporting country have not been specifically informed of the proposed visit.

vide its response. The fact that an authority realizes after verification that it needs further explanation does not mean that the verification took place too early. Indeed, as a full understanding of the information is necessary for an accurate determination of whether dumping measures are warranted, authorities should not be discouraged from asking follow-up questions, provided that they observe the requirements of Articles 6.1 and 6.2.

B. Where Authorities Collect Information After Verification, Members do not have an Obligation to Provide a Second Verification

19. Turkey also alleges that Egypt declined Turkey's offer to permit an additional verification of the information collected after the initial verification.[11] Not being familiar with the facts of this case, the United States takes no position as to whether Turkey can establish a breach of Article 6.2 in light of any such refusal. The United States would like only to make clear that collection of information after verification does not obligate a member to conduct a second verification. Nor does it require a Member to make other arrangements for an oral explanation of the information submitted.

20. As noted above, Article 6.7 does not require an authority to conduct verification at all. Article 6.7 states that authorities *may* carry out verifications in the territory of other members provided that the appropriate procedures are followed. It follows that interested parties in anti-dumping proceedings do not have a right to verification. Moreover, even where verification is conducted, Article 6.7 does not require verification of every piece of information submitted. Indeed, such a requirement would make verification extraordinarily burdensome to all involved. Rather, as the express purpose of Article 6.7 is to "verify" information, and to "obtain further details", authorities must be free to focus on those portions of the response which appear to raise issues of accuracy or clarity. Thus, the Agreement gives to authorities the latitude to determine whether to verify any information submitted, including information solicited after verification.

21. Further, while verification permits the authority to "obtain further detail", in light of the fact that verification is optional, the possibility of verification does not relieve interested parties of the obligation, in their written submissions, to explain clearly the information provided. Ultimately, it is the interested parties, and not the authority, who are in possession of the necessary information and, as that information relates to their own business, are in the best position to explain it. Moreover, Article 6 makes clear that, while opportunities for oral presentations are necessary, the primary means of providing evidence in a dumping investigation is in writing. For example, while Article 6.2 gives interested parties certain rights to present information orally, Article 6.3 prohibits authorities from taking such information into account unless it is subsequently reproduced in writing and made available to other interested parties. The emphasis in the

---

[11] *Turkey First Submission*, section IV-D (pp. 58-59).

Agreement on written evidence is not only important for the investigating authority, it is vital for the other interested parties to permit them to understand the case and to defend their interests. Thus, the Panel should be wary of reading the Agreement in a way which would place heavy reliance on oral presentations rather than on written submissions.

22.   More importantly for purposes of dispute resolution, to the extent the written submissions of fact by the exporters were unclear on their face, and could not be understood except through a subsequent oral explanation, evaluation of the facts is particularly difficult. The Panel must take such lack of clarity into account in weighing whether establishment of the facts was proper and their evaluation unbiased and objective under Article 17.6(i).[12]

IV.   THE TIME LIMIT CONTAINED IN THE FIRST SENTENCE OF ARTICLE 6.1.1 DOES NOT APPLY TO ALL REQUESTS FOR INFORMATION

23.   Turkey asserts that in its request for information after the verification, Egypt did not provide the full 30 days, plus 7 days for mailing, as required for questionnaires by Article 6.1.1, and footnote 15.[13] While not taking any position on the factual dispute, the United States would like to reiterate that not every request for information constitutes a "questionnaire" for which a 37-day response period must be provided. Indeed, Turkey makes a point of alleging that Egypt's request for information was not a mere supplemental question, but rather "amounted to an entirely new cost questionnaire".[14]

24.   The Agreement distinguishes between the deadlines for questionnaires, and the deadlines for supplemental requests for further explanation. Article 6.1.1 requires authorities to allow 30 days (plus 7 for mailing) for responses to "questionnaires". By contrast, Annex II, paragraph 6 addresses subsequent requests for further explanation. That provisions requires only that, with respect to such requests, authorities provide a "reasonable period" for response, "due account being taken of the time limits of the investigation".

25.   This distinction is an important one for the Panel to recognize. If authorities were required to grant 37 days to respond to every request for information, they would be severely constrained in the ability to seek clarification. This would

---

[12]   See, *United States – Anti-Dumping Measures on Stainless Steel Plate in Coils and Stainless Steel Sheet and Strip from Korea*, Panel Report, WT/DS/179/R, adopted 1 February, 2001 ("*United States – Stainless Steel*"), DSR 2001:IV, 1295, para. 6.26-6.31 (where unclear facts before the authority pointed to two possible conclusions, panel limited its factual analysis to the issue of whether an unbiased and objective authority *could* properly have made the determination at issue).

[13]   The United States notes that, although Turkey makes arguments about Article 6.1.1 of the Agreement in section VI-C of its First Submission (pp. 56-58), it only asserts a breach of Articles 6.1, 6.2 and Annex II, para. 6. It is unclear whether this is a typographical error, or whether Turkey is actually asserting a claim under Article 6.1 rather than Article 6.1.1.

[14]   *Turkey First Submission*, Section IV-C, para. 2 (p. 56). As noted above, Egypt disputes this assertion. *Egypt First Submission*, section IV.A.7 (pp. 51-55).

disadvantage all parties and result in less accurate determinations of dumping. Such a rule would also greatly increase the likelihood that authorities would have to take the full 18 months allowed by Article 5.10, and could even result in an increase in breaches of that provision.[15] For this reason, the deadline for requests for "further explanation" is flexible; it gives the authority the discretion to establish a deadline to reflect: 1) the amount of further explanation being requested; and 2) the time-limits of the investigation.

26.   Moreover, where the supplemental request under Annex II, paragraph 6, amounts to a second opportunity to provide information that has already been requested, in assessing the "reasonableness" of the deadline, the Panel must bear in mind that the respondent has already had at least 37 days to respond, and has not done so adequately.

27.   This is not to say that there are no limits on the deadlines which authorities may set for responding to requests for information other than questionnaires. Such deadlines must be "reasonable" under Annex II, paragraph 6. Further, the overall procedure may be reviewed by a Panel for consistency with Articles 6.1 and 6.2.[16]

V.   PARTIES MUST SPECIFY IN THEIR SUBMISSIONS THE PROVISIONS OF THE AGREEMENT WHICH THEY BELIEVE TO HAVE BEEN BREACHED

28.   As a final matter, the United States would like to underscore the importance that complainants state clearly the provisions of the Agreement they contend have been breached. For example, although section IV-H of Turkey's First Submission (pp. 69-70) refers to Article 2.4 and paragraph 7 of Annex II, Turkey does not clearly assert that either of those provisions has been breached. Similarly, section IV-I (p. 72) does not assert that any particular provision has been breached.

29.   Without such clarity it is difficult for the Panel and for other parties to address the arguments. Third parties face a particular problem when the specific claims are not clear in the first submissions, because they may not have the opportunity to participate later in the dispute when the issues are clarified. Finally, given that the AD Agreement represents a series of carefully negotiated and de-

---

[15]   For this reason, Annex II, para. 6, states that the deadline for providing "further explanation" must be set with due account being taken of the time-limit of the investigation.

[16]   Turkey also alleges that its requests for extension of the time to respond to Egypt's supplemental request for information was denied, and addresses the second sentence of Article 6.1.1 which states, "[d]ue consideration should be given to any request for an extension of the thirty day period and, upon cause shown, such an extension should be granted whenever practicable." *Turkey First Submission*, Section IV-C, paras. 3 and 4 (pp. 56-57). In this regard, the United States emphasizes only that the second sentence of Article 6.1.1 simply does not impose a specific obligation upon authorities to grant extensions

lineated obligations, whether a Member has breached an obligation can only be reviewed in relationship to the text of specific provisions of the Agreement.[17]

---

[17] Turkey cites individual members' comments to the Committee on Anti-Dumping Practices during the Article 18.5 review process. See *Turkey First Submission*, footnote 107 (p.55). These comments represent solely the views of an individual Member, and are not appropriate authoritative guidance for the Panel.

ANNEX 12-2

THIRD PARTY ORAL STATEMENT OF THE UNITED STATES

I.   INTRODUCTION

1.   Thank you, Mr. Chairman, and members of the Panel. It is our sincere pleasure to appear before you today to present the views of the United States in this proceeding. The purpose of this oral statement is to highlight certain aspects of our written statement, particularly in light of issues raised by other third parties, and briefly to present our views on certain other issues.

2.   As we stated in our written submission, not being a party to the underlying administrative proceedings, the United States' familiarity with the facts of this case is necessarily limited to the assertions made in the submissions of the parties. Thus, the United States limits its arguments to issues of legal interpretation.

II.   CONSIDERATION OF EXTRA-RECORD EVIDENCE

3.   As a preliminary matter, we would like to highlight a dispute over certain documents cited in Turkey's brief. In its submission, Egypt has argued that the documents in question were not presented to the investigating authority in the underlying proceeding, and thus should not be considered by the Panel.

4.   The Anti-Dumping Agreement, as illuminated by past panel and Appellate Body reports, is clear on this point: information not presented to the investigating authority is not relevant to a panel's consideration of whether a Member has acted in accordance with the standard set forth in Article 17.6(i). That provision establishes the standard to be applied in the Panel's "assessment of the facts of the matter". The chapeau of Article 17.6 makes clear that the "matter" covered by that Article is the same as the "matter" addressed in Article 17.5.

5.   Article 17.5, in turn, establishes that, in examining a matter presented to a Panel, the facts upon which its examination must be based are those which were presented to the investigating authority. Thus, Article 17.6(i) can only be understood by reference to Article 17.5(ii). As explained by the Appellate Body in *Thailand – Anti-Dumping Duties on Angles, Shapes and Sections of Iron or Non-alloy Steel and H-beams from Poland*:

> "Article 17.6(i) must be read in conjunction with Article 17.5(ii) of the Anti-Dumping Agreement, which requires that a panel must examine the matter based upon the 'facts' made available to the in-

vestigating authorities in accordance with appropriate domestic procedures".[1]

6.   The issue of the range of evidence which the Panel is entitled to examine has been addressed in prior disputes. For example, the Panel in *Mexico – Anti-Dumping Investigation of High Fructose Corn Syrup (HFCS) from the United States*[2] summed up this range of relevant evidence under Article 17.5(ii):

> "Mindful of the standard of review and Article 17.5(ii), we note that we may consider in our examination of this issue only what was actually available to the investigating authority at the time of the initiation in evaluating the consistency of the initiation with Article 5.3, and must consider whether SECOFI's establishment of the facts was proper and its evaluation of those facts was unbiased and objective".

7.   Similarly, the panel in *United States – Anti-Dumping Measures on Certain Hot-Rolled Steel Products from Japan*[3] stated:

> "It seems clear to us that, under this provision, a panel may not, when examining a claim of violation of the AD Agreement in a particular determination, consider facts or evidence presented to it by a party in an attempt to demonstrate error in the determination concerning questions that were investigated and decided by the authorities, unless they had been made available in conformity with the appropriate domestic procedures to the authorities of the investigating country during the investigation. . .

> That Article 17.5(ii) and the DSU provisions are complementary does not diminish the importance of Article 17.5(ii) in guiding our decisions in this regard. It is a specific provision directing a panel's decision as to what evidence it will consider in examining a claim under the AD Agreement. Moreover, it effectuates the general principle that panels reviewing the determinations of investigating authorities in anti-dumping cases are not to engage in *de novo* review".

8.   Thus, Article 17.5(ii) is fully applicable, and the Panel should disregard information which was not presented to the Egyptian authorities.

9.   Finally, the EC imagines a situation in which information was improperly rejected by the authority, and argues that the Panel may be required to review the information itself in that situation. While the United States does not necessarily

---

[1]   Appellate Body Report on Thailand – Anti-dumping Duties on Angles, Shapes and Sections of Iron or Non-alloy Steel and H-beams from Poland, WT/DS122/AB/R, adopted 5 April 2001, DSR 2001:VII, 2701, para. 17.
[2]   Panel Report on *Mexico – Anti-Dumping Investigation of High Fructose Corn Syrup (HFCS) from the United States*, WT/DS132/R and Corr.1, adopted 24 February 2000, DSR 2000:III, 1345, para. 7.105.
[3]   Panel Report on *United States – Anti-Dumping Measures on Certain Hot-Rolled Steel Products from Japan*, WT/DS184/R, adopted 23 August 2001, DSR 2001:X, 4769, para. 7.6.

agree with this assertion, we note that the EC admits that improper rejection of the information Turkey has presented is not an issue in this case, and thus the Panel need not address this issue.

III. INJURY ISSUES

10.   The United States will now turn to the injury issues arising in this dispute. The United States will address the following subjects: (1) the obligation to examine the impact of the dumped imports under Article 3.4, (2) the obligation to examine price undercutting under Article 3.2, (3) the examination of causal link between imports and injury under Article 3.5, and (4) the determination of the period of investigation for injury analysis.

> A.   *The Requirements of Article 3.4 to Consider all Relevant Economic Factors should not be Confused with the Separate Obligation Contained in Article 3.5 of the Agreement*

11.   Turning first to the obligation under Article 3.4, Turkey argues that the Egyptian authorities failed properly to consider the factors listed in Articles 3.4 and 3.5 of the Anti-Dumping Agreement.[4] The United States agrees that an investigating authority must evaluate the critical factors listed in *Article 3.4* (or other relevant economic factors, not listed) in its consideration of the impact of dumped imports on the domestic industry, so that it may be discerned how imports affect, *inter alia*, the industry's sales, prices, its share of total domestic production, its profitability, financial performance, or the overall condition of the industry. Without such an analysis, the investigating authority would fail to comply with Article 3.4 of the Anti-Dumping Agreement. This issue is well settled by now, having been addressed by panels in the *High Fructose Corn Syrup* and *Bed Linens* disputes and by the Appellate Body.

12.   The United States disagrees, however, with Turkey's assertion that investigating authorities are required to identify specific lost sales. In evaluating Article 3.4 factors, the investigating authority is required by the Anti-Dumping Agreement to examine any actual and potential decline in sales, but the authority is not required to investigate whether specific sales were lost by the domestic industry to unfairly traded imports. While there may be certain types of investigations involving large capital goods or custom-made goods ordered under contract in which the loss of a single sale or a few specific sales could prove indicative of injury, there is nothing in Article 3.4 of the Agreement that specifically obligates a Member to investigate specific lost sales in determining the impact of dumped imports on the domestic industry.

---

[4]   First Written Submission of Turkey at 3 and 8-19.

B. The Determination of Price Undercutting under Article 3.2 Need not Always be Made on a Delivered-Price Basis

13.   Turning to the issue of price undercutting under Article 3.2, the United States agrees that injury determinations under Article 3 must be based on positive evidence and must involve an objective examination of not simply the volume of dumped imports but also the effect of those imports on prices in the domestic market. Article 3.2 provides that, in determining the effect of dumped imports on prices, the investigating authorities shall consider whether there has been significant price undercutting by the dumped imports as compared with the price of a like product of the importing Member, or whether the effect of such imports is otherwise to depress prices to a significant degree or prevent price increases, which otherwise would have occurred, to a significant degree. Turkey argues (at 3 and 20-21) that by not ensuring that the comparison of domestic and imported prices was conducted on a comparable, delivered basis, the Egyptian authority's finding of price undercutting was based on a flawed price comparison. However, there is no legal requirement under the Anti-Dumping Agreement that an authority make its price comparison only on a delivered price basis. In fact, in many instances sales are made on an FOB basis and converting them to a delivered basis is both unnecessary to obtain comparable prices and potentially distorting to commercial realities.

C. The Article 3.5 Obligation

14.   With respect to Turkey's argument about Article 3.5, it appears that none of the parties–dispute that the Anti-Dumping Agreement does not prescribe a specific methodology to be used by Members to establish the requisite causal link between subject imports and the injury suffered by a domestic industry. The Appellate Body confirmed in *Hot-rolled Steel* that Article 3.5 leaves open to Members the means employed to fulfill the non-attribution requirement.

15.   Although the United States agrees with Turkey's assertion that consideration of the Article 3.4 factors is mandatory, we do not agree with the implication that consideration of the factors listed in Article 3.5 is also mandatory. By failing to differentiate between the analysis required under Articles 3.4 and 3.5, Turkey has left the erroneous impression that the factors referenced in paragraph 5 of Article 3 must be examined and considered in every determination. The plain language of that provision makes clear that is not the case.

16.   Although Article 3.5 directs Members to "examine any known factors other than the dumped imports which at the same time are injuring the domestic industry . . .", the nature of this obligation is different from the requirement in Article 3.4 that all relevant economic factors be examined. In particular, Article 3.5 states that the authorities' demonstration of the causal relationship between dumped imports and injury shall be based on an examination of all relevant evidence before them. The specific factors that are listed in Article 3.5 are not mandatory, but simply illustrate the type of factors which may be examined by the investigating authority. Article 3.5 specifically refers to causal factors which

"may be relevant" in this respect.[5] Moreover, the scope of an investigating authority's obligation under Article 3.5 extends only to "known" factors.

17.   More fundamentally, Article 3.5 does not require investigating authorities to demonstrate that there are no other factors also causing the domestic industry's injury or to investigate any factors other than those which are known to the investigating authority. Accordingly, a complainant does not satisfy its *prima facie* case requirement simply by suggesting that there *may* be other unidentified factors contributing to the injury.

D.   The Periods of Investigation for Dumping and Injury Analyses

18.   With respect to the proper period(s) of investigation for determining dumping and injury, the Anti-Dumping Agreement does not prescribe any specific time period(s) for the purpose of data collection. In light of the requirement in Article 3.5 that it "be demonstrated that the dumped imports are, through the effects of dumping . . . causing injury", the United States submits that both the dumping and injury components of the investigations must be contemporaneous such that an investigating authority can substantiate the requisite causal link, or lack thereof, between the allegedly dumped imports and any alleged injury, or threat of injury. This is not to state, however, that the two periods must be exactly the same. In fact, the injury investigation may reasonably include a substantial period of time either prior to or subsequent to (or both prior to and subsequent to) the dumping investigation, and be of sufficient length to allow investigating authorities to examine various industry and import trends.

IV.   THE DUMPING DETERMINATION

19.   The United States would now like to address certain of the legal issues presented to the Panel in connection with Egypt's determination of dumping. As stated, the United States will confine its comments to issues of legal interpretation and procedure.

20.   First, as mentioned in our submission, in reviewing the amount of time to respond to a request for further information made after the initial questionnaire, the deadlines established in Article 6.1.1 are simply not relevant. Such supplemental requests for information are not "questionnaires" within the meaning of that term as used in Article 6.1.1. As the EC points out in its submission, several provisions of the Agreement provide for requests for information other than questionnaires. Most importantly, where an investigating authority does not believe evidence or information is acceptable, it must request further explanation, and provide a "reasonable" period to respond to such request, "due account being taken of the time-limits of the investigation".

---

[5]   Panel and Appellate Body Reports on Thailand - Anti-Dumping Duties on Angles, Shapes and Sections of Iron or Non-Alloy Steel and H-Beams from Poland, WT/DS122/R, WT/DS122/AB/R, adopted 5 April 2001).

21.   However, while the United States does not believe that the time limit established in Article 6.1.1 is relevant to subsequent requests for information, we agree with Japan that the Panel may review the period to ensure that the party has had "ample opportunity" to present its evidence, as required by Article 6.1, and has had a full opportunity for defense of its interests, as required by Article 6.2. However, the Panel must bear in mind, in determining whether the investigating authority has acted reasonably, that the needs and circumstances of the responding party are not the only relevant consideration. Authorities must weigh those needs and circumstances against the deadlines for investigations established in Article 5.10, and the time needed by the investigating authority to make an accurate, well-reasoned and well-explained analysis.

22.   The United States would also like to clarify one point about collection of information after the verification – not only is collection of further information after verification permitted under the agreement, the right of investigating authorities to do so is also highly desirable as it fosters more accurate determinations. To the extent authorities realize that they need clarification on some point after verification is conducted, it is in the interest of accuracy that they be permitted to request such clarification, provided that they establish a reasonable deadline.

23.   Paragraph 7 of Annex I in no way limits the authority of Members to collect further information after verification. As noted in our written submission, that provision applies only to questionnaires, and not to supplemental requests for information. That provision is aimed against the abusive practice of conducting an on-the-spot investigation of a respondent's business practices before the respondent has even been informed of the information required, and before it has had an opportunity to formulate its response. Thus, paragraph 7 relates to the timing of verifications, rather than the timing of requests for information.

24.   In this regard, the United States would also like to point out the potential for confusion in the way some parties have used the term "verification". Turkey has objected to what it terms "mail order" verification by Egypt. Japan has picked up this term, and argued that because on-the-spot verifications are provided for, any other type of "verification" is prohibited. This mis-use of the term "verification" could be highly misleading. Verification is not required under Article 6.7. Rather, on-the-spot verification may be conducted by the investigating Member if it perceives some benefit from doing so, and the exporting Member permits it. Responding parties do not have a right to rely on a verification being conducted in order to provide necessary information. Whether a verification is conducted or not does not alter the obligation of responding parties to provide requested information and support the claims they make. Requests for such support are not "verification".

25.   The anti-dumping investigation process is a demanding process, both for the investigating authority, and for the responding party. Making the required determinations, while meeting the obligation to ensure accuracy under Article 6.6 and at the same time meeting the deadlines under Article 5.10, requires a large amount of information in a short amount of time. In determining whether

an investigation has been conducted in accordance with the Agreement, the Panel must bear in mind one important fact: the necessary information is in the possession of the responding party. Although investigating authorities must provide a full opportunity for interested parties to defend their interests, ultimately there is a burden on responding parties. The quality of the determination is directly related to the extent to which responding parties have been promptly forthcoming. Insistence that those parties provide requested information should not be dismissed as "mail order" verification. There is nothing improper about asking responding parties to provide documentary evidence to establish the accuracy of claims they have made. Indeed, the Agreement requires it.

26.   The United States appreciates this opportunity to address the Panel on these points, and would welcome any questions.

ANNEX 12-3

THIRD PARTY RESPONSES OF THE UNITED STATES
TO QUESTIONS FROM THE PANEL

Q1. **What role does the US foresee for an investigating authority in an anti-dumping investigation establishing the existence of "other known factors" under Article 3.5, and what is the legal basis for its position?**

Reply

1.   Article 3.5 of the Agreement on Implementation of Article VI of the General Agreement on Tariffs and Trade 1994 ("Anti-Dumping Agreement") directs Members to "examine any *known* factors other than the dumped imports which at the same time are injuring the domestic industry. . .". The use of the word "known" is significant as it is not used anywhere else in the text of Article 3 to describe factors relevant either to injury or causation. In fact, the inclusion of the term "known" in Article 3.5 is one of the principal changes regarding causation made between the text of the Tokyo Round Anti-Dumping Agreement and the WTO Anti-Dumping Agreement. Its use exclusively in connection with factors other than dumped imports that may be causing injury unmistakably distinguishes the investigative authorities' responsibilities associated with such factors from the other factors referenced in Article 3. The ordinary meaning of the term "known" makes clear that the investigating authorities' responsibility in this regard extends only to the examination of factors of which the investigating authorities possess knowledge or with which they are made familiar or become acquainted.[1]

2.   There is no textual requirement, express or implied, that the investigating authorities affirmatively seek out information about other possible alternative factors that are not "known" to them that may be causing injury. Thus, factors will be known to the investigating authorities by virtue of any relevant information already in their possession in the applicable record or by reason of information provided by the participants in the investigation. In this connection, we agree with the European Communities' observation[2] regarding the pertinence of the findings by the Panel in *Thailand - H Beams* that

> "We consider that other "known" factors would include those causal factors that are clearly raised before the investigating authorities by interested parties in the course of an investigation. We are of the view that there is no express requirement in Article 3.5 that investigating authorities seek out and examine in each case on their own initiative the effects of all possible factors other than im-

---

[1]   The Shorter Oxford English Dictionary, 1993 ed.
[2]   Third party Oral Statement of the European Communities, 27 November 2001, para. 4.

ports that may be causing injury to the domestic industry under investigation".[3]

3.   The factors identified in the last sentence of Article 3.5, moreover, are merely illustrative of the factors that, if known to the investigating authorities, are to be examined in ensuring that no injury caused by factors other than subject imports is attributed to such imports. That this list is illustrative only is indicated by the introductory language, which states that the factors *may* be relevant. Therefore, the factors set forth in Article 3.5 do not constitute a mandatory list of matters that the investigating authorities must in each investigation examine. Investigating authorities may rely on interested parties to bring relevant "known" factors to the authorities' attention.

Q2.   Is there a different obligation borne by an investigating authority in an anti-dumping investigation with regard to establishing "other known factors" in terms of Article 3.5 of the Anti-Dumping Agreement, compared with the establishment of "all relevant factors" in terms of Article 4.2(b) of the Safeguards Agreement and, if so, what are the different obligations and the legal bases for these obligations?

Reply

4.   The United States submits that quite different investigative obligations are established by the text of the Anti-Dumping Agreement and the Safeguards Agreement, as befits the distinct objectives of those agreements, the particular rights and obligations contained, respectively, in them, and the significant textual differences in the language of the two Agreements. By virtue of the use of the term "known factors" in Article 3.5 of the Anti-Dumping Agreement investigating authorities have no obligation under Article 3.5 to seek out causes of injury other than dumped imports. Given, in particular the absence of the same term "known factors" from the text of Article 4.2 of the Safeguards Agreement, that Article is not useful to inform the nature of the responsibilities of the investigating authorities under the Anti-Dumping Agreement, the pertinent issue before this Panel.

5.   Further, the Safeguards Agreement's specific reference to a competent authority's consideration of "all relevant factors" of an objective and quantifiable nature having a bearing on the situation of that industry appears in Article 4.2(a), which concerns the determination of serious injury, rather than in Article 4.2(b), which concerns causation. The provision in the Anti-Dumping Agreement most directly comparable to, but not identical with, Article 4.2(a) of the Safeguards Agreement, is not Article 3.5, but Article 3.4.

---

[3]   Panel Report in *Thailand - Anti-Dumping Duties on Angles, Shapes and Sections of Iron or Non-Alloy Steel and H-Beams from Poland*, WT/DS/122/R, adopted 5 April 2001, as modified by the Appellate Body Report, WT/DS122/AB/R, DSR 2001:VII, 2741, para. 7.273.

Q3   The US view seems to be that the reference in Article 17.5(ii) to facts "made available" during an investigation means facts "presented" to the Investigating Authority. In the US view, by whom, how and when would such information be presented?

Reply

6.   In the view of the United States, Article 17.5(ii) limits the review of the panel to facts that were presented to the investigating authority, either through submission by some person, as discussed below, or through its own investigative activities. The reference to facts "*made* available" is significant in that it eliminates from consideration facts which, although theoretically "available," were not actually presented to the authority.

7.   The Panel's question is answered in a general way by the language of Article 17.5(ii) itself, which states that, even if facts were "made available," they are only relevant to the Panel's consideration if they were made available "in conformity with appropriate domestic procedures". This phrase reserves to each member the authority to determine by whom, how and when information may be presented during an investigation.

8.   This is not to say that such authority is unfettered. For example, although domestic procedures may specify who has a right to present information, such procedure must meet the requirement of Article 6.11 which defines interested parties as including:

(i)   an exporter or foreign producer or the importer of a product subject to investigation, or a trade or business association a majority of the members of which are producers, exporters or importers of such product;

(ii)   the government of the exporting country; and

(iii)   a producer of the like product in the importing country or a trade and business association a majority of the members of which produce the like product in the importing country.

9.   Similarly, Article 6.12 requires investigating authorities to permit industrial users and representative consumer organizations to provide information which is relevant to the investigation regarding dumping, injury and causality.

10.   Although the question of *who* may provide information is subject to fairly clear guidelines, the question of *when* is more vague under the Agreement. Members have the authority to establish deadlines. One clear limit on that authority, however, is the requirement under Article 6.1.1 that authorities allow at least 37 days for questionnaire responses. Deadlines for submission of information may also be reviewed for consistency with Article 6.1, to ensure that interested parties have been provided ample opportunity to present in writing all evidence which they consider relevant. Finally, to the extent the investigating authority does not intend to accept information submitted, under Annex II, paragraph 6 authorities must provide a "reasonable period, due account being taken of the time limits of the investigation", for parties to provide further explana-

tions. However, Article 6.14 counters these limitations on deadlines by making clear that a member is free to proceed expeditiously. This concept is reinforced by the relatively short deadlines of Article 5.10.

11.   Finally, on the question of how information is to be provided, the Agreement is largely silent. Information must be provided in writing, or otherwise reduced to a form which can bee seen under Article 6.4. There must be an opportunity for a hearing under Article 6.2. Additionally, a party who has provided confidential information must furnish a non-confidential summary. Apart from those requirements, the authority is free to establish appropriate procedures for parties to submit information.

***

12.   The United States would also like to take this opportunity briefly to present its views on one of the questions presented to Japan.

Questions to Japan

Q3   How does Japan interpret Article 2.4, in its context?

Reply

13.   It is the view of the United States that the first sentence of Article 2.4 cannot be divorced from the context of the remainder of Article 2.4. While the first sentence of Article 2.4 establishes the requirement to make a "fair comparison", the remainder of Article 2.4 *defines* how "this comparison" is made.

14.   The predecessor to Article 2.4, Article 2.6 of the Antidumping Code, also defined what was required "*[i]n order to effect* a fair comparison" (emphasis added). The "in order to effect" language of this provision was ambiguous. One possible reading of this language was that the fair comparison was not required, but if a Member wished to make one, it should do so as instructed in Article 2.6. Thus, all of Article 2.6 could have been read as non-mandatory. In other words, Article 2.6 clearly mandated *how* to make a fair comparison, but the fair comparison itself was not clearly mandated.

15.   That ambiguity was eliminated in the current Agreement by adding the first sentence of Article 2.4, which makes explicit the requirement to make a fair comparison. However, the remainder of Article 2.4, like its predecessor, defines the comparison. Thus, Article 2.4 of the current Agreement is clearly mandatory – it requires members to make the fair comparison, and instructs them how to do it. This interpretation of Article 2.4 is also consistent with its drafting history. In what is known as the "Dunkel Draft", Article 2.4 read:

> "A fair comparison shall be made between the export price and the normal value. *The two prices shall be compared* at the same level of trade... " (Emphasis added).

16.   Arguably, that formulation was ambiguous as to whether the requirement to make a fair comparison was free standing. In the final draft, however, the language was amended to read:

> "A fair comparison shall be made between the export price and the normal value. *This comparison* shall be *made* at the same level of trade... " (Emphasis added).

17.   Substitution of the phrase "this comparison" establishes a reference back to the subject of the prior sentence, *i.e.*, a fair comparison, which is what is being defined.

18.   Further support for this reading of Article 2.4 is found in the first sentence of Article 2.4.2 which refers to "the provisions governing fair comparison in paragraph 4". The plural term "provisions," as well as the reference to "paragraph 4," rather than "the first sentence of paragraph 4", make clear that this clause refers to the entirety of Article 2.4. Further, this clause clarifies that the entirety of Article 2.4, and not just the first sentence, constitutes the provisions which "govern fair comparison".

19.   In light of the object and purpose of the AD Agreement, there is no basis for an interpretation of Article 2.4 that divorces the obligation in Article 2.4 to make a fair comparison from the allowances required to establish price comparability. In accordance with Article 2.1, a dumping analysis is based on a comparison of prices for sales in the export market to prices for sales in the home market. By requiring due allowance for all factors affecting price comparability, Article 2.4 assures that the prices used to establish dumping in Article 2.1 are "comparable," *i.e.* a comparison of such prices is fair. There is simply no logic in asserting that even where transactions in the two markets are rendered comparable in all respects affecting price, comparing them in a dumping analysis could be unfair.[4] The concept of fairness and the concept of comparability are inseparable.

---

[4]   Similarly, holding the requirement of a fair comparison separate from the requirement of comparability implies that a comparison of two prices which are not comparable could be fair, clearly an absurd result.

ANNEX 13

SUPPLEMENTAL WORKING PROCEDURES OF THE PANEL CONCERNING CERTAIN BUSINESS CONFIDENTIAL INFORMATION

1.   Egypt shall submit to the Panel six copies and to Turkey one copy of the *Confidential Injury Analysis,* as referred to in its written response to Question 5 of the Panel, dated 7 December 2001.

2.   Egypt shall mark the cover and/or first page of the document containing business confidential information, and each page containing such information to indicate the presence of such information. Specifically, the information in question shall be placed between double brackets, as follows: [[xx,xxx.xx]]. The first page or cover of the document shall state "Contains business confidential information on pages xxxxxx", and each page of the document shall contain the same notice at the top of the page.

3.   As required by Article 18.2 of the DSU, Turkey shall treat as confidential the information in the *Confidential Injury Analysis* that has been designated as business confidential under these procedures; i.e., Turkey shall not disclose the information contained therein without the formal authorization of Egypt. Turkey shall have the responsibility for all members of its delegation, which, for the purposes of these supplemental procedures only, shall not include any employee of any private entity that was an interested party in the anti-dumping investigation. In particular, no member of Turkey's delegation shall disclose to any person outside the delegation any information designated as business confidential under these procedures, and any such information must only be used for the purposes of submissions and argumentation in this dispute and for no other purpose.

4.   Any party referring in its written submissions or oral statements to any information that has been designated as business confidential under these procedures, shall clearly identify all such information in those submissions and statements. All such written submissions shall be marked as described in paragraph 2, above. A non-confidential version, clearly marked as such, of any written submission containing business confidential information shall be submitted to the Panel simultaneously with the confidential version. In the case of an oral statement containing business confidential information, a written non-confidential version shall be submitted within a day after the statement has been made. Non-confidential versions shall be redacted in such a manner as to convey a reasonable understanding of the substance of the business confidential information deleted therefrom.

5.   The Panel engages not to disclose, in its report, or in any other way, any information designated as business confidential under these procedures. The Panel may, however, make statements of conclusion drawn from such information.

6.   Submissions containing information designated as business confidential under these procedures will, however, be included in the record forwarded to the Appellate Body in the event of any appeal of the Panel's Report.

Cumulative Index of Published Disputes

Argentina – Definitive Anti-Dumping Measures on Imports of Ceramic Floor Tiles from Italy

Complaint by the European Communities (WT/DS189)

Report of the Panel .... DSR 2001:XII, 6241

Argentina - Measures Affecting Imports of Footwear, Textiles, Apparel and Other Items

Complaint by the United States (WT/DS56)

Report of the Appellate Body .... DSR 1998:III, 1003

Report of the Panel .... DSR 1998:III, 1033

Argentina - Measures Affecting the Export of Bovine Hides and the Import of Finished Leather

Complaint by the European Communities (WT/DS155)

Report of the Panel .... DSR 2001:V, 1779

Award of the Arbitrator under Article 21.3(c) of the DSU .... DSR 2001:XII, 6013

Argentina - Safeguard Measures on Imports of Footwear

Complaint by the European Communities (WT/DS121)

Report of the Appellate Body .... DSR 2000:I, 515

Report of the Panel .... DSR 2000:II, 575

Australia - Measures Affecting Importation of Salmon

Complaint by Canada (WT/DS18)

Report of the Appellate Body .... DSR 1998:VIII, 3327

Report of the Panel.. DSR 1998:VIII, 3407

Award of the Arbitrator under Article 21.3(c) of the DSU .... DSR 1999:I, 267

Report of the Panel - Recourse to Article 21.5 of the DSU....... DSR 2000:IV, 2031

Australia - Subsidies Provided to Producers and Exporters of Automotive Leather

Complaint by the United States (WT/DS126)

Report of the Panel .... DSR 1999:III, 951

Report of the Panel - Recourse to Article 21.5 of the DSU....... DSR 2000:III, 1189

Brazil - Measures Affecting Desiccated Coconut

Complaint by the Philippines (WT/DS22)

Report of the Appellate Body .... DSR 1997:I, 167

Report of the Panel .... DSR 1997:I, 189

Brazil - Export Financing Programme for Aircraft

Complaint by Canada (WT/DS46)

Report of the Appellate Body .... DSR 1999:III, 1161

Report of the Panel .... DSR 1999:III, 1221

Report of the Appellate Body - Recourse to Article 21.5 of the DSU .... DSR 2000:VIII, 4067

Report of the Panel - Recourse to Article 21.5 of the DSU.......DSR 2000:IX, 4093

Report of the Panel - Second Recourse to
Article 21.5 of the DSU ....DSR 2001:XI, 5481

Decision by the Arbitrators - Recourse to Arbitration by Brazil under
Article 22.6 of the DSU and Article 4.11 of the SCM Agreement...DSR 2002:I, 19

Canada - Certain Measures Affecting the Automotive Industry
Complaint by the European Communities (WT/DS142);
complaint by Japan (WT/DS139)
Report of the Appellate Body ....DSR 2000:VI, 2985
Report of the Panel .... DSR 2000:VII, 3043
Award of the Arbitrator under Article 21.3(c) of the DSU .... DSR 2000:X, 5079

Canada - Certain Measures Concerning Periodicals
Complaint by the United States (WT/DS31)
Report of the Appellate Body ....DSR 1997:I, 449
Report of the Panel ....DSR 1997:I, 481

Canada - Export Credits and Loan Guarantees for Regional Aircraft
Complaint by Brazil (WT/DS222)
Report of the Panel...DSR 2002:III, 849

Canada - Measures Affecting the Importation of Milk and the Exportation of Dairy Products
Complaint by New Zealand (WT/DS113); complaint by the United States (WT/DS103)
Report of the Appellate Body .... DSR 1999:V, 2057
Report of the Panel..DSR 1999:VI, 2097
Report of the Appellate Body - Recourse to Article 21.5
of the DSU .... DSR 2001:XIII, 6829
Report of the Panel - Recourse to Article 21.5 of the DSU.... DSR 2001:XIII, 6865

Canada - Measures Affecting the Export of Civilian Aircraft
Complaint by Brazil (WT/DS70)
Report of the Appellate Body ....DSR 1999:III, 1377
Report of the Panel ....DSR 1999:IV, 1443
Report of the Appellate Body - Recourse to Article 21.5
of the DSU ....DSR 2000:IX, 4299
Report of the Panel - Recourse to Article 21.5 of the DSU.......DSR 2000:IX, 4315

Canada - Patent Protection of Pharmaceutical Products
Complaint by the European Communities (WT/DS114)
Report of the Panel .... DSR 2000:V, 2289
Award of the Arbitrator under Article 21.3(c) of the DSU ....DSR 2002:I, 3

Canada - Term of Patent Protection
Complaint by the United States (WT/DS170)
Report of the Appellate Body .... DSR 2000:X, 5093
Report of the Panel ....DSR 2000:XI, 5121

Award of the Arbitrator under Article 21.3(c) of the DSU ......DSR 2000:IX, 4537

Chile - Taxes on Alcoholic Beverages
Complaint by the European Communities (WT/DS87), (WT/DS110)
Report of the Appellate Body ....DSR 2000:I, 281
Report of the Panel ....DSR 2000:I, 303
Award of the Arbitrator under Article 21.3(c) of the DSU .... DSR 2000:V, 2583

European Communities - Anti-Dumping Duties on Imports of Cotton-Type Bed Linen from India
Complaint by India (WT/DS141)
Report of the Appellate Body .... DSR 2001:V, 2049
Report of the Panel ....DSR 2001:VI, 2077

European Communities - Customs Classification of Certain Computer Equipment
Complaint by the United States (WT/DS62); complaint by the United States – Ireland (WT/DS68); complaint by the United States – United Kingdom (WT/DS67)
Report of the Appellate Body .... DSR 1998:V, 1851
Report of the Panel .... DSR 1998:V, 1891

European Communities - Measures Affecting Asbestos and Asbestos-Containing Products
Complaint by Canada (WT/DS135)
Report of the Appellate Body .... DSR 2001:VII, 3243
Report of the Panel .... DSR 2001:VIII, 3305

European Communities - Measures Affecting the Importation of Certain Poultry Products
Complaint by Brazil (WT/DS69)
Report of the Appellate Body .... DSR 1998:V, 2031
Report of the Panel .... DSR 1998:V, 2089

European Communities - Measures Concerning Meat and Meat Products (Hormones)
Complaint by Canada (WT/DS48); complaint by the United States (WT/DS26)
Report of the Appellate Body ....DSR 1998:I, 135
Report of the Panel (Canada) .... DSR 1998:II, 235
Report of the Panel (United States) ....DSR 1998:III, 699
Award of the Arbitrator under Article 21.3(c) of the DSU .... DSR 1998:V, 1833
Decision by the Arbitrators under Article 22.6 of the DSU (Canada) ....DSR 1999:III, 1135
Decision by the Arbitrators under Article 22.6 of the DSU (United States) ....DSR 1999:III, 1105

European Communities - Regime for the Importation, Sale and Distribution of Bananas
Complaint by Ecuador; Guatemala; Honduras; Mexico; and the United States (WT/DS27)
Report of the Appellate Body .... DSR 1997:II, 589

Report of the Panel (Ecuador)..DSR 1997:III, 3

Report of the Panel (Guatemala, Honduras)..............................DSR 1997:II, 695

Report of the Panel (Mexico)...DSR 1997:II, 803

Report of the Panel (United States)...DSR 1997:II, 943

Award of the Arbitrator under Article 21.3(c) of the DSU ....DSR 1998:I, 3

Decision by the Arbitrators under Article 22.6
of the DSU (US)..DSR 1999:II, 725

Report of the Panel - Recourse to Article 21.5 of the DSU
(European Communities) ....DSR 1999:II, 783

Report of the Panel - Recourse to Article 21.5 of the DSU
(Ecuador) ....DSR 1999:II, 803

Decision by the Arbitrators under Article 22.6
of the DSU (Ecuador) ....DSR 2000:V, 2237

European Communities – Trade Description of Scallops

Complaint by Canada (WT/DS7); complaint by Chile (WT/DS14); complaint by Peru (WT/DS12)

Report of the Panel (Canada) ....DSR 1996:I, 89

Report of the Panel (Chile, Peru) ....DSR 1996:I, 93

Guatemala – Anti-Dumping Investigation Regarding Portland Cement From Mexico

Complaint by Mexico (WT/DS60)

Report of the Appellate Body ....DSR 1998:IX, 3767

Report of the Panel ....DSR 1998:IX, 3797

Guatemala - Definitive Anti-Dumping Measures on Grey Portland Cement from Mexico

Complaint by Mexico (WT/DS156)

Report of the Panel ....DSR 2000:XI, 5295

India – Measures Affecting the Automotive Sector

Complaint by European Communities (WT/DS146,) complaint by the United States (WT/DS175)

Report of the Appellate Body ....DSR 2002:V, 1821

Report of the Panel...DSR 2002:V, 1827

India - Patent Protection for Pharmaceutical and Agricultural Chemical Products

Complaint by European Communities (WT/DS79); complaint by the United States (WT/DS50)

Report of the Appellate Body (United States)...................................DSR 1998:I, 9

Report of the Panel (European Communities)............................DSR 1998:VI, 2661

Report of the Panel (United States)..DSR 1998:I, 41

India - Quantitative Restrictions on Imports of Agricultural, Textile and Industrial Products

Complaint by the United States (WT/DS90)

Report of the Appellate Body ....DSR 1999:IV, 1763

Report of the Panel...DSR 1999:V, 1799

Indonesia - Certain Measures Affecting the Automobile Industry
Complaint by European Communities (WT/DS54); complaint by Japan (WT/DS55, WT/DS64); complaint by the United States (WT/DS59)
Report of the Panel...DSR 1998:VI, 2201
Award of the Arbitrator under Article 21.3(c) of the DSU ......DSR 1998:IX, 4029

Japan - Measures Affecting Agricultural Products
Complaint by the United States (WT/DS76)
Report of the Appellate Body ....DSR 1999:I, 277
Report of the Panel ....DSR 1999:I, 315

Japan - Measures Affecting Consumer Photographic Film and Paper
Complaint by the United States (WT/DS44)
Report of the Panel ....DSR 1998:IV, 1179

Japan – Taxes on Alcoholic Beverages
Complaint by Canada (WT/DS10); complaint by the European Communities (WT/DS8); complaint by the United States (WT/DS11)
Report of the Appellate Body ....DSR 1996:I, 97
Report of the Panel...DSR 1996:I, 125
Award of the Arbitrator under Article 21.3(c) of the DSU ....DSR 1997:I, 3

Korea - Definitive Safeguard Measure on Imports of Certain Dairy Products
Complaint by the European Communities (WT/DS98)
Report of the Appellate Body ....DSR 2000:I, 3
Report of the Panel ....DSR 2000:I, 49

Korea – Measures Affecting Imports of Fresh, Chilled and Frozen Beef
Complaint by Australia (WT/DS169); complaint by the United States (WT/DS161)
Report of the Appellate Body ....DSR 2001:I, 5
Report of the Panel ....DSR 2001:I, 59

Korea - Measures Affecting Government Procurement
Complaint by the United States (WT/DS163)
Report of the Panel .... DSR 2000:VIII, 3541

Korea - Taxes on Alcoholic Beverages
Complaint by the European Communities (WT/DS75); complaint by the United States (WT/DS84)
Report of the Appellate Body ....DSR 1999:I, 3
Report of the Panel ....DSR 1999:I, 44
Award of the Arbitrator under Article 21.3(c) of the DSU .... DSR 1999:II, 937

Mexico - Anti-Dumping Investigation of High Fructose Corn Syrup (HFCS) from the United States
Complaint by the United States (WT/DS132)
Report of the Panel .... DSR 2000:III, 1345
Report of the Appellate Body - Recourse to Article 21.5
of the DSU .... DSR 2001:XIII, 6675

Report of the Panel - Recourse to Article 21.5 of the DSU.... DSR 2001:XIII, 6717

Thailand – Anti-Dumping Duties on Angles, Shapes and Sections of Iron or Non-Alloy Steel and H-Beams from Poland
Complaint by Poland (WT/DS122)
Report of the Appellate Body .... DSR 2001:VII, 2701
Report of the Panel .... DSR 2001:VII, 2741

Turkey - Restrictions on Imports of Textile and Clothing Products
Complaint by India (WT/DS34)
Report of the Appellate Body .... DSR 1999:VI, 2345
Report of the Panel .... DSR 1999:VI, 2363

United States - Anti-Dumping Act of 1916
Complaint by the European Communities (WT/DS136); complaint by Japan (WT/DS162)
Report of the Appellate Body .... DSR 2000:X, 4793
Report of the Panel (European Communities)........................... DSR 2000:X, 4593
Report of the Panel (Japan).. DSR 2000:X, 4831
Award of the Arbitrator under Article 21.3(c) of the DSU .... DSR 2001:V, 2017

United States-Anti-Dumping and Countervailing Measures on Steel Plate from India
Complaint by India (WT/DS206)
Report of the Panel... DSR 2002:VI, 2073

United States - Anti-Dumping Duty on Dynamic Random Access Memory Semiconductors (DRAMS) of One Megabit or Above from Korea
Complaint by Korea (WT/DS99)
Report of the Panel .... DSR 1999:II, 521

United States – Anti-Dumping Measures on Certain Hot-Rolled Steel Products from Japan
Complaint by Japan (WT/DS184)
Report of the Appellate Body .... DSR 2001:X, 4697
Report of the Panel .... DSR 2001:X, 4769
Award of the Arbitrator under Article 21.3(c) of the DSU ...... DSR 2002:IV, 1389

United States – Anti-Dumping Measures on Stainless Steel Plate in Coils and Stainless Steel Sheet and Strip from Korea
Complaint by Korea (WT/DS179)
Report of the Panel .... DSR 2001:IV, 1295

United States – Definitive Safeguard Measures on Imports of Circular Welded Carbon Quality Line Pipe from Korea
Complaint by Korea (WT/DS202)
    Report of the Appellate Body .... DSR 2002:IV, 1403
    Report of the Panel .... DSR 2002:IV, 1473
    Award of the Arbitrator under Article 21.3(c) of the DSU .... DSR 2002:V, 2061

United States – Definitive Safeguard Measures on Imports of Wheat Gluten from the European Communities
Complaint by the European Communities (WT/DS166)
    Report of the Appellate Body .... DSR 2001:II, 717
    Report of the Panel .... DSR 2001:III, 779

United States – Import Measures on Certain Products from the European Communities
Complaint by the European Communities (WT/DS165)
    Report of the Appellate Body .... DSR 2001:I, 373
    Report of the Panel .... DSR 2001:II, 413

United States - Imposition of Countervailing Duties on Certain Hot-Rolled Lead and Bismuth Carbon Steel Products Originating in the United Kingdom
Complaint by the European Communities (WT/DS138)
    Report of the Appellate Body .... DSR 2000:V, 2595
    Report of the Panel .... DSR 2000:VI, 2623

United States - Import Prohibition of Certain Shrimp and Shrimp Products
Complaint by India (WT/DS58); complaint by Malaysia (WT/DS58); complaint by Pakistan (WT/DS58); complaint by Thailand (WT/DS58)
    Report of the Appellate Body .... DSR 1998:VII, 2755
    Report of the Panel .... DSR 1998:VII, 2821
    Report of the Appellate Body - Recourse to Article 21.5
    of the DSU (Malaysia) .... DSR 2001:XIII, 6481
    Report of the Panel - Recourse to Article 21.5
    of the DSU (Malaysia) .... DSR 2001:XIII, 6529

United States - Measure Affecting Imports of Woven Wool Shirts and Blouses from India
Complaint by India (WT/DS33)
    Report of the Appellate Body .... DSR 1997:I, 323
    Report of the Panel .... DSR 1997:I, 343

United States - Measures Treating Export Restraints as Subsidies
Complaint by Canada (WT/DS194)
    Report of the Panel .... DSR 2001:XI, 5767

United States - Restrictions on Imports of Cotton and Man-made Fibre Underwear
Complaint by Costa Rica (WT/DS24)
    Report of the Appellate Body .... DSR 1997:I, 11
    Report of the Panel .... DSR 1997:I, 31

United States – Safeguard Measures on Imports of Fresh, Chilled or Frozen Lamb Meat from New Zealand and Australia

Complaint by Australia (WT/DS178); complaint by new Zealand (WT/DS177)

Report of the Appellate Body ....DSR 2001:IX, 4051

Report of the Panel ....DSR 2001:IX, 4107

United States - Section 110(5) of the US Copyright Act

Complaint by the European Communities (WT/DS160)

Report of the Panel .... DSR 2000:VIII, 3769

Award of the Arbitrator under Article 21.3(c) of the DSU .... DSR 2001:II, 657

Award of the Arbitrator under Article 25 of the DSU................. DSR 2001:II, 667

United States - Sections 301-310 of the Trade Act of 1974

Complaint by the European Communities (WT/DS152)

Report of the Panel .... DSR 2000:II, 815

United States – Section 211 Omnibus Appropriations Act of 1998

Complaint by the European Communities (WT/DS176)

Report of the Appellate Body .... DSR 2002:II, 589

Report of the Panel... DSR 2002:II, 683

United States – Standards for Reformulated and Conventional Gasoline

Complaint by Brazil (WT/DS4); complaint by Venezuela (WT/DS2)

Report of the Appellate Body ....DSR 1996:I, 3

Report of the Panel ....DSR 1996:I, 29

United States - Tax Treatment for "Foreign Sales Corporations"

Complaint by the European Communities (WT/DS108)

Report of the Appellate Body ....DSR 2000:III, 1619

Report of the Panel ....DSR 2000:IV, 1675

Report of the Appellate Body - Recourse to Article 21.5
of the DSU ....DSR 2002:I, 55

Report of the Panel - Recourse to Article 21.5
of the DSU ....DSR 2002:I, 119

Decision by the Arbitrator under Article 22.6 of the DSU
and Article 4.11 of the SCM Agreement...................................DSR 2002:VI, 2517

United States – Transitional Safeguard Measure on Combed Cotton Yarn from Pakistan

Complaint by Pakistan (WT/DS192)

Report of the Appellate Body .... DSR 2001:XII, 6027

Report of the Panel .... DSR 2001:XII, 6067